Encyclopedia of Development Methods

Dedication
For Janet, Sophie and Gregory

Encyclopedia of Development Methods

Andrzej Huczynski

Gower

Published by
Gower Publishing Limited
Gower House
Croft Road
Aldershot
Hampshire GU11 3HR
UK

Gower Publishing Company
131 Main Street
Burlington VT 05401–5600
USA

Andrzej Huczynski has asserted his right under the Copyright, Designs and Patents Act 1988 to be identified as the author of this work.

British Library Cataloguing-in-Publication Data

Huczynski, Andrzej
    Encyclopedia of Development Methods. – 3rd edn
    1. Management – Encyclopedias
    I. Title
    658′.003

The Library of Congress Control Number is pre-assigned as: 2001089559

ISBN 0 566 07920 8

Typeset in Ehrhardt by Acorn Bookwork, Salisbury, Wiltshire, and printed in Great Britain by T J International Ltd., Padstow.

Contents

Preface

Soap and education are not as sudden as a massacre, but they are more deadly in the long run.
Mark Twain

The room for improvement is the biggest room in the world.
Anon.

This publication updates and integrates my two earlier encyclopedias which were published as separate volumes. The first of these, the *Encyclopedia of Management Development Methods*, originally appeared seventeen years ago, while the second, the *Encyclopedia of Organizational Change Development Methods*, will soon be celebrating its thirteenth birthday. In the intervening years, many changes have taken place in the fields of organizations, management, education and technology, and many more are occurring at present. In this preface, I indicate some of the major issues, themes, developments and opportunities, and consider their relevance to methods of management development and organizational change.

Organizational developments

The Association for Management Education and Development (AMED), a leading body composed of management trainers, lecturers and consultants, has identified seven key issues facing business, and has considered their implications for those responsible for developing managers and their organizations. In his article, Murray (1998) presents AMED's development themes for the new millennium, and suggests the contribution developers should make to each of these. This is a useful framework with which to begin a discussion of management development and organizational change methods. Let me first summarize each of Murray's seven themes.

The humanizing of work

Murray argues that the ruthless search for efficiency during the last thirty years with its goal of maximizing shareholder value, coupled with technological change, has resulted in reduced employee morale and commitment. Downsizing, outsourcing, business process re-engineering, short-term employment contracts, flattened structures and disappearing career ladders have all had their impact. He suggests that the role of developers should be to persuade business leaders to humanize work, giving it meaning, value and purpose beyond the pay-packet. In response to the inexorable process of change, their task is to help ensure that jobs in the future are performed in constructive work environments, helping to build a humane society.

Globalization

The prospect of a global economy generates equal amounts of fear and excitement. Moreover, it means different things to different people, from 24-hour Internet shopping via trans-border financial flows to manufacturing in the lowest-cost locations. The desirability of these developments is subject to debate. Will foreign competition heighten the efficiency of domestic produ-cers, or will power be concentrated in the hands of a few companies which will dominate the world market? Murray argues that, at the organizational level, developers should be helping companies improve their performance, develop their ability to learn and become more agile, both operationally and strategically. At the societal level, companies entering a new country should be encouraged to respect its citizens, as well as its employees back home. To these suggestions, one might add the contribution of the management educator working with under-graduates who might become the global company's new recruits. Helping them to understand what working for a global company might mean, both professionally and personally, as well as providing them with the knowledge and skills to do so, seem to be important and worthwhile objectives.

Stakeholders and management

Murray's third theme is the challenge to the long-held belief that companies are the sole property of their shareholders and should be run entirely in their interest. Discussions about 'stakeholding' at both national and organizational levels have become increasingly common. Organizational stakeholding has been discussed in terms of questions about corporate govern-ance and environmental policy, among many others. The prospect that legislation might take account of multiple stakeholder interests has also been mooted. Murray's view is that develop-ers should help companies identify their key relationships and the critical factors within them, and to develop stakeholder strategies. At the organizational level, this will involve helping the company discover what its internal and external stakeholders are thinking and feeling. At the individual level, it will involve managers exploring different aspects of their role.

Sustainability

Sustainable development in advanced economies raises questions about the direction, pace and means of development. Pollution, environmental disasters and company policies to relocate production to countries with more relaxed health and safety regimes are just some of the issues facing organizations under this heading. Short-term financial gains may be made at the cost of long-term reputation loss, as several international companies have already found. For Murray, developers should help companies confront these issues, which many find uncomfortable. The first step is to encourage them to discuss and agree a philosophy or approach to the question, and the second is to assist them to translate these good intentions into corporate behaviour and individual employees' work styles.

High performance

The maximization of performance at the organizational and individual level has been a primary objective of organizational change and management development activities in the past, and will continue to be so in the future. What is different today is that this is being demanded with fewer and fewer resources. It needs to be achieved in a way that retains and expands the commitment of companies' personnel (in a 'humane' way, as Murray puts it), and what counts as high performance may need to be redefined. In this sphere, the role of developers, according to Murray, should be twofold: first, to identify the skills required by managers and leaders to raise their own performance and that of their work teams; second, to help them redefine performance objectives, and to take steps to achieve these.

Working across boundaries

Boundaries – whether between teams, units, departments, plants or organizations – can both encourage healthy competition and produce barriers to co-operation, co-ordination and communication. Senior management decisions to restructure through privatization, spin-off companies or mergers often unconsciously create what Murray calls 'boundary behaviour'. This has been exacerbated by the effects of power-building, sectional interests and divisive accounting practices. For this reason, effective boundary management, at whatever level, has become an increasing priority. The key role for developers, says Murray, is to break down such barriers and promote effective working across boundaries. However, one might add that drawing companies' attention to the potential boundary problems that may result from their restructuring decisions would be even more useful, addressing the causes of the problem rather than its consequences or symptoms.

Ethics in organizational life and development

Business, professional and organizational ethics have gained prominence through accounts by the media of wrongdoing by individuals, companies and governments around the world. New technologies raise critical ethical questions, such as bio-engineering (gene modification) and computing (personal privacy). These matters are discussed in the context of corporate social responsibility and corporate reputation.

Murray points to four areas in which management development and organizational change experts can contribute to a company's ethical development:

1   helping to produce a company code of conduct or corporate philosophy which is developed in a way which involves a wide range of different company members, and which gains their commitment
2   working with management to ensure that there are internal company communication channels that allow employees to voice their concerns about ethical issues without fear of retribution
3   providing training to help company employees working abroad to resist extortion; act with integrity; and be sensitive to issues of harassment and discrimination
4   assisting senior management to conduct an ethical or social audit which would provide them with information on which to base their future strategy and planning.

The seven themes outlined above currently provide the 'big picture' within which development activity at the management or organizational level takes place. When engaged in the often emotionally demanding and exhausting process of face-to-face interaction with managers and students, developers can lose sight of the fact that the methods they use in their work are only means to an end, not ends in themselves. While the method may be considered innovative or challenging by its users, the customer is more likely to be interested in the outcomes achieved than the techniques employed. These issues are constantly changing: new ones come to promi-nence while older ones disappear. Unless trainers, lecturers and consultants recognize and prioritize the main problems and opportunities, and are able to 'deliver the goods', however this is defined by companies or government, then they are unlikely to be rewarded by offers of repeat business or increased resources. One purpose of this encyclopedia is to offer developers a toolkit with which they can address the opportunities and problems described in Murray's article.

Managerial developments

Most commentators agree that change is the normal state of affairs in organizations, and that the challenge for managers is to manage constant change. The two areas, management development and organizational change, have historically come together in management development programmes. Historically, company trainers have run in-house courses for junior management staff, while external consultants have run courses for middle and senior managers. Recent developments have resulted in changes in this area. The competencies movement has defined what managers need to be able to do in different areas and at different hierarchical levels. For the first time there is a marriage between the academic offerings of educational institutions and the management performance requirements defined by organizations. A progression of management qualifications has been established from certificate, through diploma and on to Master's degree level. In-company courses are now accredited by local universities, and can count towards a university qualification. In addition, for many years now, university business schools have run company-based MBA programmes. The consequence of all this is that university education has become more like executive development of the past, and executive development activities now resemble university programmes.

Educational developments

Many changes have also taken place which affect the providers of business management education within higher education. There are now more than 100 universities in the UK. They all offer business management programmes at undergraduate and postgraduate level, while many have established separate business schools. The number of students entering higher education has risen substantially. Thus both old and new universities which were established and built at a time of much smaller student numbers now have to cope with hundreds instead of scores of students. Some of the issues to be addressed at the undergraduate level were identified by Mutch (1997). They are perhaps most neatly summarized by the title of one of the sections in his article: 'Successes and strains'. These developments in the British higher education system have influenced the choice of teaching and learning methods that can be used. The system of regular evaluation of the quality of teaching at these institutions has been established by the various Higher Education Funding Councils. In addition, the Association of Master Business Administration (AMBA) conducts its own regular accreditation of business schools. Both bodies grade departments on a set of criteria. Among these, attention is paid to the range of teaching and learning methods used at each institution, focusing particularly on innovative approaches.

Perhaps an even greater influence on university teaching has been the impact of research assessment exercises, also conducted by the Higher Education Funding Councils. Whereas teaching quality assessments have resulted in a grade and, on occasion, extra funding of student numbers, research quality assessments directly affect the income of the parent university and the department assessed. The effect of this has been to increase the importance of research and publication at the expense of teaching. If academics consider teaching and preparing teaching materials a 'waste of valuable time', then they will be looking for ways to deliver their teaching more efficiently. This in turn will have an effect on their choice of instructional techniques. We have also seen growing competition among higher education institutions in general, and among business management programmes in particular. At the national level, several British universities have established 'branch offices' in the form of campuses located away from the centre. The major US and UK business schools recruit students globally, holding information days at hotels all around the world. Joint MBA programmes involving two or more university-level institutions located in different continents are now commonly advertised. Since the content of most business management programmes is similar, especially at the MBA level, the competing business schools use their teaching and learning methods to differentiate themselves from their competitors and attract potential students. Advertisements draw attention to the use of the case study method, small group working, project methods, internships, outdoor training, and so on.

In the context of business education provision in higher education, one contribution this encyclopedia can make to those business management academics for whom research rather than teaching is a priority is to suggest ways they can work 'smarter rather than harder'. Equally, for those instructors who gain most of their work satisfaction through teaching and interacting with students, this encyclopedia can provide a source of new approaches to try out. Finally, for the business school or management studies department seeking to differentiate its MBA programme from its competitors', the encyclopedia provides a choice of approaches which can help them do this. A few business schools are closely associated with pioneering a distinctive and consistent approach to their programmes. The Harvard Business School is perhaps the prime example of this in its use of the case study method. During the 1970s, the Manchester Business School pioneered the use of Joint Development Activities as an instructional design. At about the same time, the Architectural Association School was associated with the project method of student learning. From the 1980s, business schools have established programmes based on learning contracts and individually negotiated programmes of study, on action learning principles, and on integrated overseas visits or periods of study at collaborating institutions. Thus, in marketing terms, the method of instruction has come to be a business school's unique selling proposition (USP).

Technological developments

Developments in technology have also had a tremendous impact. Students in the classroom will have noticed that their lecturers now support their lecture presentations with *Powerpoint* presentations using a laptop PC. Their textbooks may contain a CD-ROM. In addition, their courses will use computer-assisted learning (CAL) materials available on the department or faculty server, or via the Internet. Groupware allows them to interact with their instructor and fellow students, and video-conferencing is being more frequently used. Entire courses and entire programmes of courses leading to the award of a degree can now be presented over the Internet. Over the past two decades, a great deal has changed in how education is delivered and consumed.

Despite all these changes, the objective of this encyclopedia remains the same: to provide a source of information and ideas for the educational decision-maker. This term encompasses students, course designers, tutors, teachers, company training personnel, human resource management specialists, external consultants – indeed anybody who has to make a decision about any learning event or organizational change intervention they are about to embark on or design.

It is perhaps easiest to talk about the company trainer to illustrate the types of decisions that must be made. In tackling an organizational problem, the first decision is whether a training intervention or an organizational intervention is most appropriate.

If a training intervention is required, then trainers have the choice of doing the training themselves by designing their own course and teaching it, or sending the manager concerned on an externally run course. They can buy a training package together with a consultant to run it on an in-company basis, or buy a package which they run themselves. If they believe that an off-the-shelf training package may be the answer, then this encyclopedia describes some of the most popular ones, together with supplementary reading which can help them make their final choice. If, on the other hand, trainers decide to run a course in-house, they can choose from a bewildering variety of teaching and learning methods. The encyclopedia suggests some of the criteria that need to be considered when making such a choice.

If an organizational intervention is required, it is still necessary to decide who is to conduct it. Increasingly, trainers have been taking the role of internal consultants or facilitators, working with line managers to define the problems and consider the appropriate level of organizational intervention. At other times, they have brought in outside consultants, judging that their perceived independence or possession of special skills will increase the chances of a successful outcome. These consultants, in turn, can either offer customized approaches, working with the client through a cycle of problem definition, alternatives generation, solution selection and implementation, or can introduce a standard package to implement some technique desired by the customer.

While management development and organizational change is an innovative field in terms of its adoption of new techniques, developments have taken place in other areas. For this reason, the encyclopedia includes descriptions of teaching, learning and organizational intervention methods taken not only from management education, but also from other areas such as medicine, biology, geology, languages, physics and community development. These approaches are selected in the belief that they have a potential application to the work of developers. In the encyclopedia, readers will find entries at five levels of application:

1   methods which can be applied by the trainer or consultant following a reading of the description with no further preparation
2   methods which, although directly applicable, nevertheless require the trainer or consultant to do some reading of the recommended literature to gain greater familiarity with the objectives and the steps involved
3   methods which, if they were to be applied personally by the trainer or consultant themselves, would require them to have gained first-hand experience of them in a learner or employee role; alternatively, they should be used by the trainer or consultant under the guidance of someone skilled in their use
4   methods which require the engagement of an experienced professional, because the trainer or consultant lacks the necessary skill, knowledge or experience, or does not wish to develop such expertise
5   packaged or copyrighted training programmes run by an outside consulting company which may do the training or provide the consultancy advice on an in-company basis. This category would include not only the standard organizational change packages offered by the large consultancy companies, but also university business school MBA programmes tailored to the needs of managers in that company or industry.

As a general rule, where the training or change methods focus on affective issues – those concerned with people's feelings, values and emotions – the trainer or consultant will need to have developed the relevant skills to lead such a learning activity successfully.

The following brief description of the content of each of the chapters may help readers select those which are of most immediate relevance to them.

In Chapter 1, 'Defining the field', the concepts of management development and organizational change are defined, contrasted, and distinguished from the related field of organizational development.

Chapter 2, 'Management development method classification', focuses on management development methods and, in particular, on presenting different bases for classifying these. Different taxonomies are presented in the form of frameworks, and the reasons why a development methods selection system is unlikely ever to be developed are set out. The chapter ends with an analytical framework designed to help practitioners analyse the management development methods they are using or planning to use.

Chapter 3, 'Organizational change method classification frameworks', complements Chapter 2, but this time concentrates on organizational change methods. Seven different taxonomies are presented in increasing levels of sophistication and complexity. As before, the aim is to group together similar methods and relate them to key dimensions of organizational problems.

The 'Directory of methods' constitutes the main body of the encyclopedia. Each entry gives a brief description of a management development and organizational change method, together with some of the alternative names by which it is known. References are given both to related methods and to further reading.

Appendix

The appendix provides details of books, journals and other sources of information about teaching, training and facilitation materials.

References

Murray, D. (1998) 'Seven Development Themes for the 21st Century', *Organisations and People*, vol. 5, no. 1, pp. 4–18.

Mutch, A. (1997) 'Re-thinking Undergraduate Business Education', *Management Learning*, vol. 28., no. 3, pp. 301–12.

Invitation to readers

The purpose of this encyclopedia is to produce a comprehensive source of references on management teaching, learning and organizational change methods for colleagues in the field of management. Despite careful research, it is inevitable I will have omitted some, and new approaches are constantly being developed. In order to keep the encyclopedia as comprehensive and up-to-date as possible, I should welcome input from readers who use (or have had used on them) any methods in their work which significantly differ from those described in this encyclopedia. Method descriptions, where possible including references to published descriptions of their uses as well as further reading references, can be e-mailed to me at:

A.A.Huczynski@mgt.gla.ac.uk

I shall undertake to collate and edit these contributions, which will be included in any future editions of the encyclopedia, and the help of contributors who have taken the trouble to do this will be acknowledged.

Andrzej Huczynski

Acknowledgements

I should like to express the debt I owe to the individuals who developed and described the teaching and learning and organizational change methods contained in this encyclopedia. I hope I have not distorted their ideas in the process of summarizing them to make them more widely available.

My editor at Gower Publishing was Malcolm Stern, who supplied both advice and encouragement. I am also grateful to Janie Ferguson of Glasgow University Library, who provided valuable assistance in checking the many references cited in this encyclopedia.

The following publishers were kind enough to give their permission to reproduce their material:

Addison-Wesley Publishing Company Inc., Reading, Massachusetts, for Figure 3.8, 'The Consulcube', from Blake, R.R. and Mouton, J.S., *Consultation*, 1983, p. 11, Figure 1.1, and figure on page 315, 'Responsibility chart', from Beckhard, R. and Harris, R.T., *Organizational Transitions: Managing Complex Change*, 1977, p. 78.

Bantam Books Inc., New York, for figure on page 274, 'Parallel career ladder', and for figure on page 335, '7-5 Framework (modified)', from Clifford, D.K. and Cavanagh, R.E., *The Winning Performance: How America's High Growth Midsize Companies Succeed*, 1985, p. 14 and p. 114 respectively.

Blandford Press for figure on page 58, 'Algorithmic approach to sales training', from Jinks, M., *Training*, Blandford Management Series, 1979.

Centre for Leadership Studies, Escondido, California, for figure on page 20, 'Interaction influence analysis model', and figure on page 340, 'Situational leadership prescriptive curve' from Hersey, P. and Keilty, J.W., 'Developing one-to-one OD communication skills', in Burke, W. and Goodstein, L.D. (eds), *Trends and Issues in OD: Current Theory and Practice*, 1982, San Diego, CA: University Associates Inc., pp. 257 and 260.

Falmer Press for figure on page 311, 'Relational diagrams', from White, R. and Gunstone, R., *Probing Understanding*, 1992.

Dr K. Macharzina for Figure 1.2, 'Hierarchy of management decision-making', from Burgoyne, J.G. and Cooper, C.L., 'Research and Teaching Methods in Management Education: Bibliographical Examination of the State of the Art', *Management Education Review*, 1976, vol. 4, no. 1, pp. 95–192.

MCB University Press, Bradford, Yorkshire, for figure on page 233, 'An enlarged portion of the MORT Analytical Tree', in Conger D.S., 'Using MORT as an OD tool', *Leadership and Organization Development Journal*, vol. 3, no. 5, 1982, pp. 10–15.

McGraw-Hill Book Company (UK) Ltd for figure on page 130, 'Example of a decision table', from Davis, I.K., *The Management of Learning*, 1981, p. 143.

Prentice-Hall Inc, Englewood Cliffs, New Jersey, for Figure 3.4, 'OD interventions classified by two independent dimensions: individual vs group dimension and task vs process dimension'; Figure 3.5, 'Typology of interventions based on target groups'; Figure 3.6, 'Intervention typology based on principal emphasis of intervention in relation to different hypothesized change mechanisms'. These came from French, W.L. and Bell C.H., *Behavioural Science Interventions for Organizational Improvement* (3rd edn), 1984, pp. 130, 131, 132 and 247.

Sage Publications, for Figure 3.7, 'The depth of various group or organizational interventions', *Journal of Applied Behavioural Science*, vol. 6, April–June, pp. 181–202.

University Associates Inc, San Diego, California, for Figure 3.9, 'The OD cube: A scheme for classifying OD interventions', in Schmuck, R. and Miles, M.B. (eds), *Organizational Development in Schools*, 1971, pp. 8–9.

Index of methods

1 Defining the field

Identifying the boundaries between the different stakeholders interested in the general field covered by this encyclopedia is both difficult and not very fruitful. A few years ago, a conference took place on the topic of emergent fields in management. The flyer advertising it was interesting in that it demonstrated the breadth of the field. It contained a diagram with the labels 'Management Learning', 'Human Resource Development', 'Training and Development', 'Management Education' and 'Management Development'. Below the diagram, it read:

> Learning has emerged in recent years as a central concept in relation to management and organizations. It is seen as crucial to both organization success (the 'learning organization idea') and individual employment changes in globalizing, knowledge-based economies. Learning, knowledge, information, training and development, education and people are now more actively managed than ever before and numerous masters programmes have sprung up to 'educate', 'develop' and credentialize the professionals concerned with managing them. (Fox and Grey, 1997)

In practice, when thinking about change in organizations, most managers approach the topic in a narrower way. Management development methods have been used by company trainers and training consultants to help organizations to adapt to change, and to become more effective and efficient. Where management development ends and the development of organizations begins is difficult to establish. Indeed, the distinction may be an artificial one. That is why my previous two works, the *Encyclopedia of Management Development Methods* and *Encyclopedia of Organizational Change Methods*, have been integrated into a single volume and updated and expanded.

Jones and Woodcock (1985) offered a general model which relates the various methods of management development, management education, management training and of organizational development (see Figure 1.1). The core of their model is based on their belief that effectiveness is based on a manager's ability to 'take care of him or herself' (self-development). Beyond that, depicted by ever widening concentric circles, is their need to manage subordinates, to manage the relations between their department and others in the company; and then manage the relationships with those outside their organization. Jones and Woodcock argue that these four levels of a manager's responsibility demand different types of knowledge and skill. One might also add that there are different ways to acquire such knowledge and skill, and different methods with which to manage the aforementioned relationships. Later in the same book, Jones and Woodcock (1985, pp. 62–3) make a useful distinction between *management* development (MD) provided through training, and *organizational* development (OD), highlighting the main similarities and differences. They feel it is the differences which have implications for guiding the assessment of managerial training needs.

The similarities between management development and organizational development include the following:

1   The two activities have the same meta-goal – improved organizational functioning.
2   Both activities focus on balancing concerns between individual needs and organizational demands.
3   They are both subsumed under the umbrella of 'human resource development'.

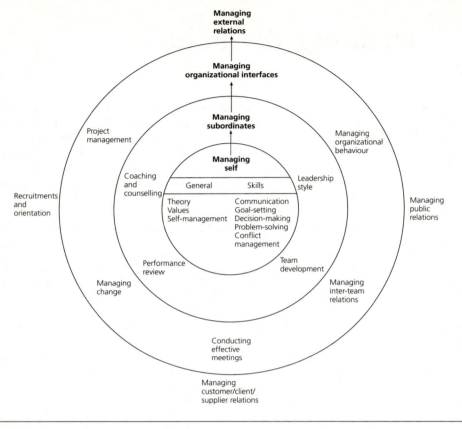

Figure 1.1   Definition of management development methods
Source: Jones and Woodcock (1985, p.55)

4   Both training and OD feature applications of behavioural science to human and systems problems.
5   The two types of effort have a common value base.
6   They are very often carried out by the same people.

There are a number of differences between the two, including:

1   The 'target' for MD is the individual manager; in OD it is groups of people and systems.
2   MD requires that its practitioners have skills in presenting and facilitating learning; OD calls for skills in system assessment, problem identification, problem–solving and intervention.
3   The role of the professional in MD is that of a 'shaper' of learning, but the primary role of the OD practitioner is process consultation.
4   MD specialists engage in training needs assessment, designing and conducting courses; OD practitioners involve themselves in action research and consulting with groups and individuals about problems.
5   The content of MD courses centres on simulated problems, but OD focuses exclusively on real ones.

Some writers see 'method' as referring to a series of teacher-directed activities that result in learning. Since method is a process, it consists of several steps. Many of the elements or steps used in a particular method may also be used in other methods – hence the overlap between educational programme designs, structured programme designs and organizational development activities. Educational psychologists have also argued that methods are tutor-initiated, and are based on an educational philosophy which states the values to be achieved, and on a theory of how people learn. They are said to list a set of learning principles which have relevant applications in the classroom, and indicate the behaviour that the teacher should maintain in order to make effective use of these principles. While a method consists of several steps or elements, it is the tutor who combines or synthesizes the elements into an effective process. Wallen and Travers (1963) have written that research into teaching methods is the study of the consistencies in the behaviour of teachers and the effect of these consistencies on the learning process. Teacher behaviour which might be considered could include the amount of information provided by a teacher, the emphasis placed on assessment, and so on. These writers use the terms 'teaching method' and 'pattern of teacher behaviour' interchangeably. Burgoyne and Stuart (1978), who investigated the relationship of learning theories to teaching methods, reported that:

> the idea that one teaching method always embodied the same learning theory was wrong. We found, rather, that different learning theories illuminated different aspects of the same teaching methods, and that different applications of teaching methods 'implemented' assumptions from different learning theories, depending on the manner or style of application of the method by the person applying it.

To date, attempts to classify different teaching and learning methods have met with little success. Those offered by Wesley and Wronski (1965) and Joyce and Weil (1980) either tend to omit many of the entries described in this encyclopedia altogether, or else place them into categories where experience and common sense suggest they do not belong. Simplistic categorization systems are likely to fail for at least two reasons. First, a method label carries no agreed indication of the interactions it is likely to describe, and second, in order to produce any classification system one needs criteria with which to establish the categories. Numerous such criteria are possible, but after one's interest is stated, it is then impossible to apply a single-criterion classification system universally. Given these difficulties, one needs to ask: what is the purpose of classifying these methods in the first place? At one level, the answer may be to indicate to readers which methods are operationally similar to each other so they can choose from several that are likely to achieve similar objectives, or else those which are similar in their mechanics but which can be used to achieve a variety of objectives. At another level, the purpose may be to indicate that the entries in the encyclopedia differ qualitatively from each other. Some are learning principles, while others might be described as recipes, interaction rules, feedback systems, and so on. This would allow the tutor to reflect on the suitability of any particular method in relation to the objectives and participants being worked with. For this reason, an analytical framework is offered in preference to a classification system (see Chapter 3).

About half the methods described in this encyclopedia seek to develop managers as individuals. Morris (1971), for example, saw it as 'the systematic improvement of managerial effectiveness within the organization assessed by its contribution to organizational effectiveness'. Ashton and Easterby-Smith (1979) identified a number of perspectives within management development which they viewed as an organizational function within which 'activities such as training, coaching, career planning, appraisal, job rotation might all have some part to play'. These writers saw management development as involving the continuing education of the individual manager at all stages of their career. Thus management development was considered as being concerned not only with education and training, but also 'with a broader concept of development which implies improvement'. The breadth of this definition allows one to use it to refer to a wide range of different activities. It can be used to apply to both in-company and extra-company development programmes, to short as well as to long courses, to periods of training and education, to those which lead to formal qualifications as well as those which do not. It is an all-embracing concept of management development which is being used in this book. A more detailed examination follows of what is included under the label 'management development'.

Burgoyne and Cooper (1976) conducted a study on the research that had been carried out into management teaching methods and identified journal references concerned with teaching methods. In doing this, they produced a hierarchy of decisions concerning management education which was what they used as a basis for classifying the research studies they found. Their five-level hierarchy is summarized in Figure 1.2.

1 Policy – decisions on issues concerning national approaches to education.
2 Strategy – decisions on issues concerned with management education at the institutional or departmental level.
3 Programme design – choices of approaches relevant to learning objectives and to how people learn.
4 Choice of methods – within-programme choices between different teaching/learning methods.
5 Intra-method decisions – 'here-and-now' choices made by tutors during the teaching session itself.

Figure 1.2 Hierarchy of management decision-making
Source: Burgoyne and Cooper (1976)

While the authors did not explicitly define their term 'teaching method', they nevertheless presented a useful framework with which to begin to sort out some of the confusion which surrounds the use of terms such as 'management development', 'education' and 'organizational development'. They achieved this by raising the terms 'management education' and 'development' to an abstract level, and in their place referred to different types of programme designs. Their description of a branching hierarchy of decisions is shown in Figure 1.3.

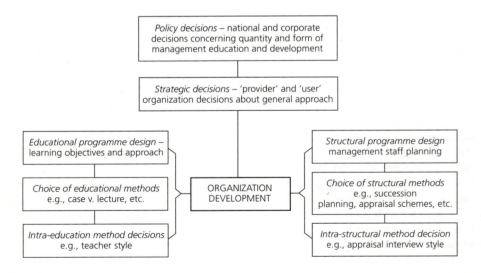

Figure 1.3 Branching hierarchy of management education decisions

The attractiveness of the Burgoyne-Cooper hierarchy is that it sidesteps the arid debate over nomenclature referred to earlier. It is based on decisions to be taken by different people at different levels. In terms of methods or 'what people actually do', there is likely to be a high degree of overlap between what happens in educational programmes and in structural programmes. This encyclopedia focuses on two educational and structural programme designs on levels 3, 4 and 5. Burgoyne and Cooper see organizational development activities as deriving from both these strategies. However, the encyclopedia does not attempt to deal explicitly with organizational development methods, although some of these OD techniques are included if they are capable of being extracted and used outside their usual OD context. Similarly, psychotherapies are excluded, other than those which have already established themselves in management development (such as Transactional Analysis). Such therapies have been dealt with in great detail in other books (Winn, 1980; Clare and Thompson, 1981).

What exactly does the term 'method' refer to in the context of teaching and learning? Wesley and Wronski (1965) commented on the lack of specificity in the use of the word. They quoted a study in which students were asked to list the methods they knew. In addition to listing traditional, well-known ones such as the lecture and seminar, other methods listed included curricular materials, organization schemes, activities and devices. All these were equated with the term 'method'. A brief survey of the literature on teaching and learning methods in management development can show whether the connotations of the word 'method' are equally broad in this field. In Burgoyne and Cooper's (1976) article, the authors produced a 'list of teaching methods' which consisted of the following: lecture, texts, programmed instruction, role-playing, case studies, games and simulations, projects, packages, T-group/social skills training and 'specials'. In a second paper on teaching and learning methods in management development, Burgoyne and Stuart (1978) discussed lecture, seminar, business game, encounter group, T-group, joint development activities, action learning, autonomy lab, learning community, guided reading and programmed instruction. The final example is taken from some work by Pedler (1978) on negotiating, which will be referred to in greater detail later. In discussing the teaching of information or situational knowledge, he argued that 'the more traditional methods of teaching or training would seem to apply best'. He went on to list these as being lectures, talks, seminars, films, books, handouts and discussions. From these few examples, it is clear that the term 'method' is used in the same broad way in management development as elsewhere. Being such a difficult concept to pin down, it is not surprising that there has been little success in producing a meaningful method classification system. According to Wesley and Wronski (1965), such a task is impossible:

> the complex and inclusive nature of method defies epigrammatic condensation. It is composed of diverse elements and is scarcely susceptible to logical analysis.

Nevertheless, the attempt to classify or group different methods in some way is useful in that, as the same authors state:

> it clearly demonstrates the futility of devoting oneself wholly to one method. It appears desirable not only to use different methods, but to take care that those grounded in different bases are employed. And the analysis also furnishes an inclusive viewpoint that will prevent one from assigning undue merit or inclusive qualities to any one method.

Definition of organizational change methods

Jones and Woodcock (1985) do not explicitly define their use of the term 'organizational development'. They appear to use the label to refer to activities that are focused on the organization as a system, rather than on individual managers. However, for over fifty years the term 'organizational development' (or OD), has had a specific meaning, which includes what Jones and Woodcock refer to, but goes beyond it. Organizational development originated in the USA after 1945. Richard Beckhard (1969, p. 9) defined it as: 'an effort, planned, organization-wide, and managed from the top, to increase organization development and health through planned interventions in the organization's "process", using behavioural science knowledge'. This definition does not differ greatly from Jones and Woodcock's. However, Buchanan and Huczynski (1997, p. 489) note that in pursuing these objectives, OD has a clear and prescriptive value orientation. OD values relate to an individual's experience of employment and the way the organization treats and relates to its members. They quote the underpinning OD values which were listed by Robbins (1986, p. 461):

1   The individual should be treated with respect and dignity.
2   The organization climate should be characterized by trust, openness and support.
3   Hierarchical authority and control are not regarded as effective mechanisms.
4   Problems and conflicts should be confronted, and not disguised or avoided.
5   People affected by change should be involved in its implications.

It is clear that this 'human-centred' agenda is not shared by all managers. Thus some company change programmes will reflect these values, while others will not. One can read books and articles which describe an 'OD' way of implementing management-by-objectives (MBO) programmes or staff appraisal meetings. This implies that non-OD approaches to implementing change exist and are based on a different set of values. Thus, it does not seem appropriate for a book which deals with changing organizations to restrict itself to a class or category of approaches, irrespective of how important they may be. A second reason for going beyond OD is the renewed interest in improved organizational performance, as reflected by the growth in 'excellence literature'. This was initiated by the research of Peters and Waterman (1982), the findings of which are contained in their book *In Search of Excellence*. This book has been a stimulus to the identification of new work and organizational practices that have been described in different books (Peters and Austin, 1985; Goldsmith and Clutterbuck, 1985; Clifford and Cavanagh, 1986). The author felt it was appropriate to capture the ideas contained in this field. For both these reasons, the term 'organizational development' has been used to refer to a certain US-based approach to organizational change. It therefore represents only one of many such approaches – though among the most influential – used during the last twenty years. Throughout the encyclopedia, 'organizational change' is used as the generic term to refer to all change strategies, including OD ones. The aim of this book is to provide the organizational decision-maker with information and ideas about ways of changing an organization. For this reason, the more general label of 'organizational change methods' is used both here and in the description of the methods. Although many OD techniques are indeed included, the encyclopedia does not restrict itself to them.

Most of this encyclopedia focuses on these organization-wide approaches towards *implementing change*. The interventions described tend to be components of a change strategy which has its own specific objectives. That change strategy may deal with changing people, organizational goals, technology, organizational structures, or a combination of all four. Such a definition cannot exclude management education and training activities, since these will form part of any people-change approach.

Among organizational change methods, it is useful to distinguish between *development approaches* and *proprietary programmes*. A development approach is an organizational technique that can be adopted and implemented by any company without payment to its originator. A development approach is often based on some theory of human behaviour generated through research. One example of a well-known development approach is job enrichment, based on Frederick Herzberg's 'motivation hygiene' theory. Any manager can read about the theory, learn about its implications for the design of jobs, and then implement a job-enrichment programme. Other examples of development approaches include quality circles, management-by-objectives and briefing groups. Over 90 per cent of the organizational change methods described in this encyclopedia fall into the category of development approaches.

Despite this high percentage, it is important to distinguish development approaches from proprietary programmes, which are 'off-the-shelf', ready-to-use organizational change courses. These frequently consist of a package of materials, such as videos, workbooks, leader's guides, role plays and instruments. These materials are copyrighted and the user buys them or obtains a licence to use them. Such programmes may be run by the selling company's own consultants or by the buying organization's staff. Among the best-known examples of such programmed packages are Grid Development (Blake and Mouton) and the Kepner-Tregoe Problem Solving Programme.

Traditionally, the direction of organizational change has been towards greater productivity, quality and, hence, profitability. At the same time, it has been observed that some of the most successful changes also increase employee participation and satisfaction. But who are these organizational decision-makers? The term is intended to include *senior company managers* who have to make decisions about implementing proposed organizational changes. Many of these changes may be fundamental and have long-term implications: for example, giving staff status to all employees. Also included are the *staff advisers* such as management training and development managers and personnel managers, who are responsible for advising senior executives about the options currently available to them. Another category of decision-maker is the *management development adviser*, who often acts as an internal company consultant with responsibility for implementing any organizational change policy. Finally, one might also mention the *external consultant*, brought in to advise a company and act as an independent third party during the implementation of some change programme. All these people are likely to find the encyclopedia useful as a source of ideas and reference as to what change strategies are available.

Every so often, most companies realize that, in order to perform better, or in some cases to survive, they need to change the way they function *as an organization*. Then a company looks beyond the development of its employees at the shop-floor, supervisory or management level, and considers its aims and objectives, its current organizational structure, the way its technology is organized, its sensitivity to aspects of its environment, and so on. Such a review may lead senior management to decide that some changes at the organizational level are appropriate. A gap then opens up between the way the company operates at present, and the way it should ideally operate in the future. The techniques described in this book represent a means for moving from the present state to the desired future state. They also describe the way of operating in that new state: for example, survey feedback can be used to obtain the views of employees about proposed new types of work schedules. The survey represents a means to an end state (some improved arrangement of working hours), while the introduction of a flexitime work schedule represents that new desired end state.

The objectives of the changes will be decided by the company concerned. The choice of change approach will depend on what the organization is trying to achieve, what theory of change its managers hold, and what constraints apply. Some managers may hold a theory of change which says that the way to achieve their desired objective is to change the behaviour of their employees. In such a situation, the choice of change strategies will be restricted to *people approaches*, such as staff selection, team development, leadership training, and so on. In contrast, a senior manager who believes that change can be brought about by changes in organizational structures will emphasize *structural approaches*, such as job redesign, task force assignments, the creation of matrix teams, and so on. Each manager has their own theory of change, which will guide their selection and adoption of organizational change methods.

British companies, with the exception of some of the largest, have generally shied away from the use of US organizational development (OD) techniques. However, some have given the person who holds the position of internal consultant the job title 'OD Adviser'. During the past decade, the quest for survival and improvement led many companies to look for specific ways to change their internal operations. Inevitably, these companies looked to see what others had done. This is another reason for compiling this encyclopedia. The author has reviewed books and articles, and talked to managers to discover what methods and approaches they are using to implement change. Each method is described briefly, and further references are included where they exist. No attempt has been made to offer any evaluation of these techniques.

References

Ashton, D. and Easterby-Smith, M. (1979) *Management Development in the Organization*, Macmillan.

Beckhard, R. (1969) *Organization Development*, Addison Wesley.

Buchanan, D.A. and Huczynski, A.A. (1997) *Organizational Behaviour: An Introductory Text* (3rd edn), Prentice-Hall Europe.

Burgoyne, J.G. and Cooper, C.L. (1976) 'Research on Teaching Methods in Management Education: Bibliographical Examination of the State of the Art', *Management Education Review*, vol. 16, no. 4, pp. 95–102.

Burgoyne, J.G. and Stuart, R. (1978) 'Teaching and Learning Methods in Management Development', *Personnel Review*, vol. 7, no. 1, pp. 53–8.

Clifford, D.K. and Cavanagh, R.E. (1986) *The Winning Performance: How America's High Growth Midsize Companies Succeed*, Sidgwick and Jackson.

Clare, A.W. and Thompson, S. (1981) *Let's Talk About Me*, BBC Publications.

Fox, S. and Grey, C. (1997) leaflet, 'Conference Announcement and Call for Papers: A Collaborative Conference Organised by Lancaster and Leeds University'.

Goldsmith, W. and Clutterbuck, D. (1985) *The Winning Streak*, Penguin Books.

Jones, J.E. and Woodcock, M. (1985) *Manual of Management Development*, Gower.

Joyce, B. and Weil, M. (1980) *Model of Teaching* (2nd edn), *Prentice-Hall*.

Morris, J. (1971) 'Management Development and Development Management', *Personnel Review*, vol. 1, no. 1, pp. 30–43.

Pedler, M. (1978) 'Negotiating Skills Training Part 4: Learning to Negotiate', *Journal of European Industrial Training*, vol. 2, no. 1, pp. 20–5.

Peters, T.J. and Austin, N. (1985) *A Passion for Excellence*, Penguin Books.

Peters, T.J. and Waterman, R.H. (1982) *In Search of Excellence*, Harper and Row.

Robbins, S.P. (1986) *Organizational behaviour: Concepts, Controversies, Applications*, Prentice-Hall International.

Wallen, N.E. and Travers, R.M.W. (1963) 'Analysis and Investigation of Teaching Methods', in Gage, N.L. (ed.) *Handbook of Research on Teaching*, Rand McNally.

Wesley, E.B. and Wronski, S.P. (1965) *Teaching Social Sciences in the High Schools*, D.C. Heath.

Winn, D. (1980) *The Whole Mind Book*, Collins/Fontana.

2 Management development method classification frameworks

Introduction

It is important to stress the difference between a classification system and a selection system. We use classification systems to group together phenomena which share common characteristics, such as plants. We then have to use our own judgement to decide (select) where any particular plant should be located in the garden. Plants can be classified according to their colour, height, scent, ability to tolerate drought or damp, speed of growth, and many other criteria. A single plant will appear in different places on different lists, depending on the chosen criteria for classification. In the end, it is the responsibility of the gardener, once provided with different classifications tables, to select the plant that is most suitable for a given garden location.

There are a number of useful classification systems that can focus the thinking of management developers. Similarly, there are a number which appear attractive, but which, on closer inspection, are not. This chapter begins with a consideration of several method classification systems, and ends with an analytical framework.

There are numerous criteria on the basis of which one can classify the management development methods to be found in this encyclopedia. The methods themselves can be considered rather like a pack of cards: how they are sorted and which ones are used depends on the criteria you apply and the game you are playing. This chapter will describe four bases for classifying the management development methods listed in this book, and give examples of methods for each of the different categories.

'Learning objectives' framework

Consideration of the objectives of education and training provides an important basis for differentiating between management development methods. The aim, goal, purpose or objective of any learning situation – whether defined by the tutor, the students, or by both – constitutes one of the guiding considerations. While stating the objectives of learning is universally considered a good thing, there has been less agreement on the classification system to be used or on the degree of specificity which is relevant and appropriate. The attempt to produce a comprehensive list of educational objectives has a long tradition in educational psychology which goes back to the 1950s. Best-known, perhaps, are the taxonomies developed by Bloom and his collaborators (Bloom et al. 1956; Krathwohl et al., 1964) and added to by Simpson (1966). Bloom identified three areas or domains of learning (see Figure 2.1): the *cognitive*, which is concerned with knowledge, facts and their manipulation (see Figure 2.2); the *affective*, which deals with feelings, emotions and values (see Figure 2.3), and the *psychomotor*, which is concerned with movement (see Figure 2.4). Within each of the three domains, the objectives are arranged in increasing levels of complexity or sophistication from level 5 or 6 at the bottom

Cognitive	Affective	Psychomotor
Concerned with knowledge, facts and their manipulation	Concerned with feelings, emotions and values	Concerned with movement
1 Evaluation 2 Synthesis 3 Analysis 4 Application 5 Comprehension 6 Knowledge	1 Characterization by value(s) 2 Receiving 3 Responding 4 Valuing 5 Organization	1 Complex overt response 2 Mechanism 3 Guided response 4 Set 5 Perception

Figure 2.1   Bloom's three domains of learning

	Label	Definition	Examples of methods
1	Evaluation	The ability to detect logical fallacies in arguments, to recognize inappropriate criteria used in a given situation, to detect various types of errors, to identify means–end relationships, and to make judgements based on the information provided.	Appraisal module Argumentation Book reviewing Buberian dialogue Debate Jurisprudential model PIT technique Reaction paper
2	Synthesis	The ability to draw upon parts of elements, and arrange them into a new structure or pattern not clearly present before.	Chronology charting Dissertation proposal Fortune lining Re-framing Student-designed companies
3	Analysis	The ability to break down material into component parts. It involves identifying parts, and defining the relationships between parts.	Case study method Concept mapping
4	Application	The ability to apply knowledge, experience and skill to new situations presented in a novel manner. The method of solution is not implied in the question.	Group investigation model Students as school tutors Student-consulting companies
5	Comprehension	The ability to translate data from one form to another (e.g., verbal and mathematical), to interpret or deduce the significance of data, and to solve problems in which the mode of solution should be familiar (e.g., calculation).	Company file project Data approach method Description–Prediction–Outcome–Observation
6	Knowledge	The ability to recall facts, nomenclature, classification, concepts, practical techniques, laws or theories.	Drill and practice Mind Mapping Rote learning Self-tests

Figure 2.2   Bloom et al.'s six cognitive domain levels with examples of methods

	Label	Definition	Examples of methods
1	Value	Learners' hierarchies of values have been internalized so that they can be characterized as holding a particular value or set of values.	Corporate culture training Brainwashing
2	Organization	Learners successively internalize multiple values and organize them into a system which allows certain values to exercise greater control.	Moral philosophy approach
3	Valuing	Learners display behaviour with sufficient consistency in appropriate situations to be perceived as holding a particular value.	Values-clarification Confluent education
4	Responding	Learners respond in ways that go beyond merely attending to phenomena, but doing so actively.	Achievement motivation training
5	Receiving	Learners are willing to attend to certain phenomena and stimuli at three levels – awareness of phenomena, willingness to receive phenomena, and selective attention to phenomena	Apperception–interaction method

Figure 2.3   Krathwolhl et al.'s five affective domain levels with examples of method

	Label	Definition	Examples of methods
1	Complex overt response	Individual is capable of performing a complex motor skill efficiently and smoothly with minimum expenditure of time and effort.	Demonstration–performance method
2	Mechanism	Having achieved confidence and skill in task performance, the act is part of the repertoire, and is available as a response.	Alexander Technique
3	Guided response	This is the overt behavioural act of an individual under the guidance of another.	Behaviour modelling Mathetics
4	Set	This involves the preparatory adjustment for a particular action or experience. The three distinct aspects of set are mental, physical and emotional.	Action profiling
5	Perception	The first step in performing a motor act is to become aware of objects, qualities or relations through the senses.	Awareness training Confidence-building training

Figure 2.4   Simpson's five psychomotor domain levels with examples of methods

Cognitive	Inter-personal	Psychomotor	Affective	Self-knowledge
Thinking abilities distinguished according to level, from knowledge, comprehension, application, analysis and synthesis to evaluation.	This is a blend of specific cognitive, affective and even psychomotor skills focused on dealing with people.	Behavioural skills, traditionally manual. However, now include para- and non-verbal communication.	This concerns feelings, emotions values and beliefs.	Better self-understanding, in particular personal knowledge of one's own strengths and weaknesses.
Problem-based learning	Role-playing	Non-verbal encounters	Confluent education	Psychodrama Feedback

Figure 2.5   Pedler's five domains of management development objectives with examples of methods

Level of learning	Description	Learning methods	
		Off-the-job	On-the-job
1 Memory	Learners can recall facts, definitions, procedures, actions, behaviours. They can identify, define and describe.	Lectures Talks Programmed learning	Algorithms Checklists Information maps
2 Understanding	Learners have grasp of concepts, ideas procedures and techniques. They can explain, compare and justify.	Talks Discussions Case studies Business games In-tray exercises Incident studies Action mazes Information mazes Group feedback analysis	Assignments Projects
3 Application	Learners can use the concepts, ideas, techniques, etc. in standard situations. They can use or apply them in the 'correct', prescribed way.	Demonstration and practice Role-plays Some case studies Simulations In-tray exercises Discussions	Demonstration and practice Supervised practice Coaching Assignments Projects Job rotation
4 Transfer	From all the concepts, ideas, procedures and techniques ever learned, learners can select the one most appropriate to a new, non-standard situation. They can modify or create new theories, ideas or tools to cope with unique situations where there are no 'right' answers.	Experimental learning situations Discovery learning Brainstorming Discussions Dialogues Group exercises Sensitivity training Diagnostic instruments and feedback	Counselling Job rotation Assignments Self-diagnosis instruments Process consultations Discovery learning

Figure 2.6   Pedler's learning methods by level of learning

Domain	Definition	Examples of methods
Cognitive	Knowledge of procedures, rules and regulations at various levels, issues at stake, etc.	Rote learning
Affective	Feelings and beliefs about the issues, your case, other side's case, fairness, justice, etc.	Values-clarification
Inter-personal	Ability to express self clearly, respond appropriately to other parties, develop trust and understanding with own team and other team.	Team-building
Self-knowledge	Knowledge of own behaviour under different conditions, strengths and weaknesses, likes and dislikes, etc.	Laboratory training

Figure 2.7   Analysis of negotiating behaviour by domains with examples of methods

to level 1 at the top. A study of Bloom's taxonomy, or the less elaborate one developed by Gronlund (1971), well repays the time and effort spent.

Simpson (1966) offered a taxonomy of objectives in the psychomotor domain, distinguishing five different levels (see Figure 2.4).

Pedler (1978) offered his own classification of objectives which were particularly relevant to types of field of management education and training. His schema adds two new domains, and merges some of the levels presented previously (see Figure 2.5).

In addition to revising the domains of learning, Pedler simplified and amended Bloom's six levels within the cognitive domain described earlier, to emphasize the four objectives most commonly sought by management educators in that domain: memory, understanding, application and transfer. Figure 2.6 shows how Pedler defines each of the four cognitive objectives; and offers a classification which relates the objectives to learning methods.

Pedler (1978) went on to provide an example of how a complex managerial behaviour such as negotiating spanned a number of learning objectives. To his example we can add examples of methods that could be used to help learners develop in these four areas (see Figure 2.7).

Despite some overlaps, Pedler's classification scheme helps one think about related learning objectives. When considering a typical manager's behaviour or competency, a number of these separate learning areas come together. Gage and Berliner (1979) made this point when they wrote:

> None of these kinds of behaviour is isolated from the others. While we are thinking, engaged in intellectual activity, we also experience emotions and display certain movements. When we are lost in feeling, swept away by a symphony or a poem, we are nonetheless thinking and posturing, i.e. engaged simultaneously in certain cognitive and psychomotor behaviours. And whenever we perform certain bodily movements - such as high diving or piano playing - we also think about how we move and have feelings about our performance.

'Number of learners' framework

Student numbers can impose severe limitations on the methods which can be used and the learning objectives that can be achieved. This is an important dimension on which to classify teaching and learning methods. Gage and Berliner (1979) referred to the 'quantitative and

Number	Label	Examples of methods	Description
1–2	Individual/dyad	Coaching Independent study Mentoring One-to-one learning	A few individuals have a learning need, e.g. a head of department needs to learn a foreign language.
3–16	Small group	Group project Role-playing Tutorial	Upper limit determined by number of groups which can report back during a 60-minute class.
17–24	Large group	Case study method Experiential exercise Short talks by students	Upper limit related to ease of face–name association, seating limitations and eye contact.
25+	Aggregate	Large groups as small groups Lecture Panel discussion Symposium meeting	Nameless faces and lecture seating constraints impede interactions between instructors and students.

Figure 2.8   Gage and Berliner's classification by group size with examples of methods

powerful determiner or at least correlate of teaching methods, namely, group size'. The focus of the work of these authors is on the US secondary school system. In management development, the numbers involved tend to be smaller. For this reason, Gage and Berliner's classification by group size has been somewhat adapted and is summarized in Figure 2.8. Classifying methods on the basis of student numbers can be carried out in combination with a classification based on the objectives to be achieved.

'Student autonomy level' framework

A third criterion for choice of method is the instructor's desired degree of student autonomy. In the 1960s, Wallen and Travers (1963) argued that 'probably on no other dimension do teaching methods differ more than on the matter of the exercise of control'. Within management development, the interest in this idea can be traced back to the early 1980s with the work on 'self-development approaches' (Boydell and Pedler, 1981). This has been paralleled in other areas of higher and post-experience education with discussions on how to increase autonomous student learning. The emphasis of these movements has been away from teaching towards placing greater responsibility on students for their own learning. Boud (1981) wrote: 'Autonomous learning is not an absolute standard to be met but a goal to be pursued; what is important is the direction – towards student responsibility for learning – not the magnitude of the changes in a given direction.' A framework for considering the degree of autonomy is provided by Percy and Ramsden (1980), which sets out the dimensions of freedom of choice available to students when they are confronted with a defined learning situation. The dimensions provide a straightforward way of analysing learning methods to determine the degree of freedom, and thus autonomy, they offer to the learner. They conceptualize the relationship between individualized and 'independent' study, and degrees of student independence, suggesting four linked stages:

1   Pace – Students can work at their own pace and choose the times (and sometimes the places) at which they find most appropriate to learn.

2   Choice – Students choose to work or not to work at a course, or at a part of a course.
3   Method – Students can decide the most suitable method of learning.
4   Content – Students choose what they want to learn according to their own goals and interests.

The notion of student control over content and method in the above schema necessarily subsumes that of control over pace and choice. The four dimensions – pace, choice, method and content of study – are those which immediately come to mind whenever student autonomy is discussed. There are, however, several others, which have been mentioned by Cornwall (1981) but which were omitted by Percy and Ramsden.

Cornwall suggested a hierarchy of independence in learning (see Figure 2.9). He suggested a number of levels relating to the provision of choice in different aspects of the curriculum. Each of these was likely to require a reorganization of a conventional 'teacher-prescribed, teacher-presented, teacher-paced and teacher-assessed course'. He was primarily concerned with learning in traditional institutions such as universities, but his hierarchy offers a set of questions which can assist in the categorization of student autonomy in general. Cornwall's levels are presented in increasing order of autonomy, level 1 being the highest.

The key differences in Cornwall's scheme are at the top and bottom of the hierarchy. At the bottom, managers may have little or no choice in becoming involved in a management develop-

	Definition	Question	Explanation	Examples of methods
1	Criteria for success	What should be the criteria for my success or failure?	Is the learner involved in setting criteria, or does someone else judge whether the person has done well or not?	Self-generated scaling
2	Assessment methods	How do I wish these objectives to be assessed?	Is the assessment system employed open for discussion and negotiation between staff and learners, or is it unilaterally imposed?	Appraisal module
3	Study objectives	What specific objectives will I pursue in my study?	What influence does the learner have in specifying the knowledge, attitude and skill learning objectives to be pursued?	Independent study
4	Mode of study	In what way will I study?	Is there a choice about learning methods or learning resources to be used?	Distance education Residential
5	Pace of study	How fast and when will I study?	Is the course fixed in time, or can the learner take a longer or shorter period to study?	Keller plan Individualized learning
6	Decision to enrol	Shall I join the course? Shall I participate in the activity?	The most basic level is concerned with choice in participation. In universities and companies, the question is whether the course is compulsory, or whether the learner can choose to attend.	

Figure 2.9 Cornwall's levels of student autonomy with examples of methods

ment exercise. They may be sent, or else pressured to 'volunteer'. At the top of the hierarchy, the references are to criteria to be used for assessing success. To what extent are learners involved in setting and agreeing such criteria and in choosing how they wish to be assessed? These crucial elements appear to be missing in Percy and Ramsden's listing.

Learning theories framework

In an article exploring the possibility of a grand, unified theory of learning, Burgoyne (1999) provides a valuable taxonomy of development methods based on the theories, models, principles, technologies and understandings of learning. First, he explains that each theory, approach or perspective suggests a certain 'model' of the learning process which guides professional practice in helping learning to occur. This practice is further guided by distinct 'principles of learning' – propositions about how learning should take place, and what instructors should do to ensure that it occurs. A particular understanding of how learning is believed to take place is contained within the descriptions and discussions of learning and teaching methods and techniques themselves; it underpins the discussion of the skills of training, educating and developing that are believed to be required (as well as their descriptions); and it is also implicit in assumptions about and discussions of technology and learning, most often information technology, and particularly computer-assisted learning.

Figure 2.10 shows schematically how these two types of decisions are related. The macro-decisions are shown on the vertical axis. It is the theoretical 'understandings' of learning by an

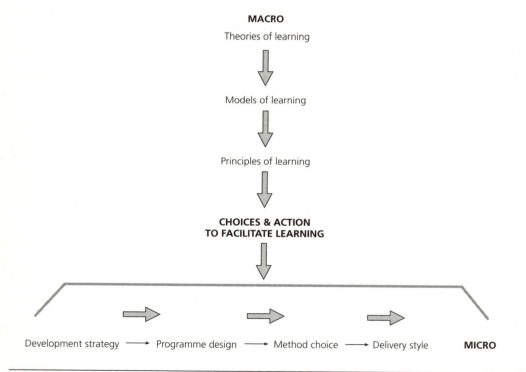

Figure 2.10 Locations of understandings of learning
Source: Burgoyne (1999)

individual or an institution that are embodied in these macro-level decisions. For example, a macro-level decision would be to use or reject distance-learning approaches, a resource-centre strategy or engage in outdoor training. These decisions shape the context in which the micro-level decisions are made, and are shown on the horizontal axis. They are concerned with detailed matters of exactly how managers are to be developed; when and for how long teaching will take place; how and where it will be done; and in what manner and by whom. Thus, the penultimate micro-decision in Burgoyne's schema is a person deciding between running an experiential exercise, organizing a role-play or showing a film. These micro-level decisions serve to implement the macro-level ones. An example of this is provided by the Harvard Business School, which espouses a theory of learning (macro-decision) that sets a learning context in which the case study method and its variants and associated methods (micro-decisions) predominate over all others.

A modified version of Burgoyne's model is presented in Figure 2.11, which distinguishes ten formal schools of thought or learning theories that an instructor, a training department or an entire organization might subscribe to. Each theory-school, and its adherents, has its own view of what learning is and the process through which it occurs. Building on Burgoyne's schema, we can summarize his definition of each theory-school's process and product, and then use this to suggest the type of teaching and learning methods (micro-level) that would implement the understanding (macro-level) for that school-theory. Some examples are shown in a new, fourth column, which complements Burgoyne's first three.

Conditioning

The conditioning school represents the behavioural psychology approach. It considers learning to be the establishment of a linkage between a stimulus and response in perception and behaviour. This approach sees the product of learning as habit, and the process as requiring the instructor to establish associations using positive and negative reinforcements. Numerous learning methods require learners to respond to stimuli which may be in the form of a question, problem or information requiring a decision. Students then receive feedback as to whether their answer, solution or choice was correct or not, and they are rewarded or penalized in terms of high or low marks awarded, or profit increases or reductions. Typical methods to be used here would be action maze, programmed simulation or business game. The common feature of all the methods in this category is that correct behaviour – whether in the form of answers or decisions – is rewarded, while incorrect behaviours are punished, and both responses are based on timely feedback provided to learners.

Trait modification

Trait modification theory sees learners as possessing a given set of characteristics, some of which may be changed by their involvement in learning. As a theory, it is more specific about learning as a product than learning as a process. In the management and organizational context, 'knowledge', 'skills' and 'attitudes' are the three broad trait categories which define learning goals and outcomes. It involves measuring people's traits and comparing their job profiles. The recently popular 'competency' approaches to managing learning are implicitly or explicitly based on this trait modification perspective. This theory necessarily raises debate over which individual characteristics are genetically determined, fixed and hence incapable of modification; and which might be changeable through the process of learning. It holds that not only are people different, they also learn in different ways. The methods in this category are

School of thought – learning theory	Learning process	Learning product	Examples of methods
1 Conditioning	Association Reinforcement	Habit	Action maze Business game Programmed simulation Synergogy
2 Trait modification	Learning style	Personality characteristic	Action profiling Instrumented laboratory Resource centre Keller plan
3 Information transfer	Memory	Public knowledge	Advance organizers Circulated lecture notes Mind Mapping Study skills training
4 Cybernetic/ Autopoietic	Adaptation	Survival	Behavioural simulation Team role theory Game Learning community
5 Cognitive	Gestalt information-processing	Personal knowledge	Repertory grid Gestalt techniques Concept mapping Cognitive-behavioural therapy Self-efficacy training
6 Humanistic/ Developmental	Growth, discovery	Development	Androgogy Rogersian counselling Values-clarification Moral development approach
7 Social influence	Socialization Identification	Identity, self-concept	Awareness training Career life planning Consciousness-raising group Role analysis technique Sociodrama
8 Psychoanalytic	Conscious/unconscious dynamic	Integration	Co-counselling Tavistock Conference Method Psychoanalytical approach Psychodrama Transactional Analysis
9 Existential	Action choice	Being, meaning	Creativity training Dramatic skit Music for learning Play for learning
10 Situated learning	Apprenticeship	Communal knowledge	Apprenticeship On-the-job learning Role-modelling

Figure 2.11 Modified version of Burgoyne's learning theories and schools of thought with examples of methods added

thus likely to fall into two categories: those which allow the learner and instructor to identify the traits possessed, such as action profiling, team role theory and instrumented laboratory; and those which offer different learning environments, allowing students to choose their own preferred approach from such radically different learning contexts as self-development, resource-centre and Keller Plan.

Information transfer

This approach treats the learning process as consisting of the transmission, communication, organization, storage and retrieval of information; and the product of learning as objective, truthful, publicly owned knowledge. The stress is on learning as memory, and pedagogical issues revolve around how learners can best be helped to input this information, internalize and organize it, store it, and retrieve it when required. The methods here emphasize the knowledge possessed by the instructors, and their responsibility to communicate it effectively to students. The student's role is to acquire such knowledge, develop ways to retain it in the memory, and then re-present it when required. It also extends to ways of applying such knowledge in various ways in different contexts. The methods listed from this perspective would emphasize efficiency and effectiveness of information coding and its transmission by the instructor, and its decoding, retention and reproduction by the learner: for example, advance organizers to set the context of the course content, circulated lecture notes to structure transmission, Mind Mapping to assist material retention, and study skills training to help students reproduce the material in the examination context.

Cybernetic/autopoietic

This approach goes beyond seeing the learner as a system interacting with their environment and adapting to it. It also contains the concept of autopoiesis, whereby the learner-as-a-system modifies their environment to their own benefit. The methods based on this theory of learning share the common feature of creating a learning environment, which may be artificial or real. In the past, these were predominantly business games, but more recently, with the help of advanced computer software and increased processing power, virtual organizations, virtual communities, virtual economies and virtual worlds have been developed. Learners explore their virtual environments, make changes to aspects of them, then observe the consequences. Also included under this heading would be methods which use the concept of interdependencies, of the relation of the parts to the whole, and of the need to adapt to the environment.

Cognitive

This school of thought sees the learning process as one in which learners develop their own mental model or cognitive map of themselves in their own situations, modify them to make sense of their experience, and act to achieve their goals. In this way they are using their own knowledge to regulate their own behaviour. From this learning perspective, the product of learning is subjective, personal knowledge. The common feature of methods in this category is that they elicit from the learner their personal, internal view, in terms of values, perceptions, beliefs, and then go on to either represent them back to the learner, or more commonly, to compare them with the views of others. The best-known of these methods is probably repertory grid, while concept mapping has found popularity both as a research and a learning tool. In terms of applying the mental models and maps, cognitive behavioural therapy and self-efficacy training have been offered by a number of companies.

Humanistic or developmental

This school of thought acknowledges an emotional, affective dimension to learning, while retaining a focus on the intellectual and cognitive one. It sees learning as helping individuals to move towards a 'fully developed' personal state which will allow them to lead a full, fulfilling life. Some writers within this school have gone beyond the affective domain to address personal, moral and ethical issues. The common feature of methods in this category are that they do not restrict themselves to the cognitive domain of learning which was defined and described earlier. Instead, they attempt to blend cognitive with other domains – mainly, but not exclusively, the affective. The school and its methods aims to help learners achieve a balance between differing internal states, such as male and female attributes, right brain and left brain, yin and yang, and so on. Examples of methods which demonstrate such an integrating function include androgynous management, Rogerian counselling, values clarification, and the moral development approach.

Social influence

The sociological and social psychological perspectives reject the individual, psychologistic orientation of the earlier schools of thought, and views learners as a product of their social context. The common feature of methods in this category is that they consider how an individual's identity – individual and professional – is perceived and shaped by others. Stress is placed upon learners' self-concept formation and on their perceptions of those around them. The methods provide the tools with which the focal person can explore themselves in relation to those around them, and also receive information from these others. The concept of socialization, as a process and as an outcome, is a prime focus in this perspective. Beyond personal identity, methods concentrate on the acquisition of technical skills as a way of securing or enhancing an occupational role, but in terms of reputation rather than actual task performance. Thus, career life-planning exercises can provide a vehicle for self-reflection and help answer not only the question 'Who am I?', but also 'How did I get here?' Similarly, role analysis techniques permit an exploration of an organizational role. Both methods pay as much attention to contextual factors as to the individual.

Psychoanalytic

The common feature of methods based on the psychoanalytical school of learning is that they all, in some way, use the concept of the unconscious, and of various forces and sources of energy, to offer interpretations of experience and behaviour. This school provides a theoretical basis for a whole class of therapeutic programmes which tend to originate in the clinical area, but subsequently cross over to the managerial field. Another aspect of this school is the explanation of leadership styles and organizational performance in terms of managerial personalities. Methods which emphasise assisted individual exploration, one-to-one counselling and certain types of group-based experiences, mainly those provided by the Tavistock Institute, would come under this heading.

Existential

As a philosophical point of view, existentialism challenges the traditional assumptions about learning which hold that ideas, beliefs, thoughts and decision-making precede and determine action. Sartre's existentialism proposes that action *precedes* and *generates* meaning. From this perspective, learning and creativity are closely allied. Wilful action in a domain not pre-structured by existing meaning and habits generates new meanings. Perhaps the creativity-focused methods, as well as those which emphasize play, drama, humour and music, would fall most appropriately into this category.

Situated learning

This school stresses the collective, local and informal nature of much learning, emphasizing 'communities of practice'. From this perspective, learning outcomes exist in 'communities of practice' that share a way of doing things. Individuals come to share this collective learning through a process of 'legitimate peripheral participation' from which they are slowly incorporated into collective practice and community membership. Apprenticeship, on-the-job learning, socialization and role-modelling would be typical methods.

Will there ever be one best way of classifying development methods, let alone a way of selecting the most appropriate ones for a task? It is unlikely for at least two reasons. First, the selection of a method is based on the personal philosophy of the teacher. Burgoyne and Stuart (1978) noted that the 'design of management development programmes is usually seen by practitioners in the field as a matter of choosing the methods appropriate to the content of what they want to teach or the learning they hope to bring about'. Burgoyne's more recent work cited above (Burgoyne, 1999) distinguishes these personal philosophies in terms of different theories and schools of thought, and reinforces his earlier point that development methods are merely ready-made assumptions about learning processes, and that these assumptions can be varied by the manner in which the methods are applied. Thus, for trainers and instructors, the methods are not 'out there', to be chosen from some sort of list or menu, but are instead 'inside them', waiting to be implemented when a suitable opportunity arises.

A second reason why a simple framework for selecting methods is unlikely to be developed relates to the nature of learning in general, and to the many-faceted tasks of management in particular. The competency research reminds us that the behaviours required of a successful manager are complex, and span the different learning domains and the different levels within each domain. It is therefore impossible to select a single appropriate method; many are likely to be needed. Gage and Berliner (1979) wrote:

> Not all teaching methods are equally appropriate for helping students to attain all instructional objectives ... The question – what method of teaching is best? – really has no answer unless one specifies the characteristics of the students and the objectives of the teaching. The student's age, intelligence, motivational background of previous learning and achievement in the subject matter of the teaching are important factors to consider.

This comment hints at the possibility of selecting methods on the basis of the preferred learning styles of the students, which certainly has an intuitive, customer-orientated, common-sense appeal. Reynolds (1997) defines this process of method–student matching as the 'simplistic proposition that if a learning style can be measured, it should be possible to provide a consistent teaching method. Thus someone who scores high on "abstract conceptualization" will thrive on books and lectures, while someone who has a high score on "concrete experience" will learn best from practical projects or experiential activities' (Reynolds, 1997, p. 130). In the USA, Kolb has produced a Learning Styles Inventory (LSI), while in the UK, Honey and Mumford (1992) have developed a Learning Styles Questionnaire (LSQ) to establish individuals' learning preferences. LSQ results are used to identify each learner as an Activist, Reflector, Theorist or Pragmatist. Development methods are then selected which match that preferred style. One can envisage how, using this approach, course members would be selected on the basis of questionnaire results to produce a homogeneous group of each type (Honey and Mumford, 1992). Thus, there would be four different types of 'Introduction to Leadership' course, one to match each of the four preferred learning styles (Mumford, 1998a, 1998b).

Reynolds goes on to provide a convincing critique of such an approach. Among the points he makes are the following. He notes the failure of Kolb's LSI instrument to distinguish between people's learning approaches, and he points to an empirical mismatch between LSI profiles and expressed preferences for teaching methods. He discusses the educational value of creating a conscious, creative mismatch between preferred learner style and learning method, and is doubtful whether learning is a process independent of external factors. He challenges the notion that students possess inherent, invariant styles of learning, and suggests that more attention should be paid to the social and institutional environment created for education and development. Finally, he challenges the view that a person's experience of, or reaction to, a particular method is either uni-dimensional or predictable. Reynolds' critique reminds us how simple, intuitively appealing approaches to the choice of methods each bring their own problems and that, in the end, it is the judgement of the instructor or tutor, based on internal and external factors, which determines which method is chosen.

Analytical framework for assessing management development methods

This analytical framework is not a taxonomy. It does not present general category labels such as interaction rules, learning theories or schools of thought, under which one might group the entries in this encyclopedia, since this was covered in the previous section. Nor does the analytical framework seek to relate one development method to another. What it does provide is a tool which helps instructors to think about the methods they use in their work. The framework presented here was developed by Alex Main and Andrzej Huczynski.

Introduction

The analytical framework is built around three dimensions: 'Content', 'Process' and 'Setting' (see Figure 2.12). To identify the primary content focus of a teaching or learning method, one asks the question: 'What have I designed or adopted the method for?' There are likely to be several answers to this question, but it is the most important of these which constitutes the primary focus. The first column of Figure 2.12 presents ten possible content foci, from which the primary one would be chosen.

In a similar way, an indication of the primary process focus of one's method can be obtained by asking the question: 'What does the method stress in its execution?' In this case, eight possible process foci are suggested. The concern is with how things are done. The third and final dimension is concerned with the ethos of the method of organization. One's view or personal philosophy about how people learn and develop colours the setting in which the

Content* focus	Process focus	Setting focus
Subject	Individual learning	Teaching
Task	Self-learning	
		Learning
	Group learning	
	Group facilitation	Counselling
Learning		
Experience	Teacher/trainer	Inspirational
	Community	Apprenticeship
Structures	Resource-based	Discipleship
	Feedback system	Revelatory
Modelling		
Mirroring		
Procedures		
Practices		
Principles		

Figure 2.12   Framework for analysing management development methods
Note: *Also labelled 'Objectives' or 'Levels of understanding'

learning or teaching takes place. Seven potential setting foci are listed, to help tutors reflect on their own ethos. The function of the framework is to help individual tutors or teachers reflect on the methods and approaches they use in their work, and this personal reflection is structured around the foci of Content, Process and Setting. Whenever instructors are asked to describe a learning situation they have designed, their descriptions are likely to include a reference to the content of the method ('What it was used to teach') and to its process ('How things happened'). After further questioning, they are likely to reveal their philosophy of learning ('How they believe people learn'). It is therefore argued that a method-in-use, as opposed to some abstract or 'ideal type' definition of it, can be described in terms of its three primary foci (see Figure 2.13).

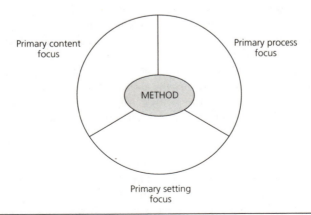

Figure 2.13   Management development methods defined by primary foci

Primary content focus

A teaching or learning method is not an abstract entity, but something that relates to actual *content*. Method can relate to content in at least two ways: first, in terms of subject content (for example, in the study of finance, organizational behaviour, interviewing, etc.); a second type of content is concerned with what you have designed or adopted the method for. This might be described as the content of the method. Looking at the 'Content' column in Figure 2.12, a number of items in it would, in the eyes of many teachers, belong more properly in the 'Process' column. In using the framework, trainers can ask whether their content objectives for a particular session are reflected in the process of the method – in their involvement and that of their students. Modelling, for example, makes many assumptions about the appropriate types of activity and levels of involvement. In deciding on the primary content focus of a teaching or learning method, one needs to ask the question: 'What does the method stress in its concepts and activities?' This has to be answered with respect not only to concepts, but also to activities.

To omit activities would mean not accepting the assumption made here, that the very content of a method is bound up with its activities – those in which you are actually involved. Similarly, one's learning objectives must always be part of what one is doing, rather than being perceived as being somehow 'out there'. The idea of a content focus is not intended to imply that content is separate from process or from setting; rather, as one takes each dimension in turn and considers it with respect to a method used, it is possible to identify the way the particular method will emphasize a particular feature. In doing this, one gets away from considering the dimensions as being mutually exclusive lists and begins to view them in terms of relative emphasis. Behind each *primary* content focus in the list there is also usually a *secondary* focus, and one needs to decide whether a given focus is primary or secondary. A number of possible content method foci are presented below.

Subject and task
It is possible to differentiate a subject-focus from a task-focus in content. This is a familiar distinction in management education and training. A teaching method which concentrates on 'that which people have to do' would be task-focused, whereas one which stressed 'that which people must understand or must assimilate into their knowledge structures' would be subject-focused. When a tutor devises a learning activity, among the earliest decisions is whether to deal with people's behaviour or with helping them to learn knowledge or acquire understanding. There is no claim that these two foci are mutually exclusive but, in terms of primary focus, such a distinction may be valid. Task is content, in that if one uses a learning or teaching method to help people perform or do something as opposed to know or accept something, then the primary content focus of the whole effort is the task they are going to perform, even though they may not necessarily perform that task using the learning method. It is important to check that the process mirrors the content. For example, on training courses for new university staff, when a tutor lectures, they are obviously using the teaching method 'lecture'. When that lecture is about lecturing, then it is about task – the primary content focus of the lecture as a teaching method is the task of lecturing. The process itself is the task, and the content is the task. They mirror each other and come together well. However, on the same course one may have a person lecturing about student learning. That is no longer task-focused, but becomes instead subject-focused. The same would be true with counselling. When one lectures people about a university counselling system, then it becomes a subject. If I lectured to you about counselling itself, the focus would remain the subject if you were not a counsellor, nor intended to be one, and your only interest in the topic was as a subject of

study. However, if one learns about counselling and develops counselling skills through being counselled, then the focus becomes the task. Whenever a task is elevated into a 'bit of knowledge', one shifts from a task-focus to a subject-focus.

Experience and learning
One can see experience and learning as one step removed from subject and task. Learning is one step away from subject, while experience is one step away from task. Learning is to subject what experience is to task. It is as if content had veered away from the specific subject matter towards a whole set of activities which surrounded the subject. This would be people's (personal) learning about the subject. In the same way, when they perform a task they develop experience. Experience develops out of task activity. Therefore, the primary content focus of a method may be experience rather than task, or learning rather than subject.

In a simulated group problem-solving task such as the Lego-man building exercise, the primary content focus for the observers is either on learning or experience, depending on how the activity is designed by the tutor. In their role as observers, the teaching method as it applies to them is concentrating on experience and learning, not on task or subject. The primary content focus of most debriefing sessions will be learning. An important point to mention is that in using a particular teaching method there may be different phases in the use of that method in which the primary content focus changes. Thus, in this list of proposed contents, the individual entries are not necessarily alternatives, but may be foci which flow into each other. The relationship between subject, task, learning and experience has been described, and one can see these four foci as constituting a single grouping which can be distinguished in qualitative terms from the next focus: structures.

Structures
'Structures' refers to any kind of link, framework or logistical diagram whose purpose is to help organize knowledge into some meaningful pattern for the learner. A structures-focus in content may be concerned with the examination of the structures that have evolved in the student's learning, or those links which may have evolved within a working group. It is possible to conceive of subject moving out to learning and then moving out still further to structures. A similar progression may be observed with task, through experience to structures, as shown in Figure 2.14.

In a debriefing, one can concentrate the learner's mind on the structures of the learning that have been evolved. One can examine how knowledge has taken on a certain format in the learner's mind, and question how relevant that is for a particular situation. Equally, the experiences participants have derived from tasks can be examined in terms of their structures because

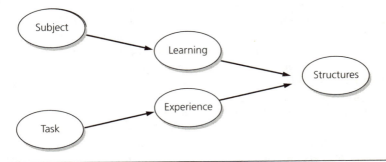

Figure 2.14   Relationship of subject, learning, task and experience foci to structures

one's experience relates to other people's, as in the case of a group or dyad. Equally, the experiences of a person as a student, and that of another as a teacher in a teaching learning situation can be structured, and examining these structures may be important for further learning and development. In many experiential learning situations, there are members who say that they enjoyed the activity, found the experience involving, learned a lot, but that their learning was very fragmented. In essence, they are saying that they did not have a framework or structure within which to integrate their new knowledge. Without this, they are unable to relate it to anything else, and are therefore unable to make further use of it. In such situations, there would be a need for a debriefing session with the persons concerned, which could help them explore the possible links or logistics, and provide them with an opportunity to both reflect on the learning and to integrate it.

Those participants who found a session enjoyable and useful but who felt unable to apply the learning may have 'blocked' on it – they may have taken part in an exercise which was so far removed from their daily activities that they were unable to make the necessary link between the two. They may need help to approximate to their work situation through finding metaphors and parallels in their own sphere of activity. Such activity concentrates almost entirely on the structures of knowledge and the structure of teaching, as opposed to experience gained through doing a task or the learning which surrounds a particular subject.

Modelling and mirroring

There is a second grouping of contents which is qualitatively different from the first, which contained subject, task, learning and experience. In discussing modelling and mirroring, it is clear that one could easily be discussing a process, and people usually use these terms in that way. For example, in modelling, one learns by copying someone else, and in mirroring, one learns by observing oneself doing something and making an analysis of it. However, in the present list, modelling and mirroring are seen as content foci. This is because when a teacher devises a learning situation, they are frequently conscious of whether the whole thing is centred on an assumption about modelling or mirroring. For example, if one gives a lecture on the topic of lecturing, for most of the time one demonstrates the method, although one also talks about the method and hopes that the demonstration of the method harmonizes with what is being said about it. However, confusion can arise concerning the teacher's intentions. Do they want the audience to look at them and say, 'That's how I should lecture,' or should they be thinking, 'Is the way he is lecturing the way I ought to be doing it?' In the first case, the content is modelling, while in the second it is mirroring. When the two elements are in harmony, there is no problem, but when they become separated – as when the lecture runs over time, the overhead projector fails to work or when the teacher cannot be heard at the back of the room – it is necessary to be clear about one's aims. Did the teacher want the audience to use them as a model, or did they want the listeners to take in the ideas presented? The point here is that it is not what teachers *do*, but the *content of what they do* which is the modelling situation. It is the content which focuses on the modelling. Moreover, it is not just the content of the teacher's lecture presentation which is being modelled, but also its structure, its ethos, its value structure and the preparation that went into it.

There are methods of teaching other than the lecture where the primary content focus is not modelling but mirroring. For example, a trainer may put individuals into a group and ask them to do certain things and take part in certain activities. Here, the participants are not being asked to model, but rather to mirror by saying things and doing things to each other. The teacher creates a situation in which the primary content focus is the mirroring the participants do for each other. One example might be a group task which involves persons taking leadership roles. During the exercise, members might reflect on whether the leadership behaviour being exhibited by another individual was the same as or different from their own. All of this is being achieved through the content of the method, not the process, because the facilitator has not explicitly stopped the activity to look at what has happened. It is content because, in constructing the situation, the tutor allowed the participants to concentrate on seeing themselves, observing themselves and judging themselves.

A relevant question to ask here is whether the difference between modelling and mirroring in method content terms is dependent on the conscious design of the tutor, or on what the learner chooses to take away from the activity. A response might be that what the learner takes away is more dependent on the process than on the actual content. Content can be viewed as the conscious design of the teacher. When a subject is taught in a traditional way, such as how to use a pocket calculator, what the learner takes away from this interaction is the result of the process, not the content. The actual content is what the teacher puts in, and in a sense is still there whether the student takes it away or not. Consider another example. A method such as guided group problem-solving contains the potential for mirroring rather than modelling. Most group situations, especially those in universities, tend to have modelling as the primary content focus. The group leader, usually a lecturer, wants people to behave according to their model of the 'good contributor'. In contrast, in the group problem-solving situation, there is the opportunity for participants to mirror their problem-solving skills.

Procedures, practices and principles

These form the third grouping in the list of primary content foci. The distinction between procedures, practices and principles can be clarified by analogy. The *procedures* of the law concern the way in which the law is actually discharged. The focus is on how individuals are charged, how people are called to account, how they are dealt with in the courts, and so on. The *practices* of the law are one abstract step away from the procedures, but they are not yet the *principles* of the law. The practices have to do with the judgements that people make regarding the application of the principles. They are not, however, concerned with the 'hands-on' aspects of the procedures. When one uses a particular teaching method, it is possible to concentrate a great deal on the procedures people will have to go through, as opposed to emphasizing the element of making judgements and seeing these judgements reach an action point. Equally, some teaching methods take principles as their primary content focus, and thereby move towards a subject- or structures-focus.

In any subject, be it chemistry, physiology or psychology, one can separate out procedures, practices and principles. Consider the operation of some problem-solving programmes which use a problem-solving laboratory. The students who attend the programme will be exposed to a number of different primary content foci. Some of the teaching methods used, especially the more didactic ones that will precede some of the activity-oriented ones, will concentrate on the principles and theories of creative problem-solving. They may stress the use of certain problem-solving strategies. Other approaches in the programme will use interactive methods, whereby students examine problems together and observe each other's attempts to reach a solution. These would have practices as their primary content focus, since they would be looking at how students have understood some of the principles and how they see them as relating to the particular subject matter or problem. In contrast, a third set of activities in the programme would involve the actual solution of problems and the testing of alternative solutions to problems. This would demonstrate a *procedures*-focus, since what was being dealt with there would be the actual 'bits of equipment' that were not working, or with paper-and-pencil tests, circuit diagrams, chemical bonding or whatever the subject content was.

Primary process focus

The second column in Figure 2.12 considers the Primary Process Focus of a teaching or learning method. The concern is with *how* things are done, and the question is asked: 'What does the method stress in its execution?' Process is concerned with 'doing'.

Individual learning and self-learning

In individual learning, the primary process focus is on the person *learning for themself*, but usually in a situation which has been structured by others. It is this emphasis on 'for themself' that distinguishes this process from other group learning situations, where one may be learning *through* a group, *for* a group or even *with* a group. Individual learning can be contrasted with self-learning, which is characterized by the student *learning by themself*. In individual learning, the tutor may have devised some materials which the learner then uses to work on their own, whereas in self-learning, the learner goes out and searches for the material themself. The material will not have been structured for them. The two foci may flow into each other. An example of self-learning may be a manager who wishes to understand which type of leadership style they ought to use. They observe different managers working, note their different styles and identify their different interactional behaviours. Having done this, they may then indulge in individual learning in order to place their observations into some framework, or perhaps in order to identify the different organizational contexts in which a particular leadership style might be most effective. To do this, they may be supplied with notes, guided reading or a programmed text which they complete on their own.

Group learning and group facilitation

Counselling skills may be acquired through group learning. For example, managers may take part in different experiential activities where they find out a great deal about themselves through the group. Group learning is distinguished from group facilitation by the fact that in the latter, one becomes able to do certain things and acquires certain skills, not through taking part in experiential group activities, but by being part of a group which facilitates one's learning. For example, membership of a certain workgroup may allow a manager to develop certain diagnostic skills rapidly. In group facilitation, the group concerned would not deliberately set out to teach its members specific skills or knowledge. The member would learn these informally through group membership.

Teacher/trainer

There is a well-known process in which a teacher or a trainer is in command, and it is they who direct and carry out a learning/teaching activity. Under this heading, one could include not only didactic processes ('Get up and tell them'), but also those forms of group activity where the primary process is the trainer, not the group. In such circumstances, the trainer is not asking the group 'How is it?', but is saying, 'Do this, do that.' Examples of this primary process focus would include micro-labs, tutorials and seminars. In these cases, the group learning or group facilitation focus may be the secondary one.

Community

This term is intended to include activities such as teaching by learning and study service, where the focus is on the community at large. It may involve students leaving the classroom situation to undertake an activity which is outside their learning. Community as a primary process focus is intended to be broadly defined. It takes in practical activities such as placement, and some aspects of 'sitting by Nellie', as represented in the training of health visitors and district nurses. A community-focused process usually involves a larger group of people than merely the learners themselves. Moreover, it has to be a larger group to whom the learners relate in some structured way. All examples of community-focused methods come from service occupations where the training demands a lot of feedback from those to whom the service is being provided. Doctors, for example, are community-trained, even though the community concerned may be the hospital.

Resource-based

There are methods where the primary process focus is on the resources, not on activities or experiences. Some rigid forms of Keller plan teaching exemplify a situation where the resources take over completely and thereby de-emphasize the actual activities and interactions involved. Another example would be programmed learning, which overlaps a little with what has been described as an individual learning focus.

Feedback system

Since feedback systems are involved to some degree in all the previous foci described, they have been left until last. There are some teaching and learning methods where the primary focus is on the feedback, not on the group or the trainer or on the resources. For example, many forms of counselling training fall into this area, as does inter-personal process recall, video confrontation, micro-teaching and instrumented laboratory.

Primary setting focus

The third column in Figure 2.12 considers the primary setting focus. This concerns the *ethos* of the method of organization, and the orientation of its organizers and designers. It has to do with the way in which one puts things together, and the philosophy and values which underlie that choice.

Teaching

The values inherent in the way you organize a teaching/learning situation can focus a great deal on teaching. There is a whole educational philosophy which says, 'I teach you something.'

Learning

On the other hand, there is another philosophy which says, 'You learn, and I will facilitate that learning.'

Counselling

Yet another philosophy says, 'I listen and try to understand your learning needs and help you to identify not only those needs, but also the resources which can help you fulfil those needs.'

Inspirational

Over and above the teaching ethos, it is possible to construct situations in which people really become motivated, not necessarily by the form of the teaching, although this is possible, but by the *dynamics* of the teaching. For example, there are some forms of confrontation and example-building that can inspire people to learn. Equally, there are forms of lecturing and problem-centred teaching which can be classed as inspirational.

Apprenticeship

The apprenticeship model is also an ethos, since it is underpinned by a great many assumptions about how people learn, and why they should learn in that way.

Discipleship

Discipleship is differentiated from apprenticeship as an ethos because the latter tends to be more structured, more formal, and usually has rules. Discipleship is a situation in which the learner attaches themself to a particular person, 'school of thought' or group. There is the idea of 'following the leader'. At one time, medical education had a discipleship ethos, when each consultant had their own following. It was not apprenticeship, because consultants did not deign to show their followers how to do things. They followed in the consultant's wake and tried to ape and imitate, but to also go beyond. Discipleship is an ethos which is usually characterized by uncritical involvement of the learner.

Revelatory

A revelatory ethos is common in many group learning situations such as counselling training or in group therapy. The ethos underlying this form of teaching is that there is no rigid pattern to people's learning, but there is an implicit belief that people will have insight. It stems from the idea that a lot of learning comes from sudden flashes of inspiration and insight. This ethos can be seen in those modern learning methods which deal in experience and sharing, and where people have revelations about what they ought to do next.

Let us illustrate the point that a management development method is defined more by the form of its use by its user than by the innate characteristics of the method itself. Four different methods are selected from the encyclopedia are random. Since lecturers or trainers are likely to use the same methods in different ways, each one has to be asked the three questions listed in Figure 2.15, to elicit their different intentions about method application.

Question	Primary focus
What did the method emphasize most in terms of its concepts and activities?	Content
What did it stress in its execution?	Process
What was the ethos of its organization and the orientation of its user?	Setting

Figure 2.15 Management development methods: focus and question

If, as is likely, they used the same methods differently, their answers to the three questions will be different, and hence the 'profile' of their particular method-in-use is likely to differ. Thus, for one of the trainers questioned about how they used the four methods listed, their answers might yield the profile shown in Figure 2.16. Another trainer, using the same four methods might, if questioned, reveal a totally different profile.

The purpose of the framework and its questions is not to group similar methods together on the basis of some criteria, but to test the internal consistency of a method which one may be already using. Instructors can refer to the definitions of the three primary foci – content, process and setting – and familiarize themselves with the options under each. They can then think back over a method which they used during a recent session and ask themselves the

Method	Content focus	Process focus	Setting focus
Study skills training	Learning	Individual learning	Counselling
One-to-one learning	Experience	Feedback system	Apprenticeship
Trigger film	Modelling	Group facilitation	Revelatory
Role-play	Experience	Group learning	Revelatory

Figure 2.16 Management development method profiles

questions listed in Figure 2.15. Their answers will reveal their distinctive profile of method usage, and can indicate the effectiveness or lack of effectiveness of a method. For example, a trainer may believe that they are being inspirational, but on analysis may discover that they are in fact being highly teaching–oriented, and that they place great emphasis on themself as the trainer and on structures. In such a situation, it is possible to understand why the trainer was unable to motivate their trainees to either change or innovate.

The three columns suggest a complementary relationship. There are certain limited combinations of complementary content, process and setting mixes, but there are many other combinations which are incompatible. The triple column listing does not have the characteristics of the well-known 'random buzz word generator', where all mixes are possible. The reader is invited to consider which mixes are feasible. In the analytical framework described, other dimensions may be possible which have not been included. The framework is merely offered as a tool which tutors and trainers can use to reflect on the teaching/learning methods they use in order to help their students learn.

This analytical framework also suggests why it is very unlikely that any useful management development method schema will ever be developed, and hence why there is no attempt to provide one in this book: knowing what precisely is meant by the term 'group discussion' or 'lecture' well enough to be able to classify it is rare. On its own, each label says nothing about the nature of the interactions between the persons involved. Two lectures on quality management may be conducted in two such radically different ways that it would be wrong to refer to these two activities using the same label. Binstead et al. (1980) reported that management teachers tended to perceive the same teaching method label in different ways. The same is likely to be true of organizational change facilitators and consultants. Binstead et al. held that the label we give to a management development approach or teaching method is insufficient to convey the detail or the spirit of the event, and that this spirit is itself a function of the particular teacher or facilitator and their audience. While this observation is generally valid, it is nevertheless also true that when confronted with the terms 'lecture' or 'group discussion', most teachers recognize both the denotation of each word or phrase and some of its connotations. Each term does conjure up in their minds a picture of specific activities and behaviours which are guided by certain communication sequences and interaction rules. However, beyond this very general level there is unlikely to be sufficient agreement between different people to produce a useful framework for selecting methods.

References

Binstead, D., Stuart, R. and Long, G. (1980) 'Promoting Useful Management Learning: Problems of Translation and Transfer', in Beck, J. and Cox, C. (eds) *Advances in Management Education*, Wiley.

Bloom, B.S., Engelhart, M.B., Furst, E.J., Hill, W.H. and Krathwohl, D.R. (1956) *Taxonomy of Educational Objectives. The Classification of Educational Goals Handbook 1: Cognitive Domain*, Longmans Green.

Boud, D.J. (ed.) (1981) *Developing Autonomy in Student Learning*, Kogan Page.

Boydell, T. and Pedler, M. (eds) (1981) *Management Self-Development: Concepts and Practices*, Gower.

Burgoyne, J.G. (1999) 'Learning: Conceptual, Practical and Theoretical Issues', unpublished manuscript.

Burgoyne, J.G. and Stuart, R. (1978) 'Teaching and Learning Methods in Management Development', *Personnel Review*, vol. 7, no. 1, pp. 53–8.

Cornwall, M. (1981) 'Putting It Into Practice: Promoting Independent Learning in a Traditional Institution', in Boud, D.J. (ed.) (1981) *Developing Autonomy in Student Learning*, Kogan Page.

Gage, N.L. and Berliner, C. (1979) *Educational Psychology* (2nd edn), Rand McNally.

Gronlund, N.E. (1971) *Measurement and Evaluation in Teaching*, Macmillan.

Honey, P. and Mumford, A. (1992) *Manual of Learning Styles* (3rd edn), Honey Publishing.

Krathwohl, D.R., Bloom, B.S. and Masia, B.B. (1964) *Taxonomy of Educational Objectives, Handbook 2: Affective Domain*, David McKay.

Mumford, A. (1998a) 'Choosing Development Methods', *Organisations and People*, vol. 5, no. 2, pp. 32–8.

Mumford, A. (1998b) *How to Choose the Right Development Method*, Honey Publishing.

Pedler, M. (1974) 'Learning in Management Education', *Journal of European Training*, vol. 3, no. 3, pp. 182–94.

Pedler, M. (1978) 'Negotiating Skills Training Part 4: Learning To Negotiate', *Journal of European Industrial Training*, vol. 2, no. 1, pp. 20–5.

Percy, K. and Ramsden, P. (1980) *Independent Study: Two Examples from English Higher Education*, Society for Research into Higher Education.

Reynolds, M. (1997) 'Learning Styles: A Critique', *Management Learning*, vol. 28, no. 2, pp. 115–33.

Simpson, E.J. (1966), 'A Slightly Tongue-in-cheek Device for Teacher Cognition', *Illinois Teacher of Home Economics*, vol. 10, no. 4, Winter.

Wallen, N.E. and Travers, R.M.W. (1963) 'Analysis and Investigation of Teaching Methods', in Gage, N.L. (ed.) *Handbook of Research on Teaching*, Rand McNally.

3 Organizational change method classification frameworks

It is possible for organizational change methods to involve a company-wide programme of management training and development courses. However, they are more likely to use a different set of approaches which are frequently referred to as 'interventions'. Consultants are brought in to intervene in the way the organization is currently working, and to make changes designed to move it in the direction considered desirable. Frameworks for classifying different organizational change methods can be based on:

- the general problem or opportunity being addressed
- the form of the intervention itself
- the target of the intervention effort
- the specific issue at which the intervention is being focused
- a combination of any of these.

With respect to organizational change interventions, one can note that a number of attempts have been made by different authors to classify them. The objective of these different frameworks is to help the manager or consultant select the most appropriate change approach. The problem with any classification scheme is that the placing of anything as ambiguous as an organizational change technique will inevitably be approximate. As long as this is borne in mind, the frameworks described in this chapter will be useful.

A number of different frameworks for classifying organizational change are presented below, arranged broadly in terms of increasing complexity.

Business issues framework

A business issues framework simply lists the key concerns of companies at a point in time, and identifies intervention methods that might be relevant. The Preface referred to Murray's (1998) summary of the seven current business issues identified by the Association for Management Education and Development (see Figure 3.1). The problems or opportunities to be tackled suggest a grouping of intervention methods. These are the tools that trainers, lecturers and consultants would apply to deal with the issue specified. For illustrative purposes, following Murray's description, the author has suggested a few of the available management development and organizational change methods that might be employed.

Leavitt framework

Harold Leavitt (1964) suggested that organizations could be viewed as complex systems which consist of four mutually interacting independent classes of variables: task, technology, structure and people (see Figure 3.2). All of these were affected by the organization's environment, such as the economic, political and social situation.

Business issue	Examples of methods
1 Humanizing work	Confidence-building training Job design Product familiarization programme
2 Globalization	Diversity training Overseas project Cross-cultural sensitivity training
3 Stakeholders and management	Customer interface meeting Organizational mirror Role analysis Development of a new management/operating philosophy
4 Sustainability	Attitude-changing Behaviour modification Corporate culture training Ideological change
5 High performance	ACHIEVE model Benchmarking Self-development
6 Working across boundaries	Manager exchange Intervisitation Inter-organizational information-sharing
7 Ethics in organizational life and development	Moral philosophy approach Participative design On-going feedback system Assessment of the organization as a system

Figure 3.1   Murray's 21st-century development themes with examples of change methods

Leavitt also argued that change could be directed at any one of the four variables. He called these the *entry points* for interventions to bring about organizational change. In practice, a number of different entry points are used in combination. Nevertheless, the distinction he makes is useful, and offers an intervention methods classification system. Managers and consultants who wish to introduce organizational change in a conscious and planned way can intervene at the task, technology, structure or people levels.

Task interventions

The task, goal or mission of an organization is the reason for its existence. The task may range from manufacturing computers to refining and selling oil to curing patients.

Technology interventions

Technology is not a personal computer or an assembly line. An organization's technology consists of *apparatus* (tools, machines); *techniques* (skills, methods, procedures, routines) and *social arrangements* (factories, teams, units). Technologically–based intervention strategies can

Variable	Examples of change methods
Task	Developing a new management/operating philosophy
	Ideological change
	Strategic management
	Strategic planning process
Technology	Quality circles
	Customer interface meeting
	Deming method
	Skunkworks
Structure	Autonomous workgroups
	Matrix design
	Job enrichment
	Job descriptions
People	Team-building
	Sensitivity training
	Role-negotiation
	Career counselling

Figure 3.2   Leavitt's four-variable framework with examples of change methods

involve all of these. For example, internal team communication and development can be facilitated by means of an intranet. Equally, the management of quality can be facilitated by the use of quality circles, customer interface meetings or the use of the Deming method. Finally, social arrangements can be devised which foster creative activity away from the mainstream working arrangements.

Structure interventions

An organization's structure refers to the pattern of authority relationships, the distribution of responsibilities among employees, and the design of the communication and work flows within a company. In the past, structural modification has been a popular intervention strategy. Managers and consultants have made changes to job definitions, the design of jobs, role relationships, areas of responsibility and spans of control. Both communication patterns and decision-making processes can be altered. Organizations can either decentralize or centralize decisions, giving more or less autonomy to their junior staff. The effects of a structural alteration are to change a person's job responsibilities, and change their relationship with other members of the organization. The consequence, at the individual level, is to alter the employee's experience within the company. Examples of structural interventions include job enrichment programmes and autonomous workgroups.

People interventions

The people in an organization are its workforce – managers, technical staff, secretaries, shop-floor personnel. They constitute the organizational members or employees. People interventions are probably the most popular organizational change strategy. This popularity stems from the belief that changing people is the least disruptive strategy for the organization, even though it may not be the easiest or the most straightforward. The various techniques used claim to be able to change people's behaviour, attitudes, inter-personal skills, values and motives. The many different people-modification approaches can be combined in different ways to achieve the change objective. Most of the techniques which form the organizational development toolkit are people-change ones.

The organizational change approaches described in this encyclopedia generally fall into one of these four areas. It is usual for a single change programme to consist of a number of related interventions. The change intervention point selected will depend partly upon what it is that triggers the original change idea. Buchanan and Huczynski (1997) distinguished three such types of change triggers:

1   **External triggers** – Here, the stimulus for change comes from outside the organization, for example through foreign competition, environmental considerations and developments in information technology.
2   **Internal triggers** – Senior management may decide that there is a need to motivate its staff or instigate a change in attitudes. The stimulus for the change comes primarily from inside the company, even though it may be related to factors in the environment.
3   **Proactive triggers** – Senior management may seek to anticipate events and trends by making changes to position the company strategically to meet future challenges. The types of change required to achieve this strategy may be fundamental and can take a great deal of time to put into effect. Nevertheless, one sees daily examples of task modification by companies in the form of mergers, joint ventures and plant closures.

Pugh framework

Derek Pugh provides a framework which contains two dimensions (Buchanan and Huczynski, 1997, p. 493). In Figure 3.3, four different organizational levels are set out on the vertical axis – organizational, inter-group, group and individual – while the horizontal axis considers the types of problems which might be encountered at each level – behavioural factors, organizational structural factors and wider contextual factors. Each of the resulting twelve cells contains a cluster of change interventions which might be used to address the issue described.

French and Bell framework

In their book on organizational development, French and Bell (1984) offer three typologies of change methods: an individual group and task process typology, a target group typology, and a change mechanism typology.

Individual group and task process typology

The first typology is based on two questions which constitute dimensions (see Figure 3.4). First, who or what is the *target* of the intervention – is it the individual or the group? Second, is the *focus* of technique on the task issue (on what is being done), or is it on a process issue (how the task is being accomplished)?

	Behaviour *What is happening?*	Structure *What is the system?*	Context *What is the setting?*
Organizational level	Poor morale, pressure, anxiety, suspicion, weak response to environmental changes *Survey feedback* *Organizational mirroring*	Inappropriate and poorly defined goals, strategy unclear, inappropriate structure, inadequate environmental scanning *Structure change*	Geography, product market, labour market, technology, physical working conditions *Change strategy, change location, change conditions, change culture*
Inter-group level	Sub-units not cooperating, conflict and competition, failure to confront differences, unresolved feelings *Inter-group confrontation,* *Role negotiation*	No common perspective on task, difficult to achieve required interaction *Redefine responsibilities, change reporting relations, improve liaison mechanisms*	Differences in sub-unit values and lifestyles, physical barriers *Reduce psychological and physical distance, exchange roles, arrange cross-functional attachments*
Group level	Inappropriate working atmosphere, goals disputed, inappropriate leadership style, leader not trusted or respected, leader in conflict with peers and superiors *Process consultation, team-building*	Task poorly defined, role relations not clear, leader overloaded, inappropriate reporting structures *Redesign role relations, autonomous groups, socio-technical system redesign*	Lack of resources, poor group composition, inadequate physical facilities, personality clashes *Change the technology, change the layout, change group membership*
Individual level	Individual needs not met, frustration, resistance to change, few learning and development opportunities *Counselling, role analysis, career planning*	Poor job definition, task too easy, task too difficult *Job restructuring or redesign, job enrichment, clear objectives*	Poor individual–job 'fit', poor selection or promotion, inadequate training, inadequate recognition and reward *Improve personnel procedures, improve training, align recognition and rewards with objectives*

Figure 3.3   Pugh's organizational change method framework with examples of methods

Target group typology

The second typology offered by French and Bell is based on the identification of the organizational unit which is the target of the change intervention (see Figure 3.5).

Change mechanism typology

The third of French and Bell's typologies is based on the underlying dynamics of the technique, which are the probable causes of its effectiveness (see Figure 3.6).

Figure 3.6 distinguishes between different intervention methods on the basis of their hypothesized change mechanism. Thus, *feedback* concerns two closely related aspects: the first

Individual v. group dimension

	Focus on the individual	Focus on the group
Focus on task issues	Role analysis technique Education: technical skills; also decision-making, problem-solving, goal-setting, and planning Career planning Grid OD phase 1 (see also below) Possibly job enrichment and management by objectives	Techno-structural changes Survey feedback (see also below) Confrontation meeting Team-building sessions Inter-group activities Grid OD phases 2 and 3 (see also below)
Focus on process issues	Life planning Process consultation with coaching and counselling of individuals Education: group dynamics, planned change Stranger T-groups Third-party peacemaking Grid OD phase 1	Survey feedback Team-building sessions Inter-group activities Process consultation Family T-group Grid OD phases 2 and 3

(Left axis label: Task v. process dimension)

Figure 3.4   OD interventions classified by two independent dimensions: individual vs group and task vs process dimension

Source: French and Bell (1984)

is the acquisition of new information about oneself, other people, or the processes that occur in the organization as a whole; the second aspect is its use by individuals in their decision–making and behaviour.

The second broad change mechanism identified by these writers is changing the *socio-cultural norm*. The belief is that one can change the behaviour of people by changing their norms. This category of change approach seeks either to make members aware of what the old norms are, or to modify them in some new direction.

Interaction- and communication-based techniques form French and Bell's third category. The underlying idea here is that increased interaction and communication between people affects both their attitudes and their behaviour. The interventions in this grouping seek to increase the communication between people in order to counteract tunnel vision, and thereby allow them to compare their perceptions to see if they are valid and shared.

As a change mechanism, *confrontation* rests on a different underlying belief. The confrontation-type interventions address the differences between individuals and groups in terms of their values, attitudes, feelings and beliefs. The objective is to remove the obstacles that impede effective interaction between people. The confrontation process aims to identify these obstructing issues, so that they can be worked on in a helpful way.

Target group	Types of intervention
Interventions designed to improve the effectiveness of INDIVIDUALS	Life- and career-planning activities Role analysis technique Coaching and counselling T-group (sensitivity training) Education and training to increase skills knowledge in the areas of technical task needs, relationship skills, process skills, decision-making, problem-solving, planning, goal-setting skills Grid OD phase 1
Interventions designed to improve the effectiveness of DYADS/ TRIADS	Process consultation Third-party peacemaking Grid OD phases 1 and 2

Interventions designed to improve the effectiveness of TEAMS and GROUPS	Team-building
	   – Task-directed
	   – Process-directed
	Family T-group
	Survey feedback
	Process consultation
	Role analysis technique
	'Start-up' team-building activities
	Education in decision-making, problem-solving, planning, goal-setting in group settings

Interventions designed to improve the effectiveness of INTER-GROUP RELATIONS	Inter-group activities
	   – Process-directed
	   – Task-directed
	Organizational mirroring (three or more groups)
	Techno-structural interventions
	Process consultation
	Third-party peacemaking at group level
	Grid OD phase 3
	Survey feedback

Interventions designed to improve the effectiveness of the TOTAL ORGANIZATION	Techno-structural activities Confrontation meetings Strategic planning activities Grid OD phases 4, 5 and 6 Survey feedback

Figure 3.5 Typology of interventions based on target groups
Source: French and Bell (1984)

Finally, French and Bell suggest *education* as a fifth category. As a causal mechanism, education seeks to improve people's knowledge and concepts, change those beliefs and attitudes which are no longer relevant, and upgrade their skills. As a strategy, education-based techniques can be used in job redesign and in inter-personal relationships management.

In evaluating these three classifications, French and Bell consider all three to contain fundamental weaknesses. Commenting on the individual group/task process typology, they refer to the overlap of categories, and highlight the way in which a single intervention can focus on task at one point and on process issues at another. Their main criticism of their target group

Hypothesized change mechanism	Interventions based primarily on the change mechanism
Feedback	Survey feedback T-group Process consultation Organizational mirroring Grid OD instruments
Awareness of changing socio-cultural norms	Team building T-group Inter-group interface sessions First three phases of Grid OD
Increased interaction and communication	Survey feedback Inter-group interface sessions Third-party peacemaking Organizational mirroring Management by objectives Team-building Techno-structural changes
Confrontation and working for resolution of differences	Third-party peacemaking Inter-group interface sessions Coaching and counselling individuals Confrontation meetings Organizational mirroring
Education through: 1　New knowledge 2　Skill practice	Career and life planning Team-building Goal-setting, decision-making, problem-solving, planning activities T-group Process consultation

Figure 3.6   Intervention typology based on principal emphasis of intervention in relation to different hypothesized change mechanisms
Source: French and Bell (1984)

typology is the redundancy and overlap it contains. The same intervention appears in several of their categories. Finally, their third typology, based on the underlying dynamics of the intervention, suffers from the fact that different authors might hypothesize different causal dynamics. French and Bell note that only recently has research become available to help students understand the underlying mechanisms of change interventions.

Harrison framework

Harrison (1970) offered a framework for selecting interventions on the basis of their *depth* (see Figure 3.7). By 'depth', he meant the extent to which the change was targeted on the formal organizational system, the informal organizational system or the individual. This continuum of choice is based on accessibility and individuality. 'Accessibility' refers to the extent to which data are publicly available rather than being private or hidden. It also includes the ease with which the skills needed to implement the change can be learned. 'Individuality' refers to the

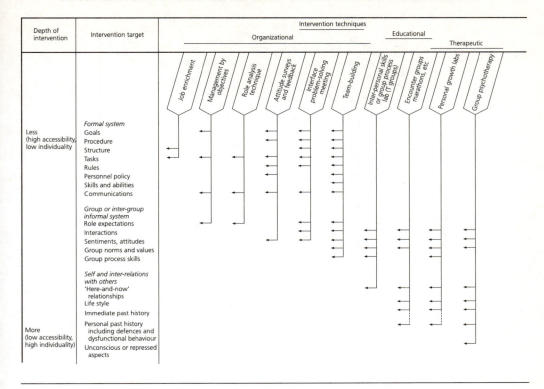

Figure 3.7 The depth of various group or organizational interventions
Source: Harrison (1970)

extent to which the change affects the individual rather than the organization. The more self-focused the technique, the more it affects the person's emotions and values. The guiding principle Harrison suggests is that the change should be attempted at a level no deeper than that required to ensure a solution to the problem. Quite how one can make such a judgement before the intervention is selected is not clear.

Blake and Mouton framework

Blake and Mouton's (1983) discussion of the consultation process includes a definition of 'intervening', by which they mean the taking of action to help clients solve their problems. Such problems, say the writers, while they may be varied and diverse, have common underlying features which enable them to be slotted into a common framework. Blake and Mouton have drawn up a framework called the Consulcube. As Figure 3.8 shows, it is composed of three dimensions: the kinds of intervention, the focal issues for intervention, and units of change. The aim of the Consulcube is to allow a descriptions of what the consultant *does* (kinds of intervention), *what issue* or problem is addressed (focal issues), and *who* is the target of the intervention (units of change). Each dimension will now be examined briefly in turn.

Kinds of intervention

Blake and Mouton identify five main types of intervention:

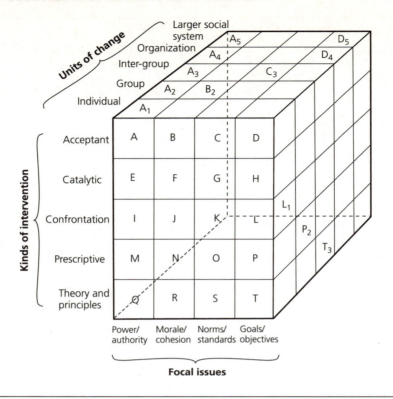

Figure 3.8   Consulcube
Source: Blake and Mouton (1983)

1   **Acceptant** interventions aim to give the client a sense of personal security, and enable them to express their personal thoughts. Clients are assisted to resolve their own problems.
2   **Catalytic** interventions help the client to collect information so they can reassess their perception of the situation around them. Here, the purpose is to help the client achieve a clearer understanding of their problem and how it might be handled.
3   **Confrontation** interventions challenge the client to re-evaluate the basis of their thinking, which may be distorting the way they perceive situations.
4   **Prescriptive** interventions involve the consultant telling the client what has to be done in order to sort out their problem, or even doing that sorting out for them.
5   Interventions based on **theories** and **principles** help the client internalize the systematic and empirically tested ways of understanding. The effect of using theories is to let clients see their situation in a more analytical, cause-and-effect way. This allows them to diagnose the problem, and enables them to plan more effectively.

Focal issues for intervention

Blake and Mouton identify four main change issues. First, there is the exercise of *power and authority* in organizations. Some job redesign strategies suggest sharing power with shop-floor employees. A second dimension refers to *morale and cohesion*. Change approaches may be initiated because of perceived falling morale in the company. The third issue relates to problems which can arise from *standards* or *norms* of behaviour. For example, an absenteeism problem would fall into this category. Finally, there are issues concerned with *goals and objectives*. These can relate to the question: 'Where do we go, and how do we get there?' The focal issue is defined as the one which causes the client the difficulty. Blake and Mouton acknowledge that when change is initiated in one of these four focal issues, changes can be observed in some of the other three. The focal issue is likely to suggest the appropriate type of intervention.

Units of change

The target of change can be an *individual*, a *group* or *team*, an *inter-group relationship*, an entire *organization*, or a *larger social system*, such as a community or a city. The problem lies in determining who the client is. There may be a choice as to which unit in the organization the change technique is aimed at. The decision about who the client or target of the change effort is will depend on senior management's definition of the situation and/or the consultant's preferred approach.

The three dimensions which form the Consulcube together produce a hundred–cell framework. Each cell defines the characteristics of a particular kind of change intervention, specifies the target at which that intervention is being directed, and identifies the class of problem being addressed. In Blake and Mouton's terms, it describes 'what the consultant *does*, *what issues* it is intended to resolve, and *to whom* he does it'.

Schmuck and Miles framework

The final change method classification to be considered here is that proposed by Schmuck and Miles (1976). They call their framework the OD Cube (see Figure 3.9). While it uses the same three dimensions encountered previously, the precise category labels used within each dimension differ. The authors distinguish eight broad categories or families of intervention.

The seven organizational change typologies described here, plus many others that could have been mentioned, all represent useful attempts to classify interventions, and thus assist in the process of selection. However, in practice, the choice of intervention will depend on the personal theory of organizational change held by the manager or the consultant involved in implementing the improvements. This is similar to the personal theory of learning or school of thought encountered earlier with respect to management development methods. 'Theory of organizational change' may seem a somewhat grand title for the set of values, hunches, beliefs, attitudes and perceptions that each of us carries around, and which we use whenever we wish to change an individual or a situation. Many of these we hold in the form of folksy axioms, such as: 'If you want to achieve increased output, you need to change workers' attitudes' or 'To get your way, you have to manipulate group attitudes.' While these may constitute a ragbag of bits and pieces, they nevertheless form the basis on which we each think about organizational change, and on which we carry it out.

A few examples will serve to illustrate this point. If our personal theory of change leads us to see organizational problems in terms of the individuals concerned (people with 'wrong' attitudes), then our preferred change strategy will be to use one of the individually focused interventions such as counselling or behaviour modification. On the other hand, consultants who believe that individual behaviour is the outcome of group performance are likely to select group-focused approaches such as team-building or group norm modification. If you, as a

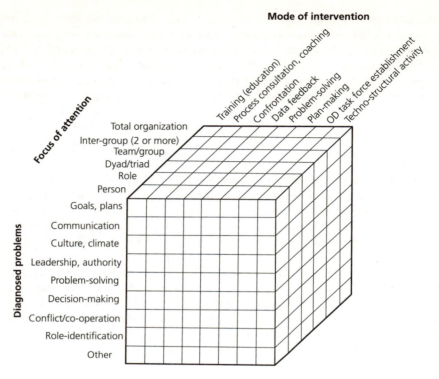

1 Training or education: procedures involving direct teaching or experience-based learning. Such technologies as lectures, exercises, simulations, and T-groups are examples.
2 Process consultation: watching and aiding on-going processes, and coaching to improve them.
3 Confrontation: bringing together units of the organization (persons, roles or groups) which have previously been in poor comunication: usually accompanied by supporting data.
4 Data feedback: systematic collection of information, which is then reported back to appropriate organizational units as a base for diagnosis, problem-solving and planning.
5 Problem-solving: meetings essentially focusing on problem identification, diagnosis, and solution-intervention and implementation.
6 Plan-making: activity focused primarily on planning and goal-setting to re-plot the organization's future.
7 OD task force establishment: setting up ad hoc problem-solving groups or internal teams of specialists to ensure that the organization solves problems and carries out plans continuously.
8 Techno-structural activity: action which has as its prime focus the alteration of the organization's structure, work flow, and means of accomplishing tasks.

Figure 3.9   The OD cube: a scheme for classifying change interventions
Source: Schmuck and Miles (1971)

manager, believe that the job a person does defines their performance, then you will probably opt for a technological change strategy, such as job redesign, or for a structural intervention, such as a task force team or a collateral organization. Many management consultants have a preferred working style or approach: some are experts in team-building, while others specialize in redesigning organizational structures, running T-groups or setting up quality circles. Those who · offer some packaged problem solution, in the form of a course or development programme, can similarly be restricted in their approach. This is not necessarily a criticism of what they offer. Managers need to define their problem carefully, and state the objective of the organizational change. They can engage a consultant to assist them in this process of definition, but they need to be aware that the consultant who offers interventions or training courses will have their own preferred way of viewing a situation. What may be needed is for the manager to engage an independent expert who is not wedded to any particular intervention approach. This person will not be concerned with the follow-up change programme, and can therefore help the manager choose the most suitable consultant or consultancy firm for the problem at hand. While individual managers and consultants may use their personal theories of organizational change to select interventions, Gray and Starke (1984, p. 231) have pointed out:

> although some OD programmes have a theoretical base (job enrichment for example), many do not. Instead they are designed and sold on a normative basis ('this is how things should be done') rather than on an objective assessment of whether the programme is appropriate for a given organization. This practice has led to failures, as well as dissatisfaction with programmes that do not deliver all that was promised.

A general theory of organizational change which can go beyond the personal theories of individual managers is clearly needed. In the 1950s, Litwick wrote:

> We cannot do without theory. It will always defeat practice in the end for quite a simple reason. Practice is static. It does well what it knows. It has however no principle for dealing with what it doesn't know ... Practice is not well adapted for rapid adjustment to a changing environment. Theory is light footed. It can adjust itself to changing circumstances, think out fresh combinations and possibly, peer into the future.

While the frameworks presented in this chapter can help us clarify our thinking about approaches to change, they are no substitute for a comprehensive theory of organizational change method selection which can indicate the intervention that is the most appropriate for a given set of circumstances.

References

Blake, R.R. and Mouton, J.S. (1983) *Consultation*, Addison Wesley Longman.

Buchanan, D.A. and Huczynski, A.A. (1997) *Organization Behaviour: An Introductory Text* (3rd edn), Prentice-Hall.

French, W.L. and Bell, C.H. (1984) *Organization Development: Behavioural Science Interventions for Organization Improvement* (3rd edn), Prentice-Hall.

Gray, J.L. and Starke, F.A. (1984) *Organizational Behaviour: Concepts and Applications*, Charles E. Merrill.

Harrison, R. (1970) 'Choosing the Depth of Organizational Intervention', *Journal of Applied Behavioural Science*, vol. 6, April–June, pp. 181–202.

Leavitt, H.J. (1964) 'Applied Organizational Change in Industry: Structural, Technical and Human Approaches', in Cooper, W.W., Leavitt, H.J. and Shelley, M.W. (eds) *New Perspectives in Organizational Research*, Wiley, pp. 53–71.

Murray, D. (1998) 'Seven Development Themes for the 21st Century', *Organisations & People*, vol. 5, no. 1, February, pp. 4–18.

Schmuck, R. and Miles, M.B. (eds) (1971) *Organization Development in Schools*, University Associates Inc Books.

Abercrombie method (associative discussion group)

This is a structured teaching method whose objective is to develop thinking and judgement skills among students. It was originally developed in the 1960s by Dr M.L.J. Johnson Abercrombie, who taught anatomy to medical students at University College London. Abercrombie defined judgement as: 'making a decision or conclusion on the basis of indications and probabilities, when the facts are not entirely ascertained'. It involves selecting from presented information, interpreting it in the light of information already possessed, and making a prediction about the future. She did not feel that existing scientific teaching developed students' abilities to solve problems.

Abercrombie defines 'free' or 'associative' discussion groups as ones which are organized to enable each participant to become aware of the tacit assumptions which are relevant to the topic at hand. Groups of six to twelve students meet for about one-and-a-half hours in a series of eight or more weekly meetings. The first three of these deal with seeing (perception), while the next ones consider language, classification, evaluation of evidence, and causation. The final meeting reviews the course.

In the first session, she provided each student with two X-ray photos (radiographs) which they had to compare and interpret. They wrote down their reactions to this stimulus, which served as the basis for group discussion. Members were free to participate as they wished, and to follow up their own and others' associations with the topic. Each participant could then see how their past experience and habitual ways of reacting to the content influenced their own process of perception and interpretation of current events. Students analysed their own individual reactions, and compared and contrasted them with those displayed by other members within their group, then modified their own if they chose.

Abercrombie emphasized 'free discussion', in which students talked among themselves and not to the instructor, who instead became a listener and guide. Through such discussion, students become aware of the discrepancies between different members' interpretation of the same stimulus, and begin the process of weighing evidence in favour of alternative interpretations. Any job or profession which requires the exercise of judgement can benefit from Abercrombie's approach. It seeks to counter the habit of 'jumping to conclusions' without first testing assumptions, obtaining different information, sifting evidence and weighing alternatives. Above all, it forces students to make the unconscious influences on their judgements conscious. The free group discussion process facilitates this. Its ultimate aim is to improve judgement.

Abercrombie, M.L.J. (1979) *Aims and Techniques of Group Teaching* (4th edn), Society for Research into Higher Education.

Abercrombie, M.L.J. (1981) 'Changing Basic Assumptions About Teaching and Learning', in Boud, D.J. (ed.) *Developing Autonomy in Student Learning*, Kogan Page.

Abercrombie, M.L.J. (1989) *The Anatomy of Judgement: An Investigation into the Processes of Perception and Reasoning*, Free Association Books.

Abercrombie, M.L.J. and Nias, J. (eds) (1993) *The Human Nature of Learning: Selections from the Work of M. L. J. Abercrombie*, Open University Press.

Abercrombie, M.L.J. and Terry, P.M. (1978) *Talking to Learn: Improving Teaching and Learning in Small Groups*, Society for Research into Higher Education.

See also: Case study method; Creative dialogue; Group discussion; Lateral thinking; Small-group teaching

Absenteeism/turnover task force

Absenteeism represents a major cost to industry, but it does not attract the same amount of attention in the media as strikes, for example. The visible costs of absence include money paid out of the company's and the government's sickness schemes. However, there are more important invisible consequential costs, including unnecessarily high staffing levels, overtime working, lost production and orders, general disruption, and reduced employee morale.

Companies which recognize this problem and take it seriously have established task forces to deal with it. These temporary groups first establish adequate record-keeping so that the magnitude of the absence problem can be established and its manifestation in different parts of the company determined. Next, they move to consider the causes and problems associated with absence within the company. Finally, they select the most appropriate absence control technique from the many that are currently available.

Evans, A. and Palmer, S. (1997) *From Absence to Attendance*, Institute of Personnel and Development.

Goodman, P.S. and Atkin, R.S. (1984) *Absenteeism: New Approaches to Understanding, Measuring and Managing Employee Absence*, Jossey-Bass.

Grundemann, R.W.M. (1997) *Preventing Absen-*

teeism in the Workplace, Commission of the European Communities.

Horn, P. (1994) *Employee Turnover*, South-Western Publishing.

Morris, S. (1995) *Managing Attendance*, The Industrial Society.

Rhodes, S.R. and Steers, R.M. (1990) *Managing Employee Absenteeism*, Addison Wesley Longman.

Tylczak, L. (1990) *Attacking Absenteeism*, Kogan Page.

See also: Alcohol recovery programme; Multiple management; Problem-solving groups; Skunkworks

Accepting positions of responsibility in community associations/university societies

A number of companies encourage managers to take up positions of responsibility such as chair, secretary or treasurer in civic, community, church, social or political organizations, and some give staff time off to attend these organizations' meetings. The belief is that such involvement can help managers develop a broader view of situations which will have long-term benefits for their job performance. This can become a much more valuable learning experience if managers are told to look for certain things, keep a log of their experiences, try out different strategies, and so on.

Companies may view these types of activities as learning opportunities which can be used by their employees to develop their skills and broaden their outlook. Managers, on the other hand, may view them as a social duty or a social occasion. Students, too, can become presidents, treasurers and secretaries of university clubs and societies. This gives them experience of working with others, setting objectives, organizing events, solving problems, making decisions and managing money.

See also: Assignment to community organization; Assignment to customer as representative; Assignment to government body study group; Diary exercise; Logging critical incidents; Secondment; Service in professional organizations

ACHIEVE model (ACHIEVE system)

The ACHIEVE model was designed as a tool to facilitate the attainment of short-term task objectives and long-term development objectives. The developers of this approach hold that managing people comprises three major functions: setting goals for staff members, coaching by giving them day-to-day feedback, and evaluating their performance over a given period. It aims to help managers determine why performance problems occur, and helps them to develop a change strategy to solve them.

Hersey and Goldsmith identify seven variables which they claim are necessary for effective performance: Ability, Clarity (of role), Help (organizational support), Incentive (the motivational factor), Evaluation, Validity and Environmental fit – hence the acronym ACHIEVE, which is synonymous with performance.

Managers can use the ACHIEVE model by evaluating how each of the seven factors will affect either present or future performance. They then do what is necessary to deal with the causes of any performance problem. The authors list each of the seven factors, along with their problem-solving alternatives. One example will serve to illustrate their approach. Clarity represents the second dimension of the ACHIEVE model. It refers to the employee's understanding of their job or role perception. It concerns employee knowledge and acceptance of what to do, and how and when to do it. To be able to perform a job well, the employee needs to be clear what the main goals are, what the priorities are among these goals, and how the goals should be accomplished. Staff may have problems in developing clarity about their goals, and verbal acceptance of what is required may be insufficient. The model suggests that the manager should ensure that all objectives are formally recorded, and that employees are encouraged to ask questions until they are sure they understand what is required of them.

The ACHIEVE model can be used to analyse almost any performance situation. The manager looks at the situation and decides which factor may be responsible for the performance problem, although some performance problems may be caused by more than one factor.

Hersey, P. and Blanchard, K.H. (1984) *Management of Organizational Behaviour* (4th edn), Pearson Education.

Hersey, P. and Goldsmith, H.M. (1980) 'The ACHIEVE System: A Human-Performance Problem-solving Model', in Burke, W.W. and Goldstein, L.D. (eds) *Trends and Issues in OD: Current Theory and Practice*, Pfeiffer/Jossey-Bass, pp. 266–74.

See also: Assessment of the organization as a system; Benchmarking; Diagnostic activities; Feedback; Functional administrative control technique; Goal-setting; Interviewing; Looking for trouble; Management audit; Management by objectives; Organizational analysis; Overhead value analysis; 7-S framework

Achievement motivation intervention

The work of David McClelland identified a motivation which he called 'need for achievement' (nAch). This led to the creation of a theory-based intervention designed to increase an individual's capacity for achievement. The advocates of this technique claim that such changes in motivation translate into improved performance and achievement at work. The search for personal achievement can act as a continuing stimulus for financial progress.

Achievement motivation interventions begin with participants being taught how people who possess a high need for achievement think, talk and act. They are also shown how achievement motivation is revealed in imaginative stories, as well as in personal goal-setting. High achievers, for example, prefer to plan and personally take the actions which can lead to successful or unsuccessful outcomes. They enjoy stretching their capabilities, but avoid setting goals which are virtually unattainable. They prefer work situations in which they receive continuing feedback on their performance. Thus, achievement motivation interventions seek to stimulate participants to set higher, but carefully planned and operational work goals, and ensure that they receive feedback on their progress towards them.

Another feature of the intervention is small-group discussion work, during which participants evaluate and criticize each other's achievement motivations. In these discussions, individuals are obliged to explain to other group members why the goals they have set for themselves are realistic in terms of their particular situation, aptitude and performance. The group members may then comment on these goals if they consider them to be either too high or too low. Such discussions are intended to stimulate a broader, shared discussion of the life goals of achievement.

Achievement motivation intervention aims to free participants from their old habits and attitudes. The small-group atmosphere is intended to produce cohesion between the members, which creates a climate of mutual encouragement and support for future striving. The promoters of this intervention claim that, as long as the participants have gained a sound and systematic understanding of the dynamics of achievement motivation, it is possible for them to increase their motivation to achieve. McClelland argues that the important deterrents to achievement motivation are the cultural norms and attitudes which surround an individual. If these are stagnant or negative, then the chances of achievement motivation interventions being successful are lower than if the motivation to achieve within the culture is high.

Abouserie, R. (1995) 'Self-esteem and Achievement Motivation in Determining Students' Approaches to Studying', *Studies In Higher Education*, vol. 20, no. 1, pp. 19–26.

Aronoff, J. and Litwin, G.H. (1971) 'Achievement Motivation Training and Executive Advancement', *Journal of Applied Behavioural Science*, vol. 7, no. 2, pp. 215–29.

McClelland, D.C. (1961) *The Achieving Society*, Van Nostrand.

McClelland, D.C. (1965) 'Achievement Motivation Can be Developed', *Harvard Business Review*, November–December, pp. 6–24 and 178.

McClelland, D.C. (1984) 'That Urge to Achieve', in Kolb, D.A., Rubin, I.M. and McIntyre, J.M. (eds) *Organizational Psychology: Readings in Human Behaviour in Organizations* (4th edn), Pearson Education, pp. 73–80.

McClelland, D.C and Burnham, D.H. (1976) 'Power is the Great Motivator', *Harvard Business Review*, March–April, pp. 100–10.

See also: Assertiveness training; Awareness training; Confidence-building training; Ideological change; Intrapreneurial group; Norm-clarification; Norm-formation; Norm-modification; Power management; Self-efficacy training; Simulated entrepreneurship

Acting assignment

In an acting assignment, a manager is given a temporary role for a fixed period: for example, a production department manager may be attached to the human resources staff team during a period when a major work re-design project is taking place. Alternatively, the assignment may be subject to time limits, with acting managers waiting to see what problems arise while they are occupying the position.

See also: Assertiveness training; Assignment to manager with high development skills; Confidence-building training; Development assignment; Expanding job assignment; Exposure to upper management; Job rotation; Job swop; Manager exchange; Manager shadowing; Planned delegation; Research assignment; Rotation training; Sick leave/holiday replacement assignment; Understudy

Action Centred Leadership

Action Centred Leadership (ACL) courses were developed by John Adair on the basis of what he calls the 'functional approach' to leadership. His ideas developed out of the deficiencies he saw in the 'qualities approach' to leadership, which held that 'leaders were born'. Adair claimed that research had revealed no common list of personality traits which indicated who might be a good leader. Adair also felt that the 'situational approach', which emphasized the importance of the situation in which leadership was carried out as well as the task being performed, was equally unhelpful since it implied a need for a constantly changing leadership to match constantly changing tasks.

Adair's 'functional approach' is based on the identification of the functions that need to be performed in a team if it is to be successful. He lists three different sets of needs. First, there are task needs. Since a workgroup comes together to achieve certain objectives, it has a need to move towards the achievement of those objectives. If some measure of success is not achieved, the group may disintegrate. Second, there are group needs. The co-operation of team members is necessary if the group's goals are to be achieved. For this reason, motivation and group morale need to be maintained. Finally, there are the individual's needs. In taking part in groups, individual members seek to fulfil their own unique needs. Failure to meet these individual needs may lead to members withdrawing their support from the team or perhaps leaving the group altogether. Adair views these needs as interdependent, and sees the leader's role as ensuring that all three sets of needs are met. The development of this form of leadership is the objective of Action Centred Leadership courses.

ACL courses consist of a series of group tasks in which the objectives are specified and feedback on success or failure is clear. Group members take up and relinquish leadership roles as they work on the task, depending on their personal characteristics. Debriefing sessions focus on the extent to which individual, group and task needs were met, the degree of task success, communication problems and the problem-solving approaches adopted.

Adair, J. (1979) *Action Centred Leadership*, Gower.
Adair, J. (1983) *Effective Leadership*, Gower.
Adair, J. (1989) *The Action Centred Leader*, The Industrial Society.
Smith, E.P. (1975) 'Action Centred Leadership', in Taylor, B. and Lippitt, G.L. (eds) *Management Development and Training Handbook*, McGraw-Hill.

See also: Grid development; Situational leadership; 3-D management effectiveness seminar

Action enquiry

Action enquiry is similar to action research, except that it places greater emphasis on service to the practitioner and on the collaborative effort between the researcher and the practitioner team. The inquiry team collaborates with the client or client group to define the goals in all the phases of the research, and the change strategies to be adopted.

The approach is based upon a belief in collaboration. It holds that people will support that which they have helped to create, so the emphasis is on the researcher–practitioner joint problem-solving process, which is concerned with defining the problem to be addressed, the research methods to be used, the relevant hypotheses to be tested, and the evaluation of the action.

Fisher, D. and Torbert, W.R. (1995) *Personal and Organizational Transformation*, McGraw-Hill.
French, W.L. and Bell, C.H. (1984) *Organizational Development: Behavioural Science Interventions for Organization Improvement* (3rd edn), Pearson Education, p. 90.
Havelock, R.G. (1969) *Planning Through Dissemination and Utilization of Knowledge*, Institute for Social Research, University of Michigan.

See also: Action research; Attitude survey; Data-based interventions; Survey feedback interventions

Action learning

The action learning approach was developed and popularized by Professor Reg Revans. It involves groups of managers coming together regularly to work on real-life organizational problems. They form a group which is assisted by a 'set adviser', who acts as a facilitator or resource person to each group.

Although action learning seeks to develop the individual manager, it uses organizational problems as the vehicle for the learning. Action learning follows a number of principles: the person best qualified to solve any problem is the person who has it; the best opportunities to develop managers occur in their own organizations; a self-help approach based on groups can encourage the solution of problems. Most importantly, action learning is concerned with *taking actions*, not merely making *recommendations* for actions.

Action learning aims to develop managers' abilities to pose entirely new questions, seeks to help them to recognize the value of their experiences, and prepares them to deal with future problems. Its effect is to change organizations by helping managers to recognize their strengths and weaknesses, and to create a momentum to help them deal with future problems through a continuous process of learning and development. Some business schools, including Ashridge and Sundridge Park, now offer programmes with an action learning element.

Beatty, L., Bourner, T. and Frost, P. (1993)

'Action Learning: Reflections on Becoming a Set Member', *Management Education and Development*, vol. 24, no. 4, 205, pp. 350–67.

Boshyk, Y. and Mercer, S. (eds) (1999) *Strategic Executive Development and Action Learning*, Macmillan.

Inglis, S. (1994) *Making the Most of Action Learning*, Gower.

Mumford, A. (ed.) (1997) *Action Learning at Work*, Gower.

Peattie, K. (1996) 'Action Learning in Action: The Teaching Company Scheme', *Management Learning*, vol. 27, no. 1, pp. 87–112.

Pedler, M. (1997) *Action Learning in Practice* (3rd edn), Gower.

Raelin, J.A. (1997) 'Individual and Situational Precursors of Successful Action Learning', *Journal of Management Education*, vol. 21, no. 3, pp. 368–94.

Vince, R. and Martin, L. (1993) 'Inside Action Learning: An Exploration of the Psychology and Politics of the Action Learning Model', *Management Education and Development*, vol. 24, no. 3, pp. 205–15.

Wallace, M. (1990) 'Can Action Learning Live Up to its Reputation?', *Management Education and Development*, vol. 21, no. 2, pp. 89–103.

Weinstein, K. (1998) *Action Learning: A Practical Guide* (2nd edn), Gower.

See also: Agenda method; Consulting assignment; Context training; Experience-based learning; Illuminative incident analysis; Intervisitation; Job swop; Joint development activity; Learning history; Manager exchange; Problem-solving groups; Project-based management development; Prompt list; Real-life entrepreneurial project; Self-help group; Student-planned learning

Action maze (mulage)

An action maze is a description of an incident for analysis which is followed by a list of alternative actions. Each action choice taken by a learner directs them to a new page which gives them the results of their action and presents them with a new set of alternatives from which to choose. The results the learner receives after each step may give them more information, as well as providing a reaction to their action choice. It is possible that this set of choices may lead learners to a dead end and send them back to make another choice from another set of alternatives.

Action mazes borrow ideas from programmed learning – although they differ significantly – in particular the notions of scrambled pages (which are not read consecutively) and selecting one choice from a number of alternatives (each leading down a different path). Programmed learning involves teaching a correct response both through reinforcement when the correct response occurs and by re-teaching when an error is made. Although some aspects of management may be susceptible to that approach, the attitudes and behaviours which compose the major elements in management training and development are not.

Action mazes usually come in book form, but the individual pages can be duplicated, placed in pocket files and distributed around the floor of the training room or on tables. Increasingly, mazes are being displayed on multi-media PCs. Individual trainees work their way through the maze and report their route as well as their exit point (of which there may be several) to the instructor. Groups can be formed consisting of learners who take different routes, who discuss the reasons for their choices. An alternative approach is to display each page on an overhead transparency for group discussion, both at the 'decision-making' and 'debriefing' stages.

Since learners receive immediate feedback on their progress, students frequently find action mazes interesting, and they tend to provoke intense discussion. Mazes reflect real-life decision-making, and confirm that we have control only *before* we take action: once action has been taken, it provokes reaction, which in turn creates new situations that demand responses.

Mazes have been developed for topics such as dealing with a regular work absentee and disciplining staff. When an action maze is used in medical education and, for example, involves practice sessions where medical or nursing students have a patient to assess and manage, it is known as 'mulage'.

Elgood, C. (1980) 'Use of Business Games in Management Training', *The Training Officer*, vol. 16, no. 12, pp. 332–4.

Zoll, A.A. (1969) *Dynamic Management Education*, Chapters 11–12, Addison Wesley Longman.

See also: Behaviour modification; Experiential exercise; Feedback; Game; Guided design approach; In-basket exercise; Problem pack; Programmed simulation; Simulation; Surrogate client

Action profiling

This approach is based on the idea that every individual may be considered to have three modes of operating: *Thinking*, *Acting* and *Feeling*. It was originally formulated in 1928 by Rudolph Laban to describe and capture a person's rhythmic patterns by a system of notation, but it developed into a means for recording the movement and energy of those observed. It was subsequently used by a consultant in the 1940s to train women to do work previously done by men. He wanted to use film to carry out time and motion studies, but war shortages prevented this. When working with Laban, Warren Lamb used his notation method to analyse how managers and supervisors used their energy. Focusing on their rhythmic patterns, he found that the same ones demonstrated at a meeting or interview were used by them in their job.

Pamela Ramsden has carried out research on the action profile as a way of understanding a manager's behaviour. She found that the profiling process also revealed a person's motivation (not just their aptitude) to take initiative during the three stages of decision-making identified by Lamb: *attention* ('I can see something I want to do'), *intention* ('I am going to do it') and *commitment* (actually doing it). Each requires a different type of effort.

The first type of effort is *giving attention*. This may involve answering a query or presenting a problem. Before decisions can be made, attention needs to be given. The second type of effort is *forming an intention*. This is the building of resolve; a basis of purpose and determination on which to proceed. The last stage is the effort of *making a commitment* to pass through a moment of decision to a point of no return.

This approach suggests that each individual has a preference for one or other of these stages and energises him or herself in that way. Individuals' energy preferences are labelled 'action motivations'. The energy preference is held to be a motivating force because of its compelling nature and the satisfaction reported by people as they act in their preferred ways. The action profiles of individual managers are assessed, and each manager, it is claimed, has their own unique pattern of strengths in action motivation which is called their 'action profile'. This action profile is diagrammatically described by allocating '100 units of energy' on criteria which are unclear, across the three action stages of 'attending', 'intending' and 'committing'.

The action profile does not measure a manager's performance, but the basic motivating forces within their personality. It has been used as a basis to develop individual managers, teams and individuals within teams.

Lamb, W. (1982) 'The Recruiter's Responsibility for Judging People: The Need to Observe Body Movement', *Journal of Management Development*, vol. 1, no. 1, pp. 63–74.
Lamb, W. and Watson, E. (1985) *Body Code: The Meaning of Movement*, Routledge.
Ramsden, P. (1973) *Top Team Planning: A Study of the Power of Individual Motivation in Management*, Associated Business Programmes/Cassell.
Ramsden, P. and Zacharias, J. (1993) *Action Profiling* (2nd edn), Gower.
Rose, C.L. (1978) *Action Profiling: Movement Awareness for Better Management*, MacDonald and Evans.

See also: Alexander Technique; Neurolinguistic programming; Non-verbal encounters; Non-verbal exercise; Process analysis; Team role training

Action project

The aim of this method is to encourage undergraduates to progress from rote recall of theories to conceptualization, and finally to application. It does this by encouraging students to apply abstract thinking to effect small-scale changes in their life and environment. The focus of an action project is not restricted, and students are encouraged to innovate and experiment. However, chosen projects tend to fall into one of four main categories. *Individually focused* projects seek to change the behaviour of individuals: for example, tutoring youngsters with learning difficulties; or working with individual students from disadvantaged backgrounds to help them win a college place and stop them dropping out. *Group-focused* projects include raising sponsorship for a charity or developing team spirit and motivating a school football team. *Product-focused* projects involve groupwork to design, develop and test a product such as a university student handbook, a company training manual or a retirement plan for a small company. Finally, *organization-effectiveness* projects include altering restaurant practice by training waiters, changing inventory procedures and modifying work times and table responsibilities, or devising and implementing a plan to recover overdue payments from customers.

An action project is divided into three parts, each of which is submitted by the student at a different time during the term or semester. First, at the start of the course, students write down the objectives of their project, together with the need or rationale that underpins it. The individuals or groups involved in or affected by it are identified, and background information is also included. The instructor assesses each project's feasibility, suggests resources, and encourages some students to expand and others to restrict the scope of their project.

The second stage occurs about a third of the way into the semester or term, and deals with planning and action strategies under five headings. The first is a force field analysis of driving and restraining forces; alternative actions and their consequences; and the prioritization of these. The second breaks the general plan down into specific steps which describe in detail how each will be carried out. The third requires students to describe an alternative strategy in case the first one turns out to be unfeasible. The fourth asks students to list what they need to succeed, in terms of people and other resources, and also how they intend to secure such support. The fifth consists of a chart which specifies what will be done by when.

The third and final part of the project is submitted towards the end of the period, and is itself divided into three sections. The first describes in detail the action taken by the students in the preceding six to eight weeks. This may take the form of a narrative essay; a diary or journal; or a time-line with appended notes. In the second, each student answers four questions: 'On what criteria would you evaluate your project?'; 'What insights or personal learning have you gained, and what generalizations can you make about human nature/management from completing this project?'; 'If you were to repeat the project with what you now know, what would you do differently, and why?', and 'What recommendations do you have as to what should happen next?' The third section of the third stage includes the relevant theory from the course, which includes an explanation of how and why it is relevant to the project. The assessor assumes that the theory is not relevant, and it is up to the student to demonstrate, through their argument and examples, that it is valuable in either analysing the problem, revealing causes, assisting solutions or guiding actions.

Whitcomb, S.W. (1981) 'Bridging the Gap From Theory to Application: The Action Project', *Exchange: The Organizational Behaviour Teaching Journal*, vol. 6, no. 4, pp. 39–41.

See also: Concept uncovery; Force Field Analysis; Group project; Project method

Action research

The origin of action research is often traced back to two independent sources: John Collier and Kurt Lewin. Collier was a Commissioner for Indian Affairs in the US Government from 1933 to 1945. His job involved diagnosing problems and instituting action to help race relations. He found that making changes in the area of ethnic relations was difficult, and that it required a joint effort between the researcher, the practitioner and the client. He called this form of activity 'action research' because taking effective action on important problems and issues required information based on research. The solutions that were proposed needed to be both feasible and relevant, and this was what the research was intended to establish. Lewin was also interested in applying social science to prac-

tical problems. He used the principles of action research on subjects such as inter-group relations and changing wartime eating habits.

Action research is not a single approach, and four different variants have been identified: in *diagnostic action research*, the scientist considers the problem and makes a recommendation for remedial action which is intuitively derived and has not been tested, but comes from the scientist's own experience or knowledge. The recommendation is then put into effect by the client group. In *participative action research*, the people who are to take the action participate in the entire process. This ensures that those who will be implementing decisions are involved from the start, and that the proposed actions are both feasible and workable. In *empirical action research*, participants keep systematic notes about what they did and what effect it had. *Experimental action research* focuses on the relative effectiveness of different intervention techniques. Several different ways of solving a single problem are implemented, and all are evaluated.

Atweh, B., Weeks, P. and Kemmis, S. (eds) (1998) *Action Research in Practice*, Routledge.
Bennett, R. and Oliver, J. (1988) 'How to get the Best from Action Research: A Guidebook', special issue of *Leadership and Organization Development*, vol. 9. no. 3.
Clark, P.A. (1972) *Action Research and Organizational Change*, Harper and Row.
Cunningham, J.B. (1993) *Action Research and Organizational Development*, Praeger.
Elden, M. and Chisholm, R.F. (eds) (1993) 'Action Research', special issue of *Human Relations*, vol. 46, no. 2, February, pp. 121–298.
Lewin, K. (1946) 'Action Research and Minority Problems', *Journal of Social Issues*, vol. 2, no. 4, pp. 34–46.
McNiff, J. (1992) *Action Research: Principles and Practice*, Routledge.
McNiff, J. (1992) *Teaching as Learning: An Action Research*, Routledge.
McNiff, J. (1996) *You and Your Action Research Project*, Routledge.
Stringer, E.T. (1996) *Action Research*, Sage.

See also: Action enquiry; Attitude survey; Data-based interventions; Focus groups; Organizational climate analysis; Organizational mirror; Self-generated scaling; Survey feedback interventions

Action training

Action training was originally developed to help new managers learn the social skills required for appraising and counselling their subordinates. It evolved from dissatisfaction with the existing lecture approach (which dealt only with knowledge about appraisal) and role-playing (which dealt with skills in an artificial and unreal situation).

In action training, classroom situations are created in which managers can be themselves and are able to explore and develop the desired social skills. Subsequently, this same approach came to be used in the development of group skills. Action training requires a trainee in a group to deal with behaviour by working at a task which is carried out under time pressure and which stimulates excitement, frustration and curiosity. It relies on a systematic approach which includes a regular review, and it encourages participants to learn by experience. An action training course usually lasts between two and three days, has between 15 and 18 participants, and is conducted by two instructors.

Drinkwater, A. (1972) 'Group Training and Consulting Approaches in IBM', in Berger, M.L. and Berger, P.J. (eds) *Group Training Techniques*, Gower.
Peach, L. (1979) 'Developing High Fliers at IBM', *Personnel Management*, vol. 11, no. 9, pp. 32–5.

See also: Appraisal; Coverdale Training; Role-playing; Structured social skills seminar

Action training and research

In recent years, the term 'action training and research' (ATR) has been used to refer to a method of organizational development which was pioneered by Neely Gardener during the 1960s and has become a classic methodology for implementing change within public sector institutions.

ATR represents a means of changing hierarchically structured public organizations whose managements have a vested interest in the status quo. It emphasizes changing to participative styles of management, devolving managers' power to promote innovation, adapting to customers' changing needs, and promoting efficient, clear and practical decision-making.

Wyman, S.M. and Bruce, R.R. (1998) *Changing Organizations: Using Action Training and Research*, Sage.

See also: Conference Model; Fast-cycle, full-participation work design; Future search; Open space technology; Participative design; Real-time strategic change; Real-time work design; Search conference; Simu-Real; Strategic planning process; Work-Out

Administrative interventions

These types of organizational change interventions focus on a company's policies and procedures, its staffing procedures, including the promotion of personnel, and remuneration policies (salary and fringe benefits). Administrative interventions may include redesigning an organization's structure and its relationship with its environment.

See also: Functional Administrative Control Technique; Job descriptions; Outplacement counselling; Recruitment; Reward systems

Advance organizer

Developed by David Ausubel, the advance organizer (AO) is designed to strengthen learners' cognitive structure: both their knowledge of a given subject and its mental organization. The latter will determine how well new material is acquired and retained by the learner, and how meaningful it will be to them.

The learner is 'prepared for learning' by being exposed to advance organizers which consist of introductory material, presented ahead of the learning task, which is at a higher level of abstraction than the learning task that follows it. The purpose of this material is to explain and differentiate the existing, old, material from the new, and link the two together. The best advance organizers have been found to be familiar terms, concepts, propositions, illustrations and analogies. The advance organizer is analogous to showing a traveller a map half-way through their journey. The map is an abstract representation of reality. It shows where the traveller has been, where they are going, and how the future terrain relates to that which has been traversed.

Joyce and colleagues describe the three phases involved in integrating the advance organizer into a lesson. First, the phase's aims are clarified, the advance organizer itself is presented, its defining attributes are identified, examples are given, and the context is provided. The learner thus becomes aware of their experience and knowledge which is relevant to the learning task ahead. Next, the new material to be learned is presented in such a way that the learner understands the order in which it is to be learned. The instructor's presentation of the new material is related to the advance organizer presented earlier. The last phase involves strengthening the student's cognitive organization of the total material, both old and new.

Ausubel recommends promoting integration by reminding learners of the 'big picture', by encouraging them to summarize the main features of the newly learned material, by repeating precisely any definitions, by asking them to highlight differences between parts of the new material, or by asking them to explain how the new material relates to and supports the organizer. Additional strategies are also possible. Learning can be improved by asking students to provide additional concepts and propositions in the learning material; by encouraging them to verbalize, using their own terminology and frame of reference, the essence of the material, and by having them examine the material from different viewpoints. A critical approach to the subject matter can be fostered by asking students to attend to the assumptions or inferences they may have made in learning the material, and encouraging them to judge and challenge these, while reconciling any contradictions between them. Finally, the learning can be consolidated by inviting them to clarify their ideas and test them while they apply them. Ausubel's model is designed to increase learners' abilities to learn. It encourages them to look for organizing ideas and to reconcile information.

Ausubel, D.P. (1960) 'The Use of Advance Organizers in the Learning and Retention of Meaningful Verbal Material', *Journal of Educational Psychology*, vol. 51, pp. 267–72.

Ausubel, D.P. (1968) *Educational Psychology: A Cognitive View*, Holt, Rinehart and Winston.

Ausubel, D.P. (1968) *The Psychology of Meaningful Verbal Learning*, Grune and Stratton.

Ausubel, D.P. (1980) 'Schemata, Cognitive Structure and Advance Organizers: A Reply to Anderson, Spiro and Anderson', *American Educational Research Journal*, vol. 17, no. 3, pp. 400–3.

Joyce, B., Weil, M. and Showers, B. (1992) *Models of Teaching* (4th edn), Allyn and Bacon, pp. 181–95.

Lawton, J.T. and Wanska, S.K. (1977) 'The Effects of Different Types of Advance Organizers on Classification Learning', *American Educational Research Journal*, vol. 16, no. 3, pp. 223–39.

Melton, R.F. (1984) 'Alternative Forms of Preliminary Organizer', in Henderson, E.S. and Nathenson, M.B. (eds) *Independent Learning in Higher Education*, Educational Technology Publications.

Righi, C. (1991) 'Using Advance Organizers to Teach BASIC Programming to Primary Grade Children', *Education Training Research & Development*, vol. 39, no. 4, pp. 79–90.

See also: Concept mapping; Large groups as small groups; Mind Mapping; Pre-course learning; Rote learning

Advanced seminar

The term 'advanced seminar' is used here to refer to a particular type of seminar design which was first described by Nisbett. Its distinguishing characteristic is the alternation of a session in which students enjoy a relatively high degree of freedom with one in which there exists a greater degree of discipline.

The design of the seminar programme proceeds along traditional lines: topics for study are selected, and students in the group are then allocated to a seminar topic. However, one difference is that while each student has a single topic, they are allocated two consecutive seminar sessions, and are responsible for providing material for them. Each topic is organized along the following lines. The student begins by deciding on six 'statements worth making' about the subject which have the following characteristics: they are clear, specific and important, they are controversial enough to need careful discussion before being accepted or rejected by the group, and they represent the student's personal belief, based on their study experience and reflection. These statements must avoid triviality and vagueness, must not be platitudes, nor should they be mere opinions based on the student's ignorance or the type of assertions which are likely to win agreement without further discussion. The student then circulates their list of statements to the other seminar participants at least one week before the first of the two meetings, along with a list of reading references.

During the first meeting, the author of the statements devotes about a quarter of an hour to introducing each statement in turn, explaining its meaning and justifying their belief that it is 'a statement worth making'. The group discussion which follows is concerned with clarifying the meaning of the statements and testing the responses of group members to the list in a generally unstructured and freewheeling way.

The second meeting is more disciplined because it is more task-orientated. The group must arrive at a consensus on the six statements or any modifications of them. Because the original statements were controversial, it is rare for there to be initial agreement on any of them. Individuals in the group become involved in a process of mutual persuasion, in which the statements must be modified to satisfy objectors while retaining the support of those who originally agreed with them. At the end of this process of negotiation, the ensuing list of statements must continue to conform to the criterion of what constituted 'a statement worth making'.

When group unanimity is impossible, the dissenting minority group produces a reasoned report to the majority statement. At any time during the second seminar, statement supporters have to assess the relative advantage of pursuing their own viewpoints versus giving up some of them in order to gain unanimous agreement on a statement which is close to their own but which may not exactly resemble it. Agreement is reached by disciplined discussion. The instructor's involvement is crucial here. Since consensus depends both on members stating their case and on having their views considered by others, the instructor must foster a climate in which receiving and considering views is accorded equal status with giving them.

Advanced seminars offer students a number of benefits. The selection of the original six statements is an exercise in individual learning. Students are required to read, think about their reading, and exercise their judgement. The two contrasting types of sessions allow students to consider the advantages and disadvantages of each. In the open discussion of the first seminar, there are similarities to a brainstorming group, where new ideas and perspectives are evolved. In the second, there is a need for greater self-discipline and group management if the learning task is to be achieved. In addition to developing skills in reasoned argument, it develops members' group/committee skills as well as influencing skills, especially in negotiating and bargaining situations, where it may be necessary to check tactfully how far apart the positions of the two sides are and to assess the degree to which differences have a substantive, emotional or semantic base.

Nisbett, S. (1965–6) 'A Method for Advanced Seminars', *Universities Quarterly*, vol. 20, June, pp. 349–55.
Nuffield Foundation (1976) *Small Group Teaching* (selected papers), Nuffield Foundation.

See also: Brainstorming; Group discussion; Mediation; Seminar; Small-group teaching; Tutorial

Advocacy

Teaching through advocacy is concerned with persuading another to accept your reasoning or views on a subject. Advocacy refers to not only presenting a position, but arranging facts in such a way as to persuade an audience. The skills of fact-gathering, selecting, sequencing and verbal delivery all offer the potential for learning.

Bateman, N. (1995) *Advocacy Skills*, Gower.
Munkman, J. (1991) *Techniques of Advocacy*, Heinemann-Butterworth.
Spacks, P.M. (1996) *Advocacy in the Classroom: Problems and Possibilities*, St Martin's Press.

See also: Argumentation; Case debate; Debate; Jurisprudential model; Mock trial; Short talks by students; Visiting lecturer

Affirmative action (managing integration; managing diversity)

Affirmative action is the practice of explicitly considering race, gender, national origin or some other characteristic governed by legislation in making an employment decision. It seeks to counter the lingering effects of prior intentional or unintentional discrimination by individuals or employers. It also seeks to create a workforce that is more representative of the gender and ethnic make-up of the qualified labour market for the positions in the organization. Prejudice and discrimination can result from conscious and unconscious preconceptions. Such behaviours arouse strong feelings in those who attempt to change them, and even stronger feelings in those who resist. Change therefore requires energy and persistence.

In affirmative action, the organization adopts the view that change is a process to be managed by members of staff who have experience of 'exclusion'. In most Western countries, legislation can alter social structures in fundamental ways. Such reforms can change our definitions of organizations and the roles of the managers within them. In some companies, the responsibility for meeting affirmative action goals has been incorporated in the managers' performance, evaluation and reward system. In US organizations, the move from a segregated to an integrated workforce is managed through the staff affirmative action function, rather than through line management.

Ackerman, R.W. (1973) 'How Companies Respond to Social Demands', *Harvard Business Review*, vol. 51, no. 5, pp. 88–98.
Horne, G. (1992) *Reversing Discrimination: The Case for Affirmative Action*, International Publishers.
Innes, D. et al. (1994) *Reversing Discrimination: Affirmative Action in the Workplace*, Oxford University Press.
Morley, E. (1980) 'Managing Integration', in Burke, W.W. and Goodstein, L.D. (eds) *Trends and Issues in OD: Current Theories and Practice*, Pfeiffer/Jossey-Bass, pp. 124–49.
Thomas, R.R. (1996) *Redefining Diversity*, AMACOM.

See also: Androgynous management; Cross-cultural sensitivity training; Diversity training; Employee assistance programme; Let's-talk-it-over programme

Agenda method

The agenda method is one of several autonomous learning approaches available to students. In this technique, most of the course sessions take place in the instructor's absence. The teacher attends in order to hand out and define the task, and returns later to receive reports of the solutions or decisions that have been arrived at, and to lead a discussion on them.

The agenda method gives students a great deal of autonomy, but it nevertheless features a firmly directed line of enquiry, content and activity. The instructor's skill lies in defining the task for the group and helping it work through the different stages, and their role is similar to that of the set adviser in the action learning approach. In using this method, group members obtain the satisfaction of reaching solutions and making decisions without the instructor's involvement.

The greatest difficulty of this approach lies in choosing a suitable task for the group to work on. If the instructor is to avoid taking a directing role, the task must contain some mechanism that gives the students feedback on their progress. A suitable task for a group of college students might involve designing a question paper for their end-of-year examination.

See also: Action learning; Audio tutorial method; Autonomous group learning; Creative dialogue; Instrumented team learning; Learning cell; Media-activated learning group; Parrainage; Structuring seminars; Tutorium

Alcohol recovery programme

Many millions of working days are lost every year because of alcohol-related problems. The cost to industry is considerable. Employees who have a drink problem are three times as likely to be absent from work as the average employee. In most companies, 3–5 per cent of the workforce have a drink problem, and in particular industries, such as catering and brewing, this figure is much higher.

While many companies acknowledge the problem, few are prepared to risk attracting unwelcome publicity by tackling it. Moreover, the staff with the main responsibility for dealing with the problem – occupational health workers and company doctors – almost always lack the influence to approach it constructively. A charity called ACCEPT (Addictions Community Centres for Education and Treatment) has tried to encourage companies to act, instituting a Drinkwatchers programme which seeks to teach the skills of sensible drinking.

The most effective strategy appears to be to encourage organizations to talk about their alcohol policies. This can bring the problem into the open and remove the associated guilt. All those concerned – employees, managers and doctors – can then discuss the range of drinking behaviour without feeling threatened. The company can establish ground rules which make it clear that it will treat alcohol dependence as an illness, that it will help problem drinkers to obtain medical treatment and, if possible, will keep their job open for them without penalty.

Beaumont, P.B. (1981) 'The Problems of Alcoholism in Industry', *Employee Relations*, vol. 3, no. 4, pp. 21–4.

Beaumont, P.B. (1982) 'The Problem of Diffusing Organizational Change: The Case of Alcohol Policies', *Leadership and Organizational Development Journal*, vol. 3, no. 2, pp. 13–16.

Beaumont, P.B. (1983) 'Trade Unions, Organizations and Alcohol Policies', *Industrial Relations Journal*, vol. 14, no. 3, Autumn, pp. 68–75.

Gardner, A.W. (1982) 'Identifying and Helping Problem Drinkers at Work', *Journal of Society of Occupational Medicine*, vol. 32, pp. 171–9.

Guppy, A. and Marsden, J. (1997) 'Assisting Employees with Drinking Problems', *Work and Stress*, vol. 11, no. 4, October–December, pp. 341–50.

Scanlon, W.F. (1991) *Alcoholism and Drug Abuse in the Workplace*, Praeger.

Trice, H.M. and Beyer, J.M. (1982) 'Job-based Alcoholism Programmes: Motivating Problem Drinkers to Rehabilitation', in Pattison, E.M. and Kaufman, E. (eds) *Encyclopedic Handbook of Alcoholism*, Gardner Press.

Weiss, R.M. (1980) *Dealing With Alcoholism in the Workplace*, Conference Board.

See also: Absenteeism/turnover task force; Counselling; Discipline without punishment; Early retirement; Employee assistance programme; Executive family seminar; Job support; Psychodrama; Psychotherapy; Stress management; Wellness programmes

Alexander Technique

The Alexander Technique is a method for correcting destructive habits such as bad posture and bad breathing. Certain actions, such as tensing the whole arm instead of just the wrist, can become so habitual that they end up as automatic reactions, and we are unaware of them. The Alexander Technique aims to make people conscious of their bad habits, thereby helping to control them. The approach was developed by F.M. Alexander (1869-1955), an Australian actor. While observing himself in the mirror one day, he noticed that

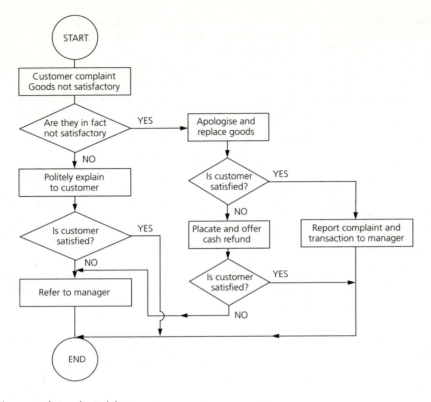

Algorithmic approach to sales training

when he spoke he involuntarily jerked back his head and made a gasping sound through sucking in his breath. By controlling his head movement, he found he could improve his breathing and the functioning of his larynx.

In management training, the Alexander Technique aims to overcome what is held to be the biggest obstacle to learning in adults: their habitual patterns of behaviour, which prevent them from responding in new ways to both new and familiar situations. It seeks to develop our ability to gain conscious control over ourselves by means of the teacher using their hands to communicate directly how this conscious control can be developed through the sensory system. Unlearning precedes new learning. Once managers discover the habits that are hindering their ability to learn something new, they can go on to remove these and become more effective.

Alexander, F.M. and Maisel, E. (1989) *The Essential Writings of F. Matthias Alexander*, Lyle Stuart.

Brennan, R. (1997) *Alexander Technique*, Element Books.

Craze, R. (1996) *Alexander Technique*, Hodder and Stoughton.

Drake, J. (1996) *Alexander Technique in Everyday Life*, Thorsons.

Gelb, M. (1994) *Body Learning*, Aurum Press.

Hodgkinson, L. (1996) *The Alexander Technique*, Piatkus Books.

Stevens, C. (1996) *Alexander Technique: An Introductory Guide to the Technique*, Constable.

See also: Action profiling; Behaviour modification; Bio-energetics; Re-evaluation counselling

Algorithm

Algorithms are recipes or sets of instructions, usually presented in the form of a 'family tree', which can be used to present complex rules and procedures. Any set of rules can be represented diagrammatically, though it is best when the number of interactions or outcomes is limited. Provided the necessary information is accurate, a correct end point will be reached.

Although they may become unwieldy if they become very large, algorithms have proven very useful in organizations, providing systematic plans which reduce problem-solving to a series of comparatively simple operations and indicate, for a variety of contingencies, the order in which the operations should be carried out. It is only necessary to work through the part of the procedure that is directly relevant to the problem, so the time spent on decision-making is reduced and process is simplified.

Creating algorithms can itself be a valuable learning experience, but one of the dangers of using algorithms for instruction is that the learner can arrive at the right answer without understanding how or why. For this reason, they are often called 'anti-teaching devices'. They can be very useful as long as one does not assume that the learner is necessarily doing more than following a simple, usually dichotomous, route map.

Cook, M.H. (1980) 'Algorithmization: A Shortcut to Learning (and to Savings) Parts 1 and 2', *Training and Development Journal*, vol. 34, no. 4, pp. 4–8 and vol. 34, no. 6, pp. 4–7.

Keyworth, R. (1977) 'Communicating Complex Information', *Industrial and Commercial Training*, vol. 9, no. 11, pp. 455–61.

Landa, L. (1974) *Algorithmization in Learning and Instruction*, Educational Technology Publications.

Landa, L. (1976) *Instructional Regulation and Control: Cybernetics, Algorithmization and Heuristics in Education*, Educational Technology Publications.

Manber, U. (1989) *Introduction to Algorithms: A Creative Approach*, Addison Wesley Longman.

Ralston, A. and Neill, H. (1997) *Algorithms*, Teach Yourself Books.

Skiena, S.S. (1997) *The Algorithm Design Manual*, Springer Verlag.

Tavernier, G. (1981) 'Algorithms: Helping Trainees Think Like Experienced Workers', *Management Review*, vol. 70, no. 4, April, pp. 45–9.

See also: Decision table; Flowchart; Heuristic

Alternative dispute-resolution (private arbitration)

Alternative dispute-resolution (ADR) developed out of companies' dissatisfaction with rising legal costs, which were often twice the amount of any compensation the company might be required to pay. Part of this can be attributed to the time-consuming adversarial litigation or arbitration system, in which lawyers are paid for their time, not the end result. Companies in the USA spend about $100 billion a year on litigation, including pre-trial procedures. Any approach which reduces this sum is worthy of careful consideration.

ADR consists of a carefully prepared session in which the two parties in a dispute are represented by company managers who occupy a sufficiently senior position in the organizational hierarchy to be able to decide on the matter without having to refer back. These managers are accompanied by their specialist staff and lawyers. The ADR session is chaired by a neutral party, often a former judge, law professor or practising lawyer. The person chosen for this neutral role might equally have been selected to act as an arbitrator, but their role in an ADR is quite different. The sessions themselves have – somewhat incorrectly – been called 'mini-trials'. While lawyers may present the case for their clients, no trial of any sort takes place.

A typical ADR meeting lasts a couple of days, but it might go on for two weeks. Clarification of issues for the managers may take place after the initial discussion, before agreement has been reached, or even before the chair's summing up. Initially, the aim is to identify and clarify the facts and issues, and the law as it relates to these. A period of questioning takes place, plus short discussions on different matters, in which the managers and staff participate. It is not the aim of this phase to reach a settlement. In the second phase, the chair sums up the presentations and the outcomes of the discussions, and speculates on the relative prospects for the two parties should the dispute be brought to court. An opinion may also be expressed on how long it will take for one party to win, and what order of compensation and costs can be anticipated. This is the first objective of ADR: to provide an estimate of the likely costs of litigation. However, it can be taken a stage further.

The parties to the dispute can ask the chair to suggest a solution, although this is not binding in the way that an arbitration award might be. After listening to the chair's comments, the two sides may retire to separate rooms, and discuss the relative advantages of continuing the dispute by arbitration, litigation, or by settling. Frequently, this is the first time the managers have heard the other side's case in full, so they begin to understand how it developed into a dispute in the first place. The two sides may then reconvene to discuss possible settlements. Rather than an adversarial, legalistic, win–lose approach, ADR allows more leeway in problem-solving, and aims to find a solution acceptable to both parties which will ideally help to develop their business relationship.

ADR can be adapted to meet the particular characteristics of each issue and the degree of trust or confidence the parties have in each other. It does not prejudice any future litigation or arbitration. However, the parties may agree that certain disclosures or partial agreements can be used in subsequent litigation, or they may agree that the neutral chair can make a recommendation, and the party refusing to accept it will pay a stipulated fine if the recommendation is later confirmed in a court of law.

Acland, A. (1995) *Resolving Disputes Without Going to Court: A Consumers' Guide to Alternative Dispute Resolution*, Century Business Books.
Freeman, M. (ed.) (1995) *Alternative Dispute Resolution*, Dartmouth Publishing.
Hibbard, P.R. (1996) *Alternative Dispute Resolution in Construction Contracts*, Blackwell Science.
McDermott, E.P. and Berkeley, A.E. (1996) *Alternative Dispute Resolution in the Workplace*, Quorum.
Trachte-Huber, W. and Huber, S.K. (1997) *Alternative Dispute Resolution*, Anderson Publishing.
York, S. (1996) *Practical Alternative Dispute Resolution*, Longman Law.

See also: Employee assistance programme; Lets'-talk-it-over programme; Mini-trial; Mediation; Ombudsman; Rent-a-judge; Sensitivity bargaining

Analogy teaching

Whenever instructors tell students that something is similar in form or function to something else, yet remains somehow different – for example, that the brain is like a computer, or that the eye is like a camera – they are engaging in analogy teaching. Analogy pervades all our thinking, and for that reason can be used to support the process of learning.

A formal definition of an analogy is: 'a non-literal comparison between superficially dissimilar knowledge domains'. Using an analogy in teaching involves counterposing a new concept (e.g., human nervous system) alongside a familiar one (e.g., computer game). The hope is that the old example will help students conceptualize the new. Analogies are particularly useful in teaching theoretical concepts, where the provision of first-hand experience is not possible.

In addition to helping learners acquire understanding, analogies are also useful to counter misconceptions. Although much of the research and application in the use of analogies has been carried out in the field of natural science, the findings are equally relevant to management education, which is replete with abstract social science concepts.

There are five steps in analogizing. First, analyse the subject, asking what you most want the learners to understand about it. Second, brainstorm the potential analogies, identifying which of the concrete items proposed share the important features that you have identified. Third, choose the analogy which offers the best combination of the following four characteristics: *familiarity* (will the learners recognize the analogy?); *accuracy* (does the analogy accurately reflect the identified feature?); *memorability* (is the analogue vivid enough so the learner will remember it?), and *concreteness* (is it something that can be directly perceived?). The fourth step involves describing the connector and the ground – explaining how the subject and the analogue are alike and different. Finally, the analogy is evaluated in terms of whether it works with the intended audience.

Brown, D.E. (1992) 'Using Examples and Analogies to Remedy Misconceptions in Physics: Factors Influencing Conceptual Change', *Journal of Research in Science Teaching*, vol. 29, pp. 17–34.
Duit, R. (1991), 'On the Role of Analogies and Metaphors in Learning Science', *Science Education*, vol. 75, no. 6. pp. 649–72.
Halprin, D.F., Hansen, C. and Reifer, D. (1990) 'Analogies as an Aid to Understanding and Memory', *Journal of Educational Psychology*, vol. 82, pp. 298–305.
Iding, M.K. (1997) 'How Analogies Foster Learning from Science Texts', *Instructional Science*, vol. 25, pp. 233–53.
McAuliffe, J. and Stoskin, L. (1994) *What Colour is Saturday?: Using Analogies to Enhance Creative Thinking in the Classroom*, Zephyr Press.
Newby, T.J., Ertmer, P.A. and Stepich, D.A. (1995) 'Instructional Analogies and the Learning of Concepts', *Educational Technology Research & Development*, vol. 43, pp. 5–18.
Peattie, K. (1990) 'Pretending to Understand Business Policy', *Management Education and Development*, vol. 21, no. 4, pp. 287–300.
Stepich, D.A. and Newby, T.J. (1988) 'Analogical Instruction Within the Information Processing Paradigm: Effective Means to Facilitate Learning', *Instructional Science*, vol. 17, pp. 129–44.
Stepich, D.A. and Newby, T.J. (1988) 'Analogizing as an Instructional Strategy', *Performance and Instruction*, vol. 27, no. 9, pp. 21–3.
Venville, G.J. and Treagust, D.F. (1996) 'The Role of Analogues in Prompting Conceptual Change in Biology', *Instructional Science*, vol. 24, pp. 295–320.
West, C.K., Farmer, J.A. and Wolff, P.M. (1991) *Instructional Design: Implications from Cognitive Science*, Merrill/Pearson Education.

See also: Concept analysis; Concept Attainment Model; Concept mapping; Concept formation; Metaphor approach; Reframing

Androgynous management

The development of an androgynous management style is based on the belief that successful leadership draws on the best of the 'male' and 'female' characteristics within all of us. Sargent calls this 'androgyny': having the characteristics of both genders. The key to her use of the term is balanced coexistence. Leaders and managers need both logic and intuition, to recognize both facts and feelings, and be both competent and caring.

The androgynous leadership model considers the traditional view of the leader as a highly competent, power-driven person whose feelings are submerged as being inappropriate to modern needs. It also considers the perspective of women and ethnic minorities, who represent groups new to management roles, and for whom the male model of leadership has presented difficulties. The conclusion is that neither model is adequate for successful leadership. Rather than women imitating men, they should adopt the best features men have to offer, and men should do the same with the contributions that women bring. Both groups in the organization would thus possess male and female characteristics. Sargent claims this is desirable because it increases organizational effectiveness and efficiency. In order to achieve this objective, Sargent outlines an intervention which includes self-analysis through various instruments, awareness-raising, role-playing and leadership style development.

Appelbaum, S.H. and Shapiro, B.T. (1993) 'Why Can't Men Lead Like Women?', *Leadership and Organization Development Journal*, vol. 14. no. 7, pp. 28–34.

Blanchard, K. and Sargent, A.G. (1984) 'The Androgynous Manager is a One Minute Manager', *Training and Development Journal*, vol. 38, no. 5, pp. 82–5.

Cooper, C.L. and Lewis, S. (1995) 'Working Together: Men and Women in Organizations', *Leadership and Organization Development Journal*, vol. 16. no. 5, pp. 29–31.

Knowles, M.S. (1984) *Andragogy in Action*, Jossey-Bass.

Sargent, A.G. (1983) *The Androgynous Manager*, AMACOM.

See also: Affirmative action; Diversity training; Gestalt techniques; LIFO method

Apperception-interaction method

This is a projective approach to learning. The instructor begins by identifying problem themes in the daily lives of learners. This may be done through interviews, group discussion or an analysis of essays completed by learners on an appropriate topic. On the basis of these results, a set of learning materials focusing on the themes identified is prepared. These may consist of a provocative picture, an open-ended drama or a brief story. Learners begin by relating their own feelings and experiences to the photograph or story ('apperception') and then go on to explore a particular problem projected in the narrative through a group discussion ('interaction'). The role of the instructor is that of a discussion leader, helping learners to explore the options open to the characters in the story or photograph.

This approach assists learners to work in the affective domain of learning (values, feelings, emotions, beliefs) while having a relatively strong cognitive base. It encourages learners to think for themselves and to explore creative solutions to problems and issues that are uppermost in their minds. The learning materials contain multiple stimuli in the form of motives, situations and characters and visual material. For example, an important current issue is that of women in management. The course designer might interview actual and potential managers of both genders within a company to identify the relevant issues and concerns. Male managers may express views regarding interaction with a female colleague of equal status, their perception of the role of women in society, their capability with regard to their role, and so on. Female staff may express their reluctance to apply for managerial and supervisory positions, or their anxieties about 'being the only woman there'. The instructor can then write a few brief vignettes describing some of the situations described, obtain photographs of female world leaders, collect relevant feminist literature, and so on. This method combines well with some of those listed below.

See also: Confluent education; Drawing for learning; Gestalt techniques; Group discussion; Jurisprudential model; Posters; Psychodrama; Role-playing; Trigger film; Values clarification

Application discussion group (praxis group)

In an application discussion group, students are encouraged to draw relationships between experiences in the group and similar training experiences outside it. In 1947, after Kurt Lewin and his colleagues had stumbled across the T-group method of training, action groups (A-groups) were established to consider this question of application. While these quickly died out in the US model, A-groups or application study groups continue to be a regular feature of the Tavistock Institute of Human Relations' 'Leicester Conferences'.

See also: Post-course follow-up; Sensitivity (T-group) training; Tavistock conference method; Training evaluation as learning; Training transfer training

Application of principles

Joyce and colleagues explain that 'application of principles' is the third element in the inductive thinking model (after 'concept formation' and 'interpretation of data'). The model was developed by Hilda Taba, and can be used separately from the other two elements.

Learners are encouraged to apply the principles they have learned in order to explain new phenomena. 'Application of principles' involves three steps. First, learners are given data and taught principles. Using these, they are required to predict consequences, given initial position descriptions. They explain unfamiliar data and hypothesize what would happen in given circumstances. For example, given the financial details of a company, and given the principles of effective financial management, they are asked to predict the company's future policy or problems. In step two, learners are required to explain or support their predictions. They have to determine the causal links which lead to their prediction. In the final step, learners answer the question, 'What would it take for this prediction to be true or probably true?', to establish the conditions that would be necessary for their predictions to be borne out.

Joyce, B., Weil, M. and Showers, B. (1992) *Models of Teaching* (4th edn), Allyn and Bacon, pp. 119–20.
Taba, H. (1967) *Teacher's Handbook for Elementary Social Studies*, Addison Wesley Longman.

See also: Concept formation; Description-prediction-outcome-explanation; Group investigation model; Interpretation of data

Appraisal (job performance review; performance management; performance review; staff appraisal)

The need for some kind of systematic evaluation or assessment of personnel arose at the beginning of the twentieth century. The term 'appraisal' came to the UK from the USA but, even there, it was probably not used much before the Second World War. Since that time, it has largely superseded the term 'merit rating'.

Appraisal is the systematic evaluation of individual employees' performance on the job and their potential for improved performance and development. It usually takes place within the context of a formal company performance management system which frequently prescribes the structure of the discussion between employees and their managers and the timing of the appraisal meeting during the year. Appraisal and feedback are considered essential for the survival of an organization.

During the appraisal interview, the manager and subordinate jointly set goals for the latter to achieve, review critical work-related incidents, and set performance standards for the future. After the interview, the manager may encourage the employee to analyse their own performance and set their own objectives in line with job requirements. The superior acts in a helping and counselling role. From a learning viewpoint, and depending on the way it is carried out, appraisal can offer employees feedback on their performance. For such information to be of value, it must be reliable, the assessment must be related to a common standard, the whole scheme must be taken seriously by all concerned, and in its final form the information must be usable. Most importantly, all employees must feel that they are being treated as individuals (despite the formal and all-embracing nature of most staff appraisal schemes), and they should all receive sufficient feedback to enable them to know where they stand, and be able to give their own view before major decisions are made regarding their careers.

The staff appraisal scheme can be divided into three elements: the *reward review*, which relates to the employee's pay, power, status and self-fulfilment; the *potential review*, which predicts the level and type of work the individual will be capable of doing in the future, and how long they will take to achieve this, and the *performance review* itself, which focuses on improving the performance of staff in their present jobs. There is a strong argument for carrying out these three reviews separately.

While appraisal discussions have the potential to promote learning, it is rare for significant learning to result from them. There are a number of things an appraiser can do to increase appraisal's benefits for the appraisee. First, it is important to ensure that the feedback provided about the appraisee's performance is related to standards and criteria that have been defined earlier, and which are specific. The appraisee's likely reaction to the appraisal discussion must be anticipated, in particular the part of the interview which deals with their needs for further development. Appraisers must monitor the impact they are having on their appraisees in the course of their discussion. Is it an attack–defend interchange or a mutual problem-solving discussion? What depth of discussion is appropriate? Is it a matter of the appraiser suggesting useful training courses, or could the two openly discuss the failure of the appraisee to accept increased responsibility in the job? Finally, the appraiser might wish to discuss the possibility of agreeing with the appraisee that certain issues will not be recorded on the appraisal form.

Appraisal can be considered part of an organization's change activities. Traditionally, appraisal occurs between an employee and their line manager. It has been argued that appraisal fits into an organizational development programme if it focuses primarily on the work team and is conducted in a participative and transactional manner. 'Transactional' in this context means that, when goals are being set, individuals are given the chance to make their own contribution. Moreover, when a review is carried out, it should not consider an individual's performance in isolation, but should include the influences which affect that performance. These may include the impact of the person's manager, the team in which they work, and the company situation as a whole. Some management-by-objectives programmes stress team leadership, and this has generated interest in team appraisal. Others emphasize a one-to-one style while stimulating interest in self-appraisal – an approach where employees carry out their own evaluation of their performance.

Armstrong, M. and Baron, A. (1998) *Performance Management*, Institute of Personnel and Development.

Edis, M. (1995) *Performance Management and Staff Appraisal*, Kogan Page.

Fisher, M. (1996) *Performance Appraisals*, Kogan Page.

Fletcher, C. (1997) *Appraisal: Routes to Improved Performance* (2nd edn), Institute of Personnel and Development.

Gillen, T. (1997) *The Appraisal Discussion*, Institute of Personnel and Development.

Latham, G.P. and Wexley, K.N. (1981) *Increasing Productivity Through Performance Appraisal*, Addison Wesley Longman.

Laud, R.L. (1984) 'Performance Appraisal and its Link to Strategic Management Development', *Journal of Management Development*, vol. 3, no. 4, pp. 3–11.

Newton, R. and Findlay, P. (1996) 'Playing God: The Performance of Appraisal', *Human Resource Management Journal*, vol. 6, no. 3, pp. 42–58.

Wynne, B. (1997) *Performance Appraisal*, Financial Times/Pitman.

See also: Active learning; Assessment centre method; Feedback; Goal-setting; Goal-setting and planning groups; Job descriptions; Management by objectives; Measuring performance; Periodic planning conference; Position charter; Positive feedback; Self with peer appraisal; Team appraisal; 360-degree appraisal

Appraisal module

The appraisal module is a useful method for structuring group discussion where the task to be performed is the evaluation of something, perhaps an object (e.g., a PC), an event (e.g., staff appraisal), a statement (e.g., from the government) or a proposal (e.g., from the managing director).

There are two elements involved in this activity. The first is the acquisition of a *warrant*: a proposition that serves to support or justify the evaluation of the thing as good or bad, desirable or undesirable, fair or unfair. In some cases, the warrant will be the same as the criteria for evaluation. The second element consists of a *set of facts* that connect whatever is being evaluated to the warrant, and thus support the evaluation of it.

Taking a proposal as the focus of the exercise, the warrant might be: 'any staff selection technique that predicts high employee performance and success in the job should be used as a basis for recruiting people to the company'. The set of facts would be those which showed the validity of a certain selection technique in predicting employee performance. Applying the warrant and the facts to the question of whether a particular technique should be used or not serves to structure the discussion.

Let us consider another application: carrying out an appraisal. A group of trainees prepares a check-list/appraisal form against which the performance of an individual or a group of individuals can be judged, first working individually and then in groups. One member of the trainee group then does something which is appraisable, for example giving a short talk, interviewing a job applicant or giving a stranger directions, and the other trainees appraise the volunteer's performance. Individual assessments can then be compared and discussed.

This method can be useful either to highlight the important elements for success in performing certain tasks, or to emphasize the subjectivity and consequent variability in assessing performance. The exercise can be applied to setting objectives, appraisal for improvement, appraising someone else's performance, and so on.

Meux, M.O. (1963) 'The Evaluating Operation in the Classroom', in Bellack, A.A. (ed.) *Theory and Research in Teaching*, Bureau of Publications, Teachers College, Columbia University.

Stewart, V. and Stewart, A. (1978) *Managing the Manager's Growth*, Gower.

Stewart, V. and Stewart, A. (1978) *Practical Performance Appraisal*, Gower.

See also: Argumentation; Jurisprudential model; Management audit; Mock trial; Training evaluation as learning

Apprenticeship

The apprenticeship process is one of the oldest known forms of education, and has produced skilled craftspeople for hundreds of years. It is ideally suited to transferring information, and produces high levels of student motivation.

The key element of the information transfer process is being placed in the charge of a skilled and experienced practitioner. By observation and imitation, the apprentice assists the practitioner in their duties, learning the relevant skills and repaying the practitioner by assisting them. In this learning situation, the apprentice is exposed to certain key concepts, and the practitioner can directly observe the behaviour of the apprentice, determining whether those key concepts have been acquired. The practitioner can give immediate corrective instruction if the apprentice's performance reveals differences in their understanding of task performance. The apprentice is motivated because they know that the practitioner can provide the type of assistance that will allow them to make rapid progress on learning tasks, enabling them to progress to increasingly complex ones, thereby gaining recognition, positive reinforcement and increased self-esteem. Finally, the apprentice develops positive inter-personal relationships with the practitioner, thereby increasing their commitment to the learning task.

The term 'apprenticeship' is also used loosely to describe any form of on-the-job experience, and is sometimes wrongly equated with 'sitting by Nellie'. However, as the description above highlights, the practitioner's role in apprenticeship is active, not passive.

As a management learning and development approach, apprenticeship can be, and has been, used on occasions when an individual takes over the job of another person. Before taking over, the new incumbent works as an understudy to the person they will succeed.

Hasluck, C. (1997) *Modern Apprenticeship*, The Stationery Office.
Mainiero, L.A. (1986) 'Muddling Through: The Anguish of Apprenticeship', *Leadership and Organization Development Journal*, vol. 7. no. 5, pp. 3–7.
Organization for Economic Co-operation and Development (1995) *Apprenticeship: Which Way Forward?*, OECD Publications.
Revans, R.W. (1968) 'The Management Apprentice', *Management International Review*, vol. 8, no. 6, pp. 29–42.
Sinclair, S. (1997) *Making Doctors: An Institutional Apprenticeship*, Pavilion.
Williams, G. (1977) 'Apprenticeship Revisited', *Journal of Further and Higher Education*, vol. 1, no. 2, pp. 65–73.

See also: Assignment to manager with high development skills; Development assignment; Expanding job assignment; Exposure to upper management; Internship; Manager shadowing; Mentoring; One-to-one learning; On-the-job training; Parrainage; Rotation training; Student placement; Structured tutoring; Understudy

Argumentation

'Argumentation' refers to a process, rather than its outcome. Spoken and written argument is a feature of both debate and formal discussion, and the argumentation approach focuses on the process or action of arguing.

The terms 'reasoning' and 'argumentation' are often either used synonymously or are confused. *Argumentation* refers to the entire activity of making claims, challenging them and backing them up, while *reasoning* is more narrowly restricted to presenting reasons in support of a claim. Hence, reasoning can be viewed as a sub-area of argumentation.

There are four elements to argumentation training: first, a focus on *claims*, which are the assertions made or positions taken by the arguer; second, the *grounds*, which are the foundation for those claims, frequently offering a proof of some kind; third, *warrants*, which justify a link between the claim and the grounds for it, and fourth, the *backing*, which is the general body of information that is presupposed by the warrant and is appealed to by the arguer.

The study of arguments and argumentation itself have become a distinct teaching approach in which the different elements of arguments used in different subject fields are explored and the variety of forms argument takes becomes the focus of study, particularly, but not exclusively, in higher education.

Andrews, R. (1989) *Narration and Argument*, Open University Press.
Andrews, R. (1995) *Teaching and Learning Argument*, Cassell.
Andrews, R. (1997) 'Reconceiving Argument', *Educational Review*, vol. 49, no. 3, pp. 259–69.
Phelan, P.J. and Reynolds, P.J. (1995) *Argument and Evidence*, Routledge.
Thompson, A. (1996) *Critical Reasoning*, Routledge.
Warburton, N. (1996) *Thinking from A to Z*, Routledge.

See also: Advocacy; Appraisal module; Buberian dialogue; Case debate; Debate; Jurisprudential model; Mock trial; PIT technique; Short talks by students

Assertiveness training

Assertiveness training was developed by Andrew Salter in 1949, and has established itself firmly in management development and training. The approach aims to help people to avoid embarrassment in communicating their legitimate grievances to others: for example, returning unsatisfactory goods to a shop or complaining to neighbours about excessive noise.

The purpose of assertiveness training is to help participants take account of their own and other people's feelings, and in so doing preserve their self-esteem. The training method involves roleplays of situations in which they find it difficult to assert themselves. It illustrates how we can allow ourselves to be manipulated into feeling guilty, giving in to unreasonable requests and then harbouring hostilities and resentments. It teaches people to change their expectations and behaviour by encouraging a more assertive approach. Lack of assertiveness can result from a fear of upsetting people and provoking resentment. Some managers may find this type of training helpful in workplace transactions such as disciplinary interviews, staff appraisals and interdepartmental communications.

Gillen, T. (1997) *Assertiveness*, Institute of Personnel and Development.
Huczynski, A. (1996) *Influencing Within Organizations*, Pearson Education Europe, Chapter 10.
LeMon, C. (1997) *Assert Yourself*, Gower.
Morris, S. and Willcocks, G. (1996) *Putting Assertiveness to Work*, Pitman.
Rakos, R (1992) *Assertive Behaviour: Theory, Research and Training*, Routledge.
Townhead, A (1991) *Developing Assertiveness*, Routledge.

See also: Achievement motivation training; Acting assignment; Awareness training; Confidence-building training; Consciousness-raising group; Motivation achievement training; Role-playing; Self-efficacy training

Assessment centre method (development centre; management centre)

Assessment centres are used by companies for staff selection, to assess the potential of managers for promotion, and to identify managers' development needs. The candidates are given a series of tests, and they participate in an interview, a group discussion and a number of similar events. While they perform their tasks, a group of managers trained as observer-judges rank their relative performance.

The assessment centre method involves exercises, case studies and simulations to stimulate behaviour which would either not normally occur during the course of a job, or if it did, would not lend itself to observation and measurement. For this reason, the technique is most commonly used to identify an individual's potential for significant career change. Many engineers, salespeople and scientists who have attended assessment centres have gone on to become managers, and junior and middle managers have progressed to senior management positions. Some companies also run graduate assessment centres which provide information about candidates to supplement personality and intelligence tests.

Assessment centres were first used in the UK during the Second World War, in order to meet the special selection needs it created. While the Civil Service has continued to rely on them, the technique was developed further in the USA, where it has become a popular means of measuring managerial potential, and has enjoyed a greater degree of acceptance than in the UK.

What makes an assessment centre a developmental tool rather than just a method of selection is the feedback candidates receive about their performance, and the opportunities for development which are subsequently provided for them. Allowing candidates to apply for the assessment centre experience and promoting some of them serves to create openness and mobility within a company.

Recently, experiments have been carried out on team selection of candidates for posts, which allows companies to identify and meet the development needs of their employees. Assessment centres have also been used as a research tool. Douglas Bray, who conducted longitudinal studies into managerial characteristics and careers at AT&T, used the approach in this way.

Ballentyne, I. and Povah, N. (1995) *Assessment and Development Centres*, Gower.
Forester, A. and Iles, P. (1994) 'Development Through Assessment Centres', *Organizations and People*, vol. 1, no. 3, pp. 7–11.
Dalziel, S., McDougall, M., Barclay, J. and Nimmo, R. (1993) 'Introducing Development Centres into Management Education', *Management Education and Development*, vol. 24, no. 2. pp. 280–92.
Goodge, P. (1992) 'Development Centres for the

90s: Third Generation Design', *Organizations and People*, vol. 1, no. 3, pp. 18–20.

Iles, P. (1992) 'Centres of Excellence? Assessment and Development Centres, Managerial Competence and Human Resources Strategies', *British Journal of Management*, vol. 3, no. 2, pp. 79–50.

Jackson, R.P. (1992) 'Development Through Assessment Centres', *Organizations and People*, vol. 1, no. 3, pp. 13–17.

Jansen, P. and de Jonge, F. (1997) *Assessment Centres*, Wiley.

Woodruffe, C. (1997) *Assessment Centres*, Institute of Personnel and Development.

See also: Appraisal; Feedback; Realistic job previews; Self with peer appraisal; Team appraisal

Assessment of the organization as a system

This approach, developed by Joseph H. Hand and Melvin E. Allerhand, assesses an organization or department as an operating system in order to identify both the sources of the problems and the people who can deal with them. Such an assessment may take nine or ten hours, and consists of seven stages. The consultant considers the system as a whole, to establish a baseline view, then each of the following systems is studied in turn: leadership/decision-making, communication/information, resources, inter-personal relationships and review/evaluation.

In the first stage, the system is considered as an organism, and is tested to ensure that each of its parts exists, and that they are effective. Then follows the identification of members in the organization who tend to be the sources of thinking, feeling, listening, digesting, action, blocking, expenditure of energy and energy consumption. In the second stage, the leadership/decision-making system is considered. How are decisions made and implemented? How do power groups operate in the organization? The third stage considers the communication/information system. Who collects the information? What is it used for? What information is specific to the organization, and what are the patterns of the information flow? In stage four, the resource system is considered. What resources are available to carry out work tasks? Which are available for growth? What is the best way to pull them together? Stage five studies the inter-personal relationship system. What is the past history of mutual support and of conflict? Who is open with their views, and who is resistant to change? Stage six considers the review/evaluation system. Who carries out evaluation, how often, and does it make a creative impact on the organization? The final stage is to communicate the assessment results to the managers. Having checked the information with company staff, the consultant extracts up to ten or so important aspects of each of the subsystems studied, and presents these in the assessment report, which contains conclusions and recommendations for action.

Merry, U. and Allerhand, M.E. (1977) *Developing Teams and Organizations*, Addison Wesley Longman, pp. 39–46.

See also: ACHIEVE model; Benchmarking; Diagnostic activities; Functional Administrative Control Technique; Interviewing; Looking for trouble; Management audit; Organizational analysis; Overhead value analysis; 7-S framework

Assignment attachment

Assignment attachments provide a framework for giving students feedback on written assignments. Instructors inform students about the evaluation criteria beforehand, such as 'ability to specify the question' or 'adequate definition of key terms', and provide written and oral feedback on each of them.

Their second and equally important task is to standardize the grades awarded, by listing the different aspects of the assignments which will be considered, to ensure that different markers assess them according to an agreed set of criteria. For instance, if a course is being taught by a team and assignments are given out by different team members to different seminar or syndicate groups within the course, it is important that marks or grades and feedback criteria are standardized, because these are the learning objectives for the exercise. To some extent, therefore, assignment attachments force instructors to specify learning objectives.

See also: Essay; Feedback

Assignment to community organization

In this form of development, a manager may be seconded to a civic, community, voluntary or social organization for a continuous period of up to a year. For example, a major international electronics company has lent managers with development potential to certain organizations to solve inner-city problems. While there are no financial benefits to the organization, the individuals concerned return to their posts having learned something, and the company has served as a good corporate citizen. The problem is to ensure that the employees involved are clear about their learning goals, and do not allow these to be compromised by the demands of their new job or the glamour of being involved in a (necessarily) rare form of staff development.

With this approach, the company must ensure that the secondment is not just a matter of good public relations, but will prepare the managers for whatever role the company intends them to play in future, or whatever the managers have in mind for themselves. For example, there would be little point in a college seconding one of its teaching staff to the local authority's social services department to learn counselling skills unless the college intended to expand the counselling services it offered its students, and intended making that a bigger part of the staff member's job in future.

Ashridge Management College (1998) *Making Community Investment Work*, Ashridge Management College.

Badeaux, L.M. (1982) 'Volunteer Organizations Serve as Leadership Labs for Business Persons', *Leadership and Organizational Development Journal*, vol. 3, no. 4, pp. 23–6.

Kelly, E. and Jackson, D. (1998) *Corporate Responsibility, Community Involvement and Social Entrepreneurship*, Tranman, c/o Pat Robson, 78 Clifton Rd, Prestwich, Manchester M25 2HR.

Lovell, G. (1994) *Analysis and Design: A Handbook for Practitioners and Consultants in Church and Community Work*, Burns and Oates Publishers.

Paton, J. (1992) *Making the Most of Employee Community Volunteers*, National Centre for Volunteering.

Watkins, T. et al. (1997) 'Recycling: A Structured Student Exercise', *Journal of Management Education*, vol. 21, no. 2, pp. 244–54.

See also: Accepting positions of responsibility in community associations/university societies; Assignment to customer as representative; Assignment to government body study group; Development assignment; Employee volunteering; Job swop; Secondment; Service in professional associations

Assignment to customer as representative

In this form of development, a manager may be assigned for a certain period to work closely with one of the company's major customers. The customer benefits by having its particular problems examined in depth by a representative of its supplier, and the manager benefits by being placed in a new and challenging work environment.

This approach avoids some of the difficulties of assignment to a community organization because

the manager is almost certain to develop in a way which will benefit their own firm on their return.

Whitehead, M. (1997) 'Mind the Gap', *People Management*, 9 October, pp. 40–2.

See also: Accepting positions of responsibility in community associations/university societies; Assignment to community organization; Assignment to government body study group; Development assignment; Job swop; Service in professional associations; Staff exchange

Assignment to government body study group

Managers may sometimes be invited to serve on a governmental or quasi-governmental committee which is investigating a particular problem or issue because such bodies require their specialized knowledge. With this approach, the company involved needs to be clear about the developmental needs of its own staff, but when such requests come from the government or its agencies, political considerations may make it difficult to refuse.

In the UK, such a study group was formed under the leadership of a Cabinet minister following a period of rioting in inner-city areas. On this occasion, representatives of leading investment institutions were invited to participate, and banks, insurance companies and pension funds lent the services of chief executives, chairs of boards of trustees and senior property executives. When, as in this case, the issue is politically contentious, both companies and individual managers may feel uneasy about their involvement.

See also: Accepting positions of responsibility in community associations/university societies; Assignment to community organization; Assignment to customer as representative; Development assignment; Job swop; Secondment; Service in professional associations

Assignment to manager with high development skills

Within an organization, certain managers may be identified as having the skills, knowledge, ability and temperament to develop their subordinates to a higher degree or at a faster rate than others. Such individuals may possibly, although not necessarily, be 'plateaued' managers, who are not expected to progress up the career ladder, but developing a junior staff member may itself be considered a developmental activity for the senior manager concerned. Managers who take on this role must be clear about their responsibilities, and may require training and development themselves to carry out their new role.

How does one identify an individual with such skills? Managers who are good, conscious developers of their staff are capable of drawing out the strengths and weaknesses of their subordinates, rather than suppressing them. They reward their subordinates both materially and psychologically for the risks they take in attempting to develop themselves. They identify learning opportunities for their staff, and they devote time to their development – for example, reviewing and analysing an activity for learning purposes. They involve their subordinates in some of their own important tasks, rather than simply delegating trivial ones. They share some of their problems and anxieties with their staff to promote their development, rather than simply to seek relief for themselves. They listen rather than talk. They do not say or imply, 'Be more like me.' They are willing to take risks regarding the desired results of their unit in pursuit of relevant learning opportunities for their staff.

Leigh, D.R. (1966) 'Development or Developers: Developing Others as a Management Development Method', *Training and Development Journal*, November, pp. 42–6.
Mumford, A. (1980) *Making Experience Pay*, McGraw-Hill, p. 4.

See also: Acting assignment; Apprenticeship programme; Coaching; Development assignment; Expanding job assignment; Exposure to upper management; Internship; Manager shadowing; Mentoring; Parrainage; Rotation training; Sick leave/holiday replacement assignment; Structured tutoring

Attitude survey

An attitude survey is a systematic investigation of the attitudes and feelings of the workforce. Since behaviour is related to attitudes, managers may seek to identify employee attitudes in order to change them if they do not match company goals.

An attitude survey seeks to overcome the weaknesses of some of the other attitude-collecting techniques which lack objectivity and which represent only the views of the vocal minority. Properly conducted, it can gauge the views of the entire workforce, either by asking each person individually or by obtaining a representative sample of views. Some large organizations run a regular survey, while others carry one out when there is a specific problem to diagnose or explain. Such a survey can also act as a communication device to gather the ideas of staff in a way that other, more traditional channels cannot. A survey allows

managers to monitor attitude trends, can forewarn them of problems, and allows them to take action in good time.

Attitude surveys have been used extensively in change implementation programmes. Two aspects are particularly important in this context. First, they can be used in assessing the potential reaction to proposed changes. Second, they permit management to consider employees' attitudes at the start of the programme, thereby minimizing the suspicions that such change can cause.

The survey process can be thought of as consisting of eight stages: defining the objectives, communication with employees, survey design, piloting the survey instrument, administration, analysis, feedback and action.

While companies can use their own staff to conduct an attitude survey, there are advantages in calling on independent researchers or consultants who can provide managers with the survey expertise they lack, since a badly conducted survey will produce misleading results. Respondents may also be concerned that their answers could be used against them by management, and are more likely to give honest responses if those asking the questions and running the survey are independent of the company, giving a greater guarantee of confidentiality and objectivity.

French, W.L. and Bell, C.H. (1984) *Organization Development: Behavioural Science Interventions for Organization Improvement* (3rd edn), Pearson Education.
Walters, M. (1996) *Employee Attitude and Opinion Surveys*, Institute of Personnel and Development.
White, M. (1980) 'Getting the Drift of Employee Attitudes', *Personnel Management*, January, pp. 38–42.

See also: Action enquiry; Action research; Corporate culture training; Data-based intervention; Drawing for learning; Focus group; Ideological change; Metaphor approach; Myth-making interventions; Organizational climate analysis; Questionnaires; Self-generated scaling; Survey feedback

Audience reaction/watchdog team (concept moderators)

When conducting a meeting which involves a number of platform speakers and a large audience, inviting members of the audience on to the platform to serve as a reaction or watchdog team can promote involvement. An *audience reaction team* simply listens to the presentation and then gives its reactions, either in a series of statements or through a panel discussion, whereas an *audience watchdog team* monitors language or concepts it thinks members of the audience might not fully understand, and may interrupt the presenter at any time to ask for clarification. If the people selected to serve on the team are a representative cross-section, the audience will identify psychologically with the interaction on the platform.

One application of this idea, *concept moderation*, has been developed by de Winter Hebron. If a large group, such all those attending a conference, is working in a number of small sub-groups and the organizer suspects there may be valuable points for a watchdog team to consider – for example, how particular labels are being used by group members – one participant in each sub-group can be given the additional role of looking out for these as the sub-group's work progresses. In addition, one or more persons can be assigned to go round all the sub-groups, visiting their individual meetings. In this way, each group has a concept moderator who knows the whole of the group's work, and also one or more concept moderators who know some of what has been going on in all the sub-groups. These moderators then meet and examine which problems run through the whole of the conference and which are specific to particular sub-groups, report their findings to the whole conference in a plenary session about half-way through the proceedings, and this is followed by a discussion. The sub-groups then reform and continue working, having clarified and shifted their perceptions of what is being said.

See also: Colloquy meeting; Controlled discussion; Forum meeting; Interrogation of experts; Listening team; Reaction panel

Audio for learning

Audio in teaching can take at least two forms: audio cassettes may be played in the lecture or training room, or they may be used as an adjunct to self-study and computer-based learning. Audio tapes can be used either as a method of breaking up a period of lecturing or to stimulate and provoke students in a seminar or small-group discussion.

Audio tapes are easy to prepare beforehand, and since the instructor controls the content, they have many potential applications. For example, an item such as an interview with a politician or a union representative can be extracted from a current affairs programme and replayed to the lecture class or small group, but it needs to be short enough to have an immediate impact. In a lecture class, the teacher can comment on the views expressed and then ask for audience reaction through votes of

agreement or disagreement. Alternatively, buzz groups can be asked to discuss the views expressed. In small-group discussion, more in-depth questioning techniques can be used. Many other stimuli for discussion can be put onto a tape, such as short dramatic sequences (similar to trigger films), a scripted discussion between two people with opposing views on a key issue, analysis of telephone conversations, and so on. Audio is also a feature of self-instruction approaches. Originally, these took the form of a book with a cassette, but this approach is being replaced by computer-based courseware delivered through CD-ROMs, or over the Internet in the form of 'streamed audio'.

Aarntzen, D. (1993) 'Audio in Courseware: Design Knowledge Issues', *Education and Training Technology International*, vol. 30, no. 3, pp. 354–66.

Engel, C.E. (1971) 'Preparation of Audio Tapes for Self Instruction', *Medical and Biological Illustration*, vol. 21, no. 1, pp. 14–18.

McDonald, R. and Knights, S. (1979) 'Learning from Tapes: The Experience of Home Based Students', *Programmed Learning and Educational Technology*, vol. 16, no. 1, pp. 46–51.

Rahmlow, H.F. and Langdon, D.G. (1977) 'Ubiquitous Audio', *Programmed Learning and Educational Technology*, vol. 14, no. 1, pp. 9–12.

Rowntree, D. (1994) *Teaching With Audio in Open and Distance Learning*, Routledge.

See also: Audio tutorial method; Group buzz; Media-activated learning group; Tape-assisted learning programme; Tape stop exercise; Television programme; Trigger film

Audio tutorial method

Although the original technology has been superseded, with PC-based presentations replacing cassette tapes and slides, the general concept of the audio tutorial method (ATM) remains valid. For individual learners, ATM will involve individual work in carrels or cubicles, group working and attending lectures. The key factor is the balance between the different activities in which the learner engages.

ATM is used mainly where it is not feasible to make all the resources available at a certain time or continuously. It consists of administrative techniques and procedures which allow slow and active learners to absorb course material, while freeing rapid learners to proceed as quickly and in as much depth as they are able. In an ATM course, each cohort of students works through the same set of materials in the same order. However, individual learners can take as much time as they feel necessary to complete the work, although everyone is expected to finish the same work in a given amount of time, equal to a 'grading period'. The grade is related to the amount of material covered as verified by criterion tests, which are often of the objective test type.

Courses organized primarily on an ATM model frequently include large-group meetings from time to time so that learners will feel less isolated and can have face-to-face contact with the 'voice from the machine'. Optional or compulsory discussion groups or quiz sessions may also be scheduled. Although formal lectures are often integrated into the course, these are not mentioned in the self-instructional material. The software tends to be a guide only to what is in the computer, carrel or audio tutorial lab. A printed study guide is also very common, and contains objectives, questions, spaces for answers, diagrams, and so on. The value of this is that the student can retain it as a record of the audio tutorial session.

Carre, C.G. (1969) 'Audio Tutorials as Adjuncts to Formal Lecturing in Biology Teaching at Tertiary Level', *Journal of Biological Education*, vol. 3, no. 1, pp. 57–64.

Garland, P.B., Dutton, G.J. and MacQueen, D. (1977) 'Audio Tutorial Aids for Teaching Biochemistry', *Studies in Higher Education*, vol. 2, no. 2, pp. 167–71.

Koumi, J. and Daniels, J. (1994) 'Audio Guided Learning With Computer Graphics', *Education and Training Technology International*, vol. 31, no. 2, pp. 143–56.

Meyer, C.R. (1972) 'Audio-tutorials: An Overview', in Simpkins, W.S. and Miller, A.H. (eds) *Changing Education: Australian Viewpoints*, McGraw-Hill.

Postlethwait, S.N. and Hurst, R.N. (1972) 'The Audio Tutorial System Incorporating Mini-courses and Mastery', *Educational Technology*, September.

Postlethwait, S.N., Murray, H. and Novak, J. (1972) *The Audio Tutorial System: An Integrated Experience Approach to Learning*, Burgess.

Pressey, S.L. (1964) 'Audio-instruction: Perspectives, Problems, Potentials', in Hilgard, E.R. (ed.) *Theories of Learning and Instruction: 63rd Yearbook of the National Society for the Study of Education*, University of Chicago Press.

See also: Audio for learning; Autonomy lab; Autonomous group learning; Block method; Computer-assisted learning; Info bank; Language laboratory; Learning through discussion; Mastery learning; Media-activated learning group; Personalized system of instruction; Self-instructional model and interactive group; Tape-assisted learning programme

Autonomous group learning

Autonomous group learning (AGL) combines programmed instruction and the participative group activity of the case study method to provide an environment to motivate managers without relying on formal instruction. An AGL session usually consists of two eight-hour days, each of which is made up of two learning cycles of approximately four hours. This gives learners a sense of achievement and completion when they finish each stage. A typical sequence consists of a personal welcome by the instructor, an audio-visual presentation indicating the objectives and methods which will be used, a quiz to be completed individually, individual work, an audio-visual lecture and a case study group discussion.

AGL sees instruction as a means of controlling and manipulating a sequence of events to produce a change of behaviour, relying on simple technology such as books, papers and audio cassettes, although nowadays multi-media PCs may also be used. There is no formal instruction. Learning takes place in an environment which neither directs nor teaches learners, but draws on the ability of the group to stimulate and react to them in conditions of self-discovery and mutual help. The learning process is designed to be a cyclical and rhythmic activity of information input and application clearly relevant to the learner's business environment which rewards them by providing continuous group activity and knowledge of results, thereby motivating them to continue. The design incorporates the element of surprise, with tests and quizzes to challenge the learners and reward them.

Boland, R.G.A. (1977) 'The Design of the Autonomous Group Learning System', *Programmed Learning and Educational Technology*, vol. 14, no. 3, pp. 233–9.

See also: Audio tutorial method; Autonomy lab; Case study method; Guided group problem-solving; Independent study; Instrumented team learning; Mastery learning; Media-activated learning group; Personalized system of instruction; Programmed learning; Self-directed learning; Self-instructional model and interactive group

Autonomous workgroups (autonomous work teams; high-performance teams; self-managing workgroups; self-managed teams)

An autonomous workgroup is a group of employees who operate without a manager and who are responsible for a complete work process or segment that delivers a product or service to an external or internal customer. Autonomous workgroups resemble problem-solving teams in that they consist of small numbers of workers from the same department. Groups can develop their own culture, can adapt their behaviour patterns to individual group needs, and can implement any solutions they develop to overcome work problems.

This form of work organization developed from research on socio-technical systems. Focusing only on the technical factors of a job means that important social needs and the functioning of the social group tend to be ignored. The Hawthorne studies of the 1920s and 1930s and the socio-technical systems research of the 1960s highlighted the need to understand the influence groups can have on productivity. The thrust of systems research has been the development of autonomous – that is, self-governing – workgroups in place of individual effort. Rather than assembly lines, some companies have begun to organize work around group efforts, with a team leader instead of a supervisor or foreperson. The specialization of labour is minimized, and this affects the job design.

The autonomous workgroup approach attempts to restore a family-like atmosphere in larger organizations by giving employees the opportunity to identify with the smaller group. While circumstances differ, each group may conduct a number of tasks. It plans and operates within a budget, sets goals to meet production schedules, assigns work to individual team members, operates in assigned production roles, sets overtime schedules, selects a team leader or establishes a shared leadership process, assists in the selection of new team members, applies discipline within the group, and maintains communication with other teams. Members often cross-train each other so that each is able to perform the variety of tasks assigned to the team. Productivity gains are attributed in part to the exercise of considerable flexibility in scheduling and work rules. Because of the high degree of self-sufficiency these teams develop, they have been described as 'self-managed'.

Autonomous workgroups are found in non-union environments, and the training programmes associated with them emphasize team-building skills and quality control techniques. Individual group members' wages are often related to their level of knowledge.

US experience of autonomous workgroups suggests that they are easier to implement in production facilities in which assembly work is done in a circular or rotary arrangement than on a traditional assembly line. It appears that the process of selecting new workers must be geared to selecting employees who are able to work in unsupervised, self-directed settings.

Barry, D. (1991) 'Managing the Bossless Team', *Organizational Dynamics*, Summer, pp. 31–47.

Chang, R.Y. and Curtain, M.J. (1995) *Succeeding as a Self-managed Team*, Pfeiffer/Jossey-Bass.

Colenso, M. (1998) *High Performing Teams*, Institute of Management/Butterworth Heinemann.

Ford, R.C. and Fottler, M.D. (1995) 'Empowerment: A Matter of Degree', *Academy of Management Executive*, vol. 9, no. 3, pp. 21–8.

'HR Change at British Steel: A Cast Iron Success Story?', *IRS Employment Trends*, no. 655, May 1998, pp. 11–16.

Kemp, N.J., Wall, T.D., Clegg, C.W. and Cordery, J.L. (1983) 'Autonomous Work Groups in a Greenfield Site: A Comparative Study', *Occupational Psychology*, vol. 56.

Parker, S.K. and Wall, T.D. (1996) 'Job Design and Modern Manufacturing', in Warr, P. (ed.) *Psychology at Work* (4th edn), Penguin, pp. 333–58.

Torres, C. and Speigel, J. (1995) *Self-directed Work Teams: A Primer*, Pfeiffer/Jossey-Bass.

Trist, E.L., Susman, G.I. and Brown, G.R. (1977) 'An Experiment in Autonomous Working in an American Underground Coal Mine', *Human Relations*, vol. 30, pp. 201–36.

Wilson, P. (1996) *Empowering the Self-Directed Team*, Gower.

Yeatts, D.E. (1998) *High Performing Self-managed Work Teams*, Sage.

See also: Collateral organizations; Greenfield plants; Group technology; Independent product teams; Integrated support functions; Intrapreneurial group; Job enrichment; Job rotation; Likert's level meetings; Linked subcontracting; Matrix designs; Participation; Quality of working life; Socio-technical systems design; Structural interventions

Autonomy lab (creativity laboratory)

The autonomy lab (also known as the 'laboratory in autonomy, initiative and risk-taking') is an educational event used to encourage autonomous learning, based on the view that managers are neither born nor 'made' by others, but create themselves. Throughout the lab, individuals are encouraged to find their own motives, strengths, interests and patterns of development. These decisions help them to choose and learn from the wide variety of materials which characterize the lab.

A unique aspect of this programme is the absence of the constraints on learners which tend to feature in most other teaching/learning situations. Labs are designed according to the principle that participants should be in control of their own learning, that the design should allow them to choose activities they consider appropriate (based on their experience, background, method and speed of learning), and should cater for learners' own needs, motives and values. Finally, there should be an acceptable level of risk-taking, and hence stress, for each learner.

The physical features of the autonomy lab may include a wide range of learning resources, such as exercises, books, games, audio cassettes, case studies, handouts, articles and questionnaires. Participants are also encouraged to see themselves, other participants and their instructors as learning resources. The instructor's role is to guide learners to the resources that are available and give advice on how they can be used to the greatest effect.

The lab may begin with a brief introductory talk, and there will be a daily full-group meeting in which everybody shares experiences and assesses progress. Labs are usually run on a residential basis and last three to seven days. Participants are encouraged to take risks, set personal goals and take initiatives about their own development without depending on instructors. An additional facet is the encouragement of 'learning how to learn': developing a framework for solving hitherto unmet problems.

Harrison, R. (1973) 'Developing Autonomy, Initiative and Risk Taking Through a Laboratory Design', *European Training*, vol. 2, pp. 100–17.

Megginson, D.F. (1975) 'An Autonomy Lab in Identifying Training Needs', *Youth in Society*, November/December.

See also: Audio tutorial method; Autonomous group learning; Community of enquiry; Independent study; Instrumented feedback; Instrumented laboratory; Instrumented team learning; Learning community; Learning organization; Media-activated learning group

Awareness training (self-awareness training)

This is a generic term for any programme of instruction, approach or course whose objective is to increase participants' self-knowledge. In addition, students develop alternative behaviour patterns for their personal and social development. This approach is based on psychologists' and educators' views that self-awareness is essential to productive personal and inter-personal functioning. The self-knowledge such training seeks to promote lies in the areas of personal values, cognitive style, inter-personal orientation, personal, interests, leadership style, and so on.

Knowledge about one's self comes from two sources – internal and external. *Internal self-knowledge* is gained through trainees completing and interpreting self-assessment questionnaires. The most popular starting point for such self-exploration is the Myers Briggs Indicator of personality type. Students complete their questionnaires and interpret their meanings in the context of the theory, research or models presented by the instructor. They then compare and discuss their scores, both against some norm provided by the instructor, and also in groups with other course members. The scores are meaningless in themselves: they must be compared to others'.

External self-knowledge is gained from other people by engaging in activities such as role-plays, exercises, in-baskets, where participants' behaviour is observed and they are given feedback about it. The insights and interpretations which arise may challenge their own self-concept, and thereby raise their self-awareness. Beyond the course context, such diverse feedback has been institutionalized in the form of team appraisal and 360-degree feedback, where each person in a team or department receives feedback on aspects of their performance and behaviour from those above, around and below them.

When originally used during the 1960s in the USA, awareness training, in its myriad forms and flavours, was considered controversial. Now, its principles and methods have been incorporated into more traditional approaches, and are used at various educational levels, including secondary schools. Joyce and colleagues cite the FIRO model developed by William Schutz as an exemplar of this educational approach. What Schutz's and the many similar methods have in common is that they seek to increase personal awareness and happiness. They also share a two-step sequence: the learners engage in a game or perform a task while the instructor or facilitator gives directions and ensures that the environment is safe. Once they have completed the game or task, the learners discuss their reaction to it. This discussion has three ground rules: taking responsibility for your own actions, focusing as much on your feelings as on thoughts, and being prepared to give and receive feedback. We will consider each of these in greater detail, since they are common aspects of other awareness-raising methods.

First, learners must acknowledge that they, and not others, are responsible both for any sources of their difficulties and for doing something about them – that they must be proactive, taking decisions for themselves, and not rely on others. This is reflected in the language they are encouraged to use, such as saying 'I won't' rather than 'I can't.' Second, focusing on feelings reflects the fact that the game or task is designed to provoke not only a cognitive but also an emotional response.

People may become angry, annoyed or satisfied. The discussion seeks to make them aware of their feelings and direct experience, not just their thoughts and reasons. Finally, the discussion emphasizes giving and receiving feedback. Providing information about how others experience you, and how you experience them, is a key aspect of awareness. Effective feedback is specific, direct and timely. Awareness training seeks to promote honesty and openness.

Fisher, J.D., Silver, R.C., Chinsky, J.M., Goff, B. and Klar, Y. (eds) (1990) *Evaluating a Large Group Awareness Training: A Longitudinal Study*, Springer Verlag.
Joyce, B. and Weil, M. (1980) *Models of Teaching* (2nd edn), Allyn and Bacon, pp. 187–206.
Schutz, W. (1958) *FIRO: A Three Dimensional Theory of Interpersonal Behaviour*, Rinehart and Winston.

See also: Achievement motivation training; Assertiveness training; Classroom meeting model; Co-counselling; Confidence-building training; Instruments; Instrumented laboratory; Open encounter; Questionnaires; Self- with peer appraisal; 360-degree feedback

Basic encounter (Rogersian group method)

Basic encounter was developed by Carl Rogers and his colleagues in Chicago. Participants usually sit on chairs throughout, and there is little or no physical interaction. The leader, who is called a *facilitator*, offers no techniques and does not have to adopt any particular role except that of an open participant ready to reveal their feelings and show interest, care and involvement in the talk and actions of group members. Facilitators may also share their intuitions or fantasies about other members – not as truths about other people, but as truths about what is going on in the group.

Rogers formulated three requirements for facilitators: they show *acceptance* of other people and the way they are – not judging or evaluating them; they cultivate *accurate empathy* – trying to sense feelings that are just below the surface; they display *genuineness* – being aware of what is going on inside themselves and doing justice to it.

Basic encounter is a good starting experience for someone who has never taken part in an encounter group. Participants will not be pushed into extreme experiences before they are ready, and they can progress at their own pace.

Rogersian groups tend to be very 'slow' but sure. Whatever happens in them – little or much – is very real, and there is no tolerance of insincerity.

Rogers, C. (1961) *On Becoming a Person*, Houghton Mifflin.
Rogers, C. (1967) 'The Process of Basic Encounter', in Bugental, J.F.T. (ed.) *Challenges of Humanistic Psychology*, McGraw-Hill, Chapter 28, pp. 261–76.
Rogers, C. (1970) *Encounter Groups*, Penguin Books.
Rogers, C. (1990) *The Carl Rogers Reader*, Constable.

See also: Cluster laboratory; Cousin laboratory; Encounter group; Gestalt techniques; Human relations laboratory; Instrumented laboratory; Open encounter; Organizational laboratory; Sensitivity (T-group) training; Tavistock conference

Basic practice model

The basic practice model of teaching is based on learning theory, and is the most common approach to teaching. It has been described by Joyce and colleagues as consisting of five main phases.

In the first phase, *orientation*, the instructor establishes the content of the lesson, reviews previous learning, describes the lesson's objectives, and sets out the procedures for the lesson. In the second phase, *presentation*, the instructor explains or demonstrates the new concept or skill, provides a visual representation of the task, and checks learners' understanding. Phase three consists of *structured practice*: the instructor leads the learners through practice examples, and they respond with questions while the instructor corrects any errors and reinforces correct practice. The fourth phase involves *guided practice*: the learners practise the skill or apply the knowledge, and while they do this, the instructor moves among them, monitors their progress, and provides feedback and praise. In the fifth phase, the learners *practise independently* at home, possibly over an extended period, and the feedback they receive is delayed.

Joyce, B., Weil, M. and Showers, B. (1992) *Models of Teaching* (4th edn), Allyn and Bacon, pp. 299–323.

See also: Behaviour modelling; Behaviour modification; Interaction management

Behaviour analysis

Behaviour analysis involves taking any content-focused activity – such as a lecture, discussion, business game or staff meeting – and allocating time for the group to consider how problems are being solved and roles allocated.

Participants discuss issues such as the suitability of their methods for resolving differences of view, whether individuals are dominating the conversation, and whether the meeting is being handled well. The aims are to help the group overcome the limitations of being orientated exclusively on a particular task, and to cultivate process awareness and process skills. Discussing the ways group members react to one another allows participants to gain greater insight into their own and others' behaviour, and can also help them relate more effectively to each other.

When behaviour analysis is applied to the lecture situation – for example, if a teacher wishes to review the structure and approach of their lecture – verbal behaviours are analysed using a speech classification system whose categories might include proposing, building, supporting, disagreeing, giving information and seeking information. Every time a person speaks, an observer decides which category their utterance falls into, and at the end of the discussion they will have drawn up a record of who spoke and what kind of contribution they made.

Buchanan, D.A. and Huczynski, A.A. (1997) *Organizational Behaviour: An Introductory Text* (3rd edn), Prentice-Hall, pp. 223–5.

Honey, P. (1990) *Face to Face Skills*, Gower.

McCredie, H. (1991) 'Behaviour Analysis Revisited: Some New Perspectives', *Management Education and Development*, vol. 22, no. 4, pp. 315–22.

Mumford, A. (1976) 'Management Development and the Powers of Observation', *Personnel Management*, vol. 8, no. 10, pp. 26–9.

Rackham, N. and Morgan, T. (1977) *Behaviour Analysis in Training*, McGraw-Hill.

Rackham, N., Honey, P. and Colbert, M. (1970) *Developing Interactive Skills*, Wellens Publishing.

See also: Controlled pace negotiation; Coverdale training; Group development laboratory; Group dynamics laboratory; Interactive skills training; Process analysis; Sociometry

Behaviour modelling (social learning theory)

At Stanford University, Albert Bandura developed an elaborate theory of imitation, identification and modelling in teaching which he called *social learning*.

In teaching by modelling, teachers behave in ways they want their students to imitate. Three outcomes were identified by Bandura: the *modelling* effect, whereby the learner acquires new kinds of response patterns (for example, teachers show students how to listen empathetically by listening empathetically themselves); the *inhibitory/disinhibitory* effect, whereby the learner increases/decreases the latency/intensity of previously acquired responses (for example, the teacher shows students that it is/is not approved behaviour to express their feelings openly, thus inhibiting or disinhibiting an old response), and the *eliciting* effect, whereby students receive from the model a cue which releases a response that is neither new nor inhibited (for example, the teacher models the art of giving and receiving feedback by inviting students to criticize their own performances in helpful ways).

A number of management training packages draw upon behaviour modelling theory. Positive modelling (showing how something should be done) is held to be more effective than negative modelling (showing how not to do something). The aim is to increase individuals' behavioural repertoire by providing them with examples of alternative, more effective behaviours in a variety of situations relevant to their jobs. Behaviour adaptation can be encouraged by role-playing, through which participants gain some experience of the application and effectiveness of different approaches to a problem or situation. The usual pattern is for trainees to observe a model of effective behaviour on a video or audio tape, then role-play it themselves before applying it in the work situation.

In the field of management development, managers and colleagues provide role models for recruits to emulate, based on their *actions* – what they do rather than what they say. This may be a conscious or unconscious process, and all managers need to be aware that they teach their staff by example. Staff may copy others' behaviour in expectation of reward or for fear of punishment, and it may or may not have positive outcomes: for example, a recruit may notice that their boss asks them and their departmental colleagues for ideas about a problem, and may try to emulate this behaviour; on the other hand, a recruit may observe that their boss does not share information with others, and may model this behaviour.

Atkinson, J., Dolan, M., Pettigrew, N. and Hyndley, K. (1994) *Jobsearch: Modelling Behaviour and Improving Practice*, Institute for Employment Studies.

Bandura, A. (1986) *Social Foundations of Thought and Action*, Prentice-Hall.

Decker, P.J. (1985) *Behaviour Modelling Training: Principles and Applications*, Harcourt Brace.

Decker, P.J. (1986) 'Social Learning Theory and Leadership, *Journal of Management Development*, vol. 5, no. 3, pp. 46–58.

Johnson, P.D. and Sorcher, M. (1976) 'Behaviour Modelling Training: Why, How and What

Results', *Journal of European Training*, vol. 5, no. 1, pp. 62–70.

Jones, L. (1981) 'Behaviour Modelling – Training by Demonstration', *Education and Training*, vol. 23, no. 2, pp. 39–41.

Kraut, A.I. (1976) 'Developing Managerial Skills via Modelling Techniques: Some Positive Research Findings – A Symposium', *Personnel Psychology*, vol. 29, no. 3, pp. 325–8.

Latham, G.P. and Saari, L.M. (1979) 'Application of Social Learning Theory to Training Supervisors Through Behaviour Modelling', *Journal of Applied Psychology*, vol. 64, pp. 239–46.

Manz, C.C. and Sims, H.P. (1981) 'Vicarious Learning: The Influence of Modelling on Organizational Behaviour', *Academy of Management Review*, vol. 6, no. 1, pp. 105–13.

Moses, J.L. and Ritchie, R.J. (1976) 'Supervisory Relationships Training: A Behavioural Evaluation of a Behaviour Modelling Programme', *Personnel Psychology*, vol. 29, no. 3, pp. 337–43.

Porras, J.I., Hargis, K., Patterson, K.J., Maxfield, D.G., Roberts, N. and Bies, R.J. (1982) 'Modelling-based Organizational Development: A Longitudinal Assessment', *Journal of Applied Behavioural Science*, vol. 18, no. 4, pp. 433–6.

Smith, P.E. (1976) 'Management Modelling Training to Improve Morale and Customer Satisfaction', *Personnel Psychology*, vol. 29, no. 3, pp. 351–9.

Snell, R. (1993) 'More Than Meets the Eye: Adopting a Management Style Through Modelling', *Leadership and Organization Development Journal*, vol. 14, no. 5, pp. 3–11.

See also: Basic practice model; Behaviour modification; Brainwashing; Human process approach; Interaction influence analysis; Interaction management; Manager shadowing; Role modelling; Role-playing; Self-efficacy training

Behaviour modification (organizational behaviour modification; reinforcement techniques; behaviour management)

Behaviour modification has its roots in the psychological theory of behaviourism which was championed by B.F. Skinner, who distinguished between respondent or reflexive behaviour, which is the result of classical conditioning, and operant behaviours and those which result from operant conditioning.

In operant conditioning, whose key elements include reinforcement, conditioning and extinction, the subject must 'operate' on the environment to obtain a desired outcome or reward. When applied to human beings, the technique is known as behaviour modification, and will be familiar to any parent.

The theory holds that people are most likely to engage in desired behaviour if they are rewarded for doing so (*positive reinforcement*). Rewards are most effective if they immediately follow the desired behaviour response, and behaviour which is not rewarded or which is punished (*negative reinforcement*) is less likely to be repeated. Since punishment is known to have many undesirable side effects, negative reinforcement is often less efficient than positive reinforcement in developing the desired behaviour. Individuals may be rewarded every time they behave in a desired way, or only occasionally (*intermittent reinforcement*), and evidence suggests that the latter method produces behaviour changes more rapidly. Linking the reinforcement of different desired behaviours allows a much larger behaviour pattern to be established.

Behaviour modification seeks to change the behaviour of a person in a particular direction through a process called *behaviour therapy*, which focuses on changing actions and responses, rather than identifying and analysing their underlying causes. Following its initial success in the mental health field, where it produced dramatic changes in the behaviour of patients, the technique was applied to school classrooms and child management problems. Then in the 1970s it began to be applied to the management of human relations in the workplace. For example, if a manager consistently solves a worker's problems, the worker will learn that the best way to solve problems is to bring them to their boss. The manager will reinforce this problem-bringing behaviour by continuing to provide solutions, but by a process of negative reinforcement (telling employees to solve their own problems) or positive reinforcement (congratulating employees if they solve problems for themselves), the manager can seek to eliminate the undesired behaviour.

The basic premise of organizational behaviour modification is that organizational behaviour is a function of its consequences, and can be portrayed in a five-step problem-solving model. Step one involves identifying the behaviours that have a significant impact on performance (selling goods, servicing customers). The next step is to measure these behaviours and derive a baseline frequency by determining the number of times they are occurring under present circumstances. Step three entails a functional analysis of the behaviours. Here, the antecedent conditions (the cues which elicit the behaviour and sometimes control it), and the consequences (which currently maintain the behaviour) are identified as a prelude to designing an effective intervention strategy. In step four, the intervention strategy is developed, with the aim of strengthening and increasing desired behaviours through positive reinforcement, or weakening and decreasing undesired behaviours. The final step is to evaluate the intervention to check whether performance has been improved.

Behavioural engineering using these techniques has been criticized on ethical grounds, some claiming that it manipulates behaviour, whereas proponents of the approach argue that managers attempt to manipulate the behaviour of their employees all the time (in subtle and less subtle ways). Other applications of behaviour modification include teaching machines and programmed learning.

Andre, R. and Bannister, B.D. (1987–8) 'The Self-shaping Project as a Tool for Teaching Managerial Uses of Behaviour Modification', *Organizational Behaviour Teaching Review*, vol. 12, no. 4, pp. 94–101.

Bandura, A. (1969) *Principles of Behaviour Modification*, Holt, Rinehart and Winston.

Cox, C. and Makin, P. (eds) (1994) 'Behavioural Approaches to Organizational Change', special issue of *Leadership and Organization Development Journal*, vol. 15, no. 5.

Feeney, E. J. (1973) 'At Emery Air Freight, Positive Reinforcement Boosts Performance', *Organizational Dynamics*, vol. 1, no. 3, Winter, pp. 41–50.

Gullett, C.R. and Reisen, R. (1975) 'Behaviour Modification, A Contingency Approach to Employee Performance', *Personnel Journal*, vol. 54, no. 4, April.

Hammer, W.C. and Hammer, E.P. (1976) 'Behaviour Modification on the Bottom Line', *Organizational Dynamics*, vol. 8, no. 1, Summer, pp. 42–50.

Honey, P. (1987) *Solving People Problems*, McGraw-Hill.

Makin, P.T. and Hoyle, D.J. (1993) 'The Premack Principle – Professional Engineers', *Leadership and Organization Development Journal*, vol. 14, no. 1, pp. 16–21.

Marr, J.N. and Roessler, R.T. (1994) *Supervision & Management: A Guide to Modifying Work Behaviour*, University of Arkansas Press.

Martin, F. and Pear, J. (1996) *Behaviour Modification*, Prentice-Hall.

Miltenberger, R.G. (1996) *Behaviour Modification: Principles and Procedures*, Wadsworth Publishing.

Schloss, P.J. and Smith, M.A. (1998) *Applied Behaviour Analysis in the Classroom*, Allyn and Bacon.

Sundel, S.S. (1993) *Behaviour Modification in the Human Services*, Sage.

Sutherland, V. et al. (1995) 'Quality Behaviour for Quality Organization', *Leadership and Organization Development Journal*, vol. 16, no. 6, pp. 10–15.

Zirpoli, T. and Melloy, K.J. (1996) *Behaviour Management: Applications for Teachers and Parents*, Prentice-Hall.

See also: Action maze; Alexander Technique; Basic practice model; Behaviour modelling; Brainwashing; Discipline without punishment; Feedback; Human process approach; Interaction management; Norm formation; Norm modification; On-the-job training; Positive peer culture; Reinforcement environment analysis; Role prescription; Self-management

Behavioural simulation

Behavioural simulations aim to reproduce individual and collective behaviours, including normal political, cultural and conflict activities that typify organizational life, and usually last between one and three days. Activities include role-plays, experiential exercises, assessment centre exercises and individual in-basket exercises.

Extensive background information is provided to allow participants to interact realistically, and in-baskets are prepared for each simulated role. All these baskets are interconnected to reflect organizational conditions.

The roles participants are allocated are designed to reflect real-life settings, including top management roles in a company, and because of the time limitations, it is important that they take their roles seriously. They are expected to behave, react and interact as naturally as possible.

Gunz, H.P. (1994) 'Learning from a Realistic Behavioural Simulation', *Journal of Management Education*, vol. 18, no. 1, pp. 45–60.

Keys, B. and Wolfe, J. (1990) 'The Role of Management Games and Simulations in Educational Research', *Journal of Management*, vol. 16, pp. 307–36.

McCall, M.W. and Lombardo, M.M. (1982) 'Using Simulation for Leadership and Management Research', *Management Science*, vol. 28, pp. 533–49.

Oddou, G.R. (1988) 'Managing Organizational Realities: An Evaluation of a Semester Long Experiential Simulation', *Organizational Behaviour Teaching Review*, vol. 13, no. 2, pp. 47–54.

Randolph, W.A. and Miles, R.H. (1979) 'The Organization Game: A Behaviourally Played Simulation', *Exchange: The Organizational Behaviour Teaching Journal*, vol. 4, no. 2, pp. 31–5.

Seltzer, J. (1988–9) 'Experiences with Looking Glass', *Organizational Behaviour Teaching Review*, vol. 13, no. 1 pp. 58–65 and 66–7.

Stumpf, S.A., Dunbar, R.L.M. (1989–90) *Organizational Behaviour Teaching Review*, vol. 14, no. 2, pp. 43–62.

See also: Assessment centre method; Classroom as organization model; Experiential exercise; Game; In-basket exercise; Microteaching; Playing for learning; Programmed simulation; Role-play; Simulation; Surrogate client

Benchmarking (competitor analysis)

Benchmarking involves continuously comparing one organization's products, services, practices and performance levels with those of others, in order to identify areas for improvement. Improvements may result from the shock value of the comparison itself, or from extracting principles of best practice which can be emulated.

Benchmarking may focus on the internal or external operations of direct competitors or recognized industry leaders, the features and performances of individual products, or may be carried out as a generic process, also known as *functional benchmarking*, where non-competitors whose functions or processes are similar share data with one another.

Internal benchmarking – comparing processes within the same organization – and *competitor benchmarking* – comparing an organization with a competitor – both share the same difficulty of ensuring that one is comparing like with like. Obtaining data from competitors to enable comparisons is often a problem, although much of the relevant information is usually publicly available, and commercial sensitivity may mean that trusted, independent third parties are engaged to carry out the assessment.

Bogan, C.E. and English, M.J. (1994) *Benchmarking for Best Practices*, American Society for Training and Development Press.

Bramham, J. (1997) *Benchmarking for People Managers*, Institute of Personnel and Development.

Bramley, P. (1996) *Evaluating Training Effectiveness, Benchmarking Your Training*, McGraw-Hill.

Codling, S. (1995) *Best Practices Benchmarking*, Gower.

Codling, S. (1998) *Benchmarking*, Gower.

Cook, S. (1997) *Practical Benchmarking: A Manager's Guide to Creative Competitive Advantage*, Kogan Page.

Cox, A. and Thompson, I. (1998) 'On the Appropriateness of Benchmarking', *Journal of General Management*, vol. 23, no. 3, pp. 1–20.

Fisher, J. (1996) *How To Improve Performance Through Benchmarking*, Kogan Page.

McGonagle, J.J. and Fleming, D. (1998) 'Options in Benchmarking', *Journal for Quality and Participation*, vol. 21, no. 2, pp. 38–42.

Zairi, M. (1998) *Benchmarking for Best Practice*, Butterworth-Heinemann.

See also: ACHIEVE model; Assessment of the organization as a system; Diagnostic activity; Feedback; Management audit; Overhead value analysis; 7-S framework

Bioenergetics

Bioenergetics, one of the 'growth therapies' that has entered management training, was developed by US psychiatrist Alexander Lowen, who studied under Wilhelm Reich.

Bioenergetic therapy is based on the view that repressed anxiety or emotion express themselves internally in muscle tension. Such tension dulls individuals' feelings, and they spend a great deal of their time tensed up in an attempt to defend themselves against uncomfortable or painful emotional experiences. This unconscious tension becomes part of the person, and they may become unable to feel anything at all. A consequence of this reduction of feeling is a reduction of energy.

An important aspect of the therapy is the idea that a person's beliefs, attitudes and habits rigidly structure their thoughts, feelings and behaviour. In order to change, individuals must explore themselves at a deep level so that the 'unfinished business' from past experiences can be identified and worked on. It is believed that such unfinished business draws what exponents term the 'life energy' from the current tasks the person has to deal with, since they waste energy holding down feelings they have been conditioned not to express. The equal emphasis on the physical dimension arises out of the belief that psychological rigidities of behaviour are reflected in the body. Thus, it is argued, the training must focus on the cognitive as well as the affective dimensions.

The bioenergetic therapist suggests or conducts a series of exercises, including stress postures, breathing, sound and vigorous body movement that stretch those muscles which have become tight and locked and which restrict movement. The aim is to identify and reduce the muscular tension that prevents the energy flowing, thus promoting a feeling of wholeness and leaving practitioners more open to experience and expression. In addition to physical tensions, the exercises deal with verbal expressions of emotions and anxieties that are released along with the release of the body defences.

As with other growth therapies, bioenergetics aims to help the individual respond to change, become more self-regulating, deal better with feelings, and generally to cope better with problems.

Feldman, S. (1974) *Alexander Lowen*, Lancer Books.
Lowen, A. (1971) *The Language of the Body*, Macmillan.
Lowen, A. (1990) *Spirituality of the Body*, Pearson Education/Macmillan.
Lowen, A. (1994) *Bioenergetics: A Practical Guide*, Penguin Books.
Mukohata, Y. (ed.) (1992) *New Era Bioenergetics*, Academic Press.

See also: Alexander Technique; Cognitive behavioural therapy; LIFO method; Personal development laboratory; Psychotherapy; Re-evaluation counselling Stress management

Biography (autobiography)

Biography work seeks to help people improve their understanding of their personal life patterns, events and circumstances, and to develop a better relationship with these factors in order to plan for the future.

At the individual level, this work is capable of being integrated with management development. Its primary aim is to develop the participant, who may use the techniques repeatedly. Managers may work on the forces of professional formation and deformation, creativity, life patterns and rhythms.

In a biography seminar, participants work with other participants to explore their total life field, taking into account education, talents, profession, career, organizational culture, personal biography, marriage, family situation and health. Programme approaches include counselling, group discussion, individual reflection on personal questions, exercises and lectures.

Abbs, P. (1974–5) 'Autobiography and the Training of Teachers', *Universities Quarterly*, vol. 29 pp. 10–12.
Leary, M. (1981) 'Working with Biography', in Boydell, T. and Pedler, M. (eds) *Management Self-Development: Concepts and Practices*, Gower.
Mann, S. and Pedler, M. (eds) (1992) 'Biography in Management and Organizational Development', special issue of *Management Education and Development*, vol. 23, no. 3, Autumn.

See also: Career life planning; Historical analysis; Values clarification

Biological science inquiry model

The biological science inquiry model was developed by Schwab. Although it has its genesis in the study of biology, it is equally relevant to social science disciplines such as management.

The distinguishing feature of the biological science inquiry model is that it is designed to help students understand not only the nature of scientific ideas, concepts and facts, but also scientific methods. The model consists of three steps.

First, the student is presented with a description of research, which may be past, present or even proposed. The account includes a description of the research methods used to investigate the phenomenon or topic. Next, the research problem is structured for the student in such a way that they can identify the difficulties in the investigation, which may relate to the way the problem is defined, the way data is collected, how the variables in the experiment are controlled, how data is interpreted or the inferences that are made. Any aspect of the research process can be made the focus of attention. Finally, the student is asked to speculate on ways of overcoming the difficulty. Suggestions may involve changing the research design, replacing the research methods used, collecting the information in a different way, analysing the data differently or proposing a different interpretation.

Joyce, B., Weil, M. and Showers, B. (1992) *Models of Teaching* (4th edn), Allyn and Bacon, pp. 128–36.
Schwab, J. (1965) *Biological Sciences Curriculum Study: Teacher's Handbook*, Wiley.

See also: Dissertation proposal; Medical model

Block method

The central emphasis in the block method is the differentiated assignment, based on the assumption that students in a single class will fall into three or four relatively homogeneous ability groups.

The teacher provides a set of graded assignments, and the students are encouraged to select one of the 'blocks' or 'levels' and try to meet its requirements. A student may achieve one level during a certain term or part of a term, and advance or recede to another in the next period.

Determining what constitutes a block is a difficult process. The teacher usually proceeds on the basis of the minimum of essentials, then adds projects and other extra work. The only way to determine the difficulty of the blocks is by experience, for example:

- Block D – Test assignment and tests
- Block C – D plus four oral reports

- Block B – C plus one written report
- Block A – B plus one oral book report.

The method can have a stimulating effect on students, encouraging those of mediocre ability to aspire to the higher levels. It also provides variety in procedure and activity. There is no limit to the kinds of blocks that can be used.

See also: Audio tutorial method; Guided study; Learner contract; Skill session; Worksheet

Book reviewing

In this approach, students are asked to consider the different functions of book reviews which appear in publications such as popular magazines, newspapers, learned journals, hobby and leisure magazines. Their task is to agree a range of criteria against which a review may be judged. They then take a book that is related to the course and, using the criteria previously identified, they write a 'relevant' review of that book. If time and resources permit, the same book title may be reviewed by several students, and the similarities and differences in perceptions and judgements examined.

The approach can be also used to practise the skills of abstraction and processing information. Trainees can be given the task of preparing a précis of a book, paper or report for a given purpose: for example, a government White or Green Paper may be studied in order to discover what implications it has for the managing director. This is followed by a review and a further practice session. Few adults have any skills in précising, so the review may enhance vocabulary, concentrating on methods of skipping, page layout, marking documents, and so on.

Another aspect of the approach is reviewing information which is disagreeable or which is presented in an unpalatable way, while understanding what it says. In management education, the products of Marxist literature may be particularly suitable for this purpose: for example, an anti-capitalist guide to health and safety at work which illustrates how safety regulations are flouted in the interests of convenience. When a text such as this is given to managers to review in writing with a specified word limit, it can distinguish between those who are put off by the politics of the presentation and those who can nevertheless understand what is being said. Such an exercise can be followed by a trainer-led discussion on the subject.

Dehler, G.E. (1996) 'Management Education as Intentional Learning: A Knowledge Transforming Approach to Written Composition', *Journal of Management Education*, vol. 20, no. 2, pp. 221–35.

Gard, W. (1979) *Book Reviewing*, A.A. Knopf.

Lindholm-Romantschuk, Y. (1998) *Scholarly Book Reviewing in the Social Sciences and Humanities*, Greenwood Press.

Oppenheimer, E. (1981) *Oral Book Reviewing to Stimulate Reading*, Scarecrow Press.

See also: Essay; Guided study; Library assignment; Literature search; Reading; Reading parties; Rewriting

Bottom-up management

'The junior manager's "freedom to fail" underlies all decentralization strategies.' This phrase has become the hallmark of a philosophy which William B. Given called 'bottom-up management'. The philosophy is based on a combination of decentralization and participation.

Given was the President of the American Brake Shoe Company, where he developed and applied this philosophy to over fifty plants. Typical managers consider that those persons below them in the organization are working for *them*, and are serving their needs. The bottom-up philosophy of management reverses such traditional thinking, viewing the manager as working for *his or her employees*, and the manager's job as improving the way they service subordinates so that they can perform their own work more effectively. In a sense, managers become service providers to those below them, instead of bosses.

In order to practise bottom-up management, the company must be decentralized into functional units and federal units (separate product businesses). Authority is delegated as far down the line in the organization as possible, giving all employees the management freedom to think, plan, and to fight for their plan.

Bottom-up management encourages staff to take calculated risks and, most importantly, Given claimed, it gives them the freedom to make mistakes. In his view, if managers are to make decisions, they must have the freedom to make mistakes occasionally without feeling that their first error will either cost them their job or ruin their promotion chances. The basic assumption is that judgement deals with intangibles, and cannot therefore be completely certain. Since judgement is uncertain, managers who practise it must be given the freedom to fail. They must know that they have to make mistakes in order to learn and grow.

Managers who apply bottom-up management are as much teachers as order-givers. They help their staff learn how to lead and how to make effective decisions. In doing this, they themselves grow. Traditional top-down management is not completely ousted in this view, but has a role in dealing with broad policy and goals issues.

Clifford, D.K. and Cavanagh, R.E. (1986) *The Winning Performance: How America's Midsize Companies Succeed*, Sidgwick and Jackson, p. 213.
Given, W.B. (1949) *Bottom Up Management*, Harper and Brothers.

See also: Business teams; Empowerment; Independent product teams; Intrapreneurial group; Job support; Managerial decentralization; Reprogramming; Simulated entrepreneurship

Brains Trust

In learning, asking the right questions is often as important as obtaining the right answers. When the subject matter is uncontroversial and does not raise issues that can be discussed easily, or when students are unwilling to express their difficulties in class, buzz groups may be instructed to agree a question they wish to ask the lecturer, to write it on a sheet of paper, and pass it anonymously to the front. This technique provides teachers with feedback on their effectiveness, and provides clarification of the lecture points. It can also be used when a guest speaker is invited. Students can be asked to research and prepare questions, the answers to which form the basis of the presentation.

The Brains Trust can also be the first level of audience participation at a large meeting (as in the famous radio programme of that title). Questions are directed from the audience through a chairperson or addressed directly to panel members, who must be of high calibre and expert in their subject in order to be capable of standing up to the questioning.

The approach can be used to provide a background knowledge or a general survey of a subject. It can thus be designed to replace the general standard lecture. Within a company, it can be used to give junior staff an insight into the scientific and research aspects of the firm.

See also: Clinic meeting; Colloquy meeting; Forum meeting; Gordon seminar; Group buzz; Interrogation of experts; Interview meeting; Listening team; Panel discussion; Questioning; Reaction panel

Brainstorming

Brainstorming was developed by Alex Osborn, the founding partner in a US advertising agency. The technique was originally used in 1939 to draw up an advertising programme, but it can be tried whenever an organization or group wants to develop creativity or free-wheeling ideas, which may depart drastically from generally accepted practice.

Six to ten people are assembled in a room and asked to solve a particular problem within a fixed period. What makes brainstorming unique is the emphasis on creating an enthusiastic and non-judgemental atmosphere which gives participants the space to generate hitherto unthought-of solutions, the ideas generated being reviewed more soberly in a later session and the most valuable ones retained. To facilitate this process, the following guidelines are used.

First, during the brainstorming session itself, criticism of the ideas expressed is not permitted since it is felt that it inhibits creativity by encouraging self-censorship. Requiring group members to remain non-judgemental about the value of others' suggestions is thought to encourage creativity. Second, no idea is considered too outlandish, and participants are encouraged to call out any idea that comes to mind. Third, participants are encouraged to build upon the suggestions of others – to 'piggy-back' ideas. Stress is laid on group development and ownership of solutions, rather than on individual development and ownership. Finally, production of as many ideas as possible is encouraged, on the basis that the greater the number of ideas available, the greater the probability that a useful one will be found.

There are also a number of guidelines governing the composition of the group: one or more group members must possess the information necessary to arrive at a solution, such as the relevant knowledge and experience; the greater the need for such varied experience and knowledge to solve the problem, the greater the advantage the group will have over the individual; the group needs leadership so that its deliberations are focused on the objectives.

The brainstorming session is conducted as follows. The group is formed, and ideas are called out and written on a flipchart without consideration or criticism so that they can be evaluated at leisure. If a range of ideas is to be dealt with, then criteria must be established at the outset, so that the group can evaluate rationally without each person defending their own pet scheme. In this way, a long list can be cut down to a short one, bearing in mind that even an idea which does not immediately meet the criteria can be developed later. It may turn out to be necessary to consider a combination of two or three ideas. Thus the advantages of all of the ideas can be combined and the most suitable developed to obtain the best results.

Twenty to thirty minutes is probably the most appropriate limit for a brainstorming session on a particular subject, but changes of topic allow several almost consecutive sessions. The funda-mental method is capable of much variation. For example, there is the *waste-not* variant, in which a group is shown an apparently valueless by-product or factory waste item, and is asked to brainstorm some positive uses. In the *and also* variant, a suggestion is made and taken up by each group member with contributions that amount to 'Yes, and also this would make it more effective.' Finally, there is the *tear-down* variant, where the aim is to think of all the limitations, failings or drawbacks of a specific project. Each is then studied to identify possible remedies.

It is important that brainstorm group leaders are well trained, as failure can often be attributed to leader incompetence, either not defining the problem adequately or not paying sufficient atten-tion to testing and evaluating the ideas generated.

Despite criticisms of the approach, brain-storming has been widely used in many public and private firms. Brainstorming on its own cannot be seen as a problem-solving technique since it does not encourage analysis and value judgements. Its main purpose is to support problem-solving, and it has been incorporated in different ways in a number of problem-solving approaches.

Clark, C. (1989) *Brainstorming: How to Create Successful Ideas*, Wilshire Books.

Gallupe, R.B. (1993) 'Electronic Brainstorming and Group Size', *Academy of Management Journal*, vol. 35, pp. 351–3.

Kay, G. (1995) 'Effective Meetings Through Electronic Brainstorming', *Journal of Manage-ment Development*, vol. 14, no. 6, pp. 4–26.

Osborn, A.F. (1948) *Your Creative Power*, Charles Scribner's Sons.

Osborn, A.F. (1979) *Applied Imagination* (3rd edn), Charles Scribner's Sons.

Rawlinson, J.G. (1981) *Creative Thinking and Brainstorming*, Gower.

See also: Brainwriting; Creativity training; Down-up-down-up problem-solving method; Evaluation committee method; Kepner-Tregoe Approach; Lateral thinking; Management oversight and risk tree; Mind Mapping®; Nominal group technique; Problem-solving cycle; Questioning; Suggestion schemes; Synectics; Think tank

Brainwashing

Brainwashing is an individually focused change strategy that received most attention during the Korean War in the early 1950s. It consists of five steps.

First, the subject is *emptied of previous beliefs*. In the Korean War, for example, the captured US soldiers had their 'buddy' system broken down by only being allowed to receive mail such as 'Dear John' letters and those carrying messages such as 'Your car is being repossessed.' The aim was to persuade the prisoner that his country had forgotten and abandoned him. Next, a *vacuum* is established. After the soldier had 'confessed his sins' and rejected all former beliefs, he was left for a time to sweat it out in the terrifying condition of being without any belief system at all. The next step is the *refilling* process. The soldier was now in a receptive state, and was responsive to the teach-ings of a kindly, intelligent instructor. Finally, *reinforcement* completes the cycle. The soldier took over the process of his own re-education by parti-cipating in lengthy doctrinal sessions under the watchful eye of his instructor.

This process is relevant to business management methods because it differs little from some of the persuasion techniques that are used daily on us and by us. For instance, a car salesperson might use the technique on a customer who is loyal to another car brand. A potential car buyer who has decided on brand A drops into the salesroom filled with brand B models to check the prices in order to be able to negotiate later with the brand A sales-person. The brand B salesperson discovers the customer's brand loyalty in casual conversation. Delicately, 'because they know it is painful for the customer', they point out one of brand A's faults, thus setting off the first step in the brainwashing process, emptying of previous beliefs. Step two, establishing a vacuum, is achieved by refusing to discuss the weaknesses of brand A any further, with the excuse of 'not wishing to run down a competitor's product'. The seeds of suspicion have been planted, the belief vacuum has been created, and the customer is left to suffer, going away to think about it, taking with them salesperson B's competitive price. If the customer returns, they will allow salesperson B to take step three – extol-ling the superiority of brand B while pointing out brand A's deficiencies. Once the customer is softened up, the salesperson also points out all the areas where brand B scores over brand A. The customer then takes the final step, possibly using salesperson B's arguments in an attempt to get salesperson A to reduce the price. Intriguingly, the customer will become somewhat deaf to the efforts of salesperson A to point out brand A's advantages, and will feel insulted that the salesperson should try to mention brand B's weaknesses.

Ashanti, K.F. (1991) *Psychotechnology of Brain-washing: How to Re-programme Your Mind*, Tone Books.

Bromley, D.G. (1983) *Brainwashing/Deprogram-ming Controversy*, Edwin Mellen Publisher.

Cialdini, R.B. (1988) *Influence: Science and Practice*, HarperCollins.

Collins, A. (1998) *In the Sleep Room: The Story of CIA Brainwashing Experiments in Canada*, Key Porter Books.

Huczynski, A. (1996) *Influencing Within Organizations*, Prentice-Hall.

Lifton, R.J. (1989) *Thought Reform and the Psychology of Totalism: A Study of Brainwashing in China*, University of North Carolina Press.

Winn, D. (1984) *The Manipulated Mind: Brainwashing, Conditioning and Indoctrination*, IHSK Book Service.

See also: Behaviour modelling; Behaviour modification; Corporate culture training; Ideological change; Interaction influence analysis; Norm formation; Norm modification

Brainwriting (Method 635)

This is a creativity technique whose essential element is the pooling of ideas elicited by group members reading each other's contributions, in the belief that being presented with others' ideas, and having them available to you in a written form, helps to stimulate creative thinking.

Each of a group of six participants is given a sheet of paper on which they are asked to write down three ideas in five minutes (hence Method 635), then pass their sheet to their neighbour. They are then given another five minutes to write down their next three ideas on that sheet. This process is repeated until each participant receives their own sheet back. Since the six group members generate three ideas on each of the six rotations, a total of 108 ideas will be gathered.

Kurtz, H.-J. (1982) 'Developing a Personal and Social Policy Model', *Leadership and Organizational Development*, vol. 3, no. 2, p. 27.

See also: Brainstorming; Delphi technique; Nominal group technique

Broadbanding

The Institute of Personnel and Development defines broadbanding as: 'the compression of a hierarchy of pay grades or salary ranges into a small number of wide bands, typically four or five'.

Broadbanding is considered to be an organizational development technique rather than a personnel management measure, because it helps to remove barriers which may prevent employees contributing fully towards company goals. The reasoning is that, through re-structuring, a firm can become flatter and leaner, thereby eliminating such barriers.

Within the newly created broader bands, employees' roles can be expanded, and their skills and competences broadened. Their focus is thus changed from vertical to lateral progression. Broadbanding brings the company's reward practices into line with this strategy.

According to the IPD, the features of broadbanding include: having no more than four or five pay levels; wide pay spans; an emphasis on market relativities to define target rates; a focus on career development and skill competences; increased devolution of pay decisions to line managers; less emphasis on hierarchical labels, and more emphasis on flexibility and paying for the person rather than the job.

The benefits of the technique for companies include: increasing flexibility in making and administering pay decisions; enabling them to stress employee career development within homogeneous levels of responsibility rather than upward progression; reducing the problem of grade drift and status differentiation; allowing devolution of pay decisions to line managers; permitting a simplification of benefits, making them more flexible, and focusing on the value-adding tiers within a company.

Abosch, K.S. (1995) 'The Promise of Broadbanding', *Compensation and Benefits Review*, vol. 27, pp. 54–8.

Caudron, S. (1993) Master the Compensation Maze, *Personnel Journal*, vol. 72, p. 640.

Haslett, S. (1995) 'Broadbanding: A Strategy for Organization Change', *Compensation and Benefits Review*, vol. 27, vol. 6, November–December, pp. 40–6.

Institute of Personnel and Development (1997) *The IPD Guide on Broadbanding*, IPD.

Reissman, L. (1995) 'Nine Common Myths about Broadbands', *HR Magazine*, vol. 40. no. 8, pp. 79–86.

See also: Job enrichment; Job rotation; Reward

Buberian dialogue

In Buberian dialogue, named after the philosopher Martin Buber, people with opposing views on a subject are invited to present and discuss their views in front of a group. However, a ground rule is that no one is allowed to argue with anyone else on the panel. Participants may seek clarification of points and identify areas of common agreement, but they must accept any viewpoint presented by another panelist without contradiction or argument. The discussion is then opened up to the audience with the same ground rule: no arguments, only clarification.

Buberian dialogue helps people to understand each other's viewpoints. Everybody 'wins', and the negative competitive aspects of formal debate are minimized.

Buber, M., trans. by Friedman. M. and Smith, R.G. (1965) *The Knowledge of Man: Selected Essays*, Harper and Row.

Hazen, M.A. (1987–8) 'Learning How to Learn: An Experiment in Dialogue', *Organizational Behaviour Teaching Review*, vol. 12, no. 2, pp. 72–85.

See also: Argumentation; Case debate; Creative dialogue; Debate; Group with ground rules; Jurisprudential model; Mock trial; PIT technique; Role reversal; Think and listen session

Business game

Business games have been described as case studies with feedback and a time dimension. They are characterized by a competitive element, some form of time relation, and a simplified representation of an actual or typical business situation which provides participants with feedback regarding the consequences of their decisions and permits them to take account of their experience. They also contain elements of role-playing, which promotes the acquisition of technical competence.

Each business game uses a model of a business situation designed by its creator, often incorporating a set of mathematical relationships. They can be played by two or more teams consisting of between five and a dozen players, which represent business enterprises in competition with each other. Individual members of each team are designated to play specific company roles, such as managing director, sales manager and production manager, and each team is presented with information which must be considered before making a decision.

During the game, each team makes a great number of decisions which affect its continuing operation, regarding the purchase of raw materials, hiring and firing personnel, marketing the product, and so on. These may be fed into a computer programmed to respond to them dynamically and to determine the outcome of each decision for the well-being of each company. The results are then fed back to participants in the form of statements about their company's assets or the consequences for the total enterprise, and the teams are required to make further decisions on the basis of this information. The final objective of each team is to survive and, if possible, beat the opposition on some specified criteria, such as return on capital employed, dividend payments, achieved market share and stability of employment.

Simpler business games are non-interactive: the decisions of one team do not affect the outcomes of the others. In these cases, decision analysis and feedback may be carried out manually by the tutor.

It is difficult to draw a clear-cut distinction between a game and a simulation. It has been argued that a game compresses time so that an entire year or even five years in a company's existence may be represented by a few hours, whereas a simulation operates in real time, but there are examples of simulations which also compress time. It is sometimes said that a game features players, rules and competition, whereas a simulation represents reality, but one can argue that the quality of a business game is judged by the extent to which it represents reality, and that competition and rules are part of that reality.

Business games have proven useful in teaching concepts in business decisions, giving participants experience in relating elements together into a complex whole, and allowing them to make judgements and test assumptions about a business model. The skills of data management and logical assessment of a situation are stressed, and participants experience a high degree of involvement in the learning situation. The immediate feedback process gives them information about the adequacy of their decisions without the tutor having to be involved. The learning promoted by the games tends to be assimilated easily and transferred readily to the trainee's work situation.

Elgood, C. (1995) *Using Management Games*, Gower.

Elgood, C. (1997) *Handbook of Management Games and Simulations* (6th edn), Gower.

Ellington, H., Fowlie, J. and Gordon, M. (1998) *Using Games and Simulations in the Classroom*, Kogan Page.

Keeffe, M.J., Dyson, D.A. and Edwards, R.R. (1995) 'Strategic Management Simulations: A Current Assessment', *Simulation and Gaming*, vol. 24, no. 3, pp. 363–8.

Keys, B.J., Wells, R. and Edge, A. (1993) 'International Management Games: Laboratories for Performance-based, Intercultural Learning', *Leadership and Organization Development Journal*, vol. 14, no. 3, pp. 25–31.

Klein, R.D., Fleck, R.A. and Wolfe, J. (1993) 'A Role for Management Games in Internationalizing the Business School Curriculum', *Journal of Management Education*, vol. 17, no. 2, pp. 159–73.

Riis, J.O. (ed.) (1995) *Simulation Games in Production Management*, Chapman and Hall.

Roberts, J.M., Arth, M.J. and Bush, R.R. (1959) 'Games in Culture', *American Anthropologist*, vol. 61, pp. 597–605.

Stone, R.A. (1995) 'The Business Strategy Game: Faculty Experiences and Student Perceptions',

Journal of Management Education, vol. 19, no. 2, pp. 281–90.

Wolfe, J. (1993) 'A History of Business Teaching Games in English Speaking and Post-socialist Countries', *Simulation and Gaming*, vol. 24, no. 4, pp. 446–63.

See also: Action maze; Behavioural simulation; Classroom as organization; Controlled pace negotiation; Guided design approach; In-basket exercise; Programmed simulation; Play as learning; Role-play; Simulation

Business process re-engineering (BPR)

Business process re-engineering focuses on finding better ways to organize and structure key business processes, remove duplication and unnecessary steps, policies and procedures, and using information technology to improve work processing.

BPR is used in circumstances where product development or cycle times need to be reduced drastically. The contrast between more traditional performance-improvement methods and BPR is that while the former ask, 'This is what we currently have and do – how might we improve it?', BPR asks, 'If you could start again from scratch, how would you do it?' BPR therefore involves a large-scale overhaul of strategic, value-added business processes, favouring a radical approach rather than incremental, marginal or fine-tuning changes. A company undergoing BPR has to attend to business processes such as selling, administration and logistics, which are often neglected in comparison to manufacturing activities.

Since BPR considers any company as a set of business processes, each consisting of a set of activities that uses inputs to create value for the customer, the BPR analysis begins by studying the customer's definition of what constitutes product and service value. The analysis is usually performed by a combination of outside consultants and a specially appointed task force that represents the company's internal expertise and recommends ways to reorganize processes and reduce costs. The key decision concerns which tasks and activities are to be performed, and in which order.

Blair, H., Taylor, S.G. and Randle, K. (1998) 'A Pernicious Panacea: A Critical Evaluation of Business Re-engineering', *New Technology, Work and Employment*, vol. 13, no. 2, pp. 116–28.

Carr, D.K. and Johansson, H.J. (1995) *Best Practices in Reengineering: What Works and Doesn't in the Reengineering Process*, McGraw-Hill.

Coulson-Thomas, C. (1996) *Business Process Reengineering: Myth and Reality*, Kogan Page.

Hammer, M. (1990) 'Re-engineering Work: Don't Automate, Obliterate!', *Harvard Business Review*, July–August, pp. 104–12.

Hammer, M. (1997) *Beyond Reengineering*, Harper-Collins.

Hammer, M. and Champy, J. (1993) *Reengineering the Corporation: A Manifesto for Business Revolution*, Nicholas Brealey.

Harrington, B., McLoughlin, K. and Riddell, D. (1998) 'Business Process Reengineering in the Public Sector: A Case Study of the Contributions Agency', *New Technology Work and Employment*, vol. 13, no. 1, pp. 43–50.

Hunt, V.D. (1996) *Process Mapping: How to Reengineer Your Business Processes*, Wiley.

Jackson, M. and Twaddle, G. (1997) *Business Process Implementation*, Addison Wesley Longman.

Loh, M. (1997) *Reengineering at Work* (2nd edn), Gower.

Magnelli, R.L. (1996) *The Reengineering Handbook*, American Management Association, AMACOM.

Robson, M. and Ullah, P. (1996) *A Practical Guide to Business Process Re-engineering*, Gower.

See also: Conference Model; Conflict simulation techniques; Fast-cycle full-participation work design; Future search; Open space technology; Participative design; Real-time strategic change; Real-time work design; Strategic planning process; Search conference; Simu-Real; Work-Out

Business teams (slice teams)

A business team provides workers with the opportunity to take part in the decisions that affect product development. Each team has a vertical structure, its members ranging from shop-floor staff to senior managers, and focuses on the changing problems of the product line. A US company which has used such groups calls them 'slice teams'.

Business teams, usually consisting of eight to ten people, deal with issues such as capital expenditure, new equipment and new technology, focusing on a single product or part of the production process. Since the teams are engaged in product-business planning, contributions from headquarters and divisional staff complement those from plant managers and hourly paid workers, and some companies have experimented with integrating staff and line managers in their teams.

By including production workers, business teams differ from other matrix-type arrangements which interlink the different managerial functions on a project-by-project basis. Tasks such as engineering and quality maintenance cease to be organized by function, but are integrated into the line organization by changing the authority and communication relationships as well as the physical location of team members.

In the past, the business team concept has been used as part of the Quality-of-Work-Life programme, through which workers can contribute to all aspects of production. Several General Motors plants are divided into these business teams, which operate autonomously, and are concerned with the manufacturing, quality and cost aspects of the product.

See also: Bottom-up management; Collateral organization; Forcing device; Independent product teams; Integrated support functions; Line of business groups; Matrix design; Re-programming; Simulated entrepreneurship; Structural interventions

Career life planning

This is a family of career development intervention techniques originated by Herbert A. Shepherd which focus on the individual, usually involving career counselling or career planning. Management career development involves a continuous process of change in activities, positions and values. People may feel caught in an 'organizational trap' because their personal goals and sense of meaning have been lost, and many individuals' career problems may be symptoms of larger organizational problems such as a rigid bureaucratic structure. As individuals develop within an organization, their career paths may reach crisis points when they are faced with choosing between jobs or organizations, and some form of planning is necessary in order to determine how best to achieve their career goals.

The purpose of career development workshops is to help people focus on their life and career objectives, and assist them to take more control over their own destiny. The interventions may extend over a day or a week, during which participants gather information about themselves and analyse the data, both individually and in groups. The workshops may include evaluating participants' lives and careers to date, to identify their strengths and weaknesses as well as the choices they have made, formulating clear personal goals for the future in terms of desired lifestyle and career path, and planning actions in order to achieve these goals.

The structured activities used during such workshops include drawing up life and career inventories, discussing personal goals and objectives, assessing capabilities, developing awareness of strengths and weaknesses, and identifying areas where participants need additional training and development. In life planning workshops, individuals usually work on such tasks alone, then compare their results with others'.

Arnold, J. (1997) *Managing Careers into the 21st Century*, Paul Chapman/Sage.

Cochran, L. (1997) *Career Counselling*, Sage.

'Executive Careers', special issue of *Human Relations* (1994), vol. 47, no. 5, May.

Herriot, P. (1992) *The Career Management Challenge*, Sage.

Institute of Personnel and Development (1998) *IPD Guide on Career Management in Organizations*, IPD.

Mayo, A. (1997) *Managing Careers: Strategies for Organizations*, IPD.

Nathan, R. and Hill, L. (1992) *Career Counselling*, Sage.

Schein, E.H. (1978) *Career Dynamic Matching Individual and Organizational Needs*, Addison Wesley Longman.

Seligman, L. (1994) *Developmental Career Counselling and Assessment* (2nd edn), Sage.

See also: Biography; Early retirement; Job rotation; Motivation achievement training; Retreat; Sabbaticals; Self-improvement programme; Values clarification

Case active (active case)

Managers who participate in work-related projects during external company management development programmes often encounter pressures of work and travelling difficulties which interfere with the successful completion of their case studies. One way of overcoming these problems and making better use of their time is to instigate active case studies, allowing the business school to carry out the research beforehand on the managers' behalf.

The participants are given access to operating data, and have the opportunity to visit the site concerned and view recorded interviews with the managers involved. They are required to prepare a report of their findings and proposals, which are based on inputs received during the course as a whole and on their own detailed group study of a particular problem.

Margerison, V. and New, C. (1980) 'Management Development by Inter-company Consortium', *Personnel Management*, vol. 12, no. 11, pp. 42–5.

See also: Case conference; Case debate; Case experiential; Case history; Case incident process method; Case live; Case participative; Case personal history; Case student telling; Case study method; Case unprepared; Case with analogue; Case with role-play; Case-critical incident analysis; Case-structured analysis approach

Case conference

Case conferences are commonly used in fields such as medicine, nursing and social work to assess progress in dealing with a particular case and arrive at informed decisions on what steps to take next.

The case conference may involve eight to twelve participants, including one or more senior staff or workers with extensive experience of the problems being discussed, who each describe the work activities and problems which are causing them difficulties while the others listen and offer advice and suggestions. The same approach could be used by a group of managers to help them contribute more effectively to fulfilling an export order. While case conferences usually focus on a specific professional/work task, if some form of process review is incorporated into each case meeting this can contribute to meeting individual/group development needs.

See also: Case active; Case debate; Case experiential; Case history; Case incident process method; Case live; Case participative; Case personal history; Case student telling; Case study method; Case unprepared; Case with analogue; Case with role-play; Case-critical incident analysis; Case-structured analysis approach; Group discussion; Illuminative incident analysis; Problem-centred group; Process analysis

Case debate

Case debate may be used as an alternative to the case discussion format (in which the instructor leads the entire class) and the traditional oral presentation of a group's analysis of an assigned case. The method involves selecting two teams of three to five members, with the remainder of the class serving as an audience. It aims to create a classroom environment that motivates students to devote sufficient time and concentration to case-work by creating a positive competitive spirit between teams, generating enthusiasm, and encouraging commitment to case preparation. It places each team in a situation where they have to formulate a speedy evaluation of the opposing team's analysis and strategy, and devise and deliver a persuasive argument for the superiority of their own and the inferiority of the opposing team's. There are four stages.

First, each of the two teams in turn presents its analysis of the problem, and its proposed solution. The presentation is limited to 20 minutes, during which they must set out the key issues as they see them, the analytical framework of their proposed solutions, and their proposed strategic plans. Next, there is a 15-minute break, during which each team prepares its rebuttal, highlighting any major

areas of disagreement and deciding how to counter the other team's ideas while promoting its own. Meanwhile, the instructor and the remainder of the class prepare questions for the final question-and-answer stage. Each team then has 10 minutes for one or more of its team members to deliver its rebuttal, beginning with the team which was last to present its analysis in the first stage. They must identify the major points of difference between the two strategic plans, highlight the shortcomings of the other team's work, and argue for the superiority of their own analysis of the problem and proposed solution. Finally, each team in turn answers questions from the audience, the instructor and the opposing team which may include asking for more details about the strategic plan, seeking clarification of certain points, or challenging the team's assumptions.

Stewart, K.A. and Winn, J. (1996) 'The Case Debate: A New Approach to Case Teaching', *Journal of Management Education*, vol. 20, no. 1, pp. 48–59.

Terry, D. (1977) *Modern Debate Case Techniques*, National Textbook Company.

See also: Argumentation; Buberian dialogue; Case active; Case conference; Case experiential; Case history; Case incident process method; Case live; Case participative; Case personal history; Case student telling; Case study method; Case unprepared; Case with analogue; Case with role-play; Case-critical incident analysis; Case-structured analysis approach; Debate

Case experiential (experiential case project)

An experiential case project uses a one-to-one tutoring approach based on a particular case. At the first class of the term or semester, the tutor asks students to carry out a case study into some aspect or area of any organization with which they are familiar, to be submitted at the last class of the term or semester. Each student attends individual meetings with the tutor to discuss progress and problems, where the tutor makes comments, observations and suggestions to help the student complete their case study. The written report on the case study should contain three sections: description, analysis and concepts.

The case description includes a historical overview of the organization, particularly any changes in staff, structure, task, technology or environment which are pertinent to the situation, the financial background for the past five years, the organization's present structure, brief (anonymous) descriptions of the key individuals involved and their backgrounds, an account of the situation's development as reflected in communication between the individuals (such as memos, letters or reports) and an assessment of the current state of the situation or organization.

The case analysis addresses five questions: 'What are the problems?'; 'What are the causes of the problems?'; 'What are the alternative solutions?'; 'What is your solution?', and 'How would you implement your solution?'

The final section identifies the concepts defined and exemplified in the course textbook and discussed previously in class. Each student indicates how their named concepts relate to the case in terms of problem identification and cause analysis, solution generation and selection, or solution implementation. Finally, if the situation is not currently 'live', an addendum is included specifying what was done (or not done), and why.

Although originally developed for use in the field of general management and business organization behaviour, this approach can be adapted to any business school subject field. It has several positive aspects: it encourages students to develop analytical skills, it applies textbook learning to a realistic situation, it forces students to discuss matters with managers in the organizations they are studying, and it helps them to gain a holistic view of the organization. This last requirement – looking at the 'big picture' of the organization – is relevant even if the case study focuses on an inter-personal problem.

There may also be negative aspects which must be borne in mind – the project can take up a disproportionate amount of both the students' and the tutor's time, and some students lack business experience – but these difficulties can be overcome. The tutor should monitor how much time students are spending on the project by asking them to keep a diary, and if the case requirements are found to be excessive they can be scaled down, or if this element of the course work is being used for assessment, its weighting can be increased to match the effort and time being expended. The tutoring task can be shared with other instructors or graduate students, or groups of up to five students can attend each tutorial, rather than using the one-to-one method. Finally, although not every student may work in business, virtually all will have experience of some organization, whether governmental, educational, religious, public or private, which can serve as the subject of their case study.

See also: Case active; Case conference; Case debate; Case history; Case incident process method; Case live; Case participative; Case personal history; Case student telling; Case study method; Case unprepared; Case with analogue; Case with role-play; Case-critical incident analysis; Case-structured analysis approach

Case history

A case history is an account of a real-life situation or event. It may take the form of a straightforward report which merely records a series of occurrences, or it may serve as the basis for further study or analysis using a variety of techniques.

See also: Case active; Case conference; Case debate; Case experiential; Case incident process method; Case live; Case participative; Case personal history; Case student telling; Case study method; Case unprepared; Case with analogue; Case with role-play; Case-structured analysis approach

Case incident process method (incident process case study; incident process method)

A major disadvantage of traditional case studies is the impression they give that management problem-solving simply consists of finding answers to clear-cut questions. The case incident process method (CIPM) was developed by Paul and Faith Pigors in the belief that it is impossible to appreciate a real-life case situation fully by merely reading about it, and that asking questions rather than reading a case report emphasizes the ubiquitous nature of change and helps students experience a greater sense of involvement. CIPM aims to promote analytical thinking and reasoned judgement by focusing on the *process* of case-reporting – how the elements of the case are presented and discovered – rather than its *product* – what is discovered, or the solution chosen.

The first step in management problem-solving is to define the problem and obtain all the information that is necessary or available, but the complexity of real-life situations often makes it difficult to draw up a clear objective or case history. The next step is to consider the facts and formulate and implement a solution. Traditional case studies tend to focus on the second step, while CIPM concentrates on the first, using a six-stage approach.

First, either verbally or by handing out a memo or some other document, the tutor presents the group with a very short account of an incident or situation – for example, workers refusing to operate a new machine. Individual participants are then invited to ask the tutor any questions they think will help clarify the incident and provide the necessary background information, but forbidden to ask for the tutor's opinions. A strict time limit of half an hour is suggested for this phase, and participants should be informed of this beforehand. Tutors must ensure that they have researched the incident thoroughly, and ensure they are able to answer any relevant questions of fact. It is essential to avoid inconsistency, and they must supply only the information specifically requested. Another option is to arrange for a manager who was actually involved in the incident to respond to the questions.

At this point, there are two options regarding how to proceed. One is to ask each participant to note down their views on what should be done to solve the problem. Their notes are then collected, the replies are collated and charted by the tutor, indicating how many associated themselves with a particular line of action, and syndicates of like-minded individuals are formed. The alternative approach is to give each participant a voting slip offering only two workable but opposed solutions. Students record their votes, and syndicates are formed accordingly. Once the membership of the syndicates has been decided, they are allotted a fixed period to consider their decision in detail and prepare a report on its advantages and how it might be implemented.

The next stage is a plenary session, during which reports are presented by each group in turn, with opposing syndicates cross-examining each other.

Finally, the tutor comments on the reports, extracting more information, drawing attention to inconsistencies, any information the syndicates failed to obtain, or any unfounded assumptions.

Proponents of CIPM claim that it provides students with six types of learning: first, they discover the importance of *hypotheses*, and that questioning or requesting data must not be a random process; second, they discover that the data elicited must be *relevant*, and that a piece of information may be meaningless unless obtained at the appropriate time; third, they realize the value of integrating *concepts* into a scheme which structures the interrogation process and makes answers more intelligible; fourth, they practise *reasoning and logic skills* by developing chains of inferences and 'if-then' statements which guide further enquiry; fifth, they begin to appreciate the value of *serendipity* through chance discoveries and unexpected developments and, finally, by observing others they come to recognize that there are many *different approaches* to problem-solving.

Binsted, D., Stuart, R. and Long, G. (1980) 'Promoting Useful Management Learning: Problems of Transition and Transfer', in Beck, J. and Cox, C. (eds) *Advances in Management Education*, Wiley.

Boyd, B.B. (1980) 'Developing Case Studies',

Training and Development Journal, vol. 34, no. 6, pp. 113–17.

Odell, H.R. (1980) 'Special Challenge: A Case Teaching Technique', *Exchange: The Organizational Behaviour Teaching Journal*, vol. 5, no. 4, pp. 50–1.

Pigors, P. and Pigors, F. (1955) *The Incident Process: Case Studies in Management Development*, Bureau of National Affairs, Washington, DC.

Pigors, P. and Pigors, F. (1961) *Case Method in Human Relations: The Incident Process*, McGraw-Hill.

Pigors, P. and Pigors, F. (1963) 'Learning by the Incident Process', *Technology Review*, vol. 45, no. 4, February, pp. 27–9 and 40–1.

See also: Case active; Case conference; Case debate; Case experiential; Case history; Case live; Case participative; Case personal history; Case student telling; Case study method; Case unprepared; Case with analogue; Case with role-play; Case-critical incident analysis; Case-structured analysis approach; Interrogation of experts; Management problem laboratory; Mystery clue method

Case live (live case; living case)

Case live is distinguished from other case study methods by the fact that it focuses on a learning situation which is still in progress ('live') and which has not yet been recorded in any way for study purposes.

There are numerous variations on this theme, and in one popular version, senior business studies students are assigned to teams which help local company-owners or managers analyse their businesses and develop strategic plans. Each owner/manager studies the assigned textbook material, acts as facilitator during their team's classes, and participates in discussions with both their own team and the class as a whole.

The benefits of this approach are numerous. In terms of content, each case can be used to highlight a variety of management issues, new cases are available over the course of a single academic year, it ensures that instructors focus their cases on real-world issues and experiences, and the company-owners/managers can benefit from the assistance offered by the group. In terms of process, observing which of their proposed solutions are adopted and which are rejected by those actually running businesses can be illuminating for students, they can practise and refine their group decision-making skills, and their presentation skills can be honed by having to present their solutions.

Learned, K.E. (1991) 'The Use of Living Cases in Teaching Business Policy', *Journal of Management Education*, vol. 15, no. 1, pp. 113–20.

Reilly, A.H. (1998) 'Friday Night at the Plant: A Small Scale Application of the On-site Case Study', *Journal of Management Education*, vol. 22, no. 1, pp. 85–94.

Rude, D. E. and Branham, M. T. (1994) 'Student-centred Living Cases for Teaching Management', *Journal of Management Education*, vol. 18, no. 4, pp. 475–83.

Urban, T. and Keys, J.B. (1994) ' The Live Case Method of Creating the Learning Organization', *Journal of Management Development*, vol. 13, no. 8, pp. 44–9.

See also: Case active; Case conference; Case debate; Case experiential; Case history; Case incident process method; Case participative; Case personal history; Case student telling; Case study method; Case unprepared; Case with analogue; Case with role-play; Case-critical incident analysis; Case-structured analysis approach

Case participative

In this version of the case study method, a multi-faceted case is analysed by students working in teams. Each team is assigned a role (such as production managers, marketing managers, human resource managers, external consultants, shareholders or environmentalists), and is given the task of presenting an analysis of the case study from their role perspective at a plenary session.

This approach is helpful in demonstrating how those acting in various roles may have differing perceptions of problems and how to overcome them. Once they have each participated in the presentation, the teams can then analyse the reasons underlying these differences.

See also: Case active; Case conference; Case debate; Case experiential; Case history; Case incident process method; Case live; Case personal history; Case study method; Case student telling; Case unprepared; Case with analogue; Case with role-play; Case-critical incident analysis; Case-structured analysis approach; Management implications paper; Reaction paper

Case personal history (personal case history)

Like the case study method, case personal history develops skills in analysing complex organizational problems, but a distinctive feature of this approach is that it focuses on real cases derived from members' own experiences rather than invented situations, stressing the application of methodological patterns and conceptual frames of reference with which students are already familiar. The aim is to transfer specialized knowledge and help managers develop specific skills.

The personal case histories describe the management activities of participants who are willing to discuss and analyse their experiences with teachers and other course members. They may relate to the situation of the specific organizational unit for which the participant is responsible, or the situation in their organization as a whole.

A case personal history teaching session may last three or four days. It begins with a statement of objectives by the tutor, emphasizing that the class will be studying real situations within companies. Different personal case histories are offered for study, the most suitable ones are selected, and those who drew them up form workgroups. The next stage is to conduct a historical analysis consisting of a step-by-step case reconstruction, during which the most significant events are analysed. Following this, the groups draw up a diagnosis of the present condition of the system being studied, then produce a set of suggested actions and improvements.

Quaglino, G.P. and Testa, G. (1979) 'The Use of Personal Case Histories as a Tool of Management Education', *Management Education and Development*, vol. 10, no. 2, pp. 112–23.

See also: Case active; Case conference; Case debate; Case experiential; Case history; Case incident process method; Case live; Case participative; Case student telling; Case study method; Case unprepared; Case with analogue; Case with role-play; Case-critical incident analysis; Case-structured analysis approach; Management implications paper; Reaction paper

Case student telling

In this approach, the class is divided into small groups, and each student is asked describe a real-life business or organizational problem – perhaps an instance when they dealt unsatisfactorily with a situation, or a current difficulty at work – within a ten-minute time limit. The group may then discuss each problem, exploring the possibilities and consequences of different solutions. The case content must remain confidential within the group, case owners can terminate the discussion at any time, and they can decide whether or not to allow other group or class members to participate in dealing with their problems.

Each group then selects one case to be presented for discussion by the whole class, either by the case owner or another group member, since it is unnecessary for the class to know whose problem it is. The presenter describes the relevant facts of the chosen case, beginning with the most important, the group's analysis of it, and the pros and cons of alternative solutions. The remainder of the class then asks clarifying questions and offers additional suggestions that might resolve the problem.

Schiro, S.F. (1994) 'Introducing Case Analysis by Telling Real Cases', *Journal of Management Education*, vol. 18, no. 4, pp. 484–9.

See also: Case active; Case conference; Case debate; Case experiential; Case history; Case incident process method; Case live; Case participative; Case personal history; Case study method; Case unprepared; Case with analogue; Case with role-play; Case-critical incident analysis; Case-structured analysis approach; Management implications paper; Staff meeting assignment; Short talks by students; Storytelling

Case study method

The case study method – probably the most widely used approach in the teaching of management skills – was originally developed by the Harvard Law School in 1869, and became the dominant teaching method at the Harvard Business School. This method forms the foundation for a great many other learning approaches, but the Harvard method focuses on real-life situations, whereas others may rely on imaginary cases.

The method is non-directive, and students are expected to develop their own problem-solving skills. The instructor presents the case problem to the students, giving them sufficient time for study, and then creates an environment in which group discussion can take place, promoting debate and acting as a catalyst through the skilful use of questions which aim to draw out, direct or guide students' thinking. Because many solutions may be possible, the first step in the case discussion is often the presentation of a series of alternative ways to resolve the same problem.

The instructor may present the case study in written or filmed form, and usually concentrates on a specific aspect of a problem involving an entire organization or a single department in order to break up the whole situation into manageable or teachable units. The cases chosen tend to be sufficiently involved and detailed to produce a wide range of opinions concerning who was to blame, what caused a person to behave in a certain way, and what the best corrective action might be.

It is claimed that the case study method discourages students from making snap judgements about people and situations, or believing in a universal 'right answer'. It shows how the same set of facts can be interpreted in different ways, stresses practical thinking, developing high-level cognitive skills such as analysis, synthesis, and particularly evaluation, and can promote attitude change as long as it encourages students' personal involvement.

Other case study methods differ mainly in terms of presentation. In some, a group rather than an individual works on a problem. Cases may be filmed, and in this instance they usually present open-ended problems and offer considerable detail about real-life settings in which emotional relationships as well as facts may play a part, or they may be 'live', describing a continuing situation.

All the variations and developments of the original Harvard case study method share the same criteria for what constitutes a good case: it should be based on first-hand observation; it should present facts, not opinions disguised as facts; it should show more than it tells; it should provide organized information; it should give examples of both formal and informal relationships where appropriate, and it should describe the key people involved and illustrate the effects of change, indicating that the situation was in transition, and still developing when the observation stopped.

Argyris, C. (1997) 'Learning and Teaching: A Theory of Action Perspective', *Journal of Management Education*, vol. 21, no. 1, pp. 9–26.

Barnes, L.B., Christensen, C.R. and Hanson, A.J. (eds) (1994) *Teaching and the Case Method* (3rd edn), Harvard Business School Press.

Christensen, C.R., Garvin, D.A. and Sweet, A. (eds.) (1991) *Education for Judgement: The Artistry of Discussion Leadership*, Harvard Business School Press.

Easton, G. (1992) *Learning from Case Studies*, Prentice-Hall.

Erskine, J.A., Leenders, M.R. and Mauffette-Leenders, L.A. (1998) *Learning from Cases*, Richard Ivey School of Business, University of Western Ontario, London, Canada (available from European Case Clearing House, Cranfield University).

Erskine, J.A., Leenders, M.R. and Mauffette-Leenders, L.A. (1998) *Teaching with Cases*, Richard Ivey School of Business, University of Western Ontario, Canada (Available from European Case Clearing House, Cranfield University).

Haynes, P.J. and Helms, M.M. (1993) 'Increasing Participation in Case Method Courses', *Journal of Management Education*, vol. 17, no. 1, pp. 114–17.

Heath, J. (1998) *Teaching and Writing Cases: A Practical Guide*, European Case Clearing House, Cranfield University.

Holmes, B.H. (1993) 'Assigning Blame to Case

Characters: An Alternative to Defining the Problem', *Journal of Management Education*, vol. 17, no. 1, pp. 124–6.

Kellogg, D.M. (1991) 'Assigning Business Writing to Increase the Learning Potential of Case Courses', *Journal of Management Education*, vol. 15, no. 1, pp. 19–34.

Lundberg, C.C. and Lundberg, J. (1993) 'A Note on Linking Ideas and Facts: Exercises for Enhancing Case Analysis', *Journal of Management Education*, vol. 17, no. 3, pp. 377–85.

Monro, J.H. (1997) 'Mastering the Case Method', *Innovations in Education and Training International*, vol. 34, no. 2, pp. 84–91.

Oram, I. (1996) 'Computer Support of Learning from Cases in Management Education', *Innovations in Education and Training International*, vol. 33, no. 1, pp. 70–3.

Sicliano, J. and McAleer, G.M. (1997) 'Increasing Student Participation in Case Discussion: Using the MICA Method in Strategic Management Courses', *Journal of Management Education*, vol. 21, no. 2, pp. 209–20.

See also: Abercrombie method; Case active; Case conference; Case debate; Case experiential; Case history; Case incident process method; Case live; Case participative; Case personal history; Case student telling; Case unprepared; Case with analogue; Case with role-play; Case-critical incident analysis; Case-structured analysis approach; Guided design approach; Learning history; Reading; Socratic questioning; Step-by-step discussion

Case unprepared

This approach was discovered accidentally by an instructor when, at the start of his class, he suddenly realised that he had prepared a different case from the one he had set his students. The students had all analysed the case thoroughly, while the instructor had not even read it. After convincing the students that he was truly ignorant, he asked them to tell him about it: 'What's the problem? Who's to blame?' Every now and then, the instructor paraphrased and summarized what he had been told, saying, 'Let me see if I can correctly recap what I've learned from you so far about this organization, the people in it, and the issues.' Each review in turn provoked a new discussion.

The learning task for the student is somewhat like a child or person with a problem which they want to discuss with a parent or friend. They must identify the salient points of their problem, placing them in a logical sequence so that they can communicate them clearly to their listeners, and only then can the discussion of causes and

solutions take place. Case unprepared is therefore concerned as much with developing students' communication skills as their analytical and problem-solving ones.

See also: Case active; Case conference; Case debate; Case experiential; Case history; Case incident process method; Case live; Case participative; Case personal history; Case student telling; Case study method; Case with analogue; Case with role-play; Case-critical incident analysis; Case-structured analysis approach; Interrogation of experts; Management problem laboratory; Mystery clue method

Case with analogue

This method is used in combination with traditional case study methods to provide students with personal experience of the issues being explored. For example, a class may be divided into syndicate groups, each with a formally appointed leader, and given an hour to discuss a case concerning leadership. However, after 30 minutes, the instructor reallocates the leaders to other groups, so the students end up discussing the problems of leadership succession described in the case study while also experiencing it directly within their own syndicate group.

Providing students with a classroom experience which is analogous to the case problem they are studying can lead to clearer insights, promote deeper understanding, and give them a broader base for their case discussion.

Berg, D.N. (1987–8) 'Developing Analogues to Cases: Some Reactions', *Organizational Behaviour Teaching Review*, vol. 12, no. 2, pp. 33–5.

Molstad, C. and Levy, S. (1987–8) 'The Value of Case Analogues', *Organizational Behaviour Teaching Review*, vol. 12, no. 2, pp. 28–32 and 35–9.

See also: Case active; Case conference; Case debate; Case experiential; Case history; Case incident process method; Case live; Case participative; Case personal history; Case student telling; Case study method; Case unprepared; Case with role-play; Case-critical incident analysis; Case-structured analysis approach; Storytelling

Case with role-play

In this approach, a traditional written case study is followed by a role-play to help students explore the circumstances and the characters involved more fully.

After a conventional discussion of the case, highlighting problem symptoms, identifying the causes and exploring possible solutions, the instructor sketches a scene that could occur some time later, in which the primary case characters interact, for example confronting each other about some aspect of the case. Students are allocated roles, and asked to improvise what their character might say and do.

Finch, B. J. (1993) 'A Modelling Enhancement to Teaching Cases', *Journal of Management Education*, vol. 17, no. 2, pp. 228–35.

Lundberg, C. (1989–90) 'Case Follow Up Role Plays: One Way of Creating Realistic Action Experiences', *Organizational Behaviour Teaching Review*, vol. 14, no. 1, pp. 157–8.

Montcrief, J. (1997) *Sales Management Role Plays*, Addison Wesley Longman.

See also: Case active; Case conference; Case debate; Case experiential; Case history; Case incident process method; Case live; Case participative; Case personal history; Case student telling; Case study method; Case unprepared; Case with analogue; Case-critical incident analysis; Case-structured analysis approach; Character immersion; Inner dialogue; Role-playing

Case-critical incident analysis

In this technique, participants form into small groups, each person spends a few minutes recalling a critical incident concerning human relations in their own organization, such as a crisis in communication, decision-making or implementation, and the group members then share these experiences with one another.

One or more such incidents may be explored further through a role-play or by applying the problem-solving cycle.

Lacey, J.D. and Licht, N.C. (1980) 'Culminating Experience: A Tool for Management Training', *Training and Development Journal*, vol. 34, no. 3, p. 88–90.

See also: Case active; Case conference; Case debate; Case experiential; Case history; Case incident process method; Case live; Case participative; Case personal history; Case student telling; Case study method; Case unprepared; Case with analogue; Case with role-play; Case-structured analysis approach; Problem-solving cycle; Role-play; Sociodrama

Case-structured analysis approach

Unlike many teaching approaches which seek to develop students' theoretical understanding in conjunction with their ability to apply those theories in practice, the case-structured analysis approach assumes that students already understand theories in their abstract form, and tries to help them apply the theories to real or invented organizational situations.

This approach adopts the case study method as the basis for learning, but uses non-traditional, specially designed questions which channel students' investigations, focus their attention on specific theoretical constructs and their components, and ask them to apply any appropriate theories to the case, identifying any relevant concepts encountered during the process. For example, rather than the traditional technique of asking students to identify the main problems or issues in a particular case and how they should be solved, they are posed more specific, structured questions prepared by the instructor for each case, such as: 'What co-ordination and information-processing requirements are suggested by the case?', 'Which of the resources described in the case can be shared by departments?' and 'What strategic alternatives are available to the company?' The subsequent class discussion revolves around the company's situation. The contrasts between students' responses and interpretations are highlighted, since seemingly straightforward theories are often interpreted very differently by individual students when they are applied to an actual case.

To apply the approach, a five-step method is recommended, whereby instructors select a suitable textbook for the course, learn it thoroughly, identify the key theories and their components, select cases which illustrate those concepts and their application, and finally structure questions which ask students to apply those theoretical components directly to the cases.

Ramsey, V.J. and Dodge, L.D. (1981) 'Case Analysis: A Structured Approach', *Exchange: The Organizational Behaviour Teaching Review*, vol. 6, no. 4, pp. 27–9.

See also: Case active; Case conference; Case debate; Case experiential; Case history; Case incident process method; Case live; Case participative; Case personal history; Case student telling; Case study method; Case unprepared; Case with analogue; Case with role-play; Case-critical incident analysis

Chairman's forum (first-of-the-year meeting)

This communications strategy is used by a number of companies. The precise format may vary, and despite their title the meetings are usually held once or twice a year. All employees may be invited to attend, or a group of forty or so staff drawn from all levels in the company, from the shop floor up to middle management. Two representatives from each of any recognized unions are also invited, but unlike normal union–management encounters, negotiation and bargaining are forbidden, since the aim of the meeting is to examine the company's business position in a way that is both objective and non-threatening. Since different participants attend each meeting, they act as a growing body of opinion-formers, passing on their understanding of the commercial realities of the situation by talking to their colleagues.

Each forum begins with the company chairman reviewing the state of the organization and its past year's performance and future prospects in the context of the national and international economic situation, technological advances and the company's future direction. Guest speakers may be invited to give presentations on issues such as the impact of European legislation. Each meeting may consider a different part of the company and analyse its current and future progress in detail, or it may have a specific theme: for example, one US multinational invited the mountaineer Chris Bonington and the astronaut Alan Shepard to talk about the importance of challenge and perseverance in business.

One of the rules in a chairman's forum is that any issue can be discussed, and nothing will be deliberately withheld. The information may be more detailed than that supplied to shareholders and investment analysts and may include highly sensitive data, so confidentiality agreements are important.

Goldsmith, W. and Clutterbuck, D. (1985) *The Winning Streak*, Penguin Books, p. 72.

See also: Employee letters; Information-sharing meetings; Management information meeting; Open forums; Team briefing

Character immersion

Character immersion (CI) is a long-term role-playing exercise. It differs from traditional role-playing techniques in two ways. First, the character descriptions focus more on the role characters' personal backgrounds than on what they are or do at work. Each student is given a description of their character's childhood experiences, socio-economic class, family, background, and critical life events (e.g., death of spouse). This emphasis on personal background is designed to give students a feel for their characters as whole people, not just as members of an organization. However, little or no information is given about the character's feelings or attitudes, so allowing the student to interpret their character in their own way.

Second, CI can be used in conjunction with any other exercise, discussion or lecture. For example, students can be asked to participate in an experiential exercise as their character rather than as themselves, or they can fill in a personality questionnaire as their character.

In devising a CI exercise, an instructor can create roles using composites based on attributes and experiences of relatives, friends and acquaintances, with a degree of poetic licence. Each role character's job is described, but no information is given about where exactly it is placed in the organizational hierarchy or in which industry the organization operates. The only common factor among the different character roles is that they all work for the same fictional organization. None of the character roles reflects an unpleasant nature, and all of them have encountered problems in life.

Traditional role-plays have many benefits: they engage the emotions; as experiential exercises, they allow students to develop management skills which tend to be remembered; they encourage a higher level of understanding, and assuming the persona of a fictitious character helps to protect a student's self-esteem and ego. However, they also have disadvantages: they can be time-consuming to set up; role descriptions are limited by time, and hence tend to be sketchy; they are difficult to accommodate in a traditional fifty-minute session because of the time required to brief the students and for them to assimilate their character descriptions; motivation and much of the value is lost if the role-plays have to be continued in the next weekly session. For all these reasons, role-plays tend to be short in duration and are often disjointed.

CI overcomes many of these difficulties: if each student is 'living their character' for the duration of a semester or academic year, they can adopt the role immediately without the need for preparation, and longer and more elaborate role-playing can take place. In addition, more flexible short-term use can be made of the technique. For example, during a lecture on perception, the instructor might ask a student: 'Jane, how would your character, Mrs Wilson, see the situation I've just described?'

Little, L. (1989–90) 'Beyond the Role Play: Character Immersion in the Organizational Behaviour Classroom', *Organizational Behaviour Teaching Review*, vol. 14, no. 4, pp. 46–53.

See also: Case with role-play; Company file project; Dramatic skit; Inner dialogue; Monodrama; Role-play; Sociodrama

Chronology charting

Chronology charting was developed by Craig Lundberg to provide learners with an opportunity to review their course material by setting it in a historical context of evolving thought in their subject field.

Teaching any subject involves helping students to learn about its central concepts, ideas, theories, research findings and models, and the authors associated with them. Courses usually focus on the main themes, whereas the textbooks that support them are more likely to be organized into the major topics. Modularization has produced a greater number of shorter courses, rather than fewer longer ones. One effect of this has been the omission of lecture sessions or textbook chapters covering 'schools of thought', so students are shown neither how currents of thought in their discipline grew over time, nor how periods of intellectual development occurred within them.

Chronology charting involves asking students to work in teams to prepare a chart listing in chronological order the concepts, ideas, theories, research findings, models and authors encountered in their course, including the date of their first appearance or citation, and the corresponding page number in the textbook. A variation is to divide the chart into several columns with headings such as 'Perspectives', 'Author's Nationality', 'Schools of Thought', or some combination of these.

After a number of lecture sessions have been completed and the students have read the associated textbook chapters, the student teams pool their ideas and write each item on a self-adhesive note, mark the chosen time-lines and columns on a flipchart sheet, then place the notes in their appropriate positions. The completed charts are then displayed on the classroom walls so that all students can view them and compare them with their own. Alternatively, the charting exercise can be set as a homework activity to be completed by students individually in their own time.

Lundberg, C. (1989–90) 'Chronology Charting', *Organizational Behaviour Teaching Review*, vol. 14, no. 1, pp. 155–6.

See also: Collages; Concept mapping; Drawing for learning; Fortune lining; Illuminative incident analysis; Poster; Relational programming; Responsibility charting; Storyboarding

Circulated lecture notes

This method involves providing students with a full set of lecture notes together with questions and assignments designed to extend thinking and comprehension.

In one application of this approach, it was found that distributing notes beforehand did not discourage students from attending lectures, which focused on providing feedback on test performance rather than presenting information for the first time, and 90 per cent of the students took the tests either always or frequently.

In another application, feedback was obtained by contact with seven discussion groups during the first half-hour of the lecture period, and then by group reports followed by a general discussion.

Several variations of this method are possible. Incomplete lecture notes can be circulated, containing enough information to make the basic conceptual structure of the lecture material clear, but requiring students to add and link various pieces of information themselves. This approach is most effective with more able students. A second variation is for an instructor to attend a lecture given by a colleague, taking notes which are then made available to the students. This helps students, particularly new ones, to check on the adequacy of their note-taking style, gauge how meaningful their notes are, and gives them an insight into another person's perception of the lecture's structure. Another variation is to give individual students responsibility for taking lecture notes for use by their peers. This may include follow-up work to ensure that the notes are clear and comprehensive.

MacManaway, L.A. (1967–8) 'Using Lecture Scripts', *Universities Quarterly*, vol. 22, pp. 327–36.
MacManaway, L.A. (1969–70) 'Teaching Methods in Higher Education - Innovation and Research', *Universities Quarterly*, vol. 24, no. 3, pp. 321–9.
Pullis, J. (1995) *Speedwriting, Note-taking and Study Skills*, McGraw-Hill.
Woodward, K. (1993) *Reading and Note-taking*, Open University Press.

See also: Guided study; Handout; Tutorial-tape-document learning package approach

Clarifying educational environment

Clarifying educational environment (CEE) is an approach which exposes learners to certain elements of a simplified but real situation – people, objects and principles – to prepare them for more complex situations and activities in real life. It seeks to promote learners' abilities to explore their environment alone, and to use their acquired knowledge for subsequent learning.

CEE enables learners to assume different roles in interaction with other participants, permitting them to reflect on themselves and their relationships with others in an environment free of any pressures or other factors which are not specifically related to the learning activity.

The specific elements depend on the learner's particular activity, and they are selected and combined to give a clearly structured environment in which learners can work on a particular subject and acquire certain skills, depending on their own interests, either alone or in a group. An example of this in management might be setting up a PC lab in a university or training centre which features the types of hardware and software that are typically used in business organizations.

The CEE centre is usually organized by a teacher, who formulates one of several workplaces or projects, and who provides the materials necessary to simulate them. In the preparatory phase, the teacher informs learners about the organizational aspects of the study centre, and how they can control and structure the learning processes, later acting as an adviser, helping to solve problems related to content, technical matters or group dynamics. The work materials provided are limited to those required to carry out the designated projects. These include structured study guides which inform learners about the organization, its procedures, the subject matter of the learning situation, and their place within it.

See also: Vestibule training

Classroom meeting model

This personally oriented model which focuses on the development of self-understanding and responsibility for oneself and one's social group was developed by William Glasser. It is based on the principle that students are capable of dealing with their own problems themselves, and that problems of inter-personal relations are best addressed through a 30–40-minute classroom meeting during which students and instructors put aside content and curriculum issues and focus instead on personal, behavioural and academic problems in order to generate solutions. Joyce and Weil describe six problem-solving steps in the classroom meeting model.

First, a climate of involvement is created. Participants form warm personal relationships which allow their problems and differences to be discussed in a forthright manner. Everyone speaks for themselves and shares their opinions without blaming and evaluating others. Second, the problem to be discussed is revealed, either by a student or an instructor. They describe it, give examples of it, and predict the consequences they foresee if it continues. Third, group members identify the values and the social norms that seem

to underpin the problem behaviour, then make a personal judgement about the norm to follow, and articulate its values. Step four consists of identifying attractive courses of action. The group discusses specific alternative behaviours, and members agree on which they will follow. Fifth, participants agree on which will be followed, and make a commitment to do so. Finally, a follow-up meeting is held to examine how effective the new behaviours are, and to reinforce them for the future.

Glasser, W. (1965) *Reality Therapy*, Harper and Row.
Joyce, B. and Weil, M. (1980) *Models of Teaching* (2nd edn), Allyn and Bacon, pp. 206–17.

See also: Awareness training; Norm clarification; Norm modification; Role prescription; Sensitivity (T-group) training

Classroom-as-organization model

As its name suggests, the classroom-as-organization (CAO) model involves structuring the classroom as an organization – defined by Buchanan and Huczynski as a 'social arrangement for achieving controlled performance in pursuit of collective goals' – which allows instructors to explore the concepts of social arrangements, discuss what is meant by performance and how it might be controlled, and in the process consider which goals are collective and how they come to be so. The whole class can be considered as one organization, with syndicate groups representing departments, or it may be treated as one of several departments.

The approach allows instructors to model various business structures and processes. A number of work teams of six to eight members each can be formed and asked to recruit the remainder of the students using application forms and interviews, group leaders can be appointed formally or allowed to emerge, they can be formed into a tier of middle management, and job descriptions can be provided for class members. Each session may begin with the instructor serving as Chief Executive Officer, holding meetings with middle management to agree objectives and allocate tasks, members' performance can be appraised fortnightly or monthly, and students may be disciplined for lateness or absence, or even fired.

The CAO model can incorporate the major topics addressed in any introductory management or organizational behaviour course. Division of labour, co-ordination, leadership, group processes, team working and culture can all be demonstrated and discussed, and the course curriculum can be sequenced to parallel the students' experiences in the classroom or the chapters in the course textbook.

Balke, W.M. (1981) 'The Policy Learning Co-op: Treating the Classroom Like an Organization', *Exchange: The Organizational Behaviour Teaching Journal*, vol. 6, no. 2, pp. 27–32.

Barry, D. (1989–90) 'Twincorp: Extension of the Classroom-as-Organization Model', *Organizational Behaviour Teaching Review*, vol. 14, no. 1, pp. 1–15.

Buchanan, D.A. and Huczynski, A.A. (1997) *Organizational Behaviour: An Introductory Text* (3rd edn), Prentice-Hall Europe.

Gardner, W.L. and Larson, L.L. (1987–8) 'Practising Management in the Classroom: Experience is the Best Teacher', *Organizational Behaviour Teaching Review*, vol. 12, no. 3, pp. 12–23.

Greenhalgh, L. (1979) 'Simulating an On-going Organization', *Exchange: The Organizational Behaviour Teaching Journal*, vol. 4, no. 3, pp. 23–7.

Maranvillem, S.J. (1997) 'Strategic Ceremonial as a Pedagogical Exercise', *Journal of Management Education*, vol. 21, no. 2, pp. 97–109.

Mazoff, R., Cohen, A.R. and Bradford, D.L. (1979) 'A Dialogue on Creating the Organization as a Classroom', *Exchange: The Organizational Behaviour Teaching Journal*, vol. 4, no. 1, pp. 25–36.

O'Brien, C.D. and Buono, A.F. (1996) 'Creating a Networked, Learning Organization in the Classroom', *Journal of Management Education*, vol. 20, no. 3, pp. 369–81.

Obert, S.L. (1982) 'Teaching Micro OD Skills by Developing the Classroom Organization', *Exchange: The Organizational Behaviour Teaching Journal*, vol. 7, no. 1, pp. 23–6.

Pendse, S. (1984–5) 'E pluribus unum: Making the Classroom an Organization', *The Organizational Behaviour Teaching Review*, vol. 9, no. 4, pp. 41–51.

Putzel, R. (1992) 'Experience Base Learning: A Classroom-as-Organization Using Delegated, Rank-order Grading', *Journal of Management Education*, vol. 16, no. 2, pp. 12–23.

Rueschhoff, M.S. (1988–89) 'The Job of Student and its Characteristics', *Organizational Behaviour Teaching Review*, vol. 13, no. 3, pp. 94–6.

Trice, H.M. and Beyer, J.M. (1984) 'Studying Corporate Culture Through Rites and Ceremonials', *Academy of Management Review*, vol. 8, pp. 653–69.

See also: Behavioural simulation; Field format; Game; Simulation

Clinic meeting

A clinic meeting is perhaps best described as a short, intensive, multi-activity, large-group learning experience. The emphasis throughout is on diagnosing, analysing and solving problems arising out of the participants' fields of experience.

Clinic meetings employ a pattern of activities that may include large, general session-type meetings, small discussion groups, planning groups, problem-solving groups, skill practice groups, instructional groups, special interest groups, reading periods, individual consultations and recreational periods. The meetings may vary in length from one day to several weeks, and they are often residential.

See also: Brains Trust; Colloquy meeting; Conference meeting; Forum meeting; Institute meeting; Interview meeting; Panel discussion; Reaction panel; Symposium meeting

Closing down

Closing down an organization is a dramatic, although not unusual, instance of organizational change. Every year in Britain hundreds of companies go bankrupt, and many others close some of their plants because of lack of profitability. Managing the social consequences of such closures is a challenging task.

In one instance a community action team to help employees cope with job losses was established, working alongside trade union officials and the local social services agencies. A community-based programme was selected for several reasons: it was felt that it could offer more in the way of resources and services than the company could alone; since the community problems created would persist long after the company had ceased to operate, it was best if the long-term response was co-ordinated by the community, and it was felt that employees' resentment would reduce their involvement in programmes sponsored by the company in isolation.

The programme aimed to increase co-operation between community agencies to ensure that their services were fully used. An organization to co-ordinate the community agencies offering services and resources to the unemployed was set up, and an in-plant counselling programme was established to help workers define their problems and contact the appropriate helping agencies.

Edin, P.-A. (1989) *Individual Consequences of Plant Closures*, Almqvist and Wiksell International.

Hardy, C. (1985) *Managing Organizational Closure*, Gower.

Joyce, F.E. (1985) *Major Plant Closures: Problems and Potentials*, Gower.

Tabor, T.D., Walsh, J.T. and Cooke, R.A. (1979) 'Developing a Community-based Programme for Reducing the Social Impact of Plant Closing', *Journal of Applied Behavioural Science*, vol. 15, no. 2, pp. 133–55.

See also: Early retirement; Flexible manning; Outplacement counselling; Workforce reduction

Clozure

This method, derived from structuralist theories of semiotics, tests students' comprehension of a passage of text related to the subject they are studying by omitting, say, 1 in 10 words or random key words, and asking them to supply the missing words so that the passage makes sense. This can be done in a variety of ways: for example, by simply supplying the prepared text and instructing students to fill in the gaps or by providing a list of the missing words in alphabetical order along with the text. A sample paragraph without any omissions is sometimes supplied as background material. The task can be made more difficult by increasing the frequency with which words are omitted, for example from 1 in 10 to 1 in 5. Here is a brief example of a clozure exercise:

> When a cloze procedure is ... to reading tasks, the ... is asked to fill ... gap with a single word ... has been left out ... the text. To do ... successfully the word must ... to the rules of ..., have the correct meaning, ... be consistent with the ... and language patterns of ... author.

Clozure has a variety of applications. At its simplest, it can serve as an exercise in vocabulary training, grammar and comprehension. At a more complex level, it can be used to identify the 'gestalt' of a passage – its general pattern – and to consider how this enables one to predict what the particular statements made in the passage will be.

Boydell, T. (1981) 'Beauty and the Beast: A Participative Fairy Story', *Management Education and Development*, vol. 12, no. 2, pp. 81–4.

See also: Writing for learning

Cluster laboratory

A cluster laboratory is a variation of sensitivity (T-group) training in which the participants are all from the same organization, but work in different parts of it and thus do not have direct working relationships with one another.

French, W.L. and Bell, C.H. (1973) *Organization*

Development: Behavioural Science Interventions for Organization Improvement (3rd edn), Prentice-Hall, p. 143.

See also: Basic encounter; Cousin laboratory; Encounter groups; Gestalt techniques; Group development laboratory; Human relations laboratory; Instrumented laboratory; Laboratory training; Organizational laboratory; Personal development laboratory; Psychodrama; Sensitivity (T-group) training; Tavistock Conference Method; Transactional Analysis

Co-counselling (re-evaluation counselling; reciprocal counselling; peer counselling; exchange counselling)

This is a generic term for a group of methods concerned with promoting personal growth, problem-solving and development by developing self-awareness, based on the work of Harvey Jackins and Carl Rogers. The approach emphasizes the importance of mutual aid between individuals. The co-counsellors take it in turns to be 'client' and 'counsellor'. The core theory is that human beings suffer from restrictions and rigidities of attitude and behaviour, called *patterns*, caused by the accumulation of undischarged distresses and hurt from the past.

The client uses a variety of simple but powerful techniques to discharge the past distresses described, and thereby break up the patterns through a process of spontaneous *re-evaluation*, gaining insights into past experiences and how they relate to the present. The counsellor gives supportive attention, using standard counselling techniques such as active listening and reflecting. Although they may sometimes confront preconceptions, it is important to accept the client's values, views and emotions, and avoid judgementality. The counsellor may occasionally make suggestions about what the client could say or do, but should never offer interpretations, advice, criticism or analysis, since the client is self-regulating and in charge of the process.

Re-evaluation counselling was the original approach developed by Harvey Jackins in Seattle in the early 1950s, and he still holds the licence for it. The Re-Evaluation Counselling Communities authorize their own teachers and run training courses in the fundamentals of the technique.

Co-Counselling Community (1979) *Handbook on Co-counselling*, Co-Counselling Community.
Hoare, I.D. (1981) 'Peer Counselling for Personal Development', *Training*, vol. 7, no. 2, p. 9.
Jackins, H. (1982) *The Human Use of Human*

Beings: The Theory of Reevaluation Counselling, Rational Island Publishers.

Smith, P.B. (1980) *Group Processes and Personal Change*, Harper and Row, Chapter 9.

See also: Awareness training; Cognitive behavioural therapy; Interpersonal process recall; Learning cell; One-to-one learning; Psychotherapy; Re-evaluation counselling

Co-op/co-op

This is one of several co-operative learning models which combine team tasks that feature high levels of individual accountability and individual task specialization while generating individual and team products and pay-offs. In this model, overall team performance depends on the level of interdependence between team members, reducing the diffusion of responsibility that is a common feature of group tasks. Students come to understand that their individual performance within the team affects both themselves and their fellow team members directly.

The initial session identifies the topics, concepts and techniques to be studied. Heterogeneous teams of four to six students are then formed, and team-building activities are conducted to develop members' co-operative and commitment skills. The objectives of the course are set out, and each team is assigned a portion of the total task, with each team's task complementing the work of the others. The basis of grading is also negotiated.

Next, within each team, sub-topics are identified and allocated to individual team members. These individuals become sub-topic 'champions', and are responsible for instructing other members in their team in that sub-topic. Each team member works on their individual sub-topic, then presents their work to the other group members. The group as a whole then prepares a presentation to the rest of the class about what they have learned, evaluating individuals' contributions to the group's output.

Each team then presents its report, which is graded on the basis agreed earlier in a system structured to support the objectives set. Individual member performances are graded, and these count towards both their own and their group's final mark. In the process, team members are required to grade their fellow members' contributions (which they usually dislike doing). This course work element counts for 40 per cent of the individual student's course mark.

Kagan, S. (1985) 'Co-op/co-op: A Flexible Co-operative Learning Technique', in Slavin, R.F. (ed.) *Learning to Co-operate, Co-operating to Learn*, Plenum Press.

Lyons, P.R. (1991) 'Accelerating Team Interde-pendence with a Co-operative Learning Paradigm', *Journal of Management Education*, vol. 15, no. 2, pp. 265–7.

See also: Co-operative learning; Group project; Peer teaching; Teaching as learning

Co-operative education (work placement; sandwich education)

Herman Schneider is credited with instituting the first co-operative education programme at the College of Engineering in the University of Cincinnati in 1906. In contrast to co-operative learning, the approach focuses on co-operation between students and outside institutions. Students alternate academic periods at university with structured work experiences in study- or career-related employment outside the classroom, usually in business, government or professional organizations.

The aim of co-operative education is to complement traditional education. It seeks to help students reinforce and expand their learning, encourage their personal growth and provide them with career direction. Through work experiences, students learn about inter-personal relationships at work, supervision and how to meet responsibilities. They become self-reliant and develop confidence in their decision-making. This helps them prepare for their careers, allows them to test tentative career choices, to learn employers' needs, select appropriate future courses and acquire professional work experience.

Various models of co-operative education exist, but most are characterized by the fact that the work experience is productive, and is seen as an essential part of the overall educative process.

Co-operative educational experiences can be linked to existing university courses to provide a basis for student's learning on the work assignment, either concurrently with or before the work experience. Co-operative experience can be evaluated by means of projects or papers, by the employers, by staff members visiting students on site and by student self-evaluation.

Minimum performance standards and assessment techniques are integral to the programmes where academic credit is provided or where co-operative education is a degree requirement. The work experience should gradually grow in complexity and responsibility, matching the student's academic progress. Learning contracts have been used to provide a link between university and work periods, and to aid assessment. The contract is an agreement between the student, tutor, and frequently the employer, covering the learning goals the students are expected to achieve which will form the basis for their evaluation.

The main difference between co-operative education programmes is the placement patterns they adopt to integrate work with university experience. In the *full-time alternating pattern*, students are divided into two or three cohorts and one group works full-time away from the university while the others study full-time. In the *parallel pattern*, students attend classes for part of the day, and attend co-operative work assignments for the remainder. In the *field pattern*, students leave the campus for a specified period at least once during their undergraduate study, but no more than once in any given year. Other variations include being placed with either one or several employers – students may sometimes receive more than one period of supervised employment if it is not economical or practical for the employer to engage them for long enough to allow them a full learning experience – and also the degree to which such work assignments are optional or compulsory.

In the USA, students on professional programmes such as engineering or nursing are employed on study-related and frequently well-paid jobs.

In the UK, the term 'sandwich course' is used to describe the integration of work and study experience. Such programmes are a feature of many universities, and two bodies – the British Association for Business Studies Industrial Placements, and the Association for Sandwich Education and Training – help to promote this form of learning.

Co-operative education programmes with a primarily 'service ethic' which emphasizes community and national development are described in the entry on Study Service.

Ashworth, P. (1989) *Experiential Learning During Sandwich Degree Placements*, Sheffield Hallam University.

Ashworth, P. and Saxton, J. (1992) *Managing Work Experience*, Routledge.

Auburn, T., Ley, A. and Arnold, J. (1993) 'Psychology Undergraduates' Experience of Placement', *Studies in Higher Education*, vol. 13, no. 3, pp. 265–85.

Barbeau, J.E. (1990) *Learning From Working: Guide for Co-operative Education*, South-Western Publishers.

Calloway, D. and Beckstead, S.M. (1995) 'Re-conceptualising Internships in Management Education', *Journal of Management Education*, vol. 19, no. 3, pp. 326–41.

Conklin, N. et al. (1997) *Education Through Co-operative Extension*, Delmar Publishing.

Decant, K. (1994) 'Making the Most of Job Assignments: An Exercise in Planning for Learning', *Journal of Management Education*, vol. 18, no. 2, pp. 198–211.

Kaupins, G.E. (1989–90) 'Ideas for Integrating Organization Behaviour into Internships', *Organizational Behaviour Teaching Review*, vol. 14, no. 4, pp. 39–45.

Mason, R. (1997) *Co-operative Occupational Education and Work Experience* (5th edn), Interstate Printers and Publishers.

McCormick, D.W. (1993) 'Critical Thinking, Experiential Learning and Internships', *Journal of Management Education*, vol. 17, no. 2, pp. 260–2.

Megginson, D. (1988) 'Instructor, Coach, Mentor: Three Ways of Helping for Managers', *Management Education and Development*, vol. 19, no. 1, pp. 33–46.

Miller, A., Watts, A.G. and Jamieson, I. (1991) *Rethinking Work Experience*, Falmer Press.

Ryder, K.S. and Wilson, J.W. (1987) *Co-operative Education in a New Era*, Jossey-Bass.

Saxton, J. and Ashworth, P. (1990) 'The Workplace Supervision of Sandwich Degree Placement Students', *Management Education and Development*, vol. 21, no. 2, pp. 133–49.

Sheather, G., Martin, R. and Harris, D. (1993) 'Partners in Excellence: A New Model for Co-operative Education', *Education and Training Technology International*, vol. 30, no. 1, pp. 5–31.

Van der Vorm, P.T. and Jones, N. (1985) *Co-operative Education Across the Disciplines*, University Press of America.

Wilson, J.W. (1978) 'Patterns of Awarding Degree Credit in Co-operative Education', *Journal of Co-operative Education*, Autumn, pp. 87–92.

See also: Competence-based training; Corporate board of student directors; Experience-based training; Field project attachment; Industrial project; Internship; Learning contracts; Student placement; Study service

Co-operative learning

In contrast to co-operative education, co-operative learning is a teaching approach in which learners are encouraged to co-operate in the learning process rather than compete with their fellow class members. The class is subdivided into small, heterogeneous groups, and the grading system is designed to reward pupils for providing assistance to other members of their group.

Johnson and Johnson describe how this approach can be applied: 'In a co-operatively structured maths class, students working in small groups will be given tasks: to learn how to solve each assigned math problem; to make sure that the other members of their group know how to solve each problem; and to make sure that everybody in the class knows how to solve each problem. While working on the problems, students discuss their solutions with other group members; and explain how the problems might be solved. They listen and encourage each other to understand the solutions. When everyone in their group has mastered the solution, they look for another group to help, until everyone in the class understands how to work out the problems.'

Since students work in learning groups for a significant proportion of their class time, the approach is distinguished by a high level of interaction within and between the groups. Each student receives constant feedback and corrective instruction, and they develop personal relationships which enhance their desire to excel at the learning task.

Co-operative learning also develops interpersonal and group interaction skills, increases self-esteem and psychological health, and its advocates claim that the differentiated view of others it encourages combats prejudice.

Cavalier, J.C. Klein, J.D. and Cavalier, F. (1995) 'Effects of Co-operative Learning on Performance, Attitude and Group Behaviours in a Technical Team Environment', *Education, Training Research & Development*, vol. 43, no. 3, pp. 61–71.

Jackson, B. (1994) 'Co-operative Learning: A Case Study of a University Course in Systems Analysis', *Education and Training Technology International*, vol. 31, no. 3, pp. 166–79.

Johnson, D.W. and Johnson, R.T. (1984–5) 'Structuring Groups for Co-operative Learning', *The Organizational Behaviour Teaching Review*, vol. 9, no. 4, pp. 8–17.

Johnson, D.W. and Johnson, R.T. (1994) *Learning Together and Alone* (4th edn), Allyn and Bacon.

Joyce, B.R. and Weil, M. (1996) *Models of Teaching* (5th edn), Allyn and Bacon.

Kennett, D.J. et al. (1996) 'Co-operative Learning in a University Setting', *Studies in Higher Education*, vol. 21, no. 2, pp. 177–86.

Klein, J.D. and Pridemore, D.R. (1994) 'Effects of Orienting Activities and Practice on Achievement, Continuing Motivation, and Student Behaviours in a Co-operative Learning Environment', *Education, Training Research & Development*, vol. 42, no. 4, pp. 41–54.

Millis, B.J. and Cottell, P.G. (1997) *Co-operative Learning for Higher Education Faculty*, Oryx Press.

See also: Co-op/Co-op; Group project; Peer teaching; Teaching as learning

Coaching

Coaching has been defined as a process through which an individual supports the learning or performance improvement of another via interactive questioning and providing active support. The coaching instructor observes the learner, and provides hints, help and feedback in a positive way as required. Coaching is sometimes incorporated in on-the-job training, and can be carried out by an employee's immediate superior, another manager, a company trainer or an outside consultant who works with individuals to help them define their learning goals, see themselves as others see them, and encourages them to explore new ways of behaving in order to achieve their goals.

Coaching can be distinguished from mentoring because it emphasises training. The learner has a need to learn something specific, such as job knowledge or a new skill. The coach indicates what they want the learner to do, suggests how it may be done, follows up and corrects errors. The objective is to teach and guide the learner in the performance of their immediate task or assignment. Golf or tennis coaches or driving instructors are good examples of this approach. Mentoring, in contrast, involves providing less specific advice, with the mentor acting as a sounding board, a catalyst for new ideas, or a friend who offers constructive criticism.

Coaching can also be distinguished from counselling in the business context, which involves a discussion between a manager and subordinate regarding the latter's hopes, fears, emotions and aspirations. It may address very personal and delicate matters, so the manager must be skilled in the role. It is far less commonly used than coaching.

If managers take on the coaching role, a number of difficulties may arise. They may resent the demands made on their time, especially if they do not feel the activity has any direct benefits for themselves. Forming a productive coaching relationship with a subordinate may also pose problems for some managers, who may feel uncomfortable in the different role, while others may experience difficulty switching between the managerial and coaching roles.

Two separate coaching roles have been distinguished, which can be labelled *intensive* and *non-intensive*. Only managers who clearly have the ability and desire to carry out intensive coaching should be encouraged to do so. The non-intensive coaching role is considered less demanding. It involves discussing problems with subordinates, providing constructive feedback on their written and verbal presentations, discussing the reasons behind certain decisions they have taken, encouraging them to reflect on and analyse their experiences, and helping them recognize and overcome their weaknesses.

Of all the management development techniques, coaching requires the least staff co-ordination. It represents learning by doing, with the learners experiencing progress, and being able to see the fruits of their labours.

Buckley, R. and Caple, J. (1996) *One-to-one Training and Coaching Skills*, Kogan Page.

Colman, J. (1997) 'Coaching and Its Role in Senior Management', *Organizations and People*, vol. 4, no. 3, pp. 37–9.

Gould, D. (1997) 'Developing Directors Through Personal Coaching', *Long Range Planning*, vol. 30. no. 1.

Kinlaw, D.C. (1997) *Coaching*, Gower.

Landsberg, M. (1996) *The Tao of Coaching*, HarperCollins.

MacLennan, N. (1995) *Coaching and Mentoring*, Gower.

Parsloe, E. (1992) *Coaching, Mentoring and Assessing: A Practical Guide to Developing Competence*, Kogan Page.

Parsloe, E. and Wright, R. (1997) *The Manager as Coach and Mentor*, Institute of Personnel and Development.

Pay, P.M. (1996) 'The Coaching Challenge', *Organizations and People*, vol. 3, no. 2, pp. 36–40.

Popper, M. and Lipshitz, R. (1992) 'Coaching on Leadership', *Leadership and Organization Development Journal*, vol. 13, no. 7, pp. 15–18.

Voss, T. (1997) *Sharpen Your Team's Skills in Coaching*, McGraw-Hill.

Waldroop, J. and Butler, T. (1996) 'The Executive as Coach', *Harvard Business Review*, vol. 74, no. 6, November–December, pp. 111–17.

Whitmore, J. (1996) *Coaching for Performance*, Nicholas Brealy.

See also: Assignment to manager with high development skills; Competence-focused learning; Co-counselling; Consulting pair; Context training; Counselling; Development assignment; Facilitation; Insider-outsider consulting teams; On-the-job training; One-to-one learning; Outplacement counselling; Planned delegation; Process consultation; Prompt list; Re-evaluation counselling; Role prescription; Stress management; Supervisory counselling

Cognitive behavioural therapy (resilience training)

Cognitive behavioural therapy (CBT) is one of a number of psychotherapeutic methods adopted for management training and development from the clinical field. CBT was developed by psychologists in the USA, and aims to help people understand why they hold certain views and act in certain ways, and how to change self-destructive patterns of thought and behaviour. It was originally used as a substitute for drug therapy for anxious and depressed patients, and has been helpful in the treatment of personality disorders and schizophrenia.

In the organizational context, CBT has been used by companies such as Prudential, British Aerospace and Du Pont for sales training, stress management, career/family balancing, leadership training and to improve performance. A CBT course will usually involve groups of up to twenty staff attending weekly three-hour sessions over a seven-week period, during which they learn to identify how negative thought processes and reactions to events and setbacks can exacerbate stress and depress their activity levels, leading to poor work performance. Although CBT seeks to help people overcome negativity, it emphasizes realistic rather than positive thinking.

Cormier, B., Cormier, L.S. and Cormier, W.H. (1997) *Interviewing Strategies for Helpers: Fundamental Skills and Cognitive Behavioural Interventions*, Brookes/Cole.

Dryden, W. (1990) *Introduction to Cognitive Behavioural Therapy*, Gale Centre Publications.

Fowler, D.R. et al. (1995) *Cognitive Behavioural Therapy for Psychosis*, Wiley.

France, R. and Robson, M. (1997) *Cognitive Behavioural Therapy in Primary Care*, Jessica Kingsley Publications.

Scott, M.J., Stradling, S.G. and Dryden, W. (1996) *Developing Cognitive Behaviour Counselling*, Sage.

Sheldon, B. (1994) *Cognitive Behavioural Therapy*, Routledge.

See also: Bioenergetics; Co-counselling; Neuro-linguistic programming; Psychotherapy; Psychodrama; Personal development laboratory; Re-evaluation counselling; Transactional Analysis

Collaboratively designed course

Collaboration between teachers and students in drawing up a course can take place at two levels: the design of the course as a whole, where students contribute to the choice of content and the methods to be used; or the design of particular sessions in the course, where students specify questions they want answered, information they need or demonstrations they would like to witness.

Collaboration of this kind can range along a continuum. At one extreme, teachers may interpret students' needs without consulting them. To encourage greater involvement, they may consult the students, and design future sessions accordingly. As a further step, teachers may encourage students to design future sessions, for example by arranging for small groups to share their concerns and decide which items of content and practice they would like to be covered. At the other extreme, a 'learning community' format can be adopted, in which tutors and students collaborate fully in agreeing course aims, the content to be covered, what methods are appropriate, and how progress should be assessed.

Boud, D. and Prosser, M.T. (1980) 'Sharing Responsibility – Staff–student Co-operation in Learning', *British Journal of Educational Technology*, vol. 11, no. 1, pp. 24–35.
Huczynski, A.A. (1981) 'Self Development Through Formal Qualification', in Boydell, T. and Pedler, M. (eds) *Management Self Development: Concepts and Practices*, Gower.
Kilty, J. (1978) 'Design for Learning', British Postgraduate Medical Federation (mimeograph).

See also: Course design as learning; Learning community; Peer teaching; Student-planned learning

Collages

Collage exercises can be used to trace the cultural and emotional topography of a group or an organizational change process. They can also be useful as ice-breakers if approached in a light-hearted way, or as a unifying group experience at the end of a session or workshop. They allow people to express themselves at a fairly deep level by initially avoiding verbal expression, focusing instead on visual images of thoughts and feelings.

Individuals, sub-groups or groups can be asked to prepare a collage on a particular theme, such as 'feelings about the team', or if participants seem reluctant to 'play children's games' they can be allowed to choose the collage theme themselves. Facilitators should ensure that participants have enough space and a plentiful supply of materials, such as large sheets of paper, magazines from which words and pictures may be cut out, crayons, felt pens, glue, sticky tape and scissors. They should emphasize the importance of composing images which 'ring a bell' without thinking too deeply about how or why, and fix a firm deadline of 30–90 minutes for the exercise, to discourage excessive deliberation.

Each collage is then described to the whole group by its producer(s), followed by a discussion. Participants should not be allowed to turn these presentations into a game of interpretation, since the purpose of the exercise is to help them gain insights without putting words into each other's mouths or provoking defensive reactions. If the group includes the boss or senior managers, they should present their collages last, to avoid colouring the presentations of the more junior staff.

Huse, E.F. (1980) *Organization Development and Change* (2nd edn), West Publishing, pp. 95–6.
Fordyce, J.K. and Weil, R. (1971) *Managing With People*, Addison Wesley Longman, pp. 131–3 and 152–3.

See also: Chronology charting; Diagnostic activities; Drawing for learning; Family group diagnostic meeting; Fortune lining; Illuminative incident analysis; Interviewing; Inter-organizational information-sharing; Poster; Physical representation of organizations; Storyboarding

Collateral organization (parallel organization; reflective organization; reflective shadow structure)

Dale Zand considered a collateral organization to be a modified form of task force. He saw it as 'a supplemental organization co-existing with the usual, formal organization' which was created to deal with 'ill-structured' problems. Its purpose is to consider urgent problems or opportunities that affect the organization as a whole and involve more than one unit of the company. Such problems may be non-routine, extremely complex or focused on the future.

As an 'organization within an organization', the collateral organization is encouraged to develop a norm system which differs from that of the formal organization, and hierarchy-based relationships and attitudes are set aside to facilitate creative problem-solving. A reflective mode of working may be adopted whereby members consider the methods, goals, assumptions and alternatives they use. The intervention involves identifying a work unit within the company, or creating a synthetic group consisting of the representatives of other groups, and then setting it up so that it can operate independently of the 'old' culture. This group then develops problem-solving techniques which are not hampered by the practices or traditions of the past.

The use of collateral organizations thus appears to be a throwback to the task-oriented team-building activities which involve a change agent, data-gathering, data feedback and process consultation. One can argue that most team-building events deal with ill-structured problems and that the concepts of team-building and collateral organization overlap, so how do they differ? Zand argues that team-building activities commonly concern just one unit of a company, focusing on its problems rather than system-wide ones. In contrast, the remit of a collateral organization is wider. Its purpose is to complement the formal organization, operating in parallel with it to identify and address problems it has been unable to solve. Both organizations consist of the same people, and the output of the collateral organization represents an input to the formal one, so the success of the former is inextricably linked to that of the latter, and the formal organization must find the input useful.

The important factor is the difference in the norms that exist within the two organizations. In a collateral organization, all communication channels are connected and open and there is rapid and complete exchange of information, and this encourages careful questioning of goals, assumptions, methods and alternatives. Managers can approach and enlist the help of others in the organization to help solve problems without being restricted to choosing from among their formal subordinates.

In general terms, the creation of task forces often occurs as a consequence of team-building and inter-group activities: it can be seen as a structural intervention because such task forces support the structure of the organization and its parts. Task forces are temporary appendages to the structure of the organization, preserving its existing units and divisions, and its planning and communication systems. The collateral system represents a structural solution to the problem of gaining the benefits of group member equality while preserving the official hierarchy that reflects the inequality of power and authority in an organization – it preserves the status quo while creating an alternative to it.

Kilmann, R.H. (1996) 'Designing Collateral Organizations', in Starkey, K. (ed.) *How Organizations Learn*, Routledge, pp. 182–98.

Rubinstein, D. and Woodman, R.W. (1984) 'Spiderman and the Burma Raiders: Collateral Organization in Action', *Journal of Applied Behavioural Science*, vol. 20, no. 3, pp. 1–21.

Stein, B.A. and Kanter, R.M. (1980) 'Building the Parallel Organization: Creating Mechanisms for Permanent Quality of Life', *Journal of Applied Behavioural Science*, vol. 16, no. 3, July–September, pp. 371–86.

Zand, D. (1974) 'Collateral Organizations: A New Change Strategy', *Journal of Applied Behavioural Science*, vol. 10, no. 1, pp. 63–89.

Zand, D. (1981) *Information, Organization and Power*, McGraw-Hill, Chapter 4.

See also: Autonomous workgroups; Business teams; Independent product teams; Intrapreneurial group; Managerial decentralization; MAPS approach; Matrix designs; Parallel career ladders; Plural chief executive; Skunkworks; Structural intervention; Team action leadership

Colloquy meeting

A colloquy is a formal stage presentation to a large audience, similar to a panel discussion except it involves a greater degree of audience participation.

In a colloquy, three or four members of the audience join an equal number of experts on the stage and question them about a given subject which may have been raised or identified previously by an audience panel. The experts then respond to the audience as a whole, and the audience may or may not be permitted to participate.

The colloquy meeting technique is most helpful when a discussion needs to focus on a particular topic or problem. It can provide the audience with an opportunity to understand and explore a specific topic, stimulate their interest in it, and help them to identify and clarify the problems or issues involved. The success of the technique depends on the chair/moderator's ability, the audience's level of knowledge and the quality of the experts.

The chair/moderator must be familiar with the topic to be discussed and the background of audience members. The role involves explaining the colloquy's goals and the ground rules regarding audience participation, encouraging them to participate when appropriate, relating their questions to the goals, monitoring timekeeping and maintaining pace to ensure the topic is covered, directing discussions while remaining neutral, and providing a summary at the conclusion. 'Planting' audience participants who have been briefed to raise certain points or questions can promote debate, especially if the size of the audience is likely to inhibit discussion.

Colloquys allow large groups of people to participate, and can motivate the audience by making them feel more involved. Speakers are also more likely to stay alert if they know they will be questioned.

Epple, A. (1997) *Organizing Scientific Meetings*, Cambridge University Press.

See also: Audience reaction/watchdog team; Brains Trust; Clinic meeting; Conference meeting; Forum meeting; Gordon seminar; Institute meeting; Interrogation of experts; Interview meeting; Panel discussion; Reaction panel; Symposium meeting

Committee assignment

Managers may be requested to volunteer to serve on company committees, or may be nominated to serve on them by their bosses. When bosses receive such invitations, they may decide that staff development considerations mean it is most valuable to send either a junior manager who is expert in the subject to be discussed, or one who has little knowledge of the subject but would benefit from the experience of participating in the committee's work. Participants need training in a range of specific skills to be an effective committee chair or member, and imparting these skills is an important management development activity.

Where a committee is composed of staff from different departments or levels of seniority, the manager can gain an understanding of different perceptions and varying attitudes towards the same issue or problem. Membership of such committees may also allow the individual to build informal links with other staff in the organization that do not arise from their day-to-day work, but there are drawbacks. Committees seldom decide, and often compromise. They have a tendency to become social gatherings where those with the strongest personality make the decisions. However, if conditions are favourable, a committee assignment may promote a manager's development.

Committee assignments are most successful when an individual is assigned a specific area of responsibility and is not just an observer, or when a committee consists of a number of representatives from different functional groups.

Britzius, O. (1992) *Practical Guide to Meetings*, Butterworth-Heinemann.
Doyle, M. (1996) *How To Make Meetings Work*, Berkley Publishers.
Martin, D. (1995) *Manipulating Meetings*, Pitman.
Payne, J. and Payne, S. (1994) *Successful Meetings in a Week*, Hodder and Stoughton.
Timm, P.R. (1997) *How to Hold Successful Meetings*, Career Press.

See also: Consulting assignment; Development assignment; Evaluation audit assignment; Proposal team assignment; Research assignment; Selection board assignment; Staff meeting assignment; Study assignment

Community of enquiry (liberating structure approach)

This high-risk autonomous learning approach to teaching, which depends on skilled practice, was developed by William Torbert for a compulsory undergraduate course for 360 students. It aims to encourage students to develop a sense of shared purpose, self-direction and the importance of high-quality work.

Torbert identified what he calls the 'qualities of liberating structures' – the characteristics of the organization of educational settings which

enhance student self-direction: recognition that students will, at least initially, view the course differently from the staff and will need to be introduced to a new way of regarding learning; integration of learning products with learning processes by setting tasks that cannot be completed without reference to the processes of learning which are taking place; planning change in the structure of the course as it progresses so that students can take increasing responsibility; providing feedback in the course structure and learning tasks so that the process of learning is monitored; using the power held by the teacher to support the structure which places increasing responsibility on students; emphasizing the need for critical examination of the nature and functioning of the course itself by both teachers and students; holding teachers publicly accountable to their students for conducting the course along the lines which have been agreed, and a commitment to look for and correct any incongruities which are identified.

Recognizing the paradox in the phrase 'leadership for self-direction', Torbert consciously adopts what he calls an 'ironic approach', and achieving these goals calls for a style of leadership and organization which is simultaneously educative and productive, controlling and freeing.

Torbert, W.R. (1972) 'An Experimental Selection Process', *Journal of Applied Behavioural Science*, vol. 9, pp. 331–50.
Torbert, W.R. (1972) *Learning from Experience: Towards Consciousness*, Wiley.
Torbert, W.R. (1976) *Creating a Community of Enquiry: Conflict, Collaboration, Transformation*, Wiley.
Torbert, W.R. (1978) 'Educating Towards Shared Purpose, Self-Direction and Quality Work: The Theory and Practice of Liberating Structure', *Journal of Higher Education*, vol. 49, no. 2, pp. 109–35.
Torbert, W.R. (1987) *Managing the Corporate Dream: Restructuring for Long Term Success*, McGraw-Hill.
Torbert, W.R. (1991) *The Power of Balance, Transforming Self, Society and Scientific Enquiry*, Sage.
Torbert, W. R. and Hackman, J. (1969) 'Taking the Fun Out of Out Foxing the System', in Runkel, P., Harrison, R. and Runkel, M. (eds) *The Changing College Classroom*, Jossey-Bass.

See also: Autonomy lab; Community-building; Instrumented team learning; Large group as small groups; Learning cell; Learning community; Learning organization

Community-building

Community-building is a process developed by M. Scott Peck and the Foundation for Community Encouragement. Peck defines 'community' as: 'a group of individuals who have learned to communicate honestly with each other, whose relationships go deeper than their masks of composure, and who have developed some significant commitment to "rejoice together, mourn together" and to delight in each other, make others' conditions their own'.

Community-building aims to help groups of people operate according to the spirit and process of a community, tolerating ambiguity, dealing with difficult issues, operating with integrity and civility, and being open to experience and discovery.

Peck's model, based on his studies of groups which approached the state of community he defined, revealed that they passed through four stages: *pseudo-community*, the normal working state, characterized by low energy and denial of the inevitable differences in the group; *chaos*, an increase in energy as differences break out into the open and are then overcome by persuasion, fixing, and healing; *emptiness*, acceptance that one does not know what to do, acceptance of the differences in the group, and the search for authentic communication, and finally *community*. The normal sequence is to move between the first two stages, and breaking free of this pattern demands a willingness to express ignorance and vulnerability, as well as hopes and fears, so that the state of community can be achieved.

Sokolov has extended the community-building concept to organizations. He sees it as helpful in identifying and removing barriers between people and organizations, breaking down isolation among organization members, building synergistic work teams, and providing a framework within which to introduce 'spirit and civility' to organizations.

Kofman, F. and Senge, P.M. (1993) Communities of Commitment: The Heart of Learning Organizations', *Organizational Dynamics*, Autumn, pp. 5–23.

McTevia, J.V. and Peck, M.S. (1992) *Bankrupt: A Society Living in the Future*, Momentum Books.

Peck, M.S. (1987) *The Different Drum*, Rider.

Peck, M.S. (1993) *A World Waiting to be Born*, Rider.

Schaffer, C.R., Anundsen, K. and Peck, M.S. (1993) *Creating Community Anywhere*, Perigee Publishing.

Senge, P.M. (1990) *The Fifth Discipline*, Century Business.

Sokolov, I. (1995) 'Taking M. Scott Pecks's Community Building into Organizations', *Organisations and People*, vol. 3, no. 3, pp. 12–16.

See also: Assignment to community organization; Learning community; Learning organization

Company file project

This method involves a group of students researching an organization and drawing up a report whose headings correspond to the topics or perspectives covered in their coursework. This links classroom learning with organizational reality, and provides experience in drawing conclusions from fragmented information and diverse data, and incorporating it into a coherent report. Since they become experts on their allocated organizations, students can be called upon to describe the implications of particular lecture and discussion topics for them.

Following introductory lectures, students are assigned to groups, each of which is allocated an organization to study for half an academic year or one semester. They gain detailed knowledge about the organization through reading and sometimes through personal contacts, and are required to answer a series of questions about it by submitting a written report and giving an oral presentation.

The instructor's freedom in choosing which questions to set makes the project a flexible learning method that can be used on different courses. These are some examples of the themes that can be explored, each with one sample question (although three are usually set): social policy ('Describe an ethical dilemma currently facing your organization.'); international management ('To what extent is your organization globalized?'); corporate strategy ('List the major elements of your organization's task environment.'); managerial decision-making ('Discuss a major, non-programmed decision recently made by your organization.'); organization structure ('Describe your organization's structure.'), and human resource management ('Describe an HRM issue currently faced by your organization.').

Kirby, S.L. and Kirby, E.G. (1996) 'The Company File Project', *Journal of Management Education*, vol. 20, no. 1, pp. 135–40.

See also: Character immersion

Competence-focused training

These training programmes are built around the daily work experiences of employees, rather than focusing on topics, skills or group work. The approach is based on job standards (competencies) produced through the Management Charter Initiative (MCI), and the training uses briefing sessions, support groups, workshops and open learning materials.

Dale, M. and Isles, P. (1995) *Assessing Management Skills, A Guide to Competencies and Evaluation Techniques*, Kogan Page.

Edmonds, T. (1992) 'Management Development and the Management Charter Initiative "Competence" Approach to Management Development', *Education and Training Technology International*, vol. 29, no. 3, pp. 206–15.

Fletcher, S. (1997) *Analysing Competence*, Kogan Page.

Fletcher, S. (1997) *Competence-based Assessment Techniques* (2nd edn), Kogan Page.

Fletcher, S. (1997) *Designing Competence-based Training* (2nd edn), Kogan Page.

Hay, J. (1990) 'Managerial Competencies or Managerial Characteristics?', *Organisations and People*, vol. 3, no. 1, pp. 9–14.

Stothart, C. (1995) 'High Performance Competencies: Development Through Self-managed Learning', *Organisations and People*, vol. 2, no. 1, pp. 26–9.

See also: Coaching; Co-operative education; Internship

Competing values approach

The competing values approach (CVA) is a diagnostic tool developed by Quinn and Rohrbaugh for use in organizational change interventions. It seeks to overcome what its developers see as the main weakness of Robert Blake and Jane Mouton's Grid Management framework, which offers only a single solution to the management style problem. The CVA can be used to compare the performance of different companies since, despite similarities in goals, structures and sizes, each organization will have a different CVA profile.

The CVA is based on a framework of three different value dimensions, which were developed from studies into people's judgements about the similarity or dissimilarity of organizational performance criteria. The *organizational structure* dimension ranges from an emphasis on control to an emphasis on flexibility. The *organizational focus* dimension ranges from an internal perspective which emphasizes a co-ordination of parts to an external focus which stresses the well-being and development of the whole organization. Finally, the *organizational means and ends* dimension ranges from an emphasis on processes such as planning and goal-setting to an emphasis on final outcomes such as productivity. These dimensions are organized into a framework of performance values.

In the two-dimensional CVA figure, the three value continuums described and the two specific sets of performance criteria are mapped to produce four separate models: the *rational goal model*, *internal process model*, *human relations model* and *open systems model*. Each model highlights the values included within it while overlapping each of the other models, because each shares at least one core dimension and general value with its neighbour. Each of these models is then integrated into the whole by placing it along the three core dimensions. Quinn and Rohrbaugh argue that each of the four core quadrants or models is equally important, since a manager needs to consider all the criteria in making choices and deciding on trade-offs between them.

Quinn and Rohrbaugh report that managers are attracted to this tension-based framework, and that the idea of making trade-offs between competing value positions appeals to them. The CVA helps them discover their current organizational profile, but they are not guided to a Blake and Mouton-type *a priori* '9.9', or a Likert-type or 'System 4-type' style, and it is they who decide where to go next.

Quinn, R.E. and McGrath, M.R. (1982) 'Moving Beyond the Single Solution Perspective: The Competing Values Approach as a Diagnostic Tool', *Journal of Applied Behavioural Science*, vol. 18, no. 4, pp. 463–72.

Quinn, R.E. and Rohrbaugh, J. (1981) 'A Competing Values Approach to Organizational Effectiveness', *Public Productivity Review*, vol. 5, no. 2, pp. 122–40.

Rohrbaugh, J. (1981) 'Operationalizing the Competing Values Approach', *Public Productivity Review*, vol. 5, no. 2, pp. 141–59.

See also: Comprehensive interventions; Contingency approach; FIDO approach; Grid development; LIFO method; 3-D management effectiveness seminar

Comprehensive interventions

This is a class of organizational change and development interventions whose target or influence goes beyond a particular individual or group. Grid development is one such example, since when implemented completely it affects company employees at all levels, and does so over a number of years. The confrontation meeting developed by Richard Beckhard has this same quality, as do strategic management approaches. In this category one could also include survey feedback, since the whole of a company is usually involved in a two-stage programme of a survey followed by feedback.

Many writers would also identify Rensis Likert's System 4 Management and Paul Lawrence and Jay Lorsch's contingency approach as having a comprehensive range since, although neither is an organizational change intervention in its own right, both offer systematic guidelines on how to improve organizational performance.

See also: Competing values approach; Confrontation meeting; Contingency approach; Grid development; Likert's System 4 Management; Strategic management; Survey feedback interventions

Computer-assisted learning (computer-assisted instruction)

In computer-assisted learning (CAL), the computer serves either as a teaching medium or a learning resource. When used as a teaching medium, the computer adapts the presentation of instructional material to a learner on the basis of the individual's previous responses. This model is derived from Skinner and the programmed learning movement, where the computer is used as a tutorial teaching machine (sometimes referred to as 'computer-as-tutor'). In the USA, the term 'computer-assisted instruction' tends to be associated with the use of the computer as a teaching medium.

In its role as a learning resource, the computer provides a range of facilities for the learner, such as modelling, calculation, problem-solving, simulation and database interrogation. In this application the computer acts as a 'dry laboratory' facility, and does not necessarily teach in any direct sense at all. This model is based on the research uses of computers and their impact on subject disciplines (sometimes referred to as 'computer-as-laboratory').

In industry, CAL has been applied to a range of applications. British Airways has a CAL system incorporated in its international airline booking system to train users, and computer manufacturers are developing CAL courses to teach computing skills. It is likely that the number of 'computer-as-laboratory' applications will increase as the range of disciplines which rely on computers grows, but 'computer-as-tutor' applications are likely to be adopted more slowly in higher education because of lack of resources, and because academics are not rewarded financially or in terms of status or promotion for this type of work.

It is important to draw a distinction between CAL and computer-managed learning or, as it is often known, computer-managed instruction (CMI). CMI involves the use of the computer to manage teaching and learning, particularly where individualized learning systems are favoured. It is not a teaching/learning system itself. Under CMI, the computer performs one or more of the following four main tasks: test production, marking and analysis; 'routeing' students through an individualised course of study where the teaching is carried out not by computer, but through teachers, books, and self-instructional media; keeping classroom records, and writing reports for students, teachers and administrators.

Boyle, T. and Boyle, T. (1996) *Designing for Multimedia Learning*, Prentice-Hall.

Kafai, Y. and Resnick, M. (eds) (1996) *Constructionism: Designing Thinking and Learning in a Digital World*, Lawrence Erlbaum Associates.

Kemp. J.E., Morrison, G.R. and Ross, S.M. (1997) *Designing Effective Instruction*, Merrill.

Kommers, P.A.M., Grabinger, S. and Dunlap, J.C. (eds) (1996) *Hypermedia Learning Environments*, Lawrence Erlbaum Associates.

Littleton, K. and Light, P. (1998) *Learning with Computers*, Routledge.

Maddux, C.D., Johnson, D.L. and Wills, J.W. (1996) *Educational Computing: Learning with Tomorrow's Technologies*, Allyn and Bacon.

Newby, T.J., Stepich, D.A., Lehman, J.D. and Russell, J.D. (1996) *Instructional Technology for Teaching and Learning*, Prentice-Hall.

Schank, R.C. (1997) *Virtual Learning*, McGraw-Hill.

See also: Audio tutorial method; Info bank; Language laboratory; Mathetics; Programmed learning; Programmed simulation; Resource centre

Concentrated study

Concentrated study involves allocating a period of time to cover a theme or topic in isolation from all other aspects of a course, allowing students to devote more time to a particular subject than is normally possible on traditional study programmes. For example, a course subject normally taught in weekly one-hour blocks over a ten-week term may be compressed into two days.

It aims to change certain dimensions of undergraduate education, to encourage a more committed approach to studying, to enable students and teachers to build closer relationships, and to introduce a wider range of activities than is usually possible.

Concentrated study is a rarely used approach, and although it has been found to increase effective learning, a degree of understanding and the quality of social interactions and organizational arrangements, its advantages and disadvantages are finely balanced. Some authors propose using it selectively in otherwise traditional courses: for example, at the beginning of a degree programme as a form of induction to help people become acquainted with the subject; for the acquisition of particular skills and basic information, especially if these can be treated as an entity in their own right (e.g., computing); for the development of social skills, group relations and general morale; where understanding can be increased by bringing together experiences which would otherwise remain dispersed and unrelated; sometimes late in a traditional course as an integrating experience or, finally, as a way of stepping up the pace of a course when required.

One institution which does use concentrated study is the City University of New York, which condenses two years of Latin or Greek tuition into a single ten-week summer period. Students must abandon all other interests, including loved ones, jobs and hobbies. The regime involves seven hours of classes followed by six hours of homework. Every teacher is on 24-hour call, and they sleep with their textbooks beside their bed. After nine days, the Latin students begin reading Catullus, while Greek students need six weeks' grammar tuition before embarking on Plato, Euripides and Homer in the original text.

Gould, F. and Croome, D. (1977) 'The Foundation Course "Carousel" at PCL', *Studies in Higher Education*, vol. 2, no. l, pp. 55–68.

Hewton, E. (1977) 'The Curricular Implications of Concentrated Study', *Studies in Higher Education*, vol. 2, no. l, pp. 79–87.

Parlett, M.R. and King, J.G. (1971) *Concentrated Study: A Pedagogic Innovation Observed*, Society for Research into Higher Education.

Swanton, M. (1976) 'The Tutor Midwife: Concentrated Study in the Humanities', *Studies in Higher Education*, vol. 1, no. 2, pp. 169–78.

See also: Minicourse; Module; Networking; Residential; Retreat; Workshop

Concept analysis

A concept is defined as 'an idea of a class of objects'. Cat and dog are both concepts. One of the two specific family pets, Felix, would be placed in the former concept category, while the other, Rover, would go into the latter. Logically, classes of objects can only be established mentally by the abstraction of characteristics and relations (number of legs, shape of face, sound uttered). Any abstracted character or relation must of necessity be general – for example, power, authority, participation, right of management, motivation – and concepts represent different degrees of subtlety and complication.

An understanding of concepts is basic to all areas of study, including business management. However, many management students, especially those who are already managers, are so eager to focus on issues of application and practicality that they neglect development of this aspect. A question such as 'Is group empowerment consis-

tent with individual job responsibility?' is primarily a conceptual question, since it requires clarification of the concepts of 'empowerment' and 'job responsibility'. Such questions can be distinguished from factual ones ('Do companies run on empowerment principles make more profit?') and from value questions ('Is empowerment a good thing?').

Concept analysis is a way of clarifying and dealing with issues such as these. It is a topic in its own right, and relies on specialized techniques, eleven of which can be distinguished: *isolating questions of concept*, distinguishing conceptual questions from factual or value ones; *right answer analysis*, considering conceptual issues before moving on to those of fact or value; *model cases*, selecting examples which accurately represent an instance of the concept; *contrary cases*, selecting examples which clearly do not represent instances of the concept; *related cases*, considering related concepts (e.g., punishment and justice); *borderline cases*, focusing on cases where there is conceptual uncertainty; *invented cases*, considering theoretical examples outside students' experience; *social context*, imagining the circumstances related to the concept (Who? Why? When?); *understanding anxiety*, taking into account the moods and anxieties of the person who makes a statement or asks a question related to the concept being considered; *practical results*, exploring the down-to-earth consequences of accepting or rejecting a concept item and, finally, *results in language* – once a concept has been analysed and the range of its instances noted, making a statement regarding the most sensible and useful meaning of it.

Oastler, J. (1978) *Concept Analysis: From Socrates to Wittgenstein*, University Press of America.

Wilson, J. (1966) *Thinking With Concepts* (2nd edn), Cambridge University Press.

See also: Analogy teaching; Concept attainment model; Concept formation; Concept mapping; Concept teaching; Concept training; Concept uncovery; Mind Mapping; Person-card technique

Concept attainment model

Bruner and colleagues distinguish 'concept formation' from 'concept attainment' on the grounds that that the former requires students to decide the basis on which they will build mental categories, whereas the latter goes further by requiring them to analyse the attributes of a category that has already been formed in another person's mind. This is done by constructing and comparing examples (*exemplars*) that contain the characteristics (*attributes*) with examples that do not.

Joyce and colleagues describe the application of the three-step method of concept attainment within the teaching context. The first step involves presenting data and identifying a concept. The instructor has a clearly identified concept category in their mind (e.g., 'formal group'), and presents a mixture of twenty or so positive examples (e.g., 'football team', 'Cabinet committee') and negative (or non-) examples (e.g., 'people at a bus stop', 'a baby-sitting circle'). The students compare the two sets of examples, consider what they have in common, and identify the attributes present or absent in each set. On the basis of their assessment, they generate hypotheses and test them. They conclude by stating a definition of the concept, based on its essential attributes.

The second step consists of testing students' concept attainment. They identify additional, unlabelled illustrations, and define each as a positive or negative example of the concept being considered. The instructor confirms or refutes their hypotheses, names the concept, and re-states its definition according to its essential attributes. The students then generate more positive examples of the concept.

Finally, thinking strategies are analysed. Students describe how they thought about the task, and discuss the role of hypothesis-generation and testing in the process of understanding, and the type and number of hypotheses they generated.

Bruner, J., Goodnow, J.J. and Austin, G.A. (1967) *A Study of Thinking*, Science Editions Inc.

Joyce, B., Weil, M. and Showers, B. (1992) *Models of Teaching* (4th edn), Allyn and Bacon, pp. 141–58.

Klausmeier, H. J. (1980) *Learning and Teaching Concepts*, Academic Press.

Merrill, M.D. and Tennyson, R.D. (1977) *Concept Teaching: An Instructional Design Guide*, Educational Publishing.

Tennyson, R.D. and Cocchiarella, M. (1986) 'An Empirically Based Instructional Design for Teaching Concepts', *Review of Educational Research*, vol. 56, pp. 40–71.

Tessmer, M. and Wilson, B. and Driscoll, M. (1990) 'A New Model of Concept Teaching and Learning', *Education, Training Research & Development*, vol. 38, no. 1, pp. 45–53.

See also: Concept analysis; Concept formation; Concept mapping; Concept teaching; Concept training; Concept uncovery; Person-card technique; Reframing; Relational diagramming

Concept formation

Concept formation is the first element in the inductive thinking model developed by Hilda Taba during the 1960s, whose next two elements are *application of principles* and *interpretation of data*.

The objective of this approach is to expand the conceptual system students use to process information, by helping them form concepts they can then use to deal with new information. It requires students to decide the basis on which they will classify and form categories, since this is a basic skill which underpins higher-level ones such as analysis and synthesis.

Concept formation is a three-step process. First, students identify and enumerate data relevant to a topic or problem (e.g., a company's manufacturing costs would include wages, electricity, taxes, rates and raw materials). Next, they group the items enumerated into categories whose members have common characteristics (*attributes*). They then abstract and identify these common attributes (e.g., costs associated with people, non-human manufacturing costs). Here, the discussion focuses on questions such as 'Which item belongs in which category?', 'Can the same item fit into several categories?' and 'On what criteria is the choice based?'

Finally, labels are developed for the categories (e.g., 'human resource costs', 'promotional costs').

Bolton, N. (1977) *Concept Formation*, Pergamon Press.

Bruner, J., Goodnow, J.J. and Austin, G.A. (1967) *A Study of Thinking*, Science Editions Inc.

Joyce, B., Weil, M. and Showers, B. (1992) *Models of Teaching* (4th edn), Allyn and Bacon, pp. 116–19.

Outhwaite, W. (1990) *Concept Formation in Social Science*, Jean Stroud Publisher.

Stromdahl, H. (1996) *On Mole & Amount of Substance: A Study of the Dynamics of Concept Formation and Concept Attainment*, Coronet Books.

See also: Analogy teaching; Application of principles; Concept analysis; Concept attainment model; Concept mapping; Concept teaching; Concept training; Concept uncovery; Interpretation of data; Person-card technique; Relational diagramming

Concept mapping

A concept map depicts perceived relationships between concepts, ideas, people or abstractions (e.g., literary terms). Concept mapping can be used as a teaching method, or as a way of probing students' understanding of a subject.

This method is best suited to probing understanding of an entire discipline, or substantial parts of it, and has many applications. It can be used to discover how students link ideas and how they view the structure of a large topic, or to help teachers structure the content of a series of lessons. It can be used to explore the understanding of a certain aspect of a topic, to find out whether students understand the purpose of a lesson, to see how well they relate distinct topics, to check whether they understand which concepts are the most important, or simply to promote discussion within the classroom.

Each participant is given a pad of large self-stick labels on which they write the names of the items to be considered – usually between six and twenty – then arrange them on a large flipchart sheet. Alternatively, groups of four or five individuals can collaborate. White and Gunstone recommend a five-step approach.

First, the participants sort through their labels, putting aside any which carry unknown terms or those which appear to be unrelated to the others. Next, they arrange the remaining labels on the flipchart sheet in a way that makes sense to them. Related terms are placed together, but space is left between even those that are most closely associated. The participants now draw lines on their flipchart linking the labels they perceive to be related. Following this, they write the nature of the relationship on each line (e.g., 'comes from', 'is a', 'is based upon'). Arrows can be added to line ends to suggest causation and flow or interdependencies. Finally, they return to any labels that were set aside, decide whether they can now be integrated into their map, and place and link them as before.

Computer software now exists which presents blank 'map shells'. Users merely type in the concept names, indicate the direction of relationships and their nature, and the program draws up a concept map accordingly.

Mahler, S. et al. (1991) 'Didactic Use of Concept Mapping in Higher Education', *Instructional Science*, vol. 20, no. 1, pp. 25–47.

Novak, J.D. (1990) 'Concept Maps and Vee Diagrams: Two Metacognitive Tools to Facilitate Meaningful Learning', *Instructional Science*, vol. 19, no. 1, pp. 29–52.

Novak, J.D. and Gowin, D.B. (1984) *Learning How to Learn*, Cambridge University Press.

White, R. and Gunstone, R. (1992) 'Concept Mapping', in *Probing Understanding*, Falmer Press, pp. 15–43.

See also: Advance organizer; Analogy teaching; Chronology charting; Concept analysis; Concept attainment model; Concept formation; Concept teaching; Concept training; Concept uncovery; Fortune lining; Pre-course learning; Poster; Relational diagramming; Responsibility charting

Concept training

The purpose of this approach is to ensure that all managers understand the organizational model and share the organization's goals. Concept training can be applied to all management staff down to supervisor level, and each session usually lasts a week. It focuses on related sets of concepts relevant to management, such as power and authority, customer care, quality and empowerment Each concept is illustrated by a video or a lecture, followed by a discussion exploring evidence for the model, sometimes augmented by management games. Some time after the training, a survey of management concepts can be carried out in order to check on its effectiveness.

See also: Behaviour modification; Brainwashing; Company culture training; Concept analysis; Concept attainment model; Concept formation; Concept mapping; Concept uncovery; Ideological change; Mission cards; Norm clarification; Norm formation; Norm modification; Relational diagramming; Theory-based interventions

Concept uncovery

Many students who attend undergraduate business management courses have little experience of organizational life. Instructors can introduce concepts, theories, principles and research from textbooks, but need to demonstrate their relevance to the real world of organizations. The aim of concept uncovery is make that link, helping students to relate current business and organizational events to concepts that are considered in the course. Students select a recent article which illustrates one or more concepts covered in the course from publications such as *The Economist*, *Business Week*, *Newsweek*, The *Financial Times*, or the business sections of a Sunday newspaper, avoiding academic articles. The instructor must supervise the process of choice to ensure that no duplication occurs within the class, and the students are asked to submit a copy of the article and their two- to four-page analysis of it by a given date.

This method has several benefits for students. It ensures that they identify and locate a business publication, and read the articles in it carefully – perhaps for the first time. It illustrates that some journals and articles lend themselves more readily to analysis than others, the best being those that describe a situation in an organization but allow possible causes and deeper meanings to be explored by applying the concepts acquired on the course. It encourages them to go beyond trying to impose a concept or theory onto a situation by trial and error, and to call on what they have learned on the course to explain the phenomena described. Instructors also benefit by being updated about current events in their field.

Experience has shown that students should not be allowed to submit their report too early in the course, before they have been exposed to a reasonable number of concepts and theories. The instructor can choose not to distribute the briefing sheet until half-way through the term or semester, or to delay the date when students' choices of article will be approved.

Hunger, J.D. and Odell, H.R. (1979) 'The "Concept Uncovery" as a Teaching Device', *Exchange: The Organizational Behaviour Teaching Journal*, vol. 4, no. 3, Summer, pp. 42–3.

See also: Action project; Concept analysis; Concept attainment model; Concept formation; Concept mapping; Concept training; Relational diagramming

Conference meeting

Conference meetings may be high-powered events where members work well into the night, or less intensive social gatherings. Most conferences have a title which indicates their target audience, usually a close-knit group who consult together formally on problems in which they have a serious interest.

The number attending a conference tends to determine the communication and learning techniques that are used. A chairperson will usually set the scene, and a keynote speaker may address the participants and raise some general issues.

Conferences can provide a valuable way to meet people outside one's own work and geographical environment, and can be divided into two types: *educational conferences* and *working conferences*. Educational conferences tend to embrace a large – sometimes extremely large – number of people, and usually have a theme designed to promote a particular idea. Working conferences usually have a limited number of participants, and are technical in nature. They may include a few brief lecture sessions to stimulate participants, but papers and book lists will normally have been distributed in advance, and this conference format involves participants working hard in small groups.

Carey, T. (1997) *Crisis or Conference*, The Industrial Society.
Maitland, I. (1996) *How to Organize a Conference*, Gower
Seekings, D. (1997) *How to Organize Effective Conferences and Meetings*, Kogan Page.

See also: Colloquy meeting; Conference method; Clinic meeting; Forum meeting; Gordon seminar; Institute meeting; Interview meeting; Panel meeting; Symposium meeting

Conference method

In the conference method approach to learning, a group of twelve to twenty people with similar specific, practical work problems pool their experience and ideas, examine facts, test assumptions and decide on the best solutions. Although a leader runs the group, participants are expected to learn together, not be instructed, in an informal atmosphere which allows them to express ideas without constraints. The leader's opening remarks should emphasize this informality, and the importance of pooling ideas to build up a body of information to which all members have contributed. The open nature of the discussion is designed to help participants arrive at conclusions which can be accepted by the group as a whole.

At the beginning of the session, the leader asks individuals simple questions that are known to be of interest to all participants. It is vital to establish good working relationships between group members, and there must be rapport between them and the leader. The leader should give direct information sparingly, and only if it is not made available by other members. Leaders should encourage individuals to talk to the whole group and not just to them. All ideas and comments produced by members are charted, irrespective of their perceived value, so that group members can consider each point on its merits.

The role of the leader in stimulating and guiding the conference group is vital. They must know the objectives, and have thought them through in advance of the meeting, providing any supplementary material which may be required. They must be familiar with the personalities in the group and draw on the more experienced members, but must encourage equal participation, ensuring that a vocal few do not monopolize the discussion. They must explain problems clearly and precisely, and list the pros and cons of each course of action proposed, as well as the possible solutions, ensuring that no useful suggestion is overlooked while maintaining the group's focus if the discussion strays.

Busch, H.M. (1949) *Conference Methods in Industry*, Harper Brothers.

See also: Conference meeting; Directed conversation method; Free discussion method; Gordon seminar; Problem-solving cycle

Conference Model

Bunker and Alban describe this as a whole-system, participatory approach to work design. It was developed by Dick and Emily Axelrod to overcome the low participation rates involved in similar designs, such as socio-technical systems or business process re-engineering, and the length of time they require.

The Conference Model consists of a series of five two-day conferences held every three weeks or so over a period of four to five months, each attended by 80–90 participants.

The first in the sequence is the *Visioning Conference*, where participants develop a common vision of their preferred future organization. Next, the *Customer Conference* aims to understand customers' needs – both internal customers, such as other departments, and external customers, such as consumers. The third event, the *Technical Conference*, studies organizational flows – of work, services and of people. Problems and variances are studied in relation to the vision and needs specified earlier. The *Design Conference* takes place next, and draws on the vision, needs and information identified so far. The final event, the *Implementation Conference*, involves the units in the company carrying out the detailed work to identify the teams, roles and responsibilities that will implement the agreed goals and encourage the new behaviours specified.

The Conference Model can involve a wide range of company personnel over a protracted period by having a core group of 30 people who attend every one of the five conferences, but encouraging as many of the other employees as possible to attend at least one.

To keep the majority involved and committed, the model uses Data Assist Teams (DATs) to provide a communication channel between the whole system (all employees) and the conference attendees. Selected employees become full-time DAT members, temporarily relinquishing their job responsibilities. Their job is attend each conference, summarize what was said, and present it to 'walk through' groups of 20–30 employees in two- to four-hour sessions which are mini-conferences in themselves. They use videos of the conference proceedings to update and energize group members, whose observations are reported to the next main conference for further discussion.

What distinguishes the Conference Model from other large-group events is that it creates an open structure, facilitates purposeful communication and permits full involvement of inside stakeholders. It also involves outside stakeholders, who are not just surveyed or interviewed about their views, but can attend the conferences, not only providing better-quality information, but connecting with the rest of the company to engender greater understanding and a sense of partnership.

Axelrod, D. (1992) 'Getting Everyone Involved: How One Organization Involved its Employees, Supervisors and Managers in Redesigning the Organization', *Journal of Applied Behavioural Science*, vol. 28, no. 4, pp. 499–509.
Bunker, B.B. and Alban, B.T. (1997) 'The Conference Model', in *Large Group Interventions: Engaging the Whole System for Rapid Change*, Jossey-Bass, pp. 99–111.

See also: Action training and research; Business process re-engineering; Fast-cycle full-participation work design; Future search; Interface groups; Large-group interventions; Open space technology; Participative design; Real-time strategic change; Real-time work design; Search conference; Simu-Real; Socio-technical systems design; Strategic planning process; Work-Out

Confidence-building measures

These are steps a party in a conflict can take to build trust between themselves and another. They can be used in relations between any number of parties of any size in any situation: for example, between a husband and a wife, a manager and subordinate, a trade union and management, between different workgroups or functional departments within an organization, between organizations, between different ethnic or religious groups in a single community, or between nations. These measures typically precede any formal negotiation.

Alagappa, M. (1989) *In Search of Peace: Confidence Building and Conflict Reduction*, Kegan Paul International.
Alagappa, M. (ed.) (1990) *Building Confidence, Resolving Conflicts*, Kegan Paul International.
Desjardins, M.-F. (1997) *Rethinking Confidence Building Measures*, Oxford University Press.
Dunn, D. (1989) *Confidence Building in Communications*, HarperCollins.
Krepon, M. (ed.) (1996) *Conflict Prevention and Confidence Building*, Macmillan.

See also: Conflict-resolution techniques; Confrontation meeting; Consciousness-raising techniques; Negotiating by group members; No-lose conflict-resolution method; Third party peace-making interventions

Confidence-building training (RSI method)

This method can help students increase their self-confidence, allowing them to take a part in and gain greater benefits from all types of independent learning situations. It is based on the belief that traditional educational systems emphasize student dependency, which saps people's ability to learn on their own. In consequence, when confronted with more autonomous, self-initiated learning situations, these traditionally educated, dependent students turn off and cannot cope.

Confidence-building training consists of three elements or techniques – *relaxation, suggestion* and *imagery* – which is why it is sometimes referred to as the RSI method. Over three or four treatment sessions, participants are first helped to relax through the use of deep breathing exercises, counting, fixing their eyes on a bright object, inducing muscle heaviness or visualizing a pleasant scene. Once relaxed, the critical 'watchdog' facility of the mind reduces, and allows acceptance of suggestions which are in accordance with the wishes of the subject, so the facilitator talks to them quietly, employing a series of positively worded suggestions designed to promote increased energy, better health, improvements in ability to cope with problems, greater calmness, a sense of personal well-being, feelings of contentment, increased self-confidence and improved concentration. Through the use of imagery, the person is also encouraged to think of themselves as they would like to be.

This method can help people to gain confidence in their own power to change in whatever ways they choose, and to transcend the often unconscious limits they place upon themselves. Participant's confidence increases as they realize the power they have to control their own lives.

Blumenthal, E. (1997) *Believing in Yourself: A Practical Guide to Building Self-confidence*, Element Publishers.

Davies, P. (1994) *Total Confidence*, Piatkus.

Perino, J.G. (1995) *I Think I'm Hopeless – But I Could be Wrong*, River Press.

Schwartz, S. and Conley, C. (1998) *Building Self-confidence*, Capstone Press.

Stanton, H.E. (1980) 'The Modification of Student Self Concept', *Studies in Higher Education*, vol. 5, no. 1, pp. 7–16.

See also: Achievement motivation training; Acting assignment; Assertiveness training; Awareness training; Motivation achievement training; Self-efficacy training; Short talks by students

Conflict-resolution techniques

Conflict-resolution is a generic term for a family of intervention techniques which aim to identify and bring into the open both existing and potential conflicts between individuals and groups. The techniques used are often based on the assumption that suppressed or hidden conflict can be destructive to individuals and organizations, but that it is capable of being managed effectively. In addition, some conflict-resolution techniques acknowledge the irrationality of much behaviour.

The resolution of conflict within an organization usually begins by bringing the conflict or friction out into the open. Company personnel meet to share their feelings about people and their expectations of one another. Once conflicts are exposed in this way, joint problem-solving activity can be used to arrive at co-operative solutions.

Banner, D.K. (1995) 'Conflict Resolution: A Re-contextualization', *Leadership and Organization Development Journal*, vol. 16, no. 1, pp. 31–4.

Borisoff, D. and Victor, D.A. (1997) *Conflict Management*, Allyn and Bacon.

Constantino, C.A. and Merchant, C.S. (1995) *Designing Conflict Management Systems*, Jossey-Bass.

Crawley, J. (1997) *Constructive Conflict Management*, Nicholas Brealey.

Levine, S. (1998) *Getting to Resolution*, McGraw-Hill.

Morrill, C. (1996) *The Executive Way: Conflict Management in Corporations*, University of Chicago Press.

Schellenberg, J.A. (1996) *Conflict Resolution: Theory, Research and Practice*, State University of New York Press.

Weiss, D.S. (1996) *Beyond the Walls of Conflict*, Irwin.

Woods, M., Whetten, D. and Cameron, K. (1996) *Effective Conflict Management*, HarperCollins.

See also: Confidence-building measures; Conflict-stimulation techniques; Confrontation groups; Confrontation meeting; Criss-cross panels; Exchange of persons; FIDO approach; LIFO method; Negotiation by group members; No-lose conflict-resolution method; Planned re-negotiation; Third-party peacemaking interventions

Conflict-stimulation techniques

Much of management theory is based on the assumption that there is a simple solution to a problem or conflict, whereas contradictions, dilemmas and conflict are always part of business management – indeed, frictions can be created intentionally by managers to stimulate conflict and thus provoke a rethink of organizational practices.

Organizations may sometimes experience problems because of a *lack* of conflict or disagreement, so complacency may need to be countered by the use of conflict-stimulation techniques. Some examples include: creating a crisis by allowing a financial loss to occur; setting income, productivity or cycle time targets so high that they cannot be met by 'business as usual' approaches; sharing information about customer satisfaction and performance with employees, and stopping management 'happy talk' by discussing company problems in internal newsletters and management speeches.

De Dreu, C.K.W. and Van de Vliert, E. (1997) *Using Conflict in Organizations*, Sage.
Eisenhardt, K.M., Kahwajy, J.L. and Bourgeois, L.J. (1997) 'How Management Teams Can Have a Good Fight', *Harvard Business Review*, July–August, pp. 77–85.
Johnson, B. (1997) *Polarity Management: Identifying and Managing Unsolvable Problems*, Human Resources Development Press.
Kotter, J.P. (1996) 'Kill Complacency', *Fortune*, August, no. 15, pp. 122–4.
McKenzie, J. (1996) *Paradox: The Next Strategic Dimension*, McGraw-Hill.
Tjosveld, D. and Tjosveld, M. (1995) *Psychology for Leaders: Using Motivation, Conflict and Power to Manage More Effectively*, Wiley.

See also: Business process re-engineering; Conflict-resolution techniques; Dialogue; Open book management

Confluent education

The ideas underlying confluent education were developed by Dr George Brown at the University of California, Santa Barbara, who was awarded a grant by the Fund for the Advancement of Education of the Ford Foundation for a pilot project to explore ways to adapt approaches in the affective domain to the school curricula.

Confluent education – also known as humanistic or psychological education – involves the deliberate integration of the affective domain (emotions, attitudes, values and senses) with the cognitive domain (thought, intellect, reason) in learning, teaching and everyday practice. It allows for intellectual, emotional and physical learning, and uses the techniques and methodology of Gestalt Therapy developed by the late Dr Frederick (Fritz) Perls. In management training, it has come to known as 'emotional intelligence'.

One premise of confluent education is that people both need and want the opportunity to learn cognitively and affectively – within themselves, in relation to others, and in their relationships with the world. When we learn in this way, we are likely to become deeply rooted in the skills, values, feelings, senses, thoughts and behaviours which have traditionally been seen as important.

Confluent education has been used in disciplines as diverse as medicine, geology, English and psychology. Curricula have been designed with three broad goals: to cover traditional subject matter; to achieve non-traditional goals of personal and inter-personal or social development, and to learn process skills that will help individuals achieve their own goals.

Bowden, D.D., Seltzer, J. and Wilson, J.A. (1987–8) 'Dealing With Emotions in the Classroom', *The Organizational Behaviour Teaching Review*, vol. 12, no. 2, pp. 1–14.
Brown, G.I. (1990) *Human Teaching for Human Learning: An Introduction to Confluent Education*, Gestalt Journal Press.
Brown, J.D. (ed.) (1996) *Integrating Consciousness for Human Change: Advances in Confluent Education, Volume 1*, JAI Press.
Brown, J.D. (ed.) (1998) *Historical Foundations of Consciousness: Advances in Confluent Education, Volume 2*, JAI Press.
Castillo, G.A. (1974) *Left Handed Teaching*, Praeger Publishers.
Eiben, R. and Milliven, A. (1976) *Educational Change: A Humanistic Approach*, Pfeiffer/Jossey-Bass.
Goleman, D. (1998) *Emotional Intelligence*, Bantam Books.
Hopfl, H. and Linstead, S. (eds) (1997) 'Emotion and Learning in Organization', special issue of *Management Learning*, vol. 28, no. 1, March.
Strat, A. (1998) *Organization and Aesthetics*, Sage.
Thayer, L. (ed.) (1976) *Affective Education: Strategies for Experiential Learning*, Pfeiffer/Jossey-Bass.
Weinstein, G. and Fantini, M.D. (1970) *Toward Humanistic Education: A Curriculum of Affect*, Praeger Publishers.
Zeldin, T. (1995) *An Intimate History of Humanity*, Random House.

See also: Apperception interaction method; Gestalt techniques; Jurisprudential model; Values clarification

Confrontation groups

In this intervention, two or more groups within an organization are brought together in order to build a new relationship or repair a defective one, based on the theory that the best way in which to resolve the problems of antagonistic groups is to allow them to discuss their differences openly, raising contentious issues, letting each other know how they are perceived, and allowing them to compare their own group concepts with those of other people.

The aim of this technique is to 'clear the air' and provide a basis on which to build relationships. Each meeting usually concludes with an action phase in which the groups decide what should be done next.

See also: Conflict-resolution techniques; Confrontation meeting; Criss-cross panels; Customer interface meetings; Exchange of persons; External mirror; Fishbowl; Interface groups; LIFO method; Negotiation by group members; No-lose conflict-resolution method; Organizational mirror; Third-party peacemaking interventions

Confrontation meeting (confrontation goal-setting meeting; top team development)

Developed by Richard Beckhard, this is a one-day meeting of the entire management of a company at which the health of the whole organization is considered. Through a series of activities, the management group generates information about its major problems, analyses their underlying causes, develops action plans to overcome them, and sets out a schedule for remedial work.

A confrontation meeting has six stages. It begins with a *climate-setting* activity of between 45–60 minutes, when senior managers introduce the session and outline the purposes of the meeting. The need for free and open discussion of the issues to be considered is stressed, and it is emphasized that individuals will not be punished for speaking their minds. Such an event will also usually include an outside consultant, who may deliver a talk on the topic of organizational communication and problem-solving.

Stage two is *information-collecting*, and lasts about an hour. The participants form into groups, each of which is constituted so that it includes six managers from different functions and work situations. Such groups may contain people from different levels in the hierarchy, but it is important to avoid having a manager and their boss in the same group. Top managers meet separately, but all the groups are given the same brief, which was prepared by Beckhard (1967, p. 154): 'Think of yourself as an individual with needs and goals. Think as a person who is concerned about the total organization. What are the obstacles, "demotivators", poor procedures or policies, unclear goals or poor attitudes that exist today? What conditions, if any, would make the organization more effective and life in the organization better?' Each group works separately for an hour, then reporters from each of the groups summarize the conclusions from their deliberations.

Stage three, *information-sharing*, takes about an hour, and involves the group reporters presenting this information to the entire meeting by writing the items on flipcharts and displaying them on the walls. Once the lists of all the groups have been posted, the person leading the event categorizes the items under a few key headings. These may be related to the type of problem identified (e.g., conflict, communication), a type of relationship (e.g., trouble with suppliers) or a particular function (e.g., difficulties with the personnel department).

The next stage, which can conveniently follow a lunch break, consists of *priority-setting and group action-planning*. The group leader introduces this session by taking 15 minutes to go through a list of the items generated by the groups, trying to categorize each item so that every participant has their own listing. The participants then form into their functional or natural workgroups which reflect the way in which they are organized within the company, with each group now headed by its most senior manager, and have 75 minutes to work on the lists. They have three tasks: to identify and discuss the issues and problems related to each area, giving the problems priorities, and deciding the remedial steps which need to be taken and those to which they are prepared to commit themselves; to identify which problems they think should be priorities for top management, and finally, deciding how to communicate the results of the confrontation meeting to their subordinates.

The penultimate stage is the *immediate follow-up* by the top team. Once the other participants have left, the group of senior managers remains behind for a one- to three-hour meeting to plan the next steps in accordance with the information supplied to them during the day. Their plans are communicated to the rest of the management group during the following few days.

The final stage is a two-hour *progress review*, a follow-up meeting held four to six weeks later, at which the entire top management group is once again present to receive progress reports and review the actions which still need to be taken.

Beckhard, R. (1967) 'Confrontation Meeting', *Harvard Business Review*, vol. 45, no. 2, March–April, pp. 149–55.

Chartrand, P.J. and Johnston, C.P. (1973) 'Mark I, Mark II, Mark III', *Business Quarterly*, Autumn.

French, W.L. and Bell, C.H. (1984) *Organization Development: Behavioural Science Interventions for Organization Improvement* (3rd edn), Pearson Education, pp. 127–9.

Golembiewski, R.T. and Blumberg, A. (1967) 'Confrontation as a Training Design in Complex Organizations: Attitudinal Changes in a Diversified Population of Managers', *Journal of Applied Behavioural Science*, vol. 3, no. 4, pp. 525–55.

See also: Comprehensive interventions; Confidence-building training; Conflict-resolution techniques; Confrontation groups; Criss-cross panels; Exchange of persons; External mirror; Fishbowl;

Interface group; LIFO method; Negotiation by group members; Organizational mirror; Staff exchange

Consciousness-raising group

The goal of a consciousness-raising group is to examine – and frequently to change – the circumstances of a particular category of person in society, such as women in management. A group meeting may focus on a particular topic, with one participant sharing their personal experiences and taking responsibility for running the session. The emphasis tends to be exploring similarities and differences in participants' life experiences.

This approach encourages members to see previous adversities or problems as being caused not by their own personal weaknesses, but as inherent in current social structures. This may result in a reduction in members' depression and anxiety, and an increase in assertiveness, and such changes may be expressed either in terms of individual behaviour or political action.

Klein, A.E. (1979) *Mind Trips: A Story of Consciousness Raising Movements*, Doubleday.

Lieberman, M.A. and Bond, G.R. (1976) 'The Problem of Being a Woman: A Survey of 1700 Women in Consciousness Raising Groups', *Journal of Applied Behavioural Science*, vol. 12, pp. 363–79.

Loughlin, K.A. (1993) *Women's Perceptions of Transformation Learning Experiences With Consciousness Raising*, Edwin Mellen Press.

Parker, W.M. (1998) *Consciousness Raising: A Primer for Multicultural Counselling*, Charles C. Thomas Publishers.

See also: Assertiveness training; Confidence-building training; Self-help group

Construct lesson plan

Construct lesson plan (CLP) is a way of organizing and implementing classroom instruction which seeks to remove the inefficiency and ineffectiveness of many other group instruction methods by allowing for preparatory study undertaken by students themselves.

CLP involves a diagnostic pre-test and the teacher's lesson plan, which consists of two elements: lesson plan cards and the content outline. These allow the teacher to plan the lesson in full, but concentrate on aspects where students need further tuition. The approach does not preclude the use of other teaching methods or media.

A separate lesson plan card is prepared for each objective, organized by topic/sub-topic, giving answers to pre-test questions measuring attainment of the objectives, and including space for items such as content reminders or any media support required.

The content outline is an overview of the lesson, built around the major and minor content headings. In the margin, each of the objectives of the lesson is listed by a number which corresponds with the objective numbers and the pre-test question numbers.

The first step, defining a lesson plan according to learner objectives, is the basis for organizing, implementing and evaluating the CLP. It also provides a structure for the preliminary meeting, at which the objectives for the coming lesson are specified, students are given specific reading tasks in an effort to achieve them, and the teacher draws up a diagnostic pre-test to measure each of the objectives. The students carry out their preparatory study at home, then complete the test, which links their independent study to the classroom instruction which is to follow.

At the beginning of the next lesson, the teacher quickly reviews the results of the group as a whole to identify which areas are commonly presenting difficulty. The lesson plan cards are stacked in two piles: those objectives already achieved by students alone, and those which require classroom instruction. This allows a lesson to be assembled to meet the immediate learning needs of students.

If instruction is based only on the objectives which students working alone have failed to meet, the class will not form a cohesive learning unit. To avoid this, the content outline is used as a guide. Beginning at the top of the list, the teacher gives an overview of any objectives already mastered by students until an objective which needs classroom attention is reached. The teacher can then refer to the lesson plan card in one of the pre-sorted piles, and the objective can be dealt with in greater depth.

Langdon, D.G. (1977) 'The Construct Lesson Plan: Taking the Inefficiency Out of Group Classroom Discussion', *Programmed Learning and Educational Technology*, vol. 14, no. 3, pp. 199–206.

Langdon, D.G. (1978) *The Construct Lesson Plan*, Educational Technology Publications.

Pedrick, L. and Tarquinio, N.F. (1978) 'The Construct Lesson Plan: Evaluating the Efficiency of a New Approach to Group Classroom Discussion', *Programmed Learning and Educational Technology*, vol. 15, no. 4, pp. 257–61.

See also: Data approach method; Guided discussion; Guided group problem-solving; Self-instructional modules and interactive groups; Structuring seminars

Consultant network

Within a change or development programme which is organization-wide and affects many employees, the participants may be asked to act as consultants for one another. Such behaviour can become a group norm, and give rise to an internal consultant network. Varney argues that such a network can offer an organizational change skills bank which managers or supervisors can draw upon when they need to solve a particular problem.

Varney, G.H. (1977) *Organizational Development for Managers*, Addison Wesley Longman.

See also: Coaching; Consultation; Consulting assignment; Consulting pair; Insider-outsider consulting teams; Multiple job-holding; Shadow consultant

Consultation

'Consultation' has a great many different meanings in the context of strategies for management development and organizational improvement. A consultant has been defined as: 'a person who provides needed information, help and perspective'. Consultants may be employees of an organization (internal), or contracted to an organization (external) because of their competence, status, reputation or experience.

Consultancy work has a number of dimensions: diagnosing problems and indicating where there is a need for change; clarifying what is intended by and expected from changes; voicing concerns which cannot be raised, or have perhaps not even been noticed by the organization members themselves; assisting in formulating a change plan which consists of the details of the action components, timings, sequences, and so on; integrating the activities which result from the planning and implementation of changes, and providing continuity by keeping the flow of events in the change process running smoothly.

Consultants may provide instruction, but they more commonly help clients apply the resources required to solve a problem, be they an individual, a work team or the entire organizational system.

Consulting approaches fall into two broad categories: the *expert-technical approach* and the *organizational process approach*. In the expert-technical approach, the consultant is called in when a company encounters a problem it is unable to deal with on its own. The consultant takes the problem as described and applies their expert knowledge and techniques in an effort to find a solution. Once this is accomplished, the consultant withdraws. The strength of this approach is that the organization can buy in knowledge and skills it does not require every day, and it can attack a problem directly. However, its weakness is that the company may become dependent on consultants, shifting the responsibility for coping with difficult problems on to them, and failing to develop the new skills required by staff within the organization.

In contrast, the organizational process approach views the organization as a system. Consultants who use this approach seek to improve the organization's ability to cope with its own problems by developing an internal climate in which the resources available can be identified and developed. They see their task as helping the company to build and incorporate the skills it needs to assess its problem-solving capacity in the future. The advantage of this approach is that responsibility for change rests with the company as the client, and it can make better use of the resources it possesses. The stress is upon joint diagnosis and a collaborative approach to the problem. However, this approach may be inappropriate when a straightforward technical solution is required, and where an emphasis on process is unnecessary.

While often viewed as being in opposition, these two consulting approaches can be complementary, and the consultant may find it necessary to change from one approach to the other, depending on the client's needs.

Beckhard, R. (1997) *Agent of Change: My Life, My Practice*, Jossey-Bass.
Coghlan, D. (1987) 'Consultation on Organizational Levels: An Intervention', *Leadership and Organization Development Journal*, vol. 13, no. 3, pp. 87–93.
Greenbaum, T.L. (1994) *The Consultant's Manual*, Wiley.
Lewin, M. D. (1997) *The Consultant's Survival Guide*, American Society for Training and Development Press.
Miller, A.R. (ed.) (1997) *Management Consulting*, Harvard Business School Press.
Neumann, J.E., Kellner, K. and Dawson-Shepherd, A. (1997) *Developing Organizational Consultancy*, Routledge.
Salmon, B. and Rosenblatt, N. (1995) *The Complete Book of Consulting*, Round Lake Publishers.
Shenson, H., Nicholas, T. and Franklin, P. (eds) (1997) *The Complete Guide to Consulting Success* (3rd edn), Upstart Publications.

See also: Consultant network; Consulting assignment; Consulting pair; Facilitation; Insider-outsider consulting teams; Multiple job-holding; Process consultation; Shadow consultant

Consulting assignment

In a consulting assignment, managers are assigned to work in another department or another plant of their own company or a different one in order to give advice and help solve a problem that has been identified. Like all consultants, they have no formal authority of their own to implement any changes, and they may have to draw on a different power base if they wish their ideas to be implemented. Consulting assignments can help to establish closer relationships between staff in the same company, and develop the analytical and problem-solving skills of those involved.

Large companies sometimes help small, independent firms by seconding one of their own executives. Young, inexperienced managers may also be loaned on a full-time basis. This can expose them to a wide range of management problems they may encounter at middle or senior management level within a larger company, and allows them to develop their skills and potential quickly, with no risk to the efficiency of their 'home' organization. Consulting assignments can help to keep younger managers motivated and decrease the chances of their leaving a large company which may have stopped growing.

Following an extended period of consulting, particularly if they were assigned to another organization, managers may experience difficulties reintegrating into their previous post, and may need assistance from staff specialists and line supervisors to prepare them for their return, or even the support of a dedicated tutor.

Cockman, P., Evans, B. and Reynolds, P. (1998) *Consulting for Real People*, McGraw-Hill.
Margerison, C. (1996) *Managerial Consulting Skills*, Gower.
Prinder, M. and McAdam, S. (1994) *Be Your Own Management Consultant*, Pearson Education.
Thomas, M. and Elbeik, S. (1996) *Supercharge Your Management Role: Making the Transition to Internal Consultant*, Jossey-Bass.

See also: Action learning; Committee assignment; Consultation; Consulting network; Consulting pair; Development assignment; Evaluation audit assignment; Insider-outsider consulting teams; Job swop; Multiple job-holding; Proposal team assignment; Research assignment; Selection board assignment; Shadow consultant; Study assignment; Task force assignment

Consulting pair (manager in a consulting pair)

On many occasions, managers can benefit from being paired with an expert consultant from outside their own department or organization with whom they can develop a close and continuing relationship. The consultant should be someone the manager trusts, who is willing to learn about the manager's department or organization and its problems, and can help a manager identify problems early and help develop solutions to them. One advantage of this pairing relationship is that, as an 'outsider', the consultant can often see some of the trends and obstacles within the organization better than the manager, who is constantly inside it. In certain circumstances, it may be appropriate for a member of the personnel department to form a consulting pair with a line manager.

See also: Coaching; Co-counselling; Consultation; Consulting assignment; Consulting network; Context training; Insider-outsider consulting teams; Process consultation; Shadow consultant

Context training

Context training was developed by the late Hawdon Hague, who believed that managers develop only when they take the initiative, that they develop only in real-life situations, and that self-development does not just happen, but requires assistance from a *catalyst*, who may be another manager or a trainer. The method is based on the idea that individuals' jobs are the most powerful work influence, together with the help and reactions they receive from their bosses, so changing their jobs or coaching them in their work therefore offer important ways to train them.

The catalyst works with an individual manager, teaching on the job and working on whatever blocks to self-development arise during a series of visits, making suggestions, checking progress and developing a dialogue while ensuring that managers take responsibility for making decisions.

The context training approach can be applied to individual or group projects, or to a whole organization and its climate, in an effort to remove the constraints, real or imagined, that commonly make managers feel that they have neither the room nor the encouragement to change. The catalyst helps individuals develop by dealing with actual situations as they arise, and by undertaking the sort of organizational rethinking exercises normally carried out by consultants.

Project teams are an example of this approach, where a company's own executives tackle major problems, in the process experience self-development, and are more likely to implement the ideas produced.

Daley, P. and McGivern, C. (1972) 'The On-going Management Situation as the Training Vehicle',

Industrial and Commercial Training, vol. 4, no. 3, pp. 137–41.

Hague, H. (1974) *Executive Self-Development*, Macmillan.

Hague, H. (1977) 'Getting Self Development To Happen', *Journal of European Industrial Training*, vol. 1, no. 5, pp. 24–9.

Hague, H. (1978) 'Tools for Helping Self Development', *Journal of European Industrial Training*, vol. 2, no. 3, pp. 13–15.

See also: Action learning; Coaching; Consulting pair; Self-development

Contingency approach

Many recent theories in behavioural science rely on contingency, acknowledging the interdependence between factors and the uncertainty in outcomes. Unlike their predecessors which offered prescriptions claiming universal validity, contingency theories stress the importance of specific individual characteristics and organizational circumstances. For example, Fiedler (1967) developed a contingency model of leadership which stated that the most effective leadership style depended on certain characteristics of a particular leader in a particular situation.

The contingency approach has been further refined and developed by Lawrence and Lorsch, influencing the way organizational effectiveness is perceived and, by implication, the types of organizational change efforts that are considered appropriate. Their research revealed that different company environments required different organizational structures, and that effective organizations achieved a good 'fit' between their structure and their environment, while less effective organizations did not. By 'organizational structure' Lawrence and Lorsch meant the way roles and responsibilities are divided up and co-ordinated within an organization, and by 'environment' they meant those parts of the world with which the organization interacts, which may be certain or unstable, predictable or unpredictable, diverse or homogeneous.

Although a specific intervention technique has not been developed from this theory, a series of exercises based on elements of contingency thinking have been developed and are widely used to help senior managers consider their business strategy in relation to their unique organizational environment: the SWOT analysis, which considers a company's Strengths, Weaknesses, Opportunities and Threats.

Contingency theory has been a guiding principle in the choice of change strategies and interventions. The theory is used to analyse and conceptualize an organization, and the implications of this analysis are then translated into a series of interventions, such as cross-functional task forces, project teams, confrontation meetings and matrix team arrangements.

Beer, M. and Huse, E.F. (1972) 'A Systems Approach to Organizational Development', *Journal of Applied Behavioural Science*, vol. 8, no. 1, pp. 79–101.

Dowling, W.F. (1975) 'To Move an Organization: The Corning Approach to Organizational Development', *Organizational Dynamics*, Spring, vol. 3, pp. 163–4.

Fiedler, F.E. (1967) *A Theory of Leadership Effectiveness*, McGraw-Hill.

Huse, E.F. and Beer, M. (1971) 'Eclectic Approach to Organizational Development', *Harvard Business Review*, vol. 49, September–October, pp. 103–12.

Lawrence, P.R. and Lorsch, J.W. (1967) *Organization and Environment*, Harvard University Press.

See also: Competing values approach; Comprehensive interventions; Job design; Open systems planning; Strategic management

Controlled discussion

Most teachers hold a question-and-answer session after a lecture, but the success of this technique depends on how stimulating the lecture was. Moreover, since not all members of a large lecture class will be able to contribute, misunderstandings and interesting viewpoints may not be revealed, and more vocal members of the audience may dominate. It is difficult to ensure that the points raised permit a balanced consideration of the subject, and frequently what develops is not a discussion, but a series of one-to-one interactions with different students.

A better atmosphere for discussion can be created if the teacher asks for questions but does not reply to the points raised, instead asking for further contributions from the audience, but keeping control of the general direction of the discussion.

Bligh, D.A. (1972) *What's the Use of Lectures*, Penguin Books.

See also: Audience reaction/watchdog team; Directed conversation method; Guided discussion; Listening team; Reaction team

Controlled-pace negotiation

This is a method used to train negotiators which can be applied to other spheres. Its purpose is to slow down the pace of negotiation interactions, thereby giving time for participants to reflect.

The trainer divides the class into two groups, A and B, installs them in different rooms, and presents them with a problem which requires mutual agreement, such as: 'There is only a limited amount of beer available in the bar after the session. How can we best share out what there is?' The problem can be more work-oriented if desired, but it must be genuinely relevant to the parties involved. After the problem is stated, each person in group A is given three minutes to write down the message they wish the trainer to carry to group B. When all the individual members of group A have finished, the whole group must choose one individual's message for the trainer. They are not allowed to write a new, composite group message.

The trainer delivers the message to group B, which goes through the same process, and the exchange of messages between the groups continues. While the trainer is out of the room, each group can discuss strategy and tactics. Alternatively, the trainer may set the group the task of classifying the messages it sends and receives according to a simple list of categories such as: 'helpful suggestion', 'seeking information'.

Debriefing after the exercise can take place either at the individual level to explore personal negotiation style, at the group level to discuss tactics and negotiation strategy, or at the perceptual level to examine why messages classified by senders as 'helpful suggestions' may be perceived as 'attacks' by the receivers.

A variation of this approach can be used by individual managers in their day-to-day dealings with others, especially those with whom they have a difference of opinion. When discussing a topic, they need to ensure they fully understand what the other person is saying before putting their own point. They can control the pace of their own interaction with the other person by taking time to listen objectively to the speaker and summarize their understanding of what they believe the other person has said.

Fleming, P.R. (1998) *Successful Negotiating*, Institute of Management/Hodder and Stoughton.

Fuller, P. (1995) *Manager's Negotiating Answer Book*, Prentice-Hall.

Kozicki, S. and Malouf, D. (1998) *Creative Negotiating*, Adams Publishers.

Rackham, N. (1972) 'Controlled Paced Negotiation as a Technique for Developing Negotiation Skills', *Industrial and Commercial Training*, vol. 4, no. 6, pp. 266–75.

Robinson, C. (1997) *Effective Negotiating*, Kogan Page.

Shister, N. (1998) *Ten Minute Guide to Negotiating*, Prentice-Hall.

See also: Coverdale Training; Experiential exercise; Game; Interaction skills training; Process analysis

Corporate culture training (company culture; organization culture)

Corporate or organizational culture is the pattern of assumptions a given group has invented, discovered or developed to cope with external adaptation and integration problems. These assumptions are taught to new members as the 'correct' ways to perceive, think and feel in relation to such problems. Corporate culture training acknowledges that this phenomenon exists, that it can contribute to improved performance, and that a company's existing culture is capable of being modified in a desirable direction.

While the concept of 'organizational culture' has been around for some time, the notion of managing it is relatively new and somewhat controversial. 'Culture management' refers to the manipulation of an organization's goals, rituals and heroes that together characterize the company's style of operation, in order to improve productivity.

The interest in company culture is based on the belief that it is possible for management to affect its strength, direction and values content, and originated from the shaking of American dominance and pride in the business field by the Japanese during the 1970s and 1980s. Proponents argued that cultural differences accounted for the shortcomings of American managers. Moreover, the shift away from goods to more intangible services led many service companies to explore new ideas of how to structure work and motivate their employees. Examples exist in the successful transformations of traditional commercial banks into merchant and investment banks.

Corporate culture training consultants argue that no strategic move by a company can take place successfully without a corresponding change in its culture. What is more, a company's strategy need not be limited or restrained by its current culture: both can be manipulated until they become synchronized. If the culture is given the right stimulus, the response will fulfil the strategic goals. The consultants analyse an organization's culture, diagnose those elements that have strategic relevance, often using an employee attitude survey, then report their findings to senior management.

An American leader in the field of culture management has suggested a six-point change agenda: build knowledge of the cultural issues to make them explicit, develop a shared vision of why the change is necessary, determine the desired change in belief, translate these values into the correct behaviours, re-orient power to support these new values and, finally, harness the high-impact management systems to ensure implementation.

Ban, C. (1995) *Management Style and Organizational Culture*, Jossey-Bass.

Barclay, L.A. and York, K.M. (1996) 'The Scavenger Hunt Exercise: Symbols of Organization Culture', *Journal of Management Education*, vol. 20, no. 1, pp. 125–8.

Cooper, C.L. (1999) *Dynamics of Corporate Cultures*, Kogan Page.

Goffee, R. and Jones, G. (1996) 'What Holds the Modern Company Together?', *Harvard Business Review*, vol. 74, no. 6, November–December, pp. 133–48.

Goffee, R. and Jones, G. (1998) *The Character of a Corporation*, HarperCollins.

Hampden-Turner, C. (1994) *Corporate Cultures*, Piatkus.

Harris, L. and Ogbonna, E. (1998) 'Employee Responses to Culture Change Efforts', *Human Resource Management Journal*, vol. 8, no. 2, pp. 78–92.

Lessem, R. (1990) *Managing Your Corporate Culture*, Gower.

Lundberg, C. (1996) 'Designing Organizational Culture Courses: Fundamental Considerations', *Journal of Management Education*, vol. 20, no. 1, pp. 11–22.

Ogbonna, E. and Harris, L. (1998) 'Organizational Culture . . . It's Not What You Think', *Journal of General Management*, vol. 23, no. 3, pp. 35–48.

'Organization Cultures', special issue of *Human Relations* (1995), vol. 48, no. 1, January.

Sackmann, S.A. (ed.) (1997) *Cultural Complexity in Organizations*, Sage.

Schein, E.H. (1997) *Organizational Culture and Leadership* (2nd edn), Jossey-Bass.

Sherriton, J. and Stern, J.L. (1996) *Corporate Culture, Team Culture*, American Management Association, AMACOM.

Smits, S.J., Bleicken, L.M. and Icenogle, M.L. (1994) 'The Cultural Connection: Uncovering OB Concepts in Organizations', *Journal of Management Education*, vol. 18, no. 1, pp. 61–76.

Sutton, C.D. and Nelson, D.L. (1990) 'Elements of the Cultural Network: The Communication of Cultural Values', *Leadership and Organization Development Journal*, vol. 11, no. 5, pp. 3–10.

Trice, H.M. and Beyer, J.M. (1984) 'Studying Organizational Culture Through Rites and Ceremonials', *Academy of Management Review*, vol. 8, no. 4, pp. 653–69.

Van Buskirk, W. (1991) 'Enhancing Sensitivity to Organizational Symbols and Culture: An Experiential Approach for the Classroom', *Journal of Management Education*, vol. 15, no. 2, pp. 170–92.

Warnecke, H.-J. (1997) *The Fractal Company: A Revolution in Corporate Culture*, Springer Verlag.

Williams, A. and Dobson, P. (1997) *Changing Culture: New Organizational Approaches*, Institute of Personnel and Development.

See also: Attitude survey; Brainwashing; Critical theory approach; Development of a new management/operating philosophy; Greenfield plants; Ideological change; Induction training; Information-sharing meetings; Likert's system 4 management; Management by huddle; Management strategy change; Mission cards; Myth-making interventions; Norm clarification; Norm formation; Norm modification; Organizational citizenship; Organizational climate analysis; Policy-formation; Psychological contract; Simulated entrepreneurship; Strategic management

Corporate student board of directors

A corporate student board of directors (CSBD) consists of students who have agreed to serve for at least one academic year in a capacity that shadows the board of directors of a sponsoring corporation. This gives them an opportunity to work with senior managers, observing how an organization is run on a daily basis, and how what they have learned in class is put into practice within that organization. It allows the company to receive feedback from students about its image and products while assessing their potential as future employees.

The primary activity of the CSBD is a monthly meeting chaired by the company's most senior manager, who explains their role and responsibilities within the organization, giving the assembled students an insight into how senior management functions and what a career within the sponsoring organization would involve. Students may be asked to research, evaluate and make recommendations on company policies, procedures or other current issues, but these should be of limited scope in view of their university work commitments.

To gain some experience of corporate decision-making, the CSBD may be invited to discuss and vote on a proposal recently considered by the company's actual board of directors. The chairperson can then reveal what the board decided and on what basis, and lead a discussion about any differences between the CSBD's decision and that of the actual board of directors, enabling classroom concepts and real-world company practices to be compared and contrasted.

CSBD provides students with a broader perspective on business management than is offered by co-operative education programmes, and can complement them.

Cox, A.T., Minter, R. and Thompson, A.F. (1995) 'A Model for Developing a University Business Partnership', *Journal of Management Education*, vol. 19, no. 2, pp. 23–39.

See also: Co-operative education; Manager-shadowing; Understudy

Counselling

A counsellor offers time, support and sometimes guidance to another person to help them solve their problems. Counselling should be distinguished from coaching because it focuses on hopes, fears, emotions and aspirations, often exploring very personal and delicate matters.

Counselling usually takes the form of a one-to-one discussion between a counsellor and a client which aims to help them deal with the human issues they are confronting. Marital, financial, family and legal crises are employees' most common problems. If they are not resolved satisfactorily, they can cause depression, alcoholism, physical illness and, occasionally, even death. A number of companies have provided employees with a counselling service in order to help them deal with psychological, emotional and physical problems, recognizing that they can cause poor job performance, absenteeism and increased employee turnover, resulting in higher recruitment and training costs and reduced morale. Minor mental illness such as depression and anxiety have been estimated to cost 40 million lost working days a year.

The objectives of company counselling programmes, whether in-house or run by external consultants, are to give advice and reassurance, to help clarify thinking, to allow the release of emotion, and to offer reorientation and communication opportunities. Of the different counselling approaches available, a survey showed that co-operative, non-directive counselling was the one favoured by most companies. A few companies operated an in-house counselling service. As well as reductions in absenteeism and labour turnover, this was felt to improve the quality of employees' working life, reduce workplace accidents, raise morale, improve human relations and help individuals develop their problem-solving and decision-making abilities.

Increasingly, the importance of providing on-the-job 'psychological first aid' has been recognized, and some companies have developed training programmes in such skills.

Carroll, M. (1996) *Workplace Counselling: A Systematic Approach to Employee Care*, Sage.
Carroll, M. and Walton, M. (eds) (1997) *Handbook of Counselling in Organizations*, Sage.
De Board, R. (1987) *Counselling Skills*, Wildwood House.
Institute of Personnel and Development (1997) *IPD Guide on Counselling at Work*, IPD.
Ivey, A.E. (1974) 'Counselling Technology: Micro-counselling and Systematic Approaches to Human Relations Training', *British Journal of Educational Technology*, vol. 5, no. 2, pp. 15–21.
MacLennan, N. (1998) *Counselling for Managers*, Gower.
Summerfield, J. and Van Oudshoorn, L. (1997) *Counselling in the Workplace*, IPD.
Walmsley, H. (1994) *Counselling Techniques for Managers*, Kogan Page.

See also: Alcohol recovery programmes; Coaching; Employee assistance programme; Executive family seminar; Family communication programme; Helping relationship model; Let's-talk-it-over programme; Non-directive teaching model; One-to-one learning; Outplacement counselling; Peer counselling; Planned delegation; Psychotherapy; Re-evaluation counselling; Self-improvement programme; Shadow consultant; Stress management; Wellness programmes

Course design as learning

Based on the idea that the best way to learn a subject is to teach it, this method involves a small group of students designing a course themselves. The group must decide issues such as what basic texts should be used, what supplementary reading should be specified, which topics need to be covered, and how they are to be related to one another and in which order. The students learn by reading the basic texts and evaluating them critically, and by discussing issues with other course members. The tutor acts as a consultant to the group, indicating the implications of their choices. The group's finished product is a course brochure which defines the topic, explains how it will be taught and assessed, and includes a reading list specifying recommended reading for each session.

Isaak, R. (1995) 'The Open Syllabus and the White Paper: Student Empowerment Through Benchmarking', *Journal of Management Education*, vol. 19, no. 3, pp. 342–6.
Pheysey, D. (1979) 'Spadework as Learning', *Management Education and Development*, vol. 10, no. 3, pp. 167–71.

See also: Collaboratively designed course; Learning

organization; Learning community; Peer teaching; Student-planned learning; Teaching as learning

Cousin laboratory

This is a form of T-group consisting of individuals from the same organization who do not have a direct working relationship and do not know each another.

Fordyce, J.K. and Weil, R. (1971) *Managing With People*, Addison Wesley Longman, pp. 93–7.

Johns, W. (1976) 'Another View of the Small Group – A Physical Scientist Recommends Applied Behavioural Science', *Journal of Applied Behavioural Science*, vol. 12, no. 4, pp. 567–8.

See also: Basic encounter; Bioenergetics; Cluster laboratory; Encounter group; FIDO approach; Gestalt techniques; Group development laboratory; Human relations laboratory; Instrumented laboratory; Laboratory training; Organizational laboratory; Personal development laboratory; Psychodrama; Sensitivity (T-group) training; Tavistock Conference Method; Transactional Analysis

Coverdale Training

The Coverdale organization was formed in 1965 by Ralph Coverdale, a psychologist and businessman who believes that the key to effective organization is teamwork, that all people want to be of value to each other and have the potential to achieve, and that they need to develop and use their personal skills while working with, rather than for, others in pursuit of clear and mutually agreed aims.

Coverdale Training's basic principle is that people remember and use what they learn for themselves from their own experience, and that in growing, organic organizational systems, it is better to analyse the causes of success and look for strengths in order to improve on them, rather than to look for causes of failure to put things right.

Coverdale observed that since more knowledge exists in organizations than is ever used or applied, behavioural skills to put that knowledge into practice are required, so he devised his own methods of planned behaviour improvement. Such skills can only be acquired through practice and experience, but there must be a system to ensure that people learn from experience. His aim was to develop a cycle of preparation, action and review through which skills could be learned. This itself is a skill, and a prerequisite in turning experience into advantage.

Coverdale Training is based on this 'cycle of learning', aiming to help individuals learn from experience and practise skills which are relevant in co-operating with others to achieve results. Participants work together in small groups carrying out short pieces of work called *tasks*. Some of these may involve participants leaving the study centre, for example to count the cars in the vicinity, while others may require them to produce a report.

The focus of the learning is not on the task itself, but on the interaction it engenders among participants. Consideration is given to the way in which the groups carry out their tasks, agree on an effective approach, and how they plan and combine talents and build on effective team practices. Given the learning cycle, which consists of a sequence of differing tasks, participants are encouraged to experiment with different behaviours and group structures. By repeating those which appear effective while discarding those which do not, members acquire a knowledge of human behaviour and habits of good management which they can develop in the future. The emphasis is on experiment and discovery.

Coverdale techniques are based on trial and experience, and help participants consider the establishment of aims, working methodically towards them, co-operating and winning co-operation, observing, listening, identifying and making use of others' talents, planning, leadership and authority.

Babbington-Smith, B. (1967) *Working in Small Groups*, Pergamon Press.

Babbington-Smith, B. and Sharp. A. (1991) *Manager and Team Development: Ideas and Principles Underlying Coverdale Training*, Butterworth-Heinemann.

Frank, E. and Margerison, C. (1978) 'Training Methods and Organizational Development', *Journal of European Industrial Training*, vol. 2, no. 4, pp. 19–22.

Roche, S. (1967) 'Coverdale Training – A Method for Developing Managers and the Organization', *Manpower and Applied Psychology*, Ergon Press.

Smallwood, A. (1976) 'The Basic Philosophy of Coverdale Training', *Industrial and Commercial Training*, vol. 8, no. 1, pp. 12–16.

Taylor, M. (1979) *Coverdale on Management*, Heinemann.

Waterson, J. (1979) 'Coverdale Training', in Babbington-Smith, B. and Farrell, B.A. (eds) *Training in Small Groups: A Study of Five Methods*, Pergamon Press.

See also: Action training; Behaviour analysis; Controlled-pace negotiation; Experience-based learning; Interactive skills training; Managing effective relationships; Process analysis; Structured social skills seminar

Creative dialogue

In this method, the tutor writes several questions on a blackboard or flipchart which are intended to encourage group discussion, and then leaves the room. Students then form several sub-groups and discuss the assigned topic and questions under the direction of an assigned student leader. Towards the end of the session, the tutor returns and the class reassembles to listen to what the group spokesperson reports. It has been found that creative dialogues help focus discussions and permit a more open exchange than typically occurs in classroom situations.

Tighe, M.J. (1971) 'Creative Dialogue: Teaching Students to Teach Themselves', *New Directions in Teaching*, vol. 2, no. 4.

See also: Abercrombie method; Agenda method; Buberian dialogue; Free discussion method; Leaderless group discussion; Learning through discussion; Self-directed learning

Creativity training

Creativity training is based on the belief that creativity is not a chance characteristic possessed by a handful of people, but that everyone possesses creative capacity which can be developed and brought into the open.

Arnold at the Massachusetts Institute of Technology was among the first to use this approach. His students were given problems which forced them to develop new ways of thinking. For example, they had to design cars and razors for planets with different laws of gravity and with different chemical and physical conditions.

Creativity training is therefore a generic term for a variety of approaches which rely on specific techniques or exercises whose titles are frequently as inventive as the type of thinking they attempt to engender. Such training programmes usually include the creation of a climate of creativity within an organization, overcoming personal blocks to creativity, setting objectives, problems and challenges. The exercises used to release the creativity which is deemed to be inherent in all people include: the Deferred Judgement Method; Bionics; Metaphor and Analogy; Directed Speculation; Selective and Planned Ignorance; Maintaining Forward Motion; Incubation; 'Fooling around to generate ideas'; Brainstorming; Quick Think; the Little Techniques; Systematized Directed Induction, and forcing relationships between seemingly unrelated things. Subsequent topics on such courses involve the process of evaluating ideas, especially the development of criteria against which to evaluate them, and how to weigh these in order of importance. Finally, the implementation and monitoring of new ideas are considered.

Amabile, T. (1998) 'How to Kill Creativity', *Harvard Business Review*, vol. 76, September–October, pp. 77–87.

Bentley, T. (1996) *How to Sharpen Your Team's Skills in Creativity*, McGraw-Hill.

Coade, N. (1997) *Be Creative*, International Thompson Publications.

Cook, P. (1998) *Best Practice Creativity*, Gower.

Moger, S. (ed.) (1991) 'Leadership and Personal Creativity', special issue of *Leadership and Organization Development Journal*, vol. 12, no. 6.

Proctor, T. (1995) *Essence of Management Creativity*, Prentice-Hall.

Quinlivan-Hall, D. and Renner, P. (1990) *Sixty Ways to Guide Your Problem Solving Group*, American Society for Training and Development Press.

Ricchiuto, J. (1996) *Collaborate Creativity: Unleashing the Power of Shared Thinking*, Oak Hill Press,.

Rickards, T. and Moger, S. (1999) *Handbook for Creative Team Leaders*, Gower.

Robinson, A.G. and Stern, S. (1997) *Corporate Creativity: How Innovation and Improvement Actually Happen*, Berrett-Koehler.

Stacy, R. (1996) *Complexity and Creativity in Organization*, Berrett-Koehler.

Steven, K. (1990) *Essence of Creativity*, Oxford University Press.

See also: Brainstorming; Forcing device; Invitation to discover; Kepner Tregoe approach; Lateral thinking; Playing for learning; Synectics

Criss-cross panels

Accomplishing a task often requires collaboration by several groups within an organization, and inter-group relations can both cause difficulties and stimulate change. The criss-cross panel can be thought of as a variation of Negotiation by Group Members. It is designed to improve relationships between two or more groups within an organization by providing a method of choosing representatives. The matters to be discussed by the panel can vary from substantive issues which affect both groups to more emotive issues which may be at the heart of the inability of the groups to work together.

Each group develops a list of nominees they consider are qualified to represent their views. The basis for this selection can be determined beforehand by the group leaders or a third party. Each group then selects from the other's list those individuals who will be members of the panel or negotiating team. The outcome of this procedure is that the negotiators simultaneously represent each group, reducing the fear that they may be accused of not arguing for their group's position strongly enough. It addition, the approach allows participants to identify with the entire problem, or at least reduces the parochialism which impedes many negotiations.

This method is effective in situations where the groups are not totally hostile to each other, where they share a history of working through common difficulties in the past, where there is a general willingness to work through current problems and reach an acceptable solution, and where it is relatively easy to get each group to commit itself to solutions reached by the panel.

See also: Conflict-resolution techniques; Confrontation groups; Confrontation meeting; Exchange of persons; Fishbowl; LIFO method; Negotiation by group members; No-lose conflict-resolution method; Staff exchange; Third-party peacemaking interventions

Critical theory approach

In the field of management studies, one can distinguish two, contrasting approaches: *managerialist* and *critical theory*.

The managerialist approach has historically dominated the teaching of knowledge and skills to managers and students on MBA programmes and executive development courses. Crudely summarized, it accepts managers' right to manage, treats organizations and their structures and procedures as given, and sees the role of management education as making managers and their organizations more efficient and effective by improving techniques and practices. Its most extreme manifestation is perhaps found in US-published management textbooks, where the activities of American corporations are not only reported, but unashamedly celebrated. One commentator even suggested that the corporations mentioned should sponsor the relevant textbook chapters.

In contrast, the critical theory approach is significant by its absence in management education and training. It is most often encountered in final-year undergraduate management or organizational sociology courses. It also focuses on managers in organizations, but takes a perspective which is more questioning, and hence more critical of established practices. It focuses on power relations, the role of ideology and change, and does so in ways that the managerialist approach prefers to ignore.

The term 'critical theory' originated in the collective philosophy or social theory of the original members of the Frankfurt School, whose most frequently cited representatives include Adorno, Benjamin, Fromm, Habermas,

Horkheimer and Marcuse. More recent contributions have come from authors such as Derrida, Ferguson, Foucault, Lyotard and Zimmer.

Four themes are central to the critical theory approach – social construction, power and ideology, totality, and praxis – and a brief explanation of each, with examples from management and organizations, will reveal how it differs from the more common managerialist stance.

Prasad and Caproni's succinct summary of critical theory explains that it holds that organizational reality is neither objective nor unchanging, but is *socially constructed*. Organization members, owners, managers and workers collectively create, reinforce and revise reality through social negotiation and by assigning and reassigning meanings. At any point in time, one 'definition of the situation' will predominate, and will appear to be the objective reality. Critical theory questions the assumptions of managerialism, and examines how the dominant reality is constructed. Corporate culture and organizational socialization are an example of these different construction approaches. The managerialist approach, for example, accepts the link between a strong corporate culture and increased employee commitment, believing that it improves productivity and increases profits. It therefore focuses on techniques through which a strong culture can be developed, communicated to employees and sustained over time. The critical theory approach in contrast, questions that link, and goes further, challenging the notion that there can be a single corporate culture, and considering how management's emphasis on culture can serve to promote its ideology and impose a covert form of control over employees.

Critical theory holds that the social construction of reality is influenced by *power* relations, and hence stresses the importance of the objectives of the power elite within and outside organizations in an effort to understand the reality-creation process. Work is thus considered within the context of media, educational and political institutions. The concept of *ideology* used by critical theorists refers to the elements of a shared world view that provides order and meaning for its members, but at the cost of creating false expectations, and limiting their possibilities of action and aspiration. Thus dominant ideologies dictate members' expectations about work relations, level of personal success, managerial effectiveness. Such ideologically based expectations are rarely questioned by managerialist approaches.

The third theme, *totality*, refers to the fact that to understand organizations and management, the two need to be viewed holistically and historically, with a stress on interrelatedness and complexity. Thus the success or failure of quality management, industrial democracy or business process re-engineering requires a socio-historic analysis. In contrast, the managerialist approach tends to focus on the present and the future, adopting a narrower view which typically lacks a wider, historical dimension.

Finally, critical theory has a commitment to *praxis*, defined as: 'the on-going construction of social arrangements that are conducive to the flourishing of the human condition'. One can contrast this with the implicit managerialist commitment to maximizing efficiency and organizational performance.

Both the managerialist and critical theory approaches imply an action imperative, but critical theory relies on an ideology-based critique with reflective strategies for social change. It not only challenges the social realities it discovers in organizations, it also identifies ideological issues, and unmasks systems of domination.

From Prasad and Caproni's summary, it is easy to understand how a critical theory approach to teaching management differs from a managerialist one. At undergraduate level, instructors typically adopt a predominantly managerialist tone, with interspersed critiques informed by and based on the critical theory tradition.

Alvesson, M. and Willmott, H. (eds) (1992) *Critical Management Studies*, Sage.
Alvesson, M. and Willmott, H. (1996) *Making Sense of Management: A Critical Introduction*, Sage.
Caproni, P.J. and Arias, M.E. (1997) 'Management Skill Training from a Critical Perspective', *Journal of Management Education*, vol. 21, no. 3, pp. 292–308.
Frost, P. (1980) 'Towards a Radical Framework for Practising Organization Science', *Academy of Management Review*, vol. 5, pp. 501–8.
Frost, P. (1997) 'Building Bridges Between Critical Theory and Management Education', *Journal of Management Education*, vol. 21, no. 3, pp. 343–60.
Hollway, W. (1991) *Work Psychology and Organizational Behaviour*, Sage.
Jermier, J.M. (1985) 'When the Sleeper Awakes: A Short Essay Extending Themes in Radical Organization Theory', *Journal of Management*, vol. 11, pp. 67–80.
Nord, W. (1974) 'Failure of Current Applied Behavioural Science', *Journal of Applied Behavioural Science*, vol. 10, pp. 557–78.
Prasad, P. and Caproni, P.J. (1997) 'Critical Theory in the Management Classroom: Engaging Power, Ideology and Praxis', *Journal of Management Education*, vol. 21, no. 3, pp. 284–91.
Prasad, P. and Cavanaugh, J.M. (1997) 'Ideology and Demystification: Tom Peters and the Management (Sub-)Text: A Experiential Exploration of Critique and Empowerment in the Management Classroom', *Journal of Management Education*, vol. 21, no. 3, pp. 309–24.
Rosen, M. (1987) 'Critical Administrative Scholarship, Praxis and Academic Workplace', *Journal of Management*, vol. 13, pp. 573–86.
Thomas, A.B. (1993) *Controversies in Management*, Routledge.
Thompson, P. and McHugh, D. (1999) *Work Organizations* (2nd edn), Macmillan.

See also: Corporate culture training; Dialectic enquiry; Historical analysis; Literary criticism; Theory-based interventions

Critiquing

A critique may occur spontaneously during a meeting when a member may say, 'Hold it, we're going too fast. We haven't decided on our objectives,' or a working group may plan to critique its own performance by asking each member at the end of a meeting to comment on the process of information-sharing, the quality of the decision-making, the liveliness of the event, and how future meetings might be improved.

Critiquing is a simple and quick way to obtain feedback. Moreover, it distributes the responsibility for improving effectiveness among all the participants, rather than loading it all on to the group leader or chairperson. Critiques need not be limited to the conclusions of events. They can be scheduled to occur throughout them, as in the case of a lengthy management course. This can help the manager or tutor assess the effectiveness of the content and presentation of their material in time to make any necessary changes.

To be most effective, it is recommended that critiques be kept short: one minute is considered ideal, and two minutes is the maximum. Time needs to be reserved for critiques, and people should be encouraged to participate, but not pressurized to do so. Once critiquing has been institutionalized as a normal part of a group's process, the members can feel free to comment on the group's process as it happens, rather than waiting for a pre-specified time.

If critiquing raises a need for certain changes, and these are then not implemented, it will come to be seen as a futile exercise. The purpose of critiquing is to obtain individual feedback about a group's process in order to improve it, not just to allow people to let off steam.

Fordyce, J.K. and Weil, R. (1971) *Managing With People*, Addison Wesley Longman, pp. 160–2.

See also: Family group diagnostic meeting; Getting acquainted; Going round the room; Inter-group team-building; Likes and reservations; Non-verbal encounters; Polling; Sub-grouping

Cross-cultural sensitivity training

Diversity training is concerned with helping managers make the most of a workforce which may be mixed in terms of ethnic background and general and physical capabilities. Cross-cultural sensitivity training involves raising the awareness of managers who travel to other cultures, whether briefly or for an extended period, about the social, cultural, economic and political differences they are likely to encounter. At the minimum, such training may help participants avoid unpleasantness and embarrassment, and at best it can help them be more effective and successful while abroad.

In the management classroom, undergraduates often need to be taught, at various levels of sophistication, about the values and traditions of other societies. The more isolated the student group, the more basic the training required. Thus, in one report from a US business school, students had to be taught the names of the countries in Central and South America that they were likely to visit.

Dennis, L.E. and Stroh, L.K. (1997) 'A Little Jeitinho in Brazil: A Case Study in International Management', *Journal of Management Education*, vol. 21, no. 2, pp. 255–61.

Pruegger, V.J. and Rogers, T.B. (1994) 'Cross Cultural Sensitivity Training: Methods and Assessment', *International Journal of Intercultural Relations*, vol. 18, pp. 369–87.

Richards, D. (1997) 'Developing Cross-cultural Managerial Skills: Experiential Learning on an International MBA programme', *Management Learning*, vol. 28, no. 4, pp. 387–407.

Sullivan, S.E. and Duplaga, E.A. (1997) 'The Bafa Bafa Simulation: Faculty Experiences and Student Reactions, *Journal of Management Education*, vol. 21, no. 2, pp. 265–72.

Sullivan, S.E. and Tu, H.S. (1996) 'Developing Globally Competent Students: A Review and Recommendation', *Journal of Management Education*, vol. 19, pp. 473–93.

See also: Affirmative action; Diversity training; Overseas project

Customer interface meeting

There are various ways a company can obtain feedback from customers about its performance and encourage them to work with it to help it provide a better service for them and other customers.

One company ran an *internal management development seminar* for its senior staff. It invited a number of senior representatives from a customer company to attend, and to take part in a panel presentation on what they did and did not like. A facilitator encouraged the visitors to concentrate on the latter, and asked them to assess the company's products in terms of their cost, quality and reliability. In addition, he asked them to specify what the company would have to do to keep them as customers.

Technical conferences are attended by the technical staffs of several customer companies. At these events, the participants are asked to present any problems they may have with the products to a company group. Such conferences are helpful to the customers because they give them direct assistance, and allow them to obtain ideas from others which can help them to improve their own business.

Another approach is the *buyer seminar*, where purchasing staff from both current customer and potential customer companies attend a meeting at which company services and products are displayed. This is designed as an educational event, since these seminars often lead to the application of new ideas by the visitors, and the company may gain new customers.

If a company is in the packaging business, another strategy is the *packaging service laboratory*. These meetings provide an opportunity to test new approaches and techniques on customers.

Finally, there are *executive visits*, in which senior members of the company visit customers frequently to establish how well their current needs are being satisfied and to assess their future needs.

Bee, R. and Bee, F. (1997) *Customer Care*, Institute of Personnel and Development.

Clifford, D.K. and Cavanagh, R.E. (1986) *The Winning Performance: How America's Midsize Companies Succeed*, Sidgwick and Jackson, pp. 213–14.

Franz, R.S. (1998) 'Whatever You Do, Don't Treat Your Students Like Customers!', *Journal of Management Education*, vol. 22, no. 1, pp. 63–9.

James, J. (1998) *Peopletalk: The Skills of Positive Communication and Customer Care*, Stylus Publishing.

Watson, J. (1997) *Managing Quality in Customer Care*, Butterworth-Heinemann.

See also: Confrontation groups; External mirror; Interface groups; Inter-group team-building; Organizational mirror; Product familiarization programme; Quality awareness training; Quality management; Sensing; Staff exchange

Dalton laboratory plan

Originated by Helen Dalton of Massachusetts during the 1900s, this approach rejects traditional class teaching methods in favour of individual work. It provides education for self-development and social co-operation, addressing the problem of how to cater for students' varying rates of progress. The approach is based on the principles of freedom, responsibility and co-operation. Students are free to continue their work unhampered by timetable interruptions. The year's work is divided into monthly assignments or *contracts*, and each contract is divided into daily units of work. Each student must sign a contract and take responsibility for organizing their own work. They decide how to allocate time to several subjects at their own pace and in their own way with the help of a *topic sheet* which sets out the general nature of the topic to be studied, the sections to be read in particular books, a series of problems to be attempted, and recommended reading for reference and follow-up work. If the assignment fails to meet the student's needs, it can be discarded and another tried. Students are encouraged to confer with others engaged on similar tasks, to clarify and plan procedures. On completion, the student gains a sense of achievement, having experienced individual development through collective effort.

Dewey, E. (1922) *The Dalton Laboratory Plan*, Dent.
Parkhurst, H. (1923) *Education on the Dalton Plan*, Bell and Scott.

See also: Learning contract; Work sheet

Data approach method (data response method)

The data approach method (DAM) is a form of guided learning developed by Trotman-Dickenson to teach economics, but the general approach has wider applications, and can be adapted to any course which involves statistics. It is a simple method which requires no prior knowledge of mathematics and which seeks to improve students' numeracy, familiarize them with data, develop skills in selecting relevant material and give them practice in analysing and interpreting figures. It is particularly useful for students who are not mathematically minded, and it can serve as an introduction to a quantitative methods course in most subjects.

In teaching economics, DAM is usually organized as a seminar. Students are given an economic problem and a package of DAM materials providing comprehensive data on an individual economy with international comparisons. The key data listed under each discussion question provide a signpost to factual information which should be considered in the search for an answer. Once a framework has been constructed by the students on the basis of the tables indicated, they fill in the gaps with data of their own choosing. The completed picture is then presented by the students at the seminar itself, followed by a general discussion, since other class members may be familiar with the same material but may have arrived at different conclusions. The problems presented in successive seminars are linked, so that by the end of the course the students should have built up an overall view of the economy.

DAM does not just involve giving references to statistical sources and occasional handouts of economic data, it is a structured method of instruction which emphasizes the integration of material. Once students are familiar with the data in tabular form, they are encouraged to present it in different ways which may convey it more effectively for specific purposes – for example, bar and pie charts, index numbers and graph drawings – and compare the merits of the various data presentation methods. Computer software packages can also be used to assist the learning process.

Trotman-Dickenson, D.I. (1969) *Economic Workbook and Data*, Pergamon Press.
Trotman-Dickenson, D.I. (1978) 'The Use of Data Response in the Teaching of Economics', *British Journal of Educational Technology*, vol. 9, no. 3, pp. 201-4.

See also: Construct lesson plan; Interpretation of data; Library assignment; Re-writing; Self-instructional modules and interactive groups; Structuring seminars; Tutorial-tape-document learning package approach

Data-based interventions

This is a family of intervention methods which, in different ways, use data to help bring about organizational change. Research on data-based organization change and theories about how information affects behaviour in organizations have shown that data can be used to initiate, facilitate and monitor change. The use of such data depends on several discrete but interrelated steps, including the preparation of data collection, data analysis, data feedback and follow-up, of which data feedback is perhaps the most crucial.

The way data is structured and implemented has a considerable effect on its ultimate usefulness. A number of different data feedback designs have been developed, and their structures depend primarily on three variables: the *composition and membership* of the groups in which the feedback meetings are held (e.g., whether they are natural workgroups or groups created specifically to receive and work on the feedback); the *sequence* in which the data are presented to different individuals and groups in the organization (e.g., is the data given to managers first, then cascaded down the hierarchical layers, or does it go from the bottom up, or is the feedback given to a number of levels at the same time?), and finally, the *type of consultant* employed and the type of role they play is important.

Nadler, D. (1977) *Feedback and Organization Development Using Data Based Methods*, Addison Wesley Longman.

See also: Action enquiry; Action research; Attitude survey; Delphi technique; Family group diagnostic meeting; Focus group; Instrumentation; Instrumented laboratory; Likert System 4 Management; Nominal group technique; Organizational climate analysis; Questionnaires; Survey feedback interventions

Debate

In a traditional debate, participants are assigned specific standpoints to argue from. In management education, this technique can be used to help students understand complex theoretical frames of reference, such as the differences between Fox's 'unitarist' and 'pluralist' perspectives on organization.

One way of enlivening such an exercise is to simulate a television debate. The class is divided into three groups: management, unions and the TV production team. The topic, 'Are workers and managers more equal today?', is specified, and the management group is asked to argue from a unitarist perspective, while the union members couch their argument in pluralistic terms. The production team plans the seating, questions, question order and appoints a compere, and the two groups each appoint two representatives who must be ready to respond to any question the compere may ask them, with the remaining members acting as the studio audience.

Another modified form of debate has been useful in training supervisors. The tutor selects some problems in supervisor–employee interaction, such as senior management's failure to recognize supervisors' contributions and meet their needs for self-development, in which the title of the debate might be: 'What does it mean to be a supervisor?' From these problems, four or five pro and con statements are derived – for example, pro: 'As supervisors, we help to increase company profits by ensuring production targets are met. We gain nothing else from it.'; con: 'As

supervisors, we help colleagues achieve their own aims, and develop our own skills and abilities in the process.'

The 'pro-and-con' debate begins with a short presentation of the standpoints by the tutor, who provides any supplementary information required. The participants then individually rate the standpoints on a scale of plus 2 to minus 2. The choice of rating scale is important: for example, very different results will be obtained if it runs from 'Completely true' to 'Completely false' compared to 'Strongly agree' to 'Strongly disagree', or if it is rephrased to the conceptually similar but affectively different 'Just how I feel' to 'Not my opinion at all'. The individual ratings are collected and presented to the whole group on a flipchart. The group members then divide into two sub-groups, those with a mainly 'pro' rating making up the pro group, and the others the con group. Each group discusses its standpoint before meeting once again in a plenary session to develop a joint perspective on the role of the supervisor.

This type of debating session can raise role-awareness, and the extreme nature of the pro and con statements may challenge participants to reflect more deeply on the situation. This technique demands that participants develop their own standpoints and defend them, and the preparation and debate processes also encourage interaction. The debate can be videotaped and used for later evaluation.

Freeley, A.J. (1990) *Argument and Debate* (7th edn), Wadsworth.
Karmel, B. (1979) 'Big Class, Hot Room, Students Sleepy? Have a Debate', *Exchange: The Organizational Behaviour Teaching Journal*, vol. 4, no. 2, p. 48.
Mesch, D.L., Harris, M.M. and Williams, M.L. (1994) 'Debating: Managerial Skills Building Through Contest', *Journal of Management Education*, vol. 18, no. 2, pp. 258–64.
Moore, L.F., Limerick, D.C. and Frost, P.J. (1989–90) 'Debating the Issue: Increasing Understanding of the "Close Calls" in Organizational Decision-making', *The Organizational Behaviour Teaching Review*, vol. 14, no. 1, pp. 37–43.
Russell, L.G. and Scherer, R.F. (1995) 'Debating Ethical Issues: Using the Forensic Model for Analysis and Presentation', *Journal of Management Education*, vol. 19, no. 3, pp. 399–403.
Sheckels, T.F. (1984) *Debating*, Longman.

See also: Advocacy; Argumentation; Buberian dialogue; Case debate; Jurisprudential model; Mock trial; PIT technique; Short talks by students

Decision table

Like algorithms, decision tables can be used to present complex rules, procedures and instructions in such a way that selection of a correct solution is guaranteed if the necessary information is accurate. The example of a decision table below is in fact simpler than it may appear, since only two conditions (rules 2 and 3) disqualify and, if these do not apply, all other permutations and decisions must apply.

Decision tables provide a simple way of setting out questions and the decisions which must be taken on the basis of their answers. They permit a serial or sequential search through information to be carried out while disregarding particular elements or areas which are irrelevant. Decision tables ensure that every eventuality is explored, and minimize the possibility of errors due to oversights. They help to define the problem and clarify causal and effectual relationships between conditions and actions. They are one of the few strategies available which allow amendments to the logic of an instruction to be carried out without introducing unforeseen and undesired consequences.

Grad, B. (1961) 'Tabular Form in Decision Logic', *Datamation*, vol. 7, no. 7.

Magee, J.F. (1964) 'Decision Trees for Decision Makers', *Harvard Business Review*, July–August.

See also: Algorithm; Flowchart; Heuristic

Decroly method

In 1901, a Belgian physician, Decroly, founded a school for children with learning difficulties based on his concept of 'learning through living', and in 1907 he applied the same principles to teaching children in general. His school was located in natural surroundings that allowed children to observe nature and manifestations of life in plants, animals and human beings. Classes were restricted to 20 students, and the classrooms themselves were furnished as laboratories or studies.

The distinguishing feature of the Decroly method is the organization of the curriculum into a 'programme of associated ideas' divided into two parts: the study of living creatures, including humans; the study of the surrounding universe, including society. Individual academic subjects are not studied, but instead a number of important 'centres of interest' (e.g., food, protection against the elements) are examined. The school is organized as a miniature community, social learning is emphasized, and students' marks are not compared with others', but are used to gauge individual progress.

There are two main precepts in the Decroly method. The first is *direct observation* by the learner. Lessons in observation and comparison mean that an overemphasis on verbal aspects of the curriculum is avoided. Verbal instruction is necessary to extend learners' knowledge of facts not directly accessible to them in time and space,

CONDITION STUB		CONDITION ENTRIES					
Q1	Were the contributions paid late?	No	Yes	Yes	Yes	Yes	Yes
Q2	Were the contributions paid before the death of the subject of the claim?	—	No	Yes	Yes	Yes	Yes
Q3	Is the insured person alive?	—	—	No	No	No	Yes
Q4	Were the contributions paid before the insured person died?	—	—	No	No	Yes	—
Q5	Have the contributions already been taken into account for a claim for a widow's or retirement pension?	—	—	No	Yes	—	—
ACTION STUB		ACTION ENTRIES					
Death grant is payable.		*			*	*	*
Death grant is NOT payable.			*	*			
Rules		(1)	(2)	(3)	(4)	(5)	(6)

Note: A dash in the condition entry column indicates that either a yes or no answer is acceptable. In other words, the answer to the question does not affect the final outcome.

Example of a decision table

but these facts are made meaningful by being compared and associated with those learned through direct observation. The second precept is the completion of a period of study by some form of expression: either concrete, such as model-building or drawing, or abstract, such as reading, speaking or writing.

See also: Learning community; Outdoor training; Project method

Delphi technique

The Delphi technique is used to assess current needs, predict the future, and gain expert consensus while reflecting minority opinions. The technique was developed by Helmer and associates at the Rand Corporation in the early 1950s to obtain group opinions about national defence problems.

Named 'Delphi' after the Greek oracle, the method is designed to gather and develop expert opinion anonymously by means of a series of questionnaires, avoiding some of the weaknesses of group decision-making involving face-to-face inter-action, where certain individuals often dominate the discussion and inhibit the voicing of useful ideas by less aggressive group members. Each expert respondent knows that other experts are taking part in the project, hence they are likely to treat the various viewpoints expressed with respect. The technique can be used both as an organizational change tool and as a teaching method. It has been adopted by government establishments to forecast technological breakthroughs and food consumption trends, and to analyse educational needs.

The first step is to recruit a responding panel of experts on the basis of their reputation, status and knowledge. Up to 150 experts have been used, but 15–20 may be adequate, provided they are carefully selected for the issue under consideration. The initial questionnaire should contain only a limited number of questions, and respondents may be asked to give numerical estimates. Their replies are restricted to four lines. Subsequent questionnaires will be longer and more detailed, but ensuring a rapid turnaround (no longer than ten days between distributing a questionnaire and receiving the responses) will maintain momentum, and e-mail and other electronic forms of communication can be useful, reminders being sent to those who have not responded by the deadline. The raw data from the first questionnaire is edited and tabulated so that it reflects the experts' opinions, which are then offered for rating in the second questionnaire in the form of a summary showing the average, median and range of responses. The experts are asked to refer to the summary and

make another estimate. The third questionnaire is often the most complex, so it is useful to offer the respondents sample responses to help them with their task. The final reports from the data usually contain a ranking of priorities which indicates the degree of consensus for each statement, but minority opinions are also included.

In undergraduate and postgraduate teaching (as opposed to organizational development), the Delphi method can be used to explore course issues, either separately or sequentially. First, the panel of experts – every student in the class – is briefed about the task. Next, a questionnaire is circulated to the class members, and their written responses (possibly including their supporting reasons) are obtained. The data is summarized and tabulated so that the responses become anonymous, and these are fed back to the class, forming a basis for discussion. A second round of data-collection now takes place, using the same or a modified question, which allows class members to reconsider their original responses in the light of the data and discussion. This process may be repeated until the results stabilize or a pre-deter-mined schedule, for example three reiterations, has been completed.

The Delphi technique is less time-consuming than the popular alternative, the nominal group technique (NGT) because there is less verbal interaction. It is sometimes productive to combine the two techniques. Since NGT tends to produce themes that are not fully stated in operational terms and differences in opinions among groups, the weighted lists phase of NGT can be used as a starting point for the Delphi technique.

Each NGT task group refines its most valued objectives, then sends a representative to a staff group, which then eliminates duplicate items, pools the remaining items into a questionnaire, and designs a Likert questionnaire evaluation system. The questionnaires are circulated to all students, and the summaries are then fed back for class discussion, incorporating the reasons underlying the points. The narrowed items are then re-administered individually and tabulated to produce a final ordering.

This method ensures that every student becomes cognitively if not emotionally involved in the key questions asked, the range of viewpoints is broadly defined because the alternative possibilities are systematically processed, and every student has an equal responsibility for considering and evaluating the question-related data. The evaluative decision-making process forces students to interpret the data and come to conclusions, and they gain a deeper and more personalized understanding of a subject than can be provided through a case study or group discussion. Direct experience of the technique means they acquire operational skill and understand its practical applications, feeling more competent to apply it in their future work situations.

Bunning, R.L. (1979) 'The Delphi Technique: A Projection Tool for Social Inquiry' in Jones, J.E. and Pfeiffer, J.W. (eds) *The 1979 Annual Handbook for Group Facilitators*, Pfeiffer/Jossey-Bass.

Cook, C.W. (1980) 'Nominal Group Learning Methods Enrich Classroom Learning', *Exchange: The Organizational Behaviour Teaching Journal*, vol. 5, no. 3, pp. 33–6.

Dalkey, N.C. and Helmer, O. (1963) 'An Experimental Application of the Delphi Method to the Use of Experts', *Management Science*, vol. 10, April, p. 102.

Delbecq, A.L., Van de Ven, A.H. and Gustafson, D.H. (1973) *Group Techniques for Programme Planning: A Guide to the Nominal Group Technique and Delphi Processes*, Scott Foresman & Co.

Linstone, H.A. and Turoff, M. (eds) (1975) *The Delphi Method: Techniques and Applications*, Addison Wesley Longman.

Mitroff, J.J. and Turoff, M. (1975) 'Philosophical and Methodological Foundations of Delphi', in Linstone, H.A. and Turoff, M. (eds) *The Delphi Method – Techniques and Applications*, Addison Wesley Longman.

Paliwoda, S.J. (1983) 'Predicting the Future Using Delphi', *Management Decision*, vol. 21, no. 1, pp. 31–8.

Rohrbaugh, J. (1979) 'Improving the Quality of Group Judgement: Social Judgement Analysis and the Delphi Technique', *Organizational Behaviour and Human Performance*, vol. 24, pp. 73–92.

See also: Attitude survey; Brainwriting; Data-based interventions; Focus group; Nominal group technique; Open systems planning; Policy formulation; Questionnaires; Scenario planning; Search conference; Strategic management; Survey feedback interventions; Talking wall; Think tank

Deming method

W. Edwards Deming was a statistician and management guru who, after the war, helped the Japanese improve the quality of their products. Deming's philosophy of improvement consists of 14 points: (1) create a consistency of purpose towards the improvement of product and service, (2) adopt the new philosophy 'We are in a new economic age', (3) no longer depend on mass inspection to achieve quality, (4) end the practice of awarding business on the basis of the price tag, (5) constantly and forever improve the system of production and service – the system includes people, (6) institute training on the job, (7) practise leadership, to help people and machines do a better job, (8) drive out fear, (9) break down barriers between departments, (10) eliminate slogans and targets for zero defects and new levels of productivity, (11) eliminate work standards and management by objectives, (12) remove barriers that rob people of their right to pride in the quality of their work, (13) set up a vigorous programme of education and self-improvement, and (14) put everybody in the company to work to accomplish the transformation.

Gartner, W.B. (1993) 'Dr Deming Comes to Class', *Journal of Management Education*, vol. 17, no. 2, pp. 141–58.

Gartner, W.B. and Naughton, M.J. (1988) 'The Deming Theory of Management', *Academy of Management Review*, vol. 13, no. 1, pp. 138–42.

Price, F. (1990) *Right Every Time: Using the Deming Approach*, Gower.

Simcox, J. (1997) 'Deming: A Role Model for Productivity and Metanoia', *Organisations and People*, vol. 4, no. 1, pp. 28–32.

Walton, M. (1992) *Deming Management Method*, Mercury Management Books.

See also: Quality circles; Quality management; Total quality management

Demonstration-performance method (tell-show-and-do approach)

A well-planned and skilfully executed demonstration appeals to all the senses, provides practice, stimulates interest and maintains attention. Taking the 'tell-and-show' approach of the lecture-demonstration a stage further to become 'tell-show-and-do' (which might alternatively be described as an 'acted-out lecture'), the demonstration performance method involves explaining procedures or operations, then giving learners the opportunity to practise them under supervision. Learning to use computer software packages in a PC lab uses this approach.

The method is effective for groups of 25 or less: beyond that number the group must be subdivided, with a separate leader for each sub-group. Planning a demonstration involves breaking up the skill/activity into the various steps, arranged in a logical order. Following the demonstration, learners practise the skills while the tutor observes, spotting and remedying incorrect techniques before they become established habits. After all learners have had an opportunity to practise, the tutor conducts a summary or review.

Taylor, C. (1988) *Art and Science of Lecture Demonstration*, Adam Hilger Ltd.

See also: Discovery method; Drill and practice session; Lecture; Lesson-demonstration; Mathetics

Description-prediction-outcome-explanation

The description-prediction-outcome-explanation (DPOE) model was originally developed in the field of science teaching, but with only minor modifications can be applied to any other subject. After having studied a subject – its concepts, ideas, theories, research findings and models – students are presented with a short *description* of a situation, a real or invented mini-case or vignette which should be no more than a paragraph long, for example: 'Four individuals are employed as Saturday staff in a shop, and the manager discovers that occasionally but regularly the day's takings do not balance, and that one of the four employees is a thief. He distributes Eysenck's personality questionnaire to each one.'

In the *prediction* stage, the students are asked, 'What happened next?', and are given two to five options: in this case, 'Which of the four Saturday employees is most likely to be the thief?' It may be necessary to provide additional information at this time, such as that the personality questionnaire revealed that employee A was a stable introvert, employee B was an unstable introvert, employee C was a stable extrovert, and employee D was a unstable extrovert. Individually or in small groups, students are asked to select the most likely option, and to justify their choice, based on their understanding of the course concepts, theories and research findings. There may be several equally valid answers. In the *outcome* stage, the instructor states what actually happened, or was most likely to happen. Finally, the instructor provides a brief *explanation* of why this outcome occurred, linking it to the course material, and perhaps confirming, rectifying or clarifying the suggestions made by the students. In the example cited, students' knowledge of the traits possessed by each of the four personality types might suggest that the employee who was a risk-taker, impulsive, irresponsible, calm, had a low sense of guilt and sought self-esteem was most likely to be the thief.

White, R. and Gunstone, R. (1992) 'Prediction-Observation-Explanation', in *Probing Understanding*, Falmer Press, pp. 44–64.

See also: Application of principles; Fortune lining; Vignette analysis

Development assignment

There are many varieties of development assignments, but they usually accentuate individual development. In the past, these have received bad publicity because they were used as gimmicks and were touted as cure-alls. There are two basic prerequisites in their use: first, any required skill training must precede the assignment. If a production manager is to work in the finance department on a development assignment, then they must be taught the financial and accounting skills they will require to fulfil the task; second, any development assignment presumes that one-to-one coaching of the manager undertaking the assignment will be available. Line managers should use their own experience to decide what development assignments will be useful to their staff, perhaps enlisting guidance from the company's training specialist.

Daley, P. and McGivern, C. (1972) 'The On-going Management Situation as a Training Vehicle', *Industrial and Commercial Training*, vol. 4, no. 3, pp. 137–41.
Honey, P. (1976) 'On-the-job Management Training', *Industrial and Commercial Training*, June, vol. 8, no. 6, pp. 229–35.
Zeira, Y. (1973) 'Introduction of On-the-job Management Development', *Personnel Journal*, vol. 52, December, pp. 1049–55.

See also: Acting assignment; Apprenticeship programme; Assignment to customer as representative; Assignment to community organization; Assignment to government study group; Assignment to manager with high development skills; Coaching; Committee assignment; Consulting assignment; Evaluation/audit assignment; Expanding job assignment; Manager exchange; Manager shadowing; Proposal team assignment; Research assignment; Rotation training; Secondment; Selection board assignment; Sick leave/holiday replacement assignment; Staff meeting assignment; Study assignment; Task force assignment

Development of a new management/operating philosophy

Working out a new philosophy of management is both a rare and a radical approach to dealing with the problems of change. One company which has been in the news in this area for nearly three decades is Shell.

During the 1960s, Shell embarked on a widely publicized change of philosophy to guide managerial decision-making in the face of increasing technological change and to act as a stabilizing influence during a period of growing industrial unrest. The approach was based on the view that higher productivity could not be obtained through conventional bargaining procedures which sought to enhance productivity by offering financial incentives. Instead, in the long term it sought to change employees' attitudes to the point where a climate of mutual trust and confidence existed between them and management, encouraging them to become fully committed to the company's objectives so that they would maximize efficiency and productivity. Effective management, it was argued, could only be practised with the consent of those being managed. Certain standards were set for this new philosophy. It had to be acceptable to all levels of management, to the workers and to their union representatives. The second theme concerned establishing conditions under which genuine productivity bargaining could take place, which would change the company's relationship with its hourly paid employees.

In 1998, Shell received negative publicity, first with respect to its environmental policy in the controversy over the proposed dumping at sea of the Brent Spar oil-drilling platform, then concerning its operations around the globe, particularly in Nigeria. Its UK head went on radio to publicly confirm Shell's ethical policy and business principles in a number of fields, including environmental protection, bribery and its subcontractors' work practices, and he challenged observers to monitor the company's adherence to these standards.

Such changes in a company's operating philosophy are often triggered by the need to identify ways to adapt to technological, political or environmental changes under conditions of increasing complexity and uncertainty. Many companies believe that they can retain their cohesion and move in an appropriate direction only if the majority of their employees subscribe to a common set of values. Explaining this set of relevant values, examining how these affect the different fields in which the company operates and considering how the company meets the needs of its employees, customers and the public requires the formulation or reformulation of a statement of philosophy. The statement will usually postulate the existence of both social and economic company objectives, and consider how the two interact, and may often be disseminated to all company stakeholders by means of conferences and news briefings.

Blacker, F.H.M. and Brown, C.A. (1980) *Whatever Happened to Shell's New Philosophy of Management?*, Gower.
Goffee, R. and Jones, G. (1998) *The Character of a Corporation*, HarperCollins.
Hill, P.J. (1976), *Towards A New Philosophy of Management*, Gower.

Roeber, J. (1975) *Social Change at Work*, Duckworth.

See also: Corporate culture training; Greenfield plants; Ideological change; Likert's System 4 Management; Managerial strategy change; Mission cards; Myth-making interventions; Organizational climate analysis; Policy formulation; Strategic management

Diagnostic activities

These are a range of fact-finding techniques designed to ascertain the state of an organization, the nature of any problems and the 'way things are' in order to generate information which can be used to plan the implementation of feasible and workable improvements. Diagnostic techniques can use face-to-face contacts or the visual representation of situations.

Among the best-known of the interventions in this category are the *manager's diagnostic meeting* and the *manager's team diagnostic meeting*. In the former, the learning group consists of the manager, an outside consultant who acts as a resource person, and a person with organization-wide responsibility such as a personnel or training manager, focusing on diagnosis of the manager's work team. The group considers the need for change or improvement in an environment which is non-threatening to the manager concerned. The team diagnostic meeting, in contrast, involves the 'organizational family' – the manager and his immediate workgroup. The diagnosis may centre on specific tasks and problems, or it may have a broader remit, addressing questions such as what it is that group does best and worst.

French, W.L. and Bell, C. H. (1984) *Organization Development: Behavioural Science Interventions for Organization Improvement* (3rd edn), Pearson Education, p. 102.

See also: ACHIEVE model; Assessment of the organization as a system; Benchmarking; Collages; Drawing for learning; Family group diagnostic meeting; Family group team-building meeting; Focus group; Industrial dynamics; Interviewing; Looking for trouble; Management audit; Organizational analysis; Overhead value analysis; Physical representation of organizations; Questionnaires; 7-S framework; Sensing; Survey feedback interventions

Dialectical enquiry

Dehler and Welsh describe their dialectical enquiry (DE) approach to the study of abstract topics in management and organizational behaviour as being designed mainly to teach 'ways of thinking' rather than facts, while at the same time retaining the inherent complexity and paradoxical nature of organizational life.

DE is particularly suitable to the study of management and organizational behaviour topics because so many of them are dichotomous in character. A dichotomy is a presentation of a concept as a dimension with contradictory anchors (e.g., temperature, with high at one end and low at the other). The anchors at the ends serve as a fundamental premise (*thesis*) and as a contradictory position (*antithesis*). The majority of management textbooks present their core concepts in dichotomous form (e.g., systems as open or closed; environments as complex or simple; personality approaches as nomothetic or idiographic; motivation theories as content or process; learning as behaviourist or cognitive). Using dichotomies provides a basis for explaining and discussing management concepts in a way which develops students' skills of critical analysis. The dynamic relationship between the concepts is then illuminated by dialectic enquiry, and the process of organizational change is also amenable to dialectic interpretation. The DE approach uses the *thesis-antithesis-synthesis* progression.

First, students concentrate on contrary perspectives which they use to develop an understanding of the key concepts and processes being studied, and the relationships between them. They select and define their chosen concept (e.g., 'organization structure') and distinguish its opposite forms to create a dichotomy (e.g., structure as mechanistic and organic). Developing dichotomies provides them with a way of identifying isolated individual concepts by contrasting their end points, thereby establishing thesis and antithesis. Instructors can encourage students to go further and elaborate each dimension by posing questions which will force them to explore the area between the two anchors. Each represents an absolute or an ideal form, which rarely exist in real life. Real examples – in this case, of organizational structure – are only matters of degree.

In the second stage, a dialectic debate takes place in the classroom, during which the extreme positions or anchors are scrutinized and dissected. The underlying assumptions on which they rest are exposed and challenged: for example, if an organization is operating in a dynamic, uncertain environment, what types of control should it have, which technology should it use and what should its structural form be? The concepts of environment, technology and structure are presented visually in dichotomous forms, and a discussion follows.

The DE model focuses on differences, rather than achieving a conflict-free consensus, so the final stage is a constructive discussion and debate (*synthesis*) which helps students understand the richness of the concepts being considered, and their relevance to managing real-world organizations. It thus allows them to generate different – albeit equally valid – solutions.

The instructor's aim is to encourage students to acknowledge the dilemmas posed by seemingly incompatible requirements in organizational life, and then to search for managerial responses which can effectively reconcile them. Students are required to describe organizations objectively, and then go on to generate more subjective conclusions. By the end of the session, they come to see the same process from diametrically different perspectives, and thus acquire individual interpretations. Awareness of paradox and conundrum facilitates their appreciation of the integration between organizational variables and managerial actions. It also acts an antidote to the current penchant for 'one-best-way', quick-fix, universally applicable solutions to management problems.

Benson, J.K. (1977) 'Organization: A Dialectic View', *Administrative Science Quarterly*, vol. 25, pp. 72–88.

Churchman, C.W. (1991) *The Design of Enquiry Systems: Basic Concepts of Systems and Organization*, Basic Books.

Dehler, G.E. and Welsh, M.A. (1993) 'Dialectical Inquiry as an Instructional Heuristic in Organization Theory and Design', *Journal of Management Education*, vol. 17, no. 1, pp. 79–89.

Kilmann, R.H. (1994) *Beyond the Quick Fix*, Jossey-Bass.

Meyer, A.D., Snow, C.C. and Miles, R.E. (1982) 'Teaching Organization Theory', in Freedman, R.D., Cooper, C.L. and Stumpf, S.A. (eds) *Management Education*, Wiley.

Orton, J.D. and Weick, K.E. (1990) 'Loosely Coupled Systems: A Reconceptualization', *Academy of Management Review*, vol. 15, pp. 203–23.

Zeitz, G. (1980) 'Inter-organizational Dialectics', *Administrative Science Quarterly*, vol. 22, pp. 1–21.

See also: Critical theory approach; Historical analysis; Theory-based interventions

Dialogue

'Dialogue' refers to both an educational philosophy and a way of conversing within that approach. As a philosophy, it encourages person-centred interaction in which each individual meets another in an attitude of *mutuality*, *reciprocity* and *co-inquiry*. Hazen described a course underpinned by this concept of dialogue, and in this context 'mutuality' means that each course member views others as capable of developing and changing, rather than as obstacles to be overcome, 'reciprocity' relates to the belief that each member can both teach and learn from others, while 'co-inquiry' stresses that all the course members are part a single system, and only collectively can they understand that system and their place within it.

Dialogue is concerned with integrating learning from the individual, inter-personal and organizational levels. As a way of conversing and thinking together, it aims to overcome barriers and to create organizational cultures that are distinguished by collaboration and partnership. It widens information arteries so that employees at all levels begin to think along leadership lines and take responsibility for how their actions affect the whole organization. In this context, diversity becomes a resource and conflict an opportunity.

Bohm, D. and Factor, D. (1996) *Unfolding Meaning: A Weekend of Dialogue with David Bohm*, Routledge.
Bohm, D. and Nichol, E. (1994) *Thought as a System*, Routledge.
Bohm, D. and Nichol, L. (eds) (1996) *On Dialogue*, Routledge.
Dixon, N.M. (1998) *Dialogue at Work*, Lemos and Crane.
Gerard, G. and Ellinor, L. (1998) *Dialogue: Rediscover the Transforming Power of Conversation*, Wiley.
Hazen, M.A. (1987–8) 'Learning How to Learn: An Experiment in Dialogue', *The Organizational Behaviour Teaching Review*, vol. 12, no. 2, pp. 72–85.
Tannen, D. (1998) *The Argument Culture: Moving from Debate to Dialogue*, Random House.

See also: Conflict-stimulation technique; Creativity training; Socratic dialogue; Team briefing

Dialoguing

Dialoguing is a group communication process which tries to create an organizational culture based on team spirit: collaboration, fluidity, trust and commitment to shared goals. Formal dialoguing sessions may be conducted during off-site retreats.

In discussion, the objective is usually to state one's point of view and persuade the other party to accept and adopt it. In an organizational context, this might lead to divisiveness and polarization within teams. In contrast, dialoguing asks participants to suspend their attachments to a particular viewpoint so that a deeper level of listening, synthesis and meaning can evolve within the group. Individual differences are acknowledged and respected, but rather than trying to decide who is right or wrong, the group searches for an expanded, collective perspective.

Gerard, G. and Teurfs, L. (1995) 'Dialogue and Organizational Transformation', in Gozdz, K. (ed.) *Community Building: Renewing Spirit and Learning in Business*, New Leaders Press, pp. 142–53.
Schein, E.H. (1993) 'On Dialogue, Culture and Organizational Learning', *Organizational Dynamics*, Autumn, pp. 40–51.

See also: Feedback

Diary exercise

Diary exercises, a variation on the self-assessment approach, are based on Rosemary Stewart's studies into how managers spend their time. They are a feature of virtually all books on time management, but have much wider potential as a learning tool.

Diary exercises may consider the whole range of a manager or employee's job, or may focus on a few training needs in greater depth. Participants are asked to record their daily work activities over, say, ten to fourteen days, logging how much time they devote to each one. They then discuss and review their diaries with a trainer or their line manager, either individually or in a group. The aim is to develop and implement an action plan if the diary shows that they are using their time unproductively or need to adopt a different approach to their job. Those who are about to attend a training course may also be asked to keep a diary so that trainers can refer to them when discussing particular topics, such as communication or the type of interactions managers experience.

Designing a diary involves the following steps. First, conduct a pilot investigation to identify the appropriate training objectives. Second, design the diary so that it records the duration of each activity, indicating what demands are being placed on a manager. Third, within each designated activity, allocate one code for the activity itself, and another for contacts, etc., so that entries can be made as quickly and simply as possible; fourth, draw up clear instructions on how to fill in the diary. It is vital to explain the purposes of the diary and what will happen to the information gathered: for example, will the data be examined individually or as part of a group?

Allan, J. (1997) *Sharpen Your Team's Skills in Time Management*, McGraw-Hill.
Bird, P. (1998) *Time Management*, Hodder and Stoughton.
Croft, C. (1996) *Time Management*, Routledge.
DeNisi, A.S., Robbins, T. and Cafferty, T.P.

(1989) 'Organization of Information Used for Performance Appraisals', *Journal of Applied Psychology*, vol. 74, pp. 124–9.

McEvoy, G.M. (1996) 'Student Diary Keeping: A Tool for Institutional Improvement', *Journal of Management Education*, vol. 20, no. 1, pp. 206–20.

Roesch, R. (1998) *Time Management for Busy People*, McGraw-Hill.

Stewart, R. (1988) *Managers and Their Jobs*, Macmillan.

See also: Accepting positions of responsibility in community organizations/university clubs; Case-critical incident analysis; Instrumented feedback; Journalling; Logging critical incidents

Directed conversation method

The directed conversation method (DCM) developed from teachers' observations that during formal class discussions students tend to self-censor their contributions, but they often contribute in a much less inhibited fashion either before or after the formal class session. Hence DCM tries to encourage learning by blurring or redefining the formal session time boundaries and establishing an informal atmosphere for group discussions. For example, during a course a trainer feels that junior staff are not receiving the help and guidance from their bosses they require for their development, but is reluctant to confront the senior staff about this for fear of a hostile reaction. The trainer decides to apply DCM by arriving before the formal session is scheduled to begin and engages a couple of participants in conversation, raising the problem and expressing the hope that something can be done about it. Then, as other course members arrive they are likely to join in the discussion, which can be continued during the first half of the time slot, with the tutor directing the conversation in such a way that the participants themselves suggest ways to overcome the problem. During the second half of the session, the conference method can be used to chart, build upon and agree implementation strategies for ideas produced in the first stage.

See also: Conference method; Controlled discussion; Free discussion method

Directed private study

Directed private study (DPS) evolved from correspondence education (also known as 'distance learning' or 'distance education'), which relies on set reading, the use of records, audio tapes and videotapes, exercises and tutor marking, but rarely includes face-to-face tuition. In contrast, DPS combines oral and postal tuition with continuous interaction with a tutor.

A typical DPS course consists of three stages. Stage one involves two weeks of intensive class contact, during which, in addition to the usual teaching, students are given information about stage two so they understand what will be required of them. One of the main aims of this first stage is to motivate the students over the long second stage, which may consist of up to twenty months' study by correspondence. During stage two, a number of study units, each with an estimated work time allocation, may be set each month, plus written tests. The third stage may include a second period of about six weeks' oral tuition, and the final week is usually devoted to examinations.

Eagle, F.H. (1976) 'Directed Private Study in the Docks', *BACIE Journal*, vol. 30, no. 9, October, pp. 166–8.

Jones, L.H. (1968) 'Directed Private Study', in Robinson, J. and Barnes, N. (eds) *New Media and Methods in Industrial Training*, BBC Publications.

Jones, L.H. (1977) 'Directed Private Study', *BACIE Journal*, vol. 31, no. 2, February, pp. 31–2.

See also: Distance education; FlexiStudy; Open learning

Discipline without punishment

Rather than relying on punishment meted out in response to violation of rules, the discipline without punishment approach requires individuals to accept responsibility for their own behaviour. Recognizing that employees must discipline themselves, the approach does not involve reprimands for past misbehaviour, but aims to draw up an action plan to promote more positive behaviour in future by issuing a series of reminders rather than warnings. Warnings threaten future disciplinary action if the misdemeanour is repeated, whereas reminders restate the key elements of company rules and emphasize the individual's responsibility to uphold them.

In the first stage of formal non-punitive discipline, the *oral reminder*, a manager meets an employee to discuss a problem in an effort to persuade the employee to solve it themselves. The manager does not threaten more serious disciplinary action, but reminds the employee that they are personally responsible for meeting reasonable standards of performance and behaviour. A record of this discussion is kept by the manager, but it is made clear to the employee that it will not appear in their permanent record unless the problem recurs, which provides motivation to improve.

Should the problem continue, the manager progresses to stage two, the *written reminder*, issued at a further meeting. Again, this does not involve threats of further action, but reviews the good business reasons why the standard or rule exists, and why it should be observed. They discuss the employee's failure to abide by the agreement made during the first discussion, and the manager tries to help the employee solve the problem by devising an action plan. The manager writes a memo to the individual summarizing the conversation, and places a copy of it in the employee's file.

The aim of the first two stages in the process is to obtain the employee's agreement to change their behaviour, because they are more likely to do so in response to a personal agreement rather than a company demand. The discussion in stage two focuses as much on the employee's failure to keep their part of the bargain as on the continuing problem. Since the employee's refusal or inability to meet reasonable employer expectations is recorded, it can be used to justify dismissal if necessary.

Continued failure by the employee to improve leads to stage three, where they are obliged to take a day's paid *decision-making leave*. The rationale for this paid suspension is that it reduces resentment and the employee's need to 'save face'. It also shows that the organization is committed to trying to help the employee to change and accept responsibility for their behaviour, and does not want to lose them. The employee is instructed to use this day off to decide whether to leave the company or stay, but their continued employment depends on their making a commitment to good performance. On returning to work, the employee informs their supervisor of their decision. If they have decided to stay, the supervisor sets out specific goals, these are agreed, and action steps are planned. The supervisor expresses confidence that the person can achieve these goals, but also explains that failure to live up to the organization's expectations will lead to dismissal, and this statement is documented in a formal memo to the employee, a copy of which is placed in their file.

The compulsory day's paid leave is the only cost associated with the non-punitive approach, and other workers do not appear to resent the paid suspension of colleagues. Many companies have used this strategy successfully, and have achieved significant savings in staff replacement costs. Its proponents consider it to be a more realistic, more adult and more positive way to encourage a disciplined workforce, but to be successful the system needs to be linked to other company employee policies.

Campbell, D.N., Fleming, R.L. and Grote, R.C. (1985) 'Discipline Without Punishment – At Last', *Harvard Business Review*, July–August, vol. 85, no. 4, pp. 162–4, 168, 170, 174 and 176.
Grote, R. (1979) *Positive Discipline*, McGraw-Hill.
Grote, D. (1995) *Discipline Without Punishment*, American Management Association, AMACOM.
Huberman, J. (1964) 'Discipline Without Punishment', *Harvard Business Review*, July–August, pp. 62–8.
Huberman, J. (1975) 'Discipline Without Punishment Lives', *Harvard Business Review*, July–August, pp. 6–8.
King, J. and Johnson, R.E. (1983) 'Silk Purses from Old Pants', *Harvard Business Review*, March–April, p. 147.

See also: Alcohol recovery programme; Behaviour modification; Employee-designed rules; Goal-setting; Ideological change; Measuring performance; Norm formation; Norm modification; Reinforcement environment analysis; Supervisory counselling

Discovery method (discovery learning; inductive learning)

The discovery method is a style of teaching that allows students to learn by finding out principles and relationships for themselves, in contrast to traditional approaches which tend to emphasize memorizing what has been read in books or what the teacher has taught. The method can be applied to any field of study or level of student, and its success depends on gauging precisely at what point the student can solve a particular problem, judging how far the student can be pressed to look for general patterns, and devising a suitable discovery situation.

In the industrial training context, the term 'discovery method' tends to be applied more specifically to the approach originating from programmed instruction which was refined by Eunice and Meredith Belbin in the 1950s. Retraining British Railways steam locomotive drivers to operate diesel-electric trains involved teaching the basic principles of electricity to those who only had a vague theoretical knowledge. In pairs, learners were set progressively more complex tasks demonstrating a basic principle of electrical theory. They were given written instructions about how to assemble pieces of equipment, then required to observe what happened and draw conclusions while the instructor remained in the background and answered any questions. Trainees using the discovery method attained higher test scores than those who had been taught through traditional lectures.

Clay, M. (1980) 'Discovery Training', *Training*, vol. 6, no. 3, pp. 17–19.

Joyce, B.R. and Weil, M. (1996) *Models of Teaching* (5th edn), Allyn and Bacon.

Leutner, D. (1993) 'Guided Discovery Learning with Computer-based Simulation Games', *Learning and Instruction*, vol. 3, pp. 113–32.

Rogers, J. (1977) *Adults Learning*, Open University Press, Chapter 9.

See also: Demonstration-performance method; Drill and practice method; Learning by suggestion; Lesson-demonstration method; Mathetics; Prompt list

Discussion guide

This entry concerns people who act as discussion guides, whereas prepared outline questions or statements are described in the entry on 'Learning through discussion'. Both can be used to channel discussions in a desired direction.

Individuals may be selected to act as discussion guides on the basis of their interest in or knowledge of the subject, and they may be required to read about the subject or obtain information from others in preparation for their role. Three or four individuals may serve as guides in a single discussion meeting. The discussion leader determines the nature and timing of the guides' contribution, and each guide is given a secret cue at the appropriate point. It is important that group members do not discover that discussion guides are present, since any hint of artificiality in the situation may hinder spontaneity.

See also: Guided group problem-solving; Learning through discussion; Structuring seminars

Dissertation proposal (research proposal)

A requirement of most study programmes leading to the award of a diploma or degree is the submission of some form of research project, assignment or dissertation. However, as an alternative to this, or in preparation for it, students may be required to complete a dissertation proposal, where they begin their research but stop before the data-collection stage.

This process is less time-consuming than preparing a full dissertation, but it still develops a limited number of valuable research and learning skills by demanding that students frame the research question, search for and review the literature, specify hypotheses, and choose and defend their choice of research methods.

Bruce, C.S. (1994) 'Research Students' Early Experiences of the Dissertation Literature Review', *Studies in Higher Education*, vol. 19, no. 2, pp. 217–28.

Cryer, P. (1996) *The Research Student's Guide to Success*, Open University Press.

Duckworth, D. (1978) 'An Approach to Preparing Research Proposals', *Management Education and Development*, vol. 9, no. 3, pp. 206–7.

Fink, A. (1998) *Conducting Research Literature Reviews*, Sage.

Gash, S. (2000) *Effective Literature Searching for Research*, Gower.

Gill, J. and Johnson, P. (1997) *Research Methods for Managers* (2nd edn), Chapman/Sage.

Hart, C. (1998) *Doing a Literature Review*, Sage.

Hooper, H.M. (1998) *Synthesising Research: A Guide for Literature Reviews* (3rd edn), Gower.

Jankowicz, A.D. (1995) *Business Research Projects*, Chapman and Hall.

Saunders, M., Thornhill, A. and Lewis, P. (1996) *Research Methods for Business Students*, Pitman.

Saunders, M.N.K. and Lewis, P. (1997) 'Great Ideas and Blind Alleys? A Review of the Literature on Starting Research', *Management Learning*, vol. 28, no. 3, pp. 283–99.

Sharp, J.A. and Howard, K. (1996) *The Management of a Student Research Project* (2nd edn), Gower.

See also: Library assignment; Literature search; Research degree

Distance education (distance learning; teaching at a distance)

Originally known as 'correspondence courses', the development of information technology has radically altered distance education in recent years, and several universities, including the Open University, Heriot-Watt, Durham, Strathclyde and Sheffield Hallam, now offer their MBA programmes wholly or partly through distance learning.

In effect, these courses are a form of programmed learning. Students receive units of work which they complete and then return to a tutor, who provides feedback. The pacing depends on the particular course: some have flexible timetables and examination requirements, whereas others are very rigidly timetabled.

Learning on one's own requires much self-discipline, and tends to make anxious students – in particular older adult learners – even more anxious. Distance learners need to be relatively skilled and reasonably confident in their ability to cope with written work and books. Frequently, students experience difficulty in controlling the pace of their work, and many need to redevelop study skills they have not practised for quite some time. However, telephone support from course counsellors and fellow students can overcome problems of inexperience and isolation, and attention to the teaching materials can increase their motivation.

Many argue that, to be successful, distance learning must include and emphasize those factors which are important in a face-to-face learning situation. The quality of the materials prepared by tutors must be high, and tutors find that they improve their normal teaching materials when adapting them for distance learning courses, refining objectives, assignments and evaluation. The presentation of the material to the learner also demands careful preparation and monitoring.

A crucial element in any distance learning system is the means of communication between teacher and learner. The technology available nowadays – radio, television, audio tapes, videotapes, CD-ROMs, telephone tutoring, videoconferencing and Internet access, plus the use of satellites as costs fall – is extremely useful, but perhaps the most important element is not the technology itself, but the extent to which it enables students to control the pace and mode of study.

In North America, 'distance learning' usually refers to a formal system where there are satellite educational units located hundreds of miles away from the main university campus but controlled by it. These units may consist of four or five students who come together at a particular time and can conduct two-way conversations with a tutor at the main campus.

Bates, A.W. (1995) *Technology, Open Learning and Distance Education*, Routledge.

Brown, S. (1997) *Open and Distance Learning: Case Studies from Industry and Education*, Kogan Page.

Chute, A., Hancock, B. and Thompson, M. (1998) *The McGraw-Hill Handbook of Distance Learning: A 'How To Get Started' Guide for Trainers and Human Resource Professionals*, McGraw-Hill.

Cyers, T.E. (ed.) (1997) *Teaching and Learning at a Distance*, Jossey-Bass.

Freeman, R. (1997) *Managing Open Systems*, Kogan Page.

Harrison, N. (1998) *How To Design Self-directed and Distance Learning*, McGraw-Hill.

Lockwood, F. (ed.) (1995) *Open and Distance Learning Today*, Routledge.

Mantyla, K. and Gividen, R.J. (1997) *Distance Learning: A Step-by-step Guide for Trainers*, American Society for Training and Development, ASTD Press.

Marland, P. (1997) *Towards More Effective Open and Distance Learning*, Kogan Page.

Rowntree, D. (1997) *Making Materials-based Learning Work*, Kogan Page.

Rumble, G. (1997) *The Costs and Economics of Open and Distance Learning*, Kogan Page.

Tait, A. and Mills, R. (1996) *Supporting the Learner in Open and Distance Learning*, Pitman.

See also: Directed private study; Open learning

Diversity training

In companies whose employees come from diverse cultural backgrounds, individuals may be reluctant to shed their cultural identity in order to fit in. In this context, diversity training has two related objectives: to develop employees' awareness of their own prejudices and discriminatory behaviour, and to help the company in general, and managers in particular, turn the diverse backgrounds of their employees to commercial advantage.

To achieve the first objective, diversity training draws on a range of techniques from human relations training. These help trainees to evaluate their behaviour, in particular how it affects the performance of those around them, to identify and work through their cultural stereotypes, to improve the way they relate to people whose cultural backgrounds differ from their own, and to develop ways to overcome cultural barriers in the workplace.

To achieve the second objective, senior managers are brought together to assess whether current policies, systems and practices are preventing certain employees contributing to the company's objectives, and to explore ways of capitalizing on the diversity among the workforce.

Chemers, M.M. (1995) *Diversity in Organizations: New Perspectives for a Changing Workplace*, Sage.

Gardenswartz, L. and Rowe, A. (1994) *Diversity Teams at Work: Capitalizing on the Power of Diversity*, American Society for Training and Development, ASTD Press.

Hames, D.S. (1996) 'Training in the Land of Doone: An Exercise in Understanding Cultural Differences', *Journal of Management Education*, vol. 20, no. 2, pp. 258–64.

Hayes, R. and Russell, A.M. (1996) *The Diversity Directive: Why Some Innovations Fail and What to Do About It*, American Society for Training and Development, ASTD Press.

Kandola, R. and Fullerton, J. (1997) *Diversity in Action – Managing the Mosaic*, Institute of Personnel and Development.

Laudis, D. and Bhagat, R.S. (eds) (1996) *Handbook of Intercultural Training* (2nd edn), Sage.

McMillen, M.C., Baker, A.C. and White, J. (1997)

'Cultural Analysis: "Good Conversation" and the Creation of a Multicultural Learning Organization', *Management Learning*, vol. 28, no. 2, pp. 197–215.

Myers, S.G. (1996) *Team Building for Diverse Workgroups: A Practical Guide to Gaining and Sustaining Performance in Diverse Teams*, Sage.

Powell, G.N. (1996) *Gender and Diversity in the Workplace: Learning Activities and Exercises*, Sage.

Prasad, P., Mills, A.J., Elmes, M. and Prasad, A. (1997) *Managing the Organizational Melting Pot*, Sage.

'Teaching Diversity in the Management Classroom', special issue of *Journal of Management Education* (1998), vol. 22, no. 2.

See also: Affirmative action; Androgynous management; Cross-cultural sensitivity training; Overseas project

Downsizing

Downsizing – intentionally reducing the workforce within an organization – is a popular management technique for restructuring organizations which is perceived as a means of meeting the demands of a dynamic environment. It can result from elimination of functions, hierarchical levels or units within an organization, reduction in the amount of work, or cost-reduction measures. The downsizing options include the following: *short-time working*, reducing the number of hours employees work per week by instituting job-sharing or part-time working; *layoffs*, temporarily removing employees from their jobs, possibly over a period of months or years; *firing*, dispensing with employees permanently; *transfers*, balancing needs for staff within the company by moving existing employees to other posts, and *early retirement*, providing incentives for older or more senior staff to leave.

Appelbaum, S.H. (1991) 'How to Slim Successfully and Ethically: Two Case Studies of Downsizing', *Leadership and Organization Development Journal*, vol. 12, no. 2, pp. 11–16.

Begley, T.M. (1998) 'Teaching About the Human Side of Corporate Restructuring: A Three Stage Role Play', *Journal of Management Education*, vol. 22, no. 1, pp. 70–84.

Caplan, G. and Teese, M. (1997) *Survivors: How to Keep Your Best People on Board After Downsizing*, American Society for Training and Development, ASTD Press.

Cross, M. (ed.) (1985) *Managing Workforce Reduction*, Gower.

Darling, J. and Nurmi, R. (1995) 'Downsizing the Multinational Firm: Key Variables for Excellence', *Leadership and Organization Development Journal*, vol. 16, no. 5, pp. 22–8.

Ebadan, G. and Winstanley, D. (1997) 'Downsizing, Delayering and Careers: A Survivor's Perspective', *Human Resource Management Journal*, vol. 7, no. 1, pp. 79–91.

Gowing, M.K. et al. (eds) (1997) *The New Organizational Reality: Downsizing, Restructuring and Revitalization*, American Psychological Association.

Institute of Personnel and Development (1997) *IPD Guide to Redundancy*, IPD.

Kinnie, N., Hutchinson, S. and Purcell, S. (1998) 'Downsizing: Is It Always Lean and Mean?', *Personnel Review*, vol. 27, no. 4, pp. 296–311.

Labib, N. and Appelbaum, S.H. (1994) 'The Impact of Downsizing Practices on Corporate Success', *Journal of Management Development*, vol. 13, no. 7, pp. 59–84.

Noer, D. (1994) *Healing the Wounds: Overcoming the Trauma of Layoffs and Revitalizing Downsized Organizations*, Jossey-Bass.

Palmer, I., Kabanoff, B. and Dunford, R. (1997) 'Managerial Accounts of Downsizing', *Journal of Organizational Behaviour*, vol. 18, pp. 623–39.

Thornhill, A. and Saunders, M. (1998) 'The Meanings, Consequences and Implications of the Management of Downsizing and Redundancy', *Personnel Review*, vol. 27, no. 4, pp. 271–95.

Vollman, T. and Brazas, M. (1993) 'Downsizing', *European Management Journal*, vol. 11, pp. 18–29.

Whetten, D.A., Keiser, J.D. and Urban, T. (1995) 'Implications of Organizational Downsizing for the Human Resource Management Function', in Ferris, G.R., Rosen, S.D. and Barnum, D.T. (eds) *Handbook of Human Resource Management*, Blackwell Business, pp. 282–96.

Yemin, E. (ed.) (1982) *Workforce Reductions in Undertakings*, International Labour Office.

See also: Closing down; Early retirement; Job sharing; Outplacement counselling; Recruitment; Sabbaticals

Down-up-down-up problem-solving method

This participative problem-solving method described by Gordon consists of four steps. First, senior managers take a problem they are facing *down* through several levels in the organizational hierarchy: for example, the divisional managers may be asked to conduct meetings with their heads of departments to discuss the problem and share their views and suggestions. These departmental heads then conduct similar meetings with their own supervisors, and the supervisors hold meetings with their subordinates. In step two, all the ideas produced by these small groups are taken *up* the hierarchy to senior management. In step three, senior management delegates examination of the suggestions to a task group chaired by a functional head and another member of senior management. Their job is to assess the ideas and identify a solution which would include employees' suggestions. The proposed plan is then sent *down* the line to the groups that took part in step one. These groups evaluate the plan, and make a decision whether to accept it, reject it, or to accept it but with modifications. Finally, the decision of each of the groups is sent *up* the hierarchy to senior management, which makes the final modifications and adopts the amended plan.

Gordon, T. (1979) *LET: Leadership Effectiveness Training*, Futura Books, p. 229.

See also: Brainstorming; Evaluation committee method; Kepner-Tregoe approach

Dramatic skit (playmaking; theatre)

In traditional education, communication tends to take the form of essays or reports, answers to questions, and speech presentations. A less common format is the creation and performance of a play – playmaking, which involves the use of dialogue and action to interpret situations and events. This is similar to the popular role-play technique, in which people either play themselves or respond according to guidelines presented in a briefing. However, in playmaking there is an objective, the play usually lasts longer and involves a more fully developed plot, and students rehearse and perform from a script they have written and memorized.

Dramatic skits enable knowledge and experience to be presented in a manner which encourages the audience to become emotionally involved. Abstract concepts and theories may be clarified by portraying them in realistic situations with which the audience can identify, and the opportunity to relate to the various characters in turn helps the audience gain insights into their feelings and attitudes.

Full-length plays may be used for ambitious projects where there are no time limitations. *Situation stagings* or creations may deal with only part of a particular situation or problem, but they need to be supplemented by other methods. They lend themselves well to re-enacting courtroom dramas, conventions and legislative bodies in session. *Playlets* are small-scale productions dealing with a discrete problem area or an aspect of a larger problem. They may be used alone to prepare for exploration of a problem using other methods, or a series of playlets may be combined to portray successive stages in the development of a relationship between two or three people, and a short dialogue can develop sufficient background for a surprise or quick ending.

The Globe Theatre in London, in association with Cranfield School of Management, has offered a two-day 'Stepping into Management' course. Developing the metaphor of a manager playing different roles, this event uses the performing arts to enhance an individual's flexibility, innovativeness and ability to inspire others, and stresses the importance of team working. Although it is based on Shakespeare's texts, it neither analyses them nor teaches the participating managers acting techniques. Instead, it uses the plays as case studies to explore issues encountered by Shakespeare's characters which are also faced by contemporary managers, such as Henry V's problem of stepping into a key role and trying to unite a team around a common goal. The Royal Shakespeare Company also offers management consultancy drawing on the theatre, where acting techniques are applied to develop creativity, team-building, communication and presentation styles (including voice workshops). Agfa, Tarmac, Mindshare, WPP Group and Origin are some of the companies which have used this method.

Bentley, N., Guthrie, D. and Arnsteen, K.K. (1996) *Putting on a Play: A Young Playwright's Guide to Scripting, Directing and Performing*, Millbrook Press.

Brooks, H. (1993) *Making It: A Three Act Play*, I.E. Clark Inc.

Cook, C. (1972) 'The Play Way', in Hodgson, J. (ed.) *The Uses of Drama: Acting as a Social and Educational Force*, Eyre Methuen.

Finn, W. (1998) 'Complete Works with Shakespeare', *The Daily Telegraph Appointments*, 2 July, p. A6.

Golden-Biddle, K. (1993) 'Organizational Drama and Dramatic Stagings About Them', *Journal of Management Education*, vol. 17, no. 1, pp. 39–49.

Greenberg, E. (1995) 'Improv in the Classroom: An Experiential Exercise', *Journal of Management Education*, vol. 19, no. 4, pp. 519–22.

Greenberg, E. and Miller, P. (1991) 'The Player and the Professor: Theatrical Techniques in Teaching', *Journal of Management Education*, vol. 15, pp. 428–46.

Jackson, G. (1998) *Impro Learning*, Gower.

Kerr, M.M. (1995) 'Project 2000 Student Nurses Take the Stage with Interactive Drama to Facilitate Health Promotion', *Innovations in Educa-*

tion and Training International, vol. 32, no. 2, pp. 162–74.

Merrick, N. (1998) 'Theatrical Treatment', People Management, 22 January, pp. 44–6.

Molden, D. (1998) 'Making a Drama Out of a Crisis', Professional Manager, November, pp. 22–4.

Moore, P. (1997) Acting Out, Gower.

Murtuza, A. (1987) 'Dramatic Monologues as Surrogates for Experiential Learning', Developments in Business Simulation and Experiential Learning, vol. 14, pp. 144–6.

Pryor, N. (1994) Putting on a Play, Wayland Publishers.

Royal Society of Arts (1996) The Arts Matter: Work, Creativity and the Arts, RSA.

Rueschoff, M.S. (1990) 'Theatre in the OB Classroom: To Role Play or Not to Role Play – That is the Question', Organizational Behaviour Teaching Review, vol. 14, no. 3, pp. 105–8.

See also: Case with role-play; Character immersion; Inner dialogue; Model; Monodrama; Museum learning; Music for learning; Novels for learning; Poetry for learning; Reading aloud; Rewriting; Role-playing; Sociodrama; Storytelling

Drawing for learning

In this technique, group members are asked to produce large drawings portraying some aspect of an individual's life, such as their current situation or their hopes and desires, or an aspect of the nature of the organization. Participants may find it difficult to complete the task unless the facilitator gives clear instructions. Each drawing should focus on a limited number of subjects, and the group must understand what the activity is intended to achieve.

The drawings are then displayed on the walls, and their creators are asked to discuss them with the group, who should be encouraged to ask questions about the creator's meaning, rather than trying to engage in clever interpretations. The facilitator helps the group identify common themes and problems or significant differences of opinion, and writes these down for all to see.

This method can help to unearth group issues which may have been lying beneath the surface, such as unhelpful forms of competition or the existence of cliques, and can also be used to formulate an agenda for a team-building meeting. The information the drawings produce – a mixture of facts and feelings – can provide a useful entry into discussion of sensitive subjects.

Edwards, B.A. (1979) Drawing on the Right Side of the Brain, J.P. Tarcher Inc.

Fordyce, J.K. and Weil, R. (1971) Managing With People, Addison Wesley Longman, pp. 153–5.

Furth, G.M. (1988) The Secret World of Drawings, Sigo Press.

Goza, B.K. (1993) 'Graffiti Needs Assessment: Involving Students in the First Class Session', Journal of Management Education, vol. 17, no. 1, pp. 99–106.

McCaskey, M.B. (1977) 'Goals and Directions in Personnel Planning', Academy of Management Review, vol. 3, pp. 454–62.

Meyer, A. (1991) 'Visual Data in Organizational Research', Organization Science, vol. 2, no. 2, pp. 218–36.

Vince, R. (1995) 'Working with Emotions in the Change Process: Using Drawings for Team Diagnosis and Development', Organisations and People, vol. 2, no. 1, pp. 11–17.

See also: Apperception interaction method; Attitude survey; Chronology charting; Collages; Diagnostic activities; Family group diagnostic meeting; Family group team-building meeting; Fortune lining; Group posters tours; Illuminative incident analysis; Inter-organizational information-sharing; Interviewing; Metaphor approach; Music for learning; Novels for learning; Physical representation of organizations; Poetry for learning; Questionnaires; Responsibility charting; Storyboarding

Drill-and-practice method

Although the terms 'drill' and 'practice' are frequently used interchangeably, 'drill' refers to an activity carried out in a step-by-step manner under the immediate direction of an instructor (e.g., fire drill), whereas 'practice' refers to an activity in which the learner can engage either under instruction or alone.

The difference between knowing how an operation should be carried out and being skilled in its performance has long been recognized. People usually learn the requirements for a given activity through problem-solving, project execution and trial-and-error methods, but sometimes it may be necessary to be able to perform an act with such speed and accuracy that it is necessary to avoid reflection, so that it becomes second nature. In such cases, the use of drill may be appropriate.

Drill is the repetition of facts or activities in order to form a strong and lasting association or perfect a skill. Drilling cannot be conducted until some degree of learning has been achieved. How permanently that learning becomes fixed depends on the amount and types of drill employed. While mere repetition is not education, repetition coupled with attention may help students develop new or deeper insights, interpretations or applications. Drill itself does not teach new facts or ideas, but students may learn through their own curiosity, reassessments, explorations, mental experimentation and interesting associations that churn around their minds while performing the repetitive drill task.

Practice activities are more important than drill in adult business and industrial learning programmes. When trainees progress to the point where they can practise an entire procedure, lesson or activity, the point of the learning task becomes more apparent, the process becomes less arduous, and improvement accelerates – hence the importance of structuring practice into meaningful units. It is also useful to keep periods of instructor dominance brief and to vary their nature as much as possible.

In many educational contexts, computers are used for drill-and-practice purposes: for example, language learning. Their advantages are that they can be used interactively, presenting problems which require a student response, they can provide immediate feedback which tells students whether they are correct or incorrect, and they possess infinite patience and never get tired. An element of fun and challenge can also be introduced by turning the exercise into a game, as in some computer software designed to teach maths and grammar to children.

See also: Demonstration-performance method; Discovery method; Lesson-demonstration method; Mathetics; Rote learning

Early retirement (early retirement incentive programme)

Early retirement means leaving work before the conventional retirement age of 65. Early retirement policies usually come into operation after 55, although they may start as early as 45. Some early retirement plans are only offered for a limited period, so the decision must be made by a fixed date, frequently only a few months ahead. In the USA, less than 1 in 5 men and 1 in 10 women remain in the workforce until they are 65.

Early retirement is increasingly being viewed as an alternative to layoffs, and some people find it an attractive alternative to continuing in an unsatisfactory job. It also offers financial benefits to the company: it can make room for younger managers on substantially lower salaries. Those who retire early are paid reduced pensions – this is an important consideration for pension fund managers, since increasing longevity means that a company may find that its commitment to pension funding for some retired employees exceeds what they paid them in salaries during their career. However, these gains are balanced by the need to begin paying pensions early.

Retirement can take many forms. *Phased retirement* is a gradual progression to full-time retirement over a period of up to five years. The transition may take the form of increasingly long holidays. The advantage of this approach is that it can allow a mutually beneficial consulting and training relationship to develop, where the employee's expertise continues to be available to the company, and they can act as a mentor to younger staff while enjoying a gradual reduction in responsibility.

Phased retirement is only one of a number of options. The others include: *interrupted retirement*, where the employee takes a half-year break and then returns to another position in the same or a different organization; *semi-retirement*, where they transfer to a part-time job in the same or a different company; *consulting retirement*, where they act as a full-time or part-time consultant for the organization, and *dream retirement*, where they start a new career, perhaps in a field they have previously considered a hobby. When people retire, they often find it difficult to cope with the sudden change of lifestyle, so many employers offer retirement counselling and pre-retirement programmes.

Bermel, M. and Lazarus, H. (1985) 'America is Retiring Early', *European Management Journal*, vol. 3, no. 3, pp. 161–4.

Bradford, L.P. (1979) 'Retirement: A Concern of Organizational Behaviour', *Exchange: The Organization Behaviour Teaching Journal*, vol. 3, no. 1, pp. 21–4.

Feldman, D.C. (1994) 'The Decision to Retire Early: A Review and Reconceptualization', *Academy of Management Review*, vol. 19, pp. 285–311.

Gravitz, D.H. and Rumack, F.W. (1983) 'Opening the Early Retirement "Window"', *Personnel*, vol. 60, March–April, pp. 53–7.

Greenberg, K. (1983) 'Why Encourage Early Retirement?', *Advanced Management Journal*, vol. 48, pp. 19–20.

Hughes, K. (1992) *Retirement Counselling*, McGraw-Hill.

Reynolds, P. and Bailey, M. (1993) *How To Design and Deliver Early Retirement Training*, Kogan Page.

Riker, H.C. and Myers, J.E. (1990) *Retirement Counselling: A Handbook for Action*, Hemisphere Publishing Corporation.

Sinick, D. (1978) *Counselling Older Persons: Careers, Retirement, Death*, Human Sciences Press.

Toulson, N. (1987) *Preparing Staff for Retirement*, Ashgate Publishing.

'When the Baby Boomers Retire' (1996), special issue of *Compensation & Benefits Review*.

See also: Alcohol recovery programme; Career life planning; Closing down; Downsizing; Job rotation; Outplacement counselling; Sabbaticals

Educational visit

Educational visits – whether to a local museum, a factory or a foreign country – are a familiar feature of many people's schooldays, and can be very useful in management study courses, especially if they provide first-hand knowledge or experience of something which cannot be brought into the classroom. Such visits can help students relate theory to practice by observing objects, actions, people or problems in their natural setting. They may be able to witness procedures they may later duplicate in their own work environments, and may have the opportunity for learning by doing. In addition to providing opportunities for new experiences, going on an excursion together can also help students get to know each other better away from the relatively formal classroom environment, and may provide a valuable stimulus for discussion activities following the visit.

On the other hand, visits are usually expensive and time-consuming. Some studies suggest that video presentations or slide-illustrated lectures can be just as effective, and they are obviously considerably cheaper. The main advantages of visits seem to lie in realizing cognitive objectives to a limited extent, but more especially affective ones.

The timing of a visit during a course depends on the lecturer's objectives. It may be scheduled late in the programme to summarize and consolidate material initially presented by more traditional methods, or it can serve to introduce a subject.

Whatever the purpose of the visit, it is essential that the organizer prepares thoroughly and considers issues such as the travel plans, including departure and arrival times and locations, arrangements for meals if necessary, and any additional resources required. The students should be briefed beforehand about the cost and travel arrangements, what is expected of them, what clothing they should take, the visit's objectives, any particular points to look out for, and the nature of any follow-up activities.

Butler, B.H. and Sussman, M.B. (eds) (1990) *Museum Visits and Activities for Family Enrichment*, Haworth Press.
LeUnes, A., Christensen, L. and Wilerson, D. (1975) 'Institutional Tour Effects on Attitudes Related to Mental Retardation', *American Journal of Mental Deficiency*, vol. 79, pp. 732–5.
Perkins, D.C. (ed.) (1987) *School Visits, Tours, Outings, Holidays: A Guide*, Domino Books.
Smart, J. (1995) *Educational Visits*, Practical Management.
Upton, D.M. and Macadam, S.E. (1997) 'Why (and How) to Take a Plant Tour', *Harvard Business Review*, May–June, pp. 97–106.

See also: Field format; Field trip; Intervisitation; Management systems study; Outdoor training; Studycade

Employee assistance programme

Some companies offer employee assistance programmes (EAPs) to help their staff overcome personal and health-related problems. They developed from alcohol recovery programmes established in the USA by Kodak, Du Pont and Standard Oil in the 1940s. The range of problems addressed still includes different forms of addiction (Campbell's Soup Co., for example, offers psychiatric and substance abuse help) but now also covers such problems as sexual harassment and bullying at work. EAPs enable a company to demonstrate a tangible commitment to its staff, reduce the problems of absenteeism and sick leave and, in the USA, have cut companies' health care insurance premiums by up to 30 per cent.

Some companies set up an EAP department run by employee assistance officers whose role is similar to that of an ombudsman or counsellor, while others sub-contract an external, specialist agency. If an employee has been unable to resolve a problem, question or complaint by discussing it with their supervisor, manager, department head or district administrator, or feels uncomfortable raising the issue with their superiors, they can approach an employee assistance officer. Confidentiality is assured, and the officer will only discuss the issue with someone else if the employee gives permission.

Blum, T.C. and Roman, P.M. (1985) 'Employee Assistance Programmes and Human Resources Management', in Ferris, G.R. and Rowland, K.M. (eds) *Research in Personnel and Human Resource Management*, JAI Press.
Cunningham, G. (1994) *Effective Employee Assistance Programmes: A Guide for EAP Counsellors and Managers*, Sage.
Nicholas, G. (1991) 'How To Make Employee Assistance Programs More Productive', *Supervision*, July, pp. 3–6.
Smits, S.J. and Pace, L.A. (1992) *The Investment Approach to Employee Assistance Programmes*, Quorum Books/Greenwood Publishing.

See also: Affirmative action; Alcohol recovery programme; Alternative dispute-resolution; Counselling; Let's-talk-it-over programme; Ombudsman

Employee letters (speak-out programme; open line programme)

Many companies actively encourage their employees to write letters to management expressing their concerns or putting forward ideas. For instance, when Henry Ford II instituted his new industrial relations policy in the 1940s, one of his first steps was to write to his employees, encouraging them all to send letters directly to him, telling him what they thought of the policy. In addition to obtaining information, this approach shows employees that management is interested in their viewpoint, and that they can communicate their opinions to the very top if they wish.

The first programme inviting employees to submit letters was inaugurated in 1947 as the 'My Job Contest' by the General Motors Corporation and, in the 1980s, the Bank of America introduced a similar approach, which it called 'Open Line'. Printed forms were distributed to employees, who could address any questions they had to the Open Line Co-ordinator. Whenever a form was received, the writer's details were replaced by a number and a subject code to preserve confidentiality. The question or concern was then typed on a plain sheet of paper and forwarded to the appropriate bank official, who was required to respond within ten days. The responses were usually sent to the writer's home, but if preferred they could attend an interview with the official to discuss the answer. With the writer's permission, if the issues were of general interest, the question and answer might also be printed in the house magazine.

One way to encourage employee letters is to publish a 'rumour clinic' column in the company magazine or journal. Employees send in rumours they have heard, which are either confirmed or denied. A broader approach is a column entitled 'Answers to Your Questions' or 'Employee Letters'.

Ewing, D.B. and Banks, P.M. (1980) 'Listening and Responding to Employees', *Harvard Business Review*, January–February, vol. 81, pp. 101–14.
Foulkes, F.K. (1981) 'Top Non-union Companies Manage Employees', *Harvard Business Review*, September–October, pp. 90–6.

See also: Chairman's forum; Family communication programme; Information-sharing meetings; Let's-talk-it-over programme; Management information meeting; Open forums; Suggestion schemes; Team briefing

Employee volunteering

Nearly nine million people in the UK serve as volunteers in more than a million non-profitmaking organizations. Many do so on an individual basis, but others participate through company schemes. The 'Employees in the Community' scheme, sponsored by the charity Business in the Community, attracted 152 competitors in 1994, indicating the growing popularity of this approach among major employers such as Marks and Spencer, the Royal Mail, Whitbread and IBM UK.

Some companies establish a volunteer committee to decide which schemes they will become involved in, ranging from tree planting or pond cleaning to taking disabled children for a day out. They see this as a developmental technique because the volunteers draw on talents and skills they would not normally be able to exercise in their jobs. In return, the non-profitmaking organizations obtain free advice from the volunteers on matters such as time management, team-building, job descriptions and staff appraisal, in addition to practical assistance.

Some volunteer programmes, such as IBM's scheme, allow staff half a day's paid leave every week, but if staff act as volunteers in their own time, their managers are encouraged to be flexible. Companies can organize their training and development programmes to incorporate community projects which involve employee volunteers. This in turn can form the basis for secondments. There are also advantages in terms of increasing employee morale, improving internal communications, developing employees' skills, and promoting a caring public image of the organization.

The success of volunteer programmes depends to a large extent on the management abilities of the non-profitmaking organizations. It is important to draw up a comprehensive strategy which addresses questions such as how to attract and recruit volunteers, how to train and integrate them into the organization's structure, how to manage them, and what responsibilities they should be given. Both managers and volunteers must have a clear understanding of their respective roles and responsibilities, and they also need to be familiar with issues such as standard employment law and risk management.

Connors, T.D. (ed.) (1995) *The Volunteer Management Handbook*, Wiley.
De Pree, M. (1997) *Leading Without Power: Hope in Serving the Community*, Jossey-Bass.
Hedley, R. (1992) *Volunteering and Society*, National Centre for Volunteering.
McSweeney, P. and Alexander, D. (1996) *Managing Volunteers Effectively*, Gower.
Pidgeon, W.J. (1997) *Universal Benefits of Volunteering*, Wiley.
Platt, S. (1994) 'Charity Begins at Home', *Personnel Today*, 8 February, pp. 27–8.
Thomas, A. (1990) *On Volunteering*, National Centre for Volunteering.

Wilson, M. (1990) *You Can Make a Difference: Helping Others and Yourself Through Volunteering*, Volunteer Management Association (USA).

See also: Assignment to community organization; Secondment

Employee-designed rules

When employees participate in drawing up company rules, the workforce is more likely to internalize and comply with them. For example, some companies have invited employees to develop rules on attendance, and the appropriate sanctions against those who transgress them are determined jointly by employee and management representatives.

See also: Discipline without punishment; Employee-guided management; Information-sharing meetings; Likert's levels meetings; Norm modification; Participation; Self-generated scaling

Employee-guided management

Employee-guided management (EGM) is a participative approach which uses information obtained from employees to guide choices on management decisions and actions which affect their job security, skills, performance and attitudes. EGM incorporates the principles of participative decision-making, performance feedback and survey feedback into comprehensive employee involvement programmes which seek to provide information, formulate policy, carry out action strategies, and evaluate outcomes. EGM has been applied to such diverse activities as a workforce reduction programme, a project to monitor employee attitudes because of a morale problem, and a company relocation, and consists of eight major components.

First, it is necessary to *decide the purpose of the intervention*. EGM may be used to deal with a short-term crisis, or it can be applied as a long-term organizational change approach. It may be used to 'take the temperature' of the organization, or as an inter-personal tool to examine workgroup relations.

The second stage is to *determine the type of information to be collected*. This will vary in content (depending on whether the objectives are task or process ones), in the degree of subjectivity required (whether cognitive, affective or behavioural information is sought), in the level of aggregation (at the individual, group or organizational level), and in frequency, timeliness and specificity.

The next step is to *choose the information source*. Since each employee will have their own perceptions of the organization, and reactions to it, it will be necessary to gather data from a range of individuals and groups, including subordinates, peers, superiors and outsiders.

The fourth stage is to *decide on the data-collection method*. Any existing data-collection methods can be used, including surveys, questionnaires and interviews, usually in combination.

Once the information is obtained, the next stage is to *design the feedback process*, deciding who will receive the feedback, and in what form. The guiding principle is that feedback should be given to those who are accountable for the data and who control the factors affecting it. Feedback is most effective if it can be provided quickly, allowing the recipients to participate by asking questions and discussing the results. In some cases aggregated data will be more useful than individual comments. An important consideration is how this information will be used by those responsible for doing something about the situation. They are more likely to act on it if they accept the findings and can attribute them to factors under their control. They also need to be assured that the potential benefits exceed the costs, and that these are great enough to make the action worthwhile.

The final stages, *monitoring the process* and *identifying and measuring the relevant outcomes for evaluation purposes*, are designed to keep the EGM process running smoothly. It is vital to check that the outcomes at each stage are achieved: for example, that a clear purpose for EGM has been defined, and that feedback is being provided.

Ashford, S.J. and Cummings, L.L. (1983) 'Feedback as an Individual Resource: Personal Strategies of Creating Information', *Organizational Behaviour and Human Performance*, vol. 32, pp. 320–98.

Ilgen, D.R., Fisher, C.D. and Taylor, M.S. (1979) 'Consequences of Individual Feedback on Behaviour in Organizations', *Journal of Applied Psychology*, vol. 64, pp. 34–9.

Landen, D.L., Bluestone, I. and Lawler, E.E. (1995) 'High Involvement Organizations and Industrial Democracy', in Ferris, G.R., Rosen, S.D. and Barnum, D.T. (eds) *Handbook of Human Resource Management*, Blackwell Business, pp. 370–85.

London, M. (1985) 'Employee-guided Management: Steps for Involving Employees in Decisions and Actions', *Leadership and Organization Development Journal*, vol. 6, no. 1, pp. 3–8.

See also: Employee-designed rules; Goal-setting interface groups; Informal action group; Open forums; Participation; Suggestion schemes; Survey feedback interventions; Worker directors

Empowerment

Empowerment involves senior management creating a workplace culture which encourages all employees to take responsibility for their own decisions and actions, and to develop their full potential for the benefit of the organization. This means that the organization must trust the competence and commitment of its employees; share information freely and replace the top-down style of management with a more democratic model.

Many managers fear that this approach may lead to anarchy, and loss of authority and control over management processes. However, whether they work individually or in teams, empowered people feel a strong sense of ownership of their work and its outcomes, gain greater job satisfaction and are more highly motivated, and these factors lead to higher-quality work and a sense of achievement, creating a positive, upward spiral. Hence – paradoxically – managers who empower their staff do not give up their own power to achieve results, but enhance it.

Empowerment is not mere delegation. It harnesses the power of skilful, motivated employees, and demands that they define their purpose and their goals, and participate in creating the kind of work culture they desire. It increases their emotional investment in the organizational community, and leads to a greater commitment to its vision and goals.

Argyris, C. (1998) 'Empowerment: The Emperor's New Clothes', *Harvard Business Review*, May–June, pp. 98–105.

Brown, R. and Brown, M. (1996) *Empowered: A Practical Guide to Leadership*, The Industrial Society/Nicholas Brealey Publishing.

Cook, S. and McCauley, S. (1996) *Perfect Empowerment*, Constable.

Foy, N. (1997) *Empowering People at Work*, Gower.

Ginnodo, B. (ed.) (1997) *The Power of Empowerment: What the Experts Say and 16 Actionable Case Studies*, Pride Publications Inc.

Isaak, R. (1995) 'The Open Syllabus and the White Paper "Student Empowerment Through Benchmarking"', *Journal of Management Education*, vol. 19, no. 3, pp. 342–6.

Johnson, R. and Redmond, D. (1998) *The Art of Empowerment*, Pitman.

Kinlaw, D.C. (1995) *The Practice of Empowerment*, Gower.

Lucas, J.R. (1998) *Balance of Power: Authority or Empowerment*, American Management Association, AMACOM.

Rooke, D. and Jones, M. (1994) 'Empowerment: Lessons from Northern Telecom', *Organisations and People*, vol. 1, no. 3, pp. 21–6.

Smith, J. (1996) *Empowering People*, Kogan Page.

Wilkinson, A. (1998) 'Empowerment: Theory and Practice', *Personnel Review*, vol. 27, no. 1, pp. 40–56.

Wilson, T. (1996) *The Empowering Manager*, Gower.

Woods, M., Whetten, D. and Cameron, K. (1996) *Effective Empowerment and Delegation*, Harper-Collins.

See also: Bottom-up management; Delegation; Manager as consultant; Open-book management; Participation; Planned delegation

Encounter group

In an encounter group, participants are encouraged to say what they really feel, to feel what they are saying, hearing or doing, and generally to experience and share their own view of the world in an atmosphere of total honesty. In normal circumstances, individuals would find this too risky, since we all have aspects of ourselves we do not wish to reveal to others for fear of rejection. Proponents of this approach argue that taking this risk in a carefully controlled environment leads to improvements in self-image.

Encounter groups are often used as an individual change approach, especially as part of organizational development programmes. There are two main types, and both can be applied to organizational change: the *basic encounter* or *Rogersian* group, based on the work of Carl Rogers and his associates, and the *open encounter* group, developed by Bill Schutz at the Esalen Institute in California.

Burton, A. (ed.) (1969) *Encounter: Theory and Practice of Encounter Groups*, Social and Behavioural Science Series, Jossey-Bass.

Egan, G. (1970) *Encounter: Group Processes for Interpersonal Growth*, Brooks/Cole Publishing Company.

Rogers, C.R. (1970) *Carl Rogers on Encounter Groups*, Harper and Row.

Siroka, R.W., Soroka, E.K. and Schloss, G.A. (1971) *Sensitivity Training and Group Encounter: An Introduction*, Grosset and Dunlop.

See also: Basic encounter; Classroom meeting model; Cluster laboratory; Cousin laboratory; Gestalt techniques; Group development laboratory; Human relations laboratory; Instrumented laboratory; Laboratory training; Micro-lab; Open encounter; Organizational laboratory; Personal development laboratory; Psychodrama; Sensitivity (T-group) training; Tavistock Conference Method

Ergonomics (biomechanics; human factors engineering)

Ergonomics (from the Greek *ergon*, 'work', and *nomos*, 'law') is the study of the relationship between human beings and their work environment in order to maximize efficiency. In the USA, the term 'human engineering' is preferred.

Ergonomics developed in the Second World War, when human endurance was tested to its limits, but recent publicity and law suits concerning repetitive strain injury (RSI) have forced managers to direct their attention to how the design of equipment such as desks, chairs and computers can enhance or detract from productivity.

This is an interdisciplinary approach involving engineers, physiologists, anatomists and experimental psychologists, whose research findings have been used by organizations both to create optimal working conditions and to help design products for customers.

Although similar to motion study in some ways, ergonomics is more sophisticated since it draws on individuals' assessments of their workplace conditions and their reactions to them, identifies which parts of the body are most susceptible to injury, particularly in automated processes, and explores how they can be protected.

The main fields of study in ergonomics include: *visual tasks* (brightness, colour and gaze), *visual display* (speed and accuracy of reading symbols), *sound and hearing* (noise frequency intervals), *atmospheric conditions* (comfort, range and tolerance), *motor activities* (strength, force and speed) and *space requirements* (body measurement, machine design and location of controls).

Oborne, D.J. (1995) *Ergonomics at Work*, Wiley.

O'Neill, M.J. (1998) *Ergonomic Design for Organizational Effectiveness*, Lewis Publishers.

Ostrom, L.T. (1994) *Creating the Ergonomically Sound Workplace*, Jossey-Bass.

Shaffer, W.A. and Cross, R. (1996) *ErgoWise: A Personal Guide to Making Your Workplace Comfortable and Safe*, American Management Association.

See also: Physical interventions in organizations

Essay

Although essays tend to be considered primarily as a means of assessing students, in many subjects they constitute the principal learning medium. How much students learn by writing an essay depends not only on the degree of preparation, study and organization they devote to completing it, but also the nature and detail of the comments, both verbal and written, their tutor makes in response.

If essays are being used to promote learning rather than for assessment – that is, for formative rather than summative evaluation – the feedback to the student needs to be quite detailed. Minimal feedback consists of a grade and perhaps a short written comment at the end such as 'Quite good'. This tells students little, since they do not know precisely what 'quite good' means or what aspects it refers to. It is much more helpful if the grade is supplemented by a series of indicators in the margin which relate to more detailed comments on a separate sheet covering the overall structure of the essay, any omissions or errors, and the reasons for awarding the grade. An even more sophisticated approach would be for the tutor to discuss the essay with the student in person, perhaps pointing out alternative approaches they could have adopted. The learning opportunities can be enhanced further in several ways.

The student can be invited to select an area for study, carry out the research and draw up a draft plan for the essay which they then discuss with the tutor before completing it. An alternative is ask the student to use the essay not only as a means of learning something, but also as a way of learning how to learn by practising their research, essay planning and writing skills and exploring different ways of presenting information. A development of this approach involves the student first writing an essay on a chosen topic in the normal way. In response, the tutor offers a detailed counterpoint to some of the views and ideas expressed in the student's work, perhaps running to two or three pages. This and the original essay are returned to the student, who is then invited to respond to the tutor's comments.

Barrass, R. (1995) *Students Must Write* (2nd edn), Routledge.

Creme, P. (1996) 'Kate's Story: Helping a Student With Essay Writing', *Innovations in Education and Training International*, vol. 33, no. 3, pp. 197–202.

Creme, P. and Lea, M.R. (1997) *Writing at University: A Guide for Students*, Open University Press.

Dean, K.C. (1995) *Essentials of the Essay: Reading, Writing and Grammar*, Allyn and Bacon.

Fairbairn, G.J. and Winch, C. (1996) *Reading, Writing and Reasoning* (2nd edn), Open University Press.

Foreman, J. (ed.) (1995) *What Do I Know? Reading, Writing and Teaching the Essay*, Boynton/Cook Publishers.

Good, S. and Jensen, B. (1995) *The Student's Only Survival Guide to Essay Writing*, Orca Book Publishers.

Henderson, E.S. (1980) 'The Essay in Continuous Assessment', *Studies in Higher Education*, vol. 5, no. 2, pp. 197–203.

Lewis, R. (1993) *How To Write Essays*, Harper-Collins.

McCormick, D.W. and Smith, K.E. (1992) 'Integrating Theory and Experience in the Short Essay', *Journal of Management Education*, vol. 16, no. 4, pp. 499–502.

Nimmo, D. B. (1977) 'The Undergraduate Essay: A Case of Neglect?', *Studies in Higher Education*, vol. 2, no. 2, pp. 183–9.

Palmer, B. (1990) 'Writing and Teaching Writing: The Inner and Outer Game', *Management Education and Development*, vol. 21, no. 2, pp. 104–10.

Prosser, M. and Webb, C. (1994) 'Relating the Process of Undergraduate Essay Writing to the Finished Product', *Studies in Higher Education*, vol. 19, no. 2, pp. 125–38.

Roberts, D. (1997) *The Student's Guide to Writing Essays*, Kogan Page.

See also: Assignment attachment; Book reviewing; Examination; Literature search; Rewriting

Evaluation audit assignment (quality assessment project)

This development activity requires managers to carry out research into a subject such as an individual, a new technology or an information system, develop criteria for their evaluation, obtain the data necessary to complete it, and present a report with supporting evidence.

A popular topic for such an assignment is a company's training programme. In addition to developing their evaluation skills, it can help managers familiarize themselves with a function that is particularly relevant to increasing the performance of employees and the organization.

Bassi, L.J. and Russ-Eft, D. (eds) (1997) *What Works: Assessment, Development and Measurement*, American Society for Training and Development, ASTD Press.

Bloomfield, S.D. and Paschhke, P.E. (1997) 'Quality Assessment Projects as Teaching and Learning Tools', *Journal of Management Education*, vol. 21, no. 1, pp. 73–86.

Parry, S.B. (1997) *Evaluating the Impact of Training*, American Society for Training and Development, ASTD Press.

Phillips, J.J. (ed.) (1991) *Handbook of Training Evaluation and Measurement Methods*, Kogan Page.

Phillips, J.J. (ed.) (1994) *In Action: Measuring Return on Investment, Volume 1*, American Society for Training and Development, ASTD Press.

Phillips, J.J. (1997) *Handbook of Training Evaluation*, American Society for Training and Development, ASTD Press.

Phillips, J.J. (ed.) (1997) *In Action: Measuring Return on Investment, Volume 2*, American Society for Training and Development, ASTD Press.

Phillips, J.J. (1997) *Return on Investment in Training and Performance Improvement Programmes*, American Society for Training and Development, ASTD Press.

Rae, L. (1997) *How To Measure Training Effectiveness*, Gower.

See also: Committee assignment; Consulting assignment; Development assignment; Proposal team assignment; Research assignment; Selection board assignment; Staff meeting assignment; Study assignment; Task force assignment

Evaluation committee method

This five-step participative approach to problem-solving was developed and described by Gordon.

The first step is to obtain senior management's permission for all divisional levels to participate in generating solutions to a particular problem defined by the managing director. In step two, a consultant runs a series of 60- to 90-minute brainstorming meetings with groups of employees from each division. Step three involves choosing a representative from each of the groups to serve on an ideas evaluation committee, which should represent all levels of the company. The committee functions without a chairperson, and is authorized to make final decisions. In step four, the committee is presented with three possible solutions to evaluate. It can either implement them, reject them, or study them further and reconvene to consider recommendations. Step five consists of the committee members holding brief presentation meetings to explain to their respective groups why certain solutions were rejected while others were adopted.

Gordon, T. (1979) *LET: Leadership Effectiveness Training*, Futura Books, pp. 230–3.

See also: Brainstorming; Down-up-down-up problem-solving method; Functional administrative control technique; Kepner-Tregoe approach; Multiple management; Synectics

Examination

Formal, written examinations remain an important part of student assessment systems in most management degree courses, and they are an entry requirement in certain fields. However, some students who gain high grades in course assignments conducted in their own time with ample opportunity for reading and reflection often fail to perform well in examinations. Responding to questions intelligently, coherently and comprehensively within well-defined and frequently tight time limits may simulate certain aspects of students' future work environment, but does not necessarily reflect their ability in others. Students can be helped to improve their techniques in preparation for their final exams if they are given access to marked versions of their classroom examination scripts written under similar constraints. Furthermore, examinations can provide learning opportunities if certain approaches are adopted, two of which are described here.

Halfway through a course, students can be invited to devise a list of questions for their end-of-course exam, with the tutor retaining the final choice over which to include. As a group, they agree criteria for a 'good question', then each develops their own list. Throughout the rest of the course, some class time is devoted every week to comparing, revising and refining a list of questions on which all can agree. The students eventually draw up a list of about ten questions ranked in order of preference, from which the tutor chooses, say, three compulsory ones. Since the process of selection, discussion, evaluation and selection requires students to reflect on and revise the course material, it offers a continuous learning opportunity.

An alternative or additional method is for students to agree, first individually and then in groups, criteria for what constitutes a good essay answer, allocating marks according to a ranking of their importance. They then derive a marking scheme in collaboration with the tutor. Having completed a piece of work on a topic chosen by themselves, the tutor or jointly, they or a fellow student mark it before comparing their rating with the tutor's, and the final mark is agreed in negotiation with the tutor.

See also: Essay; Learning contract; Question production; Self-tests; Student-planned learning

Exchange of persons (exchange)

If tensions have arisen within an organization, it may be useful to exchange members of antagonistic groups or departments in an attempt to improve relationships. The rationale underlying this intervention is that face-to-face communication and personal contact can help individuals develop a greater understanding of the other group's culture, goals and problems.

Experience has shown that this method of resolving inter-group differences is more effective if the employees chosen for exchange hold neither strong negative nor positive attitudes to the other group. If they are harbouring deeply rooted feelings of hostility, the exchange will probably just confirm their stereotypes and attitudes. Neutral members are most susceptible to influence and change, and are more likely to arrive at an objective evaluation of the inter-group situation.

To ensure success, a great deal of effort should be devoted to planning the exchange and working out the details of selection and assignment. The method works best if there is an overlap in technical competencies between the individuals exchanged, as in the case of two engineering groups which need to collaborate on a task.

Individual change is more likely if those exchanged are initially given support by some members of their own group. Communication between the exchanged employee and members of the host group may be resisted if the employee feels that this will violate their own group's norms. A reference group is crucial if one is seeking to change how one perceives another group and how one relates to its members.

Experiments involving the exchange of sub-groups rather than individuals have shown that changes in a whole group's attitude are more likely when they have already taken place in a significant sub-group. However, the exchange of sub-groups can pose problems when those exchanged hold a key position in their group: day-to-day operations which depend on them may be disrupted, and feelings of loss of affiliation, or betrayal and disloyalty may arise.

Margulies, N. and Wallace, J. (1973) *Organizational Change: Techniques and Applications*, Scott Foresman, pp. 130–1.

See also: Conflict-resolution techniques; Confrontation groups; Confrontation meeting; Criss-cross panels; LIFO method; Negotiation by group members; No-lose conflict-resolution method; Third-party peacemaking interventions

Executive Family Seminar

Some organizations, such as the British Foreign Service, offer assistance to the families of employees who work abroad. Although several large companies also offer this kind of help, it may be minimal. Few such programmes, except those at top management level, take the manager's partner into account, and this may lead to domestic and personal difficulties which can affect job performance.

To address these problems, Barrie Grieff, a psychiatrist at the Harvard Business School, developed a course called the Executive Family Seminar, based on acknowledgement that couples form an equal partnership in which both individuals should be highly valued. The seminar focuses on the process as well as on the activities of their relationship. It examines the relationship between individual managers, their families and the organization, and helps couples recognize that rather than simply reacting to external events, they can be proactive in designing their individual, marital and organizational lives.

The Executive Family Seminar studies the normal, dynamic development of talented, aggressive and perceptive couples in the business world who accept a high degree of risk and mobility. It also explores the trade-offs available to couples who lead active personal and professional lives. It analyses the myths of marriage, and examines the critical points in the human life cycle, giving participants the opportunity to interact with other couples in order to share experiences. The topics it addresses include the role of women in business, business travel and job relocation, dealing with success, the impact of job loss on a family, the dual-career couple, the decision whether or not to have children, the executive living abroad, divorce, extramarital affairs, and the psychological manifestations of stress.

Grieff, B. (1976) 'Executive Family Seminar: A Course for Graduate Married Business Students', *Journal of the American College Health Association*, vol. 24, no. 4, April.
Grieff, B.S. and Munter, P.K. (1979) *Trade-offs: Executive, Family and Organization*, Simon & Schuster.
Hon, D.C. (1983) *Trade Off: For the Person Who Can't Have Everything*, Pfeiffer/Jossey-Bass.

See also: Alcohol recovery programmes; Counselling; Family communication programme; Job support; Stress management

Exhibit

An exhibit is an item used for instruction. Just as a department of mechanical engineering in a college may have a cut-away car or aeroplane engine on display which is used for teaching students, and in the field of medicine, specimens of bodily organs are preserved for study, in management education a group discussion concerning aspects of plant layout may be helped by the use of a scaled-down model.

Miles, R.S. et al. (1988) *Design of Educational Exhibits*, Routledge.
Moss, M. (1974) 'Models as an Aid to Training', *Industrial and Commercial Training*, vol. 6, no. 7, pp. 314–17.

See also: Exhibition; Fair; Festival; Model; Museum learning; Poster; Storyboarding

Exhibition (exposition; trade show)

Exhibitions are popular teaching devices. Annual *stationary exhibitions* of products and services held in major cities around the world allow interested members of the public or the trade to visit and learn about the items on display, whereas *travelling exhibitions* visit different locations.

In recent years, the Inland Revenue has mounted travelling exhibitions to inform the public about changes in tax assessment policies, and other bodies such as the Blood Transfusion Service use travelling exhibitions to inform and educate the public and recruit donors.

Belcher, M. (1993) *Exhibitions in Museums*, Smithsonian Institute Press.
Cartwright, G. (1995) *Making the Most of Trade Shows*, Butterworth-Heinemann.
Maitland, I. (1997) *How To Plan Exhibitions*, Cassell Academic.
Montgomery, R. (1994) *Meetings, Conventions and Expositions: Introduction to the Industry*, Van Nostrand/Wiley.
Sixsmith, M. (ed.) (1995) *Touring Exhibitions: The Touring Exhibition's Group's Manual of Good Practice*, Butterworth-Heinemann.
Verlade, G. (1988) *Designing Exhibitions*, Ashgate Publishing.

See also: Exhibit; Fair; Festival; Museum learning

Expanding job assignment

In this managerial job-enrichment approach, a manager is given additional responsibilities: perhaps new areas or products to look after, or more power, authority and discretion in dealing with existing job tasks. The best way to achieve this is to motivate managers to expand their own work roles by seeking their opinions, including them in decision-making processes and delegating more authority to them.

See also: Acting assignment; Apprenticeship programme; Assignment to manager with high development skills; Development assignment; Planned delegation; Rotation training; Sick leave/holiday replacement assignment

Experience-based learning

Experience-based learning is difficult to define precisely, but it could be said that the key feature distinguishing it from other forms of learning is that it arises from the learner's first-hand experiences. This is not a specialized teaching approach in itself, but is incorporated in a variety of methods such as action learning, Coverdale Training, workshop activities, educational visits, internship programmes and a host of otherwise dissimilar approaches.

Allner, D. and Tiere, J. (1976) 'Experiential Learning: A View from the Inside, Part 1', *Industrial and Commercial Training*, vol. 8, no. 1, pp. 27–35.

Allner, D. and Tiere, J. (1976) 'Experiential Learning: A View from the Inside, Part 2', *Industrial and Commercial Training*, vol. 8, no. 2, pp. 73–8.

Allner, D. and Tiere, J. (1976) 'Experiential Learning: A View from the Inside, Part 3', *Industrial and Commercial Training*, vol. 8, no. 3, pp. 114–19.

Ayal, H. and Segev, E. (1976) 'Integrating the Didactic and Experiential Approaches in Management Education', *Journal of European Training*, vol. 5, no. 5, pp. 276–83.

Boud, D. and Walker, D. (1990) 'Making the Most of Experience', *Studies in Continuing Education*, vol. 12. No. 2, pp. 61–80.

Boydell, T.H. (1976) *Experiential Learning*, Manchester Monographs No. 5, Department of Adult Education, University of Manchester.

Keeton, M.T. and Tate, P.J. (eds) (1978) *Learning by Experience: What, Why and How?*, New Directions in Experiential Education No. 1, Jossey-Bass.

Keeton, M.T. et al. (1976) *Experiential Learning: Rationale, Characteristics and Assessment*, Jossey-Bass.

Kemp, B. (1979) 'A Local Government Experience with Experiential Learning', *Personnel Management*, vol. 11, no. 6, pp. 37–41.

Kolb, D.A. (1985) *Experiential Learning: Experience as a Source of Learning*, Prentice-Hall.

November, P. (1997) 'Learning to Teach Experientially: A Pilgrim's Progress', *Studies in Higher Education*, vol. 22, no. 3, pp. 289–99.

Roskin, R. (1976) 'Learning by Experience', *Journal of European Training*, vol. 5, no. 4, pp. 181–212.

Van Eynde, D.F. and Spencer, R.W. (1987-8) 'Lecture Versus Experiential Learning: Their Different Effects on Long Term Memory', *Organizational Behaviour Teaching Review*, vol. 12, no. 4, pp. 53–8.

See also: Action learning; Co-operative education; Coverdale Training Experiential exercise; Internship

Experiential exercise (experiential learning; substitute task exercise)

In a structured experiential exercise, learners are exposed to an intensive learning experience. This usually involves half a group carrying out a *substitute task*, such as constructing a model using building blocks or ranking a number of items, while the other half observes. The important factor is not so much what is done, but how it is done, so the tasks set are deliberately simple or childlike to avoid distracting from the process. In recent years there has been a dramatic increase in the number of such exercises, which have been widely published.

Experiential exercises are structured into pre-planned steps and follow a timetable involving short periods of activity of between half an hour and three hours. They are used to provide practical experience of theories or principles, so it is important that the tutor is clear about these and what the exercise is intended to contribute to the session and the course as a whole. It is helpful if the tutor has had previous experience of the exercise, and they should devote as much effort to planning the observation and post-task debriefing as they do to organizing the task itself. Participants and observers need to be given some form of conceptual framework or background beforehand, which might be a model (e.g., of decision-making styles) or a list of functions (e.g., Fayol's managerial activities).

Boud, D. and Miller, N. (1997) *Working with Experience: Animating Learning*, Kogan Page.

Bradford, D. and Eoyang, C. (1976) 'The Use and Misuse of Structured Exercises', in Cooper, C.L. (ed.) *Developing Social Skills in Managers: Advances in Group Training*, Macmillan.

Dennehy, R.F., Sims, R.R. and Collins, H.E. (1998) 'Debriefing Experiential: Learning Exercises: A Theoretical and Practical Guide for Success', *Journal of Management Education*, vol. 22, no. 1, pp. 9–25.

Hoberman, S. and Mailick, S. (1992) *Experiential Management Development*, Quorum Books.

Milligan, J. and Griffin, C. (ed.) (1992) *Empowerment Through Experiential Learning*, Kogan Page.

Olsen, J.P. (1996) *Lessons from Experience: Experiential Learning in Administration*, Scandinavian University Press.

Sims, R.R. (1990) *Experiential Learning Approach to Employee Training Systems*, Quorum Books.

Weil, S.W. (1990) *Making Sense of Experiential Learning*, Open University Press.

See also: Action maze; Behavioural simulation; Controlled-pace negotiation; Experience-based learning; In-basket exercise; Non-verbal exercise; Programmed simulation; Simulation

Exporting for others

This is one of several ways in which large companies are experimenting in their relationships with small companies that go beyond the traditional supplier–purchaser model. For example, some large companies take up the slack in their distribution or export functions by making these services available to smaller companies with which they are already associated.

See also: Independent product teams; Investing in a small company; Merger management intervention

Exposure to upper management

In this approach, a junior manager is temporarily assigned to work with either a single top-level manager or the senior management team. This allows junior managers to observe how senior management works, and in particular how decisions are made, and in turn senior managers are given the opportunity to assess their subordinates' performance and potential for development. Thus a senior management committee reviewing an aspect of company policy may include someone who is not necessarily knowledgeable about the topic, but who may benefit from being involved. There are usually a number of candidates for this form of training, and an individual's success or failure should not blind managers to the needs of their other staff members.

Another method is to invite subordinates to represent their managers at a meeting with top management, where they may present a project, answer questions and generally take on the manager's responsibilities. In this instance, it is essential that the subordinate is coached thoroughly beforehand.

See also: Acting assignment; Apprenticeship programme; Assignment to manager with high development skills; Job rotation; Job swop; Manager exchange; Manager shadowing; Mentoring; Sick leave/holiday replacement assignment

External mirror

An external mirror is a meeting where an organization invites a number of its key contacts, such as customers or suppliers, to provide feedback in order to draw up a list of specific areas where operations, products or services need to be improved. Such meetings are probably best run by an external consultant, who will explain the purposes of the event, stressing that its objective is to help the company to relate more effectively to all the interest groups with which it comes into contact.

While the sequence of activities may differ, the guests invited to provide feedback usually work individually first, noting down their observations of the company under a number of headings, such as 'image of product', 'value for money' and 'good payer'. The precise categories will depend on the purpose of the meeting and the membership of the group. Moving from general perceptions to specific instances, the guests then note down the basis for their judgements. Working in groups, they synthesize and organize the material before presenting it to the company representatives, who should listen to and absorb the feedback without becoming defensive, asking questions to ensure they understand what is being communicated.

After the guests have left, the company representatives hold discussions to formulate action plans to address the concerns that have been raised.

See also: Confrontation groups; Confrontation meeting; Customer interface meeting; Interface groups; Inter-group team-building; Organizational mirror; Sensing

Facilitation

Facilitation is the process of guiding a group, using a learner-centred mode of instruction. The facilitator can also be considered to be a group member. Many company trainers are reducing the emphasis on presenting information and giving instruction, placing greater stress on stimulating trainees to develop their own insights and learn for themselves. Many external consultants also see themselves as facilitators when working on organizational development projects.

Bee, R. and Bee, F. (1998) *Facilitation Skills*, Institute of Personnel and Development.
Casey, D., Roberts, P. and Salaman, G. (1992) 'Facilitating Learning in Groups', *Leadership and Organization Development Journal*, vol. 13, no. 4, pp. 8–13.
Clements, P. and Spinks, T. (1993) *A Practical Guide to Facilitation Skills*, Kogan Page.
Hackett, D. and Martin, C. L. (1993) *Facilitation Skills for Team Leaders*, Kogan Page.
Havergal, M. and Edmonstone, J. (1999) *The Facilitator's Toolkit*, Gower.
Heron, J. (1993) *Group Facilitation*, Kogan Page.

Howell, J.L. (1995) *Tools for Facilitating Team Meetings*, American Society for Training and Development, ASTD Press.

Hunter, D., Bailey, A. and Taylor, B. (1998) *The Facilitation of Groups*, Gower.

Kaner, S. et al. (1997) *The Facilitator's Guide to Participative Decision-making*, American Society for Training and Development, ASTD Press.

Rees, P. L. (1990) 'The Role of the Facilitator in Management', *Leadership and Organization Development Journal*, vol. 11, no. 7, pp. 11–16.

Robson, M. and Beary, C. (1995) *Facilitating*, Gower.

Wilson, J.B. (1995) *Applying Successful Training Techniques: A Practical Guide to Coaching and Facilitation Techniques*, Kogan Page.

See also: Coaching; Consultation

Fair

Traditional fairs are touring markets with a fixed schedule of visits to the same places each year, often including exhibits, amusements and other activities. In the past, some of these were 'hiring fairs', where employers and prospective employees could meet and negotiate terms for the year ahead. These ideas have been adapted to the business world in a variety of ways: for example, some companies run *graduate recruitment fairs*, business schools hold *MBA fairs* to attract potential students, and *trade fairs* can be used as a showcase and market for firms' goods and services. Fairs can also serve to generate publicity, promote standards of excellence, display the results of activities, demonstrate processes, engage community support or enlist new members for organizations. Fairs can be very effective in reaching people who do not read publications, listen to broadcasts or attend meetings or courses. As a learning opportunity, they are too transitory to achieve educational objectives in much depth, but they are probably one of the most effective methods for arousing interest.

Popli, R.S. (1990) *Trade Fair Management and Exhibit Marketing*, Deep and Deep Publications.

See also: Exhibit; Exhibition; Festival; Model; Museum learning

Family communication programme

An employee's work performance may be affected by a number of influences, the main one being family concerns. Family communication pro-grammes aim to integrate the employee's family into the organization's information network, and a number of strategies have been adopted to achieve this. A common practice is to mail the annual report, special letters from management or the company magazine to employees' homes so that family members can read them if they are interested. Some company publications have special pages for spouses and family members but, to be effective, the content of the articles must relate directly to the company. Organizing an 'open house' is another popular way to involve families, and this is particularly useful if they are normally unable to visit the workplace. In addition to these, American companies have a long tradition of holding picnics to allow families and staff to mix in an informal atmosphere.

See also: Alcohol recovery programme; Counselling; Employee letters; Executive Family Seminar; Greenfield plants; Job support; Stress management

Family group diagnostic meeting (diagnostic team meeting; manager's diagnostic team meeting)

In a family group diagnostic meeting, a manager and their immediate workgroup – their 'family' – conduct a general critique of their performance as a group. The main aim is to bring issues and problems to the surface so they can be considered. This method is usually used in preparation for a family group team-building meeting, and allows a group to identify both its weaknesses and its strengths.

The manager, who acts as facilitator, may suggest some topics, such as 'What do we do well?', 'What do we do badly?' and 'What is preventing us achieving our goals?' Participants may be informed of these beforehand to give them time to collect their thoughts.

Two meetings of two to four hours' duration are usually held every year, although in the case of newly created groups it may be necessary to meet more frequently at first. Participants should be clear that their purpose at this stage is to identify rather than to solve problems.

There are a number of ways of deriving the diagnostic data, such as holding a group discussion with all participants providing input. Since this approach can be used with groups of up to thirty people, the group may be divided into sub-groups to allow deeper discussion to take place, followed by a report-back session to the whole group. At the end of the meeting, the facilitator collects and organizes the data into themes for further consideration.

Fordyce, J.R. and Weil, R. (1971) *Managing With People*, Addison Wesley Longman, pp. 98–100.
French, W.L. and Bell, C.H. (1984) *Organization Development: Behavioural Science Interventions for Organization Improvement* (3rd edn), Prentice-Hall, pp. 141–2.

See also: Attitude survey; Collages; Critiquing; Data-based interventions; Diagnostic activities; Drawing for learning; Family group team-building meeting; Interviewing; Inter-organizational information-sharing; Organizational analysis; Organizational climate analysis; Organizational mirror; Overhead value analysis; Management audit; Physical representation of organizations; Questionnaires; Survey feedback interventions; 7-S framework

Family group team-building meeting

This intervention involves a 'family group' – in this context, a manager and their immediate workgroup – exploring ways to improve their performance. It can be used with established groups to help maintain open communication between members, or with newly formed ones to help members get to know each other quickly and establish the necessary norms for effective joint working. This approach can promote commitment to group goals, improve working relationships and increase group cohesion, but all participants should be prepared to acknowledge and deal with their differences and accept possibly unpleasant feedback.

While they have some similarities to staff meetings, family group team-building meetings differ in a number of ways. They tend to be much longer, lasting between two and five days, and may take the form of a retreat. They aim to develop an atmosphere of trust in which both feelings and opinions about aspects of the organization which affect the behaviour of group members can be aired. They are usually facilitated by an outsider, typically a management consultant or a group leader. Most importantly, the meetings and follow-up activities are planned collaboratively to ensure that all group members are committed to the outcomes. The meetings generally follow a four-stage process.

Setting objectives: in addition to the general objective of evaluating its working processes to improve performance, more specific objectives are likely to be set, such as establishing goals for the next year or so. This is carried out jointly by the group members, the manager and the facilitator.
Data collection: the team draws on information generated by its own members and collated by the

facilitator. A variety of data-collection tools may be used, such as questionnaires, instruments, interviews, collages or drawings, or the data may be gathered at a family group diagnostic meeting. *Conducting the meeting:* once the facilitator has processed and presented the data, the whole group or a sub-group produces an agenda of items to be considered, perhaps in priority order. The group then works through the issues they have identified as hindering effective performance. This stage concludes with drawing up an action plan and clarifying who is responsible for carrying out specific tasks by agreed deadlines. *Follow-up:* after the meeting, progress must be monitored to ensure that the actions agreed have been taken.

Beckhard, R. (1972) 'Optimizing Team-building Efforts', *Journal of Contemporary Business*, vol. 1, no. 3, Summer, pp. 23–32.
Bell, C.H. and Rosenzweig, J. (1978) 'Highlights of an Organization Improvement Programme in a City Government', in French, W.L., Bell, C.H. and Zawacki, R.A. (eds) *Organization Development: Theory, Practice and Research*, Business Publications.
Dyer, W.G. (1977) *Team Building: Issues and Alternatives*, Addison Wesley Longman.
Fordyce, J.R. and Weil, R. (1971) *Managing With People*, Addison Wesley Longman, pp 117–23.
French, W.L. and Bell, C.H. (1984) *Organization Development: Behavioural Science Interventions for Organization Improvement* (3rd edn), Prentice-Hall, pp. 142–6.

See also: Diagnostic activities; Drawing for learning; Family group diagnostic meeting; FIDO approach; Follow-up; Getting acquainted; Interviewing; Inter-group interventions; Looking for trouble; Retreat; Self- and peer-appraisal; Sensing; Team-building activities

Fast-cycle full-participation work design

Fast-cycle full-participation (FCFP) is a large-groupwork design method developed by Bill Pasmore, Gary Frank, Al Fritz and Mary Pasmore. It builds on the socio-technical systems approach, and involves six steps.

First, at an *orientation event* organized into one large group or a series of sub-groups, the goals and implications of the work redesign are communicated to everyone in the company, and employees are informed about their responsibilities in terms of participating in the new work culture and the new behaviours required.

Next, at a two-day conference, participants are encouraged to generate a number of *visions of the future*, and as many as thirty or forty may be produced. The participants represent the whole system that is to be redesigned, and up to a third of the workforce may be involved, the remainder being kept informed through newsletters, videos, and so on. A modified version of the future search approach is used to examine the company's past achievements and future global trends, and the predictions inform the draft design for the new company structure.

The third step is a one-day *stakeholder expectations meeting*. If the new structure is to be effective, it is essential to satisfy external stakeholders' expectations, and FCFP assumes that the way the internal technical work system interacts with the external environment can always be improved. All internal and external stakeholders may be invited to send representatives, including customers, suppliers, regulators, and perhaps even competitors, and up to several hundred may attend. The stakeholders are seated at tables in mixed groups, where they are interviewed to discover their current and future needs and expectations of the organization, and their current relationship with it. This is followed by a brainstorm on better ways to meet the stakeholder requirements identified.

The fourth step is a two- to three-day *technical work systems analysis meeting* to reveal implications for the new work design, involving both the internal stakeholders and those who actually carry out the work. The systems identified may be routine, consisting of predictable steps which are used to manufacture a product or provide a service, or non-routine, where the process is different each time it is performed.

The penultimate step is a one-day *work life analysis meeting* attended by members of the entire system. The most positive and negative aspects of current jobs are identified. The positive features – those which help to make the work meaningful to those performing it, permit social interaction, and increase workers' self-esteem – are used as templates for the new company structure.

Finally, four days are allocated to *implementing the new design*. The large-scale context for the new organization work design is specified, beginning with a reminder of the visions of the future created earlier. Working in groups, individuals imagine their preferred future organization, and distil common themes. The essential core work is specified, the sub-systems needed to support it are identified, the boundaries are established, and the administrative requirements are specified. The detailed implementation of the new design is delegated to the new units, which are responsible for establishing jobs, roles and responsibilities.

Bunker, B.B. and Alban, B.T. (1997) 'Fast Cycle Full Participation Work Design', in *Large Group*
Interventions: Engaging the Whole System for Rapid Change*, Jossey-Bass, pp. 113–21.
Pasmore, W.A. (1994) *Creating Strategic Change: Designing the Flexible, High Performing Organization*, Wiley.

See also: Action training and research; Business process engineering; Conference Model; Future search; Large-group interventions; Open-space technology; Participative design; Real-time strategic change; Real-time work design; Search conference; Socio-technical systems design; Strategic planning process; Simu-Real; Work-Out

Feedback

Feedback is the process of providing information to individuals or groups about the consequences of their actions or responses. A number of very simple but effective interventions to increase productivity are based on people's need to know how well they are doing and how their performance compares to others'. This need was first identified by psychologist Leon Festinger, whose theory of social comparison held that most people evaluate their performance by comparing themselves with others, rather than by using any absolute standard of measurement.

Feedback is obviously essential to learning and improving performance and quality, but it has specific business applications in increasing employee motivation, encouraging them to try harder or persist longer at a task. Individuals not only want and need feedback, they actively seek it out: if denied information about their performance, they may become frustrated and lose interest in the task. The behaviourist explanation of this phenomenon is that feelings of satisfaction at a positive outcome represent rewarding feedback, whereas dissatisfaction at a negative outcome serves as punishing feedback. On the other hand, cognitive theorists maintain that goals are significantly related to behaviour, and feedback not only influences the goals which are set, but is also a vital component in the goal–performance relationship.

A number of guidelines have been suggested for providing feedback: it should be delivered as soon as possible after the action or performance; it should be frequent (e.g., restricting it to the yearly appraisal is unlikely to be adequate); the greater the amount of feedback supplied the better and, finally, it should be specific, telling the employee in detail what they did well or badly.

Firms use this technique in a number of ways: Texas Instruments, Intel and Dana hold regular peer review groups; many firms provide comparative performance information to sales groups and productivity teams; Procter & Gamble operate a policy of internal competition, and an increasingly popular approach is to use computerized feedback systems to offer employees information in confidence about their previous day's performance, both in absolute terms and in relation to the past day's average.

The American food wholesaler Fleming uses a system whereby each warehouse worker about to start a task inserts a card into a computer terminal which gives an estimate of how long management think the job should take. Once the task is completed, the worker reinserts the card: if they beat the target, the screen flashes up 'Good Job'; if they don't, they are informed how far they fell below expectations. This system allows managers to keep a close check on workers' performance: if they consistently beat the target times, their workload can be increased; if they consistently fail to achieve them, they can be given extra training. In this instance, the company is using the approach to achieve a mixture of motivation and control, and there have been significant improvements in performance. For the worker, it helps to turn a routine job into a sort of game, and those who perform best have their names posted on the staff bulletin board. The system has generated a great deal of enthusiasm among employees, who voluntarily use part of their lunch break to obtain printouts detailing their previous day's performance.

In a similar application, a factory manager posted notices detailing the attendance and lateness records of all employees on a day-to-day basis. The result was a decline in absenteeism and an improvement in timekeeping.

Ashford, S.J. and Cummings, L.L. (1983) 'Feedback as an Individual Resource: Personal Strategies of Creating Information', *Organizational Behaviour and Human Resources*, vol. 32, no. 3, pp. 370–98.

Bee, R. and Bee, F. (1997) *Constructive Feedback*, Institute of Personnel and Development.

Hathaway, P. (1998) *Giving and Receiving Feedback*, Crisp Publications.

Hill, J. (1997) *Managing Performance: Goals, Feedback, Coaching, Recognition*, Institute of Personnel and Development.

Ilgen, D.R., Fisher, C.D. and Taylor, M.S. (1979) 'Consequences of Individual Feedback on Behaviour in Organizations', *Journal of Applied Psychology*, vol. 64, no. 4, pp. 349–71.

Larson, E. (1998) 'Feedback: Multiple Purposes for Management Classrooms', *Journal of Management Education*, vol. 22, no. 1, pp. 49–62.

Larson, J.R. (1984) 'The Performance Feedback Process: A Preliminary Model', *Organizational Behaviour and Human Performance*, vol. 33, pp. 42–76.

Nadler, D.A. (1979) 'The Effects of Feedback on Task Group Behaviour: A Review of the Experimental Research', *Organizational Behaviour and Human Performance*, vol. 23, pp. 309–38.

Russell, T. (1994) *Effective Feedback Skills*, Kogan Page.

Serey, T.T. (1993) 'When Things Go Wrong: Using Feedback to Manage Classroom Climate', *Journal of Management Education*, vol. 17. no. 2, pp. 243–52.

See also: ACHIEVE model; Action maze; Appraisal; Assessment centre; Behaviour modification; Benchmarking; Follow-up; Goal-setting; Instrumented laboratory; Interaction management; Likert's level meetings; Management by objectives; Measuring performance; Ongoing feedback system; Periodic planning conference; Position charter; Positive feedback

Feedback classroom

The term 'feedback classroom' can refer both to the physical location in which a particular type of teaching takes place (e.g., a specially equipped lecture room), and to computerized or other audio-visual support systems used in this teaching situation. In this entry, it will be used to refer to the entire learning situation created by means of such equipment, either as a teaching aid or for examination purposes.

One early, pre-computer version catering for up to 18 students employed a remote-controlled slide projector to present multiple-choice questions, although they could also be presented by means of a blackboard or overhead projector. Each student was provided with a handset connected to a master console controlled by the teacher or operator, providing a separate response system resembling those used in some television programmes for audience polling. Each handset had six switches, allowing up to six alternative answers. When each student indicated their choice of answer by pressing the appropriate switch, a correct response was rewarded by a green light appearing on both the handset and the master console, whereas an incorrect choice was greeted with red lights. A large meter displayed the overall percentage of correct responses, and it could also show the percentage of the class which had chosen each answer.

When used as a teaching aid, the feedback classroom can present questions to test students' understanding, and if a certain proportion fail to give correct responses about any aspect of the course material covered so far, the teacher can give further instruction before proceeding with the planned lesson. Since it is also possible to determine which answers have been selected by each student, those with problems can be identified and can be offered tutorial assistance. Alternatively, it can be used to administer programmed learning, making it possible for a technician to conduct the lesson and record the results, rather than a teacher. An additional advantage of this approach is that deriving a series of questions forces teachers to structure their courses more systematically.

When used to conduct examinations, the feedback classroom eliminates the need for marking, provides immediate feedback to students and teachers, and its efficiency means that the whole syllabus can be covered. It can also be used to assess a student's suitability for a particular course.

As a form of group programmed learning, the feedback classroom shares the advantages and disadvantages of the Skinnerian system on which it is based. Proponents of the approach claim it has a number of benefits: it improves teacher training; it enables teachers to cope with larger classes; it reduces the time required to cover the syllabus; it offers improved methods for selecting students for courses; it increases student motivation by encouraging active involvement in learning, and it reduces the cost of educating each student. Advances in multi-media technology, including personal computers, CD-ROMs and materials based on the World Wide Web, can easily be incorporated to update applications.

Bailey, G.D. (1983) *Teacher Designed, Student Feedback: A Strategy for Improving Classroom Instruction*, National Educational Association, USA.

Holling, K. (1964) 'Feedback Classroom', *Programmed Learning*, vol. 1, no. 1, pp. 17–20.

Larsen, E. (1998) 'Feedback: Multiple Purposes for Management Classrooms', *Journal of Management Education*, vol. 21, no. 1, pp. 49–62.

Twelker, P.A. (1967) 'The Teaching Research Automated Classroom (TRAC): A Facility for Innovative Change', *Programmed Learning and Educational Technology*, vol. 4, pp. 316–23.

See also: Assignment attachment; Construct lesson plan; Instrumented laboratory; Programmed learning; Self-tests

Festival

A festival may be a period set aside for celebration or religious observance, or a secular programme of special events and performances, providing companies with opportunities to gain publicity through sponsorship and display their wares. When festivals commemorate significant occasions from the past – joyful, dramatic, heroic or sorrowful – they can act as rather grand learning events, serving as reminders to those who may have witnessed them, and educating those who did not.

See also: Exhibit; Exhibition; Fair; Model; Museum learning

FIDO approach

This is a rational problem-solving process which can also serve as a conflict-resolution tool. Relying on a combination of role negotiation, team-building and conflict-resolution, it views problem-solving as an exchange of relevant information, and the factors represented by the acronym FIDO – Feelings, Information, Decision and Outcomes – should be considered as a hierarchy of priorities rather than as stages in a process.

When one starts to address a problem, it is difficult to decide what information should be exchanged until the decision to be made has been clarified, and this in turn depends on identifying the desired outcomes. However, priorities often change once the information and the decision have been defined. Since decisions are affected by emotions, ideas and preferences, feelings are incorporated into the model and are treated as the highest priority, whereas outcomes are accorded low priority. When there is a conflict at any priority level, it is resolved at the next level up. A hierarchy of feelings and outcomes may also be identified, so the whole model looks like this:

1 Feelings
  a Feelings arising from values (general beliefs)
  b Feelings arising from assumptions about the other person
  c Feelings arising from the present process
2 Information
3 Decisions
4 Outcomes
  a Outcomes arising immediately out of the present process
  b Outcomes pursued as planned objectives
  c Outcomes in the form of a distant ideal

Dick, B. (1983) 'Conflict Resolution Skills and Techniques in Management Development, Part 1', *Journal of Management Development*, vol. 2, no. 3, pp. 42–54.

Dick, B. (1983) 'Conflict Resolution Skills and Techniques in Management Development, Part 2', *Journal of Management Development*, vol. 2, no. 4, pp. 15–31.

See also: Competing values approach; Conflict-resolution techniques; Cousin laboratory; Family group team-building meeting; Hearing; Implementing the organizational renewal process;

Kepner-Tregoe approach; LIFO method; Negotiation by group members; No-lose conflict-resolution method; Role prescription; Third-party peacemaking interventions

Field format

The field format approach was originally developed to teach the topic of organizational culture, but it can be applied to any situation where hidden aspects of the organization are to be explored, and where tools are required to analyse the raw data obtained.

The aim of this approach is to allow students to experience for themselves phenomena they are studying 'in the field'. For example, an introductory lecture explaining how organizations use socialization for control might be followed by a period of observation of the goals and socialization processes in the companies they are studying, in tandem with consideration of socialization within their course and educational establishment.

Students may work alone, but are usually organized into groups of two to three called *cadres*, who study and sit together throughout the course. The classroom sessions consist of lectures which provide background material, as well as discussions of research methods and fieldwork problems. The students conduct original research into a given subject using the classroom-as-organization model. Since each course has its own unique culture, rules, structures, modes of communication and goals, it shares many features of any organization, and these are available for study.

Hurish, B. and Borzak, L. (1979) 'Toward Cognitive Development Through Field Studies', *Journal of Higher Education*, vol. 50, no. 1, pp. 63–78.

McCarthy, S. and Trice, H.M. (1985–6) 'Teaching About Organizational Cultures: The Field Format', *Organizational Behaviour Teaching Review*, vol. 10, no. 3, pp. 19–30.

Powell, G. and Graves, L.M. (1987–8) 'Predicting Organizational Behaviour from Office Environment: A Field Exercise', *Organizational Behaviour Teaching Review*, vol. 12, no. 1, pp. 114–16.

Zajdel, M.M. and Vinton, K.L. (1987–8) 'For Members Only: Assigning Ethnographies in an Organizational Behaviour Class', *Organizational Behaviour Teaching Review*, vol. 12, no. 1, pp. 119–21.

See also: Classroom-as-organization model; Educational visit; Field trip; Intervisitation; Management systems study; Outdoor training; Studycade

Field project attachment

In this approach, students spend a period 'attached' to a department or unit in a private company or public enterprise in order to carry out a particular task or project. The chosen activity should give rise to personal learning which is directly related to the course.

Field project attachments on a modest scale are possible in the context of a full-time one-year course, but the success of this approach depends on finding institutions which are large enough and present a challenge. They need to be sufficiently well staffed to be able to provide support for the project in the form of expert supervision and enough time for a worthwhile piece of work to be concluded.

Porras, J.I. (1982) 'A Field Project Approach to Teaching OD', *Exchange: The Organizational Behaviour Teaching Journal*, vol. 7, no. 1, pp. 27–31.

See also: Co-operative education; Industrial project; Internship; Overseas project; Project method; Real-life entrepreneurial project; Student placement

Field trip (study tour; study visit; fieldwork; field study)

Whereas educational visits are usually brief, perhaps lasting a single day or at most two, field trips are usually longer in duration and may involve more extensive travel. Groups of managers regularly go on study (or field) visits to factories abroad to compare their own organizational methods and approaches with those of the foreign companies. Because the purpose of a field trip is to obtain first-hand information about the phenomena being studied, it can be considered an application of experience-based learning or the laboratory method.

The different phases in a student field trip – preparation and information-gathering, the visit itself, drafting a report and discussing its findings – can achieve different learning objectives, but this relies on careful planning.

The company chosen should present a striking example of an initiative or situation, such as a take-over, a production innovation or a radical human resources approach. The field trip must have clear objectives, and these should be explored in pre-visit briefing sessions, describing the general situation to be visited, points to look out for, and any connections with previous and future study. Guest speakers may also be invited to address the group. The students should prepare thoroughly by studying the company's reports, analysing its environment and noting any problems it might be experiencing so that they can prepare questions and topics for discussion and exploration. Since the most interesting issues are normally strategic ones, it is most important that students have the opportunity to discuss policy-making with top management.

Students should prepare a report recording the company's situation and any problems observed, together with suggestions on how to tackle them. Once the report has been discussed and revised, a copy should be sent to the company.

Allen, D. and Young, M. (1997) 'From Tour Guide to Teacher: Deepening Cross-cultural Competences through International, Experience-based Education', *Journal of Management Education*, vol. 21, no. 2, pp. 168–89.

Porth, S.J. (1997) 'Management Education Goes International: A Model for Designing and Teaching a Study Tour Course', *Journal of Management Education*, vol. 21, no. 2, pp. 190–99.

Watson, C.W. (1995) 'Case Study: Fieldwork in Undergraduate Anthropology: For and Against', *Innovations in Education and Training International*, vol. 32, no. 2, pp. 153–61.

See also: Educational visit; Field format; Intervisitation; Management systems study; Outdoor training; Studycade

Film

The use of feature films for instruction is covered in the entry on Movies, whereas this entry will deal with training films produced for sale or hire by companies such as the BBC, Fenman, Gower and Video Arts, nowadays usually supplied on video. They can be used either as a supplement to other training methods or as the main vehicle of learning, and the instructor's notes which accompany the films often suggest role-plays and associated case studies.

Training films can serve to help motivate students, extend their range of experiences, introduce new material, enhance retention of information, clarify perceptions and concepts, encourage further reading and study, and promote group discussions. They can reinforce other learning methods, encouraging desirable attitudes and behaviour, clarifying processes and procedures, increasing the amount of material that can be learned within a specified period, and helping poor readers.

Four different types of management training films can be distinguished. *Didactic films* (also known as 'message films') emphasize facts and aim to communicate specific points to the audience,

such as how to run a meeting or how to approach a customer. *Point-of-view films* take a particular viewpoint on a subject and provide evidence to support that perspective: for example, that management and workforce share common interests. *Attitude shaping films* try to either reinforce, counter or modify the audience's preconceptions. *Open-ended films* present a case study, and often have an abrupt ending.

Baddock, B. (1996) *Using Films in the English Classroom*, Prentice-Hall/Phoenix ELT.

Gloia, D. and Brass, D.J. (1985–6) 'Teaching the TV Generation: The Case for Observational Conditioning', *Organizational Behaviour Teaching Review*, vol. 10, no. 2, pp. 11–15.

Marchant, H. (1977) 'Increasing the Effectiveness of Educational Films: A Selected Review of Research', *British Journal of Educational Technology*, vol. 8, no. 2, pp. 86–96.

Nolan, J. (1980) 'The Use and Misuse of Films in Management Training', *Training and Development Journal*, vol. 34, no. 3, pp. 84–5.

Suessmuth, P. (1978) *Ideas for Training Managers and Supervisors: Useful Suggestions, Activities and Instruments*, Chapter 27, Pfeiffer/Jossey-Bass.

Teather, D.C.B. (1974) 'Learning From Film: A Significant Difference Between the Effectiveness of Different Projection Methods', *Programmed Learning and Educational Technology*, vol. 11, no. 6, pp. 328–34.

Teather, D.C.B. and Marchant, H. (1974) 'Learning from Film with Particular Reference to the Effects of Cueing, Questioning and Knowledge of Results', *Programmed Learning and Educational Technology*, vol. 11, no. 6, pp. 317–27.

Unwin, D. (1979) 'Production and Audience Variables in Film and Television: A Second Selected Bibliography', *Programmed Learning and Educational Technology*, vol. 16, no. 3, pp. 232–9.

See also: Audio for learning; Movie; Music for learning; Television; Trigger film; Video for learning

Fishbowl

The fishbowl activity can be used whenever a group requires feedback on its immediate, current working processes. The group members arrange themselves in two concentric circles. Those in the inner circle (the 'bowl') take the active role and engage in a group activity. The outer circle act as observers, listening and make a note of what they observe. A general discussion follows, in which the observers comment on what they observed during the group's interaction. In a more sophisticated method, those in the inner circle also state what they felt was happening. The differences between the two views may highlight perceptual and affective discrepancies, thereby providing a very useful insight into the subjective nature of perception.

This method is useful if the size of a group means that a whole-group discussion is likely to be fragmented and be dominated by a few more vocal participants. These could be invited to sit in the 'bowl' to hold a livelier and more coherent discussion observed by the others, and the roles could be reversed after a while. Fishbowls can also be used in debriefings for syndicate work, with one member of each group entering the 'bowl' to report on what their syndicate has done.

The fishbowl can also be a useful organizational change technique: for example, a newly formed team which is to embark on a new company project may form into a fishbowl to discuss their task and objectives while being observed by management.

The method is also appropriate where one group needs to develop information and transmit it to a second group, which is directly involved but at this stage simply needs to listen and observe. An example of this may occur when two units of the same organization come together to try to improve their working relationships. A sub-group of members of both units is formed into a fishbowl and set the task of settling the issues causing conflict while others observe. After fifteen minutes, the activity may be stopped to allow the observers to assess the fishbowl members' efforts to move towards resolving the problem.

The advantages of the fishbowl technique are its spontaneous quality and its capacity to generate and maintain interest. It gives the members of the outer circle the opportunity to listen to and understand those inside the fishbowl, it combines the efficiency of small-group working with the delivery of information to a larger group, and being under observation encourages those inside the fishbowl to stick to the point.

Despite these advantages, a fishbowl is not suitable when a clearly planned presentation is required. The facilitator should check regularly that the observers can hear and see what is going on within the fishbowl, and everyone needs to be clear about the objective and the role they are expected to play. Some participants are uncomfortable about being the focus of attention, and the observers may become frustrated unless they are able to participate at some point. One way of overcoming this is to include one empty chair in the fishbowl so that any observer who wishes to make a contribution can become a temporary member of the fishbowl and do so. If the fishbowl activity suggests points for future action,

these can be written down and displayed for all to see.

Fordyce, J.R. and Weil, R. (1971) *Managing With People*, Addison Wesley Longman, p. 165.

See also: Confrontation groups; Confrontation meeting; Criss-cross panels; Group with ground rules; Inter-group team-building; LIFO method; Negotiation by group members; Organizational mirror; Process analysis

Flexastudy (learning by appointment; learning on demand)

Flexastudy is an individualized, college-based open learning system in which the student buys blocks of time to use the facilities of a college or tutor. It should be distinguished from FlexiStudy, which is mainly conducted at home.

The flexastudy system is self-pacing: each course allows students to decide how quickly they wish to progress through their studies, depending on their aptitude, their motivation and the length of time they wish to spend at college. There are no lectures, and students have a great deal of discretion in deciding when and for how long they wish to join a class. Written work schemes are used to structure the student's learning and provide information, and individual tutorial supervision and assistance are provided to reinforce the students' motivation and to ease their learning difficulties. Although the emphasis is on individual tuition, facilities are usually provided for tutors to arrange group learning in seminars.

Students enrolling on a flexastudy scheme select a course from the range on offer, the level of the examination for which they want to study, the date they wish to begin attending, and the duration of the programme. Study takes place in open-plan rooms which may have forty or so desks. Each student is allocated a desk they will use throughout the course, and supplied with a normal weekly timetable divided into set periods for certain subjects or private study.

Each subject tutor visits each student during the relevant period. At their first meeting, the tutor suggests a suitable scheme of work for the course. A bank of work schemes needs to be built up for each subject. To allow this, each course is divided up into modules. Individual topic areas combine to make up a module, and the tutor gives written instructions about what the student needs to do to cover each topic. They then agree a date for completion of the first topic, when the student will be given a work assignment to test their understanding. After this has been completed and assessed, the next topic is tackled, and so on. During the intervening period, the tutor checks if the student is having any problems. If a number of students are experiencing similar difficulties, the tutor may decide to hold a general seminar.

With the student's agreement, the pace of study may be altered by varying the period spent on particular topics.

Albrecht, A. and Spencer, D.C. (1976) *Flexastudy: The Professional Tutorial System Operated at Redditch College*, Coombe Lodge Case Study, Information Bank No. 1,119.
Morris, J.H. (1978) 'Flexastudy', *Industrial and Commercial Training*, vol. 10, no. 7, pp. 288–90.
Scott, G. (1996) 'The Effective Management and Evaluation of Flexible Learning Innovations in Higher Education', *Innovations in Education and Training International*, vol. 33, no. 4, pp. 154–70.

See also: Directed private study; FlexiStudy; Learning contracts; Networking; Open learning

Flexible staffing (flexible manning)

Firms may seek flexibility in staffing through functional flexibility, which means being able to deploy employees quickly and smoothly between activities; and numerical flexibility, which allows the total number of workers to be increased or decreased quickly in response to short-term changes in the demand for labour. At the start of 1999 in the UK, 3.9 per cent of the total workforce – nearly one million employees – were on temporary assignments.

Four approaches to flexible staffing have been distinguished: changing the employee–company relationship; establishing production flexibility agreements; combining production with front-line maintenance engineering and technical resources, and encouraging workers to become multi-role and multi-disciplinary.

The change of employee–company relationship approach involves a reduction in the total workforce in the traditional way, combined with setting up four new categories of workers: *core group workers* are full-time, permanent career employees, such as managers, designers, sales staff and quality control staff; *peripheral groups* consist of full-time employees with less job security and access to career opportunities, such as clerical staff and supervisors; *contracted workers* are engaged on finite contracts, and *external workers* may be specialists whose jobs are not company-specific, such as systems analysts or office cleaners, often self-employed, subcontracted or hired on a temporary basis through an agency.

Production flexibility agreements involve promoting the core trades to form mechanical and electrical instrument craft jobs. In addition, a division can be established between front-line maintenance and the central engineering services. Combining production with front-line maintenance engineering and technical resources entails establishing a common management structure by forming multi-skilled teams which consist mainly of single-disciplined craft and production workers. Since current high levels of unemployment among craft workers mean many of them have been applying for production jobs, production and front-line maintenance resources can be integrated further by developing multi-role, multi-disciplinary craft workers and user-maintainer jobs.

Atkinson, J. (1985) 'The Changing Corporation', in Clutterbuck, D. (ed.) *New Patterns of Work*, Gower.
Beard, K.M. and Edwards, J.R. (1995) 'Employees at Risk: Contingent Work and the Psychological Experiences of Contingent Workers', in Cooper, C.L. and Rousseau, D.M. (eds) *Trends in Organizational Behaviour, Volume 2*, Wiley, pp. 109–26.
Coates, G. (1992) 'Towards the Use of Employees as a Resource, Not a Cost', *Education and Training Technology International*, vol. 29, no. 2, pp. 169–79.
Horning, K. et al. (1995) *Time Pioneers, Flexible Working Time and New Lifestyles*, Polity Press.
Meade-King, M. (1995) *Employer's Guide to Flexible Working*, Parents at Work Publications.
Nollen, S. and Axel, H. (1995) *Managing Contingent Workers*, American Management Association, AMACOM.
Olmstead, B. and Smith, S. (1994) *Creating a Flexible Workplace* (2nd edn), American Management Association, AMACOM.
Pettinger, R. (1998) *Managing the Flexible Workforce*, Cassell.
Sherer, P.D. (1996) 'Towards an Understanding of the Variety in Work Relationships', in Cooper, C.L. and Rousseau, D.M. (eds) *Trends in Organizational Behaviour, Volume 3*, Wiley, pp. 99–122.
Simmons, S. (1996) *Flexible Working: A Strategic Guide to Successful Implementation and Operation*, Kogan Page.
Stredwick, J. and Ellis, S. (1998) *Flexible Working Practices*, Institute of Personnel and Development.

See also: Closing down; Flexitime; Integrated support functions; Intrapreneurial groups; Job sharing; Multiple job loading; Network organizations; Part-time working; Structural interventions; Teleworking; Work schedule restructuring

FlexiStudy

FlexiStudy is a locally based open learning system. It should be distinguished from Flexastudy, because in FlexiStudy the student works at home but maintains regular contact with the college.

FlexiStudy was originally developed for mature students who did not wish to follow traditional degree-level courses, but felt the need for face-to-face contacts both with each other and with teaching staff. It has parallels with the design of Open University courses, and it shares many of that organization's approaches and ideas.

Traditional college-based courses tend to offer little flexibility in terms of their admission dates, duration and how frequently students are required to attend. FlexiStudy tries to address these problems by combining distance learning with local learning, combining study at home with occasional seminars and tutorials held in a neighbourhood college. Students may be given help to develop their study skills before being allocated carefully structured and referenced distance learning material. The combination of college tutorials and communication with individual students aims to provide full and rapid feedback and advice on both their study approach and the subject matter, to make the best use of the resources available in the college.

The FlexiStudy system is now being operated from a number of local colleges throughout the country, and has been updated to take advantage of technological developments.

Davies, T.C. (1977) *Open Learning Systems for Mature Students*, Working Paper 14, Council for Educational Technology, London.
NEC (1978) *FlexiStudy: A Manual for Local Colleges*, National Extension College Reports, Series 2, No. 4, National Extension College, Cambridge.
Sacks, H. (1980) 'FlexiStudy – An Open Learning System for Further and Adult Education', *British Journal of Educational Technology*, vol. 11, no. 2, pp. 85–95.

See also: Directed private study; Flexastudy; Learning contract; Networking; Open learning

Flexitime

As its name implies, flexitime is a flexible approach in which employees have to work a certain number of hours each week, including set core hours each day, but are free to decide for themselves how to structure the rest of their work time. Flexitime is limited to jobs that can be performed by the employee independently (e.g., computer programming and clerical work). They are not suitable where constant interaction with other employees in the same or other departments is necessary, where work flow requires tight schedules, or where specialists must be available continuously to oversee functions.

The usual system is that the office or factory is open between 6.00 a.m. and 6.00 p.m. Employees must be at work during the core hours 9.00 a.m.–3.00 p.m., allowing for a lunch break, but beyond that they may vary their work time within certain limits as long as they accumulate two hours' work either before or after each day's core period.

The adoption of flexitime has been found to improve employee motivation and morale, reduce absenteeism (since workers can achieve a balance between their work and non-work responsibilities) and to help companies recruit employees from a wider labour pool of those who would find it difficult to fit into the normal regime of fixed working hours.

More recently, it has become part of a wider debate about working patterns, and Torrington and Hall list a growing range of approaches adopted by companies, of which flexitime is only one, including normal-week working, shift working, part-time working, compressed hours, annual-hours contracts and zero-hour contracts.

Daiton, D.R. and Mesch, D.J. (1990) 'The Impact of Flexible Schedules on Employee Attendance and Turnover', *Administrative Science Quarterly*, June, pp. 370–87.
'Flexing the Clock Part 1: The Use of Annual Hours, *IRS Employment Trends* (1998), no. 654, April, pp. 4–11.
'Flexing the Clock Part 2: Experiences of Annual Hours, *IRS Employment Trends* (1998), no. 655, May, pp. 6–10.
Krause, M. and Hermann, E. (1991) 'Who is Afraid of Flexitime? Correlates of Personal Choice of a Flexitime Schedule', *Applied Psychology: An International Review*, vol. 40, pp. 315–26.
Kush, K.S. and Stroh, L.K. (1994) 'Flexitime: Myth or Reality', *Business Horizons*, September–October, p. 53.
Lee, R.A. (1983) 'Hours of Work: Who Controls and How?', *Industrial Relations Journal*, vol. 14, no. 4.
Torrington, D. and Hall, L. (1998) *Human Resource Management*, Chapter 10, Prentice-Hall.

See also: Flexible staffing

Flowchart

Flowcharts are a means of representing choices or actions in a systematic or diagrammatic form. They are often used as an aide-memoire, to describe tasks, or to explain the steps required to carry them out. For example, a university computer laboratory may display flowcharts on its walls to guide users in how use the equipment – from how to switch the computers on to how to access certain programs – eliminating the need for the continual presence of an instructor. An example of a flowchart indicating the stages in the production of a computer program is shown below.

Brien, R. and Lagana, S. (1977) 'Flowcharting: A Procedure for the Development of Learning Hierarchy', *Programmed Learning and Educational Technology*, vol. 14, no. 4, pp. 305–14.

Dewar, D.L. (1992) 'The Process Flowchart and Continuous Improvement', *Journal of Quality and Participation*, vol. 15, pp. 56–7.

See also: Algorithm; Decision table; Heuristic

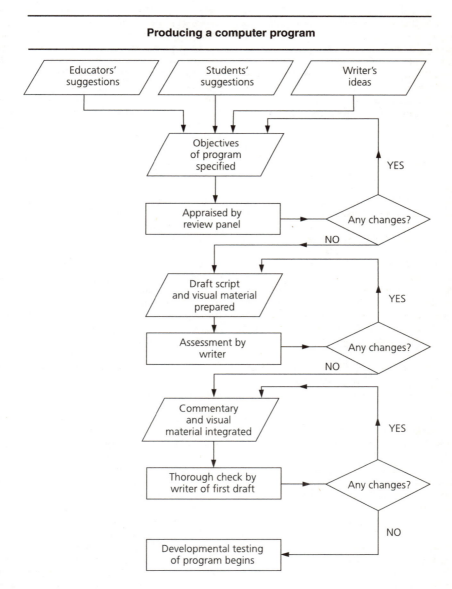

Producing a computer program

Example of a flowchart

Focus group

Focus groups first became popular in the field of marketing, where researchers sought to obtain potential customers' views on products or services. More recently, they have been used by political parties and the government to test public reaction to policies before decisions on their final launch are made.

Focus groups can be used to gather any type of data for any purpose. Since their two-way communication flow allows continuous improvements, focus groups often form part of organizational change and development work. They are conducted before, during and after a major change programme. Some companies have even adopted focus groups to complement or replace organization-wide surveys of employees' views. For example, BT Organization Development has used such research to obtain qualitative data on how changes in the company are affecting people, and how new company initiatives are likely to be received.

BT Employee Communications (1997) *Focus Groups: Involving Employees Creatively to Influence Decisions*, Industrial Society Press.

Krueger, R.A. (1988) *Focus Groups: A Practical Guide for Applied Research*, Sage.

Krueger, R.A. (1997) *Moderating Focus Groups*, Sage.

Morgan, D.L. (ed.) (1993) *Successful Focus Groups: Advances in the State of the Art*, Sage.

Morgan, D.L. (1997) *Focus Groups as Qualitative Research*, Sage.

Morgan, D.L. (1998) *Planning Focus Groups*, Sage.

Stewart, D.W. and Shamdasani, P.N. (1990) *Focus Groups: Theory and Practice*, Sage.

Vaughn, S. et al. (1996) *Focus Groups Interview in Educational Psychology*, Sage.

See also: Action research; Attitude survey; Data-based interventions; Delphi technique; Survey feedback interventions

Follow-up (follow-through)

Most organizational meetings conclude with a decision on future action, and follow-up sessions are necessary to ensure that agreed plans and proposals are being implemented effectively, to consider their consequences, and to explore any further action that might be necessary.

One way of structuring such events is to display the plans of the last meeting on a flipchart, together with the name of the person who accepted responsibility for each matter. Individuals then take turns to report back to the whole group what progress has been made, identifying areas that require further discussion or study.

Fordyce, J.R. and Weil, R. (1971) *Managing With People*, Addison Wesley Longman, pp. 134–6.

See also: Family group team-building meeting; Feedback; Goal-setting; Interaction management; Management by objectives; Measuring performance; Organizational mirror

Force field analysis

Force field analysis is a model and a technique originated by Kurt Lewin to diagnose and implement change. It describes and analyses the various forces that operate on social systems to keep them either in a state of balance or in a state of change.

Lewin proposed that two sets of forces operate in any social system: those that drive change forward, and those that impede it, which he called the 'resisting forces'. If the two sets of forces are equal in strength, the system remains in equilibrium. A force field analysis consultant will help a client recognize the forces in their field, understand the consequences of manipulating certain ones, and provide whatever support is necessary to take action.

The first step is to identify an unsolved current problem, the people concerned (their status and their relationship to the problem and the client) and any other factors that might help to understand the situation.

Next, the consultant and client list all the resisting forces – factors that make the problem worse or prevent it improving – plus all the driving forces – those which make the problem better or prevent it getting worse. It is important to understand that driving forces are not simply the opposite of resisting forces: the two are qualitatively different. For example, a driving force for change may be the high cost of unit production, but it is unlikely that the corresponding resisting force will be workers' desire to keep the unit cost high; it is more likely to be anxiety about losing their jobs because of any automation introduced to reduce output cost.

Once all the forces have been listed, a weighting is assigned to each. It is unlikely that all the forces will be of equal importance, so this involves making judgements about priorities and the intensity of each force identified.

The next step is to conduct an analysis to decide on the most effective changes that can be made. A number of questions need to be answered. Which forces does the manager have personal control over? Which forces are under the influence of other people with whom the manager has or could have direct contact? Which forces are under the influence of external agents, or people with whom the manager has no contact (e.g., the economy, law)?

Finally, having answered these questions and assessed the relative importance of the different forces, the task is to specify how the manager can change or manipulate any of the forces in order to solve the problem.

Some writers argue that this is a risky change strategy because it merely increases the driving forces. They prefer an approach that will reduce one or more of the main resisting forces.

Bennis, W.G., Benne, K.D. and Chin, R. (eds) (1985) *The Planning of Change* (4th edn), Rinehart, Holt and Winston.

Fordyce, J.R. and Weil, R. (1971) *Managing With People*, Addison Wesley Longman, pp. 106–8.

Lewin, K. (1951) *Field Theory in Social Science*, Harper and Row.

Maier, N.R.F. (1965) *Psychology in Industry*, Houghton Mifflin, pp. 432–3.

Morris, W.C. and Sashkin, M. (1976) *Organization Behaviour in Action*, West Publishing.

See also: Action project; Industrial dynamics; Open systems planning; Scenario planning; Search conference; Strategic management

Forcing device (forced coupling)

This approach involves creating situations in which separate ideas, needs, solutions and problems can be brought (or 'forced') together to see whether it is possible to marry them together to produce innovations in the organization.

Peters and Waterman describe one application of the forcing device in IBM's Fellow Programme, where employees are given a free hand and the support to do whatever they want, provided they 'shake up the system' in some way. In addition, Texas Instruments runs an Individual Contributor Programme, 3M has set up a New Business Venture Division, and United Technologies gives awards for inter-divisional technology transfer.

Some companies have established experimental units to stimulate ideas: Datapoint has set up technology centres, where people from different disciplines and functions can come together to innovate, and General Electric has established a 'toy shop', where staff can observe and rent robots in order to encourage them to develop factories of the future.

Galbraith, J.R. (1982) 'Designing the Innovating Organization', *Organizational Dynamics*, Winter.

Peters, T.J. and Waterman, R.H. (1982) *In Search of Excellence*, Harper and Row, pp. 222–3.

See also: Business teams; Creativity training; Independent product teams; Intrapreneurial group; Management by walking about; Physical interventions in organizations; Synectics

Fortune lining

Fortune lining was invented by Laurence Rush to help in the teaching of English. Case studies, novels, plays, poems, music and histories of every kind present a story that unfolds as series of events. For example, White and Gunstone (1992, p. 108) illustrate how the 'Little Red Riding Hood' fairy tale can be divided into ten scenes:

1 Little Red Riding Hood sets off from home.
2 Little Red Riding Hood enters wood.
3 Little Red Riding Hood meets wolf.
4 Little Red Riding Hood escapes from wolf, continues through forest.
5 Little Red Riding Hood comes to grandma's house.
6 'What big eyes you have.'
7 'What big ears you have.'
8 'What big teeth you have' – wolf unmasks, pursues.
9 Hunter enters, kills wolf.
10 Grandma found unhurt in cupboard.

Fortune lining probes learners' understanding of a story by requiring them to estimate and draw a graph of one or more dimensions as they vary from scene to scene, such as happiness, peace of mind, kindness, interest or power.

Fortune lining allows instructors to focus students' attention on a particular aspect of a case story, such as the relationships between the employees described. It forces students to think about each scene in terms of the specified theme, encouraging them to link events, to analyse what is changing in each scene, and to read the case from the point of view of different characters. Drawing up a graph makes them consider the balance between different elements as the story progresses, and different students' results can be compared and discussed.

In the case of material where there are specific correct and incorrect answers, fortune lining can also be used for assessment purposes, to check whether or not students have understood the themes examined.

Rush, L.N. (1988) 'Fortune Lines: A New Probe of Understanding in the Humanities', unpublished Master of Education Studies project, Monash University, Melbourne, Australia.

White, R. and Gunstone, R. (1992) *Probing Understanding*, Falmer Press, Chapter 7.

See also: Chronology charting; Collages; Concept mapping; Description-prediction-outcome-explanation; Drawing for learning; Illuminative incident analysis; Poster; Responsibility charting; Story-boarding

Forum meeting

A forum is a meeting in which members of the audience are invited to ask questions and make comments. As part of a formal stage presentation, such a meeting may be called a *lecture forum*, *symposium forum* or *panel forum*, and usually follows a presentation from a lecturer or symposium member. The advantage of this method is that the presentation may stimulate audience members to think of issues which they then have the opportunity to clarify by asking questions.

Before the formal presentation begins, the audience should be made aware that they will have the opportunity to ask questions or make responses afterwards. The success of the forum depends on the chairperson's ability to encourage their participation. If the audience is large (over a hundred people), 'planting' a few questioners can help.

See also: Audience reaction/watchdog team; Brains Trust; Clinic meeting; Colloquy meeting; Conference meeting; Institute meeting; Interview meeting; Listening team; Panel discussion; Reaction panel; Symposium meeting

Foyer training (vestibule training)

At one time, new employees in industry were trained in a 'vestibule school': a small area away from the work site where trainees could practise their skills using the same equipment and materials they would encounter once they began productive work. Nowadays, this approach is known as 'foyer training'. Foyer training is similar to on-the-job training, but provides an environment in which mistakes do not have major consequences either for trainees or the company. Another feature which distinguishes foyer training from on-the-job training is that the trainer is a full-time instructor, rather than a supervisor or co-worker. For example, the Nissan motor car company in Tyne and Wear has created a separate training production line where trainees participating in the government's New Deal Programme produce axles and other components in preparation for working on the real production facility.

The effectiveness of foyer training depends on how closely the equipment and processes match reality, and how well trainees adapt to the simulated work setting. Its disadvantages include the expense of employing professional instructors, providing space, materials and equipment solely for training, and paying wages for a period when employees are not contributing to the company's production efforts.

Foyer training provides instructors with an environment away from the normal workplace interruptions and pressures, where they can explain an operation to the trainees, observe each trainee as they practise performing it, and provide feedback, making corrections and reinforcing the correct behaviours. Each instructor may train several employees at a time, depending on their needs and the degree of sophistication of the skills being taught.

Casio, W.F. (1991) *Applied Psychology in Personnel Management* (4th edn), Prentice-Hall.
Goldstein, I.L. (1986) *Training in Organizations: Needs Assessment, Development and Evaluation* (2nd edn), Brooks/Cole.
Saul, F.E. and Knight, P.A. (1988) *Industrial/Organizational Psychology*, Brooks/Cole.

See also: Clarifying educational environment; Drill-and-practice method; Lesson demonstration method; Mathetics; Simulation

Free discussion method

In an academic context, the free discussion method provides a learning situation in which the topic and direction of the discussion are controlled by the student group, while the tutor observes and very occasionally comments on the process. It can be used to encourage changes in attitudes and feelings.

In a training context, the free discussion method may be integrated with the conference method and the problem-solving cycle, its distinctive features being the way the discussion topics and questions are raised, and the nature of the involvement of senior management. Once a series of discussions is completed, the group may choose to formalize its suggestions by presenting a written summary of its ideas and conclusions.

The idea underlying the free discussion method is that people learn by participating effectively, although this view has been challenged by those who consider group work of any kind to be of doubtful value. Nevertheless, it provides a practical and specific way of developing more effective teamwork and improving communication between different organizational levels.

Barber reported on the use of the free discussion method with groups of a dozen supervisors on a problem-solving training course. First, a list of questions relevant to the supervisors' daily work was circulated, including 'To what extent is a supervisor free to deal with a shop floor employee problem on his own? and 'What advice and assistance does the Personnel Department give a supervisor in taking on a new recruit?' These were based on interviews carried out on the job by training staff and senior management, and the supervisors were invited to choose which questions they wanted to discuss, plus any additional ones of their own.

A briefing session followed where the purpose of the training was explained, the topics chosen for discussion were revealed, and participants were asked to be frank and free with their comments during the forthcoming course. Once the trainer had opened the session, a member of senior management took the chair for the rest of the day, and the trainer's role changed to acting as a catalyst in discussions and maintaining an atmosphere of openness. The senior manager presented the problem or question and asked for comments and ideas, resisting the desire to put forward a personal viewpoint since their task was to listen to comments and report them to colleagues. (The role of chair may be taken by another member of senior management the next day.)

This method is quite demanding for the trainer, who must know about the firm in detail and be able to lead the discussion competently while remaining neutral. Free discussion demands a lively and informal atmosphere, and one way to establish this is to ask participants to introduce themselves and state what they find most satisfying and least satisfying about their job. With the group's permission, these observations can be noted and passed on to senior management, emphasizing its interest in seeking improvements.

Barber, J.W. (1968) 'Free Group Discussion Method in the Training of Supervisors', in Robinson, J. and Barnes, N. (eds) *New Media and Methods in Industrial Training*, BBC Publications.

Barnett, S.A. (1958) 'An Experiment with Free Discussion Groups', *Universities Quarterly*, vol. 12, pp. 175–80.

See also: Abercrombie method; Conference method; Creative dialogue; Directed conversation method; Group discussion; Leaderless group discussion; Problem-solving cycle; Small-group teaching

Functional administrative control technique

The functional administrative control technique (FACT) is a computer-assisted tool that allows management to develop positive change strategies based on a thorough evaluation and quantification of organizational processes. FACT uses a combination of time management, value engineering, organizational development and creative group processes to specify the appropriate corrective action.

A consultant or facilitator trains members of a unit and helps them administer the technique, taking them through its five phases: information, creativity (determining the different ways in which the functions can be provided), evaluation, planning and implementation. Each phase is fully described and illustrated with checklists, diagrams, time logs, reports, etc.

The *information* phase examines what the organization does, what it costs to do what it does, and the acceptance or worth of what it does. The *creativity* phase explores whether organizational functions could be performed in different ways. The *evaluation* phase considers how each of the ideas generated in the creativity phase could be turned into workable concepts, and how they could be evaluated in terms of the company's legal criteria, policies and procedures and their impact on the organization. Once the concepts have been evaluated and suitable ones identified for implementation, the *planning* phase involves drawing up implementation plans. These normally include a schedule, training requirements and individual responsibilities. Finally, the *implementation* phase itself incorporates computerized FACT reports. These can also be used in organizational budgeting, wage and salary analysis and organizational comparisons.

Higgins, B.K. and Dice, C.M. (1984) 'Quantifying White Collar Functions', *National Productivity Review*, vol. 3, no. 3, Summer, pp. 288–302.

See also: ACHIEVE system; Administrative interventions; Assessment of the organization as a system; Evaluation committee method; Looking for trouble; Management audit; Open systems planning; 7-S framework

Functional role analysis

Functional role analysis is a structured observational technique that can be used by managers to categorize and analyse behaviour. Many different formats exist, using a variety of structures and behaviour categories. One of the earliest of these, the Functional Role Analysis Method, was developed by Benne and Sheats in 1948. The authors' hypothesis was that effective problem-solving groups demonstrate behaviour along two dimensions: *task behaviour* (getting on with the job in hand) and *group maintenance behaviour* (maintaining member involvement, satisfaction and cohesion), and both types of behaviour are essential if the group is to be effective. The findings from this analysis can be used to identify the predominant roles that occur in successful problem-solving groups, so these can be encouraged in others.

Benne and Sheats identified six task roles. The *Information Giver* offers facts or generalizations which are authoritative or which relate to the speaker's own experience pertinent to the group problem. The other task roles are: *Information Seeker*, *Opinion Giver*, *Opinion Seeker*, *Clarifier* and *Elaborator*.

Five group maintenance roles were identified. The *Harmonizer* mediates between members in disagreement and attempts to reconcile them. The other maintenance roles are: *Encourager*, *Gate Keeper*, *Group Observer* and *Compromiser*.

These categories can be used to classify the roles members play in a particular group, and to decide which roles need to be encouraged or developed.

Benne, K.D. and Sheats, P. (1948) 'Functional Roles of Team Members', *Journal of Social Issues*, vol. 4, Spring, pp. 42–7.
Margulies, N. and Wallace, J. (1973) *Organizational Change: Techniques and Applications*, Scott Foresman, pp. 30–2.

See also: Interaction influence analysis; Process consultation; Role analysis technique; Role prescription; Team mapping

Future search

Future search is a large-group intervention method developed by Weisbord and Janoff which aims to create a vision of a desired future for a department, company or community. It explores possible agreements between people with divergent views and interests, and helps them to search for common ground and plan consensually. This approach is particularly suited to addressing complex problems within large systems.

Future search relies on the following principles: it gathers together the whole system, or a representation of that system, in one room at one time; the work is conducted in the context of the larger environment; common ground is emphasized; groups are self-managing; there are no external experts, and future search is not a problem-solving conference.

The technique usually involves 40–80 stakeholders working together for a total of 18 hours over three days, and experts are excluded. Participants form into small heterogeneous or homogeneous sub-groups to perform a series of six tasks.

In the first task, 'Focus on our history', groups consider global, organizational and personal changes. Sheets of paper representing decades are displayed on the walls, and participants write down their memories on them. The aim is to emphasize the historical context and build a common data base. Once completed, heterogeneous sub-groups of eight interpret one of the wall charts, looking for patterns and insights. This helps group members work together and gain confidence in each others' abilities.

The second task is 'Focus on the present: current trends'. A wall map is created, with the company or issue at its centre, and members of the whole group are invited to call out the trends or factors they believe are currently affecting the organization or issue. The resulting map is often overwhelming: members begin to realize that their preferred solution will not work, that they are all interdependent, and that they need others to find a solution. Participants then vote to identify what they consider the most important factors affecting the organization or issue, and highlight about half a dozen of these. Finally, sub-groups select one of these to work on in greater detail, considering what they currently do and what they would like to do.

During the third task, members discuss their 'prouds' and 'sorries' – they consider what they feel proud or sorry about in relation to the conference theme, and then consider the implications of this.

The fourth task, 'Focus on the future', signals a change in direction. Heterogeneous groups develop and present role-plays of desired future scenarios.

The fifth task, 'Discover common futures', is to identify themes that are common to the various role-plays and integrate them into a single list, which is then reviewed by the whole group.

The final task, 'Take action', can take one of several forms. In one version, stakeholder sub-groups agree on actions to take given their strategic goals, and share these with the whole group. In another, individuals self-select the future initiatives they want to work on, and form task groups to plan short- and long-term action steps.

Bunker, B.B. and Alban, B.T. (1997) 'Future Search', in *Large Group Interventions: Engaging the Whole System for Rapid Change*, Jossey-Bass, pp. 43–60.
Weisbord, M.R. (1987) *Productive Workplaces*, Berrett-Koehler.
Weisbord, M.R. (1992) *Discovering Common Ground*, Berrett-Koehler.
Weisbord, M.R. and Janoff, S. (1995) *Future Search*, Berrett-Koehler.

See also: Action training and research; Business process re-engineering; Conference Model; Fast-cycle full-participation work design; Large-group interventions; Open-space technology; Participative design; Search conference; Socio-technical systems design; Strategic planning process; Real-time strategic change; Real-time work design; Simu-Real; Work-Out

Gestalt techniques (gestalt therapy)

The gestalt form of psychotherapy was developed by Frederick ('Fritz') Perls. *Gestalt* in German means 'an organized whole', and the gestalt approach considers the human being as an organism which functions as a whole, rather than as a set of fragmented parts. People therefore possess both positive and negative characteristics which need to be acknowledged and expressed, and difficulties occur when people operate in a fragmented way, not accepting themselves, and attempting to conform to others' demands and expectations.

Gestalt therapy aims to help people achieve integration, maturation, authenticity, awareness and behaviour change to develop 'wholeness' or 'completeness'. Lack of wholeness is considered to be a personality 'hole' caused by a blockage at some point along the way to maturity. Once this hole is identified, the client and therapist can try to deal with the blockage. Perls's view was that talking about it, as in psychoanalysis, was not effective. What was needed was an active and directed approach. Perls stressed the need to take responsibility for one's actions, the need to experience and live in the present, and to stop blocking off awareness and authenticity through dysfunctional behaviour. The approach therefore consists of three basic elements: emphasis on the present (the 'here and now'); self-awareness and self-regulation and the integration of new insights, plus self-acceptance, thereby leading to the possibility of personal change.

Gestalt techniques have long been used in clinical and educational settings, and underlie encounter groups and confluent education. Their influence on management training can be traced back to the 1970s, and they have also been used in organizational development activities and team-building interventions.

Gestalt therapy relies on a great many of the techniques of Jacob Moreno, who is best remembered for the development of sociodrama. In the *two chairs technique*, the client first sits in the 'hot seat', moving to the other chair when enacting another person or another part of themselves. The *role-reversal technique* involves the client enacting their own subjective reactions and taking the role of an adversary. The consultant's task is to prevent the client rationalizing or escaping in some other way from the here-and-now activities that aim to develop some aspect of the client's personality which has not been completed because it was blocked. Clients find relief in doing things they fear in fantasy and have therefore shied away from, and in some respects gestalt therapy resembles Frank's logotherapy and Wolpe's desensitization techniques.

Although gestalt therapy has been applied to organizational and management development, this has mainly happened in the USA, where its application to organizational change interventions, such as team-building, was pioneered by Stanley Herman, a management consultant with TRW Systems. He used a form of team-building that worked with a group of people but focused on the individuals within it, the objective being to make them stronger or more authentic. When applied to leader–subordinate relations, the primary objective is not to build a stronger work team, but to help individuals develop and experience their own potency and ability to cope with the world inside the organization. The activities and interactions are geared to helping participants to identify ('get in touch with') their own feelings, deal with them to conclusion (rather than avoiding relations with other people), and accept their individual strengths and weaknesses.

Burke, W.W. (1980) 'Systems Theory, Gestalt Theory and Organization Development', in Cummings, T.G. (ed.) *Systems Theory for Organization Development*, Wiley.

Herman, R.L. (1971) 'Towards a More Authentic Manager', *Training and Development Journal*, October.

Herman, R.L. (1974) 'Goals of Gestalt Therapy', *Professional Psychology*, May, pp. 178–84.

Herman, S. (1975) 'A Gestalt Orientation in Organizational Development', in Burke, W.W. (ed.) *New Technologies in Organization Development 1*, Pfeiffer/Jossey-Bass.

Herman, S. and Korenich, M. (1977) *Authentic Management: A Gestalt Orientation to Organizations and their Development*, Addison Wesley Longman.

Passons, W.R. (1975) *Gestalt Approaches in Counselling*, Holt, Rinehart and Winston.

Perls, F. (1969) *Gestalt Therapy Verbatim*, Penguin Books.

Perls, F., Hefferline, R.F. and Goodman, P. (1976) *Gestalt Therapy*, Penguin Books.

Polster, E. and Polster, M. (1973) *Gestalt Therapy Integrated*, Brunner/Mazel.

Stevens, J.O. (1978) *Gestalts*, Bantam Books.

See also: Androgynous management; Apperception-interaction method; Basic encounter; Cluster laboratory; Confluent education: Cousin laboratory; Encounter groups; Group development laboratory; Human relations laboratory; Illuminative incident analysis; Instrumented laboratory;

Laboratory method; Monodrama; Non-verbal exercise; Open encounter; Organizational laboratory; Personal development laboratory; Sensitivity (T-group) training; Sociodrama; Tavistock conference method; Values clarification

Getting acquainted

This technique can be used to bring to the surface issues that are hidden in a group, or to establish a new atmosphere when a meeting is going badly because of distrust or competition between members. It can also be used as an 'ice-breaker' to enliven a session and give participants a chance to influence what will happen during the course of it, or to rekindle interest between people who have worked together for a long time.

At the beginning of an organizational change activity, the facilitator should explain the procedure in advance so that everyone knows what is going on and what is expected of them. Participants then pair off with someone they do not know well, and they question each other about a number of personal issues, such as what aspects of the job they like and dislike. After this, the group re-forms and the members introduce their partners. The interview questions need to be chosen carefully to ensure they are appropriate, both in terms of what the group is doing and the level of trust that exists within it. The facilitator needs to observe and listen carefully: if participants do not like the questions, there may be good reasons.

To speed up the process, the activity can also be conducted using trios or small groups of people, with the group membership being reshuffled and the task repeated until all participants have been introduced to all the others. In this case, it is best if the questions are less personal and narrower in scope, and they can be restricted to building an agenda for the meeting, for example: 'What do you hope to get out of this meeting?' Suggestions for the agenda should be displayed on flipcharts, and those supplying significant information should be rewarded.

Fordyce, J.R. and Weil, R. (1971) *Managing With People*, Addison Wesley Longman, pp. 170–2.

See also: Critiquing; Family group team-building meeting; Going round the room; Likes and reservations; Non-verbal encounters; Polling; Subgrouping

Goal-setting

Goal-setting is a systematic intervention approach. Assigning an employee a specific task, objective or deadline was first practised by the adherents of scientific management, who used time and motion study coupled with incentive payments to increase shop-floor workers' output. The same idea was later revised and applied to managers, in which case it is known as management by objectives.

There are eight steps in goal-setting: the employee's key job tasks are identified; specific and challenging goals are established for each one; deadlines for each goal are specified; the employee is encouraged to participate; the goals are prioritized; they are rated in terms of difficulty and importance; feedback mechanisms are built in to assess progress and, finally, rewards are linked to goal attainment.

Locke and Latham used goal-setting as a motivational tool to improve employee performance. They argue that whether work goals are set unilaterally by a supervisor or in collaboration with employees, they increase the level of production significantly, and contribute to a reduction in absenteeism and injuries. Their research suggests that employees assigned difficult goals perform better than those assigned easy ones, and those who have specific, challenging goals generally outperform those with vague ones. In addition, Locke and Latham found that pay and performance incentives lead to improved performance only when they lead the individual to set higher goals. They recommend that where the work itself is meaningless and boring, introducing a goal that is difficult but attainable serves to increase the challenge of the job as well as making it clear to the worker what is expected of them.

Goal feedback can give workers a sense of achievement, recognition and accomplishment. It enables them to check their progress against past performance, and also compare themselves with others. The result may be that workers not only expend greater effort, but also devise better or more creative tactics for attaining the goal.

Farh, J.-L. and Bedeian, A.G. (1987) Understanding Goal-setting: An In-class Experiment', *Organizational Behaviour Teaching Review*, vol. 12, no. 3, pp. 75–9.

Ivancevich, J.M., McMahon, J.T., Streidl, J.W. and Szilagyi, A.D. (1978) 'Goal Setting: The Tennaco Approach to Personal Effectiveness and Managerial Development', *Organizational Dynamics*, Winter, pp. 158–80.

Latham, G.P. and Bales, J.J. (1975) 'The "Practical Significance" of Locke's Theory of Goal Setting', *Journal of Applied Psychology*, vol. 60, pp. 122–4.

Latham, G.P. and Kinne, S.B. (1974) 'Improving Job Performance through Training in Goal Setting', *Journal of Applied Psychology*, vol. 59, pp. 187–91.

Latham, G.P. and Locke, E.A. (1979) 'Goal

Setting: A Motivational Technique that Works', *Organizational Dynamics*, vol. 8, pp. 68–80.

Latham, G.P. and Yukl, G.A. (1975) 'Review of Research on the Application of Goal Setting in Organizations', *Academy of Management Journal*, December, vol. 18, no. 2, pp. 824–45.

Locke, E.A. (1978) 'The Ubiquity of the Technique of Goal Setting in Theories and Approaches to Employee Motivation', *Academy of Management Review*, July, vol. 3, no. 3, pp. 594–601.

Locke, E.A. and Latham, G.P. (1984) *Goal Setting: A Motivational Technique that Works*, Prentice-Hall.

Locke, E.A. and Latham, G.P. (1990) *A Theory of Goal Setting and Task Performance*, Prentice-Hall.

Locke, E.A., Cartledge, N. and Koeppel, J. (1968) 'Motivational Effects of Knowing Results: A Goal Setting Phenomenon?', *Psychological Bulletin*, December, vol. 70, no. 6, pp. 428–33.

Marsch, T.W. et al. (1995) 'Improving Safety Behaviour Using Goal Setting and Feedback', *Leadership and Organization Development Journal*, vol. 16, no. 1, pp. 5–12.

Wilson, S.B. (1993) *Goal Setting: Worksmart Guide*, American Management Association, AMACOM.

See also: ACHIEVE model; Appraisal; Discipline without punishment; Feedback; Follow-up; Goal-setting and planning groups; Job descriptions; Likert's level meetings; Management by objectives; Measuring performance; Ongoing feedback system; Periodic planning review; Position charter; Positive feedback; Self- with peer-appraisal

Goal-setting and planning groups

Goal-setting and planning groups undertake a systematic review of performance leading to the setting of targets or goals that are the products of mutual commitments. Progress towards the goals will also be jointly reviewed. The groups may be pairs of superiors and subordinates, or family teams (a group of employees reporting to the same manager) throughout the company.

See also: Appraisal; Goal-setting; Goal-setting interface groups; Interface groups; Informal action group; Job description; Management by objectives; Measuring performance; Ongoing feedback system; Periodic planning review; Position charter

Goal-setting interface groups

Goal-setting interface groups enlist representatives from several related groups in a company to set action or change goals, usually on very specific issues. The basic work is done in mixed sub-groups consisting of five or six members. Each of these represents a department or unit, and the mix encourages an exchange of ideas and assists in the collection of information and the setting of goals. The sub-groups report back to the other participants, and a procedure which has been previously discussed and agreed is used to integrate the results: for example, group inputs may be incorporated into a decision to be made by a manager, or a committee consisting of a representative from each group may prepare a report for all the participants or for senior managers.

See also: Employee-guided management; Informal action group; Informal management team; Goal-setting and planning groups; Matrix designs; Non-conforming enclave; Scenario planning; Search conference; Strategic management

Going round the room

This technique can be used a number of times during any meeting, and simply consists of asking each participant in turn to describe their current opinions and feelings about the matter being considered. It can be particularly useful in discussions on difficult and contentious issues or if a meeting becomes deadlocked. It may reveal a general attitude or mood within the group which was not previously apparent. If a few participants have dominated the meeting so far, low contributors can be asked to speak first.

The method has a number of advantages. It allows the facilitator or chairperson to obtain contributions from the more reticent participants and prevents a vociferous minority dominating the meeting. It can be used to channel the discussion in more productive directions, or to check where the group is in its deliberations. It can also help a group uncover solutions to problems it is discussing, but it is most useful as a way of ending a meeting, when it may bring to the fore any issues which members have been hesitant to raise earlier.

Fordyce, J.R. and Weil, R. (1971) *Managing With People*, Addison Wesley Longman, p. 159.

See also: Critiquing; Getting acquainted; Likes and reservations; Non-verbal encounters; Polling; Sub-grouping

Gordon seminar

Gordon seminars are named after the late Dr Neil Gordon, a chemistry professor at Johns Hopkins University. Gordon was dissatisfied with the standard ways of transmitting scientific information, which relied on learned journals or conference meetings organized by and for academics. Instead, he wanted a small group of scientists to meet in a secluded, relaxed atmosphere that fostered an attitude of give and take.

Gordon seminars have several unique features. The formal sessions are only held in the mornings and evenings. Afternoons are reserved for recreation, private study – and above all, talk. Journalists are banned, as are tape recorders; and no papers or reports are available. Accommodation is intentionally spartan, and formal dress (including ties) is banned. The resulting structure and atmosphere fosters collaboration between participants. Researchers often re-order their priorities or completely redesign their experiments, and information exchange is freer without publicity or the pressure to publish.

Toufexis, A. (1980) 'Dr Gordon's Serious Thinkers', *Time*, 25 August, p.45.

See also: Brains Trust; Colloquy meeting; Conference meeting; Conference method; Institute meeting; Interview meeting; Panel discussion; Reaction panel; Symposium meeting

Greenfield plants

When a company wants to make a fresh start in order to make major changes in working methods and to revise its organizational culture from the top down, it may choose to set up a new plant away from urban areas, in a so-called 'greenfield site'. Because the labour pool in such locations will usually have no experience of the industry concerned and less interest in unions, the firm can break free of entrenched attitudes to work that might obstruct the introduction of new ideas and technology. For example, an organization may want to establish a participatively managed operation with a minimum of formal supervision, relying on autonomous or self-managed teams, or developments in new technology and trade union resistance may lead a company to set up a completely new facility, complete with a revised agreement on trade union rights.

Many of the innovations at greenfield sites are based on the belief that people want to work, they want to know that their work is effective, they want to be recognized for their individual contributions, and they work better if they can participate in decisions regarding work methods. It is felt that if people can see the task as a whole and recognize the importance of their individual contribution to the group effort, job demarcation will be less important, except in terms of acquired skills and safe working practices.

Where this approach has been tried, emphasis has been placed on the process of selecting new workers, especially if group-based methods are to be used, and in some cases prospective workers' families may be invited to tour the plant. Training tends to be an important part of the set-up period, and the new structure allows managers to arrange the production processes, the physical plant layout, and the machinery so that they gain from the team approach.

Greenfield plants tend to use cross-trained workers. Job classifications are few, and job rotation is maximized to reduce the need for specialists. Team members are encouraged to take on indirect work functions such as setting up machines, inspecting parts and ordering materials. The effect is that teams become multifunctional, and are frequently salaried, with pay rises related to increases in skill and knowledge. Participative team-building techniques are used, and the self-managing nature of the work team often means that traditional supervisors take on an advisory role, assisting with team meetings, advising on the selection of replacement staff, and approving team designs and projects.

Guest, D. and Hoque, K. (1996) 'National Ownership and Human Resource Practices in UK Greenfield Sites', *Human Resource Management Journal*, vol. 6, no. 4, pp. 50–74.

Kemp, N.J., Wall, T., Clegg, C.W. and Cordery, J.L. (1983) 'Autonomous Work Groups in a Greenfield Site', *Occupational Psychology*, vol. 56, pp. 271–88.

Leopold, J.W. and Hallier, J. (1997) 'Start Up and Aging in Greenfield Sites', *Human Resource Management Journal*, vol. 7, no. 2, pp. 72–88.

Smith, C. and Elger, T. (1998) 'Greenfields and "Wilderbeasts": Management Strategies and Labour Turnover in Japanese Firms in Telford', *Employee Relations*, vol. 20, no. 3, pp. 271–84.

See also: Autonomous workgroups; Company culture training; Development of a new management/operating philosophy; Family communication programme; Ideological change; Managerial strategy change; Mission cards; Myth-making interventions; Organizational climate analysis

Grid Development (grid OD; managerial grid; grid management training)

The management Grid Development programme was developed by Robert Blake and Jane Mouton. Over a period of three to five years, the programme addresses development issues at the individual, group, inter-group and organizational level, considering both managerial style and corporate strategy. It is frequently conducted by organization members who have been trained in a wide variety of approaches and techniques which allow managers, both individually and in groups, to assess their strengths and weaknesses and move towards becoming 'team managers'.

The programme uses a two-dimensional schema to examine and improve individual managers' practices. A questionnaire helps them to identify their *concern for people* on one dimension and their *concern for production* on the other. The most effective managers are held to be those who score highly on both dimensions – in grid terminology, those who have a '9.9' management style, reflecting the philosophy: 'Work accomplished is from committed people; interdependence through a "common stake" in organizational purpose leads to relationships of trust and respect.'

The grid programme consists of one preliminary seminar and six main phases. In the preliminary stage, the company managers who are to act as programme instructors attend a week-long grid seminar themselves. The main purpose of this event is to enable them to decide whether the approach is likely to be appropriate for their organization and, if so, how to conduct the programme. They assess their own managerial styles using grid instruments and the two-dimensional schema, develop team action skills, and learn techniques to improve their abilities to solve problems, give feedback and communicate. They also learn to analyse team and organizational culture.

In the first phase, the programme instructors organize a seminar for all company managers where they pass on the knowledge they gained in the preliminary seminar.

The second phase focuses on team development. Participants learn how to analyse and manage their team's culture by working on real problems and issues of interest to them, with the aim of developing the team's planning, objective-setting and problem-solving skills. Managers receive feedback on their individual and team behaviour, giving them an insight into how others see their strengths and weaknesses.

Phase three concentrates on the dynamics of inter-group co-operation and competition in order to develop more constructive inter-group relations. Each group's desired relationship with others is identified, and this information is shared. The groups consider ways of achieving these goals, and action plans to be implemented by group members are agreed.

The development of a strategic corporate model constitutes the fourth phase of the process. A top management group designs an ideal strategic corporation model which describes what the company would be like if it were excellent. Ideas and contributions from all members of the organization can be sought and incorporated. Comparing the existing organizational structure and processes with the ideal gives managers an indication of what changes are desirable. This process can take up to a year.

In the penultimate phase, planning teams are appointed to examine what changes are necessary in their part of the organization to realize the model's objectives, and these are then carried out.

The last phase consists of a systematic critique of the preceding five phases to identify achievements, barriers that need to be overcome, and any new opportunities.

Bernardin, H.J. and Alvares, K.M. (1976) 'The Management Grid as a Predictor of Conflict Resolution Method and Managerial Effectiveness', *Administrative Science Quarterly*, vol. 21, no. 1, pp. 84–92.

Blake, R.R. and McCanse, A.A. (1991) *Leadership Dilemmas: Grid Solutions*, Gulf Publishing.

Blake, R.R. and Mouton, J.S. (1968) *Corporate Excellence Through Grid Organization Development*, Gulf Publishing.

Blake, R.R. and Mouton, J.S. (1969) *Building a Dynamic Corporation Through Grid Organization Development*, Addison Wesley Longman.

Blake, R.R. and Mouton, J.S. (1975) 'Managerial Grid in Practice', in Taylor, B. and Lippitt, G.L. (eds) *Management Development and Training Handbook*, McGraw-Hill.

Blake, R.R. and Mouton, J.S. (1979) *The New Managerial Grid* (3rd edn), Gulf Publishing.

Blake, R.R. and Mouton, J.S. (1985) *The New Managerial Grid III*, Kogan Page.

Blake, R.R., Mouton, J.S., Barnes, L.B. and Greiner, L.E. (1964) 'Breakthrough in Organization Development', *Harvard Business Review*, vol. 42, November–December, pp. 133–55.

Clark, G. (1974) 'Managerial Grid Training: An Application in ICI Pharmaceuticals Division', in Berger, M. and Berger, P. (eds) *Group Training Techniques*, Gower.

Hart, H.A. (1974) 'Grid Appraised: Phase 1 and 2', *Personnel*, vol. 51, September, pp. 44–59.

Keller, R.T. (1978) 'A Longitudinal Assessment of a Managerial Grid Seminar Training Programme', *Group and Organizational Studies*, vol. 3, no. 3, pp. 343–55.

Smith, P.B. and Honour, T.F. (1969) 'The Impact of Phase 1, Managerial Grid Training', *Journal of Management Studies*, vol. 6, pp. 318–30.

Strauss, G. (1972) 'Organizational Development: Credits and Debits', *Organizational Dynamics*, vol. 1, no. 3, Winter, pp. 2–19.

Williams, A.P.O. (1971) 'The Managerial Grid: Phase 2, Case Study of a Top Management Team', *Occupational Psychology*, vol. 45, nos 3 and 4, pp. 253–72.

Group buzz (buzz groups)

Buzz groups consist of two to six persons who discuss an issue or problem for a short period during a lesson or lecture. They do not require a great deal of preparation, and the flexibility of the method means it can be used with very large classes, either formally or informally, with each session lasting as little as five minutes. Although buzz groups tend to be popular with students, it may be necessary to exercise care when introducing them to learners who are more accustomed to didactic methods.

Buzz groups offer a number of advantages. They allow tutors to check students' understanding by setting problems for each group to solve, and also provide feedback on the effectiveness of their teaching. They can help to consolidate learning if the task involves relating different parts of the lecture or buzz group members' common experiences. Applying information and analytical, evaluative or critical thinking can be encouraged by setting questions such as 'What are the advantages of ...?' or 'What is the difference between ...?' They can encourage reticent students to put forward their ideas and views. They help to foster a cohesive class spirit and, last but not least, they can give the tutor a breathing space.

There are a number of ways of organizing buzz groups, but groups of three should be used when individual viewpoints are likely to be expressed. In a lecture hall, a row of students can be asked to discuss an issue with those in the row behind, or two or three people in the same row can be asked to form a group. The buzz group idea can also be developed into a 'pyramid' or 'snowball' process. In this variation, a question or problem is first discussed by students in pairs, then fours, then a group of eight. A spokesperson can be appointed from each buzz group to report back to the whole group in a plenary session.

Bligh, D.A. (1972) *What's the Use of Lectures?*, Penguin.
University Teaching Methods Unit (1976) *Improving Teaching in Higher Education*, University Teaching Methods Unit, University of London.

Group circular interviewing

In group circular interviewing, participants sit in a circle, and each group member interviews the person opposite them about a given topic for a set period. The interviewer and interviewee roles then rotate around the group until everyone has had an opportunity to take on both. The advantages of this method are that it provides a non-threatening context in which participants can ask and answer questions without worrying about appearing foolish, and it can serve as an opener or ice-breaker, encouraging participants to talk to each other.

Group cross-overs (cross-over group; square root group)

Cross-over groups provide a quick way of familiarizing a large group with its individual members' ideas and opinions. They can be used as an ice-breaking activity at the start of a course or conference, or after a brief question-raising lecture.

The whole group is divided into a number of sub-groups in such a way that the number of people in each sub-group is the square root of the total number participating. Any extra participants can act as observers. Each sub-group then discusses for a fixed period a topic or question set by the tutor. After a predetermined interval, one member from each sub-group transfers to another one, being replaced by someone from another sub-group. The new members are briefed on what was discussed before their arrival, and they share information on the opinions and ideas from their previous sub-group. This process of discussion followed by transfer is repeated until only one person remains in their original sub-group.

Group line-ups; Group Phillips 66 technique; Group poster tours; Group pyramids; Group rounds; Group syndicate method; Group with ground rules; Small-group teaching

Group development laboratory (group dynamics laboratory)

In a group development laboratory, participants learn to diagnose and intervene in group processes. They explore how a group's structure and culture develop, how its character can be analysed and its norms changed through the actions of its members, and how groups can be organized to achieve specific tasks. Such laboratories frequently use exercises to explore group problem-solving and decision-making.

Friedlander, F. and Brown, L.D. (1977) 'Research on Organization Development: A Synthesis and Some Implications', in Burke, W.W. *Current Strategies in Organization Development*, Human Sciences Press.

Margulies, N. and Wallace, J. (1973) *Organizational Change: Techniques and Applications*, Scott Foresman, pp. 69–70.

See also: Basic encounter; Behaviour analysis; Bioenergetics; Cluster laboratory; Cousin laboratory; Encounter groups; Gestalt techniques; Human relations laboratory; Instrumented laboratory; Laboratory training; Personal development laboratory; Organization laboratory; Process consultation; Psychodrama; Sensitivity (T-group) training; Tavistock conference method; Transactional Analysis

Group discussion

Group discussions may be conducted in a wide variety of ways, but they usually centre on a specific problem, and some kind of agenda will have been agreed beforehand. Research suggests that most people work harder when they work together, and that groups are superior to individuals in some problem-solving tasks. Many people learn more rapidly in groups, and can transfer group experiences back to their individual work. However, more able students have not been found to benefit from group learning, and the social processes involved may actually inhibit their learning. Group discussions are not particularly well suited to realizing lower-order cognitive objectives. They are more appropriate for achieving higher-order cognitive objectives as well as affective ones, such as improving motivation and changing emotions and attitudes.

In order to increase the effectiveness of the approach, it is sometimes useful to put all the low contributors in one sub-group and all the high contributors in another. However, if participants are divided into sub-groups, it is important to allocate sufficient time for a plenary session where ideas can be shared under the guidance of a chairperson or tutor to ensure that all groups are given equal opportunity to contribute.

Andrews, D.J.W. (1980) 'The Verbal Structure of Teacher Questions: Its Impact on Class Discussions', *Professional and Organizational Development Quarterly*, nos 2, 3 and 4, pp. 129–63.

Christensen, C.R., Garvin, D.A. and Sweet, A. (1991) *Education for Judgement: The Artistry of Discussion Leadership*, Harvard Business Review Press.

Diamond, N.J. (1972) 'Improving the Undergraduate Lecture Class by the Use of Student Led Discussion Groups', *American Psychologist*, vol. 27, pp. 978–81.

Elbe, K. (1976) *The Craft of Teaching*, Jossey-Bass.

Ewens, W. (1985–6) 'Teaching Using Discussion', *Organizational Behaviour Teaching Review*, vol. 10, no. 3, pp. 77–80.

Hyman, R.T. (1980) *Improving Discussion Leadership*, Teachers College Press.

Jaques, D. (1991) *Learning in Groups* (2nd edn), Kogan Page.

Thorley, L. and Gregory, R. (eds) (1996) *Using Group-based Learning in Higher Education*, Kogan Page.

See also: Abercrombie method; Advanced seminar; Apperception-interaction method; Case conference; Free discussion method; Group buzz; Group circular interviewing; Group cross-overs; Group five minutes each way; Group line-ups; Group Phillips 66 technique; Group poster tours; Group pyramids; Group rounds; Group syndicate method; Group with ground rules; Problem-centred group; Seminar; Small-group teaching

Group dynamics laboratory

This form of training focuses on the evolving structure of groups and the ways their character can be diagnosed (by means of behaviour analysis) and changed through the actions of group members. The idea of dynamics is important, because this approach does not concentrate on the static structure of a group or the individual, interpersonal or organizational determinants of behaviour, but regards each group as a unit in a state of flux.

Exercises can be used to explore group decision-making, group problem-solving and the way in which group cultures and structures develop. In addition, participants examine how group norms change and how a group might organize itself to accomplish specific tasks.

Hunter, D., Bailey, A. and Taylor, B. (1996) *The Facilitation of Groups*, Gower.

See also: Behaviour analysis; Human relations laboratory; Laboratory training; Microlab; Organizational laboratory; Personal development laboratory; Power laboratory; Process analysis; Tavistock conference method; Team laboratory; Sensitivity (T-group) training

Group five minutes each way

One problem with paired group discussion methods is that participants may fail to be sufficiently intellectually rigorous and may shy away from difficulties and complexities, especially of a personal nature. This technique asks each person in a pair to take turns to think about a topic out loud for five minutes. Their partner should not interrupt, but listens intensively and keeps time, bringing the speaker back to the topic if they wander off. The challenge is for the speaker to keep going for the full five minutes, and it is important that if they do 'dry up', the listener does not bale them out.

The topics for the monologue can be tailored to a particular course or session, such as 'My experience of perception concepts in advertising' or 'Problems I experience working in a group'.

The method can be used either as a session-opener to encourage participation, in the middle of a session to encourage reflection, or as a closing activity to encourage people to take stock of what they have learned or explore how they might apply it.

See also: Group buzz; Group circular interviewing; Group cross-overs; Group discussion; Group line-ups; Group Phillips 66 technique; Group poster tours; Group pyramids; Group rounds; Group syndicate method; Group with ground rules; Small-group teaching

Group investigation model

The group investigation model is based on the philosophy of co-operative learning, emphasizing a democratic approach to decision-making, requiring a real puzzle for groups to focus on, and placing the instructor in the role of counsellor/facilitator.

Proponents of co-operative learning believe that group learning settings are more motivating and produce greater synergy than individual, competitive ones. They maintain that people learn from each other, and interacting with others produces

cognitive and social complexity which creates intellectual learning. Co-operative learning is also held to reduce alienation and loneliness, to increase self-esteem by encouraging feelings of being respected and cared for by others, and to develop participants' ability to work in a team.

Coupled to the notion of co-operation is that of inquiry and knowledge: Herbert Thelen felt that inquiry is stimulated by being confronted with a problem, and that knowledge results from that enquiry. The model consists of five stages.

First, students encounter a puzzling situation – perhaps something they discover themselves (unplanned) or which is found and presented by the instructor (planned). Next, they collectively explore their reactions to it before formulating their study task and preparing for it by defining the problem and assigning roles. Having done this, they undertake both independent and group study. Finally, they analyse their progress on their task, and the process of their working style, before beginning the whole process again by finding another puzzling situation.

Johnson, D.W. and Johnson, R.T. (1975) *Learning Together and Alone*, Prentice-Hall Europe.
Joyce, B., Weil, M. and Showers, B. (1992) *Models of Teaching* (4th edn), Allyn and Bacon, pp. 29–52.
Thelen, H. (1960) *Education and the Human Quest*, Harper and Row.

See also: Application of principles; Incident process analysis; Inquiry training model

Group line-ups

This is a group discussion method that engages participants both physically and mentally, since they are asked to commit themselves to a view on an issue by literally taking position on a line which represents that view. Topics that are controversial and can be stated clearly but briefly in the form of a motion are best, such as: 'Conflict in organizations is a problem, and should be avoided' or 'The importance of leadership in company success has been overrated.' Line-ups require little preparation beyond thinking up a topic, provide participants with many issues to talk about, need only take a few minutes to run, and can be adapted for use with large groups.

The learning that arises from this method does not come from the process of voting as such, but because participants need to talk to those next to them to establish their colleagues' views. This usually generates much spirited debate, and amendments can be made to focus on more detailed or subtle issues: for example, '*Inter-personal* conflict in organizations is a problem, and should be avoided' or 'The importance of *charismatic* leadership in company success has been overrated.'

Holmes, B.H. (1997) 'Want Participation? Have Them "Vote with their Feet"', *Journal of Management Education*, vol. 21, no. 1, pp. 117–20.

See also: Group buzz; Group circular interviewing; Group cross-overs; Group discussion; Group five minutes each way; Group Phillips 66 technique; Group poster tours; Group pyramids; Group rounds; Group syndicate method; Group with ground rules; Small-group teaching

Group Phillips 66 technique (Phillips 66 technique)

Developed by J. Donald Phillips, the Phillips 66 technique involves dividing a large group into sub-groups of six persons to discuss an issue for six minutes – hence the technique's name. It can be used with groups of ten or twenty, or several hundred, and is a quick way to obtain a large number of ideas, suggestions, attitudes or recommendations. Although it may be used as an ice-breaker, it is not intended to serve as a meeting in its own right, but to supplement other group discussion methods.

The sub-groups are formed with as little movement of chairs as possible, and in a lecture hall with fixed seating, a group of three can turn to face the three people in the row above them. Each sub-group is encouraged to take a minute or two to get acquainted and select a chairperson or 'scribe'. The nature of the questions posed is crucial in this form of exercise, so a clear and concise statement of a problem or issue is given, worded in such a way as to encourage specific single-statement answers. The six-minute discussion period then begins. When each member has expressed an opinion, the sub-group selects the best one or two answers for its report. Finally, if there are ten or fewer groups, the whole group reconvenes and calls for reports from each of the groups.

Andrews, J.D.W. (1980) 'The Verbal Structure of Teacher Questions: Its Impact on Class Discussion', *Professional and Organizational Development Quarterly*, vol. 2, nos 3 and 4, pp. 129–63.

See also: Group buzz; Group circular interviewing; Group cross-overs; Group discussion; Group five minutes each way; Group line-ups; Group poster tours; Group pyramids; Group rounds; Group syndicate method; Group with ground rules; Small-group teaching

Group poster tours

One way to collect syndicate group reports is to ask each group to produce a summary poster. Apart from its novelty value, this provides a tangible, visible output compared to rather ephemeral verbal reports, and it has been used at academic conferences as a quick way of sharing research findings.

This technique develops participants' visual communication skills, because the debriefing simply involves displaying their posters while others tour them, viewing each one. Variations include stationing one syndicate member by their poster to answer questions, or placing a blank sheet of paper next to each poster so that reactions or comments can be recorded.

See also: Drawing for learning; Group buzz; Group circular interviewing; Group cross-overs; Group discussion; Group five minutes each way; Group line-ups; Group Phillips 66 technique; Group pyramids; Group rounds; Group syndicate method; Group with ground rules; Large groups as small groups; Poster; Small-group teaching; Talking wall

Group project (team project)

This is a generic term for one of the most popular learning approaches in the field of education. Typically, students are assigned a topic or set a question to answer, but the learning involved concerns the process of investigation and the nature of team working as much as the subject matter itself. They learn that while teams can achieve more than individuals, they demand attention to problems such as division of labour, generating and maintaining motivation, developing commitment and establishing appropriate leadership.

It is now rare to find an educational programme of any substantial length that lacks a group project element with a specific objective, structure and process. The role of the instructor is to be aware of the main group working problems and to anticipate them, and to allow students to gain the maximum benefit from their experience.

Daly, J.P. and Worrell, D.L. (1993) 'Structuring Group Projects as Miniature Organizations', *Journal of Management Education*, vol. 17, no. 2, pp. 236–42.

Drexler, J.A. and Larson, E.W. (1985–6) 'Survey Research Project: A Highly Interdependent Group Task', *Organizational Behaviour Teaching Review*, vol. 10, no. 4, pp. 39–47.

Fisher, C.D., Shaw, J.B. and Ryder, P. (1994) 'Problems in Project Groups', *Journal of Management Education*, vol. 18, no. 3, pp. 251–5.

Lerner, L.A. (1995) 'Making Student Groups Work', *Journal of Management Education*, vol. 19, pp. 123–5.

Liden, R.C., Nagao, D.H. and Parsons, C.K. (1985–6) 'Student and Faculty Attitudes Concerning the Use of Group Projects', *Organizational Behaviour Teaching Review*, vol. 10, no. 4, pp. 32–8.

Verderber, K.S. and Serey, T.T. (1996) 'Managing In-class Projects: Setting Them Up To Succeed', *Journal of Management Education*, vol. 20, no. 1, pp. 23–38.

See also: Action project; Co-op/co-op; Co-operative learning; Group syndicate method

Group pyramids (snowball groups)

This group discussion technique involves students initially working alone to generate ideas or answers in response to a task set by the instructor, such as a simple question, a case study, or an initial view of a problem in a case study. Group pyramids work best if the tasks students work on are varied in terms of their abstractness, complexity, length and topic. The instructor manages the process by briefing students on each stage and keeping a note of the time.

After about five minutes of individual thinking and writing, the students pair up to discuss their individual responses. This helps them develop the confidence to present their thoughts within a larger group. After a quarter of an hour, the pairs can be combined into groups of four or six, and this is the optimum size of group for this exercise, providing a range of different ideas. Allowing about half an hour for this stage should give all members the chance to contribute, then ten minutes can be devoted to inter-group sharing and an overview.

See also: Group buzz; Group circular interviewing; Group cross-overs; Group discussion; Group five minutes each way; Group line-ups; Group Phillips 66 technique; Group poster tours; Group rounds; Group syndicate method; Group with ground rules; Small-group teaching

Group rounds

The purpose of a group round is to allow each member to speak briefly in a non-threatening environment in order to encourage them to participate again. This is based on the observation that the longer someone waits before contributing to a group discussion, the more difficult they find it to speak.

Participants may sit in a circle or around a table.

Each person should have the opportunity to contribute before anyone is permitted to speak a second time, but they should be allowed to 'pass' at any point if they wish.

The process can begin by asking each participant to respond to a prompt such as: 'One thing that has confused me about this topic is ...' or 'A valuable text for this topic was ...'. Although useful as ice-breakers, group rounds can also be held at different points in a meeting or tutorial. In the middle, participants could be asked to complete observations such as: 'An issue we seem to have omitted so far is ...' or 'To summarize the discussion so far, I would say ...'. At the end, the prompts could include: 'The most useful thing I've learned today is ...' or 'As a result of today's discussion, I intend to...'.

See also: Group buzz; Group circular interviewing; Group cross-overs; Group discussion; Group five minutes each way; Group line-ups; Group Phillips 66 technique; Group poster tours; Group pyramids; Group syndicate method; Group with ground rules; Small-group teaching

Group syndicate method (syndicate group method)

The term 'syndicate discussion' is often applied in very general senses to any situation where groups of managers come together to discuss a question, followed by group reports and a plenary, or any situation where a large class is divided into small groups to discuss a topic.

However, this entry refers to a specific approach originally developed at the Administrative Staff College in Henley. In this purest form, a group of managers is given a subject brief or an agenda for discussion. One of the syndicate members is required to act as chairperson. There is usually an oral and written report, and each group's report is discussed at a plenary session run by the instructor. The knowledge and experience of syndicate group members is supplemented by exposure to reading, films and lectures on the relevant subjects. This approach relies on the ability and willingness of people to learn from each other, and appears to be most successful in modifying attitudes.

When adapted to a wider educational context, the approach involves linking the subject matter of lectures to group projects assigned to syndicates of about six members each. Each syndicate selects a chairperson, plus a scribe who will draft the report with the participation of all members. Representatives are then nominated to make a presentation to the entire class.

If a series of syndicates is working simultaneously on a set of different problems, or even if they are working on different versions of the same problem, it is possible to vary their membership by holding meetings at which a member from one syndicate gives a demonstration or presentation which members of any syndicate group can attend and participate in.

In the Henley model, the composition of the syndicates is changed from time to time to provide stimulus, give members an opportunity to work with different people and bring together or rotate those with specialist knowledge and/or experience.

Although the method can help people accept disagreements and learn from them, the generalized nature of the discussions, the ineffectiveness of many chairpersons and the lack of involvement this provokes has led it to be described as 'organizing an exchange of ignorance'.

Adams, J. (1975) 'The Use of Syndicates in Management Training', in Taylor, B. and Lippitt, G.L. (eds) *Management Development and Training Handbook*, McGraw-Hill.

Bertcher, H.J. and Maple, F.F. (1977) *Creating Groups*, Sage Human Services Guide, Sage.

Collier, G. (1983) *The Management of Peer Group Learning: Syndicate*, Methods in Higher Education, Society for Research into Higher Education.

Collier, K. (1965–6) 'An Experiment in University Teaching', *Universities Quarterly*, vol. 20, no. 3, pp. 336–48.

Collier, K. (1968–9) 'Syndicate Methods: Further Evidence and Comment', *Universities Quarterly*, vol. 23, no. 4, pp. 431–6.

Evans, C. (1980) 'The Use of Student Led Groups or Syndicates in French Literature Classes', *British Journal of Educational Technology*, vol. 11, no. 3, pp. 185–200.

Lawrence, G. (1972) 'The Syndicate Method', in *Varieties of Group Discussion in University Teaching*, University of London Institute of Education.

See also: Group buzz; Group circular interviewing; Group cross-overs; Group discussion; Group five minutes each way; Group line-ups; Group Phillips 66 technique; Group poster tours; Group project; Group pyramids; Group rounds; Group with ground rules; Problem-centred group; Small-group teaching

Group system of studying

This approach was developed by Sanderson, who was appointed headteacher of Oundle School in 1892 at the age of 35, and held the post until 1922. He reformed maths and science teaching in the school by organizing pupils into groups to work on problems. The out-of-school interest in science grew and, in a 'Science Conversazione', groups of students displayed experiments and collections which they had co-operated to produce.

This group system spread to other classes. Plays were not studied from annotated editions, but were acted out, and questions of language and interpretation were dealt with in relation to the production. Similar changes were introduced to the study of literature and history.

Following a preliminary survey of a new class, its members were divided into groups and allocated problems to solve. Working as a group increased interest in studying, and helped develop creative and co-operative work skills for later life.

The Official Life: Sanderson of Oundle, Chatto and Windus (1923).

See also: Co-op/co-op; Co-operative learning

Group technology (part family machining)

Group technology is a policy of grouping workers and their equipment in a way that harnesses many of the positive attributes of group activity by altering some of the basic aspects of technical organization.

At its simplest, group technology tries to ensure that work is diverse in character. Among its advantages is that, unlike older methods or production lines, it encourages workers to feel responsible for a complete unit of work. This can improve motivation, and provide scope for job enrichment and job enlargement.

In technical terms, group technology (sometimes referred to as 'part family machining') involves selecting components which are technologically similar, and which thus have the same machining requirements. Several systems are available for analysing components, such as Opitz and Brisch's, and machines are grouped accordingly. The approach is seen chiefly as a means of raising productivity in factories engaged in unit and batch production.

A characteristic of factories using group technology is that they are usually organized on a traditional functional basis, with different classes of machine, such as lathes, grinders and milling machines, grouped together. The supervisors of the groups of equipment are highly skilled in a particular trade. Considerable flexibility is possible, but this often involves intricate scheduling, long journeys of components, delays and the costs of frequently setting up for new jobs.

NEDO (1975) *Group Technology*, National Economic Development Council, London.

See also: Autonomous workgroups; Integrated support functions; Job design; Job enlargement; Job enrichment; Work simplification

Group with ground rules

This is a form of small-group discussion in which the participants establish certain ground rules with the aid of a facilitator to make them more aware of certain aspects of their interactional styles. Commonly used rules include that participants must speak in the first-person singular ('I was amazed when you ...' rather than 'It was surprising ...'), and that they must categorize each comment they make (e.g., 'proposal', 'summary', 'request').

Heron, J. (1973) *Experiential Training Techniques*, Department of Adult Education, University of Surrey, Guildford.

See also: Buberian dialogue; Fishbowl; Group buzz; Group circular interviewing; Group crossovers; Group discussion; Group five minutes each way; Group line-ups; Group Phillips 66 technique; Group poster tours; Group pyramids; Group rounds; Group syndicate method; Process analysis; Small-group teaching; Think-and-listen session

Guided design approach

The guided design approach (GDA) is an educational strategy that not only teaches students subject matter, but also develops their group working, information-gathering, problem-solving and decision-making skills, and increases their self-confidence. Although it has similarities to the popular, 'Lost in the Desert' (or 'jungle' or 'moon') group consensus task which is used on many management courses, the GDA approach can completely replace a traditional course.

The basic elements of GDA are a series of paired instruction-feedback activities sequenced to cover the course subject matter. GDA learning materials seek to develop students' skills in three areas. First, *active research to gain knowledge*: GDA uses both group work and a realistic problem situation to be solved. This motivates and puts pressure on individual group members to acquire relevant knowledge before coming to the class. Each member's desire for their group to succeed, as well as peer pressure for each to play their part, ensures that students study the course textbook and assigned readings. This means that instructors using GDA need to prepare a comprehensive study guide for students. The second set of skills developed by GDA is *decision-making and creative problem-solving*: by shifting the focus to problems to be solved, GDA dramatically alters the

instructor–student relationship. Rather than listening passively to lectures, students become active solution-seekers. Third, GDA helps demonstrate the *workability* of the knowledge they have presented: the course materials, particularly the feedback, stress how textbook knowledge can be applied to problem-solving. The group's solution may be better or worse than the expert feedback they receive after each decision point. By comparing their solution with the instructor's feedback, they can rate their performance in dealing with the course content against an average answer provided. In this way, they gain confidence in independent problem-solving.

The class is divided into groups of four to seven students who collaborate to make decisions during the scheduled class meetings. Although traditional lectures are replaced by group meeting sessions, students typically study the same amount of subject matter. The instructor may choose to present a mini-lecture at any time if it is felt that additional inputs are necessary and could enhance the group working process.

First, the instructor gives an introductory presentation setting out the aims and objectives of the course. The students are given notes which set the context for the first problem to be worked on, describing a specific situation, such as 'You are lost with colleagues in a boat near a tropical island' or 'You are responsible for planning a building on the university campus.' This problem forms the basis of the students' study of course content outside the class and their decision-making activities within it.

Each problem is open-ended, since the experience of trying to solve such problems emphasizes that few have a single solution, and that when working within a team the opinions and values of other members must be taken into account. By focusing both on decision-making and the acquisition of knowledge, GDA highlights the process of active minds seeking orderly solutions to complex problems.

The problems relate to the subject field being taught, matching the relevant learning objectives, and are structured into a sequence of steps, each of which requires a decision to be made. The groups must deal with the steps in order, and are not permitted to progress to the next step until they have considered and dealt with the previous one.

The classwork is organized around discussing the best decision, and the instructor prepares feedback documentation for each step which guides students through to an acceptable solution. The instructor also checks the availability of the resources the students are likely to seek in the library, reading room or resource centre, and some may have to be put on restricted loan.

In the beginning, students think about the

problem individually and make a personal choice before discussing it with their colleagues. The instructor moves from group to group, visiting each one briefly, listening, asking questions, encouraging students to participate in the decision-making process, and providing suggestions and guidance so that no group gets completely lost.

The groups quickly discover that certain information and skills are necessary to make an appropriate decision, and these need to be anticipated and planned for. An individual member might be assigned to go to the library to find the necessary data. Students also receive reading assignments from the instructor to be completed outside class meetings which inform and contribute to the decisions that will be made in their groups.

Once a group choice has been made, the instructor supplies a feedback sheet which lists some of the possible solutions, allowing the group to compare its choice with that of an experienced decision-maker. The importance of this written feedback is that it gives students a clear frame of reference for the subject matter being discussed within the class. In addition, it provides them with a unified starting point for the round of discussions that will occur in the next step of the problem-solving process. Without such feedback, there is a danger of the groups becoming disoriented and the instructor losing a sense of 'where each one is'. The instructor must control the flow of written feedback strictly because students have a tendency to try to shortcut the decision-making process by asking for the feedback page before demonstrating an adequate level of understanding of each problem-solving step.

Once the final feedback sheet has been distributed, the instructor can choose to highlight some of the events that have occurred in the case problem, or decide to discuss them later. When a highly constructive or creative solution is presented by a group, one that differs significantly from that described in the feedback sheet, the instructor may choose to share it with all the other groups.

Each group then receives instructions about the next step in the problem, and the process continues. Each problem may take between one and five weeks to complete, with students meeting regularly inside and outside the class during that period, and several problems will be covered during the semester or year-long course.

Amano, M.M. (1978) 'Applying the Guided Design System to Management Education', *Exchange: Organizational Behaviour and Teaching Journal*, vol. 3, no. 1, pp. 25–30.

Bailie, R.C. and Wales, C.E. (1975) 'Pride: A New Approach to Experiential Learning', *Engineering Education*, vol. 65, no. 5, February.

Tseng, M.S. and Wales, C.E. (1972) 'Effects of Guided Design Course Pattern on Student Personality Variables', *Engineering Education*, vol. 62, no. 7, April.

Wales, C.E. and Stager, R.A. (1978) *The Guided Design Approach*, Educational Technology Publications.

Wales, C.E., Stager, R.A. and Long, T.R. (1974) *Guided Engineering Design*, West Publishing.

See also: Action maze; Case study method; Critical incident approach; Game; Personalized system of instruction; Problem-centred approach; Problem-solving group; Programmed simulation; Simulation

Guided discussion

This method combines private learning with group development and criticism. The emphasis is on common exploration and discovery, based on strenuous co-operation and personal contribution. It is one of the most varied, flexible and effective teaching methods available. It can fulfil cognitive, inter-personal and role requirements to a high degree, and lends itself to the development and reinforcement of values. It is an efficient instrument for making full use of the experience, knowledge and expertise that exists in a particular group.

Twelve to fifteen is the optimum size for a guided discussion group. An effective group demands commitment from individual members as well as meticulous preparation by the tutor. The group's work also needs to be recorded continuously and copies circulated to group members, providing them with feedback material so that progress can be measured against the agreed scheme, plus a permanent record of what they have achieved.

Learning arises from comments made by group members and the tutor. However, although the tutor plans and directs the group's work, the discussion is not guided by the tutor's interventions while it is taking place – indeed, discussions may be held by students in the absence of the tutor altogether. It is guided by the self-feedback mechanism and by the fact that the group members know that they have to work to a specific timescale and to a specific plan. Tutors should restrict themselves to encouraging students' contributions in accordance with the agreed structure.

The value of guided discussion depends largely on the students' prior knowledge of the material to be discussed. At each group meeting, personal study and experience are pooled, shaped and then re-focused on the next stage of individual work, which will be discussed at the next meeting.

See also: Controlled discussion; Construct lesson plan; Self-instructional module and interactive groups; Step-by-step discussion; Tutorial-tape-document learning package approach

Guided group problem-solving

This is a non-traditional teaching strategy developed at Purdue University, whose full title is the Purdue Three Stage Model for Course Design. It helps students to learn basic concepts, principles and theories, and generally fosters the development of higher-order cognitive abilities.

Each stage of the Purdue model is based on different theoretical concepts and instructional approaches. Stage one is related to Keller's personalized system of instruction; stage two draws on Wales and Stager's guided design approach, small-group dynamics theory and problem-solving concepts, and stage three emphasizes critical thinking and individual problem-solving. Stage two is of most interest to us here, since it concerns teaching and learning strategies that take place in classroom settings and are designed to help students attain three major goals: learning the basic knowledge and theory of a discipline; learning problem-solving skills for applying knowledge to the solution of realistic problems, and learning the social skills necessary to work effectively in small, task-oriented decision-making groups.

Stage one involves covering the basic subject matter, concentrating on knowledge and comprehension. Facts, terms, concepts and principles are acquired, and the student is helped to become a self-directed learner. The knowledge-comprehension objectives for each content unit must be mastered by students before they begin the in-class activities related to a given unit. Reading for this stage is directed by a Self-Instruction Guide (SIG) that helps students prepare for mastery quizzes of subject content which make significant contributions to the in-class discussions involved in stage two and the individual work in stage three. Stage one activities may include programmed instruction, audio-tutorials, units, and taped and live lectures.

Stage two involves applying the basic knowledge to realistic questions which require students to develop high-order cognitive abilities and interpersonal skills. All the instruction is carried out by students working in small groups within the class setting. Occasionally, a group will have to meet outside class time to conduct a project. The group is directed by a Group Instruction Guide (GIG) for each task that consists of an introduction, a statement of objectives, and a delineation of the task/product to be completed.

Stage three requires students to demonstrate their ability to use the knowledge and skills developed during the first two stages in solving realistic problems on their own. These activities are guided by a set of instructions called Procedures for Individual Projects.

Ames, R. and Linden, K.W. (1978) *Small Group Problem Solving Activities for Applied Educational Psychology: A Three Stage Model Approach*, Waveland Press Inc.

Ames, R., Linden, K.W. and Feldhusen, J.F. (1977) 'Guided Group Problem Solving in the Purdue Three Stage Model of Instruction', *Educational Technology*, vol. 17, no. 8, pp. 12–16.

Feldhusen, J.F., Linden K.W. and Ames, R. (1975) 'Using Instructional Theory and Educational Technology in Designing College and University Courses: A Three Stage Model', in *Improving College and University Teaching Yearbook 1975*, Oregon State University Press, pp. 64–9.

See also: Autonomous group learning; Construct lesson plan; Discussion guide; Instrumented team learning; Self-instructional module and interactive groups; Structuring seminar; Personalized system of instruction

Guided study (guided learning)

Because guided study arose in response to the unsatisfactory conditions and results of home study, it often emphasizes the development of study skills. It is usually combined with other methods. Specific provision is made for study periods under the guidance of a tutor, who demonstrates analytical thinking, active reading, outlining and other key study skills. Guided study offers an unusual opportunity to provide for both rapid and slow learners, since the tutor can modify assignments to fit their needs. Problems may be studied or drill-and-review sessions proposed as necessary.

The tutor produces annotated booklists, and then develops these into a programme of assignments which specifies the learning requirements and the date for completion. The materials may take the form of a study pack giving precise references to books and other sources of information, or the students may seek references themselves. The tutor may distribute notes on points of difficulty or confusion, and sets some practical or written work to be completed by a target date. In the classroom, the tutor's role is to present a brief review of the material to be covered, to expand and develop the subject, and to encourage group discussion.

Baum, T. (1980) 'Reference Lists for Students', *Programmed Learning and Educational Technology*, vol. 17, no. 3, pp. 175–6.

Collier, K.C. (1968) *New Dimensions in Higher Education*, Addison Wesley Longman.

Fowler, R.L. and Barker, A.S. (1974) 'Effectiveness of Highlighting for the Retention of Text Material', *Journal of Applied Psychology*, vol. 59, no. 3, pp. 358–64.

Keen, T. and Reid, F. (1977) 'Guided Learning: A Discussion', *Programmed Learning and Educational Technology*, vol. 14, no. 1, pp. 26–32.

See also: Book reviewing; Block method; Circulated lecture notes; Handout; Library assignment; Literature search; Text; Tutorial-tape-document learning package approach

Handout (note)

Circulating information about the content of a lecture can allow more time for discussion or other activities, or ease the pressure of a crammed syllabus. Handouts may be used to give factual information before a lecture, thus acting as a 'leveller' to ensure that students have a common basic background in the subject before it is elaborated or developed. They provide a means of teaching more details than could normally be absorbed in a lecture, and permit complex concepts to be built on more simple ones which would have been unfamiliar without the handout. Handouts can also be used to prepare students for problem-solving lectures. Their function here is to relieve students of the need to absorb new information, thus freeing them to think about application, validity or relationships to other topics. To be most effective, this form of handout must be distributed a week in advance, with a system of headings and subheadings to help students absorb new information. There are a number of other types of handout.

Teaching objectives handouts are distributed before the first lecture, listing the course objectives and sensitizing students to what is to be learned. They are often included in students' course booklets. *Lecture guide handouts* prepare students for difficult lectures by giving them an overview of a whole topic before any single facet is considered. These should be given out well in advance and contain blank spaces for students to insert their own notes. They allow even the least able students to take away an accurate record of the major points. *Note-taking handouts* summarize lectures to discourage students from taking their own notes, and are also useful when it is difficult for them to do so, for example during a video presentation. *Handouts for thinking* consist of questions, tests or theoretical issues designed to stimulate thought. *Reading handouts* aim to stimulate and guide reading, and can be issued in advance. By means of a carefully structured programme of reading handouts in the course of a set of lectures, it is possible to show students through practical experience that lectures are only one of many sources of information that are available to them. It is also possible to train students to use books for research by initially providing very precise reading references (including chapters, paragraphs and page numbers) related to clearly defined parts of the course, then gradually supplying less detail until eventually they are just given a list of books to choose from.

Barker, L. and Lombardi, B. (1985) 'Students' Lecture Notes and their Relation to Test Performance', *Teaching of Psychology*, vol. 12, no. 1, pp. 28–32.

Fry, R. (1997) *Take Notes*, Kogan Page.

Hartley, J. (1976) 'Lecture Handouts and Student Note Taking', *Programmed Learning and Educational Technology*, vol. 13, no. 2, pp. 58–64.

Hartley, J. and Davies, I.K. (1978) 'Note Taking: A Critical Review', *Programmed Learning and Educational Technology*, vol. 15, no. 3, pp. 207–24.

Hartley, J. and Marshall, S. (1974) 'On Notes and Note-taking', *Universities Quarterly*, vol. 28, pp. 225–35.

Helweg-Larsen, B. (1979) 'Teaching the Technique of Patterned Note Taking', *British Journal of Guidance and Counselling*, vol. 7, pp. 107–13.

Howe, M.J.A. and Singer, L. (1975) 'Presentation and Students' Activities in Meaningful Learning', *British Journal of Educational Psychology*, vol. 45, pp. 52–61.

Isaacs, G. (1989) 'Lecture Note-taking, Learning and Recall', *Medical Teacher*, vol. 11, nos 3–4, pp. 295–302.

Isaacs, G. (1994) 'Lecturing Practices and Note-taking Purposes', *Studies in Higher Education*, vol. 19, no. 2. pp. 203–16.

Kiewa, K.A. (1987) 'Note-taking and Review: The Research and its Implications', *Instructional Science*, vol. 16, no. 3, pp. 233–49.

MacManaway, L.A. (1967-8) 'Using Lecture Scripts', *Universities Quarterly*, vol. 22, no. 3, pp. 327–36.

McDougall, I.R., Gray, H.W. and McNicol, G.P. (1972) 'The Effect of Timing of Distribution of Handouts on Improvement of Student Performance', *British Journal of Medical Education*, vol. 6, pp. 155–7.

See also: Circulated lecture notes; Guided study; Personalized system of instruction; Text; Tutorial-tape-document learning package approach

Harmonization

Harmonization is the adoption of a common approach to pay and conditions for different categories of employee, usually staff and manual workers.

Harmonization should be distinguished from *staff status* programmes, whereby manual and craft employees gradually receive staff terms and conditions of employment, usually upon reaching some qualifying standard such as length of service. In the process of harmonization, staff employees may have to accept some of the conditions of service of manual employees.

Harmonization also differs from *single-status* programmes, which involve removing differences in basic conditions of employment to give all employees equal status. Some organizations take this further by putting all employees on the same pay and grading structure and, in the case of small companies, even on the same rate of pay. This is known as *equalization*.

Many British companies are following the American model and introducing single-status and harmonization programmes in the belief that they can help to eliminate divisive conflicts within the organization. However, the strength of the concept of status which is conferred on management and staff means that the transition can be difficult, and certain groups in the workforce are likely to want their differentials to be restored.

Mullins, T. (1986) 'Harmonization: The Benefits and the Lessons', *Personnel Management*, March, pp. 38–41.

Rail, R.E. (1986) 'Harmonization', *Management Services*, vol. 30, no. 3, March, pp. 8–12.

Roberts, C. (ed.) (1985) *Harmonization: Whys and Wherefores*, Institute of Personnel and Development.

'Single-status Working: The Key to Harmonious Industrial Relations?', *IRS Employee Trends* (1998), no. 668, November, pp. 7–12.

See also: Greenfield plants

Hearing

This intervention can be used at any formal meeting, as well as one designed specifically to improve communications between group members. It can help to break up wandering or injurious discussions, and may even convert controversy into co-operation. It helps to develop members' hearing skills as well as the group's ability to confront 'social deafness'. It may also bring quiet members into the discussion. However, it takes time to apply, and it may initially be resisted.

The technique can be used when two people are arguing and each is talking but not listening to the other. The facilitator gets their attention, challenges them to say that they are really listening to each other, then asks them to prove it. Each combatant is asked to repeat the other's last statement to that person's satisfaction, and then talk about their feelings for a while. If the two people concerned are unable to do this, the other group members are invited to offer their view of the disagreement or to role-play the situation.

Fordyce, J.K. and Weil, R. (1971) *Managing With People*, Addison Wesley Longman, pp. 172–4.

Helgesen, M. and Brown, S. (1995) *Active Listening : Introducing Skills for Understanding*, Cambridge University Press.

Manby, A,. (1997) *Listening and Speaking*, Harcourt Brace.

Waistell, M. (ed.) (1993) *Executive Listening*, Nelson.

Wolff, F.I. (1993) *Perceptive Listening*, Saunders/Harcourt Brace.

See also: FIDO approach; LIFO method; Meetings for two; Monodrama; Process consultation; Sociodrama

Helping relationship model

Developed by Gerard Egan, the helping relationship model seeks to improve helpers' effectiveness by developing their skills. The model can be applied by all those in the helping professions, including teachers, and it works as well in groups as in one-to-one relationships.

Egan sees the helper and the person being helped as being in temporary interaction, sharing responsibilities with the aim of changing behaviour. Egan lists a set of helping skills, and divides the helping relationship into a set of interdependent, sequenced phases described in Joyce et al. (1992).

In the first phase, *clarification*, the person being helped is engaged in searching and exploring their problem, and the helper attends to them, both physically and psychologically, by being with them and demonstrating respect. *Problem-solving* is the second phase. Here, the person being helped postulates, evaluates, decides and plans, and the helper's role is to model, disclose, confront and structure, without allowing any of their own biases and values to intrude. The final phase, *action*, involves the person being helped making and implementing their plans. They take the risk of changing their behaviour, and the helper encourages, supports and advises them.

Egan, G. (1998) *The Skilled Helper: A Problem-management Approach to Helping* (6th edn), Brooks/Cole.

Joyce, B., Weil, M. and Showers, B. (1992) *Models of Teaching* (4th edn), Allyn and Bacon.

See also: Counselling; Non-directive teaching model; Peer counselling

Heuristic

Heuristics can be used to present complex rules, procedures and instructions. However, unlike algorithms or decision tables, heuristics do not guarantee that a correct solution will be selected, since they involve trial-and-error discovery learning.

A systematic plan – a hierarchy of instructions giving the order in which a series of operations is to be carried out – which is sure to work may take too long or cost too much. In contrast, a heuristic plan is often cheap and quick, although it may sometimes fail to produce the intended result. A heuristic strategy is effective when the number of possible outcomes is very large, when the number of possible interactions is very large, and when relationships are complex. It is also appropriate when the underlying structure of the task is unknown and the risks resulting from an incorrect solution can be accepted.

When our car fails to start in the morning, we tend to implement a heuristic fault-finding plan. When a large number of choices are involved, a heuristic strategy becomes the only practicable method for accomplishing a task, since any other strategy would involve a systematic search through an enormous number of alternatives until the correct one had been identified. Thus a computer may be given some 'tips' or heuristics to avoid searches through billions of possibilities.

Groner, R. (ed.) (1983) *Methods of Heuristics*, Lawrence Erlbaum Associates.
Landa, L. (1976) *Instructional Regulation and Control: Cybernetics, Algorithmization and Heuristics in Education*, Educational Technology Publications.
Miller, G.A., Galanter, E. and Pribram, K.H. (1960) *Plans and Structure of Behaviour*, Henry Holt.

See also: Algorithm; Decision table; Flowchart

Historical analysis

Many subjects use history as a means of learning: for example, some courses on the history of psychology and sociology trace the development of themes within the subject. This approach involves studying either primary or secondary source material, examining the prevalent ideas, the political and economic causes of actions, the role of key figures, and their influence on events.

The fairly recent development of the history of ideas as a specific area of study has had important implications for historical analysis. It has provided students with a series of explicit methodologies for dealing with historical analysis, and it has highlighted the pitfalls which conventional historical analysis courses rarely consider. Furthermore, the history of ideas as a subject area is essentially interdisciplinary, whereas many historical analysis courses are only single- or double-discipline.

A number of texts covering the history of industries and of individual organizations which are suitable for this form of study exist, as do biographies and autobiographies of numerous managers. In addition, many management theorists, such as Frederick Winslow Taylor and Elton Mayo, have expounded their philosophy of management, which could be used for historical analysis purposes.

Crainer, S. (1995) *Key Management Ideas: Thinking that Changed Management*, Pitman.
Crainer, S. (1998) *The Ultimate Book of Business Gurus*, Capstone Publishing.
Crainer, S. and Hamel, G. (1997) *Ultimate Business Library*, Capstone Publishing.
Huczynski, A.A. (1993) *Management Gurus*, Routledge.
Jacques, R. (1995) *Manufacturing the Employee: Management Knowledge from the 19th to 21st Centuries*, Sage.
Lloyd, H. (1964) *Biography in Management Studies*, Hutchinson.
Warner, M. (ed.) (1998) *The IEBM Handbook of Management Thinking*, International Thompson Business Press.
Wren, D.A. (1994) *Evolution of Management Thought*, Wiley.
Wren, D.A. (1998) *Management Innovators*, Oxford University Press.

See also: Biography; Critical theory approach; Dialectic enquiry; Process analysis; Reading; Theory-based intervention

Human process approach

Human process interventions focus on people in the organization, as well as on the organizational processes such as communication, problem-solving and decision-making through which they accomplish their own and the company's goals. This orientation to organizational change is rooted in the academic fields of psychology, social psychology, sociology and anthropology. It also draws on the applied behavioural disciplines such as group dynamics and the human relations movement.

Consultants who use a human process approach tend to emphasize the fulfilment of human needs, believing that improved organizational performance will result from improved human functioning. They use survey feedback techniques in which groups of company personnel discuss diagnostic data and plan action steps, group development activities which seek to enhance the group's ability to accomplish its task, and inter-group development work which emphasizes improved management of the interfaces between the different groups. What all these approaches have in common is the belief that sharing information can be valuable, particularly when it has remained hidden up to that time but has nevertheless influenced what has gone on in the organization. A second assumption is that by confronting and working through their differences, people who must work together can enhance collaboration. Finally, the human process approach values participation in decision-making, and believes it can lead to increased commitment.

See also: Behaviour modelling; Behaviour modification; Interaction management; Laboratory training; Managing for productivity

Human relations laboratory

'Laboratory learning', in the psychological rather than the scientific sense, describes a process of learning about oneself and others, and about the groups and organizations to which one belongs. This is achieved through direct experience of participating in groups – *laboratories* – which have been formed specifically for this purpose. The focus of the learning in each different type of laboratory is specified in its title, so a human relations laboratory will concentrate on exploring and understanding inter-personal relationships, whereas group dynamics laboratories explore group issues, and power laboratories consider organizational issues.

In a human relations laboratory, participants are given opportunities to generate inter-personal data, diagnose the situation, and develop their skills in enhancing communication, creating rapport and providing help in inter-personal problem-solving and in resolving conflict. Participants in these laboratories may be strangers or may have met each other on previous occasions. This type of approach also represents a way of building links between people who have some kind of working relationship. The laboratory may be composed of a diagonal slice of the organization – employees who occupy different positions of seniority in the company hierarchy, but none of whom are in a superior–subordinate relationship to each other. In contrast, a horizontal-slice approach would bring together employees at broadly the same level of seniority in the organization but who work in different functions and in different departments. Such participant groupings assist learning when the objective stresses inter-personal competence rather than organizational knowledge.

Bolman, L. (1970) 'Laboratory Versus Lecture in Training Executives', *Journal of Applied Behavioural Science*, vol. 6, pp. 323–36.

Cooper, C.L. (1979) *Learning from Others in Groups*, Associated Business Press.
Harrison, K. and Cooper, C.L. (1979) 'Design and Training Issues in Human Relations Groups', in Pettman, O. and Margerison, C. (eds.) *European Insights in Personnel and Training*, MCB Publications.
Lippitt, G.L. and This, L.E. (1980) 'Leaders for Laboratory Training', *Training and Development Journal*, vol. 34, no. 6, pp. 56–67.
Margulies, N. and Wallace, J. (1973) *Organizational Change: Techniques and Applications*,: Scott Foresman, p. 69.
Smith, P.B. (1980) *Personal Change and Group Processes*, Harper and Row.

See also: Cluster laboratory; Cousin laboratory; Encounter group; Gestalt techniques; Group development laboratory; Group dynamics laboratory; Instrumented laboratory; Laboratory method; Laboratory training; Micro-lab; Mini-society; Organizational laboratory; Personal development laboratory; Power laboratory; Psychodrama; Sensitivity (T-group) training; Tavistock conference method; Team laboratory; Transactional Analysis

Humour for learning

McGhee defines 'humour' as intellectual play, saying it is 'a type of play that is relatively serious in nature, and characterised by a desire to expand existing knowledge'. Effective humour comes from clever insights where surprise and acute observation connect amusingly.

Any field which involves human beings can be a source of humour. Since people tend to laugh at their own foibles and those of others, management and organizational life offers vast scope for humorous illustrations and jokes which can enhance the student learning experience. Laughter has a cathartic property but, in the management classroom, it can be used to illustrate difficult concepts or emphasize a point. However, management instructors are not usually stand-up comics, and there is a fine line between being amusing and being offensive, so it is safest if they make themselves the butt of their jokes.

Humour can be used in various ways, but should be linked to learning objectives. An instructor can collect humorous stories which illustrate relevant concepts, theories and issues from the media, colleagues or researchers and write them up. In-company field research may produce a great many of these. Such stories need not produce side-splitting belly laughs, they just need to be mildly amusing and memorable. Another approach is to use humorous films, such as cartoons, silent slapstick ones (Chaplin or Laurel and Hardy) or Monty Python, since many of these are set in an organizational context and deal with work in some way. The work of the cartoonist Scott Adams, and his 'Dilbert' strip, syndicated in 1400 publications world-wide, also provides a rich source of material which explores the absurdities of company life.

In the organizational context, humour has been associated with creativity and the promotion of a more informal, relaxed culture. One company engaged a corporate jester who, attired in clown's clothing, visited staff in their offices or at their desks. The German subsidiary of a British airline hired a radio disc jockey to teach its staff how to tell jokes, engage in banter during short flights, and even juggle. There is as yet no empirical evidence to indicate the effect of this particular organizational development intervention on the company's personnel or its customers.

Adams, S. (1996) *Still Pumped from Using the Mouse*, Boxtree.

Adams, S. (1997) *Dogbert's Management Handbook*, Boxtree.

Adams, S. (1998) *I'm Not Anti-management, I'm Anti-idiot*, Boxtree.

Firth, D. and Leigh, A. (1998) *The Corporate Fool*, Capstone Publishing.

Koller, M.R. (1988-9) 'Humour and Education: Are They Compatible?', *Organizational Behaviour Teaching Review*, vol. 13, no. 2, pp. 1–9.

McGhee, P.E. (1979) *Humour: Its Origin and Development*, Freeman.

Morrell, J. (1997) *Humour Works*, Human Resources Development Press.

Wagner, F.R. and Goldsmith, H.M. (1981) 'The Value of Humour in Teaching OB', *Exchange: The Organizational Behaviour Teaching Journal*, vol. 6, no. 3, pp. 12–17.

See also: Playing for learning

Ideological change

This is a general term for intervention strategies which attempt to change the values, norms, expectations and success criteria defined and practised by management. The underlying principle is that it is possible to change people's behaviour by altering their attitudes and beliefs.

Blanchard, K. and O'Conner, (1997) *Managing by Values*, McGraw-Hill.

Bracey, H. et al. (1990) *Managing from the Heart*, Dell Publishing.

Chakraborty, S.K. (1993) *Management by Values: Towards Cultural Congruence*, Oxford University Press.

Chappel, T. (1993) *The Soul of a Business*, Bantam Books.

Frederick, W.C. (1995) *Values, Nature and Culture in American Corporations*, Oxford University Press.

Griseri, P. (1998) *Managing Values*, Macmillan.

Louis, M.R. (1994) 'In the Manner of Friends: Learnings from Quaker Practice for Organizational Renewal,' *Journal of Organizational Change Management*, vol. 7, no. 1, pp. 42–60.

McCormick, D. (1994) 'Spirituality and Management', *Journal of Managerial Psychology*, vol. 9, no. 6, pp. 5–8.

McCoy, C.S. (1985) *The Management of Values*, Pitman.

Neal, J.A. (1997) 'Spirituality in Management Education: A Guide to Resources', *Journal of Management Education*, vol. 21, no. 1, pp. 121–39.

Nystrom, P.L. and Starbuck, W.H. (1984) 'Managing Beliefs in Organizations', *Journal of Applied Behavioural Science*, vol. 20, no. 3, pp. 277–87.

See also: Achievement motivation training; Attitude survey; Brainwashing; Corporate culture training; Developing a new management/operating philosophy; Discipline without punishment; Greenfield plants; Managerial strategy change; Moral philosophy approach; Myth-making interventions; Non-conforming enclave; Norm clarification; Norm formation; Norm modification; Ombudsman; Organizational climate analysis; Quality management; Socratic dialogue

Illuminative incident analysis

Although this method of team appraisal and personnel training was originally developed by Diana Cortazzi and Susan Roote for use with care staff such as doctors, nurses and social workers, it can be used in the field of management development and training to explore the common crises groups experience. The approach stresses the visual representation of cognitive and affective aspects. The authors argue that such representations are more direct and offer less opportunity to avoid key issues by blocking emotions.

A group of staff who work together as a team, or whose work depends on the contribution of others, select an incident from their work in which they have all been personally involved. Each person represents their own view of the incident with a simple drawing, using pin/matchstick figures to depict the sequence of events. They then put themselves in the shoes of each person in the team in turn and examine the attitudes and roles of those involved by exaggerating the initial drawing – frequently to the extent of caricature. For example, a manager might draw themself on a treadmill, or lying on the ground under attack from bosses and junior staff. This helps the group to reach the deeper human and emotional issues involved, as well as the conflicts, tensions and misperceptions that lie behind any crisis in teamwork.

The technique can reveal a great deal about how people see themselves and the people with whom and for whom they work. In addition, they may indicate how such incidents may be prevented and the team strengthened and developed.

Cortazzi, D. and Roote, S. (1975) *Illuminative Incident Analysis*, McGraw-Hill.

See also: Action learning; Case conference; Chronology charting; Collages; Drawing for learning; Fortune lining; Gestalt techniques; Group poster tours; Inter-personal process recall; Monodrama; Non-verbal exercise; Poster; Psychodrama; Responsibility charting; Sociodrama; Storyboarding; Team development; Team laboratory

Implementing The Organizational Renewal Process (ITORP)

This is a model developed by Gordon Lippitt, who believed that the most important element in organizational renewal is the organization's ability to respond to new situations. The criteria used to judge the effectiveness of the response is whether the action taken has optimized the use and development of the organization's human resources, improved the interfacing process within the organization, contributed to the maturation of the organization, and made it more responsive to its environment.

The ITORP programme consists of five half-day sessions. The first session examines the technological, economic, consumer, knowledge and moral revolutions which are going on within the organization.

The second session recognizes that organizational renewal requires confrontation, searching and coping. Participants are thus given an opportunity to confront their own needs, and to develop their skills in individual, group or organizational situations. They fill out a self-assessment instrument called the Self-growth Multiple Inventory and watch the BNA's films *Confrontation* and *Search and Coping*, then in groups of three they discuss their personal goals in improving their confrontation skills.

The third session deals with the need for teamwork. Participants view another film, *Individuality and Teamwork*, and measure key factors in the teamwork situation before going on to analyse them in detail. Implementing organizational

renewal requires group action at all levels, and will strengthen the psychological contract between the organization and the individual.

Personal plans play an important role in influencing change at the work unit level, and these are discussed in the fourth session. An attempt is made to develop participants' skill and courage in analysing, initiating and coping with changes. They are shown the film *Coping With Change*, and are helped to develop change goals and plans.

The fifth session helps organization leaders to examine ways of spreading, reinforcing and securing multiple commitments to planned change efforts.

Lippitt, G.L. (1972) 'Implementing The Organizational Renewal Process (ITORP): A Situational Approach', in Burke, W.W. (ed.) *New Technologies in Organization Development*, Pfeiffer/Jossey-Bass, pp. 90–108.

Lippitt, G.L. (1973) *Visualizing Change: Model Building and the Change Process*, Pfeiffer/Jossey-Bass, pp. 302–32.

See also: FIDO approach; Grid development; Interaction influence analysis; Interaction Management; Kepner-Tregoe approach; LIFO method; Managing for productivity; Power management; Situational leadership; 3-D management effectiveness seminar

Improshare

Improshare (Improved Productivity through Sharing) was developed in 1973 by Mitchell Fein of New Jersey, who spent over twenty years formulating it. It is one of the three best-known productivity gain-sharing plans, the others being the Scanlon and Rucker plans, both of which were devised during the 1930s.

The objective of Improshare is increased output for fewer hours of input. It integrates a number of earlier methods which aim to calculate hours and products, but an important difference is that Improshare measures performance rather than financial savings. The productivity gain is expressed as the number of hours taken to produce a specific number of units compared to a prior base period, and past average productivity is used to determine what is called the base productivity factor (BPF). The BPF is multiplied by standard hours to produce Improshare hours. The cost savings due to the reduced input hours are shared 50:50 between the firm and the employees, who receive a cash bonus as a percentage of their monthly pay. The bonus calculation takes into account differences in product lines and in the input of both direct and indirect labour.

Improshare is characterized by its simplicity,

lack of emphasis on employee involvement, and ease of installation. Adjustments can be made to improve productivity by introducing capital equipment. It need not be adopted for a whole plant, but can be applied to individual departments or small work units. It is not usually necessary to secure an employee vote of support to implement the plan, and there is apparently less need for formal management–employee co-operative structures than in similar schemes. Some users of the plan also claim that union–management relations improve as a result of the mutually beneficial incentives.

When one firm, Firestone Canada of Hamilton, introduced Improshare in 1980, the management was seeking a 20–30 per cent productivity increase, which could mean a $135 bonus per month for each employee. With union support, the plan aimed to encourage employees to work both harder and smarter, and it is claimed that it fostered a new pattern of co-operation on the part of employees. The Eastern Ontario Works Inc. of Trenton, Ontario, experienced a 30 per cent average productivity increase, and the company paid $6000 in bonuses to 30 people in a single month.

Fein, M. (1981) *Improshare: An Alternative to Traditional Managing*, Institute of Industrial Engineers, USA.

Graham-Moore, B.E. and Ross, T.L. (1983) *Productivity Gainsharing: How Employee Incentive Schemes Improve Business Performance*, Prentice-Hall.

See also: Productivity sharing; Profit-sharing; Reward systems; Rucker plan; Scanlon plan; Shared ownership

In-basket exercise (in-tray exercise)

An in-basket exercise presents the learner with samples of administrative work in the form of a manager's in-tray or post box, and requires them to decide what action to take in response to them. The method was first developed by the Educational Testing Service, Princeton, New Jersey, as a selection test for air force officers. It also offers a means of sampling learners' behaviour in response to a range of problems. The baskets' contents can be chosen to reflect the problems a particular group is having and tailored to fit the time available. In addition to their roles in assessing people or conducting research into management decision-making, in-baskets are a useful management training tool. Since the in-basket exercise is conducted in real time, it can be considered a type of simulation.

In-basket exercises are more interesting and involving if the problems posed seem realistic. Trainers can modify items from existing in-basket exercises or design their own. A typical exercise asks each participant to imagine that they have just been promoted to a certain position in a company and have come into their new office for the first time on a Sunday morning. They are in a rush because they will soon have to leave to catch a plane to New York or Birmingham, where they will be attending a conference for the next week and will thus be unavailable. Because it is Sunday, there is no one else in the office, and they cannot talk to anyone outside it. In their in-tray, each participant finds an identical pile of papers. Their task is to work through the items as if they were the manager, dealing with them as best they can within the constraints, including a time limit of 60 or 90 minutes.

Once everyone has completed the task individually, the class, led by the tutor, goes through it together to determine the most appropriate action in each instance. If the in-basket is being used as an individual development exercise, then the student needs to have a follow-up interview with their boss or training officer to discuss the answers. There is evidence that in-baskets designed specifically for the individual being trained are more effective.

In-baskets can be adapted to match individual job requirements and exercise different skills. Typical ones include management information (e.g., the manager's manual, day-to-day planner, organization chart, a welcome note from predecessor giving a thumbnail sketch of the incoming management team, budget statement), queries demanding an immediate answer (e.g., a request to substitute one staff member for another on a sales trip, a secretary requesting a day off), queries that should be delegated (e.g., a request for something to be done by next Monday) and items that should not be bothered with (e.g., a golf club nomination form).

In-baskets can vary in difficulty, highlighting technical, administrative, financial and interpersonal skills. The more complex ones expect participants to realize the hidden implications of an apparently innocuous memo, or to put several pieces of information together to reveal a more serious problem or a greater opportunity than is apparent from looking at any item in isolation.

Meyer, H.H. (1970) 'The Validity of the In-basket Exercise as a Measure of Managerial Performance', *Personnel Psychology*, vol. 23, pp. 297–307.

Stewart, V. (1981) 'Training for Managerial Effectiveness, Core Skills 2', *Journal of European Industrial Training*, vol. 5, no. 1, pp. v–viii.

Zoll, A.A. (1969) *Dynamic Management Education*, Addison Wesley Longman, Chapters 9 and 10.

See also: Action maze; Behavioural simulation; Experiential exercise; Game; Programme simulation; Simulation

Independent product teams (venture teams)

Independent product teams are self-standing, semi-independent business units which are related in a variety of ways to the parent company. Each unit has its own product charter within which it can act with great freedom. If it wishes to go beyond the charter by producing a new product or making an acquisition, it is required to prepare a strategic investment plan.

One multinational's new product board was operated by its divisions, each of which had its own budget for new ventures. If the venture was considered worthwhile, the company or one of its divisions retained the right to buy out the management, whereas if an entrepreneur felt that the company's assessment of the new venture did not reflect its true potential, they could organize a management buy-out. The aim of this structural innovation was to make a contribution to the company's growth. In addition, it could also be used to train managers in entrepreneurial thinking and keep them alert to market possibilities.

Goldsmith, W. and Clutterbuck, D. (1985) *The Winning Streak*, Penguin Books, pp. 37–8 and 112–13.

See also: Autonomous workgroups; Bottom-up management; Business teams; Collateral organization; Exporting for others; Forcing device; Intrapreneurial group; Investing in a small company; Likert's levels meetings; Line-of-business groups; Managerial decentralization; Matrix design; Multiple management; Reprogramming; Simulated entrepreneurship; Skunkworks

Independent study (independent learning; autonomous learning)

Independent study is difficult to define precisely. The Nuffield Group noted on the subject that: 'some teachers regard it solely as a method of learning whilst others see it as a situation in which students are responsible for major decisions concerning their own education'. However, it could be said that whenever there is an attempt to lessen the direct influence of the teacher on the immediate learning situation, some form of independent study is being undertaken.

Some writers have identified a hierarchy of degrees of independence in learning, ranging from decision to enrol at the bottom, to choice over pace of study, choice over mode of study, involvement in deciding objectives, participation in assessment and, at the highest level, involvement in establishing criteria by which to judge success. Each step up the hierarchy requires the educational institution to surrender increasing amounts of control.

Atherton, C. (1972) 'Lecture, Discussion and Independent Study: Instructional Methods Revisited', *Journal of Experimental Education*, vol. 40, no. 4, pp. 24–8.
Boud, D. (ed.) (1981) *Developing Student Autonomy in Learning*, Kogan Page.
Dressel, P.L. and Thomson, M.M. (1973) *Independent Study*, Jossey-Bass.
Fazy, D.M.A. and Linford, J.G. (1996) 'Tutoring for Autonomous Learning: Principles and Practice', *Innovations in Education and Training International*, vol. 33, no. 3, pp. 185–96.
Moore, M.G. (1973) 'Toward a Theory of Independent Learning and Teaching', *Journal of Higher Education*, vol. 44, no. 9, pp. 661–79.
Percy, K. and Ramsen, P. (1980) *Independent Study: Two Examples from English Higher Education*, Society for Research into Higher Education.
Robbins, D. (1988) *Rise of Independent Learning*, Open University Press.
Tait, J. and Knight, P. (1996) *Management of Independent Learning*, Kogan Page.

See also: Autonomous group learning; Instrumented team learning; Learning contracts; Media-activated learning group; Research degree; Sabbatical; Self-directed learning; Student-planned learning

Induction training (orientation training; socialization)

Induction training is used by both educational institutions and companies to help new entrants fit into their new environment.

In the educational context, institutions and students' unions offer programmes of events which are partly designed to establish social contacts, and partly to familiarize the students with the institution's geography and working arrangements.

Some company induction programmes are extensive and entail new employees being exposed to 20 hours of training during 14 sessions spread over 12 weeks. The training is mainly job-oriented, and is conducted by company staff. Its purpose is to modify any poor work habits recruits may have, and to help them understand the organization's culture and rules. During the training, the benefits of working for the company are made explicit, and the rationale for company rules and the penalties for violating them is discussed at length. Research has shown that such induction training can help to reduce levels of absenteeism.

Billing, D. (1997) 'Induction of New Students in Higher Education', *Innovations in Education and Training International*, vol. 34 no. 2, pp. 125–34.

Davis, P. (1993) *Staff Induction*, The Industrial Society.

Dean, R.A. (1983) 'Reality Shock: The Link Between Socialization and Organizational Commitment', *Journal of Management Development*, vol. 2, no. 3, pp. 55–65.

Goodman, P.S. and Atkin, R.S. (1984) *Absenteeism: New Approaches to Understanding, Measuring and Managing Employee Absence*, Jossey-Bass.

Lamb, C.H., Lee, J.B. and Vinton, K.L. (1997) 'Developing a Freshman Seminar: Challenges and Opportunities', *Journal of Management Education*, vol. 21, no. 1, pp. 27–43.

Rosen, H. and Turner, J. (1971) 'Effectiveness of Two Orientation Approaches in Hardcore Unemployed Turnover and Absenteeism', *Journal of Applied Psychology*, vol. 55, pp. 29–301.

Wanous, J.P. (1992) *Organizational Entry*, Addison Wesley Longman.

See also: Corporate culture training; Information-sharing meeting; Organizational citizenship; Parrainage; Psychological contract; Realistic job previews; Recruitment; Role prescription; Smart process

Industrial dynamics

This is a method of studying the behaviour of industrial systems to clarify inter-relations between policies, decisions, structures and delays, in order to see how these affect organizational stability and growth. Developed by Jay Forrester, a programme based on industrial dynamics was carried out at the Massachusetts Institute of Technology, and had a major impact on management systems thinking during the 1960s.

Forrester's approach, which is now widely used in operational research, was the first to identify the organization's goals and the problems involved in achieving them. It defined an information network based on five flows which Forrester considered to be basic to any business activity: money, orders, material, personnel and capital equipment, and sought to integrate the functional areas of marketing, investment, research, personnel, production and accounting.

The approach enabled controlled 'management laboratory' experiments to be conducted on management situations, in which the effect of altering certain conditions could be considered while the other variables remained constant. By modelling the significant organizational features and their relationships, it was possible to test the effects of proposed changes in order to provide guidance to managers. A specially devised computer program called DYNAMO was used to speed up the analysis.

Forrester, J.W. (1961) *Industrial Dynamics*, Wiley.

See also: Diagnostic activities; Force field analysis; Open systems planning; Organizational laboratory; Socio-technical designs; Strategic management

Industrial project (line project)

An industrial project involves a full-time student – or more commonly a group of students – working on an assignment for a company. The company usually defines the project's aims and objectives, so it takes a major role in evaluating it. For instance, it may supply a group of final-year marketing students with a product which it wishes to launch, and ask them to develop a marketing plan.

Such projects give students the opportunity to bring together the diverse skills and subject knowledge they have acquired during the course and apply them to a real-life situation. The company also gains, since for little or no cost it can obtain fresh ideas and new approaches from young minds, as well as assessing the students as possible recruits.

See also: Co-operative education; Field project/attachment; Internship; Joint development activities; Overseas project; Project method; Project-based management development; Project orientation; Real-life entrepreneurial project

Info bank

Because libraries contain such a vast amount of information, they can confuse and intimidate students. This problem can be overcome by setting up an info bank: a highly selective reference library on a particular topic, such as industrial relations or teaching reading in primary schools. The materials are more highly structured than in a traditional library, and students are given more guidance on how to use them. One reason for this is that students are expected to make use of the info bank primarily on their own, although assistance is available should they need it.

The info bank approach recognizes that students have different learning needs and learning styles. It places responsibility for learning on students themselves, and views the tutor's role as a facilitator, helping students to specify and achieve their learning goals.

To prepare an info bank, tutors collect relevant materials, catalogue them, write study guides and produce info-papers and summaries. When introducing the approach, they stress that students need to clarify their own learning objectives and have some awareness of their personal learning style. For example, do they prefer to use personal computer programs and book summaries rather than journal articles? Although each student is expected to take responsibility for their own learning process, they may consult their tutor, and support is also provided by regular group meetings to compare experiences and share ideas. The tutor must ensure that the support material in the info bank is updated regularly.

See also: Audio tutorial method; Computer-assisted learning; Language laboratory; Resource centre

Informal action group

Informal action groups are formed to achieve organizational goals that require collaboration between different functions or departments. They bring together employees who share a common concern for the organization and for one another's personal growth, in order to work on issues which transcend their formal roles. The approach was developed in a university environment, where no formal organizational mechanism was available. The group remains informal in terms of responsibilities, authority and visibility, and the primary objective is constructive action.

The optimum size for an informal action group seems to be nine people, and this allows a mature group to develop. Membership, working patterns, roles, inter-personal relationships and tasks are relatively fluid, but the group's procedures resemble many similar groups, moving from agenda-setting, data-sharing and diagnosis through to the production of ideas and agreement on action plans and steps. Such groups have been asked to devise organizational plans and policies, plan changes, and develop and extend the services provided by an organization. The group can also provide support to individual members working on their own problems and decisions. These might include matters such as the member's own development, family-related problems, future roles, career and position.

Group meetings do not follow a fixed schedule, and any member may organize a meeting when they identify a personal situation, project idea or organizational problem they would like to work on.

The success of an informal action group depends on individual commitment, strong working relationships and effective working practices. The latter in turn depend on individual competences and shared organizational goals and values. In an educational institution, for instance, these would revolve around inter-disciplinary orientations, assumptions about people, attitudes towards learning, the need for the active participation of members, and the nature of meaningful collaboration.

The informal action group's contribution to the work of the organization as a whole mainly depends on two factors. The first is the extent to which its values represent those of the majority of people in the organization. If they do not, the group's work is likely to be regarded with indifference, nervousness or hostility. Second, its influence relies on establishing links with some of the critical decision-making groups and individuals in the formal organizational structure. The group must be able to influence other parts of the organization if change is to be implemented.

Grinnell, S.K. (1969) 'The Informal Action Group: One Way to Collaborate in a University', Journal of Applied Behavioural Science, vol. 5, no. 1, pp. 75–103.
Leeds, R. (1964) 'Absorption of Protest: A Working Paper', in Cooper, W.W., Leavitt, H.J. and Shelly, M.W. (eds) New Perspectives in Organizational Research, Wiley, pp. 115–35.

See also: Employee-guided management; Goal-setting and planning groups; Informal management team; Matrix design; Networking; Non-conforming enclave; Quality circles; Study circles

Informal management team (management by huddle)

This form of decision-making structure characterizes the senior levels of some of the most successful British companies. Such teams require a clear management mission, physical proximity of the key individuals, and a form of communication that provides a management bond. Participants' awareness of the organizational culture and their common goals make discussions more productive. Committees are avoided, except those which perform a consultative function. Instead, at the top levels, there is reliance on a depth of mutual understanding and agreement on where the company is going and what is right.

Goldsmith, W. and Clutterbuck, D. (1985) The Winning Streak, Penguin Books, pp. 38–41.
Goldsmith, W. and Clutterbuck, D. (1985) The Winning Streak: Workout Book, Collins.

See also: Corporate culture training; Goal-setting interface groups; Informal action group; Multiple management; Plural chief executive

Information-sharing meetings

A number of organizations hold meetings where management shares data with supervisors, unions and employees in an effort to reduce costs and thus save jobs. Peters and Waterman found that their excellent companies had a policy of making such information available to employees, rather than keeping it secret for fear that it would be abused by them to the benefit of their competitors.

This approach has also been used to involve employees in decisions about disciplinary matters, to promote acceptance and a sense of ownership of company regulations. In the area of absence control, this is done by measuring attendance and showing individual employees how the costs incurred by their poor performance affect the company, their department and their work colleagues.

Nadler, D.A. (1981) 'Managing Organizational Change', *Journal of Applied Behavioural Science*, vol. 17, pp. 191–211.
Peters, T.J. and Waterman, R.H. (1982) *In Search of Excellence*, Harper and Row.
Reeves, K.T. (1980) 'Information Disclosure in Employee Relations', *Employee Relations*, vol. 2, no. 3.

See also: Chairman's forum; Corporate culture training; Discipline without punishment; Employee-designed rules; Employee letters; Induction training; Management information meeting; Norm formation; Norm modification; Open-book management; Open forums; Organizational citizenship; Team briefing

Inner dialogue

Traditional approaches to stress management rely on three strategies – control, escape and symptom management – to reduce fear, redirect anxiety and develop confidence. However, a fourth approach, suggested by Bolman and Deal, emphasizes the need to develop the spiritual and reflective side of the personality, drawing on one's 'inner voice' to help reduce stress. It considers that it is everyone's responsibility to take a spiritual (although not necessarily religious) journey to discover their own unique gifts, and how these can be given to those around them – subordinates, colleagues, other groups and family.

The method involves studying the inner dialogues that take place in the minds of those (fictional or real) who find themselves in positions where they must take decisions or exercise leadership. Written sources may include novels, stories, plays, poems, autobiographies, accounts of other managers' spiritual journeys or the subject's own records, and the approach also uses reflective techniques such as prayer and meditation. This provides a framework for discussing leaders' doubts, uncertainties, emotions, spiritual beliefs, values, sense of identity, and similar topics of a personal nature in the affective domain of learning.

Bolman L.G. and Deal, T.E. (1995) *Leading with Soul*, Jossey-Bass.
Ferris, W.P. (1998) 'Fear, Stress and Second-guessing in Leadership Decision Making: Using Interior Monologues, Reflective Non-fiction and Spiritual Approaches', *Journal of Management Education*, vol. 22, no. 1, pp. 26–48.
Ferris, W.P. and Fanelli, R. (1996) 'The Learning Manager and the Inner Side of Management', in Cavaleri, S. and Fearon, D. (eds) *Managing in Organizations that Learn*, Blackwell, pp. 66–96.
Kilmann, R.H. and Kilmann, I. et al. (eds) (1994) *Managing Ego Energy: The Transformation of Personal Meaning into Organizational Success*, Jossey-Bass.

See also: Case with role-play; Character immersion; Confluent education; Dramatic skit; Literary criticism; Monodrama; Novels for learning; Poetry for learning; Story-writing; Storytelling; Stress management

Inquiry training model

The inquiry training model (ITM) is based on Suchman's beliefs that all learners are naturally motivated to solve puzzles, and that we are all intuitive inquirers. The model's aim is to encourage students to think independently by increasing their consciousness of their inquiring processes and developing their ability to conduct disciplined research. The approach is more concerned with promoting awareness and mastery of the inquiry process than the content of a particular problem or puzzle situation. It is usually practised with groups of students, because Suchman holds that, since all knowledge is tentative and may be disproved by others, the process of co-operative inquiry is very important. Joyce and colleagues describe five steps in implementing the ITM. These match the research method in science, and the logical problem-solving process in management.

First, in the *confrontation* stage, the instructor presents the group with a puzzling situation. The more surprising the puzzle, the better: for example, a company reduces its products prices, but sales do not rise. The inquiry procedure is explained to the participants, who then devise a set of 'yes/no' questions to ask the instructor about the puzzle.

Next comes the *verification* stage, where participants pose their questions to the instructor. The instructor rejects any requests for explanation and asks participants to re-phrase any questions which do not comply with the 'yes/no' answer format. Each question thus becomes a mini-hypothesis which is supported or refuted by the instructor's response, teaching participants the scientific approach to verifying facts.

Experimentation is the third stage. Participants isolate the relevant variables, and consider the relationship between them. They can hypothesize by testing to see how altering one variable affects another.

Stage four involves *explanation*. Each participant organizes their observations and presents either an explanation of the puzzle, a solution to it or rules of procedure.

The final stage involves *analysing* the inquiry strategy that was used, and suggesting modifications and improvements.

Collins, S.K. (1969) 'The Importance of Strong Confrontation in an Inquiry Model of Teaching', *School Science and Mathematics*, vol. 69, no. 7, pp. 615–17.
Ivany, G. (1969) 'The Assessment of Verbal Inquiry in Elementary School Science', *Science Education*, vol. 53, no. 4, pp. 287–93.
Joyce, B., Weil, M. and Showers, B. (1992) *Models of Teaching* (4th edn), Allyn and Bacon, pp. 197–211.
Suchman, R.J. (1964) 'Studies in Inquiry Training', in Ripple, R. and Bookcastle, V. (eds) *Piaget Reconsidered*, Cornell University Press.

See also: Case incident process model; Group investigation model; Interrogation of experts; Management problem laboratory; Mystery clue method

Insider-outsider consulting teams

Lippitt and colleagues define a 'change agent' as a person who comes from outside a system and attempts to create change within it. Bennis and colleagues regard this as too narrow a view, since they feel that the essence of organizational development involves enabling change to come from within the system, allowing it to adapt and solve its own problems. Bavelas showed that change introduced at the periphery of a system from outside usually spread much more slowly than change introduced from within the system.

Current attempts at organizational change therefore require both an internal change agent and an outside one. The two collaborate as members of a team, the insider linking the outsider's knowledge to those in the organization who use it. The extensive literature on gatekeepers, opinion leaders, and more generally on the importance of linkers in the knowledge-diffusion process bears out the value of this approach in implementing organizational change programmes.

Bavelas, A. (1968) 'Communication Patterns in Task Oriented Groups', in Cartwright, D. and Zander, A. (eds) *Group Dynamics: Research and Theory*, Tavistock.
Bennis, W.G., Benne, K.D. and Chin, R. (eds) (1985) *The Planning of Change* (4th edn), Holt, Rinehart and Winston.
Havelock, R.G. (1973) *The Change Agent's Guide to Innovation in Education*, Educational Technology Publications.
Havelock, R.G. and Huberman, A.M. (1977) *Solving Educational Problems*, UNESCO.
Lippitt, R., Watson, J. and Westley, B. (1958) *The Dynamics of Planned Change*, Harcourt, Brace and World.

See also: Coaching; Consultation; Consultant network; Consulting assignment; Consulting pair; Multiple job-holding; Process consultation; Shadow consultant; Supervisory counselling

Institute meeting

The term 'institute' usually refers to a department or a division of a college or university, and here it describes one of the most frequently used forms of training meeting in adult education. Institute meetings are used to develop knowledge and skill in a specialized area of concern or practice, combining the provision of information and instruction with problem identification and problem-solving. They foster intensive learning over a short period, and can consist of a series of one-day sessions or a gathering lasting several days. Informality may be introduced by the use of buzz sessions, group projects and open discussion, as well as formal presentations.

Institute meetings usually follow a well-organized programme, with a keynote address by a speaker who defines the issues, sets the stage and tempo and inspires participants to move towards solutions of the problems at hand. Following the opening address, participants form small discussion groups with a leader in charge of each. The groups may reassemble periodically to hear further addresses or summaries of progress.

See also: Clinic meeting; Colloquy meeting; Conference meeting; Forum meeting; Gordon seminars; Interview meeting; Panel discussion; Symposium meeting

Instrumented feedback (instrumentation)

'Instrumented feedback' refers to the use of questionnaires, often referred to as 'instruments' or 'inventories', whose primary function is educational, rather than research. Each instrument is based on a theory of human behaviour or management, such as McGregor's Theory X and Theory Y or Berne's Transactional Analysis. Once completed, depending on their length and complexity, they can either be scored by an administrator or participants can be given the key so they can score themselves. Feedback is then provided to allow individuals to compare their rating with that of the group as a whole or with another database provided by the tutor. Inventories are commercially available on all the major management teaching topics, such as leadership style, motivation, communication and organizational culture. However, although many classroom questionnaires are modified versions of those used in management research, when they are used in a teaching environment it is necessary to caution group members not to place too much reliance on their individual ratings.

In education, instrumented feedback encourages active participation by promoting personal involvement. The approach can be used to introduce theories, constructs and terminology with which to categorize and describe behaviour, attitudes, values, and so on. The non-threatening nature of the feedback allows participants to develop a view of themselves in comparison to others.

One method is to use an instrument deliberately to create cognitive dissonance in order to facilitate learning. If the subject being examined is group interaction skills, the tutor may ask certain group members to fill in a questionnaire about the behaviours they feel they usually exhibit during group meetings (e.g., summarizing, asking others' views), while the rest of the group scores each individual on the basis of the behaviour they observe. A de-briefing session is then held to allow the individuals to compare their view of their behaviour with the observers', followed by a group discussion.

A wide variety of instruments are used in management training for different purposes, including helping a group to diagnose its own functioning and development, generating data for organizational diagnosis, teaching various human relations concepts through self-diagnosis, and researching the outcomes of education and training designs. The approach has frequently been used to study company morale using instruments classified according to the form of question asked: *objective questions* involve supplying multiple answers to each question, from which employees choose the most appropriate; *descriptive questions* allow them to answer in their own words, whereas *projective surveys* require them to analyse and comment on situations unrelated to their job or company. Typical organizational morale questionnaires use a blend of objective and descriptive questions.

Heller, F.A. (1970) 'Group Analysis Applied to Training', *Journal of Management Studies*, vol. 7, pp. 335–45.
'In Person: Jay Hall', *Training* (1980), vol. 6, no. 6, August, pp. 2–5.
Pfeiffer, J.W., Heslin, R. and Jones, J.E. (1976) *Instrumentation in Human Relations Training*, Pfeiffer/Jossey-Bass.
Reddin, B. (1992) *Tests for Training and Feedback*, Kogan Page.
Reddin, B. (1994) *Using Tests in Training*, Prentice-Hall.
Sykes, P. (1980) 'Guide to the Use of Instruments', *The Training Officer*, vol. 16, no. 1, pp. 22–4.

See also: Attitude survey; Autonomy lab; Database interventions; Instrumented laboratory; Instrumented team learning; Learning community; Likert System 4 Management; Management audit; Organizational climate analysis; Process analysis; Self- with peer-appraisal; Self-development; Self-tests; Survey feedback interventions

Instrumented laboratory

The instrumented laboratory was originally developed by Robert Blake and Jane Mouton to teach social psychology at the University of Texas, and subsequently became the managerial grid approach to organizational development. The earliest recorded use of this approach was by Herb Shepard, Robert Blake and Murray Horowitz at Exxon's Bayway plant in Texas.

The technique makes wide use of instruments such as questionnaires, audio tapes and video tapes to provide feedback to participants based on rating scales and the measurement of group and individual behaviour during sessions. Participants take on different roles at different points, acting as subjects, analysts, interpreters, observers and consultants. Personal discovery and experimentation are encouraged, and the information obtained gives a quantitative representation of group processes. Where a workgroup participates in such a laboratory, the instruments detect subtler forms of group behaviour which frequently remain hidden.

An important feature is that the laboratory can function in the absence of a trainer, in which case an audio tape or video may direct participants to resources and/or make suggestions about how these might be used. However, if trainers are present, they can instruct the group in how to make the best use of the data generated, what analysis techniques are available, and how to interpret the theory. The lack of reliance on a trainer makes this a cost-effective development approach, especially if the company's own staff are trained to administer the instruments.

Bass, B.M. (1966) 'A Plan to Use Programmed Group Exercises to Study Cultural Differences in Management Behaviour', *International Journal of Psychology*, vol. 1, no. 4.

Blake, R.R. and Mouton J.S. (1962) 'The Instrumented Training Laboratory', in Weschler, I.R. and Schein, E.H. (eds) *Issues in Training: Selected Readings Series 5*, National Training Laboratories, pp. 61–76.

Cox, C. (1974) 'An EGROM Workshop; What is it?', *Industrial Training International*, vol. 9, no. 9, pp. 277–9.

Margulies, N. and Wallace, J. (1973) *Organizational Change: Techniques and Applications*, Scott Foresman, pp. 70–1.

Sashkin, M. (1978) 'Interview with Robert R. Blake and Jane Srygley Mouton', *Group and Organization Studies*, December, pp. 401–7.

Shepard, H.A. (1964) 'Explorations in Observant Participation', in Bradford, L.P., Gibb, J.R., and Benne, K.D. (eds) *T-group Theory and the Laboratory Method*, Wiley.

See also: Autonomous learning group; Autonomy lab; Awareness training; Cluster laboratory; Cousin laboratory; Data-based interventions; Encounter groups; Feedback; Gestalt techniques; Group development laboratory; Human relations laboratory; Instrumented feedback; Instrumented team learning; Laboratory learning; Learning community; Learning organization; Media-activated learning group; Organizational laboratory; Personal development laboratory; Psychodrama; Sensitivity (T-group) training; Tavistock conference method; Transactional Analysis

Instrumented team learning

When introducing student-centred learning, two problems tend to arise: how to direct the students' learning in the most profitable way without assuming responsibility for it, and how to encourage a group to develop task-oriented teamwork, rather than merely serving as a social forum. Instrumented team learning (ITL) was developed by Mouton and Blake to address these issues. Although it is based on principles of student-centred rather than tutor-centred learning, it is nevertheless a structured approach, making use of the strength of the team rather than individual

work. The problem of responsibility for learning is dealt with by providing of a set of instruments and directions which structure the learning that is to be acquired by the students, providing expert guidance in the absence of a teacher. To encourage teamwork, each ITL team is given explicit goals and objectives, tasks, procedures and a way of measuring its effectiveness in terms of operational outcomes. The essential structure is provided, but control over the team's actions rests with the students themselves.

Four instruments (also known as 'designs') are currently available. The *Clarifying Attitudes Design* (CAD) focuses on attitudes, and can be used where inter-departmental relationships are involved or to clarify attitudes to work performance, legislation or training. It has been applied in sales, training, customer service and among employees in general. The *Team Effectiveness Design* (TED) considers team performance, and has been used to introduce theoretical concepts in electronics and ventilation as well as new legislation and systems. The *Team Member Teaching Design* (TMTD) can be used in any situation where theory, facts or concepts need to be learned. Finally, the *Performance Judging Design* (PJD) is used in areas requiring skill development.

Clifford, D.M. (1979) 'Instrumented Team Learning: The British Gas Experience', in *BACIE Journal*, vol. 33, no. 5, May, pp. 79–81.

'In Person: Robert Blake and Jane Mouton', *Training* (1980), vol. 6, no. 1, March, pp. 8–11.

Mouton, J.S. and Blake, R.R. (1975) *Instrumented Team Learning*, Scientific Methods Inc.

Mouton, J.S. and Blake, R.R. (1976) 'Instrumented Team Learning', *Industrial Training International*, vol. 11, no. 2.

See also: Agenda method; Autonomous learning group; Autonomy lab; Community of enquiry; Guided group problem-solving; Independent study; Instrumentation; Instrumented feedback; Instrumented laboratory; Leaderless group discussion; Learning cell; Learning through discussion; Media-activated learning group; Self-directed learning; Study circles; Tape-assisted learning programme; Transactional Analysis

Integrated support functions

In this structural design, a company tries to avoid the need for any staff units or job specialities by making the operating team responsible for activities such as maintenance, quality control, production engineering and personnel management. Each team member is responsible for routine maintenance of the equipment they operate and for keeping their own work area tidy, and the team as a whole takes responsibility for performing quality tests and meeting quality standards. In addition, team members take on personnel duties when selecting job applicants.

Huczynski, A.A. (1985) 'Designing High Commitment-High Performance Organizations', *Technovation*, vol. 3, pp. 111–18.
Walton, R.E. (1972) 'How to Counter Alienation in the Plant', *Harvard Business Review*, November–December, pp. 70–81.

See also: Autonomous workgroups; Business teams; Flexible staffing; Group technology; Independent product groups; Intrapreneurial group; Job design; Job enlargement; Job enrichment; Line of business teams; Matrix design; Structural interventions

Inter-group interventions

Inter-group interventions are fine-tuning techniques used by an organization to manage relationships between different groups, such as sales and production, line and staff groups, and customers and the company.

The behaviour of individuals, small groups and organizations can, in part, be explained by the open systems concept, which emphasizes the importance of the boundaries between different groups, and defines management's primary role as maintaining the boundary relationships between the different groups. The organization is seen as an open system of interacting groups, which are co-ordinated by some common goal or goals, and which are differentiated by a hierarchy of authority, a division of labour and the collective histories of their individual members. Each person in the system is seen as contributing to the performance of certain tasks, and occupies a position in the hierarchy while being identified with certain historically defined groups.

Alderfer, C.P. (1976) 'Group and Inter-group Design', in Hackman, J.R. and Suttle, J.L. (eds) *Improving Life at Work*, Goodyer.
Alderfer, C.P. (1977) 'Improving Long Term Organizational Communication through Long Term Intervention', *Journal of Applied Behavioural Science*, vol. 13, no. 2, pp. 193–210.
Blake, R.R., Mouton, J.S. and Sloma, R. (1965) 'The Union Management Intergroup Laboratory', *Journal of Applied Behavioural Science*, vol. 1, pp. 25–57.
French, W.L. and Bell, C.H. (1984) *Organization Development: Behavioural Science Interventions for Organization Improvement* (3rd edn), Prentice-Hall, pp. 155–62.
Margulies, N. and Wallace, J. (1973), *Organizational Change: Techniques and Applications*, Scott Foresman, Chapter 8.
Varney, G.H. (1979) *Organization Development for Managers*, Addison Wesley Longman.

See also: Family group team-building meeting; Inter-group team-building; MAPS approach; Merger management intervention; Open systems planning; Socio-technical systems design; Staff exchange

Inter-group team-building (interface team-building; inter-group relations development; inter-group building exercise)

Inter-group team-building interventions aim to increase interaction and communication between work-related groups, reduce the amount of unhelpful competition between them, and emphasize group interdependence. They may involve two or more groups from separate organizational units. Although the issues involved are similar to those dealt with in internal team-building, inter-group team-building can be extremely complicated and demanding, since it deals with phenomena such as inter-group competition, or equal or co-equal authority figures.

The intervention consists of six main steps. First, the group leaders are questioned by a consultant to find out whether they think it necessary to improve relations between themselves, and whether they are willing to engage in a process to achieve this. Only if they agree can the intervention proceed. Next, the groups meet in separate rooms, and each prepares two lists. The first covers their thoughts and feelings about the other group (or groups): how they appear, what they dislike about them, what their aims are, how they achieve these, etc. On their second list, they try to predict what members of the other group are writing about them. In step three, the groups reveal the contents of both their lists to each other. At this stage, the facilitator prevents discussion of the list items, allowing only questions seeking clarification. In the fourth step, the groups return to their separate meeting places and are given two tasks to perform. First, they are asked to consider which of the areas of friction or disagreement are based on misperceptions and miscommunication. These can be resolved through the informal sharing of lists. Each group then draws up its own prioritized list of issues which need to be resolved.

In the fifth step, the groups reconvene and compare their lists. They then draw up a joint list prioritizing the issues and problems which remain, and agree and assign responsibility for taking action to resolve them. The final step is a follow-up check to review the groups' progress on their action plans and to ensure that momentum is being maintained.

There are several variations on this procedure. In one of these, each group produces three lists: a 'positive feedback list' describing what the group values in the behaviour of the other group (or groups), a 'bug list' describing what it dislikes about the other group, and an 'empathy list' which predicts what the other group might be saying about them. After sharing this information and identifying the main issues, sub-groups made up of members of both groups work on one of the issues. One or more sub-groups may be asked to 'fishbowl' their discussion for the whole group and receive its comments.

This intervention has been found useful in a number of situations, including those where there are deep problems in the relationships between people, and where good relations are critical to efficient operation. The main individuals involved must be willing to discuss the emotive issues underlying the difficulties in their relationship. If necessary, the groups involved may agree to involve an independent third party. It is important to allow adequate time for planning, preparing and implementing the process.

Blake, R.R., Shepard, H.A. and Mouton, J.S. (1965) *Managing Inter-group Conflict in Industry*, Gulf Publishing.

Fordyce, J.K. and Weil, R. (1971) *Managing With People*, Addison Wesley Longman, pp. 124–30.

French, W.L. and Bell, C.H. (1984) *Organization Development; Behavioural Science Interventions for Organization Improvement* (3rd edn), Prentice-Hall, pp. 156–9.

Margerison, C. and Leary, M. (1975) *Managing Industrial Conflicts*, MCB Publications.

Margulies, N. and Wallace, J. (1973) *Organizational Change: Techniques and Applications*, Scott Foresman, pp. 131–2.

Merry, U. and Allerhand, M.E. (1977) *Developing Teams and Organizations: A Practical Handbook for Managers and Consultants*, Addison Wesley Longman.

See also: Critiquing; Customer interface meeting; External mirror; Family group team-building meeting; Fishbowl; Interface group; MAPS approach; Merger management intervention; Organizational mirror; Sensing

Inter-organizational information-sharing

This intervention concentrates on inter-organizational relationships. One example of its application was when a consortium of seven American theolo-

gical schools wanted to make better use of their resources and provide more developmental opportunities for staff and students. Representatives attended a workshop where the basic assumption was that differentiation of one school from another was a prerequisite for their successful integration.

The workshop consisted of four phases. In the first, the necessary working climate of openness was developed, together with the skills required. Structured exercises were used to focus participants' attention on integration, mixed teams made collages representing the consortium, and direct and clear communication was encouraged. In phase two, each representative delivered a summary of information collected about another school's needs through a questionnaire and during a campus visit. Phase three involved each school's representative identifying and sharing the issues and problems they wanted to discuss with the whole consortium, and the final phase consisted of action planning.

Brown, L.D., Aram, J.D. and Bachner, D.J. (1974) 'Inter-organizational Information Sharing: A Successful Intervention that Failed', *Journal of Applied Behavioural Science*, vol. 10, no. 4, pp. 533–54.

See also: Collages; Drawing for learning; Family group diagnostic meeting; Physical representation of organizations; Questionnaires; Survey feedback interventions

Inter-personal process recall

This technique was developed by Professor Norman Kagan and colleagues at Michigan State University to improve the way people relate to each other. Kagan observed that if an interaction between two people is recorded on a video or audio cassette and played back to the participants immediately, they are able to recall their reactions in detail. An in-depth review of these experiences is usually combined with self-evaluation, and the approach is underpinned by a learning-by-discovery model, with participants in total control of their own learning. The technique is widely used in the training of doctors and counsellors.

The participants, known as *recallers*, are provided with a remote control, and are encouraged to stop and start the playback as they choose in order to explore their underlying thoughts, feelings and motives. The method was found to be more reliable when a specially trained facilitator, or *inquirer*, encouraged recallers to verbalize their experiences and elaborate upon them. The inquirer's task is neither to teach nor to give feedback, but to facilitate self-discovery, exploration and insight.

Barker, C. (1985) 'Interpersonal Process Recall in Clinical Training and Research', in Watts, F.N. (ed.) *New Developments in Clinical Psychology*, British Psychological Society and Wiley.

Kagan, N. (1980) 'Influencing Human Interaction – Eighteen Years with IPR', in Hess, A.K. *Psychotherapy Supervision: Theory, Research and Practice*, Wiley.

Kagan, N. (1984) 'Influencing Human Interaction: Interpersonal Process Recall (IPR) Stimulated by Video Tape', in Zuber-Skerritt, O. (ed.) *Video in Higher Education*, Kogan Page.

Kagan, N. and Schauble, P.G. (1969) 'Affect Simulation in Interpersonal Process Recall', *Journal of Counselling Psychology*, vol. 16, pp. 309–13.

Marsh, J. (1983) 'The Study of Boredom – The Boredom of Study', *Management Education and Development*, vol. 14, no. 2.

Thomas, L.F. and Harri-Augstein, E.S. (1985) *Self-organized Learning*, Routledge.

See also: Co-counselling; Confluent education; Illuminative incident analysis; Micro teaching; Self-criticism; Trigger film; Video confrontation

Interaction influence analysis

The aim of interaction influence analysis (IIA) is to improve communication between leaders and followers. It draws on research into verbal and non-verbal analysis developed from the work of Amidon and Powell, Flanders, and Rackham, Honey and Colbert, and is based on the Hersey-Blanchard Situational Leadership Model. IIA divides leadership events into their behavioural elements. Participants receive feedback as to which behavioural elements they are using effectively, and they are then provided with means to develop their skills.

Situational leadership theory argues that there is no single best way to influence people, and that the appropriate style will depend on the maturity of the group one is attempting to influence. Hersey and Blanchard describe a 'prescriptive curve' which shows the appropriate style at each level of maturity – telling, selling, participating and delegating. The model proposed by Hersey and Keilty argues that attempts to influence others by using a leadership style based on follower maturity are more likely to be successful if the leader communicates in a way that matches the desired style. The aim of IIA is to provide a systematic method for doing this.

Having familiarized themselves with situational leadership theory, users learn about nine behavioural elements which they might exhibit when communicating: *directing, questioning* (open and closed), *supporting, attentive listening, accepting, rational responding, non-attentive listening, rejection* and *irrational responding*. Each behavioural element is defined by the authors. The IIA model is summarized below.

Each side of the triangle is numbered to correspond to the behavioural element definition. Starting at the top, and going clockwise, the trian-

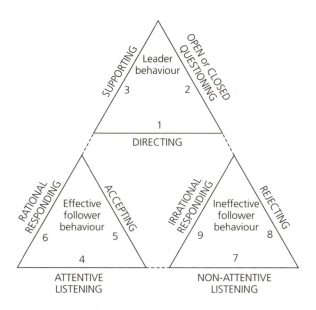

Interaction influence analysis model

gles describe leader behaviour, effective follower behaviour and ineffective follower behaviour. The observable leader elements are directing, questioning and supporting. These behaviours correspond to the first three quadrants in the situational leadership model. When the leader judges that the group's maturity has increased, they delegate leadership for that function or activity to the appropriate follower. As a result, the leader's behavioural elements shift to attentive listening, accepting and rational responding, as shown in the bottom-left triangle. How appropriate each behavioural element is will depend on the maturity of the followers, the style adopted by the leader, and the specific objectives of the leadership event. It is argued that IIA allows interactions to be analysed easily, permitting a diagnosis of interaction and the remedial action required, based on the situational leadership model.

Amidon, E.J. and Powell, E. (1969) 'Interaction Analysis as a Feed-back System in Teacher Preparation', in Nelson, L.N. (ed.) *Nature of Teaching*, Blaisdell.
Flanders, N.A. (1963) 'Intent, Action and Feedback: A Preparation for Teaching', *The Journal of Teacher Education*, September, pp. 8–12.
Hersey, P. and Blanchard, K. (1977) *Management of Organizational Behaviour: Utilizing Human Resources*, Prentice-Hall.
Hersey, P. and Keilty, J.W. (1980) 'Developing One-to-one OD Communications Skills', in Burke, W.W. and Goodstein, L.D. (eds) *Trends and Issues in OD: Current Theory and Practice*, Pfeiffer/Jossey-Bass.
Rackham, N., Honey, P. and Colbert, M. (eds) (1971) *Developing Interactive Skills*, Wellens Publishing.

See also: Behaviour modelling; Brainstorming; FIDO approach; Functional role analysis; Grid development; Implementing the organizational renewal process; Interaction Management; LIFO method; Managing for productivity; Positive peer culture; Power management; Process consultation; Situational leadership; 3-D management effectiveness seminar

Interaction Management (interaction modelling training)

Interaction Management (IM) is a training package developed and marketed by Development Dimensions International which is based on learning principles from behaviour modelling and behaviour modification. It has been defined as: 'a supervisory skills system, utilising behaviour modelling, which enables first and second level supervisors to manage critical situations (discussions) with subordinates in a manner satisfactory both to the organization and the employee'. Although it focuses on changing the behaviour of individual supervisors, it is often used as part of a wide-ranging organizational change effort. Because IM is offered as an integrated system, it may also be considered an organizational development intervention strategy.

The IM package consists of six elements: Needs Analysis, Management Reinforcement Workshops, Instructor/Programme Director Certification Workshops, Implementation of Action Plans, Interaction Management Training System, and Evaluation.

The Needs Analysis component is a diagnostic tool to determine where training should be targeted. The IM skills library consists of over forty three-and-a-half-hour modules, each relating to some critical situation faced by a supervisor, with titles such as 'Improving Work Habits' and 'Informing the Union of a Change'. Once an appropriate module has been chosen, the supervisors selected are trained in groups of six, and are shown the critical steps for handling each difficult situation successfully, including a video describing effective supervisory behaviour and action. Each participant then has the opportunity to practise the skills, and receives feedback from colleagues as well as the tutor.

A second important aspect of the approach is that the trainees' managers attend a Management Reinforcement Workshop, where they learn about the training their subordinates have received, and are taught to identify and reinforce effective behaviours in their supervisors.

Because IM programmes involve company managers being trained in the techniques and principles and then taking on the training role themselves, the Instructor/Programme Director Certification Workshops help to develop their skills as instructors.

In the Implementation of Action Plans component, preparations are made to initiate the Interaction Management Training System.

Finally, the Evaluation component involves using instruments to evaluate the package as a whole.

Byham, W.C. and Robinson, J. (1976) 'Interaction Management: Supervisory Training That Changes Job Performance', in *Personnel Administrator*, vol. 21, no. 2, pp. 16–19.
Byham, W. and Robinson, J. (1976) 'Interaction Modelling: A New Concept in Supervisory Training', *Training and Development Journal*, vol. 30, no. 2, pp. 20–33.
Byham, W.C., Adams, D. and Kiggins, A. (1976) 'Transfer of Modelling Training to the

Job', *Personnel Psychology*, vol. 29, no. 3, pp. 345–9.

Croston, B. (1983) 'Increasing the Supervisor's Contribution to Productivity Improvement', *Productivity Insights*, no. 1, October–November, pp. 4–6.

Dobbs, J.H. (1983) 'Behaviour Modelling: Training Supervisors for Results', *Personnel Executive*, October.

Roberts, D.G. (1984) 'Interaction Management: A Case Study, Part 1', *Education and Training*, vol. 26, no. 5, pp. 162–4.

Roberts, D.G. (1984) 'Interaction Management: A Case Study, Part 2', *Education and Training*, vol. 26, no. 6.

Robinson, J.C. and Robinson, L.E. (1979) 'How to Make Sure Your Supervisors Do on the Job What You Taught Them in the Classroom', *Training*, September.

See also: Basic practice model; Behaviour modelling; Behaviour modification; Feedback; FIDO approach; Follow-up; Grid development; Human process approach; Implementing the organizational renewal programme; Interaction influence analysis; LIFO method; Managing for productivity; Managing effective relationships; Role training; Post-course follow-up; Power management; Self-management; Situational leadership; Supervisory methods; 3-D management effectiveness seminar

Interactive co-teaching

Interactive co-teaching (IC) is a version of team teaching. Conventional team teaching involves two or more instructors taking it in turn to teach a class, perhaps on alternate weeks, whereas in IC each instructor is present and involved during every class session. Although one co-teacher takes primary responsibility for the topic, the other is expected to be capable of discussing all the topics in the lesson plan.

During the lecture or tutorial session, the two alternate between *initiating* and *supplementary* roles. The primary instructor initiates the topic while the secondary one observes, making interjections to supply contrary or additional information, to question, to challenge, to supplement or to provide examples. These interventions are frequently spontaneous.

The approach is best suited to presenting contrasting perspectives or views on a topic. It can engage students' interest, involves them, and encourages them to react and contribute.

Farkash, A. and Vegso, R.W. (1988-9) 'Interactive Co-teaching: Theory and Practice', *Organizational Behaviour Teaching Review*, vol. 13, no. 3, pp. 75–86.

Miller, G.V. and Wilson, P.G. (1982) 'Co-training: A Synergistic Outcome', *Training and Development Journal*, vol. 9, pp. 94–100.

See also: Team teaching

Interactive skills training

Interactive skills training aims to increase participants' awareness of their own and others' behaviour, and to develop skills in all interactive situations. The approach consists of analysing behaviour using carefully defined behaviour categories; feeding back to participants information about their behaviour, and using behavioural data to create a supportive learning environment, for example by using it to mix workgroups.

An interactive skills training programme includes consideration of behaviour analysis, non-verbal behaviour, leadership style, self-perception, Transactional Analysis and behaviour modification. The basic skills involve analysing a situation in terms of the task and people involved in it, defining the objectives to be achieved, planning in detail how to behave in order to achieve these objectives, and monitoring behaviour in order to respond to the unexpected. These skills are developed through 'learning by doing' in an environment which encourages experimentation and provides feedback before further attempts are made.

The approach is based on a number of assumptions: a manager's behaviour influences the behaviour of those with whom they interact; this behaviour is shaped more by their perception of environmental factors than by relatively constant internal factors; there is no single correct behaviour style; changing people's behaviour at all is difficult, and inferences about people's behaviour must be based on careful observations of overt behaviour in the belief that individuals are capable of planning and controlling their behaviour.

Interactive skills training can be applied to managerial behaviour in groups, or to help individual managers improve their ability to pinpoint the most important variables in their own behaviour. Following the analysis, the manager and trainer jointly decide which objectives need to be achieved in a particular context, and draw up detailed plans concerning how to behave in order to bring these about. The emphasis on monitoring one's own interactional behaviour as well as other people's enables participants to make conscious adjustments and apply behavioural antidotes as required.

Beckett, R.T., Jones, R.A. and King, S.H. (1975) 'Two Person Skills Training', *Industrial and Commercial Training*, vol. 7, no. 5, pp. 205–9.

Brewster, C.J. and Connoch, S.L. (1977) 'Interactive Skills of Industrial Relations', *Industrial and Commercial Training*, vol. 9, no. 9, pp. 377–81.

Frank, E. and Margerison, C. (1978) 'Training Methods and Organisational Development', *Journal of European Industrial Training*, vol. 2, no. 4, pp. 11–13.

Fraser, T. and Phillips, K. (1980) 'Feedback in Social Skills Training', *Industrial and Commercial Training*, vol. 12, no. 5, pp. 196–202.

Fraser, T. and Phillips K. (1980) 'The Qualities and Responsibilities of the Social Skills Trainer', *Industrial and Commercial Training*, vol. 12, no. 6, pp. 242–7.

Honey, P. (1988) *Face to Face* (2nd edn), Gower.

Morgan, T., Racknam, N. and Hudson, H. (1974) 'DIS: Three Years On, Part 1', *Industrial and Commercial Training*, vol. 6, no. 6, pp. 248–57.

Morgan, T., Racknam, N. and Hudson, H. (1974) 'DIS: Three Years On, Part 2', *Industrial and Commercial Training*, vol. 6, no. 7, pp. 318–28.

Phillips, K. and Fraser, T. (1980) 'Approaches to Social Skills Training', *Industrial and Commercial Training*, vol. 12, no. 4, pp. 158–63.

Phillips, K. and Fraser, T. (1980) 'Interaction Training in Management Training', *The Training Officer*, vol. 16, no. 12, pp. 324–8.

Rackham, N. and Morgan, T. (1977) *Behaviour Analysis in Training*, McGraw-Hill.

Rackham, N., Honey, P. and Colbert, M. (1971) *Developing Interactive Skills*, Wellens Publishing.

See also: Behaviour analysis; Controlled-pace negotiation; Coverdale training; Managing effective relationships; Process analysis; Skills practice session

Interface groups

An interface group is a very large group problem-solving exercise which may involve a hundred or more participants meeting for up to a day. The group is made up of members of different teams which need to interact, perhaps two or more different functional specialities such as sales and engineering, trade unions and management, the managements of two different plants, different organizations brought together through a merger, or internal customers and external clients. The method relies on an action research format to identify and share problems and attitudes, to establish priorities, and to assign action commitments to task forces.

There are three common types of interface group. *Mirror groups* allow an inside group such as the sales department to receive feedback from one or more of the client groups it serves: for example, suppliers, customers, or in-company users of the group's services. *Goal-setting interface groups* involve representatives from several related groups in an organization meeting to set up goals for action or change, usually on very specific issues. Finally, in *confrontation groups* two or more groups are brought together to begin to build a relationship or repair an unsatisfactory one. Each of these represents an increase in the degree of threat and complexity, so participants may require prior experience or some form of sensitivity training beforehand.

See also: Conference model; Confrontation groups; Confrontation meeting; Customer interface meeting; External mirror; Goal-setting and planning groups; Inter-group team-building; Organizational mirror; Product familiarization programme; Sensing

Interfering with the interference

This is a metaphor which underpins an approach to individual and organizational change which concentrates not on how to be different, but on how an existing pattern of behaviour is being maintained. To take the example of smoking, it does not ask how to become a non-smoker (different), but what is making someone persist in smoking (existing pattern). Interfering with what supports the existing pattern by dwelling on it, introducing diversions, interrupting it or even strengthening it may bring about the desired change.

Interfering with the interference challenges the idea of planned, linear organizational change. Putting the metaphor into practice involves various techniques, such as 'reframing' from neuro-linguistic programming, and the use of feedback, which encourage shifts in thinking patterns and habits. In the words of Tosey, it requires learning 'to see things backwards, inside out, and upside down'. It involves a shift from linear to systemic thinking, which can take three forms: part to whole, cause to process, and territory to map. *Part-to-whole thinking* means looking at a system as a single entity, not just a collection of parts. Unlike traditional, linear thinking, *cause-to-process thinking* does not search for the underlying causes of a behaviour, but relies on the concept of a circular, recursive system, in which the pattern under consideration is initiated at different points. *Territory-to-map* thinking involves understanding that to be useful, maps have to distort, codify and simplify a territory. Our mental maps, such as our beliefs and attitudes, can distort our view of reality, if we let them.

Argyris, C. and Schon, D. (1978) *Organizational Learning*, Addison Wesley Longman.

McLean, A. and Marshall, J. (1985) 'Exploring Culture as a Route to Organizational Change', in Hammond, V. (ed.) *Current Research in Management*, Frances Pinter.

O'Hanlon, B. and Wilk, J. (1987) *Shifting Contexts: The Generation of Effective Psychotherapy*, New York, Guildford Press.

Senge, P. (1990) *The Fifth Discipline*, Century Business.

Tosey, P. (1993) 'Interfering with the Interference: A Systemic Approach to Change in Organizations', *Management Education and Development*, vol. 24, no. 3. pp. 187–204.

See also: Neuro-linguistic programming

Internship

An internship programme is a period of paid or unpaid supervised work experience. The approach developed from professional schools' concern to provide a well-rounded education in fields such as medicine, pharmacy and accountancy by giving students the opportunity to apply their knowledge and skills in a work setting which balanced theory with practice. Students may be required to serve as interns after they have completed their studies and examinations but before they are awarded their qualifications or licence to practise. Alternatively, internship may be part of coursework in a co-operative education programme.

Internship programmes vary a great deal between different professions or occupations. They are a requirement of some medical courses, where this approach has been most highly developed. In the United Kingdom, once pharmacy students have been awarded their degree, they must serve a period of internship with a pharmaceutical company, hospital or retail pharmacy before they are admitted to the British Pharmaceutical Society and granted a licence to practise.

Such programmes usually last a minimum of one year, although students may be permitted to divide this period into two placements. The length of the placement allows interns to become familiar with the objectives and working procedures of the host organization, and this usually leads to their being given greater responsibility. Exposure to the normal political and administrative processes in the host organization can be a valuable part of their professional training.

As with other work experience programmes, setting up a successful internship programme requires a good deal of forethought, and it has been argued that it is this attention to planning which distinguishes internship from a sandwich course placement. Other factors which influence success are the selection of individuals, choice of organization, the type of work provided, and the degree of integration of academic work with on-the-job learning.

Internship programmes have both advantages and disadvantages for students, their university and the host organization. Interns' work experience enhances their employment prospects and enables them to make more informed career choices. The university benefits from an additional learning setting for its students, an opportunity to keep abreast of developments in professional practice, and greater communication between its students, staff and the outside world. The host organization gains access to a source of employees which can help it cope with transient increases in workload, new ideas and a pool of potential recruits.

The disadvantages are that students' graduation or licensing is delayed, and exposure to the demands of organizational life may lead to disillusionment with academic work. There is a danger that inadequate planning or unforeseen circumstances may mean that interns learn little of value and feel they have wasted their time. From the university's perspective, an internship programme represents unstructured learning, and administering it diverts staff time from academic duties. It may also be difficult to relate classroom teaching to interns' experience. Finally, the host organization may experience disruption as a result of the need to induct and train interns.

Abrahamsson, K., Kim, L. and Rubenson, K. (1980) *The Value of Work Experience in Higher Education*, Stockholm Institute of Education.

Antony, W.P. (1981) 'Using Internships for Action Learning', *Journal of European Industrial Training*, vol. 5, no. 1, pp. 11–16.

Decant, K. (1994) 'Making the Most of Job Assignments: An Exercise in Planning for Learning', *Journal of Management Education*, vol. 18, no. 2, pp. 198–211.

Huhlman, C. (1971) *Internship Concepts and Applications: A Report to the Center for Urban Affairs*, Indiana University.

RDIP (1972) *Handbook for Professional and Administrative Internships*, Resource Development Internship Project, Bloomington, Indiana.

See also: Apprenticeship programme; Assignment to manager with high development skills; Co-operative education; Competence-focused learning; Experience-based learning; Field project attachment; Industrial project; Learning contracts; Manager shadowing; Mentoring; On-the-job training; SmartProcess; Student consulting teams; Student placement; Study service

Interpretation of data

Joyce and colleagues explain that 'interpretation of data' is the second element in the inductive thinking model (after 'concept-formation' and before 'application of principles'). The model was

developed by Hilda Taba, and can be used separately from the other two elements.

'Interpretation of data' consists of three steps.
First, learners examine data, such as a company's
accounts. The instructor then asks them to identify
critical aspects of the different data items and how
they relate to each other (e.g., loans versus equity).
The final step involves drawing inferences and
speculating on what might happen in the future,
and why (e.g., a company that is too reliant on
short-term loans may have difficulty expanding).

Joyce, B., Weil, M. and Showers, B. (1992) *Models
of Teaching* (4th edn), Allyn and Bacon.
Taba, H. (1967) *Teacher's Handbook for Elementary
Social Studies*, Addison Wesley Longman.

See also: Application of principles; Concept formation; Data approach method

Interrogation of experts

In the learning process, effective questioning is one
of the key skills for both students and tutors.
Interrogation of experts combines development of
students' questioning skills with a library assignment and the introduction of expert informants in
a three-stage approach.

In the first stage, the tutor runs several sessions
to increase students' awareness of the different
purposes questions serve. These include stimulating reflective thought, developing understanding, encouraging the emergence of new
concepts, applying information, developing appre-
ciations and attitudes, developing the skills and
habit of evaluation, changing beliefs or attitudes,
focusing attention on cause-and-effect relationships, seeking background information and
creating interest. Once these have been established, the students are encouraged to draw up
criteria for distinguishing between 'good' and
'bad' questions. For example, questions should be
clearly worded and have precise objectives,
whereas vague ones such as 'What do you think
about ...' should generally be avoided, as should
leading and trick questions. Although some
questions may be clearly stated, they call for
answers which are either unavailable or demand
guesswork. However, questions such as 'When
will we achieve consistent economic growth in
Britain?' would be acceptable if the objective was
to stimulate discussion. It is also important to
avoid digressions and involved statements,
ambiguity, asking the same question more than
once in a statement, or calling for more than one
reaction at a time. At the conclusion of this first
stage, the students are informed that they will
soon be visited by an expert in a particular field
who has not been asked to make a formal presentation, but only to respond to questions asked by
class members. It may be necessary to provide
students with information about the expert's
present job, past posts, interests, and so on. In
the second stage, the students prepare lists of
questions for the visitor, either individually or in
groups, establishing their own criteria for what
constitutes a good question, and using the library
to obtain background information. The question-
and-answer session follows, and it may be helpful
to record it on video or audio cassette. The final
stage involves reviewing the session. The
students' questions are circulated and evaluated,
and the expert's responses are analysed.

Andrews, J.D.W. (1980) 'The Verbal Structure of
Teacher Questions: Its Impact on Class Discus-
sion', *Professional and Organizational Develop-
ment Quarterly*, vol. 2, nos 3 and 4, Fall/Winter.
Burton, W.H. (1962) 'Improvement in the Use of
Questions', *The Guidance of Learning Activities*,
Appleton-Century-Crofts, pp. 436–47.
Carin, A.A. and Sund, R.B. (1971) *Developing
Questioning Techniques*, Charles E. Merrill.
Sanders, N.M. (1966) *Classroom Questions: What
Kind?*, Harper and Row.

See also: Audience reaction/watchdog team; Brains
Trust; Colloquy meeting; Inquiry training model;
Invitation to discover; Library assignment;
Listening team; Management problem laboratory;
Mystery clue method; Question production;
Question searching; Questioning; Reaction panel;
Socratic group enquiry; Socratic questioning;
Visiting lecturer

Interview meeting

Interview meetings resemble some television chat
shows. Although they are held before an audience,
it plays no active role, simply listening to
exchanges between speakers on the platform or
stage. One speaker usually serves as the 'host',
introducing the other participant. If the meeting
involves additional platform speakers, it may take
the form of a symposium (a series of statements), a
panel discussion or a group interview.

See also: Brains Trust; Clinic meeting; Colloquy
meeting; Conference meeting; Forum meeting;
Gordon seminar; Institute meeting; Listening
team; Panel discussion; Symposium meeting

Interviewing

This technique can be used in preparation for a
team-building session or similar activity, encouraging the private expression of views in order to
reveal problems and opportunities within a group

or organization. The interviewer is usually not a member of the organization, and tries to uncover both positive and negative opinions and feelings about a wide variety of topics, such as the clarity of group goals or the effect of a manager's leadership style.

Each interview may last up to two hours, so the approach can be very time-consuming if there are a large number of participants. The information revealed may be so threatening to the group that they are unable to deal with it, and vent their feelings on the interviewer. However, some of these problems can be overcome if it is made clear to everyone from the start that the privacy of sources will be respected, why the information is being gathered, and how it will be used.

The information can be presented to the subsequent meeting or training session verbatim or thematically. The thematic approach protects privacy, is less threatening and makes it easier to summarize the information. One option is to introduce the themes first, then back these up with verbatim quotations. If critical views of managers are to be aired, they should be forewarned so they are not caught unprepared. The information should be distributed as handouts, while corroborating data can be displayed on a flipchart.

Cannell, C.F. and Kahn, R.L. (1972) 'The Collection of Data by Interviewing', in Margulies, N. and Raia, A.P. (eds) *Organizational Development: Values, Process and Technology*, McGraw-Hill, pp. 135–62.
Deems, R.S. (1997) *Interviewing: More than a Gut Feeling*, American Media Publishing.
Edwards, L. (1997) *Interviewing*, The Industrial Society.
Fordyce, J.K. and Weil, R. (1973) *Managing With People*, Addison Wesley Longman, pp. 140–2.
Margulies, N. and Wallace, J. (1973) *Organizational Change: Techniques and Applications*, Scott Foresman, p. 29.

See also: ACHIEVE model; Assessment of the organization as a system; Collages; Diagnostic activities; Drawing for learning; Family group diagnostic meeting; Family group team-building meeting; Looking for trouble; Management audit; Physical representation of organizations; Questionnaires; Survey feedback interventions

Intervisitation

In this approach, students visit each other's companies, plants or departments in order to gain insights into the nature of work problems, extend the diagnosis of a job group's difficulties, or observe how a method or technique introduced during a course can be used in practice. For example, if a course topic concerns are how to run meetings effectively, a student may invite fellow course members to attend the next company meeting they chair, to observe and offer feedback.

Planning for intervisitation needs to take into account the probable effects of visitors or observers at a meeting or similar event. The method is most useful when the person visited has clearly expressed their needs, when the purposes and procedures of the visit are clear to all concerned, and when the experience is explored at follow-up discussions.

Huczynski, A.A. (1978) 'Problems of Learning Transfer', *Journal of European Industrial Training*, vol. 2, no. l, pp. 26–9.
Miles, M.B. (1959) *Learning to Work in Groups: A Program Guide for Educational Leaders*, Bureau of Publications, Teachers College, Columbia University.

See also: Action learning; Educational visit; Field format; Field trip; Management systems study; Sensing; Skill practice seminar; Staff exchange; Studycade; Training transfer training

Intrapreneurship

The term 'intrapreneurship' was coined by American management consultant Gifford Pinchot III to describe an approach which aims to instil and nurture the entrepreneurial spirit of risk-taking and creativity among members of large, often bureaucratic, organizations. In the late 1970s, the Foresight Group in Sweden was among the first to apply this approach by establishing a school for prospective entrepreneurs, then helping them develop their ideas into business plans.

The first task in intrapreneurship is to set up an effective system to identify employees with the required characteristics and motivation. According to the Foresight Group's experience, these are likely to be relatively rare. The employee-entrepreneurs are then supported in their endeavours while they remain within the company. The effect is to decentralize large organizations by placing existing managers in a profit centre context. The purpose is to encourage them to think in more business-oriented terms.

Once co-operation between the individual and the company is achieved, the company acts as a friendly venture capitalist, and the individual puts their idea into practice. One benefit is that neither party has to assume the full range of risks normally associated with such an initiative. However, the company must be prepared to accept a degree of disruption to the work environment if unexpected ventures need to be catered for at very short notice. It also needs to encourage an internal climate which will be capable of seizing opportunities as they arise. The whole organization needs to become more thoughtful, more creative and more active, and the co-operation of top management is essential.

Norman Macrae introduced a related but distinct approach, which is to set up *intrapreneurial groups*. This is a structural innovation adopted by some large companies as a result of increasing dissatisfaction with traditional hierarchical arrangements. It involves creating separate workgroups which are in competition with each other. For example, cleaners can be divided into a number of groups, each of which constitutes a profit centre and organizes itself with management's help. Each group is offered an index-linked contract for a set period, such as six months. The company specifies the services it requires, and in return, each group receives a lump-sum monthly payment. The group members decide their own working hours and allocate the different tasks to individuals. They have a good deal of flexibility in this: for example, if one of them leaves or chooses to work part-time, they can either take on another member of staff or accept the increased workload and divide the salary between them. Such groups may also be allowed to tender for work in other departments or outside the company.

Atterhed, S.V. (1985) 'Intrapreneurship: The Way Forward', in Clutterbuck, D. (ed.) *New Patterns of Work*, Gower, Chapter 6.

Lessem, R. (1988) *Intrapreneurship*, Gower.

Macrae, N. (1983) 'Intrapreneurial Now', *The Economist*, 17 April.

Norburn, D., Manning, K. and Birley, S. (1986) 'Beyond Intrapreneurship', *Leadership and Organization Development Journal*, vol. 7, no. 3, pp. 21–6.

Ode, H.W. (1997) *Managing Corporate Culture: Innovation and Intrapreneurship*, Greenwood Publishing.

Pinchot, G. (1985) *Intrapreneuring*, Harper and Row.

Ressner, U. and Gunnarsson, E. (1986) *Group Organized Work in the Automated Office*, Gower.

Wainwright, J. and Francis, A. (1984) *Office Automation, Organization and the Nature of Work*, Gower.

See also: Achievement motivation training; Autonomous workgroups; Bottom-up management; Business teams; Collateral organization; Flexible staffing; Forcing device; Home working; Independent product teams; Integrated support functions; Job sharing; Likert's levels meetings; Multiple job-holding; Multiple management; Part-time working; Participation; Reprogramming; Simulated entrepreneurship; Skunkworks

Investing in a small company

This approach involves a large company making a modest investment in a promising small company to help it finance the development of mutually beneficial new products. Such venture capitalism has a long tradition. For example, the Ramtek Corporation in the USA invested $2 million in a small company called Digital Production to allow it to develop software for a powerful imaging system Ramtek needed to balance its product range.

The benefit of investing in a small company without controlling it is that it allows the development of a close but not stifling relationship, and the larger company avoids taking on responsibility for supervising what might otherwise be minor outposts of its business empire. Clutterbuck observes that this type of relationship is becoming more common in high-technology industries and among the leading service companies.

Clutterbuck, D. (ed.) (1985) *New Patterns of Work*, Gower.

See also: Exporting for others; Independent product teams; Merger management intervention

Invitation to discover

Invitation to discover is a discussion method whose primary aim is not to teach specific subject matter, but to help students learn how to make discoveries. However, the technique is tailored to match the subject being studied, such as employee relations or marketing.

A typical invitation to discover takes the form of a problem description and a set of carefully drafted questions which invite students to devise a method to solve it, make hypotheses, interpret data or identify the factors involved. It may be applied to individuals, or small or large groups.

Carin, A.A. and Sund, R.B. (1971) *Developing Questioning Techniques*, Charles E. Merrill.

See also: Creativity training; Interrogation of experts; Question production; Question searching; Questioning; Socratic group enquiry; Socratic questioning

Involvement teams

Involvement teams are voluntary groups of individuals from the same work areas who meet every week to discuss work problems. The approach recognizes that employees are the experts within their work areas, and the teams are allowed to set their own goals and work towards achieving them. Such groups have been developed and implemented by the Control Data Corporation.

Participants are first trained in the techniques of brainstorming, cause-and-effect analysis, data-gathering and making presentations to management. They then select problems from their work areas and propose solutions. The benefits of the approach include increased productivity, motivation, teamwork, job commitment and an improved quality of working life.

Tjosvold, D. (1998) 'Making Employee Involvement Work', *Human Relations*, vol. 51, no. 2, pp. 201–13.

See also: Multiple management; Quality awareness training; Quality circles; Quality management; Structural interventions; Study circles

Issue briefing (issue brief)

Issue briefings – concise yet comprehensive statements of the background and current status of a legislative issue – were developed by the US Congressional Research Service, the agency responsible for preparing information for members of Congress. In management education, they are used to help students appreciate the economic, political and social context within which organizational behaviour and business activities take place. While lectures and case studies deal with specifics, issue briefings address broader issues, demonstrating that evidence-gathering and analysis are key components of decision-making, and that policy-making in the real world is influenced by conflicting evidence, unclear value priorities, political horse-trading and the power of interest groups.

Preparing an issue briefing achieves a wide range of learning objectives. Working in groups, students learn to define the parameters of problems, develop research and analytical skills, gain experience of teamwork, practise public speaking, and acquire the ability to prepare a formal report. The approach can be used on any undergraduate or postgraduate management course which needs to take into account social and political issues such as whether the government should encourage companies to provide employer-sponsored childcare centres, whether pollution standards should be raised, or whether advertising of all tobacco and alcoholic products should be banned.

Each issue briefing consists of seven sections. The first is a short *definition of the issue*. Next, a *background and policy analysis* expands the history of the issue, explaining how it became a matter of public interest, the current state of the debate, and the main policy questions involved. This is followed by a *legislative history*, summarizing past and pending local, national and international legislation, and declarations of international conferences such as the World Summits on the environment. A short *summary of the evidence* is then presented, including testimony, synopses of committee reports, accounts of legislative debates, and the decisions of relevant agencies. Next, an *analysis of interest groups* is conducted, setting out their policy positions, membership, funding, objectives, strategies and actions. The next section consists of the group's own *policy recommendations* as a result of the analysis, and the likely implications are considered during a presentation session. If necessary, minority reports can be included. The final section is an *appendix* containing an annotated bibliography and brief abstracts of materials used in preparing the issue brief.

Wood, D.J. (1981) 'Issue Briefs: Understanding the Business Environment', *Organizational Behaviour and Teaching Journal*, vol. 6, no. 2, pp. 43–7.

See also: Historical analysis; Strategic planning process

Job description

A job description is a formal record of a job's title, reporting relationships (both upward and downward), its overall purpose, and a short description of the main activities it involves. It is helpful if the activities are arranged in terms of the key result areas. Job descriptions can contribute to organizational improvement by clarifying what is expected of employees and defining performance standards. It is preferable if job-holders write their own job descriptions and then submit them for approval by senior management, since this gives them the opportunity to participate in setting standards and resolving any problems. The company can use the job descriptions as the basis for performance reviews, job specifications, organizational structure reviews, establishing job grades and arranging whatever training is required.

As a structural intervention, job descriptions can be introduced or revised to rearrange reporting relationships between employees. This may involve increasing the authority of certain roles while decreasing that of others. The number of people assigned to each department may be changed, as may the content of the job. This process demands negotiation, and this can help develop a positive atmosphere for joint problem-solving. Some authorities recommend that such an intervention should be integrated with corporate planning, and connected to staff appraisal and development.

Armstrong, M. and Baron, A. (1997) *A Job Evaluation Handbook*, Institute for Personnel and Development.

Fowler, A. (1997) *Writing Job Descriptions*, Institute for Personnel and Development.

Pearn, M. and Kandola, R. (1997) *Job Analysis: A Manager's Guide*, Institute for Personnel and Development.

Plachy, R.J. and Plachy, S. (1997) *More Results Oriented Job Descriptions*, American Management Association, AMACOM.

See also: Appraisal; Goal-setting; Goal-setting and planning groups; Management by objectives; Management responsibility guide process; Periodic planning conference; Position charter; Psychological contract; Responsibility charting; Role analysis technique; Structural interventions

Job design (job redesign; work design; work restructuring)

This is a generic term describing a range of systematic approaches to task and role allocation which attempt to improve the quality of working life and employee performance by making work more varied and meaningful, and increasing employees' autonomy. In the USA, the term has usually been applied to approaches developed at the University of California at Berkeley, and later at the University of California at Los Angeles.

Various job design strategies are based on different theories of human behaviour, using techniques such as job enrichment, job enlargement and job simplification. The primary objective is to restructure work to improve efficiency and make greater use of individual workers' abilities, which often entails eliminating highly repetitive, monotonous jobs. Such approaches also take into account the needs of end users of modified products or services.

A number of job design studies have explored the effects of changes in the way technology is used in the task designs and assignments that make up jobs, including personal, social and organizational phenomena. For example, Frederick Herzberg's influential research into job enrichment led to a re-examination of the nature of industrial work which challenged the industrial concepts that had hitherto dominated job design. The findings showed that many job designs minimized opportunities for individual initiative, achievement and development of a sense of self-worth, and this led to a new emphasis on the quality of working life.

Parker, S. and Wall, T. (1998) *Job and Work Design*, Sage.

Parker, S. and Wall, T. (1998) 'Jobs and Modern Manufacturing', in Warr, P. (ed.) *Psychology at Work* (4th edn), Penguin Books.

Pruijit, H.D. (1997) *Job Design and Technology*, Routledge.

'Social Science and Workplace Reform', special issue of *Human Relations* (1998), vol. 51, no. 3, March, pp. 215–448.

See also: Contingency approach; Group technology; Integrated support functions; Job enlargement; Job enrichment; Quality of working life; Socio-technical systems design; Structural interventions; Work simplification

Job enlargement (horizontal job loading)

Job enlargement (also known as horizontal job loading) has been one of the more popular techno-structural change interventions within the job design family. It involves altering a particular job by giving the employee one or more additional tasks. For example, a person assembling a vacuum cleaner who had previously fitted only one component might also be required to fit others. This approach should not be confused with job enrichment, although the two are related.

The term 'job enlargement' was coined by Charles R. Walker of Yale University to describe an initiative by IBM in 1943. The company president, Thomas J. Watson, was visiting the Endicott plant when he saw a young woman idly standing by a milling machine. She explained that she was waiting for the set-up man to adjust her machine for a new operation. She was capable of carrying out the adjustment herself, but this was against plant rules. Watson decided that she and the other machine operators should make their own adjustments, and he persuaded the production managers to accept the idea. It worked well. Workers found their enlarged jobs less monotonous and tiring, tended to take more interest in their work, were absent less, complained less, and made fewer mistakes. The greater complexity of their jobs was reflected in an average 10 per cent pay increase.

One criticism of job enlargement is that it may merely give workers several boring tasks to carry out instead of just one. Nevertheless, research has shown that the variety it introduces can, in certain circumstances, benefit both the individual worker and the organization. Employees generally preferred the new arrangements, and the problems inherent in paced groups largely disappeared. Although improvements in production, costs, absenteeism, grievances or transfers were relatively rare, in many job enlargement projects it was found that significant quality improvements led to decreased labour costs. Another finding was that supervisors had to pay greater attention to the technical problems of production and worker training.

Alderfer, C.P. (1969) 'Job Enlargement and the Organizational Context', *Personnel Psychology*, vol. 22, pp. 418–26.

Davis, L.E. and Taylor, J.C. (1979) *Design of Jobs* (2nd edn), Goodyer.

Davis, L.E. and Valfer, E.S. (1965) 'Intervening Responses to Changes in Supervisor Job Designs', *Occupational Psychology*, vol. 39, no. 3, pp. 171–89.

Davis, L.E. and Werling, R. (1960) 'Job Design Factors', *Occupational Psychology*, vol. 34, no. 2, pp. 109–32.

See also: Group technology; Integrated support functions; Job design; Job enrichment; Quality of working life; Work simplification

Job enrichment

Job enrichment generally involves combining various vertically related jobs or functions to make work more meaningful by giving employees greater responsibility for achievement, challenge and growth. This may entail incorporating inspection, supervisory and other activities into a particular job. Although the approach is most commonly applied at the lowest levels in an organization, it can also be used at supervisory and managerial levels.

The approach evolved from research into individual motivation by Frederick Herzberg and colleagues, who developed the Motivator-Hygiene Theory. This held that the nature of work can be tailored to meet human needs by incorporating motivators such as opportunities for greater achievement, recognition, responsibility, advancement, task capabilities and knowledge.

Proponents of job enrichment are critical of job enlargement, claiming that it merely combines the boredom and monotony of several jobs into one. Instead, job enrichment interventions recognize that many jobs lack characteristics such as planning, control, skill variety, task identity, task significance, autonomy and feedback. To overcome these problems and increase employee motivation, it is necessary to analyse such jobs and restructure them so that employees experience *intrinsic motivation* by finding the job rewarding in itself, rather than requiring *extrinsic motivation* from an external source, such as pay. Job enrichment may be used as an organizational development tool, inviting workers to participate in work re-design, carrying out action research, team diagnosis and planning, but this need not be the case.

Job-enrichment programmes can focus either on the work of individuals or that of teams. For example, in one of the Ford Motor Company's job-enrichment initiatives, workers used statistical quality control charts, fed the line, carried out minor maintenance tasks and kept their work areas clean. Apart from using labour more efficiently, these changes resulted in workers taking greater interest and pride in their work, increasing their sense of responsibility.

Anderson, J.W. (1970) 'The Impact of Technology on Job Enrichment', *Personnel*, vol. 47, pp. 29–37.

Buchanan, D.A. (1979) *The Development of Job Design Theories and Techniques*, Gower.

Buckingham, G.L., Jeffrey, R.G. and Thorne, B.A. (1975) *Job Enrichment and Organizational Change*, Gower.

Dessler, G. (1983) *Improving Productivity at Work: Motivating Today's Employees*, Reston Publishing Company, Chapter 7, pp. 119–38.

Dettleback, W.W. and Kraft, P.(1971) 'Organizational Change Through Job Enrichment', *Training and Development Journal*, vol. 25, pp. 2–6.

Frank, L.L. and Hackman, J.R. (1975) 'A Failure of Job Enrichment: A Case Study of Change That Wasn't', *Journal of Applied Behavioural Science*, vol. 11, no. 4, pp. 413–36.

French, W.L. and Bell, C.H. (1984) *Organization Development: Behavioural Science Interventions for Organization Improvement* (3rd edn), Prentice-Hall, pp. 198–200.

Herzberg, F., Mausner, B. and Snyderman, B.B. (1959) *The Motivation to Work*, Wiley.

Luthans, F. and Reif, W.L. (1974) 'Job Enrichment: Long on Theory, Short on Practice'. *Organizational Dynamics*, vol. 2, no. 3, Winter, pp. 3–8.

Paul, W. and Robertson, K.B. (1970) *Job Enrichment and Employee Motivation*, Gower.

Paul, W., Robertson, K.B. and Herzberg, F. (1969) 'Job Enrichment Pays Off', *Harvard Business Review*, vol. 47, March–April, pp. 61–78.

See also: Autonomous workgroups; Broadbanding; Expanding job assignment; Factory of the future; Group technology; Integrated support functions; Job design; Job enlargement; Planned delegation; Quality of working life; Socio-technical systems design

Job retraining

Many organizations recognize that they underuse the talents of their workforce. Some view retraining to develop or update employees' skills as essential to survival, others see it as a way of improving performance or maintaining their competitive edge, while many feel it is important to retrain their staff to cope with continuous change. Retraining does not usually occur in isolation, but tends to be linked to investment in new technology, and in new products and processes.

Methods for selecting staff for retraining range from specially designed test batteries to calling for volunteers. Research suggests that age, previous background and skill qualifications are unreliable predictors of an individual's ability to absorb training. Although trainees may experience initial fears about their ability to cope with new technology and are often concerned about having to relearn how to learn, it can lead to increased self-confidence, improved job satisfaction and greater job security.

Fudge, C. (1986) 'Retraining for New Technology: Six Success Stories', *Personnel Management*, February, pp. 42–3.

See also: Role training

Job rotation (executive rotation)

The term 'job rotation' refers to two distinct techniques. The first is a means to reduce work boredom and increase motivation among shop-floor staff by allowing them to change tasks periodically, providing a degree of variety in otherwise repetitive jobs. The second is a popular managerial development technique which involves transferring executives between different jobs and plants, and this is the subject of this entry. Such schemes are usually co-ordinated by a senior management committee.

Job rotation differs from manager exchange in that participants do not necessarily return to their former job after a given period. Each job assignment usually lasts between six months and two years, and may represent a promotion for the individual concerned. Rotated managers are usually supported by experienced, permanent personnel, who help to keep things running smoothly and can offer assistance if there are difficulties. Their performance is evaluated by their superiors and reported back to the co-ordinating committee.

Job rotation schemes may be used to widen the range of skills and knowledge of a number of individuals, enabling them to take over each other's jobs if necessary. They can also serve to broaden the abilities of those at junior levels who possess specialist skills. The most successful schemes involve a small number of people and aim to prepare them for general management roles, rather than trying to give a large number of people experience of more than one department. They offer benefits such as breaking down departmental parochialism, injecting new ideas into different departments, and developing management strength in depth. Used selectively, they are an economical, sound way to promote learning, and provide a reliable basis for assessing managerial potential. It is vital to assess the managers' training needs in relation to their new post. Jobs in different departments, regions or countries can serve individual developmental needs: for example, a marketing manager might be moved to a production post in order to gain wider experience of the company's operations.

Frequent in-company job changes are a feature of many large companies, and may not necessarily be carried out for developmental reasons. Most job changes are straightforward promotions, but people may also be moved sideways to another function or factory/office. Although frequent changes of post may stretch managers until they learn how to cope and how to make a positive contribution, there is a danger they may grow cynical, feeling they are involved in a game of organizational 'musical chairs'.

Guerrier, Y. and Philpot, N. (1978) *The British Manager: Careers and Mobility*, Management Survey Report No. 39, British Institute of Management Foundation.

Hague, H. (1976) 'Job Rotation Beats Stagnation', *Industrial Management*, April, pp. 11–12.

Hill, R. (1974) 'Exxon Plays Global Chess With Its Managers', *International Management*, vol. 29, September, pp. 14–18.

Lord, D. (1972) 'Uniroyal Trains its Managers by Moving Them Around', *International Management*, April, pp. 59–62.

Louis, M. R. (1980) 'Surprise and Sensemaking: What Newcomers Experience in Entering Unfamiliar Organizational Settings', *Administrative Science Quarterly*, vol. 25, no. 2, pp. 226–51.

Stewart, R. (1984) 'Developing Managers by Radical Job Moves', *Journal of Management Development*, vol. 3, no. 2, pp. 48–55.

Zeira, Y. (1974) 'Job Rotation for Management Development', *Personnel*, vol. 51, July, pp. 25–35.

See also: Acting assignment; Autonomous workgroups; Broadbanding; Career life planning; Early retirement; Exposure to upper management; Integrated support functions; Job design; Job enlargement; Job enrichment; Job swop; Manager exchange; Manager shadowing; Quality of working life; Sick leave and holiday replacement assignment; Work simplification

Job-sharing (twinning)

Job-shares may develop when a full-time employee who wishes to work part-time persuades their employer to let them share their job with someone else, or two people may apply for a post as a job-share team. Proponents of job-sharing argue that it offers a number of advantages. It is attractive to women who wish to return to part-time work after having had children, to those who want to spend more time with their families, to disabled people who may find full-time work too demanding, or indeed to anyone who wishes to strike a better balance between their personal and work life. Employers often fear they will be unable to find a suitable job-share partner, but in practice this is rarely a problem. Close co-operation between the job-sharing employees is essential.

One company with a great deal of experience in this field is Barclays Bank, which has employed substantial numbers of women on a part-time basis since the 1940s. In its version of job-sharing, which is called *twinning*, the two employees work on alternate weeks. Barclays feels that this helps them retain good employees who would otherwise have to leave the company, and this is an important consideration in areas where there are severe shortages of the required skills. However, the employer's payroll costs are slightly higher (because of the need to pay two employees' National Insurance contributions and some duplication of administration) than would be the case for a full-time employee. There may also be problems finding a suitable replacement if one of the 'twins' leaves. Although twinning may be a very useful arrangement for some employees, very few gain promotion while engaged in this form of job-sharing.

Job-sharing must be distinguished from job splitting, which was an employment initiative introduced by the British Government in the 1980s. Employers were given a sum of money for each job split, and the scheme was restricted to the unemployed and those in receipt of benefit or under redundancy notice. The programme was severely criticized by the Equal Opportunities Commission and the TUC, which argued that whereas job-sharing catered for those who had made a conscious, voluntary decision to work part-time, job splitting was a way of providing employment for those who both wanted to and were able to work full-time, but could not find a job.

Russell, T. K. (1994) *Job Sharing: An Annotated Bibliography*, Scarecrow Press.
'Two Heads Are Better Than One – A Survey of Job Sharing', *IRS Employment Trends* (1998), August, pp. 6–16.
Walton, P. (1985) 'Job Sharing', in Clutterbuck, D. (ed.) *New Patterns of Work*, Gower, Chapter 10.

See also: Core working; Downsizing; Flexible staffing; Intrapreneurship; Multiple job-holding; Networking; Part-time working

Job support

Job support is a concept developed by Hans Noak, a management consultant working in the UK. Most work in companies is carried out by teams, and Noak argues that the important task of managing support systems – specifically, providing a framework which fosters mutual support at the individual, group and departmental levels – is often neglected. He identifies various categories of support: *physical*, supplying the tools, space and materials required to carry out the work; *developmental*, ensuring that employees understand what is required of them and how to carry out their tasks; *administrative and financial*, providing the job infrastructure and, finally, *moral and emotional*, which underpins the other types of support at the personal level. People usually feel more comfortable giving support than receiving it, so it is important to understand what kind of support is appropriate and to offer it in an acceptable way. Noak maintains that it is necessary to build an atmosphere of trust which encourages people to ask for support – and to see it as their *responsibility* to do so – when they experience difficulties.

Noak's approach involves holding three- or four-hour workshops for functional groups of employees from the shop floor up to boardroom level which develop the support network by means of a six-step process. In step one, the group considers the implications of inadequate support. Step two requires participants to define their personal tasks and specify the support they need, taking stock of the support they currently give and receive. In step three, they explore the quality of this support. The fourth step involves each participant drawing up a personal action plan. The fifth step charts the support network around each person. In the final step, the group agrees ways to meet the support needs identified. Review meetings are then held to deal with any problems that arise.

Kirschenbaum, H. and Glaser, B. (1978) *Developing Support Groups: A Manual for Facilitators and Participants*, Pfeiffer/Jossey-Bass.
Noak, H. (1983) 'Working at Working Together', *Data Processing*, vol. 25, no. 9, November, pp. 16–18.

See also: Alcohol recovery programme; Bottom-up management; Executive family seminar; Family communication programme; Outplacement counselling; Wellness programmes

Job swop

A job swop is a development programme which involves two managers from different organizations temporarily trading jobs to carry out a specific task. The details are defined by the participating companies but, whatever procedure is adopted, the managers concerned must have received prior training in the skills and knowledge they will require. In addition, they will need access to someone – perhaps a senior manager or trainer at one of the companies – with whom they can discuss their progress and any problems.

Working in a new environment can be a valuable experience for the participants, and the host organizations may benefit from the fresh perspectives they bring. However, managers must ensure that their training objectives are not swamped by the demands of the job. There is also a danger that participants' expectations of the experience may not be fulfilled, and they may fear being forgotten or missing opportunities in their organizations while they are away.

Although this approach can be very useful in helping managers appreciate other viewpoints, there are many practical difficulties which prevent it being widely adopted. Re-assimilating participants into their organizations at the end of the programme may require considerable time and effort, especially on the part of staff specialists and line supervisors, and the managers may find that their career and promotion prospects have been adversely affected.

Mumford, A. (1980) *Making Experience Pay*, McGraw-Hill.

Preen, D. W. (1970-1) 'Exchanging Roles', *Universities Quarterly*, vol. 25, pp. 17–19.

See also: Acting assignment; Action learning; Assignment to community organization; Assignment to customer as representative; Assignment to government study group; Consulting assignment; Exposure to upper management; Job rotation; Manager exchange; Manager shadowing; Overseas project; Rotation training; Sick leave/holiday replacement assignment

Joint development activities

This term was coined by staff at the Manchester Business School (MBS) to describe a collaborative management development approach they have adopted in working with client organizations in an attempt to break away from traditional didactic methods.

The underlying theory of joint development activities draws on the concept of 'resourceful managers' – those who are self-developed – and development functions within organizations – those concerned with developing new patterns of activity and adapting existing ones. Joint development activity projects tend to focus on identifying or creating new ideas or opportunities for the client. Together with the client firm's senior management, MBS staff form a steering group to guide a group of managers from the client organization who are working on a real organizational issue which is the main vehicle for learning. They also provide input on development needs and mechanisms, as well as resources to assist the development process.

Lupton, T., Berry, A.J. and Warmington, A. (1976) 'The Contribution of a Business School to a Joint Development Activity', *Management Education and Development*, vol. 7, no. 1, pp. 2–12.

Morris, J. (1974) 'Joint Development Activities', *Management Review and Digest*, vol. l, no. 1.

Morris, J. (1980) 'Joint Development Activities: From Practice to Theory', in Beck, J. and Cox, C. (eds) *Advances in Management Education*, Wiley.

Morris, J. (1982) 'Joint Development Activities in Practice', *Journal of Management Development*, vol. 1, no. 3, pp. 20–30.

See also: Action learning; Industrial project; Project-based management development; Project orientation

Journalling (learning diary; learning log; learning journal)

Journalling is the process of keeping a learning journal. A conventional diary usually consists of a personal account of daily events and the writer's reaction to them, whereas in a learning journal the writer reflects constructively on what they have learned about a topic, how that knowledge can be applied, or the process of learning itself. According to Cowan, learning journals enable their writers to develop generalizable capabilities. They can be particularly useful in helping students reflect on their classroom experiences.

One course-focused journal structure asks students to write down their reactions to both the course topic and the method of teaching. Apart from generating a cognitive response ('I thought it was useful'), students can also explore the affective domain ('I felt embarrassed when ...'), and both types of reactions can be related to experiences outside the classroom ('Whenever I'm out with friends, I tend to ...'). Reviewing journal entries can reveal recurring themes ('I tend to do this regularly ...'), which may increase the writer's self-awareness ('Maybe I'm the kind of person who ...').

Another popular journal framework, this time work-focused, asks students to describe a single event which occurred at work. They describe experiences at work, stating what happened, who said what, and the consequences. They then reflect on the experience, describing their feelings, reactions, questions, observations and judgements. Next, they practise conceptualization by relating any relevant concepts and theories covered in the course to the experience described, and formulate tentative conclusions, hypotheses or generalizations. Finally, they suggest any action they can take to apply or test what they have reflected upon, with a view to setting behavioural goals for similar situations.

Allan, B. and Enz, C.A. (1987) 'Journal Writing: Exercises in Creative Thought and Expression', *Organizational Behaviour Teaching Review*, vol. 11, no. 4, pp. 1–14.

Boud, D., Keough, R. and Walker, D. (1989) *Reflection: Turning Experience into Learning* (2nd edn), Kogan Page.

Coghlan, D. (1993) 'Learning From Emotions Through Journaling', *Journal of Management Education*, vol. 17, no. 1, pp. 90–4.

Coghlan, D. and Rashford, N. S. (1990) 'Uncovering and Dealing with Organizational Distortions', *Journal of Managerial Psychology*, vol. 5, no. 3, pp. 17–21.

Cowan, J. (1991) 'Opinion: Commenting on Learning Journal Entries', *Education and Training Technology International*, vol. 28, no. 3, pp. 261–4.

Estienne, M. (1991) 'A Personal Development File: Self-development Among Business Studies Students', *Management Education and Development*, vol. 22, no. 1, pp. 15–22.

Kember, D. et al. (1996) 'Encouraging Critical Reflection Through Small Group Discussion of Journal Writing', *Innovations in Education and Training International*, vol. 33, no. 4, pp. 213–20.

Laker, D.R. (1989–90) 'Management Class Journals', *Organizational Behaviour Teaching Review*, vol. 14, no. 3, pp. 73–8.

McMullen, W. and Cahoon, A. (1979) 'Integrating Abstract Conceptualizing With Experiential Learning', *Academy of Management Review*, vol. 4, no. 3, pp. 453–8.

Morrison, K. (1996) 'Developing Reflective Practice in Higher Degree Students through a Learning Journal', *Studies in Higher Education*, vol. 21, no. 3, pp. 317–32.

Sims, R. R. and Lindholm, J. (1993) 'Kolb's Experiential Learning Model: A First Step in Learning How to Learn from Experience', *Journal of Management Education*, vol. 17, no. 1, pp. 95–8.

Stevens, C. (1993) *A Book of Your Own*, Clarion Books.

Whitely, P. (1984) 'The Experience of Being Evaluated', *Management Education and Development*, vol. 15, no. 3, pp. 245–55.

See also: Diary exercise; Learning history; Logging critical incidents; One-to-one learning

Junior Achievement company

Junior Achievement (JA) is a non-profit organization that operates in over a thousand communities in the USA, providing young people with practical economic education programmes and experience in private enterprise. In the JA company programme, groups of secondary school students organize themselves into companies, appoint members to take on organizational roles, sell shares to raise capital, buy materials, manufacture and market a product, pay a dividend to shareholders and liquidate their company – all within a fifteen-month period. Similar programmes designed to encourage entrepreneurialism within the classroom have also been run in British schools for several years.

Although the pupils fill the key company roles and make the decisions, senior management students serve as advisers and teach basic commercial and economic concepts in the classroom. Each Junior Achievement company usually has four advisers, and since the programme is not a simulation but a real-life, hands-on business experience, it can also provide a useful case study for them, their university regarding their involvement as a 'special topics' course. The advisers' role is to help the pupil-entrepreneurs to direct their company profitably by determining objectives and the actions required to achieve them. They keep in close contact throughout, organizing regular feedback sessions and helping them explore options, but in no circumstances do they make decisions for the pupils. Experience has shown that faced with such responsibilities, many advisory groups develop into self-reliant, mature management teams.

Cousins, R.B., Thorn, R.G. and Benitz, L.E. (1995) 'The Junior Achievement Company', *Journal of Management Education*, vol. 19, no. 2, pp. 228–32.

Cox, A.T., Minter, R. and Thompson, A.F. (1995) 'A Model for Developing a University Business Partnership', *Journal of Management Education*, vol. 19, no. 2, pp. 233–9.

See also: Intrapreneurship; Proposal team assignment; Student-designed companies; Students as entrepreneurs; Students as school tutors

Jurisprudential model

To apply this model, a tutor arranges a discussion dealing with a situation where there is a conflict of values: for example, 'the interests of the workforce' versus 'the interests of the management'. To resolve the conflict, participants must develop a general strategy, or jurisprudential framework, by clarifying principles, establishing the facts and defining the terms they use.

Joyce and Weil specify eight intellectual operations required for this approach. The tutor must ensure that participants are clear which stage they have reached and which will come next. First, it is necessary to *abstract general rules from concrete situations* – for example, in this case, what are the values involved in management's rights? Second, participants must explore *the use of general value concepts as dimensional constructs* – for example, deciding whether there are degrees of workers' rights, or whether they are absolute. Third, they need to *identify conflicts between value constructs* – in this case, considering how management's and workers' rights are in conflict. Fourth, it is necessary to *define classes of value-conflict situations* – for example, what are the differences between management's rights and management's privileges? The fifth operation is to *develop analogies to the problem under consideration*. The sixth involves *working towards a general qualified position*. The seventh requires them to *test the factual assumptions behind this position*. The eighth entails *testing the relevance of statements*.

Collins, D. (1996) 'Distributive Justice and Capitalism: A Rawlsian Exercise', *Journal of Management Education*, vol. 20, no. 1, pp. 82–6.
Joyce, B. and Weil, M. (1996) *Models of Teaching* (5th edn), Allyn and Bacon, Chapter 8.
Oliver, D.W. and Shaver, J.P. (1966) *Teaching Public Issues in High School*, Houghton Mifflin.

See also: Apperception-interaction method; Appraisal module; Argumentation; Buberian dialogue; Confluent education; Debate; Mock trial; PIT technique; Short talks by students; Values clarification

Kepner-Tregoe Approach

Social psychologist Charles H. Kepner and sociologist Benjamin B. Tregoe evolved this problem-solving and decision-making process while carrying out research into US Air Force defence systems with the Rand Corporation in California. They patented the training materials that evolved, and set up Kepner-Tregoe Inc. to train managers in problem-solving and strategic and operational decision-making techniques. Strategic choice focuses on an organization's aims, and operational decision-making addresses the issue of how these can be achieved. The basic idea is that, in management, events proceed as planned unless some unanticipated factor or event produces an unexpected outcome.

Their studies revealed that managers generally lack awareness of their thought processes and the assumptions they make when trying to solve problems and make decisions. As a result, they sought to define the mental processes used by the most successful managers, organizing them into a conscious, logical, step-by-step approach. Their one-week training courses give managers the opportunity to apply the techniques by solving problems in an imaginary organization, providing feedback to help them identify areas for improvement. They divide the process into three stages – problem analysis, decision-making and potential problem analysis – each of which is itself divided into a series of steps.

The *problem analysis* stage consists of seven steps: developing awareness of what should be done; recognizing deviation from this standard; defining this deviation precisely; identifying other recent changes resulting from the deviation; examining these changes to determine which are relevant; deducing the possible causes, and discovering the real cause by identifying which of the possible causes explains all the facts.

Having found the problem, the next stage involves *decision-making* to determine what, if anything, needs to be done. Once again the manager goes through a series of logical steps to decide what is the best possible action to fulfil the objectives in the circumstances.

Finally, the *potential problem analysis* stage considers any possible adverse effects, how to try to prevent them, and what contingency plans can be drawn up to deal with them if they occur.

Kepner, C.H. and Tregoe, B.B. (1965) *The Rational Manager*, McGraw-Hill.
Kepner, C.H. and Tregoe, B.B. (1981) *The New Rational Manager*, John Martin Publishing.
'Learning to Make Better Decisions', *Works Management* (1983), vol. 36, no. 8, September.
O'Neill, H. (1976) 'Back to Training – with Kepner-Tregoe', *Industrial Training International*, vol. 11, no. 2, pp. 60–1.
'The K.T. Decision', *Business Management* (1969), January.

See also: Brainstorming; Creativity training; Down-up-down-up problem-solving method; Evaluation committee method; FIDO approach; Grid development; Implementing the organizational renewal process; Lateral thinking; LIFO method; Management oversight and risk tree; Managing for productivity; Nominal group technique; Power management; Problem-solving cycle; Problem-solving groups; Synectics; 3-D management effectiveness seminar

Laboratory method (practical work)

Laboratory methods explore the causes, effects or properties of phenomena by manipulating them or experiencing them under controlled conditions or in the field. This need not involve the use of a laboratory in the traditional sense, but can include field trips, interviews, visits to real-life situations and companies, and so on. In management education and development, the term 'laboratory' is most frequently associated with sensitivity (T-group) training.

Laboratory methods can be employed in any academic discipline where practical experience needs to be related to theory, but they are most useful if combined with other teaching approaches. Preparation can involve lectures, assignments or individual instruction, and the laboratory experience can be followed by a lecture summary, a debriefing session or a general discussion.

Alexander, L.T., Davis, R.H. and Kiavash, A. (1978) *The Laboratory: Guides for the Improvement of Instruction in Higher Education No. 9*, Michigan State University, Instructional Media Centre.

See also: Language laboratory; Microlab; Minisociety; Power laboratory; Structured social skills seminar

Laboratory training

In this approach, groups of individuals examine the causes and effects of phenomena such as intimacy, perception, affiliation, control and authority by experiencing and examining their own behaviour within the group. The term is sometimes used interchangeably with sensitivity (T-group) training. The original design developed by Kurt Lewin in 1946 came to be known as the human relations laboratory, and this term is still applied in group dynamics training. A large number of variations have been developed, such as the power lab, the organizational lab and the inter-personal relationships lab.

Laboratory training has long been an important element in organizational change strategies which also use other methods and approaches, including group discussion, role-play, instrumentation, and cognitive inputs to assist learning. *Stranger labs* involve participants from different organizations who usually have a wide range of backgrounds, professions and skills. *Cousin labs* bring together people from the same organization, but avoid mixing managers and their subordinates, and people from the same workgroup, whereas *family labs* include people who are related in these ways.

Each laboratory usually lasts between two days and two weeks. The general aim of the training is to help participants gain a better understanding of themselves, stressing process rather than task issues. During the laboratory, the trainer plays a number of roles, modelling desirable behaviour through personal example, introducing concepts and theories, encouraging experimentation, providing support to facilitate change, and stimulating confrontation. Participants have the opportunity to analyse their own learning processes, develop their own personal resources, and use their immediate environment in order to learn.

Benne, K.D., Bradford, L.P., Gibb, J.R. and Lippitt, R. (eds) (1975) *The Laboratory Method of Changing and Learning*, Science and Behaviour Books.
Bradford, L.P., Gibb, J.R. and Benne, K.D. (1964) *T-Group Theory and Laboratory Method*, Wiley.
Buchanan, P. (1969) 'Laboratory Training and Organizational Development', *Administrative Science Quarterly*, vol. 14, pp. 466–80.
Golembiewski, R.T. (1979) *Approaches to Planned Change, Part 1: Orienting Perspectives and Micro-level Interventions*, Marcel Dekker Inc.
Golembiewski, R.T. (1979) *Approaches to Planned Change, Part 2: Macro-level Interventions and Change Agent Strategies*, Marcel Dekker Inc.
Miles, M.B. (1959) *Learning to Work in Groups*, Bureau of Publications, Teachers College, Columbia University.
Schein, E.H. and Bennis, W.G. (1965) *Personal and Organizational Change Through Group Methods*, Wiley.

See also: Cluster laboratory; Cousin laboratory; Encounter group; Gestalt techniques; Group development laboratory; Group dynamics laboratory; Human process laboratory; Human relations laboratory; Instrumented laboratory; Organizational laboratory; Personal development laboratory; Power laboratory; Psychodrama; Sensitivity (T-group) training; Tavistock conference method; Team laboratory; Transactional Analysis

Language laboratory (learning laboratory)

Language laboratories were developed to teach foreign languages, each student having their own workstation where they can listen to exercises on headphones and practise their verbal skills, recording their responses by means of a microphone. They can either be used for individual self-instruction, or a tutor can monitor each student's progress through a central control desk and intervene to correct grammar or pronunciation, and so on. The original designs relied on audio tapes, but nowadays it is more common for materials to be presented by means of multi-media PCs and CD-ROMs, which allow greater sophistication and flexibility.

The approach has been extended to develop more generalized *learning laboratories*, which can be used in a similar way to teach almost any topic. For example, if a department wishes to introduce some form of self-paced study system, a CD-ROM combined with a worksheet often provides the simplest and most effective solution.

See also: Audio tutorial method; Computer-assisted learning; Info bank; Laboratory method; Resource centre; Rewriting

Large groups as small groups

A number of strategies have been developed to overcome the problems of teaching large groups by employing small-group learning methods. Moss and McMillan adopted one such approach to develop problem-solving skills in a class of a hundred students studying international relations. Apart from the problems of providing sufficient space for such a large class to assemble regularly, research indicated that less able students benefit from group problem-solving situations, and that people generally feel more comfortable making group decisions than individual ones. Therefore, the class was divided into four independent groups of 25, each of which was given a problem and asked to produce a set of coherent policies to present to a whole-class plenary session four weeks later. Four tutors were allocated to work with the groups, but it was felt in retrospect that this level of support was not necessary. Six one-hour sessions were timetabled for group meetings in a large seminar room, which allowed creativity exercises such as buzz groups and brainstorming to take place. Each student was supplied with an extensive reading list and basic articles, and all the reference material was available in the library.

The programme began with two keynote lectures as advance organizers. A student-centred approach was adopted, using a five-stage model. First, each group examined their problem, subgroups of four to six using buzz group or brainstorming techniques to decide how it could be subdivided into component parts. The group then evaluated the sub-groups' suggestions and identified several areas for further study. These were considered by another sub-group, which defined the problem, analysed it, then redefined it. In stage two, this process was repeated until each participant had identified and defined a topic for their own research. Stage three involved comparing

their research findings and ideas at sub-group meetings to derive a series of related policy recommendations. In the fourth stage, the sub-groups evaluated their members' contributions, drawing up a combined policy statement. In the final stage, each group reconvened to evaluate their sub-groups' results, synthesizing them into an overall proposal to present to the whole class at the plenary session.

Cowan, J., McConnell, S.G. and Bolton, A. (1969) *Learner Directed Group Work for Large Classes*, Department of Civil Engineering, Heriot-Watt University, Edinburgh.

Cotsonas, N.T., Kaiser, R.J. and Dowling, H.F. (1958) 'Adapting the Group Discussion Technique for Use with Large Classes', *Journal of Medical Education*, vol. 33, pp. 152–62.

Goldschmid, M.L. (1970) 'Instructional Options: Adapting the Large University Course to Individual Differences', *Learning and Development*, vol. 1, no. 5, pp. 1–2.

Moss, G.D. and McMillan, D. (1980) 'A Strategy for Developing Problem-Solving Skills in Large Undergraduate Classes', *Studies in Higher Education*, vol. 5, no. 2, pp. 161–71.

Northcraft, G.B. and Jernstedt, G.C. (1975) 'Comparison of Four Teaching Methodologies for Large Lecture Classes', *Psychological Reports*, vol. 36, pp. 599–606.

See also: Advance organizer; Group buzz; Community of enquiry; Learning cell

Large-group interventions (large-system interventions; whole-system interventions)

Top-down approaches and traditional forms of involvement such as representative committees or steering groups of departmental representatives often fail to generate support for organizational change programmes. Large-group interventions aim to overcome the common causes of resistance by enabling those who will be affected by the changes to develop a sense of ownership of the process.

A wide range of techniques has been developed to achieve this, using highly participative methods that help those involved to assess the current situation and understand why change is necessary, suggest options for action, and implement and support the programme. The system involved might be a department, factory, company, school, or locality, including external stakeholders. Large-group methods have been used for a variety of purposes, such as deciding on strategic directions for a companies or associations, redesigning products, introducing quality programmes, and changing companies' structures. Currently, there are twelve main large-system methods which fall into three categories: those which seek to create a desired future together, those for work design, and those for participative work designs.

Bunker, B.B. and Alban, B.T. (1997) *Large Group Interventions: Engaging the Whole System for Rapid Change*, Jossey-Bass.
Jacobs, R.W. (1997) *Real Time Strategic Change: How to Involve an Entire Organization in Fast and Far-reaching Change*, Berrett-Koehler.
Mindell, A. (1995) *Sitting in the Fire: Large Group Transformation Using Conflict and Diversity*, Lao Tse Press.
Weisbord, M.R. (1991) *Productive Workplaces: Organizing and Managing for Dignity, Meaning, and Community*, Jossey-Bass.

See also: Conference Model; Fast-cycle full-participation work design; Future search; Open space technology; Participative design; Real-time strategic change; Real-time work design; Search conference; Strategic planning process; Simu-Real; Work-Out

Lateral thinking

Lateral thinking was developed by British psychologist Edward de Bono, whose book *The Mechanisms of the Mind* identified four different ways of thinking: natural, logical, mathematical and lateral. Natural thinking flows along established patterns, while logical thinking results from training which attempts to restrain the excesses of natural thinking. In contrast, mathematical thinking translates materials into symbols which are then processed according to fixed rules. All of these in different ways stress previously acquired knowledge and habits, and lateral thinking seeks to counteract the errors and drawbacks of these approaches.

De Bono considers that problems result from the difference between what one has and what one wants. He divides problems into three basic types: those which need to be resolved by processing available information or collecting additional information, those which are not really problems at all, where it is simply necessary to accept the existing state of affairs, and those which can be solved by reorganizing information which has already been formed into a particular pattern. Lateral thinking is particularly suited to the last type of problem, while logical and mathematical thinking are appropriate for the others.

Like creativity training, lateral thinking uses a variety of techniques or tools which contravene the rules of logical thinking. There are four basic

principles to the approach. *Recognizing dominant or polarizing ideas* involves first acknowledging then abandoning old ideas which may inhibit new thinking. *Searching for different ways of looking at things* entails adopting a variety of viewpoints so that a number of approaches to a problem can be explored before pursuing any of them. *Relaxing rigid control on thinking* derives from de Bono's view that not only does vertical or logical thinking generally fail to produce new ideas, it can prevent their development because it must be right at every stage. In contrast, *lateral thinking* assumes that everything is possible, and does not demand that every stage is correct. It does not tackle every problem head-on, nor does it immediately freeze phenomena by labelling and classifying them. Because many innovations have arisen from chance occurrences, lateral thinking techniques are deliberately designed to allow these to happen.

A similar approach called *neologics* or *oblique thinking* has been developed in the USA by Theodore Cheney. It encourages participants to think obliquely, and stimulates innovation by encouraging them to engage in perfectly reasonable illogical thinking.

De Bono, E. (1970) *Lateral Thinking*, Penguin.
De Bono, E. (1975) *The Uses of Lateral Thinking*, Penguin.
De Bono, E. (1976) *The Mechanisms of the Mind*, Penguin.
De Bono, E. (1978) *Teaching Thinking*, Penguin.

See also: Abercrombie method; Brainstorming; Creativity training; Kepner-Tregoe approach; Mind Mapping; Synectics

Leaderless group discussion

Leaderless group discussion was first developed as a measurement or assessment tool, rather than a learning method. Its originator is believed to be J.B. Rieffert, who directed German military psychology from 1920 to 1931. The German Army used the technique until about 1939, and the German Navy employed it well into the Second World War. After 1945, it was used by the British Civil Service and by industry to screen job applicants.

When used as an assessment tool, a group of examinees is asked to conduct a discussion on one or more job-related topics for a fixed period. Because no discussion leader is appointed and the interaction is initially unstructured, one or more leaders must emerge to guide the group so that it can achieve its objectives. Examiners rate the performance of each examinee, but do not participate in the discussion. The technique has been used to assess candidates for posts in a wide range of professions and occupations.

As a learning method, the main aim of leaderless group discussion is to develop students' abilities to collaborate with others in solving problems. The absence of an authority figure encourages them to examine statements and opinions more critically, allows them greater freedom to explore feelings which might impede problem-solving, and gives them more leeway to practise a variety of intellectual and social skills. Instructors take part in proceedings only if the group specifically requests resources or advice, and, even then, the objectives of their involvement are clearly specified. Participation in small groups offers educational and psychological advantages, such as reducing anxiety levels and increasing participants' understanding and appreciation of arguments by providing feedback to each other. Despite this, many instructors are reluctant to employ the technique for fear that the group may fail to detect and challenge errors and fallacious arguments. Although research suggests that such objections are ill-founded, careful preparation by giving a detailed briefing and clarifying objectives is essential in order to achieve the group's learning objectives.

Ansbacher, H.L. (1951) 'The History of the Leaderless Group Discussion Technique', *Psychological Bulletin*, vol. 48, pp. 383–91.

Bass, B.M. (1949) 'An Analysis of Leaderless Group Discussion', *Journal of Applied Psychology*, vol. 33, pp. 527–33.

Bass, B.M. (1950) 'The Leaderless Group Discussion Technique', *Personnel Psychology*, vol. 3, pp. 17–32.

Bass, B.M. (1954) 'The Leaderless Group Discussion', *Psychological Bulletin*, vol. 51, no. 5, pp. 465–92.

Bass, B.M. and Norton, F.T.M. (1951) 'Group Size and Leaderless Discussion', *Journal of Applied Psychology*, vol. 35, no. 6, pp. 397–400.

Jaffee, C.L. (1967) 'The Partial Validation of a Leaderless Group Discussion for the Selection of Supervisory Personnel', *Occupational Psychology*, vol. 41, no. 4, pp. 245–8.

Powell, J.P. (1964) 'Tutorials without Tutors', *Vestes*, vol. 7, pp. 207–10.

Powell, J.P. (1981) 'Reducing Teacher Control', in Boud, D.J. (ed.) *Developing Student Autonomy in Learning*, Kogan Page.

Powell, J.P. and Jackson, P. (1963) 'Learning Through Unsupervised Discussion', *Hermathena*, vol. 107, pp. 99–105.

See also: Creative dialogue; Free discussion method; Instrumented team learning; Learning through discussion; Media-activated learning group; Tape-assisted learning programme

Learning by suggestion

Most learning involves a combination of reasoning, memorizing, and imitating others' behaviour and ideas. However, if these were the only means available, learning would often be a very slow process indeed. Learning by suggestion exploits the fact that teachers influence their students by suggestion: by the words they use, the attitudes they display, and by indirect means, such as their choice of textbooks. Their social position, prestige and knowledge means that many learners are ready to accept their suggestions uncritically, and this gives teachers a great deal of power, which must be used responsibly. For example, through suggestion it is possible to encourage students to seek truth and avoid prejudice. This approach can be linked to the discovery method in order to clarify how to pursue truth.

An indirect suggestion is usually more effective than a direct one, since it encourages learners to feel a sense of ownership of the idea: for example, asking 'Have you ever thought about trying ...?', rather than saying 'If I were you, I would try '. A suggestion is also more likely to be accepted if expressed positively rather than negatively: for example, conveying the message 'Seek a healthy lifestyle', rather than 'Don't smoke.'

Huczynski, A.A. (1996) *Influencing within Organizations*, Prentice-Hall, Chapters 12 and 13.

See also: Discovery method; Role-modelling

Learning cell

The learning cell involves co-operative learning in pairs. In preparation, students are given a piece of work to read, and each draws up a list of questions covering the key points of the topic, either from the reading itself or related materials. They are then assigned randomly to pairs, and take it in turns to ask and answer questions in order to consolidate their learning. Meanwhile, the tutor goes from pair to pair, also asking and answering questions.

In a variation on this method, students study different materials, taking it in turns to instruct their partners on the essentials, then asking them prepared questions.

Goldschmid, B. and Goldschmid, M.L. (1976) 'Peer Teaching in Higher Education: A Review', *Higher Education*, vol. 5, pp. 29–33.

Goldschmid, M.L. (1971) 'The Learning Cell: An Instructional Innovation', *Learning and Development*, vol. 2, no. 5.

Goldschmid, M.L. and Shore, B.M. (1974) 'The Learning Cell: A Field Test of an Educational Innovation', in Verreck, W.A. (ed.) *Methodolo-*

gical *Problems in Research and Development in Higher Education*, Swets and Zeitlinger, pp. 218–36.

See also: Agenda method; Co-counselling; Instrumented team learning; Large groups as small groups; Learning contract; Learning through discussion; One-to-one learning; Parrainage; Peer teaching; Short talks by students

Learning community (peer learning community)

Learning communities adopt a student-centred approach which encourages autonomous learning by emphasizing that individuals are responsible for identifying and achieving their own learning needs and helping others meet theirs by pooling resources and skills. Although tutors are available to offer support, all participants have equal status. The first task is to establish an atmosphere of openness, mutual trust and interdependence. Members' needs and the resources available in the group are then identified, and a programme is established to enable all members to meet their individual goals.

Heron, J. (1974) *The Concept of a Peer Learning Community*, Human Potential Research Project, Department of Adult Education, University of Surrey, Guildford.
Megginson, D.F. and Pedler, M. (1976) 'Developing Structures and Technology for the Learning Community', *Journal of European Training*, vol. 5, no. 5, pp. 262–75.
Pedler, M. (1981) 'Developing the Learning Community', in Boydell, T. and Pedler, M. (eds) *Management Self-Development: Concepts and Practices*, Gower.
Pedler, M. (1974) 'Learning in Management Education', *Journal of European Training*, vol. 3, no. 3, pp. 182–4.
Turner, I. (1976) 'A Course Without a Structure', *Studies in Higher Education*, vol. 2, no. 1, pp. 21–32.

See also: Autonomy lab; Collaboratively designed course; Community-building; Community of enquiry; Course design as learning; Decroly method; Instrumented laboratory; Learning conversation; Learning organization; Peer teaching; Student-planned learning

Learning contract (contract learning; learning by objectives)

A learning contract is an agreement between a student and an instructor about what will be learnt, how this will be accomplished, the time scale for the programme, and the criteria that will be used for evaluation. Although the term can be used in an informal sense, it is best if it is recorded in written form, including a precise description of the learning objectives and activities involved. The main advantage of this method is that it allows a course to be tailored to individuals' requirements by providing each with a different learning contract. Alternatively, a contract can be offered to the entire class, specifying the amount of work and types of activities that will required for different grades. Students can then choose which grade they want to work towards.

Learning contracts transform the instructors' role from subject content expert to learning facilitator, helping to develop an atmosphere of mutual discovery and decision-making. Staff find they need to develop a greater understanding of each learner's characteristics and how to apply course standards to individual learning contracts.

The approach was originated by Helen Parkhurst at Dalton, Massachusetts, in 1919. Her Dalton laboratory plan (often, but not entirely accurately, referred to as 'the contract method') was designed to cater for individual students' aptitudes and rates of progress. Each student was allocated an assignment giving detailed information concerning topics, projects, exercises, memory work and other course requirements. They were allowed to work on their assignment for as long as they wished, advancing as rapidly as their ability and inclination permitted. The instructor was available for help and guidance, and students occasionally attended group conferences. Graph cards were used to record each student's progress, and when a student completed one assignment, they would be given another.

Anderson, G. and Boud, D. (1996) 'Introducing Learning Contracts: A Flexible Way to Learn', *Innovations in Education and Training International*, vol. 33, no. 4, pp. 221–7.
Anderson, G., Boud, D. and Sampson, J. (1996) *Learning Contracts*, Kogan Page.
Barlow, R.M. (1974) 'An Experiment with Learning Contracts', *Journal of Higher Education*, vol. 45, June, pp. 441–9.
Berte, N.R. (ed.) (1975) 'Individualising Learning by Learning Contracts', in *New Directions in Higher Education*, Jossey-Bass.
Boak, G. (1998) *A Complete Guide to Learning Contracts*, Gower.
Boud, D. (ed.) (1981) *Developing Student Autonomy in Learning*, Kogan Page.
Brown, D.R. (1978) 'Learning by Objectives: A Contract Approach to Teaching Organizational Behaviour', *Exchange: The Organizational Behaviour and Teaching Journal*, vol. 3, no. 1, pp. 34–7.
Christen, W. (1976) 'Contracts for Student

Learning', *Educational Technology*, vol. 16, pp. 24–8.

Donald, J.G. (1976) 'Contracting for Learning', *Learning and Development*, vol. 7, no. 5.

Esbensen, T. (1978) *Student Contracts*, Guides for the Improvement of Instruction in Higher Education No. 17, Educational Techniques Publications.

Knowles, M.S. (1986) *Using Learning Contracts*, Jossey-Bass.

Mai, R. P. (1996) *Learning Partnerships, American Society for Training and Development*, ASTD Press.

Stephenson, J. and Laycock, M. (eds) (1993) *Using Learning Contracts in Higher Education*, Kogan Page.

Stuart, R. (1978) 'Contracting to Learn', *Management Education and Development*, vol. 9, no. 2, pp. 75–84.

Trait, J. and Knight, P. (1996) *The Management of Independent Learning*, Kogan Page.

See also: Block method; Co-operative education; Dalton laboratory plan; Examination; Flexastudy; FlexiStudy; Independent study; Internship; Learning cell; One-to-one learning; Parrainage; Position charter; Psychological contract; Role prescription

Learning conversation (self-organized learning; self-directed learning)

This approach aims to help managers become self-organized learners by conversing with themselves about the process of learning. It involves observation, search, analysis, formulation, review, judgement, decision and action using a conversational repertory grid and other procedures which enable them to examine how they structure meaning.

Brookfield, S. (ed.) (1985) *Self-directed Learning from Theory to Practice*, Jossey-Bass.

Cunningham, I. (1994) *The Wisdom of Strategic Learning: The Self-managed Learning Solution*, McGraw-Hill.

Graves, N. (ed.) (1994) *Learner Managed Learning*, Kogan Page.

Harri-Augstein, E.S. (1996) *Learning to Change*, McGraw-Hill.

Harri-Augstein, E.S. and Cameron-Webb, I.M. (1996) *Learning to Change: A Resource for Trainers, Managers and Learners on Self-organized Learning*, McGraw-Hill.

Harri-Augstein, E.S. and Thomas, L.F. (1978) 'Learning Conversations: A Person Centred Approach to Self-organised Learning', *British Journal of Guidance and Counselling*, July.

Harri-Augstein, E.S. and Thomas, L.F. (1981) 'Learning Conversations', in Boydell, T. and Pedler, M. (eds) *Management Self Development, Concepts and Practices*, Gower.

Piskurich, G.M. (1993) *Self-directed Learning: A Practical Guide to Design, Development and Implementation*, Jossey-Bass.

Rowlands, S. (1993) *The Enquiring Tutor: The Process of Professional Learning*, Falmer Press.

Thomas, L.F. (1976) 'The Self-organised Learner at Work', *Personnel Management*, vol. 8, no. 6, pp. 32–5.

Thomas, L.F. and Harri-Augstein, E.S. (1977) 'Learning to Learn: The Personal Constructs and Exchange of Meaning', in Howe, M. (ed.) *Adult Learning*, Wiley.

Thomas, L.F and Harri-Augstein, E.S. (1985) *Self-organized Learning*, Kogan Page.

See also: Learning community; Reflective learning; Repertory grid training

Learning history

'In corporate life, even when experience is a good teacher, it's still only a private tutor' – this observation by Kleiner and Roth means that in organizations people act collectively, but learn individually. While companies often repeat their mistakes, they rarely seem to repeat their successes. Although every member of an organization will usually have their own valid explanations for events, they are limited by their individual perspectives. If their views could be collected, shared, analysed, debated and integrated into a coherent whole, the organization would be able to learn from success or failure, and act more wisely in future. This is precisely the approach pioneered by the Centre for Organizational Learning at the Massachusetts Institute of Technology, which developed a form of case study called a learning history to capture institutional experience and disseminate its lessons. The centre has conducted over a dozen learning history projects in large US corporations: one explored a car manufacturer's success in breaking records for speed to market, while another reconsidered a restructuring programme which had left staff confused about the role of managers and the company's culture.

The learning history is drawn up by a small team of learning historians, which may include outside specialists in organizational learning (usually academics and consultants) as well as knowledgeable and concerned insiders (usually human resource or organizational effectiveness personnel). The team conducts a study which considers the background information, interviewing staff members, identifying recurrent themes, challenging assumptions and implications, and raising 'undiscussable' issues. Their report may be between 20 and 100 pages long, and is laid out in two columns. The left-hand column records the key events as described by those who were involved in them (managers, secretaries, shop floor staff, and so on). Each person is quoted directly, but is identified by job title only. Their individual stories are woven into an integrated, first-person account. The right-hand column carries the learning history team's analysis and commentary on the events described. Once the learning history report is completed, it forms the basis for group discussions involving both those who witnessed and participated in the events, and others who might learn from them.

The process of compiling a learning history is almost as important as the report itself, building trust by demonstrating to personnel that their opinions are being taken seriously. The opportunity for collective reflection provided by the group discussions can help to build a sense of community and overcome feelings of isolation. Furthermore, learning histories often raise issues that may otherwise be avoided because they are too sensitive or embarrassing, and they provide an effective means to transfer knowledge from one part of an organization to another.

Kleiner, A. and Roth, G. (1997) 'How to Make Experience Your Company's Best Teacher', *Harvard Business Review*, September–October, pp. 172–6.

See also: Action learning; Case study method; Illuminative incident analysis; Journalling; Survey feedback interventions; Story-writing; Storytelling

Learning organization (learning company; organizational learning)

Although its genesis can be traced back to the 1960s, Peter Senge is credited with stimulating interest in the learning organization concept in recent times. He defines learning organizations as those 'where people continually expand their capacity to create results they truly desire, where new and expansive patterns of thinking are nurtured, where collective aspiration is set free, and where people are continually learning how to learn together'. Some writers go further, stressing that the distinguishing feature of learning organizations is that they acquire, create and transfer knowledge in order to reflect on what they do and modify their behaviour to become more effective. Learning organizations seem to share a number of characteristics. They possess temporary structures which are responsive to change, and they promote employee participation in defining policy. They develop a culture which tolerates mistakes and encourages questioning. They want their staff to feel a sense of responsibility and to collaborate rather than compete with each other. They provide them with development opportunities, and reward them for improving their skills. They also make efforts to spread this ethos to their customers and suppliers.

A learning organization requires a vision which clarifies to all – both inside and outside – what it is seeking to achieve. This vision may be described in a set of values that engage employees' commitment. It also needs methods and tools to realize the values and achieve the vision, such as those described in this encyclopedia. Finally, it must have an innovative infrastructure to support these efforts, consisting of communication networks, reward systems, self-managing teams, and so on.

The term 'learning organization' is also used in the academic field to refer to a more structured version of a learning community which can be applied to part-time university courses.

Such aims are achieved by giving responsibility to students for selection of subject content and course process goals; the timing and sequencing of the content to be addressed and the selection of learning methods used. In the short term, the assessment procedures are largely outside the control of either the students or the tutors. Part-time courses demand more efficient structuring of class contact time, and this is achieved by dividing the time available into subject blocks, each of which is assigned a number of students who form a block team. The team approach is adopted to encourage participants to take responsibility for their own learning and to contribute to the learning of fellow course members. In this case, the tutor plays a slightly more prominent role than the facilitator in a learning community, but is still seen as an equal member of the organization, providing contributions and interventions only in response to the organization members' requests and with their approval.

Allan, B. (1997) *Developing the Learning Organization*, Financial Times/Pitman.

Bain, A. (1998) 'Social Defences Against Organizational Learning', *Human Relations*, vol. 51, no. 3, pp. 413–30.

Boas, S.C.F. (1997) 'Permanent Discovery or Collective Caprice?', *Journal of General Management*, vol. 23, no. 1, pp. 71–89.

Braham, B.J. (1996) *Creating a Learning Organization*, Kogan Page.

Cook, J.A., Staniforth, D. and Stewart, J. (1997) *The Learning Organization in the Public Services*, Gower.

Cook, P. (1997) 'The Learning Organization: Rhetoric or Reality?' *Organisations and People*, vol. 4. no. 1, pp. 10–14.

Coopey, J. (1995) 'The Learning Organization: Power, Politics and Ideology', *Management Learning*, vol. 26, no. 2, pp. 193–213.

Denton, J. (1998) *Organizational Learning and Effectiveness*, Routledge.

Dibella, A.J., Nevis, E.C. and Gould, J.M. (1996) 'Understanding Organizational Learning Capability', *Journal of Management Studies*, vol. 33, no. 3, pp. 361–79.

Dixon, N.M. (1999) *The Organizational Learning Cycle*, Gower.

Easterby-Smith, M., Burgoyne, J. and Araujo, L. (1998) *Organizational Learning and the Learning Organization*, Sage.

Edmondson, A. and Moingeon, B. (1998) 'Organizational Learning to the Learning Organization', *Management Learning*, vol. 29, no. 1, pp. 5–20.

Kilmann, R.H. (1996) 'Management Learning Organizations: Enhancing Business Education for the 21st Century', *Management Learning*, vol. 27, no. 2, pp. 203–37.

'Organizational Learning', special issue of *Human Relations* (1995), vol. 48, no. 7, July.

Probst, G. and Buchel, B. (1996) *Learning Organizations*, Prentice-Hall.

Senge, P. (1990) *The Fifth Discipline: The Art and Practice of the Learning Organization*, Doubleday.

See also: Autonomy lab; Community-building; Community of enquiry; Corporate culture training; Course design as learning; Instrumented laboratory; Learning community; Organizational climate; Peer teaching; Student-planned learning

Learning through discussion

This is a method for structuring group discussions by providing a cognitive map which guides participants through the logical processes involved, lists group roles and members' skills, and sets out criteria for judging the group's performance. One of its main advantages is that it allows small groups to work on selected texts without the leadership of a tutor.

Kitchener and Hurst's *Student Manual for Education Through Student Interaction* adopts a similar approach, but each participant fills in two questionnaires: one before the session, and another after it which asks them to assess the group's proceedings, allowing both the group and the tutor to monitor their progress.

Diamond, M.J. (1972) 'Improving the Undergraduate Lecture Class by Use of Student Led Discussion Groups', *American Psychologist*, vol. 27, pp. 978–81.

Fineman, S. and Hamblin, A.C. (1978) 'Teaching Organisational Behaviour through Discussion Groups', *Studies in Higher Education*, vol. 3, no. 1, pp. 46–62.

Hill, W.F. (1975) *Learning Thru Discussion*, Sage.

Northedge, A. (1975) 'Learning through Discussion in the Open University', *Teaching at a Distance*, no. 2, pp. 10–19.

Rabow, J., Charness, M.A. and Kipperman, J. (1994) *William Fawcett Hill's Learning Through Discussion* (3rd edn), Sage.

See also: Audio tutorial method; Creative dialogue; Discussion guide; Instrumented team learning; Leaderless group discussion; Learning cell; Media-activated learning group; Self-directed learning; Structuring seminars; Tape-assisted learning programme

Lecture

A lecture is an oral presentation on a particular topic for a specific purpose. Lectures are still a prominent feature of business management courses, especially in universities, partly because they are a cost-effective means of increasing staff–student contact time. However, although they can be effective in conveying certain types of information if they are organized and delivered properly, they need to be combined with other methods such as buzz groups and question-and-answer sessions if the aim is to promote thought or change or develop attitudes.

Some studies show that students' recall of lecture material rarely exceeds 40 per cent immediately afterwards, and drops to 20 per cent within seven days. Better results may be possible if the lecture's purpose and relevance to the course is made clear to students, if it is geared to their interests and learning objectives, and if the lecturer ensures that the subject matter is not too advanced for their stage of development. At the end of the lecture, time should be allowed to summarize not only the conclusions, but also the steps which led to them.

Careful preparation is essential, and lecturers should be willing to adapt their lecture plans according to requirements. For example, if a complex or controversial topic is being dealt with, a technique known as *ring lectures* can be adopted: a series of lectures on a single theme by different lecturers expressing different points of view. These can be followed by a debate between the lecturers.

While lectures are useful for imparting information, they can also be used to convey information *about* information: for instance, giving examples of how an academic argument can be structured in a lecture which itself consists of a structured argument. For this method to work, students need to be alerted to the existence of this secondary layer.

Barker, P. and Tan, C.M. (1997) 'Making the Case for Electronic Lectures', *Education and Training Technology International*, vol. 34, no. 1, pp. 11–16.

Blank, W. (1985–6) 'A Simple On-going Group Exercise for Large Introductory Classes', *Organizational Behaviour Teaching Review*, vol. 10, no. 1, pp. 85–7.

Bligh, D. (1972) *What's the Use of Lectures?*, Penguin.

Brown, D., Schermerhorn, J.R. and Gardner, W.L. (1986–7) 'Planned Fading as a Technique for Introducing Case Analysis Methods in Large Lecture Classes', *Organizational Behaviour Teaching Review*, vol. 11, no. 4, pp. 31–41.

Brown, G. (1978) *Lecturing and Explaining*, Methuen.

Brown, G. and Tomlinson, D. (1979) 'How to Improve Lecturing', *Medical Teacher*, vol. 1, no. 3, pp. 128–35.

Frederick, J. (1987) 'Student Involvement: Active Learning in Large Classes', in Weimer, M.G. (ed.) *Teaching Large Classes Well*, Jossey-Bass.

Gibbs, G. and Jenkins, A. (1992) 'Break Up Your Lectures or Christaller Sliced Up', *Journal of Geography in Higher Education*, vol. 8, no. 1, pp. 27–39.

Gregory, I.D. (1975) 'A New Look at the Lecture Method', *British Journal of Educational Technology*, vol. 6, no. 1, pp. 55–62.

Jenkins, A. and Gibbs, G. (1992) *Teaching Large Classes*, Kogan Page.

Kraft, K.L., Snodgrass, C.R. and Jauch, L.R. (1986–7) 'Teaching Strategy from Teaching Strategy: Lessons for a Large Required Course', *Organizational Behaviour Teaching Review*, vol. 11, no. 1, pp. 50–67.

McLennan, R. (1975) 'Lectures, Learning and Information Transmission', *Journal of European Training*, vol. 4, no. 1, pp. 56–66.

Miner, R. (1992) 'Reflections on Teaching a Large Group', *Journal of Management Education*, vol. 16, no. 3, pp. 290–302.

Weaver, R.L. (1983) 'Small Group Teaching in Large Classes', *Educational Forum*, vol. 48, no. 1, pp. 65–73.

Weingart, S. and Serey, T.T. (1984–5) 'Tips for Teaching Large Classes', *Organizational Behaviour Teaching Review*, vol. 9, no. 1, pp. 87–8.

See also: Demonstration-performance method; Lesson-demonstration method; Lecture-building; Preaching; Step-by-step lecture; Talk

Lecture-building

This approach provides a structure which allows students to select the subject matter to be covered in a lecture on a particular topic. It can be used at the beginning of a course to help students gain an overview of a topic that makes sense to them individually, and to construct their own conceptual framework as a foundation for future learning.

In preparation, students are informed that a lecture-building session will take place, and asked to think about the topic, study the recommended reading and reflect on what they require from the lecture. Unlike a traditional lecture, the lecturer's preparation does not involve drawing up a fixed lecture plan and listing the specific points to be covered. Instead, it is important to revise the topic in general terms and draw up a broad enough framework to accommodate the students' input.

The lecture itself usually lasts two or three hours, but it can be shortened or divided into several discrete sessions. There are six phases in the approach – production, construction, exhibition, inspection, re-working and examination – and the suggested timings given below assume that only one session will be held.

In the *examination* phase (10 minutes), the lecturer explains how the session will be organized, and students are given the opportunity to suggest amendments to the agenda. In the *production* phase (20 minutes), each student is given a blank index card and asked to address the question: 'What is important to know about topic X?' Their responses may include ideas, concepts, theories, research findings or relevant personal experiences, and can either be phrased as statements or questions. They are encouraged to make criticisms, ask questions and identify contradictions in the reading and research, referring to their notes and discussing the issues with their neighbours. Each student then chooses one idea, statement or question, writes it on their card and initials it before handing it in so that the lecturer can later call on them to clarify or elaborate their point. In the *construction* phase (30 minutes), the instructor sits in full view of the class and sorts the cards so that they form a coherent lecture plan. Meanwhile, the students are asked to complete a questionnaire about the session topic. For example, if the subject is employee selection methods, the questionnaire might ask them to rank the reliability or validity of different techniques. In the *exhibition* phase (30 minutes), the instructor delivers the lecture, seeking clarification from those who contributed specific points if necessary, but postponing any other discussion until the next phase. In the *inspection* phase (30 minutes), students are invited to challenge or add to the points made in the lecture, and they may respond to any criticisms of their inputs, or question the lecturer's use of them.

Finally, in the *re-working* phase, the lecturer may choose to ask the students to write a short paper on the session topic, and then share their conclusions with other course members.

McCorcle, M.D. (1980) 'Building Day: The "Lazy" Lecturer's Guide to Class Involvement', *Exchange: The Organizational Behaviour Teaching Journal*, vol. 5, no. 1, pp. 35–7.

See also: Lecture; Preaching

Lesson-demonstration method (tell-and-show method)

When introducing new procedures or equipment, it is usually more helpful to provide learners with an opportunity to observe them at first hand, rather than relying on oral or written descriptions of processes. This approach combines a brief introductory lecture with a practical demonstration to clarify the sequence of steps involved in a particular activity and show how a skilled practitioner carries them out. Learners may then ask questions about any aspects that are unclear before consolidating their learning by means of rehearsal, revision and testing. In some cases, they may be able to gain 'hands-on' experience of the skills themselves, although this may be limited by the amount of time and equipment available, as well as class size.

Ayres, R. (1977) *A Trainer's Guide to Group Instruction*, British Association for Commercial and Industrial Training.
Ayres, R. (1977) 'Strategies in Giving Group Instruction', *BACIE Journal*, vol. 31, no. 7, July, pp. 118–20.

See also: Demonstration-performance method; Discover method; Drill-and-practice method; Lecture method; Mathetics; Preaching; Vestibule training

Let's-talk-it-over programme

The Bank of America adopted this approach to provide a formal framework for resolving employees' problems. The programme consists of six stages. First, the employee discusses their problem with their immediate supervisor. If this does not provide a satisfactory outcome, they can refer it to their district administrator or department head. If the matter is still unresolved, they can enlist the help of the employee assistance department, whose staff act as ombudsmen, operating independently of the line hierarchy. If still dissatisfied, the employee can send a written appeal to the senior vice-president in their region or to the national departmental head of the company. The last resort is to request that the appeal be reviewed by a committee consisting of the heads of the personnel and legal departments, and the executive officer of the employee's division.

'Listening and Responding to Employees' Concerns', *Harvard Business Review* (1980), January–February, pp. 101–14.

See also: Affirmative action; Alternative dispute-resolution; Counselling; Employee assistance department; Employee letters; Ombudsman

Library assignment

In a library assignment, students are given a series of questions and asked to answer them by referring to books and other resources located in the library. The complexity and sophistication of the approach can be varied according to the tutor's objectives: for example, it may serve as an initiative test or 'speed trial', in which participants must use their ingenuity to obtain the correct answers in the shortest possible time.

Howard, M. (1968) *Library Assignments*, Edward Arnold.
Unwin, L. and Stephens, K. (1998) *The Role of the Library in Higher Education*, K.G. Saur.

See also: Book-reviewing; Data approach method; Dissertation proposal; Guided study; Interrogation of experts; Literature search; Research assignment; Rewriting; Worksheet

LIFO method

Stuart Atkins developed the life orientations (LIFO) method in an effort to overcome organizational conflict by providing a framework which gives individuals insights into their own and other people's behaviour. Atkins argues that individuals' inability to resolve conflicts with co-workers frequently results from lack of awareness of their own and others' behaviour styles, which means that they may exaggerate their habitual style to the point where it becomes self-defeating. Drawing on a simplified version of psychoanalytic theory, he describes four styles people may adopt in the normal course of events or in situations of stress or conflict: controlling-taking, conserving-holding, adapting-giving and supporting-giving. The method involves administering a questionnaire which enables individuals to develop a cognitive map of their own style, and the fact that they share the results with their colleagues helps them to avoid defensive reactions.

Those whose style is *controlling-taking* are assertive and confident in conflict situations, and rely on established behaviour patterns. Although these need not be negative qualities in moderation, their self-confidence can lead to arrogance and their firmness can degenerate into coercion without them realizing. Disagreements between those with a *conserving-holding* style do not usually take the form of open confrontation. Because these people tend to work in an orderly, systematic fashion by amassing a great deal of information, arguments tend to be logical and rational rather than emotional. Each person holds and argues from their own position, and escalation continues to a point of explosion. Although this clears the air, it may take a long time for them to repair their relationship. The similarities between those who adopt an *adapting-giving* style can also lead to conflict. Because they usually try to placate each other and gloss over their disagreements rapidly, problems tend to recur, and the tension builds again. Eventually, the situation explodes because there has been no lasting resolution of the difficulties. Finally, people who exhibit the *supporting-giving* style will be deferential to each other, having been trained to be polite and not to have public disagreements. Each will assume blame, and each will try harder. This behaviour will persist until they are overwhelmed with unexpressed anger, in which case they may either quietly drift apart or suddenly explode.

The LIFO method need not be restricted to managing conflict: it can also help individuals identify and accept the mix of behavioural styles in their particular group or team by helping them to develop a common language to discuss their similarities and differences. The ultimate aim is to establish compatibility and minimize conflict by balancing similarity and complementarity: enabling individuals to identify with others by recognizing their similarities, while acknowledging their differences and retaining their integrity.

'Helping People Deal With Their Differences – An OD Direction: An Interview With Stuart Atkins', *Journal of Applied Behavioural Science* (1977), vol. 13, no. 1, pp. 110–16.

Bergamini, C.W. (1976) 'LIFO', *Industrial Training International*, vol. 11, nos 7–8, August, pp. 239–40.

Katcher, A. (1976) 'LIFO', *Industrial Training International*, vol. 11, no. 5, pp. 138–41.

See also: Bioenergetics; Competing values approach; Conflict-resolution techniques; Confrontation groups; Confrontation meeting; Exchange of persons; FIDO approach; Fishbowl; Grid development; Hearing; Implementing the organizational renewal process; Interaction influence analysis; Interaction management; Kepner-Tregoe approach; Managing for productivity; Meetings for two; Merger management intervention; Negotiation by group members; No-lose conflict-resolution method; Power management

Likert's levels meetings (cross-functional teams)

Dowling described an initiative by General Motors in which one department, the cushion room, reorganized its 250 employees into cross-functional business teams. Likert called this arrangement the 'lateral linked team method' of organizational improvement, and it is at the centre of his System 4 Management approach.

The cushion room's production and service functions were brought together in a separate building, and were encouraged to operate as an independent enterprise, with all the employees participating in setting goals and developing strategies to achieve them. Senior managers first prepared a set of goals, then discussed their feasibility with the cushion room top team, which included a quality control specialist and staff from production engineering, plant engineering, industrial relations, materials handling and distribution. The team in turn consulted the cushion room supervisors and their teams, and held daily meetings, either at lunchtime or after work. The targets that were finally agreed in areas such as production and scrap were more ambitious than those senior management would have specified. Continuous feedback was provided, and absenteeism, scrap levels and other relevant information were charted daily. The outcome was that the department either met or exceeded its self-determined goals, and Likert points out that this result is not unusual when this approach is adopted.

Bowers, D.G. (1972) *System 4: The Ideas of Rensis Likert*, Basic Books.

Dessler, G. (1983) *Improving Productivity at Work: Motivating Today's Employees*, Reston Publishing, Chapter 5.

Dowling, N.F. (1975) 'System 4 Builds Performance and Profits', *Organizational Dynamics*, Winter.

Golembiewski, R.T. and Munzenrider, R. (1975) 'Social Desirability as an Intervening Variable in Interpreting OD Effects', *Journal of Applied Behavioural Science*, vol. 11, pp. 317–32.

Likert, R. (1975) 'Improving Cost Performance with Cross Functional Teams', *Conference Board Record*, vol. 12, no. 9, pp. 51–9.

Lorsch, J.W. and Lawrence, P.R. (1965) 'Organizing for Product Innovation', *Harvard Business Review*, January–February, pp. 109–22.

See also: Autonomous workgroup; Employee-designed rules; Goal-setting; Independent product teams; Intrapreneurship; Likert's System 4 Management; MAPS approach; Participation; Quality circles

Likert's System 4 Management

By means of questionnaire surveys which asked respondents to describe their organization's climate and processes, Rensis Likert derived a theory which describes a continuum of business management leadership styles: *System 1*, exploitative-authoritative; *System 2*, benevolent-authoritative; *System 3*, consultative-authoritative, and *System 4*, participative-group. He found that the most effective organizations consistently possessed System 4 characteristics, whereas the least effective exhibited System 1 and System 2 features. As a result, Likert concluded that in order to improve organizations, it was necessary to develop and maintain System 4 features. To achieve this, managers needed to adopt a democratic, participative leadership style which focused on attaining goals but also built existing workgroups into effective teams.

In Likert's view, System 4 Management represents the ideal model of how to run an organization. His approach can be used to guide an organization through the process of change by means of a variety of intervention techniques and programmes, such as altering work flow, amending incentive and payment systems, introducing training programmes, adopting different leadership styles and using all employees as sources of expertise. To achieve these ends, Likert advocates running training sessions for all supervisors and managers in order to increase mutual understanding, trust and teamwork, and to develop supervisors' communication, goal-setting and team-building skills. In a System 4 training group, all members participate in making decisions that affect the group, and all decisions are made by consensus.

The method uses employees' responses to locate their organization's current management structure and style on the System 1–System 4 continuum. Once this has been achieved, Likert highlights three sets of variables which demand attention: *causal* variables, which are those factors controlled by managers, such as organizational climate and leadership behaviour; *intervening* variables, such as communications, control, decision-making and motivation, and *result* variables, including productivity, costs, profits and job satisfaction. Likert argues that to achieve success, it is necessary to focus on changing managerial behaviour rather than paying direct attention to the intervening or end result variables, describing his approach as: 'based on increased involvement and innovative thinking about the management–employee relationship'.

Dowling, W.F. (1973) 'At Lever Brothers, Sales Move Towards System 4', *Organizational Dynamics*, Summer, pp. 50–66.

Dowling, W.F. (1975) 'At General Motors, System 4 Builds Performance and Profits', *Organizational Dynamics*, vol. 3, no. 3, Winter, pp. 23–38.

King, D.C. (1975) 'Selecting Personnel for a System 4 Organization', in Burke, W.W. (ed.) *New Technologies in Organizational Development*, Pfeiffer/Jossey-Bass, pp. 201–11.

Likert, R. (1961) *New Patterns of Management*, McGraw-Hill.

Likert, R. (1967) *The Human Organization*, McGraw-Hill.

Likert, R. and Likert, J.G. (1976) *New Ways of Managing Conflict*, McGraw-Hill.

Marrow, A., Bowers, D. and Seashore, S. (1967) *Management by Participation*, Harper and Row.

See also: Comprehensive interventions; Corporate culture training; Data-based interventions; Development of a new management/operating philosophy; Grid development; Instrumented laboratory; Likert's levels meetings; Managerial strategy change; Situational leadership; 3-D management effectiveness seminar

Likes and reservations (spelling out likes and reservations)

This exercise can be used as an ice-breaker in team-building meetings. Each person in turn chooses another individual in the group and makes two statements to them: 'Something that I like about you is ...' and 'A reservation I have about you is ...'. The recipient repeats each statement until the person who made it feels it has been understood correctly, but there is no subsequent discussion.

This exercise can be used to diagnose existing relationships or if the tone of the meeting appears to be shallow and the participants seem indifferent. Taking turns ensures that all members participate, and having to repeat the message stresses the need for accurate listening and counters defensiveness. It is particularly useful if group members have difficulty talking to each other about inter-personal problems. It is also quicker and more effective at exploring these areas than pre-meeting interviews, because group members choose for themselves which issues they bring to the surface. The requirement for both a positive and negative comment can increase the level of trust among the group members, but this exercise may not be suitable if they are highly competitive and tend to be over-critical of each other.

Fordyce, J.K. and Weil, R. (1971) *Managing With People*, Addison Wesley Longman, pp. 178–80.

See also: Critiquing; Getting acquainted; Going round the room; Non-verbal encounters; Polling; Process consultation; Sub-grouping

Line-of-business groups

This structural change strategy involves a company forming business groups made up of research and development staff, engineers, sales people and accountants, each of which deals with a particular market sector or product family. This specialization means that each team is able to offer a more comprehensive service to the client. For instance, in the sphere of office automation, it might be able to supply an integrated workstation rather than just a single machine – providing a *solution to a problem* rather than just selling equipment.

Procter & Gamble is one company that has used a variation of this approach. In one of its pet food plants, business teams have been created to deal with a particular product family.

Walton, R.E. (1972) 'How to Counter Alienation in the Plant', *Harvard Business Review*, November–December, pp. 70–81.

See also: Business teams; Independent product teams; Integrated support functions; Matrix designs; Simulated entrepreneurship; Structured interventions

Listening team

Listening teams may be designated to take notes and question a formal lecturer or symposium participants, or they may listen to, evaluate and question a group participating in an informal discussion. The team members need to be alert and well-informed on the subject under consideration, but must be careful to remain unbiased. A team of two or three people is usually sufficient, but up to five may be necessary in the case of a large-group discussion. Each team member tries to record the most important issues raised by the participants, but they may also be asked to summarize what has been said and highlight significant concepts and problems. They may later be called on to help a facilitator begin a discussion, or to help the group decide its objectives and aims.

Mackay, I. (1997) *Listening Skills*, Institute for Personnel and Development.

See also: Audience reaction/watchdog team; Brains Trust; Controlled discussion; Forum meeting; Interrogation of experts; Interview meeting; Panel discussion; Reaction panel

Literary criticism

A wide range of texts can be used to explore management issues, including non-fiction works, autobiographies, novels written specifically to examine the role of the manager, or those which deal with aspects of organizational life, Ken Kesey's *One Flew Over the Cuckoo's Nest* being one popular example. A variety of literary criticism techniques can be used to help students look more deeply into their reactions to such texts and the issues they portray.

First, students may be asked to practise *selection* through a series of questions, such as: 'What details in the book did you consider to be most significant? What are the reasons for your choices? Has articulating your reasons changed your choices? Which ideas or questions have you omitted from the choices you have made?' The next stage may focus on the question of *authorship*: 'Who did you assume was narrating the story? What led you to make that assumption? Does the author speak through the narrator? Is the narrator trustworthy? What is the author's view of the narrator?' The third stage may consider the text's *structure*: 'Does the author divide the information into units, such as sections or chapters? If so, why? What does this tell us about how they see the topic?' Following this, students may be asked to analyse *value and cultural issues*: 'What cultural values and other value systems are you aware of in the text? Which of these are shared by the characters described? Which values dominate the action?' The final stage may involve examining the text's *relationship to coursework*: 'Do the individuals, groups, structures or events described relate to any of the theories encountered in the course?'

Prasad, P. and Cavanaugh, J.M. (1997) 'Ideology and Demystification: Tom Peters and the Management (Sub-)Text: A Experiential Exploration of Critique and Empowerment in the Management Classroom', *Journal of Management Education*, vol. 21, no. 3, pp. 309–24.

Zajdel, M.M. and Vinton, K.L. (1987-8) 'Beyond the Story: How to Use a Literary Critic in the Organization Behaviour Class, *Organizational Behaviour Teaching Review*, vol. 12, no. 3, pp. 62–7.

See also: Critical theory approach; Inner dialogue; Novels for learning; Rewriting; Writing for learning

Literature search

The broad aim of this exercise is to familiarize students with the range of literature available in a given subject area by asking them to use their initiative to find the texts, classify them and evaluate them. Basic training in how to use the library's resources may be necessary beforehand, and the degree of guidance given by the lecturer will depend on their specific objectives. Students may be given only minimal instructions, such as the subject to be investigated and where in the library the information can be found. An alternative is to issue a reading list and set tasks, such as evaluating the books according to particular criteria.

Cooper, H.M. (1998) *Synthesising Research: A Guide for Literature Review* (3rd edn), Sage.
Fink, A. (1998) *Conducting Research Literature Reviews*, Sage.
Girden, E.R. (1996) *Evaluating Research Articles from Start to Finish*, Sage.
Hart, C. (1998) *Doing a Literature Review*, Sage.
Locke, L.F. et al. (1998) *Reading and Understanding Research*, Sage.

See also: Book reviewing; Dissertation proposal; Essay; Guided study; Library assignment; Problem-centred group; Reading; Reading party; Research degree; Rewriting

Logging critical incidents

This approach calls on individuals to describe those work-related incidents that caused them the greatest difficulty during a certain period. One method is to ask employees to keep a daily log of such incidents and review them with a line manager after a suitable interval. This provides an opportunity to identify any recurrent problems which might reveal training needs, allowing the employee and manager to decide how to meet them. This is sometimes known as 'training by exception', concentrating attention on those aspects of the job that are causing problems for a particular employee, rather than providing generic training.

An alternative approach is to interview managers, asking them to reveal the most difficult problems they have encountered over a more extended time scale. The appropriate period is usually considered to be one-and-a-half times the manager's reporting cycle: for example, if their work varies little from week to week, the review may cover the last ten days, whereas for a senior manager the review may cover the last three or four months. Having established which incident caused the greatest difficulty over the specified period, the circumstances are explored by asking a series of probing questions, such as: 'When did this happen? Was it a one-off problem? Why? Was it your problem, or someone else's? What caused it? What was the cost? Will it happen again? How was it solved? Are there any long-term effects?'

Flanagan, J.C. (1949) 'Critical Requirements: A New Approach to Employee Evaluation', *Personnel Psychology*, vol. 2, pp. 419–25.
Flanagan, J.C. (1951) 'The Use of Comprehensive Rationales in Test Development', *Educational Psychological Measurement*, vol. 11, pp. 151–5.
Mumford, A. (1980) *Making Experience Pay*, McGraw-Hill.

See also: Accepting positions of responsibility in community associations/university clubs; Diary exercise; Journalling; Management audit

Looking for trouble

This organizational diagnosis model was developed by Marvin Weisbrod, who specifies 'six places to look for trouble' in an organization. The first area he identifies is *leadership*: someone must be responsible for keeping the other five elements in balance. *Purposes* is the next: employees must know what their business involves. The third consideration is *structure*: managers must ensure that the workload is divided evenly. *Helpful mechanisms* is the fourth: an effective infrastructure to co-ordinate the technologies needs to be established and maintained. The fifth problem area is *relationships*: competing technologies and conflict between individuals must be managed. The final consideration is to check whether there are *incentives* to do all that needs to be done.

Weisbrod goes on to invite managers to explore three further areas of organizational functioning. They should check whether the boundaries of the organization have been defined, identifying its unique characteristics by listing its inputs and outputs. He then suggests that the manager should select an output and trace its relationship to the system as a whole, comparing the existing state of affairs with that which is desired. Finally, the manager needs to consider the demands of customers, suppliers, competitors and other agencies, to check whether they are having an adverse effect on any of the problem areas identified.

Weisbrod, M. (1978) *Organizational Diagnosis: A Workbook of Theory and Practice*, Addison Wesley Longman.

See also: ACHIEVE model; Assessment of the organization as a system; Diagnostic activities; Family group diagnostic meeting; Functional Administrative Control Technique; Interviewing;

Management audit; Organizational analysis; Overhead value analysis; 7-S framework

Management audit

This is a methodical review which assesses an organization's managerial performance in terms of defined criteria of good management. While other techniques examine specific procedures, processes and problems, a management audit considers broader issues covering the whole range of managerial activity: for example, whether the authority structure, communications systems and practices of all those with management responsibility produce a dynamic and well-integrated organization capable of responding rapidly to changing situations and making the best use of employees' skills and abilities.

An audit addresses two sets of performance factors. The primary elements include employees' attitudes to work (e.g., their concern for money and their social and psychological well-being), their capacity to work (the skills, knowledge and experience they possess), the support provided to enable them to work (resources and equipment), the reward systems in place, and the relevance of the tasks they carry out. These are all identified and measured, graded as either 'satisfactory' or 'unsatisfactory', and the results then provide the basis for remedial action. Assessing the secondary elements includes determining the management style being used and whether it is appropriate, examining the nature of the goals being pursued, identifying those in power and their influence on performance, defining the technology being used, and clarifying the influence of the external environment. In recent years, there has been increasing emphasis on nationally and internationally agreed criteria, such as those embodied in British Standards and ISO 9000.

There are a number of ways to conduct a management audit: for example, some organizations choose to appoint an internal or external auditor. Internal auditors usually set up an audit task force made up of organization members with a wide range of experience, the first task being to decide what information is required and how it will be collected. Having agreed what would constitute good management in this particular context, the task force draws up a checklist of questions which provides a framework to examine the organization's functioning and allow periodic reviews of management practices. Respondents may be asked to reply simply 'Yes', 'No' or 'Not sure', or they may be invited to offer more detailed comments. The audit exercise can also be related to staff appraisal systems. Once the data has been gathered, the task force analyses it and agrees what action is required, and a unit or department may be established to examine specific issues in greater detail. However, when an audit's primary purpose is to promote staff development, it is more common for individual managers to complete the audit independently, then discuss their findings. The audit report usually consists of sets of statements grouped under topic headings such as organizational structure, communications, public relations, health and safety, and personnel management, accompanied by recommendations for action.

Bennett, R. (1982) 'Auditing Performance: An Alternative Approach', *Leadership and Organizational Development Journal*, vol. 3, no. 1, pp. 5–10.

Dale, A.G. (1973) 'Management Audit', *British Hospital Journal and Social Service Review*, 26 September.

Green, D. (1997) *ISO 9000 Quality Systems Auditing*, Gower.

Leonard, W.P. (1962) *The Management Audit: An Appraisal of Management Methods and Performance*, Prentice-Hall.

Rose, T.G. (1961) *The Management Audit*, Gee.

Rothery, B. (1996) *ISO 1400 and ISO 9000*, Gower.

Santocki, J. (1974) 'Management Audit: Chance, Challenge or Lost Opportunity?', *The Accountant*, 3 January.

Woodcock, M. and Francis, D. (1998) *Management Skills Assessment: Audit for Trainers*, Gower.

See also: ACHIEVE model; Assessment of the organization as a system; Diagnostic activities; Family group diagnostic meeting; Functional administrative control technique; Instrumented feedback; Interviewing; Logging critical incidents; Looking for trouble; Organizational analysis; Overhead value analysis; Performance review; Self-appraisal; Self-criticism; 7-S framework; Task force

Management by objectives

The term 'management by objectives' (MBO) is believed to have been coined by Peter Drucker in the 1950s. George Odiorne developed its practical applications, and John Humble did much to popularize it in the UK. All organizations set objectives to guide and manage their activities, whether or not they explicitly recognize that they are doing so. MBO tries to ensure that goal-setting is a conscious process, and that employees' personal objectives are integrated with those of the organization as a whole. It does this by setting specific, demanding but achievable goals, providing constant feedback on performance, and offering rewards when goals are achieved. In the perfect

MBO system, everyone knows where they are going, why they are going there, how quickly they are progressing, and how their efforts relate to and depend on those of other employees.

The traditional approach to MBO demands that objectives are quantified wherever possible, and that goal-setting and appraisal is carried out on a one-to-one basis between subordinates and superiors throughout the management chain. In practice, organizations may adopt either autocratic or participative MBO methods, focusing either on individuals or teams. Whatever approach is adopted, the objectives should be specific and measurable. When used as a participative organizational development tool, employees collaborate with their superiors to set goals and review them, and hold regular meetings to resolve any problems. Individuals' career goals are also taken into account. If a team approach is being used, attention is paid to team culture and group dynamics, seeking to develop a co-operative rather than competitive relationship both between and within teams.

Beck, A.C. and Hillmar, E.D. (1972) 'OD to MBO or MBO to OD: Does it Make a Difference?', *Personnel Journal*, November, pp. 827–34.

Beck, A.C. and Hillmar, G.D. (eds) (1972) *A Practical Approach to Organization Development Through MBO: Selected Readings*, Addison Wesley Longman.

Beck, A.C. and Hillmar, E.D. (1976) *Making MBO/R Work*, Addison Wesley Longman.

Byrd, R.E. and Cowan, J. (1974) 'MBO: A Behavioural Science Approach', *Personnel*, vol. 51, March, pp. 42–50.

French, W. and Hollman, R. (1975) 'Management by Objectives: The Team Approach', *California Management Review*, vol. 17, Spring, pp. 13–22.

French, W. and Drexler, J. (1984) 'A Team Approach to MBO: History and Conditions of Success', *Leadership and Organization Development Journal*, vol. 5, no. 5, pp. 22–6.

Golembiewski, R.T. (1979) *Approaches to Planned Change, Part 2: Macro-level Interventions and Change Agent Strategies*, Marcel Dekker, pp. 166–79.

Hersey, P. and Blanchard, K.H. (1974) 'What's Missing in MBO?', *Management Review*, October, pp. 25–32.

Ivancevich, J.M. (1972) 'A Longitudinal Assessment of Management by Objectives', *Administrative Science Quarterly*, vol. 17, pp. 410–25.

Kerr, S. (1972) 'Some Modifications in MBO as an OD Strategy', *Academy of Management Proceedings*, August, pp. 39–42.

Levinson, H. (1972) 'Management by Objectives: A Critique', *Training and Development Journal*, April, pp. 410–25.

Likert, R. and Fisher, M.S. (1977) 'MBGO: Putting Team Spirit into MBO', *Personnel*, vol. 54, January–February, pp. 40–7.

McConkie, M.L. (1979) 'A Clarification of the Goal Setting and Appraisal Process in MBO', *Academy of Management Review*, vol. 4, January, pp. 29–40.

Murphy, J.J. (1983) 'Re-appraising MBO', *Leadership and Organization Development Journal*, vol. 4, no. 4, pp. 22–7.

Odiorne, G. (1965) *Management by Objectives*, Pitman.

See also: ACHIEVE model; Appraisal; Feedback; Follow-up; Goal-setting; Goal-setting and planning groups; Job descriptions; MAPS approach; Measuring performance; On-going feedback system; Periodic planning conference; Positive feedback; Self- with peer assessment

Management by walking around

This approach was described by Peters and Waterman, who observed that it was a key management principle in the Hewlett-Packard company. Since a primary task of all managers is to monitor what is happening, they are encouraged to establish informal control by leaving their offices and visiting employees in their workplaces to promote regular casual communication, instead of relying exclusively on written reports. The approach has grown in popularity, and the Industrial Society has promoted it in the UK, producing a management training film on the subject.

Industrial Society *See For Yourself: A Manager's Guide to Walking the Job* (video), The Industrial Society.

Peters, T.J. and Waterman, R.H. (1982) *In Search of Excellence*, Harper and Row, p. 51.

See also: Forcing device; Physical interventions in organizations; Sensing; Supervisory methods

Management information meeting

A management information meeting gives employees an opportunity to listen to reports, call senior management to account for its stewardship of the organization over the past year, and establish what plans are in place for the future. The meetings are usually held outside work time to avoid disruption. They culminate in a long question-and-answer session, and any employee who cannot attend can put their question in written form. Although a formal report responding to all the questions is circulated, the approach mainly relies on a 'cascade effect': if each participant talks to a number of other employees during the next few weeks, the information will eventually be communicated and discussed throughout the organization.

Goldsmith, W. and Clutterbuck, D. (1985) *The Winning Streak*, Penguin, p. 70.

See also: Chairman's forum; Employee letters; Information-sharing meetings; Open forums; Team briefing

Management implications paper

This is a short written assignment describing a particular management technique which a student has used or observed in the workplace. For example, if a student chooses management by objectives, they may describe its application in their own company; on the other hand, if they do not currently have a job, they can discuss the technique with friends and relatives, then summarize their observations. The paper may include an explanation of how the technique was put into practice, what the consequences were, what was done correctly or incorrectly, and any recommendations for improvements.

Clinebell, S. (1992) 'Using Managerial Implications Papers in a Principles of Management Class', *Journal of Management Education*, vol. 16, no. 1, pp. 116–18.

See also: Case live; Case personal history; Case student telling; Management problems survey method; Reaction paper

Management Oversight and Risk Tree (MORT)

The Management Oversight Risk Tree is one of a variety of analytical tools developed for fault analysis in the aerospace industry during the 1960s. Its components are: Change Analysis, which considers the past (Why did things go wrong?), the MORT Analytical Tree, which examines the present (What changes are needed now?) and the Positive Tree, which looks to the future (How can we stop things going wrong again?).

Change Analysis is a systematic approach to problem-solving which helps to identify accidental

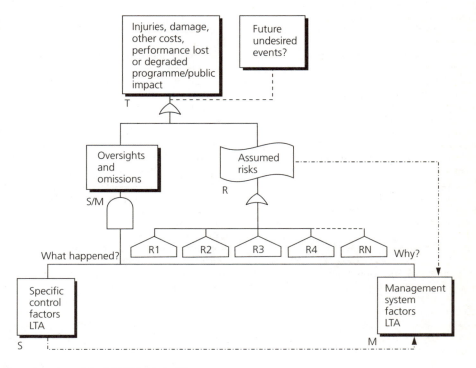

An enlarged portion of the MORT Analytical Tree

causes. Based on a simple idea – 'It used to work, but it doesn't now, so something has changed' – it clarifies what additional information is needed, identifies the potential causes of change, and draws conclusions by means of a five-step process. First, consider the past situation to identify the 'accident conditions' – what went wrong. Next, examine the prior conditions to establish what they were like before things went wrong. Then compare the accident conditions with the prior conditions to establish what had changed. Next, analyse the possible significance and implications of the changes, both individually and in combination. Finally, having identified the causal factors, recommend the action required to prevent the problem recurring.

The entire *MORT Analytical Tree* is complex. Conger presents only part of it, and this is shown on the previous page. At the top is the undesirable state one wishes to avoid, and the objective is to prevent or control any loss. The event concerned could result from oversight, omission or assumed risk. The analysed and known risks are specified, analysed and quantified as far as is practicable. The oversight and omissions branch of the tree divides into specific control factors (which answer the question, 'What happened?') and management system factors (which answer the question, 'Why did it happen?'). This information may indicate that some background aspects of the situation should be examined closely, and that there is a deficiency in the management system which needs to be rectified.

The *Positive Tree* is used to identify oversights and omissions before a system comes into operation by defining the possible critical paths from the start of events to predicted success or failure outcomes. It provides a visual record of the analytical process, highlighting the management system's weaknesses and strengths, by means of a seven-step process: defining the top event, acquiring a comprehensive understanding of the system to be analysed, constructing the Positive Tree, validating the tree, evaluating a future system by means of the Positive Tree, conducting trade-off studies, and making a rational and informed decision.

Conger, D.S. (1982) 'Using MORT as an OD Tool', *Leadership and Organization Development Journal*, vol. 3, no. 5, pp. 1–15.
Knox, N.W. and Eicher, R.W. (1977) *MORT User's Manual (SSDC-4)*, US Department of Commerce, Springfield, Virginia.
Lawrence, P.R. and Lorsch, J.W. (1969) *Developing Organizations: Diagnosis and Action*, Addison Wesley Longman.

See also: Brainstorming;   Kepner-Tregoe Approach; Nominal group technique; Problem-solving group; Synectics

Management problem laboratory

A major weakness of the traditional case study method is that case descriptions usually give all the information necessary to allow students to proceed immediately to problem-diagnosis, analysis or action, neglecting development of their data-discovery skills. The management problem laboratory is one of two techniques which have been developed to remedy this in the study of live cases, the other being the mystery clue method. Both encourage students to discover information for themselves and develop their own selective database.

Students work in teams on a single case study about a real organization which lasts most of one academic term. Although an extensive data bank about the organization is provided, the information is divided into small, self-contained modules, and students are only given access to the data they specify. There may be as many as 200 modules, covering subjects as diverse as the absenteeism rate of one class of employee, short biographies of senior managers, or several pages of financial accounts. Each module is filed by classification number, ready to be retrieved by the instructor's assistants or made available to the teams through computer terminals.

At the beginning, all students receive a one-page introduction to the organization which contains basic background information such as origin, size and location, and are shown a short video presentation about it. They then form into teams and discuss what else they need to know about the company. Each time they request data, they must provide a working hypothesis or explain how it will help in problem-identification or problem-solving. The data may be supplied immediately, or time lags of up to 24 hours may be built in. If a request is justified but the data is unavailable, the company may be asked if it can supply it. Although they are given no guidance about the contents of the data bank, the instructor may assist by suggesting that they focus on certain aspects or broaden the scope of their investigations, and students learn that certain data modules suggest other lines of enquiry. Once they have completed their work, the case organization's managers are given copies of their reports and invited to provide feedback on the practicality of each team's suggestions. Team members are also given the opportunity to meet members of the organization they have been studying, which helps to mark the culmination of their term's work together.

The requirement for teamwork over an extended period effectively transforms the classroom into a behavioural laboratory, allowing the instructor to address topics of organizational behaviour and development. Group dynamics can be considered, and team-building interventions can be introduced to improve collaboration and problem-solving skills. Teaching theory on a 'need-to-know' basis means that the instructor must be more flexible, since the neat, linear progress of the traditional course is replaced by diversions, detours and the need to backtrack at times in order to move forward. This allows concepts such as product portfolio analysis, leadership style or motivation to be introduced and explored at the very moment when students' interest in them is at its highest, and when they can apply them directly to problems they have encountered.

Cook, C. W. (1980) 'Policy Unfolding Through Data Discovery Techniques', *Exchange: The Organizational Behaviour Teaching Journal*, vol. 5, no. 4, pp. 30–4.

See also: Case incident process method; Interrogation of experts; Medical model; Mystery clue method; Project orientation; Socratic group enquiry

Management problems survey method

In this method, an instructor conducts a survey of local managers, asking them to describe their most pressing problems and concerns. The results can then be used in the classroom to design a course which covers the issues identified, rather than the traditional academic topics. The questions to be covered by the course might include: 'How would you know if you had this problem? What might have caused it? How could it be overcome? Do you have any experience of this sort of problem? What else do we need to know about it?' This allows concepts, theories, models and research to be introduced as required, enabling traditional subject matter to be covered alongside discovery, enquiry and application approaches. Another approach is to run a traditional course for two-thirds of the time, and for the remaining third, allocate small groups to consider each problem and present their recommendations to other class members using the ideas, concepts, frameworks and theories presented earlier in the course. A third application is to replace traditional group prediction-ranking tasks such as 'Lost in the Desert' or 'Lost on the Moon' with a list of what local managers consider to be their main current problems and concerns. Finally, the survey results can be used as a course icebreaker, asking students to work in groups to list what they consider to be the main management

problems and concerns, then comparing their views with those of the real managers.

Posner, B. (1985–6) 'Using Managerial Problems in the Classroom', *Organizational Behaviour Teaching Review*, vol. 10, no. 3, pp. 103–5.

See also: Focus groups; Management implications paper; Reaction paper; Survey feedback intervention

Management responsibility guide process

Developed by MRG Associates, this intervention uses a method known as the management responsibility guide (MRG) to help organizations initiate and manage change by identifying managerial practices and concepts that are in conflict with their core aims. The process involves a systematic examination of input from different levels in the organization, in order to clarify goals and job requirements, and improve accountability and communication networks.

There are three main steps in the MRG process. In the first step, managers study the capabilities and resources most affected by growth. The second step requires them to define job requirements and clarify roles and relationships, exploring how to improve co-operation. The final step is to interview staff to establish the key elements of their jobs and the factors that lead to inefficiency, identifying and overcoming barriers to effective interaction and communication.

Boulgarides, J. and Jamieson, D. (1984) 'Using OD to Improve Managerial Productivity: The Case of Culver City', in Kakabadse, A. and Mukti, S. (eds) *The Future of Management Education*, Gower, pp. 145–59.

See also: Job descriptions; Position charter; Responsibility charting; Role prescription; Role analysis technique

Management systems study

This variant of the industry study or field trip is distinguished by the fact that it lasts several weeks, considers a limited number of topics (often only one), and gives students the opportunity to visit several companies in different cultural, political and economic settings. Both the students and the companies are informed of the selected topic or topics beforehand, which may include company–vendor relationships, factors contributing to company growth, control of international operations, market research practices and employee motivation. The approach is particularly well suited to international programmes, since it allows comparison of different strategies developed to solve similar problems.

See also: Educational visit; Field format; Field trip; Intervisitation; Studycade

Manager as consultant

Since the time of Frederick Taylor, Henry Ford and Henri Fayol, management's main role has been seen as controlling and policing, and its responsibilities have been defined as planning, executing, monitoring and punishing. However, the recognition of the importance of employee empowerment and the instigation of group working practices as well as advanced information systems mean that these views have changed.

Nowadays, a manager's primary role is usually considered to be to help colleagues and subordinates fulfil their objectives. This places greater emphasis on an advisory rather than a policing-controlling function, and in this sense modern managers resemble consultants who are brought in to provide specialist assistance at specific times to achieve particular objectives. Such developments mean that managers must change their perception of their relationship to others and develop a new range of inter-personal skills.

Prinder, M. and McAdam, (1994) *Be Your Own Management Consultant*, Pitman.
Thomas, M. and Elbeik, S. (1996) *Supercharge Your Management Role: Making the Transition to Internal Consultant*, Jossey-Bass.

See also: Empowerment; Mentoring

Manager exchange

In this staff development activity, two managers in the same company swop positions for a specified period, then return to their original jobs. The managers may be located in the same plant or in different locations. Such programmes may also involve staff-to-line or line-to-staff exchanges in an effort to overcome misunderstandings and conflicts between departments.

See also: Acting assignment; Action learning; Development assignment; Exposure to upper management; Job rotation; Job swop; Manager shadowing; Rotation training; Sick leave/holiday replacement assignment

Manager shadowing

In this developmental approach, a trainee is assigned to a manager, serving as an assistant in order to learn what their job entails by observing an experienced practitioner at work. In some respects it resembles apprenticeship, but it is less formal, and the shadower is not necessarily being prepared to assume the same role as the manager.

Although the principles underlying this approach are sound, such assignments can be fraught with pitfalls: on one hand, the shadower may end up doing little more than running errands; on the other, if they are too pushy and try to assume line responsibility, serious problems can arise. However, if both the manager and the shadower are clear about their respective roles and the trainee is given adequate preparation, it can be very effective. It is helpful if the training covers systematic observation skills, including guidance to clarify the types of situations and problems the manager may encounter, and the strategies and solutions employed to deal with them. The manager should ensure that the shadower is free to gather information and interpret it, but should not delegate the supervision and direction of other staff.

Taylor, C. (1977) 'Shadowing: The Creative Approach to Supervisory Training', *Management*, vol. 24, no. 8, pp. 1–15.

See also: Acting assignment; Assignment to manager with high development skills; Behaviour modelling; Corporate student board of directors; Development assignment; Internship; Job rotation; Job swop; Manager exchange; Mentoring; On-the-job training; Prompt list; Rotation training; Sick leave/holiday replacement assignment; SmartProcess; Student placement; Understudy

Managerial decentralization

This structural intervention was pioneered by General Electric in the 1950s, and many companies have adopted the approach since in an effort to overcome the problems of bureaucracy, often adopting a cycle of management centralization followed by decentralization. It involves delegating authority down to the smallest unit that is practicable throughout an organization, the effect being to increase the importance of each subordinate's role. These decision-making units usually have a high degree of autonomy, but their efforts must be co-ordinated from the centre to ensure that they are all working towards common goals.

The philosophy underlying this approach is that managers and staff should be given the opportunity and responsibility to develop and use their own talents. To achieve this, managers need to be given the authority, plant facilities and senior management guidance necessary to take as many decisions as possible within their own sphere of operations.

Cordiner, R.J. (1956) *New Frontiers for Professional Managers*, McGraw-Hill.

Drucker, P.F. (1946) *The Concept of the Corporation*, John Day.

Drucker, P.F. (1955) *The Practice of Management*, Heinemann, pp. 178–94.

Sloan, A.P. (1964) *My Years at General Motors*, Doubleday.

See also: Bottom-up management; Collateral organization; Independent product teams; Intrapreneurship; Multiple management; Parallel career ladders; Plural chief executive; Reprogramming; Simulated entrepreneurship; Structural intervention

Managerial strategy change

An organization may attempt to change the strategy or style it adopts in managing its staff for a number of reasons. Management may have revised its assumptions or attitudes towards people and their motivations, or the loss of key managers and difficulty in recruiting suitable staff may have indicated that a new approach is necessary. Whatever the causes, any change of strategy is likely to require assistance from a consultant. Their role might involve working with senior managers, examining entrenched attitudes among middle managers and deciding how to overcome them, ensuring that subordinates have confidence in the new management structure, and minimizing any disruption to the organization's clients and suppliers. The techniques required might include organizational diagnosis, job design, goal-setting, team-building and planning.

Implementing any change in management style demands considerable time and patience. A sense of perspective is essential, and this can often be lost by the client company. The strategy must go beyond the consideration of individual managers' behaviour, and extend to the general organizational context in which that behaviour is exhibited. There are a number of questions key managers need to address in planning such a change. To what extent does the top management of other parts of the organization influence their thinking? How is conflict managed? Is decision-making power located on the basis of who has the information, or on hierarchical position? How do they deal with the rewards they control? What feedback systems exist to provide information about the state of the organization?

See also: Corporate culture training; Development of a new management/operating philosophy; Greenfield plants; Ideological change; Likert's System 4 Management; Mission cards; Moral philosophy approach; Myth-making intervention; Organizational climate analysis; Socratic dialogue

Managing effective relationships (MER training)

This form of training aims to develop participants' strategic inter-personal skills to help them form more productive and satisfying relationships with others. The method was developed by Helen Clinard, and it is based on a model called the MER Lens, which helps people choose the most appropriate inter-personal style to adopt in a particular situation. The training presents interactive skills in a behavioural framework, and participants are shown how to apply them in relevant situations.

Participants receive training in six basic skills. Giving *appreciation messages* involves commenting on the behaviour of others in a way that makes them feel appreciated and motivated. Practising *facilitative listening* entails demonstrating understanding, respect and empathy, and allows the other person to ventilate feelings, identify underlying problems and find solutions. *Constructive confrontation* deals with how to confront another person about their behaviour without causing resentment or lowering their self-esteem, encouraging them to feel co-operative. *Mutual problem-solving* is a process for finding solutions to problems or conflicts in a way that leaves everybody involved feeling respected, co-operative and motivated to make the proposed solution work. *Unsolicited consultation* shows how to give advice when it has not been asked for in such a way that the other person is willing to accept it. Finally, *solicited consultation* describes how to use influencing, counselling or helping skills when someone has asked for help in solving problems.

Clinard, H. (1978) 'Managing Effective Relationships', *BACIE Journal*, vol. 32, no. 3, p. 514.

Clinard, H. (1981) 'Developing Higher Levels of Interpersonal Communication Skills', *BACIE Journal*, vol. 35, no. 4, pp. 77–8.

See also: Coverdale training; Interaction management; Interactive skills training

Managing for Productivity

Managing for Productivity (MFP) is a programme developed by Dr George Labovitz at the Boston University School of Management. It is based on the belief that increasing productivity is the biggest challenge currently facing organizations, and that this relies on adopting the appropriate management style and improving the way work is organized and processed for employees.

The MFP programme is suited to all levels of management. It consists of ten inter-linked modules of two-and-a-half to three hours' duration which can be run at scheduled intervals. By means of video-taped presentations, case studies, role-plays, simulations, exercises and group discussions, the programme not only develops individual managers' skills, but acts as a catalyst, bringing groups of managers together to decide how to improve their organization's effectiveness. The topics addressed include the evolution of management, motivation, perception, group dynamics, morale, leadership, participation and productivity, managing change and management by objectives, goal-setting and feedback. Its aims are to increase managers' understanding of the managerial process, improve organizational communications, promote inter- and intra-departmental problem-solving within a supportive and constructive climate, clarify jobs and role descriptions, and identify and resolve performance problems quickly.

These objectives are underpinned by certain assumptions. Performance is regarded as a function of individual and group behaviour as well as the organizational environment. Management is felt to hold the key to improving productivity. Structuring employees' expectations is seen as management's most important task. Employees need to be given the opportunity to participate in decisions which affect their working lives. The selective application of participative management techniques is considered to lead to high productivity. Finally, a common language of management is seen as essential for organizational effectiveness.

Cameron, K. (1984) 'Creating a Consistent Management Style', *Productivity Insights*, no. 2, January, pp. 3–5.

Labovitz, G. (1982) 'Seeing and Believing Management Productivity', *Leadership and Organization Development Journal*, vol. 3, no. 3, pp. 2–4.

See also: Grid development; Human process approach; Implementing the organizational renewal process; Interaction influence analysis; Interaction management; Kepner-Tregoe approach; LIFO method; Power management; Releasing organizational potential; Situational leadership; 3-D management effectiveness seminar

MAPS approach

The MAPS (Multivariate Analysis, Participation and Structure) approach to organizational design was developed by Ralph Kilmann and William McKelvey in the School of Management at UCLA as an aid to designing an organic-adaptive organization which can cope with a dynamic and unpredictable environment. It does this through the systematic application of participative management, management by objectives, management of interdependencies and organizational development principles in a way that avoids the adoption of bureaucratic leadership styles and allows members to choose with whom they would like to work on what projects.

The approach consists of three basic procedures. The raw data is obtained through the administration of MAPS questionnaires, and multivariate analysis is used because the type and volume of information derived would be too complex to analyse by less sophisticated methods. First, organization members participate in defining the tasks they believe would be most effective at accomplishing organizational objectives. Second, multivariate analysis is used to separate the total set of tasks into clusters which contain the important interdependent tasks. Finally, multivariate analysis is applied again to assign members to sub-units with those who share their view of which would be the most productive tasks. This enables the selection of an appropriate organic-adaptive organizational design which allows each sub-unit to be matched up with a task cluster for each possible design solution.

When used as part of an organizational change programme, the members of each sub-unit meet to prepare a detailed statement on the objectives, scope and title of their task cluster. Information about the technology and the resources needed to implement the work is also supplied, as well as a note on the leadership structure to be employed. Next, the members of each sub-unit share their 'identity' statement with other sub-units to identify possible conflicts between the units, which emphasizes interdependencies. Methods for co-ordinating the work of different sub-units are then discussed, possibly using Likert's linking pin function concept. Team-building and inter-group team-building activities may also be necessary at this stage.

There may be differences between the existing design of the organization and that recommended by the MAPS analysis. The MAPS analysis is based on employees' perceptions, whereas the existing design reflects senior management's views. Any wide discrepancy between the two might indicate a deficit in resources, skills and motivation among employees. The current organizational design may be based on stereotyped notions of skill specialization or traditional functional areas, whereas this will not be true of the MAPS analysis's recommended design because it does not take into account the constraints imposed by the physical layout of the organization when arriving at the most effective solution. This in itself can be valuable, as it suggests that some employees should move to a different location. Finally, the MAPS design may highlight the informal organization, indicating how work is accomplished in reality, rather than how it is supposed to be carried out.

MAPS has been used in a wide range of educational and public sector organizations, both to develop new designs and to test design changes across traditional functional areas. It has been most useful in settings where employees have to work closely together to achieve organizational aims, because performance depends on effective management of the many interdependent activities involved. It is also helpful where a company has a major organizational design problem because it has large numbers of staff, tasks and sub-units – the more complex the design issue being analysed, the more useful MAPS may be. Finally, its proponents argue that the approach is applicable to those organizations which have a Theory Y form of management. This is because managers must believe that employees are capable of providing relevant and reliable information on which to base design decisions. In addition, they must also believe that the sub-units formed as a result of the MAPS analysis can take responsibility for defining and performing tasks that are in line with organizational objectives. Equally, the employees in such groups must want to assume responsibility for influencing design decisions, and subsequently for implementing the new design.

Dunphy, D.C.(1981) *Change by Choice*, McGraw-Hill.

Kilmann, R.H. (1974) 'An Effective Organic-Adaptive Organization: The MAPS Method', *Personnel*, vol. 51, pp. 35–7.

Kilmann, R.H. (1976) 'MAPS as a Design Technology to Effectively Mobilize Resources for Social and Organizational Problem Solving', in Kilmann, R., Pondy, L. and Slevin, D. *The Management of Organizational Design: Strategies and Interpretation*, North Holland Publishing, pp. 251–94.

See also: Collateral organization; Instrumented feedback; Inter-group interventions; Inter-group team-building; Likert's levels meetings; Management by objectives; Matrix designs; Participation; Physical interventions in organizations; Recruitment; Self-development; Structural interventions

Mastery learning

Mastery learning is a concept which has been incorporated into a variety of educational approaches, but mainly the Keller Plan's Personalised System of Instruction (PSI). The underlying principle is that students should have *mastered* the material to be learned in a particular instruction

unit before proceeding to the next one. This acknowledges the fact that students will exhibit different rates of progress in studying the units, but assumes that all will achieve the same standard by the end of the course. Like more traditional approaches, mastery learning incorporates regular tests, but in this case their purpose is to monitor students' progress, rather than allocating grades. The process is known as *formative testing*, because it is designed to detect specific difficulties or misunderstandings at an early stage, while students' understanding of a topic is still being formed. This avoids the frustration of trying to assimilate concepts before the underpinning principles have been grasped. To achieve this, the tests are held more frequently and earlier in the instruction process than is usually the case.

There are two ways to apply the mastery learning approach. The first, known as the Keller Plan method, involves abandoning classes altogether, allowing students to work at their own speed in their own time. Learning materials are provided to guide them through their individual studies, and they elect to be tested when they feel that they have mastered the unit. If they pass, they are allowed to proceed to the next one; if they fail, they discuss their problems with a student-proctor, who directs them to remedial instructional material. The second method involves using scheduled classes to overcome misunderstandings identified by the tests. The instructor may provide assistance by discussing generally troublesome concepts with the entire class, or by providing study guides or enrichment materials in the form of notes, audio tapes, CD-ROMs or videos.

Block, J.H. (1971) *Mastery Learning: Theory and Practice*, Holt, Rinehart and Winston.

Kulick, J.A., Kulick, C.L.C. and Smith, B.B. (1976) 'Research on Personalised System of Instruction', *Programmed Learning and Educational Technology*, vol. 13, pp. 23–30.

See also: Audio tutorial method; Autonomous group learning; Media-activated learning group; Personalized system of instruction; Proctor method; Tape-assisted learning programme

Mathetics

Thomas Gilbert is credited with developing this approach, which can be used to teach any skill which involves memorizing a sequence of tasks. It does this by breaking down procedures into stages. For example, the usual way to teach someone how to make an origami figure is to start with a blank piece of paper, demonstrate how to make the first fold, then the second, and so on until the figure is complete. The trainee is then given a piece of paper and asked to follow the instructions. However, this method might require a number of attempts before the trainee is able to complete the figure without assistance.

Mathetics adopts a different approach, which reduces the number of trials needed to learn a given procedure. The instructor gives the trainee an origami figure with only the last fold yet to be completed, and describes how to carry out this last step. Once this has been accomplished, the process is repeated, but this time with a figure which has the last two folds omitted, then the last three, and so on until the trainee is able to carry out the whole process. Gilbert called this technique 'backward chaining', and stressed the motivational value of the satisfaction produced by completing a task successfully. The learning process is reinforced by the fact that the trainee learns one new step in the procedural chain at a time while rehearsing all the others. Although research has shown that not all chains lend themselves to being taught backwards, this approach demonstrates that, in teaching, the obvious sequences may not always be the most effective.

Gilbert, T.F. (1962) 'Mathetics: The Technology of Education', *Journal of Mathetics*, vol. 1, pp. 1–73.
Mager, R.F. (1961) 'On the Sequencing of Instructional Content', *Psychological Reports*, vol. 9, pp. 405–13.

See also: Computer-assisted learning; Demonstration-performance method; Discovery method; Drill-and-practice method; Lesson-demonstration method; Programmed learning

Matrix design

In the matrix design approach to project management, specialists from different departments in an organization work as a team to tackle problems that cross functional lines. Each team member reports both to their project manager and to the manager of their particular function (e.g., marketing). The problems they address might include developing a new product, installing a new plant or initiating a new system. A single organization may have numerous projects running in parallel, each under the direction of a different project manager, and each at a different stage of completion.

Managers in the various functional departments are responsible for supervising the 'talent bank' from which team members are recruited, ensuring that the necessary skills are available for particular projects. Operating successfully in a matrix structure demands that team members curb their competitive instincts, develop a spirit of collabora-

tion and openness, and take a problem-solving rather than a blaming approach. They also need to share responsibility at daily meetings, and work cohesively with other units in the organization. They may return to their functional speciality once the project has been completed, or they may transfer to a new project team.

The American space programme has greatly encouraged the growth of matrix design, and the approach has proven popular among companies which rely heavily on research and development. It has also been adopted by colleges and universities to enable lecturers from different departments to collaborate in teaching Master's degree courses, for instance.

Carpenter, H. (1983) 'Matrix Management: A Case Study in a Management Department', *Personnel Review*, vol. 12, no. 2, pp. 3–10.
Davis, S.M. (1978) 'Matrix: Filling the Gap Between Theory and Practice', in Burke, W.W. (ed.) *The Cutting Edge: Current Theory and Practice in Organization Development*, Pfeiffer/Jossey-Bass, pp. 95–104.
Davis, S.M. and Lawrence, P.R. (1977) *Matrix*, Addison Wesley Longman.
Harris, P.R. (1984) 'Team Management Synergy', *Leadership and Organizational Development Journal*, vol. 5, no. 1, pp. 17–20.
Harris, P.R. and Moran, R.T. (1979) *Managing Cultural Synergy*, Gulf Publishing.
Hurst, D.K. (1984) 'Of Boxes, Bubbles and Effective Management', *Harvard Business Review*, vol. 62, no. 3, May–June, pp. 98–103.
Knight, K. (1977) *Matrix Management: A Cross Functional Approach to Organization*, Gower.

See also: Autonomous workgroups; Business teams; Collateral organization; Goal-setting interface group; Independent product teams; Informal action group; Integrated support functions; Line-of-business teams; MAPS approach; Skunkworks

Measuring performance

Although various management-by-objectives exercises have shown that measuring an employee's performance can serve as a powerful motivational tool, this approach is still underused. It can provide a highly effective and straightforward means to overcome a number of problems. The process is effective because simply measuring an aspect of work performance directs employees' attention to that area. It conveys to them which activities the organization considers important; it increases their acceptance of legitimate authority, and it clarifies to employees that accepting a particular performance standard, such as attendance level, is a necessary condition for participating in the system – in Katz and Kahn's words, it emphasizes 'the profound truth that the involvement of people in social systems entails generalised obligations to follow systematic demands'. The cost of the resources required to monitor and record statistics is likely to be offset by the savings that result.

Peters and Waterman reported on an initiative by AT&T in the USA which used this approach to address the problem of absenteeism. Management erected a highly visible board which displayed every employee's name, and awarded them a gold star if they came to work regularly. This led to a dramatic and rapid improvement in attendance.

Goodman, P.S. and Atkin, R.S. (1984) *Absenteeism*, Jossey-Bass, pp. 328–33.
Katz, D. and Kahn, R.L. (1966) *The Social Psychology of Organizations*, Wiley, p. 342.
Peters, T.J. and Waterman, R.H. (1982) *In Search of Excellence*, Harper and Row, p. 342.

See also: Appraisal; Discipline without punishment; Feedback; Follow-up; Goal-setting; Goal-setting and planning groups; Management by objectives; Norm modification; On-going feedback system; Periodic planning review; Positive feedback; Recognition programmes; Self- with peer assessment

Media-activated learning group

This approach provides a method to orientate and structure the activities of a group of students without the constant involvement of an instructor. In the past, the supporting media prepared by the instructor usually took the form of an audio-visual programme delivered by means of slides and audio cassettes, but nowadays it is more common to use a multi-media PC. Research indicates that the peer pressure generated by this method can overcome the major problem of learner-centred groups: students' failure to carry out the set reading.

There are six phases in this approach, but there may also be an optional phase of individual preview and review of the material. The *orientation phase* includes an oral introduction to the programme's objectives, and a written presentation of the assignments. The *stimulus phase* takes the form of a mini-lecture presenting a problem for the group to consider. The *response phase* consists of the evaluating of possible solutions, either individually or in groups. In the *confirmation phase*, the teacher gives an audio-visual or multi-media presentation of their preferred solution. The *validation phase* identifies the programme's deficiencies so that the teacher can revise the methods adopted. Finally, in the *review phase*, the teacher helps the group

conduct an analysis to assess its comprehension and interpretation of the programme's content.

Berman, A.I. (1974) 'Field Studies of Small Media-activated Learning Groups' in Verreck, W. (ed.) *Methodological Problems in Research and Development in Higher Education*, Swets and Zeitlinger.

See also: Agenda method; Audio for learning; Autonomy lab; Autonomous learning group; Independent study; Instrumented team learning; Leaderless group discussion; Learning through discussion; Mastery learning; Peer teaching; Self-directed learning; Tape-assisted learning programme

Mediation

This form of dispute-resolution relies on the participation of a disinterested third party who assists those involved in a conflict to resolve their difficulties. The mediator's role is to allow the parties to vent their feelings, help them to explore their options, and ensure that they appreciate the consequences of failure to reach an agreement. Mediation is a voluntary process, and the mediator lacks formal decision-making authority. Originally developed in the field of trade union–management negotiations, the approach is now used to settle claims between firms, and is a step in many grievance and complaint procedures.

Beer, J.E., Steif, E. and Teif, E. (1997) *Mediator's Handbook*, New Society Publications.
Kolb, D.M. et al. (1997) *When Talk Works*, Jossey-Bass.
Lewicki, R., Saunders, D. and Minton, J. (1998) *Negotiation*, McGraw-Hill.
Moore, C.W. (1996) *The Mediation Process*, Jossey-Bass.
Potter, B. and Frank, P. (1996) *From Conflict to Co-operation: How to Mediate a Dispute*, Ronin Publishers.
Zeigler, Z.W. (1997) *The Mediation Kit*, Wiley.

See also: Alternate dispute-resolution; Negotiations by group members; Ombudsman; Rent-a-judge; Sensitivity bargaining

Medical model

In the field of medicine, patients' problems are used as a major teaching tool in the classroom, integrating the skills and information which have been obtained from the separate disciplines into a coherent system. Applying the medical model to management curriculum design involves studying organizational problems in holistic, interdisciplinary fashion that focuses on practical issues. Students are taught to conceive of organizations as sub-systems that combine to make up a single large system which is part of a wider industry located in a national and international environment. In practical terms, students take on the role of 'doctors', treating organizations as 'patients': noting symptoms that indicate difficulties, determining the symptoms' causes by identifying the underlying problems, and recommending the appropriate remedies.

A four-step approach is adopted in analysing case studies or the conduct of live cases or real-life group projects. The first is to *examine the symptoms* to establish whether a problem exists. During the process of observation, students must remain objective, collect data in a non-evaluative way, and decide whether it provides evidence that the organization is not performing as well as it should. The second step is to *review the problem indicators* in the light of wider information about the organization, to establish the factors giving rise to each of the symptoms. This is essential in order to select the appropriate treatment. The third step, *diagnosis*, involves arranging the information on symptoms into a coherent pattern and prioritizing the aspects of the organization that need to be addressed in order to restore it to health. The final step is *prescribing the remedy*, deciding what action is necessary to solve or manage the problem that has been diagnosed. This includes describing a course of action and how to carry it out, considering the side-effects of the proposed remedy, and reviewing alternative treatments.

Pablo, A.L. (1995) 'Using the Medical Model in the Management Classroom', *Journal of Management Education*, vol. 19, no. 2, pp. 263–7.

See also: Action maze; Biological science enquiry model; Socio-technical systems; Surrogate client; Mystery clue method; Management problem-solving laboratory

Meetings for two

Carl Rogers advocated these meetings as a means of resolving disagreements, having analysed situations where two people were in dispute and identified four recurring elements. First, each person believed that they were right and the other was wrong. Second, a breakdown in communication had occurred, each party being unwilling to hear what the other was saying. Third, perceptions were distorted, information being shaped and trimmed to fit preconceptions, while contradictory information was conveniently ignored or twisted to make it acceptable. Finally, there was an element

of distrust, each party attributing dubious motives to the other's actions.

Rogers claimed that these elements were present in any dispute between two people, be they employee and boss or husband and wife. To resolve them, he advocated holding a meeting with the assistance of a facilitative listener, who could listen empathetically and understand the attitudes of each party.

Rogers, C. (1965) 'Dealing with Psychological Tensions', *Journal of Applied Behavioural Science*, January–March, pp. 12–14.

See also: Hearing; LIFO method

Mentoring

The term 'mentoring' derives from Greek mythology: when Odysseus left for the Trojan Wars, he entrusted his son's education to his friend, Mentor. Although mentoring is often linked to coaching, and the two roles share some of the same skills, a coach's role is restricted to providing training, while a mentor's role includes giving a junior colleague support, guidance and career advice. A manager should never serve as a mentor to an immediate subordinate, and should ideally be located in a different department.

In the USA, mentoring was adopted in response to equal opportunity legislation. It was believed that the development and advancement of female and ethic minority employees would be facilitated by personal attention from respected, well-connected senior managers. At first, the approach was restricted to new graduate recruits. The relationship was reciprocal, the recruit could provide specific knowledge which the manager lacked, while the manager could introduce the novice to the company culture and its political landscape. It was later recognized that this development method would be of equal value to non-graduates, and it was also seen as a useful way to re-motivate managers who felt their career had stagnated. The concept has also been extended to the educational sphere, where first-year students may be assigned to a more senior student who acts as their mentor, helping them adapt to the demands of the course and academic life.

Appelbaum, S.H., Ritchie, S. and Shapiro, B.T. (1994) 'Mentoring Revisited: An Organizational Behaviour Construct', *Journal of Management Development*, vol. 13, no. 4, pp. 62–72.
Clutterbuck, D. (1997) *Everyone Needs a Mentor* (2nd edn), Institute of Personnel and Development.

Clutterbuck, D. and Megginson, D. (1997) *Mentoring in Action*, Kogan Page.

Cohen, N.H. (1995) *Mentoring Adult Learners*, Krieger.

Freeman, C. (1994) 'Mentoring is for Personal Growth', *Organisations and People*, vol. 1, no. 4, pp. 32–5.

Gibb, S. and Megginson, D. (1993) 'Inside Corporate Mentoring Schemes: A New Agenda of Concerns', *Personnel Review*, vol. 22., no. 1.

Glover, D. and Mardle, G. (ed.) (1995) *The Management of Mentoring*, Kogan Page.

Lewis, G. (1996) *The Mentoring Manager: Strategies for Unlocking Employee Excellence*, Pitman.

MacLennan, N. (1995) *Coaching and Mentoring*, Gower.

Mathews, S. (1997) *Mentoring and Coaching*, Financial Times/Pitman Publishing.

McDougall, M. and Beattie, R.S. (1997) 'Peer Mentoring at Work', *Management Learning*, vol. 28, no. 4, pp. 423–37.

See also: Apprenticeship programme; Assignment to manager with high development skills; Coaching; Exposure to upper management; Internship; Manager shadowing; Role modelling; Rotation training; Self-improvement programme

Merger management intervention

Company mergers commonly provoke a range of reactions, including mutual suspicion, appeals for autonomy, hostility to head office, and competition for resources. A merger management intervention attempts to create a new, effective organization by encouraging a co-operative atmosphere. This is achieved by gathering and sharing information to combat the distrust and ignorance which result from the lack of a shared history.

In one such intervention (which followed the identification of a problem), functional workgroups of eight to ten participants were convened to study and design various possible solutions, each being evaluated by means of role-playing. The consultants focused members' attention on decision-making strategies, conflict-resolution approaches, communication barriers, and levels of trust. On occasions, they provided pre-tested solutions which allowed goals to be set for future culture-building activities. The workgroups arrived at administrative and operational solutions, and agreed policies for follow-up and action proposals.

Blumberg, A. and Wiener, W. (1971) 'One From Two: Facilitating an Organizational Merger', *Journal of Applied Behavioural Science*, vol. 7, no. 1, pp. 87–102.

Cartwright, S. and Cooper, C.L. (1994) 'The Human Effects of Mergers and Acquisitions', in Cooper, C.L. and Rousseau, D.M. (eds) *Trends in Organizational Behaviour*, Volume 1, Wiley, pp. 47–61.

Cartwright, S. and Cooper, C.L. (1996) *Managing Mergers, Acquisitions and Strategic Alliances*, Butterworth-Heinemann.

Duflin, R., Falusi, A., Lawrence, P. and Morton, R. (1973) 'Increasing Organizational Effectiveness', *Training and Development Journal*, vol. 27, no. 4, pp. 37–46.

Golembiewski, R.T. (1979) *Approaches to Planned Change, Part 2: Macro-level Interventions and Change Agent Strategies*, Marcel Dekker, pp. 190–201.

Marks, M.L. and Mirvis, P.H. (1998) *Joining Forces*, Simon and Schuster.

Mirvis, P.H. and Marks, M.L. (1991) *Managing the Merger: Making It Work*, Prentice-Hall.

Pritchett, P. (1985) *After the Merger: Managing the Shockwaves*, Dow Jones Irwin.

Prichett, P. et al. (1997) *After the Merger*, Irwin.

Schweiger, D.M. and Weber, Y. (1989) 'Strategies for Managing Human Resources During Mergers and Acquisitions: An Empirical Investigation', *Human Resource Planning*, vol. 12, pp. 69–86.

Volards, S. (1997) *Takeover*, Gower.

See also: Exporting for others; Inter-group interventions; Inter-group team-building; Investing in a small company; LIFO method

Metaphor approach

When teaching complex topics, one approach is to draw analogies, highlighting similarities between familiar concepts and novel ones: for example, pointing out that the brain's function resembles a computer, or that the eye resembles a camera. A metaphor goes one step further: rather than pointing out that something *resembles* something else, it asks students to think of it as *being* something else. For example, regarding the *Windows* computer interface as an office desktop because it serves many of the same functions.

The use of metaphors to help students understand organizations was popularized by Gareth Morgan, but Perren incorporated them into organizational change management, developing them as a diagnostic tool which can be applied in preparation for a change intervention. Perren's approach involves asking each member of a group of managers to complete the sentence 'My organization is ...' in their own words, then explain why they chose that particular metaphor. The subsequent discussions often cover themes such as ethics, barriers to growth and leadership style. Talking metaphorically serves to distance individuals from their organizational situation, and helps them to identify the key issues. From his experience of using this technique, Perren feels that metaphors can be useful in stressful situations, and they can provide a means of measuring 'organizational health'. Comparing metaphors gathered from a range of staff can be revealing, and this method can be combined with other more formal diagnostic tools, focusing managers' attention on specific problems, helping them to diagnose problems; and facilitating organizational change.

Bailey, J.R. and Ford, C.M. (1994) 'Of Methods and Metaphors: Theatre and Self-exploration in the Laboratory', *Journal of Applied Behavioural Science*, vol. 30. pp. 381–96.

Bocialetti, G. (1982) 'Metaphors: A Student's Theory of Organization', *Exchange: The Organizational Behaviour Teaching Journal*, vol. 7, no. 3, pp. 46–7.

Morgan, G. (1997) *Images of Organization* (2nd edn), Sage.

Ortony, A. (1975) 'Why Metaphors are Necessary and Not Just Nice', *Educational Theory*, vol. 25, pp. 45–53.

Oswick, C. and Grant, D. (1996) *Organization Development: Metaphorical Explanations*, Pitman.

Palmer, I. and Dunford, R. (1996) 'Conflicting Use of Metaphors: Re-conceptualising Their Use in the Field of Organizational Change', *Academy of Management Review*, vol. 21, no. 3, pp. 691–717.

Perren, L. (1997) 'Metaphors and Organizations: Practical Applications in Organizational; Diagnosis', *Organisations and People*, vol. 4, no. 3, pp. 10–15.

Perren, L. and Atkin, R. (1997) 'Is There a Link Between the Growth of the Firm and the Use of Metaphor in Owner–manager Discourse?', *Journal of Applied Management Studies*, vol. 6, no. 1.

Pondy, L.R. (1983) 'The Role of Metaphors and Myths in the Organization and in the Facilitation of Change', in Pondy, L.R., Frost, P.J., Morgan, G. and Dandridge, T.C. (eds) *Organizational Symbolism*, JAI Press.

Purser, R.E. and Moutuori, A. (1994) 'Miles Davis in the Classroom: Using the Jazz Ensemble Metaphor for Enhancing Team Learning', *Journal of Management Education*, vol. 18, no. 1, pp. 21–31.

Srivasta, S. and Barrett, F. (1988) 'The Transforming Nature of Metaphor in Group Development: A Study in Group Process', *Human Relations*, vol. 41, no. 1, pp. 31–64.

See also: Analogy teaching; Attitude survey; Drawing for learning; Reframing; Storytelling; Survey feedback interventions

Micro-lab

In a micro-lab, participants complete a selection of activities chosen from the many laboratory learning techniques which aim to help people to learn about themselves and their relationships with other individuals, with other groups, and with their organization. Each micro-lab usually lasts an hour, and may include ten or twelve five-minute activities. These might involve participants sharing their first impressions of each other (both positive and negative), telling each other the one thing they would most like other group members to know about them, and so on. Micro-lab groups are usually small, consisting of three to six participants, because the time limit would otherwise provide insufficient scope for interaction. Several groups can be run simultaneously, but unless they are of roughly equal size they are unlikely to progress through the exercises at the same speed.

The directions for the micro-lab activities can either be given by an instructor or a group member. Individuals are asked to participate in the exercises wholeheartedly, postponing an assessment of their value until later, and to avoid digressing from the suggested topics. Although some activities may involve giving feedback to others, participants are asked to avoid giving advice, but simply to listen to them, learn from them and share their own feelings and thoughts.

See also: Encounter group; Group dynamics laboratory; Human relations laboratory; Laboratory method; Mini-society; Organizational laboratory; Personal development laboratory; Power laboratory; Sensitivity (T-group) training; Structured social skills seminar; Tape-assisted learning programme; Team laboratory

Micro-teaching

Micro-teaching is mainly used in teacher training, but it can be applied to other fields. A trainee teacher is asked to provide tuition on a specific subject to a group of three or four students for five minutes, and the lesson is videotaped by a supervisor. When it is over, the students are asked to fill in a questionnaire, then leave the room. The supervisor and trainee discuss the lesson, reviewing the supervisor's notes, considering the feedback provided by the students, and viewing any relevant sections of the video recording. After a short break, the process is repeated with a new group of three or four students.

A powerful advantage of the micro-teaching approach is that it gives participants the opportunity to practise their teaching skills and master curriculum topics in a relatively realistic setting. Micro-teaching reflects the complexity of normal classroom teaching, but allows greater control over variables such as class size and time, and increases the amount and quality of feedback that can be provided.

Allen, D. and Ryan, K. (1969) *Micro-Teaching*, Addison Wesley Longman.

Brown, G. (1975) *Micro-teaching*, Methuen.

Cavaleri, S. A. and DeCormier, R. (1994) 'The Microskills System for High Speed Leadership', *Leadership and Organization Development Journal*, vol. 12, no. 4, pp. 9–12.

Falus, I. and McAlleese, W.R. (1975) 'A Bibliography of Micro-teaching', *Programmed Learning and Educational Technology*, vol. 12, no. 1, pp. 3–53.

Jesson, C.K. (1974) 'An Economic Use of Micro-Teaching Techniques to Achieve Objectives for a Basic Course in Learning Resources', *Programmed Learning and Educational Technology*, vol. 11, no. 2, pp. 87–96.

Perlberg, A. (1970) 'Microteaching: A New Approach to Improving Teaching and Training', *Journal of Educational Technology*, vol. 1, no. 1, pp. 35–43.

Perrott, E. (1977) *Micro-teaching in Higher Education: Research, Development and Practice*, Society for Research into Higher Education.

Titmar, H-G., Hargie, O.D.W. and Dickson, D.A. (1977) 'Social Skills Training at Ulster College', *Programmed Learning and Educational Technology*, vol. 14, no. 4, pp. 300–4.

See also: Behavioural simulation; Inter-personal process recall; Surrogate client; Video confrontation

Mind Mapping

Tony Buzan devised the technique of Mind Mapping to provide a visual representation of items of information and how they inter-relate. Reflecting the way the brain records, stores and connects information, Mind Mapping helps users break free from some of the constraints of traditional, linear thinking. Key words are used to trigger recall and stimulate creative thinking, and the technique has become a very popular note-taking and revision aid.

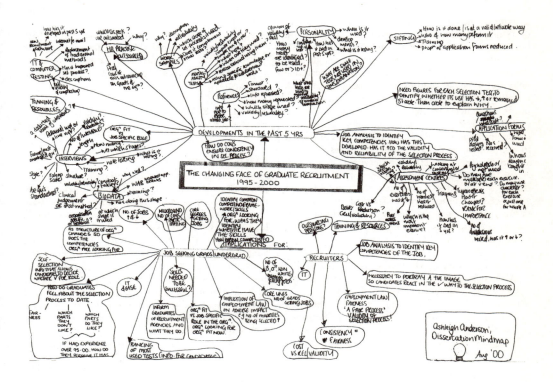

Mind map: Ashleigh Anderson

Buzan, T. (1974) *Use Your Head*, BBC Publications.

Buzan, T. and Dixon, T. (1978) *The Evolving Brain*, David and Charles.

Buzan, T. and Israel, R. (1995) *Brain Sell*, Gower.

Buzan, T. and Israel, R. (1997) *Superself*, Gower.

Malone, S.A. (1997) *Mind Skills for Managers*, Gower.

Margulies, N. (1991) *Mapping Inner Space: Learning and Teaching Mindmapping*, Zephyr Press.

Russell, P. (1979) *The Brain Book*, Routledge.

See also: Advance organizer; Brainstorming; Concept analysis; Lateral thinking

Mini-course

A mini-course is a short, self-contained, flexible course which has clearly defined objectives that can be achieved over a short time span, usually a few days or less. It is not suitable for independent study, since it depends extensively on the dynamics of small-group interaction. Each mini-course usually has a manual to provide guidance, but responsibility for co-ordinating it rests with the course leader and the group itself.

Mini-courses are based on a systems approach to curriculum development which draws on behavioural theory. Meyer described how each mini-course is based on precisely defined stimulus–response chains, with students' desirable behaviours being reinforced at the end of each response phase. These chains are organized into linear sequences of input–process–output (IPO) cycles, which in turn are combined to form a single mini-course. Each mini-course is designed to optimize some 24 conditions which research has shown to promote effective learning, including: active participation; immediacy of application; clarity of objectives; provision for reinforcement and feedback; democratic leadership; effective group work; logical, step-by-step structuring; variety of methods and media; modelling, and contiguity of elements.

Brandt, D., Ansell, M. and Cryer, N.B. (1974) 'Minicourses in a First Year Physics Laboratory', *Physics Education*, vol. 1, pp. 23–6.

Meyer, C.R. (1979) 'The Development of Minicourses (with a Basis in Educational Technology) for the In-service Education of Teachers and Trainers', *Programmed Learning and Educational Technology*, vol. 16, no. 1, pp. 23–37.

Meyer, C.R. and Jenkins, C. (1979) 'Preliminary Studies of the Effectiveness of Minicourses for In-Service Education of Teachers and Trainers', *Programmed Learning and Educational Technology*, vol. 16, no. 3, pp. 210–18.

See also: Concentrated study; Module; Residential; Workshop

Mini-learning event

A mini-learning event consists of four sequential stages which are carried out by a group of some five people working together. The stages are: diagnosis, design, implementation and review. In the *diagnosis* phase, participants identify a work problem and analyse its essential aspects. Each person then *designs* a 30-minute learning event to examine the problem identified. They will usually need to simplify their approach to allow the problem to be tackled within the time limit, and the aim is that all group members should learn something, not just the designer. Next, participants take it in turns to *implement* their learning event with the assistance of the other group members. Each event concludes with a *review*, the designer of the event receiving feedback from the other group members.

Binsted, D. and Stuart, R. (1979) 'Designing Reality into Management Learning Events, Part 1: Towards Some Working Models', *Personnel Review*, vol. 8, no. 3, pp. 12–19.

Binsted, D., Stuart, R. and Long, G. (1980) 'Promoting Useful Management Learning: Problems of Translation and Transfer' in Beck, J. and Cox, C. (eds) *Advances in Management in Education*, Wiley.

See also: Role-playing; Sociodrama; Training transfer training

Mini-society

Developed in Scandinavia, a mini-society exercise involves a fairly large number of volunteers living together in a laboratory-type setting for a certain period. As far as possible, the sample should include a wide cross-section of the population. Participants are divided into groups whose members are sociologically similar, and their interaction produces many insights into the dynamics governing society as a whole. One mini-society exercise run in the UK revealed a high degree of concern about the problem of the uneven distribution of power in society, and participants became preoccupied with this issue. In another, it was discovered that there was widespread disillusionment with traditional processes, particularly the political ones conventionally used to achieve public objectives.

Hjelholt, G. (1973) 'Group Training in Understanding Society: Mini-Society', in Cooper, C.L. (ed.) *Group Training for Individual and Organizational Development*, S. Karger, pp. 140–52.

See also: Group dynamics laboratory; Human relations laboratory; Laboratory method; Microlab; Organizational laboratory; Personal development laboratory; Power laboratory; Sensitivity (T-group) training

Mini-trial

Mini-trials were developed by TRW Inc. and Telecredit Inc. in the USA during the late 1970s as a means of resolving civil disputes between companies. The technique has grown in popularity because it provides a far less complex, time-consuming and costly alternative to pursuing matters through the normal channels, although cases whose facts are disputed, or where a legal precedent or principle is crucial to a company's future will continue to be dealt with in the courts.

The premise underlying this approach is that the parties to a dispute can settle it themselves if senior managers are shown the merits of each other's case. To achieve this, lawyers for both sides give a brief presentation of the case over the course of a day or two, senior executives from both sides having the opportunity to question the lawyers and cross-examine witnesses. A variety of formats can be adopted, including introducing a disinterested third party to act as adjudicator.

Hermann, A.H. (1984) 'The ADR Way Round the High Cost of Litigation', The *Financial Times*, 23 August, p. 23.
Hermann, A.H. (1984) 'The Competition Between ADR and Arbitration', The *Financial Times*, 30 August, p. 8.

See also: Alternative dispute-resolution; Ombudsman; Rent-a-judge; Sensitivity bargaining

Mission cards (mission statements)

Many organizations issue mission statements in an effort to clarify and reinforce their corporate culture and objectives: for example, the First Chicago Bank's states that the customer is its highest priority, that it is strategically driven, that it is committed to a standard of excellence, and that it operates through teamwork. Interest in the issue of corporate culture was originally aroused by the publication of Peters and Waterman's *In Search of Excellence* and Deal and Kennedy's *Corporate Cultures*. Some companies devote a great deal of effort to drawing up their mission state-

ment: Ford's statements took two years to develop, involved hundreds of employees and was approved by the board of directors.

Some companies, such as General Motors and Ford, have issued all their managers with as many as three glossy, pocket-sized cards to remind them of their companies' guiding principles. This practice is sometimes referred to as 'management by card'.

Deal, T.E. and Kennedy, A.A. (1982) *Corporate Cultures: The Rites and Rituals of Corporate Life*, Addison Wesley Longman.
Peters, T.J. and Waterman, R.H. (1982) *In Search of Excellence*, Harper and Row.
Schein, E.H. (1984) 'Coming to a New Awareness of Organization Culture', *Sloan Management Review*, Winter, pp. 3–16.
Thomas, M. (1985) 'In Search of Culture: Holy Grail or Gravy Train?', *Personnel Management*, September, pp. 2–7.

See also: Company culture training; Development of a new management/operating philosophy; Greenfield plants; Managerial strategy change; Myth-making intervention; Organizational climate analysis

Mock trial (courtroom model)

Acknowledging the value of role-playing and debate as teaching methods, mock trials explore controversial organizational and managerial issues by simulating courtroom proceedings. This helps students develop the ability to think quickly under pressure once they have had an opportunity to prepare their arguments (*examination* skills), and also when they must adapt their arguments according to others' responses to questions (*cross-examination* skills).

The optimum number of participants is between 10 (1 barrister and 4 witnesses per side) and 16 (2 barristers and 6 witnesses per side). If there are too few, the proceedings are unlikely to examine the issues in sufficient detail, whereas if there are too many, students' attention is less likely to be sustained. A mock courtroom may be available at a neighbouring faculty of law, but otherwise the classroom layout can be adapted to simulate one. The approach consists of ten steps, five in the pre-trial phase, and five during the trial itself.

The first step is to identify an organizational issue about which students' opinions are divided 50-50. The best way to do this is to ask the class to generate a list of issues of interest, check which produce an even split, and let them select one (e.g., 'Does good management make unions redundant?'). Next, the students are divided into two groups: the defence and the prosecution. Participants may be allowed to represent the opinion they agree with, but it may be more challenging if they are required to take the opposing view. In the third step, the prosecution draws up a charge for each witness and distributes copies to each participant. For example, in this context, one charge might be: 'Historically, unions came into being to oppose offensive management practices, and there is little evidence to believe that the situation has changed. Despite being described as a company's most valued asset, employees have little say in how it is run.' In step 4 the defence and prosecution teams now decide who will serve as their barristers and who will play the witnesses, and a list of these showing their order of appearance is circulated. In this instance, the roles might include human resource manager, chief executive, employee, union representative and plant manager. The final pre-trial step is to set a trial date, each participant working alone to prepare their part in the meantime.

The proceedings resemble a real trial as closely as possible: observers act as the jury, the barristers can raise objections, and the judge, played by the instructor, can either sustain or overrule them. Each witness prepares three questions for their own barrister to ask them, and takes the stand for 10–20 minutes. They may refer to notes, but must respond in their own words. When witnesses are not giving evidence, they may pass notes and suggested questions to their barristers. Presenting evidence in the form of exhibits is encouraged, as it enables students to introduce relevant research findings.

In step six, the judge makes the opening remarks. In step seven, the prosecution's and defence barristers each make their opening address. Step eight consists of each side's witnesses being examined by their own barristers and cross-examined by the opposition's. In step nine, the prosecution and defence barristers make their closing statements, each being allowed equal time. Finally, the judge sums up, and the jury votes to decide the verdict.

Ettinger, J.S. (1982) 'Courtroom Simulation as an Approach to Teaching Organizational Behaviour', *Exchange: The Organizational Behaviour Teaching Journal*, vol. 7, no. 3, pp. 33–6.

See also: Appraisal module; Argumentation; Buberian dialogue; Debate; Jurisprudential model; PIT technique; Role-playing

Model

Models have a wide range of applications as learning aids. They have been used throughout history to teach military personnel about battlefield tactics. Cross-sectional, cut-out models of the human body or items of equipment are commonly used in the instruction of medical or engineering students. Architects rely on scale models to work out details of their designs, and to seek approval from clients and the public.

Nowadays, computer simulations are beginning to take on some of the roles of physical models. For instance, virtual reality programs allow clients to experience what it might be like to walk through a building, any changes required can be made with relative ease and speed, and the process can be repeated until it is deemed satisfactory. However, the complexity of the design and the cost of modelling it will continue to dictate which method is adopted, and where a permanent physical record is required, traditional methods of modelling are likely to persist.

Sower, V.E. (1997) 'A Table Top Flexible Manufacturing Cell for Use in the Production/Operations Management Classroom', *Journal of Management Education*, vol. 21, no. 2, pp. 200–8.

See also: Dramatic skit; Exhibit; Fair; Festival; Museum learning; Poster

Module (modular instruction)

Although the term is often used loosely to describe any discrete course which forms part of a diploma or degree programme, a module is a self-contained cluster of concepts taught by methods which depend on the nature of the subject, perhaps as a semi-programmed and self-paced unit. Each module is usually designed to achieve highly specific objectives over a brief period – perhaps several days. It may be presented as an independent learning resource, and need not form part of a more extended course.

The basic idea of modular instruction is to offer individual units that cover the major content areas of a course. Where modules are designed for self-study, they frequently employ audio or visual media with computer support. A set of units may be completed in sequence, or students may be allowed a choice of modules at any point. Time limits may be set for the completion of each module, or students may be permitted to complete the units at their own pace. The instructor's task is to develop the modules, monitor their use and evaluate their effectiveness, as well as student achievement.

Brown, S. and Saunders, D. (1995) 'The Challenges of Modularization', *Innovations in Education and Training International*, vol. 32, no. 1, pp. 96–105.

Church, C. (1975) 'Modular Courses in British

Higher Education: A Critical Assessment', *Higher Education Bulletin*, vol. 3, no. 3, pp. 165–84.

Goldschmid, B. and Goldschmid, M.L. (1972) 'Modular Instruction in Higher Education: A Review', *Higher Education*, February, pp. 15–32.

Owens, G. (1970-l) 'The Module', *Universities Quarterly*, vol. 25, pp. 20–7.

Russell, J.D. (1974) *Modular Instruction: A Guide to the Design, Selection, Utilisation and Evaluation of Modular Materials*, Burgess.

See also: Concentrated study; Mini-course; Residential; Workshop

Monodrama

Monodrama should be distinguished from several related approaches. Whereas sociodrama examines inter-personal issues rather than intra-personal ones and psychodrama invites several group members to play roles, monodrama may also explore intra-personal conflicts, and the subject enacts the entire drama alone, the facilitator providing only guidance.

When used to explore intra-personal issues, the subject sits in a chair in a space where several other chairs are available, each symbolizing a different aspect of the self, such as ambition, indecision or greed. The first task is to decide on the different aspects to be explored during the session, assigning a chair to each of them. The subject then moves from chair to chair, enacting a dialogue between the different aspects, always speaking in the first person and identifying fully with the aspect which that chair represents. The facilitator encourages the subject to move quickly from chair to chair, maintaining spontaneity. This approach can also be used to explore conflicts between the subject's professional, domestic and other social roles.

A similar approach can be used to examine inter-personal issues, but in this case each chair represents a person, such as the subject's secretary, client or boss, rather than an aspect of the personality. The method is most effective if the monodrama portrays a problematic situation the subject has actually encountered with another person, allowing them to develop empathy with them and gain an insight into the dynamics of their interaction.

Heron, J. (1973) *Experiential Training Techniques*, Department of Adult Education, University of Surrey, Guildford.

See also: Character immersion; Dramatic skit; Gestalt techniques; Hearing; Illuminative incident analysis; Inner dialogue; Psychodrama; Sociodrama; Role-playing; Role-reversal

Montessori Method

This method was developed by Dr Maria Montessori in about 1900, when she was an assistant doctor in a psychiatric clinic at Rome University. She became interested in the teaching of children with learning disabilities, and studied the work of two nineteenth-century French doctors, Itard and Seguin. She felt that the methods they recommended could be used with other learners. In 1906, she organized her first school for infants in Rome. Today, Montessori schools are widely spread around the world, but their approach, which is based on her view of a child as having 'a body which grows and a soul which develops', remains controversial.

Montessori's guidelines for the design of learning activities and entire programmes have been developed throughout the twentieth century. Her methods emphasized learning rather than teaching, and relied on reinforcing desirable behaviour rather than punishing transgressions. She felt that images were more effective than words, showing was more effective than telling, and that learning was more likely to take place if all five senses were engaged. She also considered that too much instruction was worse than too little, and that if learners were exposed to situations which provoked anxiety, they were less inclined to experiment and be open to new experiences, reverting instead to behaviours that had been successful in the past.

Hainstock, E.G. (1997) *The Essential Montessori*, Plume Publishers.

Montessori, M. (1912) *The Montessori Method*, Heinemann.

See also: Dalton plan; Decroly method

Moral philosophy approach

This approach requires each student to develop their own managerial ethical code and set it out in a statement of about two pages in length. The codes consist of precepts to guide them through ethical dilemmas they are already facing or are likely to face in their working life: for example, one student's might be tailored to the pharmaceutical industry, and another's might be drawn up in relation to the drinks or tobacco industries. The aim is to help students reflect critically on the social values they have absorbed from those around them and the media, introduce the major ethical systems of thought developed by philosophers, and encourage them to adopt and use these as a basis for their own actions.

Ferris describes the first step as creating a 'blizzard of moral dilemmas': overloading students with management situations which create ethical difficulties in order to force them to develop a coherent ethical system to avoid being overwhelmed. In particular, new students need to be shown that they do not already have all the answers, that there are many diverse ethical issues, and that it is essential to develop some sort of personal 'moral anchor'. The second step involves reading a moral philosophy text that describes a range of ethical systems. Unfortunately, these vary in their coverage and are seldom easy to read. Next, students study corporate ethical codes which demonstrate that even senior company executives have difficulties dealing with these issues. The fourth step is to prepare a first draft of their personal ethical code and adapt it in response to feedback. The next step involves writing a paper in defence of a particular ethical position, relying on reasoned argument as much as private research. In the sixth step, pairs of students give a fifteen-minute oral presentation on an ethical issue that is currently in the news. Finally, each student submits a final draft of their personal ethical code.

Cava, A. (1990) 'Teaching Ethics: A Moral Model', *Business and Economic Review*, vol. 8, nos 2–3, pp. 117–29.
Coney, E.J. and Nelson, D.R. (1989) 'Business Law and Moral Growth', *American Business Law Journal*, vol. 27, no. 1, pp. 1–39.
Ferris, W.P. (1996) 'The Effectiveness of Teaching Business Ethics Using Moral Philosophy and Personal Ethical Codes', *Journal of Management Education*, vol. 20, no. 3, pp. 341–57.
Geet, B. (1988) *Morality: A New Justification of the Moral Rules*, Oxford University Press.

See also: Ideological change; Managerial strategy change; Retreat; Socratic dialogue

Motivation achievement training (achievement motivation training; power motivation training; attitudinal training)

While studying high achievers, David C. McClelland designed a pilot training programme to test methods for promoting motivation and entrepreneurial behaviour. His studies found that the key variable was the *need to achieve*, and group strategies based on his approach are the foundation of motivation training. It aims to teach participants how to think, talk and act like persons with a high need to achieve; to encourage them to set themselves demanding but carefully planned goals over a specific period, and to increase their self-knowledge. The objective is to foster a group spirit among participants by allowing them to learn about each other's hopes, fears, successes and fail-

ures, and by sharing an emotional experience in a retreat setting. The approach has been applied in a wide variety of situations, including training rural leaders in a UNESCO project in Honduras.

Group interaction is guided in such a way that participants reinforce each other's efforts to achieve their individual goals. The group thus constitutes one element in an ever-widening network that supports the individual need to achieve. However, change in personal behaviour takes place through introspective processes, so participants must examine their own motives, values, attitudes, fantasies and aspirations, and involve themselves in creative problem-solving and risk-taking experiences. The group acts as a mirror, providing feedback and helping individuals to examine their own behaviour and increase their effectiveness in attaining their goals.

Aronoff, J. and Litwin, G.H. (1971) 'Achievement Motivation Training and Executive Advancement', *Journal of Applied Behavioural Science*, vol. 7, no. 2, pp. 215–29.
Berlew, D.E. and LeClere, W. (1974) 'Social Intervention in Curaçao: A Case Study', *Journal of Applied Behavioural Science*, vol. 10, pp. 29–52.
Crawford, K.S., Thomas, E.D. and Fink, J.J. (1980) 'Pygmalion at Sea: Improving the Work Effectiveness of Low Performers', *Journal of Applied Behavioural Science*, vol. 16, pp. 482–505.
McClelland, D.C. (1961) *The Achieving Society*, Van Nostrand.
McClelland, D.C. and Winter, D.G. (1969) *Motivating Economic Achievement*, Free Press.
McClelland, D.C., Rhinesmith, S. and Kristensen, R. (1975) 'The Effects of Power Training on Community Action Agencies', *Journal of Applied Behavioural Science*, vol. 11, no. 1, pp. 92–115.
Miron, D. and McClelland, D.C. (1979) 'The Impact of Achievement Motivation Training on Small Businesses', *California Management Review*, vol. 21, pp. 13–28.
Reynolds P.M. (1971) 'Achievement Motivation Training in the U.K.', *Industrial Training International*, vol. 6, no. 9, p. 266.

See also: Assertiveness training; Career life planning; Confidence-building training

Movie

Feature films have long been used in management education and training to illustrate aspects of course topics and provide a basis for class discussions. Nowadays, these are usually shown on video, as this is a more flexible and convenient medium. Sometimes, an entire film may be shown, the instructor pausing the film occasionally to initiate a discussion about what has just occurred, and why. Movies that have been used in this way include *Twelve O' Clock High* to show different leadership styles, and *Twelve Angry Men* to examine group decision-making. It is often preferable to use a single scene or section: for example, the recruitment sequence at the start of *The Magnificent Seven* is popular for illustrating Maslow's hierarchy of needs theory, while a certain sequence in *Aliens* portrays the gain and loss of different types of power.

Banthin, J.M. (1993) 'Dilemmas and Choices Facing Business People as Revealed in "Nothing in Common"', *Journal of Management Education*, vol. 17, no. 1, pp. 276–85.

Comer, D.R. and Cooper, E.A. (1998) 'Michael Crichton's "Disclosure" as a Teaching Tool', *Journal of Management Education*, vol. 22, no. 2, pp. 227–41.

Daniels, J.D. (1982) 'Building a Course Around Films: A Case Example of an International Management Course', *Exchange: The Organizational Behaviour Teaching Journal*, vol. 7, no. 3, pp. 19–25.

Flores, E. (1989–90) 'The Many Different Ways to Survive the Cuckoo's Nest', *Organizational Behaviour Teaching Review*, vol. 14, no. 4, pp. 135–7.

Gallos, J.V. (1993) 'Teaching About Re-framing with Films and Videos', *Journal of Management Education*, vol. 17, no. 1, pp. 127–32.

Harrington, K.V. and Griffin, R.W. (1990) 'Ripley, Burke, Gorman and Friends: Using the Film "Aliens" to Teach Leadership and Power', *Journal of Management Education*, vol. 14, no. 3, pp. 79–86.

Hassard, J. and Holliday, R. (eds) (1998) *Organizational Representation*, Sage.

Huczynski, A.A. (1994) 'Teaching Motivation and Influencing Strategies Using "The Magnificent Seven"', *Journal of Management Education*, vol. 18, no. 2, pp. 273–8.

Kinnunen, R. and Ramamurti, R. (1987) 'Making Cases More "Real": The Use of Video Tapes to Enhance Business Policy Cases', *Case Research Journal*, Spring, pp. 1–6.

Michaelson, L.K., and Schultheiss, E.E. (1988) 'Bronson, Brenner and McQueen: Do They Have Something to Teach Us About Influencing?', *Organizational Behaviour Teaching Review*, vol. 12, no. 4, pp. 144–7.

Rappaport, A. and Cawelti, G. S. (1998) 'Cinematography and Case Videos: Some Observations on Selection and Teaching', *Journal of Management Education*, vol. 22, no. 1, pp. 104–12.

Ross, J. (1996) 'Scorsese's "Age of Innocence": An Escalation Interpretation', *Journal of Management Education*, vol. 20, no. 2, pp. 276–85.

Serey, T.T. (1992) 'Carpe Diem: Lessons About Organization and Management from "Dead Poets Society"', *Journal of Management Education*, vol. 16, no. 3, pp. 374–81.

See also: Film; Music for learning; Novels for learning; Poetry for learning; Television; Trigger film; Video confrontation

Multiple job-holding

If an individual has developed a number of marketable skills, they may decide to vary their work according to market demand and their own interests. For example, a hotel manager might supplement their income by serving as a consultant or as a specialist analyst with a stockbroking firm. This type of working pattern is becoming increasingly common, and provides a valuable resource for companies which wish to have access to a particular skill without expanding their core staff.

See also: Consultant network; Consultation; Consulting assignment; Flexible staffing; Insider-outsider consulting teams; Intrapreneurship; Job-sharing; Networking; Teleworking; Work schedule restructuring

Multiple management (junior board of executives system)

In this system, a permanent advisory committee of managers studies company problems and makes recommendations to senior management. The concept was pioneered in 1932 by Charles P. McCormick at the McCormick Company in Baltimore. Its original aim was to give junior managers the opportunity to create and screen ideas, to allow them a greater degree of participation in the company's affairs, to develop their managerial abilities, and to broaden their experience. The approach was subsequently extended to other management levels, and has proven valuable for middle managers who lack experience and may have been overlooked. McCormick also went on to develop factory boards and sales boards.

The core of the approach is the junior board of executives itself, which is given the opportunity to study any company problem and is asked to recommend courses of action. It is allowed access to company information and it sets its own rules, operating with only three constraints. First, in each succeeding term of office, some members must make way for new ones. This gives more managers the opportunity to participate. Second, all their recommendations must be unanimous.

This encourages the promotion of only the best ideas, and it also ensures that every member feels a sense of responsibility for each recommendation. Finally, no recommendation can be put into effect until the managing director or a senior management group has approved it. This ensures that top management retains ultimate control, but in practice it is seldom necessary.

All board members have the opportunity to gain knowledge and experience in aspects of business other than their own speciality. The approach can also help to identify those with executive potential: each board rates the performance of its members, and multiple judgements are used to provide a more objective assessment. Participants gain practical experience of group decision-making and team working, and the process of interaction develops respect for the views and rights of others.

Multiple management is a participative method which can benefit managers, employees, shareholders and customers. It can contribute significantly to company efficiency, productivity and human resource development, providing a relatively inexpensive means of bringing new blood into the top management structure and training people as they move up. It taps the resources of creativity which middle managers seldom have the opportunity to develop, while encouraging them to take responsibility as soon as they ready to do so. When the approach has failed, the reasons have been lack of genuine management support, or because senior executives have attended the meetings, inhibiting free discussion.

McCormick, C.P. (1938) *Multiple Management*, Harper and Brothers.
McCormick, C.P. (1949) *The Power of People*, Harper and Brothers.

See also: Absenteeism task force; Action learning; Evaluation committee method; Independent product teams; Informal management team; Intrapreneurship; Involvement teams; Managerial decentralization; Non-executive director; Plural chief executive; Problem-solving groups; Proposal team assignment; Quality circles; Quality management; Reprogramming; Task force

Museum learning

Museums are among the oldest of teaching devices. That is why so many of them are attached to ancient universities around the world, and often constitute a university department in their own right. They can be used to promote two types of learning: using the museum as a focus, and using the museum as a context.

In the *museum-as-focus approach*, the displays and reference collections are available for inspec-
tion, providing a learning medium which complements, and in some cases replaces, other pedagogical methods. Nowadays, the increasing use of computers and multi-media devices means that museums are developing into interactive learning centres.

In contrast, Cowan described a project which used the *museum-as-context approach*. Student readings and an integrative paper complemented a structured tour of an art gallery and museum. His aim was to explore management leadership concepts, not only by studying the administration of an art museum, but combining this with the context provided by history and the perceptual stimuli offered by art. Some artworks depict historical periods, and artists frequently address leadership characteristics of power, status, influence and co-operation. Cowan also used both art itself and the process of creating it (involving artists and their apprentices) to explore the concepts of imagination, innovation, guidance and mentoring.

Caulton, T. (1998) *Hands-on Exhibitions: Managing Interactive Museum and Science Centres*, Routledge.
Cowan, D.A. (1992) 'Understanding Leadership Through Art, History and Arts Administration', *Journal of Management Education*, vol. 16, no. 3, pp. 272–89.
Gardner, L. (1995) and Kozak, K. (1995) *Making an Interactive Science Museum: Hands-on Exhibits*, McGraw-Hill.
Hein, G.E. (1998) *Learning in the Museum*, Routledge.
Roberts, L.C. (1997) *From Knowledge to Narrative: Education and the Changing Museum*, Smithsonian Institute Press.

See also: Dramatic skit; Exhibit; Exhibition; Fair; Festival; Model; Posters

Music for learning

Just as videos may be shown in the classroom to illustrate certain points, music can be used to increase awareness of thoughts and feelings about different aspects of work which are likely to affect an individual's performance. A wide variety of themes may be explored using this method: for example, many songs are written from the shop-floor employee's perspective.

In one approach, the instructor first plays a recording or reads out the lyrics, which may also be displayed using an overhead projector to stress the points being made. Students are also encouraged to respond emotionally to the song's tune and arrangement. Another method is to distribute a transcript of a song, and ask students to discuss their reactions to it, either individually or in groups. As when any copyright material is reproduced or performed in public, the instructor must ensure that permission is obtained and that any fees are paid.

Powell, G.N. and Veiga, J.F. (1985-6) 'Using Popular Music to Examine Management and OB Concepts: A Rejoinder to Springsteen's Thesis', *Organizational Behaviour Teaching Review*, vol. 10, no. 1, pp. 79–81.

Rettig, J.L. (1981) 'Teaching OB With Words and Music', *Exchange: The Organizational Behaviour Teaching Journal*, vol. 6, no. 2, pp. 41–2.

Sommers, D.I. (1993) 'Team Building in the Classroom Through Rhythm', *Journal of Management Education*, vol. 17, no. 2, pp. 263–8.

See also: Dramatic skit; Drawing for learning; Film; Movie; Novels for learning; Poetry; Trigger film; Video

Mystery clue method

A major weakness of the traditional case study method is that case descriptions usually give all the information necessary to allow students to proceed immediately to problem-diagnosis, analysis or action, neglecting development of their data-discovery skills. The mystery clue method is one of two techniques which have been developed to remedy this, the other being the management problem laboratory. Both encourage students to discover information for themselves and develop their own selective database. In contrast to the management project laboratory, a mystery clue method session can last as little as half an hour, but the ideas underlying both data-discovery approaches are identical. The method involves students taking on the role of a detective who is investigating a company situation, searching for clues and linking pieces of disparate information to solve a problem.

In preparation, the instructor draws on consulting experience, media reports, existing case studies and creative writing skills to develop a case situation relating to a fictional company. This is presented on 3-inch by 5-inch clue cards, each of which carries a single piece of information about this company – perhaps a fact, a rumour, a report excerpt or an employee's observation – expressed in two or three sentences. The instructor decides how inter-related, ambiguous or complex to make the clues, depending on the session's goals and the types of students. The clues may combine to focus on a single problem, or on a range of issues of broadly equal importance.

During the session, the instructor first distributes name cards among the students, and asks them a few questions about business policy. Then, announcing 'Let's find out what policy is all about', the instructor takes out the deck of clue cards, shuffles them, and asks the students to solve a mystery: for instance, a firm's managers are concerned about the direction the company is moving in, and want to know what is really happening; what problems they should be focusing on, and what they should be doing about them. It is up to the students to find out and provide the answers. The instructor then distributes one or two cards to each student, specifying that they should not swop cards, but use only verbal exchanges to discover the critical challenge that faces the company and agree an appropriate plan of action. They are allotted 30–45 minutes to do this, during which the instructor observes without participating. Once the class has developed an interpretation of what is going on, it tests it on the instructor, and a general discussion follows.

After the class has discussed the case content, the instructor can focus on the process issues: how the class went about its task. Common themes which arise here include how leadership was exercised, the formation of cliques within the group, the methods used to solve the problem, the values and interpretations that were attached to different types of data, and the problems of information overload and how these were handled.

Although the mystery clue method was originally developed to introduce the topic of business policy, it can easily be adapted to any management topic. It need not be used merely as an ice-breaker, but can be introduced at any point in a course to discuss any relevant concepts or processes concerned with coming to grips with random data, developing a change strategy and implementing it, or indeed formulating a logically consistent policy in any area.

Cook, C.W. (1980) 'Policy Unfolding Through Data Discovery Techniques', *The Organizational Behaviour Teaching Review*, vol. 5, no. 4, pp. 30–4.

See also: Case incident process method; Inquiry training model; Interrogation of experts; Management project laboratory; Medical model; Person card technique; Problem pack; Project orientation; Socratic group enquiry

Myth-making intervention

Bumstead and Eckblad cite Peters and Waterman's book *In Search of Excellence* as evidence to support the importance of companies asking and answering fundamental questions, such as what business they are in, what they stand for, what their activities mean, and to what ends their technical and managerial competencies are directed. Peters and Waterman wrote: 'As we worked on the research of our excellent companies, we were struck by the dominant use of story, slogan and legend ... In an organizational sense, these ... appear to be very important because they convey the organization's shared values or its culture.' Appeals to such basic values and purposes can serve to energize organizations.

Exploring and articulating meaning and values is an integral part of the development of a new system of leadership. It is not a matter of simply adopting Japanese or successful company values, but requires a myth-making intervention: a systematic exploration of values and their role within the company. In this context, Peters and Waterman identified certain features in the successful companies they studied. Top management recognized and fulfilled its role of articulating and reinforcing the guiding beliefs. These beliefs were disseminated and kept alive by stories, myths, legends and metaphors which circulated informally around the organization. They did not just concern the right and wrong ways to do things, but were linked to the central functions of the organization. In different companies, these myths or stories might concern quality, innovation, or customer service. The company's central values were spelt out at a general, abstract level, and were shown to be relevant and grounded in operating decisions. Finally, the values were not boring (of the 'holier than thou' type), but emphasized excitement. They challenged and energized members to find fun and self-expression in their work. For example, the seven 'spiritual values' that Pascale and Athos found in the Matsushita company were: national service through industry; fairness; harmony and co-operation; struggle for betterment; courtesy and humility; adjustment and assimilation, and gratitude.

Boje, D.M., Fedor, D.B. and Rowland, K.M. (1982) 'Myth Making: A Qualitative Step in OD Interventions', *Journal of Applied Behavioural Science*, vol. 18, no. 1, pp. 17–28.

Bradford, L.P. and Harvey, J.B. (1972) 'Dealing with Dysfunctional Organizational Myths', in Burke, W.W. and Hornstein, H.A. (eds) *The Social Technology of Organizational Development*, NTL Institute, pp. 244–54.

Bumstead, D. and Eckblad, J. (1985) 'Meaning Business: Values in the Workplace', in Clutterbuck, D. (ed.) (1985) *New Patterns of Work*, Gower.

Jackson, N.V. and Carter, P. (1984) 'The Attenuating Function of Myth in Human Understanding', *Human Relations*, vol. 37, no. 7., pp. 515–33.

Pascale, R.T. and Athos, A.G. (1982) *The Art of Japanese Management*, Penguin Books.

Peters, T.J. and Waterman, R.H. (1982) *In Search of Excellence*, Harper and Row, p. 75.

Pondy, L.R. (1983) 'The Role of Metaphors and Myths in the Organization and in the Facilitation of Change', in Pondy, L.R., Frost, P.J., Morgan, G. and Dandridge, T.C. (eds) *Organizational Symbolism*, JAI Press.

See also: Attitude survey; Corporate culture training; Development of a new management/operating philosophy; Greenfield plants; Ideological change; Managerial strategy change; Metaphor approach; Mission cards; Norm formation; Norm modification; Organizational climate analysis

Negotiation by group members

This is one of several techniques available to improve the relationship between two or more groups. It is more appropriate for resolving substantive rather than emotive issues. Representatives of the groups come together to diagnose their difficulties, negotiate a way to reduce tension between them, and reach agreement on the issues facing each group. The success of this approach hinges on the representatives' role. They must have the power to make tentative commitments on behalf of their groups, but they must be willing to set aside their own opinions if necessary, and present their group's views even if they disagree with them. It is also important to avoid establishing a win–lose style of negotiation, since the defeat of a representative might threaten their position within their group. The members of each group must be able to deal with conflict, and a high degree of trust and support must already exist among them, so that internal group problems do impede the resolution of inter-group disputes.

Awkward, M. (1995) *Negotiating Difference*, University of Chicago Press.

Fowler, A. (1998) *Negotiating, Persuading and Influencing*, Institute of Personnel and Development.

Fowler, A. (1997) *Negotiating Skills and Strategies* (2nd edn), Institute of Personnel and Development.

Kennedy, G. (1998) *Kennedy on Negotiation*, Gower.

McRae, B. (1997) *Negotiating and Influencing Skills*, Sage.

Scott, B. (1990) *The Skills of Constructive Negotiation*, Gower.

See also: Confidence-building measures; Conflict-resolution techniques; Confrontation groups; Confrontation meeting; Criss-cross panels; Exchange of persons; FIDO approach; Fishbowl;

LIFO method; No-lose conflict-resolution method; Planned re-negotiation; Third-party peacemaking interventions

Network organizations (dynamic networks; vertically disaggregated organizations; virtual corporations)

Following the development of divisional structures during the 1920s and the matrix organizational model adopted after 1945, the networked company structure represents the third major innovation in commerce since the emergence of the company itself. Network organizations have no fixed boundaries, and no obvious headquarters or production sites – this is why they are sometimes known as *virtual corporations*. The relationships between the different parts of the company and its customers and vendors are constantly changing, so that it is not always clear who is inside and who is outside the organization. Publishers, construction firms and clothes manufacturers have always hired contractors to carry out work on their behalf. In a similar way, network organizations engage outsiders to undertake the production of their wares, improvements in communications enabling them to co-ordinate the activities and needs of suppliers and customers around the world. Some companies adopt this structure because they consider that their strengths lie not in manufacturing, but primarily in research, development, marketing, distribution or merchandising.

Adopting a network organization structure offers numerous advantages. Such firms tend to be agile and fast-moving, need less capital, have lower overhead costs and be more entrepreneurial. It also enables them to base their manufacturing functions in areas where there is a pool of low-cost labour, and to draw on specialized technology when required. The approach also has a number of weaknesses, however. Network organizations are vulnerable to competition from their suppliers, they have less control over production, and they risk losing their design and manufacturing expertise. In addition, supplies are less secure, they cannot subsidize unprofitable product lines, and their income may be subject to wide fluctuations.

In network organizations, financial and legal skills are less important than the ability to detect trends and develop and maintain strong relationships with vendors and customers. To operate successfully, such organizations must possess certain structural and cultural features. The structure must include basic rules which define operations within the network; and it must allow rapid exchange of information. In terms of culture, the partners in the network must understand how their roles combine, they must trust each other's competence, they must be prepared to share resources, particularly information, and an entrepreneurial team spirit must replace the traditional command-and-control management approach.

Birkinshaw, J. (1998) 'Corporate Entrepreneurship in Network Organizations', *European Management Journal*, vol. 16, no. 3, pp. 355–64.

Chisholm, R.F. (1997) *Developing Network Organizations*, Addison Wesley Longman.

Cox, C. (ed.) (1994) 'Organizations as Networks', special issue of *Leadership and Organization Development Journal*, vol. 15, no. 7.

Davidow, W.H. and Malone, M.S. (1992) *The Virtual Corporation*, Harper Business.

Hastings, C. (1993) *New Organization: Growing the Culture of Organizational Networks*, McGraw-Hill.

McHugh, P., Merli, G. and Wheeler, W.A. (1995) *Beyond Business Process Reengineering: Towards the Helonic Enterprise*, Wiley.

Miles, R.E. and Snow, C.C. (1995) 'The New Network Firm: A Spherical Structure Built on a Human Investment Policy', *Organizational Dynamics*, Spring.

Zeffane, R. (1995) 'The Widening Scope of Inter-organizational Networking', *Leadership and Organization Development Journal*, vol. 16, no. 4, pp. 26–33.

See also: Flexible staffing; Outsourcing; Staff exchange; Vendor excellence awards

Networking

People often form social relationships with others who share a common interest in order to provide mutual support and help each other learn how to overcome problems. These relationships may take a variety of forms, from loosely structured social groups to highly structured clubs or associations, and the processes involved may be described as *networking*. In this context, a network is an institutional model or organizational principle which might be described metaphorically as consisting of several 'threads' (relationships of communication) held together by 'knots' (individuals). Networks are particularly suitable when an objective cannot be achieved easily by a single institution, group or individual, or where regional variations mean that differing groups and forms are best suited to local needs and circumstances. For example, the Open School Project provides recurrent and remedial adult education in the Netherlands, and it is organized through a network which links educational centres, women's groups, ethnic community centres and literacy organizations, all of which provide a similar service. The Dutch government funds a network information centre which keeps these diverse groups in touch, to ensure that they are aware of each other's activities.

Baker, W.E. (1993) *Networking Smart*, McGraw-Hill.

Boe, A. and Youngs, B.B. (1989) *Is Your 'Net' Working?*, Wiley.

Hastings, C. (1993) *The New Organization: Growing the Culture of Organizational Networking*, McGraw-Hill.

Hayes, R. (1996) *Systematic Networking*, Cassell.

Huczynski, A.A. (1996) *Influencing Within Organizations*, Prentice-Hall, Chapter 14.

Krackhardt, D. (1996) 'Social Networks and the Liability of Newness for Managers', in Cooper, C.L. and Rousseau, D.M. (eds) *Trends in Organizational Behaviour*, Volume 3, Wiley, pp. 159–73.

Michelli, D. and Straw, A. (1996) *Successful Networking in a Week*, Hodder and Stoughton.

Mueller, R. (1987) *Corporate Networking*, Viacom.

Stanley, T.J. (1997) *Networking with the Affluent*, McGraw-Hill.

Yarnell, D.A. and Peterson, M.F. (1993) 'Networking in the Mid-1990s', *Journal of Management Development*, vol. 12, no. 4, pp. 37–48.

See also: Concentrated study; Flexastudy; FlexiStudy; Informal action group; Job sharing; Multiple job-holding; Self-help group

Neuro-linguistic programming

Neuro-linguistics is the study of how the brain processes and stores information. We receive raw information about the world through our senses. Language enables us to understand and structure these experiences, creating models or maps of the world. Neuro-linguistic programming (NLP) was developed in the 1970s by John Grinder, a professor of linguistics, and Richard Bandler, an information scientist, who both worked at the University of California, Santa Cruz. It explores the role of the habitual patterns and sequences (*programmes*) we adopt in our thinking, which influence our attitudes and the way we feel and behave. It is based on the belief that each individual has a preferred way of taking in information and processing it, and that by consciously and systematically changing these programmes in a natural way, we can increase our choices, flexibility and effectiveness.

NLP is based on the idea that the reality we experience is an *edited* version of what is really 'out there'. We store our experiences in the form of perceptions from our senses – sight, hearing, touch, smell and taste – relying mainly on the first three. Each of these can be defined in terms of its *sub-modalities*: for instance, for a visual perception of an object the sub-modalities might be size, position, colour, clarity and contrast; for an auditory perception of an utterance they might be the words used, the tone of voice and volume, and for a touch perception they might be position, intensity, temperature or direction of movement. Grinder and Bandler maintain that experience is conditioned and structured by the language used to communicate these perceptions to both ourselves and others. If we change the way we think about an experience, then we can change the experience itself.

In their research, Grinder and Bandler asked themselves the simple question: 'What is it that makes the difference between somebody who is merely competent at any given skill, and the person who excels at the same skill?' This question is usually answered in one of two ways: either that some people have a natural gift for that particular skill, or that practice and experience is what counts. NLP takes a different approach, focusing not on what accounts for *past* differences in two people's abilities, but on what can be done *now* to transform competent performance into excellence. For this reason, NLP has been described as, 'the study of excellence'.

Grinder and Bandler propose that there are three elements to any skill behaviour: the external behaviour (what the person actually does and says), the internal computation (what the person thinks, and how they think it) and the internal state (what and how they feel). NLP's main research, teaching and learning strategy is *modelling* – indeed, Grinder and Bandler referred to themselves as being essentially 'modellers'. Studying the behaviours, thoughts and feelings of successful performers in any area of human activity allows us to build a comprehensive model of excellent behaviour. Excellence can then be achieved by imitating the competent person's movements, internal images, voices and feelings through a set of individual practical exercises known as *patterns*.

Drawing on psychodynamics and the behavioural sciences, NLP offers a framework for understanding the underlying structures and processes of communication. The information-gathering and change strategies and interventions it embodies mean that it can help to promote creativity and improve performance, and it offers practical ways to make rapid changes in our own and others' behaviour. For these reasons, it has been applied in many areas of human activity, including education, business, sport, the performing arts, self-development and the treatment of fears and phobias.

Alder, H. (1996) *NLP for Trainers*, McGraw-Hill.

Bradbury, A. (1997) *NLP for Business Success*, Kogan Page.

Dimmock, S. (1995) *Successful Communication Through NLP*, Gower.

Garrett, T. (1997) *The Effective Delivery of Training Using NLP*, Kogan Page.

Kamp, D. (1996) *The Excellent Trainer: Putting NLP to Work*, Gower.

Knight, S. (1995) *NLP at Work: The Difference that Makes a Difference in Business*, Nicholas Brealey.

McDermott, I. and O'Connor, J. (1996) *Practical NLP for Managers*, Gower.

O'Connor, J. and Seymour, J. (1990) *Introducing Neuro-linguistic Programming*, HarperCollins.

See also: Action profiling; Cognitive-behavioural therapy; Interfering with the interference; Non-verbal encounters; Non-verbal exercise; Process analysis; Re-evaluation counselling

No-lose conflict-resolution method

There are a number of negotiation techniques which acknowledge the negative consequences that arise from a win–lose approach. The version described here, developed by Gordon, aims to bring mutual satisfaction to both parties. The steps in the process he outlined include: defining the problem, generating alternative solutions, evaluating them, seeking both parties' commitment to a particular solution, agreeing how to implement it, taking the agreed course of action and, finally, evaluating its success. Gordon argues that this approach improves the relationship between the parties, leads to better and faster decisions, and increases their commitment to carry them out.

Gordon, T. (1979) *LET: Leader Effectiveness Training*, Futura Books, Chapters 9 and 10.

See also: Confidence-building measures; Conflict-resolution techniques; Confrontation groups; Criss-cross panels; Exchange of persons; FIDO approach; LIFO method; Negotiation by group members; Third-party peacemaking interventions

Nominal group technique (N-grouping technique)

The nominal group technique (NGT) was developed at the University of Wisconsin in 1968 by Andre Delbecq and Andrew Van de Ven to encourage creativity in focusing on problems, generating ideas and making collective decisions. NGT can be used whenever a wide variety of creative individual judgements about ideas, opinions or knowledge need to be combined to resolve a problem that is too complicated for an individual to tackle on their own. Whereas other interactive group methods rely on communication between participants with a minimum of structure and control, NGT aims to minimize any negative aspects of group dynamics by only allowing verbal interaction at specified times. This encourages the involvement of all participants, enables them to have equal influence on the outcome, and promotes a wide variety of approaches to the problem.

NGT can be used in the organizational context, in which case a company facilitator selects individuals with expertise, experience and perceptions which relate directly to the problem area to be explored, or it can be applied in the classroom, in which case the instructor serves as the facilitator and the whole class participates. In both cases, an eight-step approach is adopted (where relevant, approximate timings for each step are given in parentheses). In step one, the *public orientation* phase, the facilitator gives an overview of the problem and explains participants' roles in the process. The group is divided into sub-groups of 5–8 persons, and each sub-group sits around a table and appoints one of its members to be its recorder. Step two involves *private brainstorming*. The facilitator presents each sub-group with a question, and asks each participant to define the critical elements of the problem (usually in the form of themes or brief phrases) without conferring with the others (5 minutes). Having done this, they each draw up a list of their ideas and alternatives (10 minutes). The third step is a *round robin* (10–15 minutes), in which each sub-group member in turn contributes one idea, which is recorded on a flipchart. In the fourth step, the recorder leads the sub-group in a *public discussion* to clarify the ideas, each one being summarized using examples and explanations, but not evaluated at this stage. Duplications are eliminated, and common ideas are refined into two or three themes (10–25 minutes). The fifth step involves *private evaluation*. The remaining items are discussed in turn, and each participant works alone to select what they consider to be the ten most important ones and ranks them in order of priority on the basis of criteria supplied by the facilitator (5–15 minutes). In the sixth step, *public pooling*, the sub-group tabulates and summarizes all the evaluations of its members to produce a mathematically derived sub-group decision (10–15 minutes). The seventh step involves coming to a *group decision* (15–30 minutes). A variation of this step is to conduct a preliminary vote followed by a discussion, and then a final secret vote by all the participants. In the classroom context, this may be followed by a public debriefing, during which the facilitator examines the group process and considers which factors affect group functioning, learning and the quality of the decisions, drawing comparisons with other individual and group experiences. In the eighth step, *public planning*, the group discusses how to implement the results.

In undergraduate and postgraduate teaching (as opposed to organizational development), NGT can be used to explore course issues, either separately or sequentially. Sessions can address questions such as 'What dehumanizing experiences might people experience in an organization?' or 'What should be the behavioural objectives of this course?' NGT can help students to learn by direct involvement, because it does not rely on contrived situations (e.g., 'Lost on the Moon' or 'Lost in the Desert') and all have equal responsibility for considering and evaluating the question-related data. The approach lends itself to the study of topics such as group processes and decision-making, and the systematic consideration of alternatives allowing the expression of a broad range of viewpoints. Students gain a deeper and more personalized understanding of a subject than might be provided by a case study or group discussion. The opportunity to practise the technique means that they are more likely to feel confident in applying it in their future work.

Cook, C.W. (1980) 'Nominal Group Learning Methods Enrich Classroom Learning', *Organizational Behaviour and Teaching Journal*, vol. 5 no. 3, pp. 33–6.

Delbecq, A.L. and Van de Ven, A.H. (1971) 'A Group Process Model for Problem Identification and Programme Planning', *Journal of Applied Behavioural Science*, vol. 7, no. 4, pp. 466–91.

Delbecq, A.L., Van de Ven, A.H. and Gustafson, D.H. (1975) *Group Techniques for Programme Planning: A Guide to the Nominal Group Technique and Delphi Processes*, Scott Foresman.

Sink, D.S. (1983) 'Using the Nominal Group Technique Effectively', *National Productivity Review*, vol. 2, no. 2, Spring, pp. 173–84.

Van de Ven, A. and Delbecq, A.L. (1971) 'Nominal Versus Interacting Group Processes for Committee Decision-making Effectiveness', *Academy of Management Journal*, vol. 14, pp. 201–12.

Van de Ven, A. and Delbecq, A.L. (1972) 'The Nominal Group as a Research Instrument for Exploring Health Studies', *American Journal of Public Health*, March, pp. 337–42.

See also: Brainstorming; Brainwriting; Data-based interventions; Delphi technique; Kepner-Tregoe

Approach; Management Oversight and Risk Tree; Policy-formulation; Problem-solving group; Questionnaires; Strategic management; Synectics; Think tank

Non-conforming enclave

Any complex organization may include a non-conforming enclave – a wayward group of people in positions of responsibility who refuse or fail to conform to the organizational culture and norms. This situation can be dealt with by converting the enclave into a new, legitimate sub-unit which is allowed a degree of autonomy in conducting the activity which is the focus of its non-conformity, but must otherwise adhere to organizational rules and regulations. Although those at the top of the organizational hierarchy may see this approach as a threat to their authority, Leeds calls the conversion from non-conformity to legitimacy the 'protest-absorbing process'. The organization accommodates the 'protest' or non-conformity by sanctioning an outlet for it, enabling the enclave to continue to contribute to the attainment of organizational goals. The significance of protest absorption for the organization depends on how the enclave's cause affects its core policies and practices. Historical examples of the development of non-conforming enclaves and the process of protest absorption can be found among religious groups and the armed forces.

Leeds, R. (1964) 'The Absorption of Protest: A Working Paper', in Cooper, W.W., Leavitt, H.J. and Shelley, M.W. (eds) *New Perspectives in Organizational Research*, Wiley, pp. 115–35.

See also: Corporate culture training; Goal-setting interface groups; Ideological change; Informal action group; Norm clarification; Positive peer culture

Non-directive teaching model

This educational model is based on the work of Carl Rogers and other non-directive counsellors. Rogers believed that positive human relationships enable people to grow. He developed his therapeutic approach into a learning strategy, whose basic principle is that the *relationship*, not the subject matter or thought process, should be the basis of instruction. In his approach, the teacher acts as a facilitator, drawing on interview techniques derived from non-directive counselling, such as accepting and reflecting feelings, and paraphrasing what is said. Both teacher and student share responsibility for the discussion within the interview, the teacher's role being to provide structure, to ask open questions, and to practise active listening in order to encourage the student to develop their train of thought. By developing a personal relationship, the teacher can guide the learner's growth and development, helping them to explore new ideas about their lives, their work and their relationship with others. The use of such non-directive interviewing techniques need not be restricted to situations where students are experiencing academic or personal problems. Even if they are happy and successful, the approach can help them to develop their own perceptions and evaluate their own progress and development more objectively.

Having summarized the approach, Joyce and colleagues describe a six-step sequence in applying it. The first step is to define the helping situation, with the teacher encouraging the student to express their feelings. The next step involves exploring the problem or opportunity, the teacher encouraging the student to define it while accepting and clarifying their feelings. In the third step, the teacher supports the student in developing insights during their discussions. The fourth step requires the student to make decisions and draw up plans, the teacher helping to clarify the issues and alternatives. In the fifth step, the student gains further insights and develops more positive actions with the support of the teacher. Finally, the student learns to initiate positive actions, and takes responsibility for doing so.

Joyce, B., Weil, M. and Showers, B. (1992) *Models of Teaching* (4th edn), Allyn and Bacon, pp. 261–90.
Rogers, C.R. (1995) *A Way of Being*, Houghton Mifflin.
Rogers, C.R. (1995) *On Becoming a Person: A Psychotherapist's View of Psychotherapy*, Houghton Mifflin.
Rogers, C.R. and Freiberg, H.J. (1994) *Freedom to Learn* (3rd edn), Macmillan College.

See also: Counselling; Helping relationship model; Psychotherapy

Non-executive director

A company board usually consists of full-time and part-time directors. Full-time directors have executive responsibilities in addition to their role on the board, whereas this is not usually the case with part-time directors. Like executive directors, they are subject to collective responsibility for the management and direction of the company's affairs on behalf of the company itself, the shareholders, the employees and other stakeholders, but non-executive directors' independence allows them to take a more detached and balanced view of the company's affairs, particularly where potential conflicts of interest are concerned. They can also provide skills, expertise and external contacts which might not be available among the executive directors.

Although they may be asked to take on special duties, such as serving on a committee to study a particular subject, it more common for non-executive directors to take on an advisory role. Their expertise may be useful when considering issues such as public relations, management succession and structure, executive directors' pay and the structure of the board itself, and assessing the adequacy of financial information.

See also: Multiple management; Worker-directors

Non-verbal encounters

When a meeting or group discussion is deadlocked, a variety of non-verbal techniques can be used to foster a sense of unity by relieving tensions that may be blocking communication and suppressing energy. A number of these aim to reveal the underlying feelings that divide individuals, and allow them to be expressed in constructive ways. They can be used to address issues such as feeling left out of the group, attitudes to dependence and authority, and the need to bring group members closer together at a personal level.

Fordyce, J.K. and Weil, R. (1973) *Managing With People*, Addison Wesley Longman, pp. 180–2.
Morris, K.T. and Cinnamon, K.M. (1975) *A Handbook of Non-verbal Exercises*, Pfeiffer/Jossey-Bass.

See also: Action profiling; Critiquing; Getting acquainted; Going round the room; Likes and reservations; Neuro-linguistic programming; Polling; Process consultation; Sub-grouping

Non-verbal exercise

Non-verbal exercises promote learning through methods such as using gestures, movement or dance to express ideas and feelings, or exploring individual or group fantasies by means of drawings. The idea underlying this approach is that words can both block and facilitate communication, since people generally have greater control over their verbal responses than their non-verbal behaviour. Some find the open expression of emotions threatening, and rely on verbal intellectualization as a defence. Non-verbal exercises draw on the power of silence to provide a more direct means of communication and heighten the awareness of feelings.

Because most people have little experience of this approach, it can prove unsettling. Some may feel so threatened by what they perceive as a loss of rational control that they cannot submit to the experience, and this can prevent meaningful learning. Such difficulties are not unique to this method. Sensitivity training, and indeed any approach which involves the learner affectively, may encounter similar problems. Anyone who intends to use these exercises should seek assistance from a trainer or an experienced colleague and gain first-hand experience of their application.

Watson, G. (1972) 'Non Verbal Activities: Why? When? How?', in Dyer, W.G. (ed.) *Modern Theory and Method in Group Training*, Van Nostrand Reinhold.

See also: Action profiling; Critiquing; Dramatic skit; Experiential exercise; Gestalt techniques; Illuminative incident analysis; Neuro-linguistic programming; Trust exercise

Norm clarification

Norm clarification interventions are used to help resolve tensions between groups. For example, there may be friction between two groups because each fails to understand the norms and standards the other adopts in interactions. Furthermore, even if these norms and standards are recognized, they may not be regarded as legitimate. There are two solutions to these problems. The first is to identify the existing norms and standards, and to help the groups to adjust its norms so each can carry out its tasks without antagonizing the other. The second approach is to promote collaboration between the two groups in an effort to overcome the friction between them.

See also: Achievement motivation intervention; Classroom meeting model; Corporate culture training; Concept training; Ideological change; Non-conforming enclave; Norm formation; Norm modification; Role prescription

Norm formation

Norm-formation strategies are useful where no norms exist to regulate relations between individuals or groups. For example, if management wishes to tackle absenteeism and timekeeping problems in the workforce, encouraging employees to develop group norms about these issues is likely to be more effective than imposing rules and punishments.

Blake and Mouton describe a management group's experience of a norm-forming intervention prior to a union–management bargaining round. In this example, in the absence of a rationally thought through and established organizational norm, counter-productive individual attitudes guided management's behaviour. Using a diagonal-slice workgroup design, outside consultants helped managers to explore and clarify their attitudes towards the union, and to determine whether they thought better relations could be created. The managers came to recognize the one-sided nature of their viewpoints, as well as the 'dead-end quality of hopelessness that they connoted', and the consultants encouraged them to examine why they felt this way. The intervention identified deep-seated attitudes and negative feelings, and expressing and sharing these provided a release, allowing the managers to progress to the next step. When considered from different points of view, a number of constructive concepts began to emerge. The management group realized that union–management relations could only improve if the preconceptions which obstructed problem-solving were overcome, or at least set aside for an experimental period. The group concluded that, for progress to be made, it was essential to overcome any personal antipathy towards individual union representatives, and accord them the dignity and respect warranted by their status as duly elected union officers.

The intervention provided managers with an opportunity to release their pent-up frustration, but, more importantly, it permitted the establishment of a new organizational norm. The norm of conflict which had characterized union–management relations up to that point was replaced by a new norm that allowed the management's bargaining committee to take a more collaborative stance towards the union and concentrate on problem-solving. Eventually, this led to the solution of many previously intractable problems.

Blake, R.R. and Mouton, J.S. (1974) 'The D/D Matrix', in Adams, J.D. (ed.) *Theory and Method in Organization Development: An Evolutionary Approach*, NTL Institute for Applied Behavioural Science, pp. 3–36.

Filley, A.C. (1975) *Interpersonal Conflict Resolution*, Scott Foresman, p. 78.

Moch, M. and Seashore, S.E. (1981) 'How Norms Affect Behaviours in, and of, Corporations', in Nystrom, C.P. and Starbuck, W.H. (eds) *Handbook of Organizational Design*, Oxford University Press.

See also: Achievement motivation training; Behaviour modification; Brainwashing; Concept training; Corporate culture training; Discipline without punishment; Ideological change; Information-sharing meetings; Myth-making interventions; Norm clarification; Norm modification; Role prescription

Norm modification

The sociologist George Homans defined a norm as: 'an idea in the minds of the members of a group, an idea that can be put in the form of a statement specifying what the members ... should do, ought to do, and are expected to do under certain circumstances' (Homans, 1950, p. 123). Organizations can be regarded as clusters of norms which govern the behaviour of members. Some norms may be unwritten 'rules' which group members follow, but which may not be in tune with official organizational policy. On the other hand, management may prescribe organizational norms which dictate requirements for behaviour and are adopted by the majority of the organization's members. If inter-dependent groups have radically different norms, or if a substantial minority of the organization's members hold norms that differ greatly from those of the majority, this can lead to low performance, or inter-group or organizational conflict. The aim of a norm modification programme is to identify negative norms (e.g., 'Everybody starts work late here.'), and replace them with positive ones (e.g., 'We all put in a full day's work.').

The earliest industrial example of a prescriptive intervention concerned with norms and standards was reported by Frederick Winslow Taylor. Taylor's application of his scientific management principles led to the requirement that a worker carry four times as much material as he had done before, but this time using work methods designed by the management. The fact that it took Taylor about two years to apply his methods more widely indicates that the main problem in changing work habits and practices to achieve greater productivity is not diagnosing problems or formulating solutions, but gaining individual and group acceptance of the need for change.

Underlying the need for work norm modification is the premise that organizational life in modern times is anxiety-provoking, and is characterized by high levels of distrust between members. If changes in norms are to occur, it is necessary to help employees to increase their levels of trust, so that they interact not according to implicit role requirements and norms of defensiveness, but rather as a result of spontaneous feelings or problem-solving requirements. Norm-modification interventions rely heavily on emotional release. One such approach, described by Gibb (1972), was developed by the TORI (Trust, Openness, Realisation, Interdependence) Community to help participants experience and share with one another a sense of community and relatedness.

Allen, R.F. and Pilnick, S. (1973) 'Confronting the Shadow Organization: How to Detect and Defeat Negative Norms', *Organizational Dynamics*, Spring, vol. l, no. 4, pp. 3–18.

Clapp, N.W. (1974) *Work Group Norms: Leverage for Organizational Change, Part 1: Theory*, Block Petrella.

Dunphy, D.C. (1981) *Organizational Change by Choice*, McGraw-Hill, pp. 235–8.

Gibb, J.R. (1972) 'TORI Theory and Practice', in Pfeiffer, J.W. and Jones, J.E. (eds) *The 1972 Annual Handbook of Group Facilitators*, Pfeiffer/ Jossey-Bass.

Homans, G.C. (1950) *The Human Group*, Harcourt Brace.

Wohling, W. (1970) 'Attitude Change, Behaviour Change: The Role of the Training Department', *California Management Review*, vol. 13, no. 2, pp. 45–50.

See also: Achievement motivation intervention; Behaviour modification; Brainwashing; Classroom meeting model; Corporate culture training; Concept training; Discipline without punishment; Employee-designed rules; Ideological change; Information-sharing meetings; Measuring performance; Myth-making interventions; Norm clarification; Norm formation; Role prescription; TORI community experience

Novels for learning (short stories; fiction)

Management courses based on novels have a long history. The novels may have been written specifically to illustrate points about issues such as quality management (e.g., Goldratt and Cox, 1993), or existing works of fiction can be adapted. For example, the novel *Watership Down* by Richard Adams provides a good basis for discussion of Henry Mintzberg's theory of management roles. Detective stories, such as the Sherlock Holmes series by Sir Arthur Conan Doyle, illustrate the scientific method of deduction, and can be helpful for management students conducting their own research dissertations or projects.

Bludorn, A.C. (1979) 'Winning the Race: A Report on the Use of Science Fiction in the Organization Theory Classroom', *Exchange: The Organizational Behaviour Teaching Journal*, vol. 4, no. 1, pp. 7–11.

Butler, D. W. (1987) 'The Humanities and the MBA', in Johnson, J.S. (ed.) *Educating Managers: Executive Effectiveness Through Liberal Learning*, Jossey-Bass, pp. 143–69.

Coser, L.A. (1972) 'Using Literature to Teach Business Ethics', *Journal of Business and Technical Communication*, vol. 6, no. 2, pp. 187–99.

Cowden, A.C. (1989–90) 'Mystery Novels as Organizational Context', *Organizational*

Behaviour Teaching Review, vol. 14, no. 2, pp. 93–101.

Czarniawska-Joerges, B. and Guillet de Monthoux, P. (eds) (1994) *Good Novels, Better Management: Reading Organizational Realities in Fiction*, Harwood Academic Publishers.

De Mott, B. (1989) 'Reading Fiction to the Bottom Line', *Harvard Business Review*, vol. 67, no. 3, May–June, pp. 128–34.

Goldratt, E. and Cox, J. (1993) *The Goal* (2nd edn), Gower.

Grottola, M. (1994) 'Teaching the Social Geometry of Management with Literary Narrative', *Journal of Management Education*, vol. 18, no. 1, pp. 125–8.

Guillet de Monthoux, P. (1979–80) 'A 'Novel' Approach to Management', *Journal of General Management*, vol. 5, no. 2, pp. 42–52.

Harris, C. (1991) 'Using Short Stories to Teach International Management', *Journal of Management Education*, vol. 15, no. 3, pp. 374–8.

Harris, C. and Brown, W. (1989) 'Teaching Business Ethics Using Fiction: A Case that Failed', *Organizational Behaviour Teaching Review*, vol. 13, pp. 38–47.

Hassard, J. and Holliday, R. (eds) (1998) *Organizational Representation*, Sage.

Martin, C.A. and Napier, N.K. (1989–90) 'Merging Disciplines: Methods to Madness', *Organizational Behaviour Teaching Review*, vol. 14, no. 4, pp. 1–17.

Puffer, S.M. (1991) *Managerial Insights from Literature*, PWS-Kent.

Shaw, G. and Locke, K. (1993) 'Using Fiction to Develop Management Judgements', *Journal of Management Education*, vol. 17, no. 3, pp. 349–59.

Stevenson, W.B. (1996) 'A Muse of Fire or a Winter of Discontent? Teaching Shakespeare in the Leadership Course', *Journal of Management Education*, vol. 20, no. 1, pp. 39–47.

Thompson, J and McGivern, J. (1996) 'Parody, Process and Practice', *Management Learning*, vol. 27, no. 1, pp. 21–35.

See also: Dramatic skit; Drawing for learning; Inner dialogue; Literary criticism; Movie; Music for learning; Poetry for learning; Reading; Rewriting; Storytelling; Story-writing

services, banking and financial services, and many other areas. The growing recognition that organizations have social responsibilities led to the extension of the idea to provide an internal mechanism to protect employees' rights. Although some writers have argued that managers are responsible for maintaining a balance between the interests of shareholders, employees, customers and the general public, corporate justice depends on the existence of impartial procedures for reviewing management decisions, especially where non-union employees are concerned.

The corporate ombudsman's tasks include interpreting company policy, adjudicating complaints and recommending decisions. In this sense, the ombudsman can serve as the company's conscience. Rather than simply being seen as a stage in the dispute-resolution process, the ombudsman's authority and independence must be safeguarded. Ideally, the ombudsman should be engaged on a long-term contract with substantial pay as a member of the company chairman's personal staff.

The role requires wide-ranging powers. The ombudsman should be able to investigate any written complaint by any aggrieved employee, with only a few minor exceptions, and also to dismiss a complaint at any stage, with or without a hearing, subject to the duty of stating the reasons for such a dismissal in writing. In investigating a complaint, the ombudsman should have access to all the information required, including the employee's file, and, if facts are disputed, should be able to call company witnesses to attend an informal conference in a non-adversarial setting. If this fails to resolve the issue, a more adversarial approach may be necessary, with the ombudsman acting as 'devil's advocate' for both sides. The ombudsman can also serve a very useful function beyond the resolution of disputes by drawing senior management's attention to problems among the workforce.

Silver, I. (1967) 'The Corporate Ombudsman', *Harvard Business Review*, May–June, pp. 77–87.

See also: Alternative dispute-resolution; Employee assistance department; Ideological change; Let's-talk-it-over programme; Mediation; Mini-trial; Rent-a-judge

Ombudsman

An ombudsman was originally an independent arbiter appointed to investigate individuals' complaints against government bodies. During the 1990s, this approach to resolving disputes increased in popularity, with ombudsmen being established to adjudicate complaints in local government, the health services, the Scottish legal

On-going feedback system

All organizations rely on *feedback*: information supplied to an individual, group or unit about the quality, quantity or nature of their outputs, or the processes involved in the organization's operation. An effective feedback system enables errors to be corrected, helps to identify and solve problems, clarifies goals, and improves motivation. However, this information can only have a positive effect on performance if managers are motivated and trained to use it properly. The quality of feedback relies not only on its content, but also on the process: this includes how the information is communicated, how often this takes place, and the extent to which its lessons are adopted in practice. Organizations usually possess feedback systems in the form of variance accounting, management information systems, and so on. However, the information they provide may not be relevant to the organization's main activities, feedback may not be distributed in a timely manner to the employees who would benefit most from it, and managers may not understand how to use it effectively. Despite these problems, employees often resist efforts to change their organization's existing feedback systems.

To overcome these deficiencies, Nadler and colleagues suggest an alternative design which they call the on-going feedback system. Their scheme includes information about organizational processes as well as organizational performance. Feedback measures are designed and reviewed by the system users themselves, the feedback is distributed to employees at all levels in the organization, and managers are given training in how to use the information. These principles can be applied in a variety of ways, but in all cases a great deal of attention is devoted to designing the implementation process. In one study, it was decided that a task force of ten employees would review the existing feedback system and introduce measures to improve it. The fact that members came from a variety of organizational levels meant that their initial hurdle was to work through their status differences. The group met regularly over a two-month period, deciding what information should be collected, how it should be distributed, and how much of it should be fed back along with the performance data. At times, there were disagreements about which data should be included. Having designed the feedback system, they moved on to the implementation phase, beginning with meetings to outline the objectives of the feedback system and the history of its development. The aim was to ensure that employees understood the system before being required to operate it. The final stage of the implementation phase was to train the relevant managers to use the system.

Nadler and colleagues drew a number of conclusions from their research. They argued that on-going process and performance feedback systems are potentially valuable managerial tools. Whether the effects of the feedback are positive or negative depends on how managers use it. Given the importance of management's role, the design and implementation of the on-going feedback system should emphasize motivating and training managers to apply it effectively. Finally, they felt that their experiment demonstrated the value of involving employees in designing the feedback system.

Carnmann, C. and Nadler, D.A. (1976) 'Fit Control Systems to Your Managerial Style', *Harvard Business Review*, January–February.

Lawler, E.E. and Rhode, J.G. (1976) *Behaviour and Control in Organizations*, Goodyer.

Nadler, D., Mirvis, P. and Cammann, C. (1976) 'The On-going Feedback System: Experimenting with a New Management Tool', *Organizational Dynamics*, Spring, vol. 4, no. 4, pp. 63–80.

Newman, W.E. (1975) *Constructive Control: Design and Use of Control Systems*, Prentice-Hall.

See also: Feedback; Goal-setting; Goal-setting and planning groups; Management by objectives; Measuring performance; Periodic planning review; Positive feedback; Questionnaires; Recognition programmes

On-the-job training (sitting by Nellie)

This is probably the most widespread training technique in industry, in which trainees are allocated increasingly complex work tasks as they gain experience and their skills improve. One traditional approach involves the trainee observing a skilled practitioner – 'Nellie' – carrying out a particular task. The success of this method depends on a number of considerations, the most important being that, when necessary, the person serving as 'Nellie' must have the ability and time to explain to the trainee what they are doing and why. When managerial trainees are allocated to a specific manager, this may present problems, since the manager may find it too difficult or time-consuming to explain to a trainee the complex reasoning behind a particular course of action. An alternative is to attach the management trainee to a company department and ask a more junior staff member to supervise their induction. Whichever approach is adopted, it is important to ensure that the training programme is well planned and to monitor progress.

Barron, J.M., Berger, M.C. and Black. D.A. (1997) *On-the-job Training*, W.E. Updike Institute.

Broadwell, M.M. (1994) *The Supervisor and On-the-job Training*, Addison Wesley Longman.

Institute of Personnel and Development (1997) *IPD Guide to On-the-job Training*, IPD.

Jacobs, R.L. and Jones, M.J. (1995) *Structured On-the-job Training*, Berrett-Koehler.

Lawson, K. (1997) *Improving On-the-job Learning and Coaching*, American Society for Training and Development, ASTD Press.

Marchio, D., Adnot, J. and Pulido, I. (1997) 'Synergy Between On-the-job Training and Academic Education in the Case of a Newly Created Part-time Engineering Curriculum', *European Journal of Engineering Education*, vol. 22, no. 4, pp. 401–10.

Rothwell, W.J. and Kazanas, H.C. (1994) *Improving On-the-job Training*, Jossey-Bass.

Smalley, L.R. (1994) *On-the-Job Orientation and Training*, Jossey-Bass/Pfeiffer.

See also: Apprenticeship; Behaviour modelling; Coaching; Internship; Manager shadowing; One-to-one learning; Parrainage; SmartProcess

One-to-one learning (one-to-one discussion)

This approach is related to co-counselling, and forms the basis of a complete programme of study. The one-to-one discussion sessions are brief, the subject matter is varied, and the wording of all questions, even academic ones, is open-ended: for example, asking 'What is inflation?' rather than 'What are the causes of inflation?' This is because closed questions would not allow students to work from limited information. Activities are included which build self-confidence, self-knowledge and group identity, but these are considered as steps, not objectives. One-to-one learning courses are usually ungraded, but regular attendance and a certain amount of written work are required. Students are usually asked to produce a weekly written statement or 'journal' detailing their experiences, to help them consolidate their learning and develop their writing skills, as well as to provide feedback to the tutor.

In its purest form, the method relies only on one-to-one interactions between students, there being no lectures nor group work. A group of 16 or so students is divided into one-to-one partnerships, and the tutor sets a series of questions for discussion, such as: 'What is a fact?' Each partner then takes it in turns to speak uninterrupted for three minutes while the other listens, until both have spoken twice. Once this process has been completed, further questions are set. These paired discussions are supplemented by reading tasks, but the questions chosen by the tutor are broad enough to allow students either to read the set texts or develop their own lines of enquiry and find their own answers.

A variation of the method involves mixing one-to-one work with a short lecture. As before, the tutor sets a question and the pairs discuss it, but this is followed by a five-minute lecture by the tutor to remind them of the basic content and to raise problems or suggest various alternative perspectives. Following this, the class returns to one-to-one discussion.

Potts, D. (1981) 'One to One Learning', in Boud, D.J. (ed.) *Developing Student Autonomy in Learning*, Kogan Page.

Powell, M. (1997) 'Personal Tutoring in a Vocational Discipline', *Innovations in Education and Training International*, vol. 34, no. 2, pp. 92–5.

Wheeler, S. and Birtle, J. (1993) *Handbook for Personal Tutors*, Society for Research into Higher Education/Open University Press.

See also: Apprenticeship programme; Coaching; Co-counselling; Counselling; Group buzz; Journalling; Learning cell; Learning contract; On-the-job training; Parrainage; Peer teaching; Socratic group enquiry; Tutorial

Open book management

Open book management (OBM) was developed by John Case between 1983 and 1996, while working at *Inc Magazine*. It challenges management's traditional right to make far-reaching decisions which affect all staff without being obliged to explain its actions. Recognizing that employees resent feeling that change is being forced upon them, OBM's ideology rests on two basic principles: managers and subordinates should work together, and managers should explain the reasons behind their decisions. Providing this information encourages staff to think like managers, enabling them to understand the company's finances and monitor its performance.

OBM demands that managers develop new ways to involve staff and improve their performance. Some are reluctant to adopt this approach because it makes them accountable to their staff, and any errors they make will be apparent to all. Its advantages are that it can improve company performance by harnessing the collective intelligence of the organization's staff. Establishing a system which forecasts, plans and provides key data allows everyone to check that they are moving in the right direction, and creates a culture of creativity because responsibility for success is shared by all.

Case, J. (1997) *Open Book Management: The Coming Business Revolution*, Harper Business.

Case, J. (1997) 'Opening the Books', *Harvard Business Review*, March–April, pp. 118–27.

Case, J. (1998) *Open Book Management Experience*, Nicholas Brealey.

Ivanic, C. (1997) *Open Book Management*, Crisp Publications.

McCoy, T.J. (1996) *Creating an Open Book*

Organization, American Management Association, AMACOM.

Schuster, J.P., Carpenter, J. and Kane, M.P. (1996) *The Power of Open Book Management*, Wiley.

Schuster, J.P., Carpenter, J. and Kane, M.P. (1997) *The Open Book Management Field Book*, Wiley.

See also: Conflict-stimulation techniques; Empowerment; Information-sharing meetings; Open forums; Organizational citizenship; Participation; Team briefing

Open encounter

This approach, which adopts some of the principles of gestalt therapy, was developed by Will Schutz and others at the Esalen Institute in California. It differs from Carl Rogers' basic encounter method in several ways. First, it emphasizes that people interact – often unintentionally – in physical ways. In a typical session, participants do not sit on chairs but are encouraged to remove their shoes and sit on the floor. A second difference is that the facilitator takes on a more active role: for instance, taking responsibility for setting the group's basic norms and encouraging it to progress. This makes open encounter a more intensive experience, since the norms the facilitator sets are usually more demanding than those the group would set itself, as is the case in basic encounter. There is an emphasis on energy throughout: participants' words or actions are held to be less important than the energy behind them.

Schutz, W.C. (1967) *Joy: Expanding Awareness*, Random.

Schutz, W.C. (1979) *Elements of Encounter*, Irvington Publications.

Schutz, W.C. (1982) *Here Comes Everybody*, Irvington Publications.

Schutz, W.C. (1991) *Joy: Twenty Years Later*, Ten Speed Press.

Smith, P.B. (1980) *Group Processes and Personnel Change*, Chapter 8, Harper and Row.

See also: Awareness training; Basic encounter; Encounter group; Gestalt techniques

Open forums

Open forum meetings give staff the opportunity to ask questions and make observations about any aspect of the company's operations in a relaxed atmosphere. This approach has been adopted by some furniture retailing firms. Area managers hold open forums in each of the stores under their control every month, and these are attended by representatives from all job categories in the store, including salespeople, cleaners and warehouse operatives. The area manager passes the meetings' minutes up the hierarchy through the operations manager and regional manager to the retail operators' director, who sits on the board of directors. This enables board meetings to address any issues which are particularly serious or which seem to be emerging in a definable pattern.

Goldsmith, W. and Clutterbuck, D. (1985) *The Winning Streak*, Penguin.

See also: Chairman's forum; Employee-guided management; Information-sharing meetings; Management information meeting; Open book management; Team briefing

Open learning (distance learning; teaching at a distance)

Learners may be unable to take part in traditional courses for a number of reasons: domestic or work commitments may make it impossible for them to attend at the usual times, a disability or their location may make it difficult for them to attend college, or their interests may be so specialized that there are too few students in a particular area to justify setting up a course. A wide range of flexible, student-centred learning systems have been developed to address these problems by allowing learners a measure of freedom in choosing when and where they study.

Open learning systems can be divided into three distinct types. The first and perhaps best known is *distance learning*, as adopted by the Open University, in which students receive course assignments through the post and are supported by a tutorial facility at local or regional level. Second, there are *locally based systems*, such as FlexiStudy, where students work at home while maintaining contact with the college by attending regular tutorials. Finally there are various college-based systems known as *flexastudy*, *learning on demand* or *learning by appointment*, in which students use college facilities such as libraries or self-learning programmes at times which suit them, and receive tutorial support from staff based on their individual learning needs. Although students engaged in these programmes may lack immediate access to a tutor, the support organizations provide tuition and guidance to help them plan their studies.

Brown, S. (1997) *Open and Distance Learning: Case Studies from Industry and Education*, Kogan Page.

Calder, J. and McCallum, A. (1997) *Open and*

Flexible Learning in Vocational Education and Training, Kogan Page.

Marland, P. (1997) *Towards More Effective Open and Distance Learning*, Kogan Page.

Ruble, G. (1997) *The Costs and Economics of Open and Distance Learning*, Kogan Page.

See also: Directed private study; Distance education; Flexastudy; FlexiStudy

Open space technology

Open space technology (OST) was developed by Harrison Owen after running an organizational change conference. He realized that the most valuable exchanges occurred during the coffee breaks, when people could meet, identify topics of common interest and chat freely. Bunker and Alban describe open space technology as a whole-system participative work approach, but what Owen designed is, in effect, a conference that consists entirely of coffee breaks, enabling participants to define their own agendas and focus on the issues they consider most important.

An open space technology conference consists of a relatively simple structure based on a traditional African village with a central circular 'market'. The venue must include a large, open area which can accommodate a circle of chairs several rows deep, as up to 500 people may attend the event over the course of one to three days.

The facilitator opens the conference by giving an hour-long talk to explain its purpose, how it will be run and the topics it is hoped will be discussed. This opening address sets the tone and encourages participants to identify issues within the general theme that are of concern to them, and to be prepared to take responsibility for them. Although the proceedings are loosely structured, the facilitator explains a number of ground rules. The agenda for the event is created by conference participants themselves. Any participant can offer to turn up at a particular place and time to initiate discussion about a topic, and agree to type up some notes about the discussion afterwards and deliver them to the OST news room. They register their topic title by displaying a card on the community bulletin board which covers one wall, and other participants can sign up for whichever discussions interest them. A fundamental rule is the *law of two feet*: participants may go wherever they wish, and can walk away from discussions that do not engage them in order to try to find ones that do. Flitting between groups is acceptable. OST also relies on four basic principles: *whoever comes is the right person* – the quality of interaction is what matters, not how many people turn up or who they are; *whatever happens is the only thing that could have* – people should be prepared to be

surprised by what takes place; *whenever it starts is the right time* – creativity and movement are valued above structure and continuity, and finally, *when it is over, it is over* – participants should leave when there is no more to say. The OST News Room gathers together the summaries from each session, and these are shared at half-hour Morning News and Evening News plenary sessions, during which the entire conference can share experiences, propose new topics, and raise issues of a general nature.

Bunker, B.B. and Alban, B.T. (1997) 'Open Space Technology', in *Large Group Interventions: Engaging the Whole System for Rapid Change*, Jossey-Bass, pp. 177–95.

Owen, H. (1992) *Open Space Technology: A User's Guide*, Abbott Press.

Owen, H. (1993) *Open Space Technology*, Abbott Press.

Owen, H. (1995) *Tales from Open Space*, Abbott Press.

See also: Action training and research; Business process re-engineering; Conference Model; Fast-cycle full-participation work design; Future search; Large-group intervention; Open systems planning; Participative design; Real-time strategic change; Real-time work design; Search conference; Socio-technical systems design; Strategic planning process; Simu-Real; Work-Out

Open systems planning

Open systems planning (OSP) was developed by Clark, Krone and McWhinney. Their model goes some way towards integrating the disparate aspects of organizational development by taking into account the relationships between an organization, its component systems and the changing environment. In any organization, a number of interdependent features can be identified: goals and strategies, tasks and technology, structures and procedures, people and skills, experiences and attitudes, processes such as communicating, planning, problem-solving, decision-making and evaluating, and the organization's culture and style. The OSP model suggests that for organizations to be healthy and to survive and grow in their changing environment, there needs to be a balance across these boundaries. By promoting systematic thinking that encourages people to think 'outside-in' – from the environment to the organization – OSP forces them to face current realities and draw up plans to establish priorities in the medium-term future. By a process of diagnosis, using the appropriate data-collection methods and analysis techniques, conflicts and imbalances can be detected and action plans developed.

Open systems planning stresses the importance of the environment, the core socio-technical processes, and the dynamic equilibrium within and between the internal and external domains in which these transactions take place. It calls for a five-step process. First, a *present scenario* is created by defining the external domains of the environment, as well as expectations and interactions. The same process is then carried out in terms of the organization's internal domain and identity. Finally, the transactions across the system boundary are defined. Step two draws up a *realistic future scenario* by considering the same three areas. Step three again considers these three areas, this time formulating an *idealistic future scenario*. In step four, participants *compare the two future scenarios*, identifying broad areas of consensus, controversy and total disagreement. The final step involves *planning an action programme* to address the areas identified, including timelines.

OSP can enable an organization's management to focus more clearly on its strategic goals, and to look objectively at its present responses to demands. It can also allow the projection of a likely demand system if no action is taken to bring about an ideal demand system. OSP can help to define what activities and behaviour would have to be developed for this ideal to be achieved, and provides means to analyse the cost-effectiveness of undertaking these activities.

Bunker, B.B. and Alban, B.T. (1997) *Large Group Interventions: Engaging the Whole System for Rapid Change*, Jossey-Bass.
Jayararn, G.K. (1976) 'Open Systems Planning', in Bennis, W.G., Benne, K.D., Chin, R. and Cory, K. (eds) *The Planning of Change* (3rd edn), Holt, Rinehart and Winston, pp. 275–83.
Krone, C. (1974) 'Open Systems Redesign', in Adams, J. (ed.) *Theory and Management in Organizational Development: An Evolutionary Process*, NTL Institute for Applied Behavioural Science.
Merry, U. and Allerhand, N.E. (1977) *Developing Teams and Organizations*, Addison Wesley Longman, pp. 117–24.
Mungall, D.K. (1982) 'Organizational Change on a North Sea Project', *Personnel Management*, May.

See also: Action training and research; Business process re-engineering; Conference Model; Fast-cycle full-participation work design; Future search; Large-group intervention; Open space technology; Participative design; Real-time strategic change; Real-time work design; Scenario planning; Search conference; Socio-technical systems design; Strategic planning process; Simu-Real; Work-Out

Organizational analysis

'Organizational analysis' is a generic term for a wide variety of techniques which examine aspects of an organization in an attempt to improve its performance. The analytical framework and the aspects chosen for study will depend on the individual analyst's view of what is important, and this in turn will be dictated by their preferred theory of organizational functioning.

Galbraith, J. (1973) *Designing Complex Organizations*, Addison Wesley Longman.
Galbraith, J. (1977) *Organizational Design*, Addison Wesley Longman.
Kotter, J.P. (1978) *Organizational Dynamics: Diagnosis and Intervention*, Addison Wesley Longman.
Lawrence, P.R. and Lorsch, J.W. (1969) *Developing Organizations: Diagnosis and Action*, Addison Wesley Longman.

See also: ACHIEVE model; Assessment of the organization as a system; Diagnostic activities; Family group diagnostic meeting; Looking for trouble; Management audit; Open systems planning; 7-S framework

Organizational citizenship

There are certain types of behaviour among employees which management considers desirable, but which do not necessarily form part of a formal job description. These 'pro-social' or 'extra-role' aspects combine to form a model of organizational citizenship, which can be analysed into five types of behaviour: *altruism*, *courtesy*, *civic virtue*, *conscientiousness* and *sportsmanship*. These manifest themselves in behaviours such as helping others with their work when necessary, volunteering and innovating, and not complaining or arguing. Because they are not linked to the formal reward system, such features are sometimes labelled 'good soldier syndrome'. Behaving like an organizational citizen obviously has a positive impact on company performance, so management often tries to create a work environment which encourages it, and also takes such personality aspects into account when recruiting staff.

Brief, A. and Motowidlo, S. (1986) Pro-social Organizational Behaviours', *Academy of Management Journal*, vol. 11, pp. 710–25.
Organ, D. (1988) *Organizational Citizenship Behaviour: The Good Soldier Syndrome*, Lexington Books.
Turnipseed, D. and Murison, G. (1996) 'Organizational Citizenship Behaviour: An Examination of the Influence of the Workplace', *Leadership and*

Organization Development Journal, vol. 17, no. 2, pp. 42–7.

See also: Conflict-stimulation techniques; Corporate culture training; Empowerment; Information-sharing meeting; Induction training; Open book management; Open forums; Participation; Team briefing; Role-modelling

Organizational climate analysis

'Organizational climate' is one of the most widely used but least adequately defined terms. Sometimes it is held to reflect the general pattern of managerial practices and policies, perhaps most clearly defined in Rensis Likert's Systems 1, 2, 3 and 4, of which the last is the most participative. Others who have defined the term, for example Litwin and Stringer (1968), view it as a motivational pattern among organizational members which is supported by the organizational reward system. Blake and Mouton (1969) use 'organizational climate' to refer to the way in which an organization fits into their people concern/production concern grid, claiming that a '9.9' climate (maximum concern for both people and production) results in the greatest organizational effectiveness.

In general, it can be said that organizational climate analysis is a way of measuring people's perceptions of what it is like to work in a particular environment. Research has shown that motivation affects behaviour and organizational performance. Organization climate describes a set of conditions that arouse or inhibit various motivational states. By changing the climate, the manager is able to influence employee motivation and, in turn, performance. For this reason, organization climate analysis can be considered an organizational change strategy.

Blake, R.R. and Mouton, J.S. (1969) *Building a Dynamic Corporation Through Grid Organization Development*, Addison Wesley Longman.
Hofstede, G. (1984) *Culture's Consequences: International Differences in Work-related Values, Volume 5*, Cross Cultural Research and Methodology Series, Sage.
Likert, R. (1961) *New Patterns of Management*, McGraw-Hill.
Likert, R. (1967) *The Human Organization*, McGraw-Hill.
Litwin, G.H. and Stringer, R.A. (1968) *Motivation and Organizational Climate*, Division of Research, Harvard Business School Press.
Margulies, N. (1974) 'Organization Development and Changes in Organization Climate', *Public Personnel Administration*, vol. 2, pp. 88–92.
Taguri, R. and Litwin, G.H. (eds) (1968) *Organizational Climate: Explorations of a Concept*, Division of Research, Graduate School of Business Administration, Harvard University.

See also: Action research; Attitude survey; Corporate culture training; Data-based intervention; Development of a new management/operating philosophy; Family group diagnostic meeting; Greenfield plants; Ideological change; Learning organization; Managerial strategy change; Mission cards; Myth-making intervention; Questionnaires

Organizational laboratory

Organizational laboratories simulate a range of different organizational configurations, enabling participants to analyse the consequences of each design. While maintaining the quality of involvement and reality which is integral to the success of T-groups, they focus on the relationships between groups, the causes of conflict and ways to resolve it, and the process of setting goals. Organizational laboratories are designed to deal with larger organizational systems, and can involve up to a hundred people. Their applications include preparing individuals for company mergers.

This approach differs from other types of laboratory in that an organizational laboratory consists solely of a model formulated in advance by the participants: in this sense, the model *is* the design. The model consists of a set of assumptions concerning learning about an organization, and it also establishes certain parameters, such as the time boundaries (start and endpoints) and the physical resources available. However, it does not prescribe either training exercises or detailed, timed activities within these boundaries. Underlying this design is the view that if a behavioural vacuum is created, participants will project into it their own assumptions about organizations, such as the appropriate management behaviours, decision-making processes and organizational structures. These assumptions are reflected in participants' behaviour, and are modified as a result of feedback about regarding their consequences. As with other forms of laboratory training, time is devoted to formulating theories and helping participants understand the emerging phenomena. Attention is also paid to individual and group skill development, to help participants cope with the problems encountered in the simulated organization.

Boydell, T. and Pedlar, M. (1976) 'An Organizational Laboratory in Ghana', *Industrial and Commercial Training*, vol. 8, no. 5, pp. 187–92.
Handy, C. (1974) 'Putting an Organization into the Classroom', *Journal of European Training*, vol. 3, no. 2, pp. 85–96.

Harrison, R. and Oshry, B. (1972) 'Laboratory Training in Human Relations and Organizational Behaviour', *European Training*, vol. 1, no. 2.

Harvey, J.B., Oshry, B.I. and Watson, G. (1970) 'A Design for a Laboratory Exploring Issues of Organization', *Journal of Applied Behavioural Science*, vol. 6, no. 4, pp. 401–11.

Margulies, N. and Wallace, J. (1973) *Organizational Change: Techniques and Applications*, Scott Foresman, p. 70.

Morton, R.B. and Bass, B.M. (1964) 'The Organizational Training Laboratory', *Training Director's Journal*, vol. 18, October, pp. 2–18.

Reynolds M. (1976) 'Experience-Based Designs in Organisational Development', in Cooper, C.L. (ed.) *Developing Social Skills in Managers: Advances in Group Training*, Macmillan.

Walker, H. (1975) 'Organizational Simulation in Management Training', *Industrial and Commercial Training*, vol. 7, no. 3, pp. 11–20.

See also: Basic encounter; Cluster laboratory; Cousin laboratory; Encounter group; Gestalt techniques; Group development laboratory; Group dynamics laboratory; Human relations laboratory; Industrial dynamics; Instrumented laboratory; Laboratory training; Micro-lab; Mini-society; Personal development laboratory; Power laboratory; Psychodrama; Sensitivity (T-group) training; Tavistock conference method; Team laboratory

Organizational mirror (mirror groups)

The organizational mirror was developed by Sheldon Davis and colleagues at TRW Systems Inc. to enable a unit or department within an organization – the *host* group – to obtain feedback from other departments, suppliers or customers about its performance and how it is perceived. Although the aim is to improve relations between the host group and the other groups, this intervention differs from the inter-group team-building exercise in that three or more groups can take part, and only departmental representatives are involved, rather than the whole department. This is a one-way process: the host group sees itself mirrored by the respondent groups, but it does not reflect back its own perceptions of them. The organizational mirror epitomizes the action research concept. One of its most useful characteristics is that it brings together mixed groups of data-recipients and data-producers in a problem-solving relationship in order to improve effectiveness. The relevance of the information is ensured by using it immediately to generate ideas about how to improve matters.

The intervention consists of eight steps. First, an organizational unit which is experiencing difficulties with other units asks them to send representatives to attend a meeting and provide feedback on their view of the host unit, and the consultant interviews the representatives beforehand to discover the nature and difficulty of the problems which will be raised. Next, following some opening remarks by the manager of the host group, expressing a desire to 'see ourselves as others see us', the consultant feeds back to the whole group the information obtained from the interviews. In step three, the respondents form a 'fishbowl' to discuss this data, while the representatives from the host group sit on the outside and listen but do not participate. In the next step, the roles are reversed, the host group representatives sitting in the fishbowl to discuss the comments they have heard. They seek clarification from the departmental representatives in order to ensure they have understood the information, and a general discussion then takes place to explore the issues raised, but no solutions are sought at this stage. Problem-solving occurs during the sixth step, during which mixed sub-groups made up of representatives from the host group and the repondent groups identify the most important changes which need to be made to improve the host group's functioning. In the penultimate step, the whole group reconvenes to draw up a master list in order to work out specific action plans to bring about these changes. The whole group then listens to a summary report from each sub-group, the details of action plans are finalized, participants are assigned tasks, and target dates for completion are agreed. The final step consists of a follow-up meeting to review progress.

Blake, R.R. and Mouton, J.S. (1976) *Consultation*, Addison Wesley Longman, pp. 182–3.

Fordyce, J.K. and Weil, R. (1971) *Managing With People*, Addison Wesley Longman, pp. 101–5.

French, W.L. and Bell, C.H. (1984) *Organization Development: Behavioural Science Interventions for Organization Improvement* (3rd edn), Prentice-Hall, pp. 159–60.

Margulies, N. and Wallace, J. (1973) *Organizational Change: Techniques and Applications*, Scott Foresman, pp. 32–3.

See also: Action research; Confrontation groups; Confrontation meeting; Customer interface meeting; External mirror; Family group diagnostic meeting; Fishbowl; Follow-up; Interface groups; Inter-group team-building; Product familiarization programme; Sensing

Organizational role analysis

Organizational role analysis (ORA) was developed by Bruce Reed and his colleagues at the Grubb Institute, who recognized that although role analysis may in one sense be a self-limiting technique in relation to a particular job, in another sense it provides people with a way to preserve what power they have, both inside and outside their immediate work environment. Their approach assumes that there are significant differences between what managers are supposed to do in their work (their normative role), their experience of what actually happens (their existential role) and others' observations of their behaviour (their phenomenological role).

While traditional consultancy approaches attempt to move people from where they appear to be to where they should be, ORA attempts to establish why they are where they are, and what the outcomes of change strategies are likely to be. The objective is to enable managers to derive their own basic *role idea*: a concept of how they relate to their job, which helps them to determine and regulate their own behaviour at work. The basic role idea can then be related to subsidiary role ideas, which allows the connections between these ideas and the systems, groups and individuals within the organization to be traced. This makes it possible to determine what skills, beliefs, capacities and resources can be marshalled by the role idea to improve the manager's performance. As the ORA consultation proceeds, both manager and consultant develop a clearer idea of the likely outcomes of any action contemplated. A major breakthrough occurs when managers recognize that the map of their organization they are describing reflects their own assumptions, beliefs and feelings: in attempting to describe their organization, they are – at least in part – describing themselves.

McGivering, I. (1980) 'Facilitating Re-entry Through Role Analysis', in Beck, J. and Cox, C. (eds) *Advances in Management Education*, Wiley.

Reed, B. 'Organizational Role Analysis', in Cooper, C.L. (ed.) (1976) *Developing Social Skills in Managers: Advances in Group Training*, Macmillan.

See also: Role analysis technique; Role-modelling; Role-reversal; Role prescription; Role rehearsal; Role training

Outdoor training (outdoor management development; adventure training; wilderness training)

Based on the belief that leadership is the key to effective management in general, this approach owes much to military officer training courses, where participants may be set tasks such as crossing a river using limited materials. In contrast to the more traditional classroom-bound or training centre-based forms of management development, small groups of participants usually work on practical tasks in the open air, gaining experience in understanding group dynamics and the roles of both leaders and followers. The programmes aim to increase self-confidence by promoting self-reliance and shifting responsibility on to participants, developing their awareness of their strengths and weaknesses, and enabling them to tap into latent resources.

A number of training organizations provide outdoor management training programmes, such as the Leadership Trust, Outward Bound Ltd and the John Ridgeway Adventure Centre, and a number of major British companies have used them as team-building exercises. Because they are usually run as intensive residential courses, participants often become totally immersed in the activities. They remain in their groups continuously, and the exercises tend to be physically demanding and promote emotional involvement. The activities may be preceded or followed by tutor presentation sessions to give conceptual guidance and interpret the experiences.

Bank, J. (1994) *Outdoor Development for Managers*, Gower.

Buller, R.F., McEvoy, G.M. and Cragun, J.R. (1995) 'Developing Student Skills and Assessing MBA Programme Outcomes Through Outdoor Training', *Journal of Management Education*, vol. 19, no. 1, pp. 35–53.

Burnett, D. and James, K. (1994), 'Using the Outdoors to Facilitate Personal Change in Managers', *Journal of Management Development*, vol. 13, no. 9, pp. 14–24.

Burtletson, L. and Grint, K. (1996) 'The Deracination of Politics: Outdoor Management Development', *Management Learning*, vol. 27, no. 2, pp. 187–202.

Ibbetson, A. and Newell, S. (1996) 'Winner Takes All: An Evaluation of Adventure-based Experiential Training', *Management Learning*, vol. 27, no. 2, pp. 163–85.

Institute of Personnel and Development (1998) *IPD Guide on Outdoor Training*, IPD.

Irvine, D. and Wilson, J.P. (1994) 'Outdoor Management Development: Reality or Illusion?', *Journal of Management Development*, vol. 13, no. 5, pp. 25–37.

Krouwell, B. and Goodwill, S. (1994) *Management Development Outdoors: A Practical Guide to Getting Results*, Kegan Paul.

Tuson, M. (1994) *Outdoor Training for Employee Effectiveness*, Institute of Personnel and Development.

Wagner, R.J., Baldwin, T.T. and Rowland, C.C. (1991) 'Outdoor Training: Revolution or Fad?',

Training and Development Journal, vol. 45, no. 3, pp. 51–6.

See also: Decroly method; Educational visit; Field format; Field trip; Studycade

Outplacement counselling

When an employer has to dispense with the services of an employee for whatever reason, it may offer outplacement counselling to help them come to terms with the loss of their job, and ease the transition to another work situation. Outplacement counselling can be a valuable human resource management tool. Its proponents argue that a dismissal represents a point at which the interests of the employee and the company converge, since (disregarding macro-economic factors) it reflects a failure on the part of the individual, the company, or both. Brammer and Humberger estimate that in 50 per cent of cases, employees are dismissed because they have failed to perform or to get on with colleagues, or have not developed in their job. Other reasons include organizations' failure to select, train, counsel or evaluate their employees effectively. They observe: 'Everybody wins in outplacement counselling, the organization gets rid of troublesome situations, office morale improves, and terminated employees usually get better jobs than they had before.'

Outplacement counsellors should not be confused with career guidance counsellors or those consultants who charge individuals for occupational assessment and assistance in planning their job-seeking campaigns. Outplacement counsellors do not function as job search agencies, employment experts or management recruiters, but are usually employed by organizations which are adopting the approach as part of a general strategy to increase productivity, deal with problem employees or reduce staffing levels (e.g., the American firms Weyerhauser, Pfizer, Citicorp and the Goddard Flight Centre). An important aspect of the outplacement counselling process is that it adopts a holistic approach, focusing on rebuilding employees' self-esteem, encouraging them to find new meaning in life, and helping them to get the right balance between work and family life. Its aim is to provide advice which enables people to conduct their own job-hunting campaigns or pursue retraining plans that will lead to a new job.

Brammer, L.M. and Humberger, F.H. (1984) *Outplacement and Inplacement*, Prentice-Hall.
Leibowitz, Z. and Schlossberg, N. (1980) 'Organization Support Systems as Buffers to Job Loss', *Journal of Vocational Behaviour*, vol. 17, pp. 204–17.
Meyer, J.L. and Shadle, C.C. (1994) *The Changing Outplacement Process*, Quorum Books.
Morin, W. and Yorks, L. (1982) *Outplacement Techniques*, American Management Association, AMACOM.
Pickman, A.J. (1994) *Complete Guide to Outplacement Counselling*, Lawrence Erlbaum Associates.
Silverman, E. and Sass, S. (1982) 'Applying the Outplacement Concept', *Training and Development Journal*, February, pp. 70–85.

See also: Alcohol recovery programmes; Closure; Coaching; Counselling; Downsizing; Early retirement; Job support; Recruitment; Stress management

Outsourcing

Outsourcing involves an organization subcontracting – or contracting out the production of components or the provision of services. Contracting out common company services such as catering, cleaning, delivery and information technology is a well-established practice frequently adopted to cut costs. However, in recent years strategic outsourcing has been regarded as one component in a more radical, longer-term organizational change strategy, involving an ever-increasing range of activities. Many companies see it as part of a continuing reappraisal of their core competencies in an attempt to develop their competitive advantage, but there are a number of pitfalls. The company may lose control over the manufacture of its products or the delivery of its service, leading to customer dissatisfaction. In-company expertise may be lost, and contract workers may be less committed to ensuring quality and standards of service. In addition, the savings may not be as great as was anticipated, and the costs of researching, negotiating, administering and controlling numerous subcontractors may be substantial. Moreover, unless great care is taken in choosing which core competencies to discard, there is a danger that the company may experience a long-term decline through being 'hollowed out': for instance, one radical outsourcing decision involved a company closing down its training and personnel departments to allow it to concentrate on its main business.

Burnett, R. (1998) *Outsourcing IT: The Legal Aspects*, Gower.
Institute of Personnel and Development (1998) *IPD Guide to Outsourcing*, IPD.
Johnson, M. (1997) *Outsourcing*, Butterworth-Heinemann.
Kochan, T.A., Wells, J.C. and Smith, M. (1992) 'Consequences of a Failed IR System: Contract Workers in the Petrochemical Industry', *Sloan Management Review*, vol. 33, no. 4, pp. 78–89.

KPMG (1995) *Best Practice Guidelines for Outsourcing*, Stationery Office Books.

Peisch, R. (1995) 'When Outsourcing Goes Awry', *Harvard Business Review*, May–June, pp. 24–37.

Quinn, J.B, and Hilmer, F. (1994) 'Strategic Outsourcing', *Sloan Management Review*, pp. 43–55.

Rothery, B. and Robertson, I. (1995) *The Truth About Outsourcing*, Gower.

White, R. and James, B. (1996) *The Outsourcing Manual*, Gower.

See also: Linked subcontracting; Network organizations; Staff exchange; Vendor excellence awards

Overhead value analysis

Overhead value analysis (OVA) is an intervention technique associated with the consultancy firm McKinsey & Co. Although it can be used as a problem-solving method to improve organizational effectiveness, it can also serve as a standard accounting tool, in which case it provides a powerful technique for budgetary control and organizational development. From the problem-solving perspective, this intervention is targeted at the functional level in the organization. As the OVA process develops up the line, the field of vision becomes wider, until a careful assessment is made at the highest level. Its outcome is a set of budgets and action plans to be implemented.

The application of this method requires a temporary restructuring of the company while the OVA co-ordinating team interacts with the company management committee, heads of functional units and unit managers. The OVA process consists of six steps. First, the consultant discusses the company's objectives with its directors. These are then distilled into written aims and guidelines, which are supplied to senior managers. Next, the consultant conducts a communications and training exercise to create the OVA culture. The functional unit managers then carry out a value analysis. The plans based on the results of this value analysis are presented to senior managers for approval. Finally, the plans are implemented. The most important activity in this process is the value analysis itself, which can be broken down into four activities: restructuring costs around the products and services, generating cost-reduction ideas, weighing risks against potential benefits, and selecting the most attractive ideas for action.

See also: ACHIEVE model; Assessment of the organization as a system; Benchmarking; Diagnostic activities; Family group diagnostic meeting; Looking for trouble; Management audit; 7-S framework

Overseas project (expatriate assignment)

For the purposes of this entry, the term 'overseas project' refers to an assignment undertaken by a student, whereas 'expatriate assignment' refers to one involving a manager.

With the growth of globalization, a new species, the 'Euromanager' or 'global manager', has been born. The 'year abroad' has long been a compulsory element of most undergraduate language degrees, and the need to prepare management students for the international dimension of their future work has meant that a number of business schools now have exchange arrangements with counterparts in Europe and the USA. Full-time students are often required to complete an *overseas project*, such as conducting a study or carrying out a work task in a country or culture which is unfamiliar to them, either as part of their undergraduate or Master's degree programme.

In an *expatriate assignment*, an organization posts a manager to a location in another country. This arrangement lasts for longer than a business trip and, since the manager's operational base is transferred to the foreign country, it requires that they reside there. Expatriate assignments offer a number of learning opportunities. For example, it is quite likely that the company's headquarters will want the individual to take a certain course of action, while local circumstances may dictate that this is inappropriate. This means that the managers involved usually face new and complex issues unlike any they may have encountered in their home country.

Black, J.S., Gregersen, H.B. and Mendenhall, M. (1992) *Global Assignments: Successfully Expatriating and Repatriating International Managers*, Jossey-Bass.

'Expatriation', special issue of *International Journal of Human Resource Management* (1997), vol. 8, no. 4.

Fontaine, G. (1993) 'Training for the Three Key Challenges Encountered in All Multinational Assignments', *Leadership and Organization Development Journal*, vol. 14, no. 3, pp. 7–14.

Guzzo, R.A. (1996) 'The Expatriate Employee', in Cooper, C.L. and Rousseau, D.M. (eds) *Trends in Organizational Behaviour, Volume 3*, Wiley, pp. 123–37.

Harvey, M. (1998) 'Dual Career Couples During International Relocation: The Training Spouse', *International Journal of Human Resource Management*, vol. 9, no. 2, pp. 309–31.

Prahalad, C.K. (1990) 'Globalization: The Intellectual and Managerial Challenges', *Human Resource Management*, vol. 29, pp. 27–37.

Richards, D. (1996) 'Strangers in a Strange Land: Expatriate Paranoia and the Dynamics of Exclusion', *International Journal of Human Resource Management*, vol. 7, no. 2, pp. 533–71.

Stroh, L.K. and Dennis, L.E. (1997) 'What's Fair is Fair: A Case Study in Affirmative Action on the Global Scale', *Journal of Management Education*, vol. 21, no. 2, pp. 110–16.

Tung, R.L. (1987) 'Selection and Training of Personnel for Overseas Assignments', *Journal of World Business*, vol. 16, no. 1, pp. 68–87.

See also: Cross-cultural sensitivity training; Diversity training; Field project attachment; Industrial project; Job swop; Project method; Project orientation; Real-life entrepreneurial project

Panel discussion

In a panel discussion, a small group, usually four to six people, discusses a topic of which they have specialized knowledge in the presence of an audience, which simply listens without participating. This technique is useful in clarifying or identifying problems or issues, presenting several different points of view on a given topic, or stimulating interest. Although it is relatively simple to administer, there are a number of considerations which dictate whether or not it will be successful.

The first issue to address is whether a panel discussion will provide the best way to achieve the learning objective, or whether some other technique would be more appropriate. The panel should be seated on a raised platform or stage to ensure the entire audience can see, and a public address system should be used if large numbers are attending. Much depends on the skills of the moderator or panel leader and the quality of the panel members. A skilled moderator can extract points from the panel and create an informal atmosphere, which can improve the audience's understanding and appreciation, but all too frequently each panel member is left to develop the discussion theme as they see fit, with little attention being paid to co-ordinating, integrating or summarizing their contributions. In addition, although a fairly large and diverse panel may lead to a more thorough discussion of the topic, there is a danger that the more vocal members may dominate the discussion.

See also: Brains Trust; Clinic meeting; Colloquy meeting; Conference meeting; Forum meeting; Gordon seminar; Institute meeting; Interview meeting; Listening team; Symposium meeting

Parallel career ladders (dual career ladders; vertical horizontal management)

This is a structural device designed to retain good technical and professional employees by ensuring that they are given attention, recognition and rewards equal to those of managerial staff. Its effect is to balance the rewards for line and staff personnel on the one hand, and high-achieving individual performers in non-managerial areas on the other. Those companies which operate a parallel career ladders often have some sort of 'technology council', headed by the managing director, which includes the corporate fellows as well as line managers. This approach has also been adopted in the service sector by the UK government, which has recently sought to encourage senior school teachers and nurses to remain in technical rather than managerial posts by adjusting the reward structure.

Clifford and Cavanagh describe how in one electronics company, the parallel career ladder is designed to encourage 'highly competent technical contributors to continue their career growth without the necessity of assuming line management responsibilities'. This company's dual career ladder is shown overleaf. The technical ladder is shown on the left-hand side of the figure, running upwards from the level of senior product engineer through to corporate fellow. The parallel managerial positions are depicted on the right-hand side of the chart. At the top of the organization are two kinds of leaders: managers who influence and develop others, and those who mainly serve as strategists and advocates. The latter influence the company's policy and its key decisions. In many instances, the top individual contributors earn more than their managerial counterparts.

Clifford, D.K. and Cavanagh, R.E. (1986) *The Winning Performance: How America's Midsize Companies Succeed*, Sidgwick and Jackson, p. 14.

See also: Collateral organization; Managerial decentralization; Plural chief executive; Recognition programmes; Structural interventions

Parrainage

While parrainage was originally developed in universities, a number of its aspects could be adapted to company induction programmes and employee counselling systems. In the educational context, a senior student (*parrain*) is appointed to serve as counsellor and tutor to four or five new entrants (*filleuls*) in the same department, to help them adapt to their new environment. The professors supervising the system meet regularly with the parrains to provide guidance and help them deal with problems beyond their competence, and often gain valuable feedback about general course problems. Early meetings between parrains and filleuls explain the purpose and procedures of the system, and address issues such as how to use the library and how to organize their study time. Later, more advanced topics such as note-taking skills and the course curriculum may be discussed. If requested by the filleuls, the formal, scheduled group meetings may be followed by informal or individual sessions. The Austrian Union of Students operated a version of this method which was systematic, in that the parrainage groups were also learning groups, and the senior students were given group dynamics training during the summer vacation before they took up their responsibilities as parrains.

Gentry, N.O. (1974) 'Three Models of Training and Utilization', *Professional Psychology*, vol. 5, pp. 207–14.
Goldschmidt, B. and Goldschmidt, M.L. (1976) 'Peer Teaching in Higher Education: A Review', *Higher Education*, vol. 5, pp. 9–33.
Goldschmidt, M. (1981) 'Parrainage: Students Helping Each Other', in Boud, D. (ed.) *Developing Student Autonomy in Learning*, Kogan Page.
Wrenn, R.L. and Mencke, R. (1972) 'Students Who Counsel Students', *Personnel and Guidance Journal*, vol. 50, pp. 687–9.

See also: Agenda method; Apprenticeship programme; Assignment to manager with high development skills; Induction training; Learning cell; Learning contract; On-the-job training; One-to-one learning: Peer counselling; Peer teaching; Rotation training; Teaching as learning

Part-time working

In many organizations, the 35–40-hour working week is no longer seen as the norm. In an effort to find more appropriate approaches, some companies have linked remuneration to the number of hours spent at work. In each company section, employees are required to work a certain number of hours per week averaged over a period, depending on their section's workload and customer demand. The

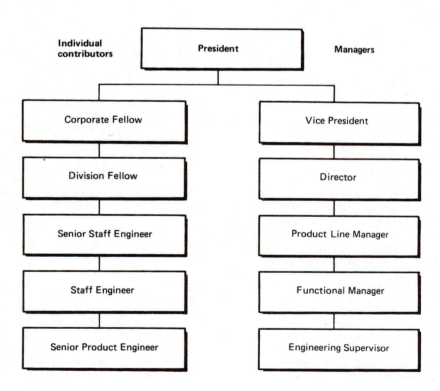

Parellel career ladder

minimum commitment is usually 35 hours, and this dictates the base salary for a particular grade of employee, which is then increased pro rata, usually up to maximum of 48 hours per week. No separate overtime or bonus payments are made. This means that employees' working hours may vary by as much as 20 per cent of their agreed commitment from day to day and week to week. The arrangements are usually reviewed every three months to ensure that a suitable balance between time and workload is being achieved and, if necessary, additional staff may be hired. The advantage of this system is that, despite its fixed costs, the company gains the flexibility to respond to peaks and troughs of product demand.

These developments illustrate that nowadays, 'full-time employment' embraces a wide spectrum of work patterns. This raises a number of issues. It highlights the benefits of including employees in business planning, moving away from an adversarial approach to one which recognizes and meets everyone's obligations to the customer. It also demonstrates that in structuring work patterns, management must try to achieve a balance between the needs of the business and those of individual employees and their families. Disputes over how long or short the working week should be reflect narrow and limited thinking on the part of both employers and employees, since it is more important to establish a system with sufficient flexibility to cope with additional jobs as the system grows, and to adapt to employees' changing aspirations. Finally, it stresses the importance of developing an integrated approach to pay, working time, staffing and customer service. The EU Working Time Directive will have an impact here.

Warme, B. et al. (ed.) (1992) *Working Part-time: Risks and Opportunities*, Praeger.

See also: Flexible staffing; Intrapreneurship; Job-sharing; Work schedule restructuring

Participation (employee consultation; employee involvement; industrial democracy; participative management)

Although the principle of involving employees is central to a variety of interventions, there is disagreement as to what constitutes genuine participation. In general, the term refers to the mental and emotional commitment which encourages an individual to contribute to group goals and feel a sense of responsibility for them. All participation programmes aim to increase employees' interest,

commitment, job satisfaction and performance by giving them some ownership – actual or psychological – of the system in which they work. However, one useful criterion which can be used to judge whether an organization is truly committed to encouraging participation in its workforce is whether management is willing to entrust some of its power and discretion to employees.

There are at least five different modes of participation. *Personal participation* refers to the extent to which an individual uses their mental and physical capabilities in their job. In *downward participation*, managers participate in the work of subordinates which has been structured by management. In *upward participation*, employees help managers in work which is considered to be mainly the managers' responsibility. *Lateral participation* involves collaboration between individuals at one or several levels. Finally, *organizational participation* occurs across the larger units of an organization, such as functions and divisions.

Participative management is a management style which has its roots in the research of Elton Mayo at the Hawthorne works in the 1930s. It gives employees more say in how they do their job and how the company operates, and requires them to make a contribution to managing the organization. In the USA, many joint committees of unions and managers have been established as part of Quality of Working Life Programmes, and their success suggests that these initiatives will be taken up more widely. Participative management can take many forms, ranging from employee suggestion schemes to placing employees on the board of directors or on works councils, which recent European Union legislation has given legal status, providing a formal mechanism for employee input into policy-making.

Biagi, M. (ed.) (1993) *Participative Management and Industrial Relations*, Kluwer: Law & Taxation.
Cotton, J.L. (1993) *Employee Involvement*, Sage.
'Employee Involvement', special issue of *Human Relations* (1994), vol. 47, no. 8, August.
Ghoshal, S. and Bartlett, C.A. (1997) *The Individualised Corporation*, Harper Business.
Heller, F. et al. (1998) *Organizational Participation: Myth and Reality*, Oxford University Press.
Hyman, J. (1995) *Managing Employee Involvement and Participation*, Sage.
Jacobs, R.W. (1997) *Real Time Strategic Change: How to Involve an Entire Organization in Fast and Far-reaching Change*, Berrett-Koehler.
Jeanquart-Barone, S. (1994) 'Participatory Management in the Classroom Setting', *Journal of Management Education*, vol. 18, no. 3, pp. 385–7.
Lawler, E.E. (1992) *Employee Involvement*, Jossey-Bass.

Lawler, E.E. (1995) *Employee Involvement and Total Quality Management*, Jossey-Bass.

The Involvement and Participation Association (1998) *Sharing the Challenge: Employee Consultation*, IPA.

See also: Autonomous workgroups; Employee-designed rules; Employee-guided management; Empowerment; Intrapreneurship; Likert's levels meetings; Linked subcontracting; MAPS approach; Open book management; Participative design; Quality of working life; Shared ownership; Suggestion schemes; Worker-directors

Participative design

Participative design is a large-group work design method devised in 1971 by Fred and Merrelyn Emery which involves workgroups redesigning their own tasks. Its distinctive features are that it is inward-looking, and bottom-up rather than top-down. The socio-technical systems approach, in which isolated design groups examine only part of the system, fails to change the structure of a company or gain the commitment of its members. In contrast, the Emerys' method is based on the principles of workplace democracy, maintaining that the people who do the work should design and manage it, rather than being controlled by their supervisors.

The Emerys' model of participative design relies on meeting six 'critical human requirements' which complement the democratic principle. *Adequate elbow room* is necessary to enable employees to make their own decisions without scrutiny from supervisors. *Constant learning* is achieved by establishing a setting in which employees can set challenging goals and receive feedback about their achievements. *Variety* is essential to reduce boredom and fatigue, allowing employees to establish a productive work rhythm. *Mutual support* engenders a sense of respect between employees, and allows them to co-operate as a group to maximize individual performance. *Meaningful work*, whose importance to a customer or community is understood by employees, increases their motivation and enhances their self-esteem. Finally, a *desirable future* in terms of a career path is necessary to promote personal growth and provide employees with incentives to increase their skills and knowledge.

The participative design process is implemented using a four-phase workshop which produces a new organizational culture and structure. In the first phase, *educational workshops* are held for senior management to help them differentiate between democratic and bureaucratic structures. A cascade approach is adopted so that management builds up a framework of minimum acceptable criteria which can be used to assess the designs that are devised. Next, each workgroup proceeds independently through the three remaining phases of analysis, design and implementation. While the views of external stakeholders are surveyed and considered by the workgroups, they do not attend the workgroup meetings. The *analysis* phase is initiated by senior managers, who explain the organizational purpose and the minimum specifications, then leave the room. The workgroup members then analyse their current jobs, considering how the six critical human requirements can be met. The skills necessary for the redesigned jobs are identified, any skill deficits are noted, and this information is later used in planning training. In the *design* phase, each workgroup analyses the company's structure and work flows, assessing the extent to which the democratic design principle operates, then suggests a design with incorporates the critical human requirements. Finally, in the *implementation* phase, workgroup members meet to learn from each other, develop goals, specify training needs, test their designs against the principles and finalize them, then negotiate with senior management about how to implement them.

Bunker, B.B. and Alban, B.T. (1997) 'Participative Design', in *Large Group Interventions: Engaging the Whole System for Rapid Change*, Jossey-Bass, pp. 137–49.

Cabana, S. (1995) 'Can People Restructure Their Own Work?', *Target*, vol. 11, no. 6, pp. 16–30.

Cabana, S. (1995) 'Participative Design Works, Partially Participative Doesn't', *Journal for Quality and Participation*, vol. 18, no. 1, pp. 10–19.

'Do It All Opts for DIY Management', *IRS Employment Trends* (1998), no. 664, September, pp. 6–9.

Emery, F. (1995) 'Participative Design: Effective, Flexible and Successful, Now!', *Journal for Quality and Participation*, vol. 18, no. 1, pp. 6–9.

See also: Action training and research; Business process re-engineering; Conference Model; Fast-cycle full-participation work design; Future search; Open space technology; Participation; Real-time strategic change; Real-time work design; Search conference; Socio-technical systems design; Strategic planning process; Simu-Real; Work-Out

Peer counselling (peer mediation; peer mentoring)

Counselling is usually carried out by someone who is either specially trained, more knowledgeable than the person being counselled, or more senior in the hierarchy. In contrast, as its name suggests, peer counselling is provided by individuals of the same age, background and seniority. This approach has been adopted in universities, colleges and even schools, with students counselling other students about a wide variety of issues.

Barker, R.T. and Pitts, M.W. (1997) 'Graduate Students as Mentors: An Approach for the Undergraduate Class Project', *Journal of Management Education*, vol. 21 no. 2, pp. 221–31.

Cowie, H. (1996) *Peer Counselling in Schools*, David Fulton Publishers.

Goodlad, S. (1996) (ed.) *Students as Tutors and Mentors*, Kogan Page.

Jacobi, M. (1991) 'Mentoring and Undergraduate Academic Success: A Literature Review', *Review of Educational Research*, vol. 61, pp. 505–32.

Phillips, M. (1993) *Developing Peer Counselling Skills*, Daniels Publishing.

Phillips, M. (1993) *Using Peer Counselling Skills*, Daniels Publishing.

Salovey, P. and D'Andrea, V.J. (1990) *Peer Counselling: Skills and Perspectives*, Science and Behaviour Books.

Simpson, C. (1997) *Coping Through Conflict Resolution and Peer Mediation*, Rosen Publishing Group.

Sturkie, J. (1988) *Listening With Love: True Stories in Peer Counselling*, Columbia Publishers.

Tindall, J.A. (1990) *Peer Counselling*, Accelerated Development Inc.

See also: Co-counselling; Counselling; Helping relationship model; Parrainage; Peer teaching

Peer teaching (peer-assisted learning; peer tutoring)

A variety of approaches involve students teaching and helping other students of approximately the same age and educational experience through activities such as leading discussion groups or participating in peer revision and autonomous study groups, using teaching staff members as consultants. In one technique, students are divided into several small groups, and each student takes it in turn to teach a topic to the other members of their group. Once a topic is completed, each peer teacher presents the whole class with a summary of how they taught the topic, highlighting the main points that were covered.

Research indicates that both peer teachers and learners benefit from the approach in cognitive and affective terms, especially if students alternate between the roles. Peer teaching methods encourage active learning by facilitating social relations between students, developing their social skills and improving the effectiveness of teaching. Participating in peer teaching programmes usually encourages students to become more self-reliant and self-confident in taking responsibility for their own learning processes. Planning and organizing others' learning processes requires peer teachers to adopt a more conscious and active approach to their own studies, and the advantages of learning by teaching have been well documented. However, to ensure high-quality teaching, the instructor should monitor the work of peer teachers very closely, and should be available to answer particularly difficult questions.

Boud, D.J. and Prosser, M.T. (1980) 'Sharing Responsibility: Staff–student Co-operation in Learning', *British Journal of Educational Technology*, vol. 11, pp. 2–35.

Collier, K.G. (1980) 'Peer Group Learning in Higher Education: The Development of Higher Order Skills', *Studies in Higher Education*, vol. 5, no. 1, pp. 55–62.

Fantuzzo, J. W., Dimeff, L. A. and Fox, S. L. (1989) 'Reciprocal Peer Tutoring: A Multimodal Assessment of Effectiveness with College Students', *Teaching of Psychology*, vol. 16, no. 3, pp. 133–5.

Goldschmidt, B. and Goldschmidt, M.L. (1976) 'Peer Teaching in Higher Education: A Review', *Higher Education*, vol. 5, pp. 9–33.

Goodlad, S. (1989) *Peer Tutoring*, Kogan Page.

Goodlad, S. (1990) *Explorations in Peer Tutoring*, Blackwell.

Goodlad, S. (1996) (ed.) *Students as Tutors and Mentors*, Kogan Page.

Magin, D.J. and Churches, A.E. (1995) 'Peer Tutoring in Engineering Design: A Case Study', *Studies in Higher Education*, vol. 20, no. 1, pp. 73–85.

McKaig, A., Rogers, C., Rushi, N. and Yound, D. (1997) 'Paired Reciprocal Peer Tutoring in Undergraduate Economics', *Innovations in Education and Training*, vol. 34, no. 2, pp. 96–113.

Muzur, E. (1996) *Peer Instruction, A User's Manual*, Prentice-Hall.

Nelson, S. (1989) *Partners in Practice: Strategies for Successful Peer Teaching*, Lake Publishing Company.

Topping, K. (1996) 'The Effectiveness of Peer Tutoring in Higher and Further Education: A Typology and Review of the Literature', *Higher Education*, vol. 23, no. 3, pp. 321–45.

Topping, K. and Ehly, S. (1998) *Peer Assisted Learning*, Lawrence Erlbaum Associates.

Topping, K. et al. (1997) 'Paired Reciprocal Peer Tutoring in Undergraduate Economics', *Innovations in Education and Training International*, vol. 34, no. 2, pp. 96–113.

Wagner, L. (1983) *Peer Teaching: Historical Perspectives*, Greenwood Press Inc.

See also: Collaboratively designed course; Co-op/co-op; Co-operative learning; Course design as learning; Learning cell; Learning community; Learning organization; Media-activated learning group; One-to-one learning; Parrainage; Peer counselling; Proctor method; Teaching as learning; Tutorium

Periodic planning conference

The periodic planning conference (PPC) was developed by Gordon to offer a radical, new approach to performance appraisal. Managers hold a PPC with each of their subordinate workgroup leaders on a regular basis, usually every six or twelve months, to agree a number of goals, such as trying to improve team members' work performance, building a better relationship with subordinates, and developing a climate of mutual trust and confidence. The approach is based on seven beliefs: that employees must change if they are to progress; that there is always a better way of doing things; that no one ever works at full capacity; that change and growth are the characteristics of an effective organization; that people are not strongly motivated to accomplish goals set by others; that they will work hard to accomplish goals they set themselves, and that individuals are happier when they are given the chance to accomplish more. In accordance with these principles, managers should allow free discussion of job problems, focus on the future, allow their subordinates to recommend their own performance goals, and give them the opportunity to resolve any conflicts in a way that is acceptable to all concerned.

When introducing the PPC approach, managers must prepare their team members by explaining its benefits and securing their approval to implement it. Next, managers must agree with each of their subordinates which tasks they are expected to carry out as part of their jobs, and how performance will be measured. The PPC is a two-way process, so the manager's goals must match those of their subordinate, and they must collaborate in working out a mutually acceptable plan for each subordinate. Having agreed the goals, the manager must provide the subordinate with the information necessary to evaluate their own progress, supplying any material, financial or personnel resources that may be required. The manager should also be available to act as a facilitator or adviser if the individual encounters difficulties.

Gordon, T. (1979) *LET: Leadership Effectiveness Training*, Futura Books, pp. 241–55.

See also: Appraisal; Feedback; Goal-setting; Goal-setting and planning groups; Job description; Management by objectives; Measuring performance; On-going feedback system; Position charter; Positive feedback; Self- with peer appraisal

Person-card technique (card sort)

This approach seeks to develop the high-level cognitive skill of *synthesis*, defined as 'putting together parts or elements so as to form a whole', in contrast to the more commonly taught skill of *analysis*, which involves taking apart and separating the elements that form a whole. Hibino and Nadler divide the process of synthesis into four stages. *Generation* involves gathering ideas. *Grouping* then sorts these ideas into arbitrary categories. *Structuring* entails developing a generalization about each group. Finally, *developing major alternatives* consists of refining and integrating each idea into a more inclusive framework of innovative concepts.

The person–card technique provides a useful aid to synthesizing generated ideas or examples. First, the student writes each idea on a card (generation). The cards are then grouped intuitively by arranging them on a large sheet of paper until the ideas are categorized into several groups or 'families' with common attributes (grouping). In order to define the essence of the idea written on each card and explore its different facets and dimensions, the student treats each one as if it were a person – hence the term 'person–card' – and talks to it, asking: 'Why did you come to this family?', 'What is your essence?' and 'What do you want to be called?' If a single idea has a number of different facets, the card can be duplicated and placed within two or more different families. Next, the student develops a person–card chart which shows the complete structure or conceptual hierarchy of all the ideas (structuring). Each idea group is circled and placed in such a way as to show mutual relationships, such as cause and effect, opposite relationships or simple relationships. In the final stage (developing major alternatives), the student considers the purposes, measures of effectiveness and regulatory conditions in order to arrive at synthesized alternatives based on "idea families".

Hibino, S. and Nadler, G. (1980) 'The "Person-card" Technique', *Training and Development Journal*, November, pp. 78–83.

Wulf, S.A. (1998) *Building Performance Values*, Human Resource Publishers.

See also: Conceptual analysis; Concept attainment; Concept-formation; Mystery clue method; Problem pack

Personal development laboratory (personal growth laboratory)

Personal development laboratories focus on the individual rather than the group or the organization, using solitary and group exercises to enable participants to explore and diagnose their own behaviour by means of feedback from others. Shepard described this form of laboratory as: 'an experimental test of the notion that mechanistic mentality and culture can be transcended. It is a re-socializing institution, providing conditions that disconfirm some mechanistic assumptions and affirm some different views of the self in relation to others.' The aim is to help participants become more aware of what they do and why they do it, developing their self-knowledge so they can identify options for change. Personal development laboratories are usually designed for 'strangers' – people who do not normally have relationships with each other outside the laboratory setting.

Argyris, C. (1972) 'Do Personal Growth Laboratories Represent an Alternative Culture?', *Journal of Applied Behavioural Science*, vol. 8, no. 1, pp. 7–28.

Margulies, N. and Wallace, J. (1973) *Organizational Change: Techniques and Applications*, Scott Foresman, p. 69.

Mill, C.R. (1976) 'Recent Developments in Experiential Group Methods: the USA', in Cooper, C.L. (ed.) *Developing Social Skills in Managers: Advances in Group Training*, Macmillan.

Shepard, H.A. (1970) 'Personal Growth Laboratories: Towards an Alternative Culture', *Journal of Applied Behavioural Science*, vol. 6, no. 3, pp. 259–66.

Wilson, J.E., Mullen, D.P. and Morton, R.B. (1968) 'Sensitivity Training for Individual Growth', *Training Development Journal*, vol. 22, pp. 47–54.

See also: Bioenergetics; Cluster laboratory; Cognitive behavioural therapy; Cousin laboratory; Encounter groups; Gestalt techniques; Group development laboratory; Group dynamics laboratory; Human relations laboratory; Instrumented laboratory; Laboratory method; Micro-lab; Minisociety; Organizational laboratory; Power laboratory; Psychodrama; Psychotherapy; Role training; Self-development; Sensitivity (T-group) training; Team laboratory; Tavistock Conference Method

Personalized reflection (reflective recall)

The discussion of reflection in Dewey's book *How We Think* is considered by many to be the most useful. Dewey defined reflective thought as the 'active, persistent and careful consideration of any belief or supplied form of knowledge in the light of the grounds that support it and the further conclusions to which it tends'. This type of reflection offers a opportunity for managers to learn from their work experiences by applying Kolb and Fry's learning cycle. It demands that managers discipline themselves to reflect on their actions so that they avoid continually repeating the same mistakes.

To apply this technique, a manager observes what happens during a first-hand experience, such as interviewing a job applicant, then uses this as a basis for reflection. For example, perhaps all the questions they asked the job applicant were answered with a 'yes' or 'no', whereas a colleague's questions produced long replies which were very revealing. This information is then used to develop some abstract concepts and generalizations: for example, that the colleague asks 'better' questions, straightforward and structured ones which are open, requiring the applicant to think divergently. Having done this, the manager tests this hypothesis by drawing up a list of similar questions and using them at the next interview.

Bayes, E.E. (1950) *Theory and Practice of Teaching*, Harper and Row.

Bayes, E.E. (1960) *Democratic Educational Theory*, Harper and Row, Chapter 12.

Burton, W.H., Kimball, R.B. and Wing, R.L. (1960) *Education for Effective Thinking*, Appleton-Century-Crofts.

Dewey, J. (1909) *How We Think*, Heath.

Hunt, M.P. and Metcalf, L.E. (1968) *Teaching High School Social Studies* (2nd edn), Harper and Row, Chapters 3 and 8.

Kolb, D.A. and Fry, R. (1975) 'Towards an Applied Theory of Experiential Learning', in Cooper, C.L. (ed.) *Theories of Group Process*, Wiley.

See also: Process analysis; Reflective learning; Self-criticism

Personalized system of instruction (Keller plan; self-paced study)

A personalized system of instruction (PSI) is a self-paced guided study programme in which the work is broken down into specially prepared modules or assignments based on existing published materials. The instructor devises a variety of tests to assess 'mastery' of the subject, which is usually defined as attaining a mark of 80 per cent or more. Students can elect to take these tests whenever they feel ready, and the instructor marks them immediately in the presence of the student. Differences in the education systems have led to the development of distinct versions of this approach in the UK and USA. The US definition is stricter: a PSI course must contain five separate elements, and must incorporate student proctors (undergraduate tutors, often advanced students in the field). The UK criteria are more flexible, the only requirement being that the course should be self-paced.

One example of PSI is the Keller plan, originally developed by F.S. Keller of Columbia University. Students generally work individually at their own pace, each unit representing about a week's work. The emphasis is on achieving competence rather than studying for a certain period. The instructor's role is to select and organize the course materials, write study guides and construct examinations. Proctors may also grade tests and offer support and encouragement. Printed study guides are used as the primary teaching devices, providing an introduction to each unit, suggesting study procedures and listing questions. A few lectures may be given by the instructor, but they are not compulsory, and examinations are not based on them. The aims of each unit are set out clearly, together with suggested ways of achieving them. Students may be advised to read a textbook chapter, together with specially prepared discussion notes, and then to work on certain practice questions. They are encouraged to co-operate and help each other with problems. When students feel that they have mastered a given unit, they present themselves for a short test, which they must pass before being permitted to proceed to the next unit, although there are no penalties for failure other than the requirement to re-sit the test. The pass mark is set by the instructor, and tends to be high. After the test, the student and instructor can discuss any problems that have arisen either in working through the unit or tackling the test itself.

Boud, D.J., Bridge, W.A. and Willoughby, L. (1975) 'PSI Now: A Review of Problems and Progress', *British Journal of Educational Technology*, vol. 6, no. 2, pp. 15–34.

Keller, F.S. (1968) 'Goodbye, Teacher ...', *Journal of Applied Behavioural Analysis*, vol. 1, no. 1.

Keller, F.S. and Sherman, J.G. (1974) *Keller Plan Handbook*, W.A. Benjamin.

Sherman, J.G. (eds) (1974) *PSI: Forty One Germinal Papers: A Selection of Readings on the Keller Plan*, W.A. Benjamin.

See also: Audio tutorial method; Autonomous learning group; Guided design approach; Guided group problem-solving; Handout; Mastery learning; Proctor method; Programmed learning; Tutorial-tape-document learning package approach

Physical interventions in organizations

Historically, the earliest organizational interventions were physical ones, those conducted in companies during the 1920s and 1930s concentrating on addressing levels of illumination, ventilation and noise. Modern approaches try to ensure that the physical work setting, be it an office or a factory, is congruent with the organization's value system or goals. The most important work in this field has been carried out by Fritz Steele. He argues that the physical setting is a key aspect of organizational culture that affects both individual and group performance, since changes in the design of plant and the architecture of buildings alter patterns of social interaction. For instance, the size of an office may lend itself to spontaneous group meetings, while its location may dictate whether a manager is either at the heart of things or hidden away at the periphery. Steele cites the example of the university lecture room seating arrangement, which emphasizes the dominant role of the lecturer and impedes interaction between the students.

Steele describes the different ways in which the physical setting reflects an organization's climate, structure and processes. His methodology includes a rating system for factors such as lights, desks, seating arrangements, and the norms relating to the use of physical settings. It emphasizes participative diagnosis to study the way people use space, how different territories are defined, the social processes generated by issues of how space is structured, distributed or organized, and choices about physical movement. This analysis of the interaction of physical and social factors is then used to develop a change strategy which aims to enhance team performance while providing privacy for the individual.

The recognition that the physical setting has a major effect on an organization's social system is illustrated by the example of a Canadian company, Life, which linked employee involvement to office refurbishment. The designers asked employees at all levels two questions: 'What do you need to do your job, and who do you need to be close to?' When the design was completed, the employees were asked to make suggestions before senior management approved the floor plans.

Becker, F. and Steele, F. (1995) *Workplace by Design: Mapping the High Performance Workspace*, American Society for Training and Development/Jossey-Bass.

'Corporate Head Offices: Places to Linger', *The Economist* (1998), 1–7 August, pp. 63–4.

Eley, J. and Marmot, A.F. (1995) *Understanding Offices*, Penguin.

Oborne, D.J. and Gruneberg, M.M. (eds) (1983) *The Physical Environment of Work*, Wiley.

Powell, G.N. and Graves, L.M. (1987–8) 'Predicting Organizational Behaviour from Office Environments', *Organizational Behaviour Teaching Review*, vol. 12, no. 1, pp. 114–16.

Smith, P. and Kearny, L. (1994) *Creating Workplaces Where People Can Think*, Jossey-Bass.

Steele, F. (1973) *Physical Settings and Organization Development*, Addison Wesley Longman.

Steele, F. (1977) *The Feel of the Workplace: Understanding and Improving Organizational Climate*, Addison Wesley Longman.

Steele, F. (1983) 'The Ecology of Executive Teams: A View From the Top', *Organizational Dynamics*, Spring, pp. 65–78.

Steele, F. (1986) *Making and Managing High Quality Workplaces: An Organizational Ecology*, Teachers College Press.

Steele, F. (1995) *Workplace by Design*, Jossey-Bass.

Sundstrom, E. (1986) *Workplaces: Psychology of the Physical Environment in Offices and Factories*, Cambridge University Press.

Turner, G. and Myers, J. (1998) *New Workspace, New Culture*, Gower.

See also: Ergonomics; Forcing device; Management by walking around; MAPS approach

Physical representation of organizations

This method can be used to bring into the open relationship problems which may be bothering group members, such as the existence of cliques, competitiveness or poor communication. A group of employees gathers in a room, and participants are asked to take up a position which reflects their perception of certain criteria. For example, if the intention is to examine the workings of the informal organization, they may be invited to stand near those with whom they feel the greatest affinity. If the issue being considered is influence, they may position themselves close to or far away from their manager, according to the amount of influence they feel they have. These exercises are then followed by discussion of the relationships revealed.

Fordyce, J.K. and Weil, R. (1971) *Managing With People*, Addison Wesley Longman, p. 155.

See also: Collages; Diagnostic activities; Drawing for learning; Ergonomics; Family group diagnostic meeting; Family group team-building meeting; Forcing device; Inter-organizational information-sharing; Interviewing; Looking for trouble; 7-S framework; Sensing

PIT technique

This technique helps students learn how to learn, while using them as learning resources within the class. PIT stands for Polemics, Inquiry and Theo-

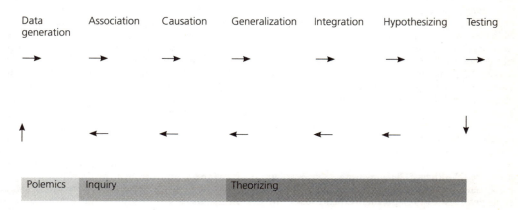

PIT cycle

rizing, the three phases of this teaching method, which consists of seven learning cycle stages, as shown on the previous page.

The first phase is *polemics*, the art of disputation, and in particular the use of aggressive argument to refute errors. A skilled polemicist is able to present an argument from any prescribed viewpoint. The class is therefore presented with two polar extreme positions on a topic (data-generation). In the *inquiry* phase, students attempt to discover relationships between the opposing viewpoints (association), considering the reasons for these connections and their implications for other related topics (generalization), and how they relate to previous learning (integration). The *theorizing* phase involves students developing possible explanations (hypothesizing), so that their understanding can be checked (testing). They also address the question of how their understanding might be applied.

In practice, two steps are necessary to prepare for a PIT session. First, the instructor prepares a carefully worded statement which reveals the critical issues raised by the article, chapter or book being considered (an entire course can be designed around a dozen or so such statements). Next, 'Pro' and 'Con' teams are selected, ideally consisting of two or three people each, the Pros being set the task of arguing in favour of the proposition, and the Cons arguing against it. The PIT session itself consist of 13 steps and usually takes about 95 minutes to complete, although it can be shortened if necessary.

In step 1, the Pro team presents its case without interruption (10 minutes). In step 2, the Con team does the same (10 minutes). In step 3, both teams collect their thoughts (5 minutes). In step 4, the Pro team responds to the Con team's points, as in a classical debate (5 minutes). In step 5, both teams collect their thoughts again (5 minutes). In step 6, the Con team rebuts the Pro team's points (5 minutes). In step 7, after each team has had an opportunity for rebuttal, questions from the audience are written up on the board. In step 8, team members respond to these questions while still defending their positions (5 minutes). A ninth optional step, in which the class provides a written assessment of the polemicists' performance, completes the Polemics component of the PIT session.

Step 10 consists of the *Inquiry* component (10 minutes). The audience assumes responsibility for this process, and the team members remain silent, now being given the option of abandoning their prescribed positions. The audience members try to make sense of the viewpoints presented, discovering links and exploring causal explanations. The instructor may assist by asking simple questions if they are failing to make progress. A few themes usually emerge, and these are developed until a tentative understanding is achieved.

The *Theorizing* component of PIT begins with step 11, in which students are asked to relate the themes in order to develop a coherent picture of the topic (10 minutes). In step 12, students are required to generate testable hypotheses, which focuses their minds and provides another level of learning (10 minutes). In step 13, the instructor adds their own input to the session, drawing out any significant themes or issues not covered earlier, and providing summary comments.

DeLuca, J.R. (1980) 'The PIT Teaching Technique', *Exchange: The Organizational Behaviour Teaching Journal*, vol. 5, no. 2, pp. 37–9.

See also: Argumentation; Buberian dialogue; Debate; Jurisprudential model; Mock trial

Planned delegation

Opportunities for temporary delegation often arise when managers know in advance that they will be absent for a certain period, for example to attend a course, but they are rarely used for staff development. Whether the manager will be absent or not, planned delegation involves providing a task which will stretch an employee beyond their previous capacity, and gives them an opportunity to learn and practise new skills. However, to ensure this will be a positive experience, it is essential that subordinates are given the necessary support to develop the skills and knowledge that will be required. In this sense, delegation can be seen as a stage of training which can follow a period of coaching, and it requires many of the techniques involved in coaching, especially listening and observation skills.

Implementing a planned delegation programme demands a high degree of organization. The manager should log their daily activities for a period, then draw up a list of those that could be delegated. The next step is to draw up a timetable for delegating each chosen responsibility, deciding which member of staff could be asked to attend a certain meeting instead of the manager, for example. The staff member's performance on the assignment should be reviewed as soon as possible after its completion.

Brown, C.A. (1997) *Essential Delegation Skills*, Gower.
Huppe, F.F. (1997) *Successful Delegation*, Career Press Inc.
Nelson, R. (1994) *Empowering Employees Through Delegation*, Irwin.
Woods, M. et al. (1996) *Effective Empowerment and Delegation*, HarperCollins.

See also: Acting assignment; Coaching; Counselling; Empowerment; Expanding job assignment; Job-enrichment; Sick leave/holiday replacement assignment

Planned renegotiation (pinch model)

Relationships within systems rarely proceed smoothly, be they between a couple, members of a group, employees within a company or members of a community. Planned renegotiation is based on a cyclical model of how social systems are established, how they stabilize so that goals can be achieved, and how change enters the system. It consists of a four-phase strategy for anticipating and controlling change.

The first phase involves sharing information and negotiating expectations, in order to reduce uncertainty. In phase two, the parties make commitments to each other, based on the understanding they have gained of their respective roles and shared expectations. Phase three draws on these commitments to establish stability and allow productive work. The final phase reflects the belief that this stability will prove to be temporary, and internal or external factors will disrupt it and trigger changes in commitments and roles. This impending disruption is signalled by a *pinch*, which is experienced by one or more of the parties involved, which may take the form of a sense of loss of freedom within their role. Unless addressed, the pinch may become a *crunch*, leading to confrontation. The approach aims to avoid this and the resultant negative effects on the relationship by renegotiating current expectations and commitments at the pinch stage, before the disruption occurs, enabling each party to exercise a greater degree of choice and control.

Sherwood, J.J. and Scherer, (1975) 'A Model for Couples: How Two Can Grow Together', *Journal for Small Group Behaviour*, vol. 6, no. 1.

See also: Role analysis technique; Negotiation by group members; Conflict-resolution techniques; Role prescription

Playing for learning (playwork)

Play is an important aspect of human interaction characterized by a number of attributes: it is voluntary, intrinsically motivating, does not depend on external rewards, involves active, often physical engagement, and includes a make-believe element. Children learn through play long before they embark on formal instruction at school. Once they attend school, playtime during morning, lunch and afternoon breaks provides an opportunity to act independently with less direct supervision by adults, to interact with their peers, and to develop friendships. Indeed, research has criticized some schools for reducing or eliminating these breaks to allow more teaching time to cover the National Curriculum and monitor disruptive pupils more closely.

Play is often regarded as something only young children do, and as an activity that can be dispensed with as individuals grow up. Yet adults spend a great deal of time, money and energy engaging in different types of play, such as sports, music and hobbies. When any learning task is defined as play, it becomes much less onerous. This fact is exploited in a number of learning approaches, and developments in computer technology and software mean that play is likely to grow in importance as a teaching method, both for children and adults.

Blanchard, K. and Cheska, A. (1985) *The Anthropology of Sport: An Introduction*, Bergin and Garvey Publishers.

Blatner, A. and Blatner, A. (1997) *The Art of Play: Helping Adults Reclaim Imagination and Spontaneity*, Brunner/Mazel.

Malone, T.W. and Lepper, M.R. (1987) 'Making Learning Fun: A Taxonomy of Intrinsic Motivations for Learning', in Snow, R.E. and Farr, M.J. (eds) *Aptitude, Learning and Instruction, 3: Cognitive and Affective Process Analysis*, Lawrence Erlbaum Associates, pp. 223–53.

Pellegrini, A.D. (ed.) (1995) *The Future of Play Theory: A Multidisciplinary Enquiry in the Contribution of Brian Sutton-Smith*, State University of New York Press.

Pellegrini, A.D. and Smith, P.K. (eds) (1995) 'School Recess: Implications for Education and Development', *Review of Educational Research*, vol. 63, no. 1, pp. 51–67.

Rieber, L.P. (1996) 'Seriously Considering Play: Designing Interactive Learning Environments Based on Blending Microworlds, Simulations and Games', *Education, Training Research & Development*, vol. 44, no. 2, pp. 43–58.

See also: Behavioural simulation; Game; Humour for learning; Reading aloud; Role-modelling; Storytelling; Simulation

Plural chief executive

Recognizing that the work of senior managers has been complicated by the growing impact of new technology, the broadening of many companies' product bases, and the scope of international operations, some companies have adopted new approaches to the post of chief executive officer

(CEO). Drawing a distinction between the position itself, the range of tasks associated with it, and the person who occupies it has led to the development of the plural chief executive concept. This involves restructuring the organization's senior management by forming a chief executive office or executive committee, which usually consists of a team of three to seven members. The approach spreads the workload, provides for succession and overcomes the sense of isolation experienced by many individual chief executives. However, it is essential to find the right people, define the committee's role in relation to the rest of the company, and set the appropriate corporate tone.

The chief executive committee's members have equal status, but may be assigned different spheres of interest. Their tasks include the usual ones of setting corporate objectives and making decisions about issues such as capital and staffing, but the team approach provides a broader base of executive judgement when this is required, for example in international business, in large capital-intensive businesses, where a broader range of judgements is valuable, and in companies which operate on a world-wide basis and consume large amounts of capital.

Daniel, D.R. (1965) 'Team at the Top', *Harvard Business Review*, March–April, pp. 74–82.

See also: Collateral organization; Informal action group; Informal management team; Managerial decentralization; Multiple management; Parallel career ladders; Structural interventions

Poetry for learning

Poetry can play a valuable role in the management classroom or training centre, where it is often used to stimulate creativity. Like dance, mask work, metaphor, painting, sculpting, storytelling and visualization, it is useful when exploring the relationships between traditional management development issues and those of self-development, psychotherapeutic concerns and spirituality.

The use of poetry has also grown in popularity in organizations and companies. For example, poets-in-residence are often engaged in schools, prisons, hospitals and universities. During the late 1990s, assisted by a National Lottery grant, a Poetry Society project sought to encourage more commercial sponsorship of poetry in the workplace, and the initiative was taken up by Marks & Spencer, Kew Gardens and the BBC. Such schemes encourage staff to develop their creative abilities and communication skills but, in addition, poems concerning the darker side of organizational life can provide both an outlet for frustration and a spur for change.

Cloves, J. (1998) 'Putting Poetry to Work', *Professional Manager*, Institute of Management, May, pp. 36–8.
Vaill, P. B. (1981) 'Thoughts on Using Poetry in the Teaching of OB', *Exchange: The Organizational Behaviour Teaching Journal*, vol. 6, pp. 50–1.
Whyte, D. (1994) *The Heart Aroused: Poetry and Preservation of the Soul in Corporate America*, Currency Doubleday.

See also: Dramatic skit; Drawing for learning; Music for learning; Novels for learning: Reading aloud; Rote learning; Storytelling; Story writing

Policy-formulation

A traditional method of introducing organizational change is to propose a new departmental or organizational policy. The initial draft of the policy is usually prepared by the individual who is most affected by the issue. The draft is submitted to the administrative or managerial staff to enable them to make comments and review it. Copies of the policy are then distributed for scrutiny by all departmental personnel. The revised policy is then promulgated throughout the organization, and this refining process continues until the policy is satisfactory to all concerned.

See also: Corporate culture training; Delphi technique; Development of a new management/operating philosophy; Managerial strategy change; Nominal group technique; Open systems planning; Scenario planning; Socio-technical systems design; Strategic management; Strategic planning process

Polling

Polling should be distinguished from voting, which is a group decision-making strategy. Polling can be used to address hidden factors which may be interfering with the progress of a meeting or the functioning of a group or organization. For example, when a group is growing uneasy or is experiencing stalemate and participants feel bored and out of tune with each other, this may indicate that there are unresolved issues which individuals find difficult to discuss. Polling provides a means to bring such problems to the surface, enabling the group to deal with them. Because group members can devise their own questions and polling procedures and have an opportunity to express their opinion, participants are more likely to accept the results. The method is most appropriate for groups of five to thirty participants.

The group is polled by asking a question that draws attention to the present situation. Some group issues may be so sensitive that members are reluctant to discuss them. In such circumstances, an outsider may be invited to ask the question or a secret ballot may be held. However, secret ballots should be a last resort, since polling should generally be restricted to issues the group is willing to confront openly. If the question is posed by an outsider, the group members may modify it until they agree that it reflects the issue they wish to address. Participants may then decide on the polling procedure. For example, if the poll aims to reveal their optimism about achieving consensus on a change goal being discussed, each could be asked to assess their degree of optimism on a scale of 1 to 5. If the scores cluster around 2.5, the group can then discuss the reasons for pessimism and decide how to overcome them.

Fordyce, J.K. and Weil, R. (1971) *Managing With People*, Addison Wesley Longman, pp. 146–52.

See also: Critiquing; Focus group; Getting acquainted; Going round the room; Likes and reservations; Non-verbal encounters; Process consultation; Questionnaires; Self-generated scaling

Position charter

A position charter is a contract between a supervisor and an employee which is drawn up during a performance appraisal discussion. It describes the employee's job responsibilities, the required standards of performance and desired improvements. This approach offers two benefits: it allows employees to negotiate the setting of their own performance standards, and it enables supervisors to receive feedback about improvements to the system which might help employees carry out their work more efficiently.

See also: Appraisal; Feedback; Goal-setting; Goal-setting and planning groups; Job descriptions; Learning contract; Management responsibility guide process; Periodic planning conference; Responsibility charting; Role prescription

Positive feedback

Providing feedback is essential to help an individual or group to improve their performance. While it is obviously necessary to give negative feedback, pointing out any errors or omissions, the role of positive feedback is often neglected. Rewarding good performance, for example with praise, increases motivation and reinforces learning. Although all feedback should be given as soon as possible after the event, this is probably even more important in the case of positive feedback, since the passage of time may reveal relatively minor shortcomings in the performance which lead to a

more negative tone. It is also vital to give ourselves positive feedback in our reflection and self-talk, rather than constantly dwelling on our deficiencies.

Blanchard, K. and Johnson, S. (1983) *The One Minute Manager*, Fontana.

See also: Appraisal; Feedback; Goal-setting; Management by objectives; Measuring performance; On-going feedback system; Periodic planning review; Recognition programmes; Self-with peer review

Positive peer culture

This long-term intervention devised by Vorrath and Brendtro can be applied to groups in general, although it has been used primarily with adolescents. When a group begins to hold regular meetings, the leader (who may be a manager) monitors the interactions between members which constitute the beginnings of a group process. Acting as a catalyst, the leader exerts influence in a variety of ways, ranging from overt confrontation to passive withdrawal, following a carefully designed sequence of passive, active and mood-changing steps. The leader's contribution to the group's process seeks to produce and enforce what society or the organization consider to be positive norms of behaviour. The leader's choice of behaviour –or *behaviour kaleidoscope*, in Vorrath and Brendtro's terminology – is made according to their reading of events during the four successive stages of guided group process identified by the authors: *casing*, *limit-testing*, *polarization of values* and *positive peer culture*. This last stage represents effective group functioning.

Vorrath, H.H. (1985) *Positive Peer Culture* (2nd edn), Walter de Gruyter.

See also: Behaviour modification; Interaction influence analysis; Non-conforming enclave; Process consultation; Reinforcement environment analysis

Post-course follow-up

Given the number of courses employees are required to attend nowadays, it is important to ensure that the results are integrated into their everyday work. To do this successfully, managers must make efforts to familiarize themselves with the course material. One approach is to ask employees to submit a report outlining what they gained from the course, and how they plan to apply their learning to improve their performance. The manager and employee can then meet to decide which ideas are feasible, and finalize an action plan to implement them. Relating theory to action in this way demonstrates to employees that their managers are interested and involved in their development.

Farnsworth, T. (1968) 'After the Course is Over: Dynamism or Despair?', *Personnel and Training Management*, February, pp. 26–8.
O'Neill, H. and Loew, H. (1975) 'The Anatomy of a Problem: Follow Up Training in Analytical Trouble Shooting', *Industrial and Commercial Training*, February, vol. 7, no. 1, pp. 27–31.
Weiss, E., Huczynski, A. and Lewis, J. (1980) 'The Superior's Role in Learning Transfer', *Journal of European Industrial Training*, vol. 4, no. 4, pp. 17–20.

See also: Application discussion group; Interaction management; Training evaluation as learning; Training transfer training

Poster

Posters are widely used in schools, training centres, offices or factories to provide information, influence attitudes using slogans (e.g., 'Our customers do the final quality control!'), warn of dangers or provide guidance on how to perform certain tasks (e.g., lifting heavy objects or running meetings). Posters often serve as one element in a broader educational programme, reinforcing messages delivered during courses or presentations by senior management.

See also: Apperception-interaction method; Chronology charting; Collages; Concept mapping; Drawing for learning; Exhibit; Fortune lining; Group poster tours; Illuminative incident analysis; Model; Museum learning; Relational diagramming; Responsibility charting; Storyboarding

Power laboratory

This is a learning design based on a theory of power dynamics developed by Barry Oshry. On arrival at the course venue, participants are divided into two groups labelled 'Haves' and 'Have nots'. Each group contains 'Ins', who have most power, and others who have less. All resources, including food, shelter, clothing, transportation and access to communications, are unevenly distributed, grossly in favour of the Haves. Moreover, the Haves are not allowed to give up their power. Over a five-day programme, about half the time is devoted to analysing the dynamics which arise under these circumstances. Participants often report significant changes in their feelings of potency and their ability to cope with the forces influencing their lives.

Oshry, B. (1972) 'Power and the Power Lab', in Burke, W.W. (ed.) *Contemporary Organizational Development: Conceptual Orientations and Interventions*, NTL Institute, pp. 242–54.

See also: Group dynamics laboratory; Human relations laboratory; Laboratory method; Minisociety; Micro-lab; Organizational laboratory; Personal development laboratory; Sensitivity (T-group) training; Tavistock Conference Method; Team laboratory

Power management

Power management aims to help managers use their power positively, both in their business and personal relationships. The model of power presented by Brewer and colleagues incorporates three dimensions – *position*, *behaviour* and *personality* – and four personality types – Bold, Expressive, Sympathetic and Technical. The authors also describe four generalized organizational environments: Active/Competitive, Willing/Steady, Precise/Systematic and Persuasive/Interactive. Their approach demands that individuals identify their own personality type, the personality types of others with whom they interact, and the organizational situation. The theory then offers a power management model which relates the personalities of both leaders and followers to four mixes of task-directive behaviour and human relationships – Directing, Developing, Co-producing and Self-pacing – enabling the individual to identify which approach will be successful in a particular organizational situation.

Bell, C. (1972) *Influencing: Marketing the Ideas that Matter*, Jossey-Bass.
Berlew, D.E. (1974) 'Leadership and Organizational Excitement', *California Management Review*, vol. 17, no. 2, pp. 21–30.
Brewer, J.H., Ainsworth, J.M. and Wynne, G.E. (1984) *Power Management*, Prentice-Hall.
Coplin, W.D. and O'Leary, M. K. with Gould, C. (1985) *Power Persuasion*, Addison Wesley Longman.
Harrison, R. (1980) 'Personal Power and Influence in Organization Development', in Burke, W. and Goodstein, L.D. (eds) *Trends and Issues in OD: Current Theory and Practice*, Jossey-Bass, pp. 15–19.
Huczynski, A.A. (1996) *Influencing Within Organizations*, Prentice-Hall.
Karp, H.B. (1985) *Personal Power: An Unorthodox Guide to Success*, American Management Association, AMACOM.
Korda, M. (1976) *Power: How To Get It, How To Use It*, Ballantine.
Monsky, M. (1976) *Looking Out for No. 1*, Pocket Books.

Ringer, R. (1976) *Winning Through Intimidation*, Fawcett World.

See also: Achievement motivation intervention; Grid management; Implementing the organizational renewal process; Interaction influence analysis; Interaction management; Kepner-Tregoe Approach; LIFO method; Managing for productivity; Situational leadership; 3-D management effectiveness seminar

Pre-course learning

Pre-course learning refers to a set of preparatory activities a student may be asked to complete before a course or programme officially begins. In most cases, the materials will be mailed to students, and they will be expected to study them either at work or at home.

Perhaps the most well-known form of pre-course learning material is a *set of objectives*, which defines what the course will try to achieve. While these can serve to focus the student's mind, there are a number of pitfalls to this approach. The objectives may be ambiguous and fail to communicate the teacher's intentions. There may be more than one path through a body of knowledge, and lists of 'what the student should be able to do' at the conclusion of the course may not reflect the structure of the knowledge being presented. Objectives may also be offputting, either because they are couched in formal language, or because they are seen as the teacher's, and not necessarily shared by the students. In order to overcome some of these problems, a number of alternative pre-course learning techniques have been developed.

A *pre-test* is a set of questions distributed to students before any formal instruction takes place, which may relate to items included in a test at the end of the course. Students may be asked to answer the questions or simply study them. The purpose of this exercise is to focus students' attention on the key concepts and material, or to serve as a model of what will ultimately be accomplished. Pre-tests have also been found to increase students' sensitivity to the learning situation, drawing their attention to issues, problems and events they will encounter during the course, and helping them to evaluate the relevance and meaning of the learning task. They help to alert and orientate students, preparing them for both the character and content of the teaching that is to follow.

An *overview* is a brief summary of what will be accomplished during the course. In general, overviews consist of continuous prose rather than lists of topics or questions, and their purpose is to familiarize students with the central arguments being presented, emphasizing key points, introducing technical terms or setting out the general structure of the material to be covered. They are usually written in the same style as the material which is to follow, and take the form of a selective precis.

Finally, *advance organizers* aim to clarify the learning task ahead. While the other pre-course learning approaches concentrate on the course's content, advance organizers focus on its processes. They are frequently pitched at a higher level of abstraction, generality and inclusiveness, providing a broad framework rather than a limited, narrow and highly specific outline. Expository advance organizers are used when the course material is likely to be completely unfamiliar to students, providing a foundation for this new material by building on the knowledge they already possess. Comparative advance organizers are used when the material is not new, emphasizing similarities and contrasts between the course content and what students already know.

Ausubel, D.P. (1965) *Educational Psychology: A Cognitive View*, Holt, Rinehart and Winston.
Davies, I.K. (1976) *Objectives in Curriculum Design*, McGraw-Hill, Chapter 10.
Hartley, J. (1973) 'The Effect of Pre-testing on Post-test Performance', *Instructional Science*, vol. 2, no. 2, pp. 193–214.
Hartley, J. and Davies, I.K. (1976) 'Introducing New Materials: The Role of Pre-tests, Behavioural Objectives, Overviews and Advance Organisers as Pre-instructional Strategies', *Review of Educational Research*, vol. 46, no. 2.
McDonald-Ross, M. (1973) 'Behavioural Objectives: A Critical Review', *Instructional Science*, vol. 2, no. 1, pp. 1–52.

See also: Advance organizers; Concept mapping; Mind Mapping; Self-help; Text

Preaching

Although preaching is usually associated with religion, its quality of earnest discourse driven by the speaker's desire to persuade the audience to accept their deeply held beliefs also has applications in the business world. Historically, the objective of preaching has been to change listeners' minds, and hence their behaviour, and this aim is shared by motivational speakers. In addition, the skills of preparing and delivering an effective sermon can be adapted to both conference and classroom presentations.

Broadus, J.A. and Stanfield, V.L. (1979) *On the Preparation and Delivery of Sermons*, Harper.
Koller, C.W. (1997) *How to Preach Without Notes*, Baker Book House.

Stott, J.R. (1994) *Between Two Worlds: The Art of Preaching in the Twentieth Century*, Wm B. Eerdmans Publishing Company.

See also: Lecture; Lecture-building; Lesson-demonstration method; Demonstration-performance method

Problem pack

A problem pack presents individual students with a series of related problem-solving exercises in the form of a pack of cards. Each card carries a clear definition of a situation and presents a series of alternative courses of action, the option chosen dictating which card is addressed next. This approach lends itself to technical subjects, and it has been used to develop medical students' diagnostic skills. For example, one card describes a patient's symptoms, and the student is given the option of requesting certain tests. They are then referred to a card which gives the test results and go on to make further decisions. Problem packs can also be used for assessment, in which case each student is given a problem pack and scored on whether they complete it with the minimum number of decisions.

See also: Action maze; Mystery clue method; Person-card technique; Problem-based learning; Problem-centred group; Problem-solving cycle; Problem-solving group; Programmed learning; Programmed simulation

Problem-based learning

Adopting a learner-centred strategy, problem-based learning presents students with significant, contextualized, real-life, ill-structured situations and provides them with resources, guidance, instruction and opportunities for reflection as they develop their knowledge of the content and their problem-solving skills. Although many variants of the approach exist, all share five distinguishing characteristics. They use a problem to provide a stimulus as a starting point. They focus on types of problems students may face after they graduate. The knowledge students are expected to acquire is organized around the problems, rather than disciplines. Students assume individual and collective responsibility for their own instruction and learning. Finally, most of the learning occurs in small groups, rather than lectures.

Alavi, C. (ed.) (1995) *Problem Based Learning in a Health Sciences Curriculum*, Routledge.

Birch, W. (1986) 'Towards a Model for Problem-based Learning', *Studies in Higher Education*, vol. 11, no. 1, pp. 73–82.

Boud, D. and Feletti, G. (1997) *The Challenge of Problem-based Learning*, Kogan Page.

Bowden, P. (1986) 'Problem-oriented Training', *Journal of Management Development*, vol. 5, no. 1, pp. 52–61.

Brown, R.B. and McCartney, S. (1994) 'Learning About Knowing, Knowing About Learning', *Education and Training Technology International*, vol. 31, no. 4, pp. 254–67.

Hoffmann, B. and Ritchie, D. (1997) 'Using Multimedia to Overcome Problems with Problem-based Learning', *Instructional Science*, vol. 25, pp. 97–115.

Margetson, D. (1994) 'Current Educational Reform and the Significance of Problem-based Learning', *Studies in Higher Education*, vol. 19, no. 1, pp. 5–19.

Reynolds, F. (1997) 'Studying Psychology at Degree Level: Would Problem-based Learning Enhance Students' Experiences?', *Studies in Higher Education*, vol. 22, no. 3, pp. 263–75.

Schmidt, H.G. (ed.). (1994) 'Problem-based Learning', special issue of *Instructional Science*, vol. 22, no. 4.

See also: Problem pack; Problem-centred group; Problem-solving cycle; Problem-solving group

Problem-centred group

The purpose of a problem-centred group (PCG) is to encourage students to think analytically or creatively by focusing on a problem set by the teacher. Solving this problem may demand that they evaluate information or apply some previously agreed criteria. A PCG usually consists of about six students. The technique can be used during a lecture by simply combining two buzz groups, or during a small-group session. In either case, the group discussion enables the teacher to gauge how well students apply the material presented in lectures or prescribed reading. As they work on the task, the teacher is available to clarify any points that are unclear.

Bligh has suggested five different types of problem that can be set for a problem-centred group. To teach the skills of *selecting and organizing literature*, the students can be set a problem which requires them to carry out research in the library; alternatively, a large range of books from which they must choose may be brought into the classroom. In order to consolidate knowledge of general principles and to illustrate how to apply them, students may be set *problems with a single correct solution*, such as identifying the cause of some phenomenon. To encourage them to understand and be aware of different viewpoints, they may be set *problems with a number of possible solutions*. To provide training in dealing with *problems that require judgement*, they may be asked to evaluate a theory. Finally, the technique can provide a framework for *revision and preparation for an examination*.

Bligh, D.A. (1972) *What's the Use of Lectures?*, Penguin Books, p. 192.

Boud, D. and Feletti, G. (1997) *The Challenge of Problem-Based Learning*, Kogan Page.

De Graaff, E. and Bouhuijs, P.A.J. (1993) *Implementation of Problem-Based Learning in Higher Education*, IBD.

Fogerty, R. (1997) *Problem Based Learning*, Skylight Publications.

Gijselaers, W.H. (ed.) (1995) *Educational Innovation in Economics and Business Administration: The Case of Problem-based Learning*, Kluwer Academic Publishing.

Glasgow, N.A. (1997) *New Curriculum for New Times: A Guide to Student Centred, Problembased Learning*, Corwin Press.

Wilkerson, L. and Gijselaers, W.H. (eds). (1996) *Bringing Problem-Based Learning to Higher Education: Theory and Practice*, Jossey-Bass.

See also: Action maze; Conference method; Group buzz; Group discussion; Guided design approach; Literature search; Mystery clue method; Person-card technique; Problem pack; Problem-based learning; Problem-solving cycle; Problem-solving group; Programmed learning; Programmed simulation; Skill session

Problem-solving cycle

The five stages of the problem-solving cycle can be taught to a large group by dividing it into task groups of four or five members. A facilitator then guides each group through the stages while they examine an incident that highlights some behavioural problem in a company, for example. The first stage involves clarifying the symptoms, and distinguishing between these and the underlying causes. The next stage is to identify all possible causes. Having done this, the group goes on to isolate the relevant causes in this case. A brainstorm is then conducted to generate a wide range of alternative solutions. The final stage is to evaluate and test the solutions in order to select the most appropriate. If all the task groups have been working on the same problem, a plenary session can then be held to collate their suggested solutions.

Flood, R.L. (1995) *Solving Problem Solving*, Wiley.

Lowe, P. (1995) *Creativity and Problem-solving*, McGraw-Hill.

Lumsdaine, E. (1995) *Creative Problem-solving*, McGraw-Hill.

Sternberg, R.J. (1994) *Thinking and Problem-solving*, Academic Press.

Woods, M., Whetten, D. and Camerson, K. (1996) *Effective Problem Solving*, HarperCollins.

See also: Brainstorming; Case-critical incident analysis; Free discussion group; Guided design approach; Kepner-Tregoe Approach; Problem pack; Problem-based learning; Problem-solving group

Problem-solving group

Some problems can be resolved without reflective thought, for example by following an algorithm, in which case the scope for learning about the wider range of problem-solving skills is limited. However, such mechanistic methods are seldom appropriate when addressing the types of difficulties individuals encounter in their working lives, such as situations in which they must make a complex decision, answer a thought-provoking question, weigh the advantages of different ways of performing an activity, draw a conclusion or inference, carry out an analysis or define relationships. All teaching methods should incorporate elements of problem-solving, whether they focus on real-life problems or ones invented by the teacher to promote learning, and the skills required can be taught and developed using a number of group approaches.

In group-problem-solving, the teacher's role is to help students identify the relevant issues and generate alternative solutions. Students should be taught to apply the conceptual steps of the scientific method: observing a chosen phenomenon, accumulating facts, noting any patterns arising from these, finding plausible explanations for the patterns by constructing hypotheses, making predictions on the basis of these hypotheses, and checking these predictions through experimentation. Understanding the processes involved is as important as selecting a correct solution in a particular instance, and guidance is often necessary to enable students to choose from the huge number of alternative solutions available. The criteria for selection can be based on three different approaches: experience, experimentation, and research and analysis. The *experience* approach assumes that our past mistakes and successes provide a reliable guide to action. However, it is often difficult to identify the reasons for our mistakes, and relying on this method alone may not enable us to address new problems, so it is important to develop more reliable ways to analyse our experiences. *Experimental problem-solving* involves applying a number of possible solutions, then examining the results. Although this approach allows us to address novel problems, it may prove time-consuming and expensive. *Research and analysis* is the most effective approach. Data is gathered about the situation, then the problem is broken down into its components so that the various factors can be studied.

Lamb, D. (1991) *Discovery, Creativity and Problem-solving*, Avebury.

Larson, L. (1986) 'Improving Management Development Through Problem-solving Groups', *Journal of Management Development*, vol. 5, no. 2, pp. 15–26.

Lowe, P. (1995) *Creativity and Problem-solving*, McGraw-Hill.

Lumsdaine, E. (1995) *Creative Problem-solving*, McGraw-Hill.

Newman, V. (1998) *Made to Measure Problem Solving*, Gower.

Rayward-Smith, V. (1996) *Adopting Decision Technologies: Modern Heuristic Methods*, Wiley.

Rickards, T. (1990) *Creativity and Problem Solving at Work*, Gower.

Robson, M. (1998) *Problem Solving in Groups* (2nd edn), Gower.

Runco, M.A. (ed.) (1994) *Problem Finding, Problem Solving and Creativity*, Ablex Publishing.

Tuma, D.T. and Reif, F. (1980) *Problem Solving and Education: Issues in Teaching and Research*, Lawrence Erlbaum Associates.

See also: Absenteeism/turnover task force; Action learning; Action maze; Conference method; Group buzz; Group discussion; Group syndicate method; Guided design approach; Kepner Tregoe Approach; Literature search; Management Oversight and Risk Tree; Multiple management; Mystery clue method; Nominal group technique; Person-card technique; Problem pack; Problem-based learning; Problem-solving cycle; Problem-solving group; Programmed learning; Programmed simulation; Skill session

Process analysis

Process analysis considers interactions between one or more members of a group, and examines the processes involved, such as determining how problems are solved and how roles are allocated. The precise approach adopted depends on the aspect and level of social interaction being addressed, and there are three distinct methodologies with different objectives.

Group analysis considers aspects of a working group, such as the amount and direction of communication between members, how norms develop and are enforced, how conflict between members is managed, and how decisions are made. Because this method focuses on the group as a whole, it limits intrusiveness and is less threatening to members because the group cannot pinpoint the individuals or relationships that are causing difficulties. Survey feedback analysis is one example of this approach, in which discussion centres on data gathered about general aspects of group functioning. *Role analysis* does allow the identification of individuals, but limits itself to studying task-oriented behaviour, including members' performance and the relationships between them in their roles within the group. For example, role negotiation addresses members' expectations of each other in performing their roles, but avoids issues of personal and inter-personal style. In contrast *inter-personal analysis* focuses explicitly on relationships, and addresses such topics as inclusion and exclusion, members' tendency to influence and be influenced, and closeness or distance between individuals. The T-group is an example of this approach.

Argyris, C. (1962) *Interpersonal Competence and Organizational Effectiveness*, Dorsey.

Argyris, C. (1970) *Intervention Theory and Method*, Addison Wesley Longman.

Falchikov, N. (1993) 'Group Process Analysis: Self and Peer-Assessment of Working Together in a Group', *Innovations in Education and Training International*, vol. 30, no. 3, pp. 275–83.

See also: Action profiling; Behaviour analysis; Case conference; Controlled-pace negotiation; Coverdale training; Fishbowl; Group dynamics laboratory; Group with ground rules; Instrumented feedback; Interactive skills training; Neuro-linguistic programming; Personalized reflection; Process consultation; Role prescription; Self-tests; Sensitivity (T-group) training; Sociometry; Structured social skills seminar

Process consultation

In this intervention, a skilled outside consultant works with individuals or groups to help them learn about social processes and deal with the problems that arise from them. The consultant observes the processes of problem-solving meetings, intervening when appropriate to enable the group to examine and improve its functioning. The roles and functions the group members fulfil reflect the group's structure, and this affects its processes, including communication, problem-solving, group norm formation, leadership, inter-group co-operation and competition.

According to Schein, process consultants can contribute in four ways. They can make *agenda-setting interventions* by asking questions about inter-personal issues, reviewing agendas, testing procedures and describing models of inter-personal processes. They can provide *feedback of observa-*

tional data, either after meetings or during work time. They can make *structural suggestions*, addressing issues such as group membership, the ways members interact and communicate, how work is allocated within the group, how responsibility is assigned, and how authority is exercised. Finally, they can provide assistance by *coaching and counselling individuals*.

The process consultation model takes the view that the consultant should serve as a resource, rather than an expert. Therefore, it is rare for them to make a specific recommendation, and they concentrate instead on providing accurate feedback and helping clients to analyse the costs, benefits and consequences of alternative courses of action, examining their feasibility, relevance and appropriateness. In this, the role of process consultant resembles that of a counsellor, since both aim to help clients to improve their ability to observe and process data about themselves, learn from feedback, and play an active role in identifying and solving their own problems. The approach also resembles team-building and inter-group team-building interventions, except that it places a greater emphasis on diagnosing and understanding process events, and the consultant tends to use more non-directive and questioning methods in order to encourage the group to solve its own problems.

Coghlan, D. (1988) 'In Defence of Process Consultation', *Leadership and Organization Development Journal*, vol. 9, no. 2, pp. 27–31.
Coghlan, D. (1988–9) 'Process Consultation Skills for Personnel Managers', *Organizational Behaviour Teaching Review*, vol. 13, no. 3, pp. 87–93.
Kaplan, R.E. (1979) 'The Conspicuous Absence of Evidence that Process Consultation Enhances Task Performance', *Journal of Applied Behavioural Science*, vol. 15, no. 3, pp. 346–60.
Reddy, W.B. (1994) *Intervention Skills: Process Consultation for Small Groups and Teams*, Jossey-Bass.
Schein, E. (1987) *Process Consultation: Lessons for Managers and Consultants, Volume 1*, Addison Wesley Longman.
Schein, E. (1988) *Process Consultation: Its Role in Organizational Development, Volume 2*, Addison Wesley Longman.

See also: Coaching; Consultation; Consulting pair; Functional role analysis; Group development laboratory; Hearing; Insider-outsider consulting teams; Interaction influence analysis; Likes and reservations; Non-verbal encounters; Polling; Positive peer culture; Process analysis; Shadow consultant; Team-building activities; Third-party peacemaking interventions

Proctor method

Proctors are undergraduate students who serve as tutors, and they play a key role in some personalized systems of instruction, in particular the Keller plan. Working under the supervision of the course lecturer, proctors may help students master course material or complete a specified unit of work, administer tests and give constructive feedback on students' results. Proctors can make a valuable contribution beyond relieving a lecturer's workload by providing feedback on the lecturer's performance, students' progress and aspects of the course which are presenting difficulties. The benefits to students include being given individual attention by a tutor who is close to them in terms of age and experience. In return, proctors gain experience and the opportunity to practise skills learnt during their own studies.

Born, D.G. (1971) *Instructor Manual for the Development of a Personalised Instruction Course*, University of Utah, Centre for the Improvement Learning and Instruction.
Rasmussen, R.V. (1981) 'Using Students as Instructors', *Exchange: The Organizational Behaviour Teaching Journal*, vol. 6, no. 4, pp. 14–18.

See also: Keller plan; Mastery learning; Peer teaching; Personalized system of instruction; Teaching as learning; Tutorium

Product familiarization programme

This approach attempts to relate employee input to product outcome by providing feedback to all employees about customers' reactions to the product they helped to produce, and how well it operated once it was installed or used by the customer. Peters and Waterman describe one application of this idea adopted by Hewlett-Packard. The company set up a series of LACE (Lab Awareness of Customer Environment) events, inviting customers to give presentations to engineers outlining their needs and their reactions to Hewlett-Packard's services and products.

Peters, T.J. and Waterman, R.H. (1982) *In Search of Excellence*, Harper and Row, p. 177.

See also: Customer interface meeting; Interface groups; Organizational mirror; Quality circles; Sensing

Productivity sharing (productivity gainsharing)

This is a generic term for a number of different pay incentive plans, many of which have implications for organizational design and culture. Productivity sharing plans are often described as a link between two separate innovations in human resources management, whereby a group incentive plan which rewards workers for productivity gains is integrated with a mechanism for worker participation in decision-making. The degree of participation depends on the type of plan adopted, but all share the aim of reducing product manufacturing costs, and the incentive takes the form of a bonus paid to employees for cost savings. The bonuses are reliant on factors employees can influence directly, so external market conditions would not be part of the equation. In deciding which would be the most appropriate productivity gainsharing intervention, management considers the level of the productivity required, and the period over which it should be achieved and then maintained. Among the most popular programmes are Improshare (with or without employee involvement), the Rucker plan and the Scanlon plan. Some programmes, such as Improshare, can be installed in either an autocratic or a participative manner. However, one means of increasing value added is to achieve cost savings through greater employee participation, and mechanisms for this include idea and problem identification programmes, productivity committees, and allowing employees to vote on whether or not to adopt the plan. Other programmes rely on the ratio of the unit of production to labour cost remaining stable, so these are likely to be useful only to small firms with a median of some 250 employees.

The *Scanlon plan*, which is the oldest and perhaps the best-known, uses historical experience in a plant to establish labour costs as a percentage of sales income. A base ratio is determined by dividing payroll by sales, plus or minus inventory, and a bonus is awarded in any month in which labour costs are less than the ratio. In the *Rucker plan*, all plant employees except the top managers share a percentage of the productivity gain. This is based on the historic relationship between the value added by US industry and its payroll costs, which has been relatively stable over time. Value added by manufacturing is measured as the difference between the costs of manufacturing the product and its sales price, and a bonus is awarded in any month in which the labour cost is less than the ratio of value added to payroll.

These productivity gainsharing programmes differ in subtle but profound ways. All the measurements try to encapsulate the ratio of labour inputs to production output. However, problems may arise because the sensitivity of the measures can be distorted by the environment and product mix factors. The differences between the formulae also have behavioural implications, but all the plans rely on a certain degree of acceptance and mutual trust.

Belcher, J.G. (1991) *Gainsharing*, Gulf Publishing Company.
Collins, D. (1998) *Gainsharing and Power: Lessons from Six Scanlon Plans*, ILR Press.
Graham-Moore, B.E., Ross, T.L. and Ross, R.A. (1995) *Gainsharing and Employee Involvement*, BNA Books.
Jackson, W.M. (1996) *Jackson Gainsharing: Boosting Productivity, Quality and Profits*, Mascotte Publishing.

See also: Improshare; Profit-sharing; Reward systems; Rucker plan; Scanlon plan; Shared ownership

Profit-sharing

Profit-sharing should be distinguished from productivity gainsharing plans, which are directly tied to production output. Profit – the amount of revenue remaining after all a business's costs have been paid, including wages, taxes and any basic return to shareholders – may be invested, ploughed back into the business or shared out among the employees, managers and shareholders. The profit-sharing approach was first adopted by a number of firms at the beginning of the Industrial Revolution, when it proved neither popular nor successful, but it gained in popularity during the period of inflation in the USA after the Second World War. Profit-sharing is not a substitute for paying reasonable wages, and such schemes should not be seen as part of an anti-union strategy. Their success does not depend on reducing employees' pay, as decreases in the basic wage are coupled to profit-sharing bonuses. Whereas basic wages, merit increases and wage incentives all recognize differences between individual employees, profit-sharing provides a means of giving concrete expression to the mutual interests that exist among employees, managers and shareholders. The main aim of such schemes is to foster a spirit of co-operation and to encourage employees to work efficiently to produce a competitive product, since there is a clear link between the company's performance and their pay. Profit-sharing workers are generally more highly motivated than workers who are only paid wages.

In recent years, profit-sharing has generated renewed interest. Some governments have seen it as a way of restructuring the relationship between capital and labour by allowing all employees to benefit from their company's growth and prosperity, and have encouraged employee share ownership schemes for the same reasons. In addition, such schemes offer macro-economic benefits. Companies traditionally agree to award each employee a pre-determined wage before the size of the company's income over a given period is known. While this offers employees a degree of financial stability, it can have a detrimental effect on the unemployed and on inflation. Widespread adoption of profit-sharing schemes would change the economics of labour: for example, companies would be more reluctant to lay employees off in lean times, and more inclined to hire them in times of plenty. It has been argued that in a profit-sharing economy, by acting in their own self-interest companies would tend to create a tight labour market, high output and low prices.

Proponents of profit-sharing recommend a number of guidelines. Such schemes should cover all employees, not just managers. They should be linked directly to profit or added value, with each company tailoring the scheme to suit its own circumstances. Once the profit-sharing formula is fixed, it should be applied consistently. Employees should be kept informed of the precise formula adopted and the level of profits, and participation should be encouraged by establishing joint councils, where employee and management representatives can discuss not just profit-sharing issues, but also development plans and employment opportunities.

However, profit-sharing schemes suffer from at least three disadvantages. The share awarded to an individual employee is not directly related to their efforts in their own job. Employees may have to wait six months or more for their reward, and there is always a possibility that there will be little or no profit to share. Finally, a number of large and multi-national companies arrange their tax-avoidance strategies in such a way that a certain number of their facilities never show a profit, even in successful years.

Baddon, L. (1989) *People's Capitalism: A Critical Analysis of Profit Sharing and Employee Share Ownership*, Routledge.

D'Art, D.J. (1992) *Economic Democracy and Financial Participation: A Comparative Study*, Routledge.

Florkowski, G.W. (1987) 'The Organizational Impact of Profit Sharing', *Academy of Management Review*, vol. 12, pp. 622–36.

Poole, M. (1989) *The Origins of Economic Democracy*, Routledge.

Poole, M. and Jenkins, G. (1991) *The Impact of Economic Democracy: Profit Sharing and Employee Shareholding Schemes*, Routledge.

Roomkin, M.J. (1991) *Profit Sharing and Gainsharing*, Scarecrow Press.

Tyson, D.E. (1996) *Profit Sharing in Canada: The Complete Guide to Designing and Implementing Plans that Really Work*, Wiley.

See also: Improshare; Productivity sharing; Reward systems; Rucker plan; Scanlon plan; Shared ownership

Programmed learning (automated teaching; individualized programme of instruction)

Programmed learning is a self-teaching approach based on B.F. Skinner's behaviourist theories which is used to convey cognitive learning: facts, techniques, principles and ideas. It demands active participation from students, they are required to make the minimum number of errors as they carry out tasks, they are given constant feedback about their performance, and they progress at their own speed. The approach gives students a certain degree of control over their own learning process, selecting a programme that corresponds most closely to their needs and interests, deciding on the timing and duration of their studies, choosing between different branches of the programme, evaluating their own learning, and taking advantage of workgroups or help from advisers. However, the programme's structure is dictated by its designer, who defines the learning goals and divides the subject matter into discrete steps, each of which follows the pattern: present the material, the student reacts, provide direct feedback.

Three kinds of programme exist: linear programmes, in which each student works through the same material in a set sequence; branching programmes, which provide a common path for those who learn quickly, and branches of remedial material for those who do not, and a variant known as mathetics, which attempts to reduce study time by analysing the learning situation carefully. Some writers argue that PL is well suited to imparting factual information on subjects which have clearly recognized procedures and 'correct' answers, but that it is difficult to write programmes in areas where the subject matter is not – or perhaps cannot be – clearly defined. Other experts regret that PL has tended to be used primarily to achieve lower-order cognitive objectives, whereas it is well suited to realizing middle-order cognitive and affective objectives, especially when integrated with flexible approaches such as computer-assisted-learning. Although commercially available materials can teach basic facts and formulae, they are often boring and uninspiring, and have led to the fallacious belief that PL can only be used in this way, whereas there are successful programmes which teach medical diagnosis, art and poetry appreciation, and listening skills.

The systems used to deliver programmed learning have developed dramatically in recent years. Originally, PL materials were presented in printed form, usually in a book. The requirement for active learning was fulfilled by requiring students to answer questions, undertake tasks or respond to the material in other ways at frequent intervals, and immediate feedback on performance was claimed to guarantee subject mastery. Nowadays, programmed material is mainly presented by means of personal computers, usually involving a range of multi-media stimuli. However, irrespective of the delivery technology, the most important aspect of programmed learning is still the quality of the programme itself: the sequencing and organization of the units of information and instruction in order to achieve the required behaviour or performance.

Comparative research suggests that traditional teaching methods are seldom more effective than programmed learning, and there is frequently no difference in their results. However, programmed learning is generally quicker and cheaper, it can be made available to large numbers of geographically dispersed students, it has standardized instruction procedures, and it can provide immediate tuition if there is a sudden increase in the intake of students.

Ely, D.P. (ed.) (1996) *Classic Writings on Instructional Technology*, Libraries Unlimited, USA.

Ivers, K.S. and Barron, A.E. (1997) *Multimedia Projects in Education: Designing Producing and Assessing*, Libraries Unlimited, USA.

Kibby, M.R. (ed.) (1994) *Computer Assisted Learning*, Elsevier/Pergamon.

Markle, S. (1969) *Good Frames and Bad*, Wiley.

Neale, M.H., Toye, M. and Belbiner, C. (1968) 'Adult Training: The Use of Programmed Instruction', *Occupational Psychology*, vol. 42, no. 1, pp. 23–31.

Newby, T.J. (ed.) (1996) *Instructional Technology for Teaching and Learning*, Prentice-Hall.

Shambaugh, R.N. and Magliaro, S.G. (1997) *Mastering the Possibilities: A Process Approach to Instructional Design*, Allyn and Bacon.

Shirley-Smith, K. (1973) *Guide to Programmed Techniques in Industrial Training*, Gower.

Tennyson, R.D. (ed.) (1997) *Instructional Design: International Perspectives: Theory, Research and Models, Volume 1*, Lawrence Erlbaum Associates.

See also: Autonomous group learning; Computer-assisted learning; Mathetics; Personalized system of instruction; Problem pack; Programmed simulation

Programmed simulation

A programmed simulation combines a simulation with programmed learning, and the approach is commonly used to teach decision-making techniques. Each member of the class is given a booklet describing a number of cases. The class then divides into groups of four. Each case consists of seven or eight stages or episodes, each of which requires participants to make a decision, perhaps by choosing from a number of options. Each group member makes their own decision before discussing the issue with the others to arrive at a group decision. The group then refers to the booklet again, which gives feedback regarding the appropriateness of their chosen course of action. Unlike the action maze, the choices made do not affect the outcome of future stages.

Elgood, C. (1980) 'The Use of Business Games in Management Training', *The Training Officer*, vol. 16, no. 12, pp. 332–4.

Elgood, C. (1996) *Using Management Games* (2nd edn), Gower.

Elgood, C. (1997) *Handbook of Management Games and Simulations* (6th edn), Gower.

Riis, J.O. (ed.) (1995) *Simulation Games in Product Management*, Chapman and Hall.

See also: Action maze; Behavioural simulation; Computer-assisted learning; Experiential exercise; Game; Guided design approach; In-basket exercise; Problem pack; Programmed learning; Self-instructional module and interactive group; Simulation

Project method

Projects have been used to promote learning since the beginning of the twentieth century. Rather than merely setting a theoretical problem to be solved, projects are integrated programmes of work built around a central situation or idea that require learners to complete a practical task, such as producing a report, a design or a computer programme. Learners may sometimes choose the project subject themselves, but it should be sufficiently demanding that they need to take initiatives, make their own decisions and take part in a variety of educational activities while producing the end product. A project may take as little as a day or as much as two years to complete, and teaching staff are involved throughout in an advisory rather than a didactic role.

Project methods offer a number of advantages. They promote active learning, enable knowledge from different disciplines to be combined, and encourage inventiveness and originality. They allow students to examine certain fields more deeply, and their flexibility means that they can be adapted to the different speeds at which individual work and learn. Projects should generate involvement, develop independent study and group work skills, and provide students with feedback on their performance and ability to communicate. Because individualized learning is not suitable for all students, some may need support from a tutor or group in order to sustain their interest and develop their ideas. Group projects may involve students from the same course or from different ones.

Abercrombie, M.L.J. (1981) 'Changing Basic Assumptions About Teaching and Learning', in Boud, D.J. (ed.) *Developing Autonomy in Student Learning*, Kogan Page.

Brown, A.D. and Neilson, A. (1993) 'The Pros and Cons of Experientially Based Projects', *Journal of Management Education*, vol. 17, no. 4, pp. 498–503.

Garrett, R. (1971) 'Project Based Education and Development', *Management Education and Development*, vol. 2, no. 1, pp. 40–9.

Harding, A.G. (1973) 'The Objectives and Structure of Undergraduate Projects, Part 1', *British Journal of Educational Technology*, vol. 4, no. 2.

Harding, A.G. (1973) 'The Project: Its Place in the Learning Situation', *British Journal of Educational Technology*, vol. 4, no. 3, pp. 216–32.

Henry, J. (1994) *Teaching Through Projects*, Kogan Page.

Kilpatrick, W.H. (1918) *The Project Method: The Use of Purposeful Act in the Educative Process*, Teachers Columbia University.

Smith, B. and Dodds, B. (1997) *Developing Managers Through Project-based Learning*, Gower.

See also: Action project; Field project attachment; Industrial project; Overseas project; Project-based management development; Project orientation; Real-life entrepreneurial project

Project orientation

Unlike the project method, where the project serves as one component in a degree or diploma course, in project orientation it comprises the entire learning programme. This educational method has been adopted in Denmark, the Netherlands and Germany, for example. It forms the basis of the entire two-year basic course at the Roskilda University Centre in Denmark, where an inter-disciplinary approach means that the subjects studied and the skills acquired by students are almost entirely dictated by the demands of their chosen project. Because no prescribed syllabus exists, the resulting curriculum relates strongly to students' own interests and motivations. There are very few formal lecture courses, although teacher-guided courses are provided if students request them to assist with their project work.

The regime at Roskilda reflects a degree of democracy which does not exist in British educational institutions, for instance. There are no schools or departments, only three inter-disciplinary faculties (humanities, natural sciences and social sciences) which are divided into social and study units called *houses*. Each house provides a work centre for 70 people, 7 of whom are teachers. Each house is allocated a budget, half of which is used to pay the teachers, while the remainder is controlled by a house finance committee. The choice of projects in each house differs. A whole house can decide to undertake a single project and divide the workload between its members; a house may agree a theme which members pursue through independent but interrelating projects, or a number of groups within a house may select their own project. It is a course requirement that projects have social and political importance, and the themes chosen in the past have included the effects of lead pollution and the implications of building a nuclear power station.

Brown D. and Goodlad, S. (1975) 'Community-related Project Work in Engineering', in Goodlad, S. (ed.) *Education and Social Action*, Allen and Unwin.

Cornwall, M. (1974) 'Authority v. Experience in Higher Education: Project Orientation in Some Continental Universities', *Universities Quarterly*, vol. 29, pp. 272–98.

Cornwall, M.G. (1978) 'A New Approach to Higher Education: Project Orientation', *Journal of Further and Higher Education*, vol. 2, no. 3, pp. 43–57.

Cornwall, M.G., Schmithals, F. and Jacques, D. (1977) *Project Orientation in Higher Education*, Brighton University and the University of London Teaching Methods Unit.

See also: Action learning; Industrial project; Joint development activities; Management problem laboratory; Mystery clue method; Overseas project; Project method; Project-based management development; Real-life entrepreneurial project; Student-planned learning

Project-based management development

Project-based management development (PBMD) is based on the same philosophy as joint development activities and action learning, with which it shares many aspects of its design and methodology.

PBMD is an in-house, part-time training activity in which a real company problem serves as the vehicle for learning. The participating managers form a project team which meets regularly with the staff team of trainers to draw up ideas to present for scrutiny by an advisory group of senior managers. The staff team's role is to help the project team develop the knowledge and skills necessary to allow them to pursue their project.

PBMD helps to overcome the problems experienced by isolated individuals attending external courses while ensuring that participants' learning is relevant to the organization's needs in terms of managerial skills, knowledge and attitudes. The design also allows senior managers to take a direct and active role in promoting and overseeing the development of their staff.

Ashton, D. (1974) 'Project Based Management Development', *Education and Training*, July–August, pp. 203–5.
Ashton, D. (1974) 'Project Based Management Development', *Personnel Management*, vol. 6, no. 7, pp. 2–8.
Ashton, D. (1982) 'Developing High-Fliers in a Multinational: The Project-based Approach', *Management Education and Development*, vol. 13, part 2, pp. 104–14.
Ashton, D. and Easterby-Smith, M. (1979) *Management Development in the Organization*, Macmillan, Chapter 6.
Fuller, J. (1997) *Managing Performance Improvement Projects*, American Society for Training and Development, ASTD Press.
Lewis, J.P. (1997) *Team-based Project Management*, AMACOM.
Smith, B. and Dodds, B. (1997) *Developing Managers Through Project-based Learning*, Gower.

See also: Action learning; Industrial project; Joint development activities; Project method; Project orientation; Real-life entrepreneurial project

Prompt list

A prompt list consists of a number of questions about a particular issue or problem. For example, on the subject of training, questions might include: 'How is training organized in this company?', 'Who is primarily responsible for it?' and 'How are the needs and priorities defined?' This is an example of the discovery learning approach, since the lists set out subjects to be explored, but leave recipients to discover the answers for themselves. Such prompt lists can be adapted to almost any subject, and can be used in a variety of ways. When an individual is attached to a manager in another department or firm, seeking the answers to

the questions can provide the basis for discussions, possibly improving their relationship with the job-holder by demonstrating informed interest. Lists can also serve as a development aid, since each question can provide the topic for an individual's project. Once a learner's strengths or weaknesses have been identified during appraisal, a prompt list can be used to guide subsequent discussions. They also have applications in team-building activities, where they provide a starting point for group feedback analysis sessions. Finally, some management training courses now rely on prompt lists instead of lengthy course notes, packaging their handouts in plastic wallets similar to those used to hold credit cards.

Barrington, H. and Beanland, D. (1978) 'The Prompt List in Training', *BACIE Journal*, vol. 32, no. 1, January.
Brassard, M. (1996) *The Memory Jogger and Featuring the Seven Management Planning Tools*, Goal/Qpc.
Roberts-Phelps, G. (1998) *Training Event Planning Guide*, Gower.

See also: Action learning; Coaching; Discovery method; Manager shadowing; SmartProcess; Work cards; Work-related exercise

Proposal team assignment (junior board)

In reviewing current working methods and future approaches, a company may establish a number of proposal teams, consisting of middle or junior management (rather than top management). These teams review existing operating procedures and policies, recommend changes and improvements. The inclusion of junior managers is favoured because they are felt to be more highly motivated to introduce improvements, whereas senior staff may be content to maintain the status quo. The team may include staff from different departments in the same organization, and may study issues such as the application of a computerized data system or the introduction of flexitime.

A related approach is sometimes known as the *junior board*. This is a participative technique designed to teach executives to deal with problems extending beyond the confines of a single function. The junior board may be a permanent group of senior managers, perhaps at a level just below the main board, or its membership may consist of a rotating pool of junior managers. In either case, they usually consider a problem that has been submitted to the main board. This approach provides training in addressing senior management problems, and can be effective in extending managers' knowledge of the company. However, one disadvantage is that, since the junior board seldom has the power to act on its proposals, its deliberations may appear rather academic. This can be overcome to some extent if the board is seen as having an advisory role, with its recommendations being presented to the board of directors.

Lazorko, L. (1972) 'Junior Boards Train Managers', *International Management*, January.

Mumford, A. (1971) *The Manager and Training*, Pitman, Chapter 8.

See also: Consulting assignment; Committee assignment; Development assignment; Evaluation audit assignment; Junior Achievement company; Multiple management; Selection board assignment; Staff meeting assignment; Task force assignment

Psychodrama

The term 'psychodrama' has at least two distinct meanings: it is used as an umbrella term for techniques such as sociodrama, role-playing and other active methods, but it is also used in a more specific sense much closer to the ideas of Jacob Moreno, who developed the technique.

When used as a generic term, psychodrama includes *monodrama* (in which the subject plays the parts of all the participants in a situation), *sociodrama* (which considers interactive situations, focusing on the collective aspects of a problem, such as the hierarchical structure of an organization's department) and *role-playing* (which allows individuals to explore how to deal with specific situations, such as attending a job interview).

Moreno's *psychodrama* is a form of psychotherapy in which the patient or subject enacts conflicts, instead of talking about them. This is usually conducted in a group setting with other people playing roles in the individual's private drama (a process known as 'alter egoing'), and the therapist or trainer taking the role of director. It has been used in a variety of settings, from therapy to superficial game-playing exercises.

The first phase of a psychodrama is *realization*, in which the subject (or *actor*) begins by acting out a situation from their everyday life. The scenes portrayed may be factual or invented. The second phase involves *replacement*, whereby trained staff assume the roles of real persons drawn from the actor's life, or imaginary ones. The final phase, *clarification*, consists of analysing the interaction and providing feedback.

Applying psychodrama in the form developed by Moreno requires a fairly large and well-trained staff. It is quite demanding for the trainer, who takes a very active role as director, social analyst and therapist, with support from auxiliary staff.

Moreno also developed the technique of *soliloquy*. Following the completion of the action in a psychodrama, the participants are asked to re-enact the scene as it happened, but this time to act out the feelings they failed to express. These previously unspoken feelings are often delivered in a softer voice, like a soliloquy in a play.

Blatner, A. (1996) *Acting In: Practical Applications of Psychodramatic Methods*, Springer Publishing.

Cossa, M., Fleischmann-Ember, S.S. and Hazelwood, L.G. (1996) *Acting Out: The Workbook – A Guide to the Development and Presentation of Issue-oriented, Audience Interactive, Improvisational Theatre*, Accelerated Development, USA.

Emunah, R. (1994) *Acting for Real: Drama Therapy Process, Technique and Performance*, Brunner/Mazel.

Holmes, H. and Karp, M. (eds) (1991) *Psychodrama: Inspiration and Technique*, Routledge.

Holmes, H., Karp, M. and Watson, M. (1994) *Psychodrama Since Moreno: Innovations in Theory and Practice*, Routledge.

Moreno, J.L. (1987) *The Essential Moreno*, Springer Publishing.

Moreno, J.L. (1991) *Psychodrama and Sociodrama in American Education*, Beacon House.

Pickering, K. (1997) *Drama Improvised: A Sourcebook for Teachers and Therapists* (2nd edn), Routledge.

Yablonsky, L. (1992) *Psychodrama: Resolving Emotional Problems Through Role Playing*, Brunner/Mazel.

See also: Alcohol recovery programme; Apperception-interaction method; Bioenergetics; Cluster laboratory; Cognitive-behavioural therapy; Cousin laboratory; Encounter groups; Gestalt techniques; Group development laboratory; Human relations laboratory; Instrumented laboratory; Laboratory training; Monodrama; Organizational laboratory; Personal development laboratory; Psychotherapy; Role-playing; Role-reversal; Sensitivity (T-group) training; Sociodrama; Tavistock Conference Method; Transactional Analysis

Psychological contract

A psychological contract is a belief system which reflects an individual's and an organization's expectations of their relationship. It can take the form of a reciprocal agreement between an employee and their company, including what individuals believe is expected of them (*performance demands*), and what they should receive in return. In the university context, instructors' expectations about the volume and quality of work required from students is mirrored by students' assumptions that they will gain personal benefits and better grades if they comply. In this sense, both employees and companies and students and universities strike a deal.

The importance of psychological contracts was highlighted during the 1980s, when downsizing, delayering and outsourcing led some companies to make many of their middle managers redundant. In large companies after the Second World War, one important aspect of the psychological contract was that if managers did whatever the company wanted, they would be guaranteed a job for life. Those involved felt that their employers had reneged on this commitment, even though it had never been formalized in written form. In recent years, these same companies have modified the terms of their psychological contracts, emphasizing employability rather than guaranteed employment. In simple terms, companies promise to give their employees the necessary experience and training to enable them to find another job even if they are made redundant.

Kotter, J.P. (1973) 'The Psychological Contract: Managing the Joining Up Process', *California Management Review*, vol. 15, pp. 91–9.
Parks, J. and Kidder, D. (1994) 'Changing Work Relationships in the 1990s', in Cooper, C. and Rousseau, D. (eds) *Trends in Organization Behaviour*, Wiley.
Rousseau, D.M. (1995) *Psychological Contracts in Organizations: Written and Unwritten Agreements*, Sage.
Zanzi, A. (1985–6) 'Psychological Contracts and Cafeteria Style Assignments', *Organizational Behaviour Teaching Review*, vol. 10, no. 2, pp. 80–90.

See also: Corporate culture training; Induction training; Job description; Learning contract; Role prescription

Psychotherapy

Psychotherapeutic techniques aim to uncover unconscious or pre-conscious factors arising from past experiences which influence current behaviour. Psychotherapy is commonly associated with mental disorders and with medical treatment by psychiatrists and other qualified therapists. Although its aim is to change individuals' attitudes and behaviour, its suitability and the ethics of applying it as an organizational change technique have been questioned. Some academics argue that since organizations are systems, system-wide changes are necessary, whereas the personality of an individual manager is only a significant property of the system in small-group situations. However, some American academic consultants do act as

psychotherapists, using hypnotic relaxation techniques, and some of the variants of T-group training used in the 1960s contained elements of short-term group psychotherapy.

Argyris and Schon argue that psychotherapy may be appropriate in situations when managers are 'conflicted': when they do not trust anyone to give them valid information. Argyris (1970) identified another circumstance in which he felt psychotherapy would be appropriate: when managers were so closed to learning that they could not learn from different environments. Stybel argues that the most promising candidates for psychotherapy exhibit the same personality traits as the most promising clients for his organizational development technique – bright, verbal, mildly anxious about their effectiveness, and in a position to control some of the events that affect them.

Stybel suggests five conditions which dictate whether psychotherapy is likely to be effective as an organizational change technique. The client should be in a position to exert legitimate change in the organization. The organization should be small enough for behavioural change at the top to have a marked impact on the whole system. The client should spontaneously identify some or all of the organization's problems as stemming from their own dysfunctional behaviour, and express a desire to change it. The consultant should have the necessary expertise and understand both personal and organizational dynamics. Finally, the consultant should make a commitment to the client, not the organization. This last requirement stresses the person-to-person nature of the therapeutic contract.

Although Stybel acknowledges that the chances of all five criteria being met are slim, he does give an example of an appropriate application from his own experience. The behavioural strategy he used sought to create a learning situation in which existing conceptual frameworks could be exposed. The client was able to test the validity of the framework and gauge its effectiveness. Having recognized that the framework was both valid and ineffective, the client could be assisted in trying out new behaviours, leading to a deliberate decision to create an alternative conceptual framework. Stybel concludes that psychotherapy is an appropriate organizational tool, but is likely to be used only rarely, in well-defined circumstances.

Argyris, C. and Schon, D.A. (1974) *Theory in Practice: Increasing Professional Effectiveness*, Jossey-Bass.
De Board, R. (1978) *The Psychoanalysis of Organizations*, Tavistock.
Kets de Vries, M.F.R. (1995) *Organizational*

Paradoxes: A Clinical Approach to Management, Routledge.

Kets de Vries, M.F.R. and Balazs, K. (1998) 'Beyond the Quick Fix: The Psychodynamics of Organizational Transformation and Change', *European Management Journal*, vol. 16, no. 5, pp. 611–22.

Kets de Vries, M.F.R. and Miller, D. (1984) *The Neurotic Organization*, Jossey-Bass.

Neumann, J. and Hirschhorn, L. (eds) (1998) 'Integrating Psychodynamics and Organizational Theory', special issue of *Human Relations*, vol. 51, no. 11, November.

Nurick, A.J. (1987–8) 'Teacher and Therapist: An Integration of Educational Roles', *Organizational Behaviour Teaching Review*, vol. 12, no. 3, pp. 91–101.

Parrott, L. (1997) *Counselling and Psychotherapy*, McGraw-Hill.

Stybel, L.J. (1981) 'Indications for Psychotherapy as an Organizational Development Technique', *Leadership and Organizational Development Journal*, vol. 2, no. 4, pp. iii–vi.

Talley, J.E. (1986) *Counselling and Psychotherapy with College Students*, Praeger.

Willcocks, S.G. and Rees, C.J. (1995) 'A Psychoanalytical Perspective on Organizational Change', *Leadership and Organization Development Journal*, vol. 16, no. 5, pp. 32–7.

See also: Bioenergetics; Co-counselling; Cognitive-behavioural therapy; Counselling; Neuro-linguistic programming; Personal development laboratory; Psychodrama; Re-evaluation counselling; Stress management; Transactional Analysis

Quality awareness training (error-free working, 'Make Certain' programme)

Many companies have extended the notion of quality circles by instigating quality awareness training programmes to ensure that employees understand the importance of quality assurance in all aspects of their work. The measures introduced include authorizing operators to stop production lines if they feel it necessary, and setting quality targets. This is coupled with the recognition that all employees have 'customers' within the company, in the sense that the outputs of their work, ranging from partly completed assembly tasks to budget reports and analyses, are supplied to colleagues, and vice versa. As a result, these programmes stress the importance of each employee ensuring that their work has been completed to a high standard before it is passed on for processing by another member of the organization.

This principle has been applied by quality management expert Philip Crosby in the 'Make Certain' programmes for white-collar and office personnel described in his book *Quality is Free*. Crosby found that up to a quarter of all non-manufacturing work has to be redone to correct errors, with many problems arising from communication breakdowns between employees. Most functions, including management, computing, clerical operations, sales and accounting, rely on the accurate transmission of information between individuals. Each person serves as a link in the communication chain, and any errors will be propagated throughout the system unless they are identified and corrected. By ensuring that each office worker carries out their tasks correctly in the first instance, it is possible to eliminate the waste associated with reworking and to increase customer satisfaction.

Capper, R. (1997) *A Project-by-project Approach to Quality*, Gower.

Crosby, P.B. (1979) *Quality is Free: The Art of Making Quality Certain*, Mentor Books.

McKinsey and Company (1996) *Quality Pays*, Macmillan.

Zink, K.J. (1997) *Successful TQM*, Gower.

See also: Customer interface meeting; Excellence training; Involvement teams; Quality circles; Quality management; Total quality management; Zero defects

Quality circles (quality control circles; quality teams)

A quality circle has been defined as a small group of employees, preferably engaged in similar work, which holds regular voluntary meetings with a leader to identify problems, analyse their causes and recommend solutions. This approach was widely used during the 1980s, when it was seen as a way to promote company loyalty by addressing employees' desire for self-improvement and their need for group recognition, group identity and a creative outlet to counter boredom. In 1985, an estimated 400–500 British manufacturing companies and 30–40 service organizations were operating an average of 20 circles each, but they have declined in popularity since then.

Adopting a participative and problem-solving style, quality circles are based on the assumptions that employees are willing to collaborate with superiors to resolve product quality problems, and that they can learn how to make the effective use of technical and process consultants if they are given appropriate training. This may include applying quality control concepts, measuring techniques and the principles of group dynamics, team leadership and inter-personal communications. Quality circles also have applications beyond improving product quality: they have been used to increase employees' motivation, cut costs, develop a sense of corporate identity, improve relationships and introduce a more participative management style.

Although a quality circle can have up to twenty members, the usual number is seven or eight, and participants are often drawn from different levels in the organization in order to bring a variety of perspectives to bear on the problems. Each circle meets for an hour or two once or twice a month, often making recommendations for management to approve, and staff experts may be asked to attend if required. Meetings may be held in company time, but if they occur outside normal working hours participants are usually remunerated, but not necessarily at standard overtime rates. On average, a circle will complete three projects per year, each leading to savings of about $5000 for the company. This figure is difficult to verify, but if accurate, represents an impressive track record.

Barra, R. (1988) *Putting Quality Circles to Work*, McGraw-Hill.

Dale, B.G. and Hayward, S.G. (1984) 'Some of the Reasons for Quality Circle Failure, Part 1', *Leadership and Organization Development Journal*, vol. 5, no. 1, pp. 11–16.

Dale, B.G. and Hayward, S.G. (1984) 'Some of the Reasons for Quality Circle Failure, Part 2', *Leadership and Organization Development Journal*, vol. 5, no. 2, pp. 28–31.

Dale, B.G. and Hayward, S.G. (1984) 'Some of the Reasons for Quality Circle Failure, Part 3', *Leadership and Organization Development Journal*, vol. 5, no. 4, pp. 27–32.

Dessler, G. (1983) *Improving Productivity at Work*, Prentice-Hall, Chapter 6, pp. 93–118.

Lawler, E.E. and Mohrman, S.A. (1985) 'Quality Circles After the Fad', *Harvard Business Review*, January–February, pp. 65–71.

Mohr, W. and Mohr, H. (1983) *Quality Circles: Changing Images of People at Work*, Addison Wesley Longman.

Robson, M. (1988) *Quality Circles: A Practical Guide (2nd edn)*, Gower.

See also: Informal action group; Involvement teams; Multiple management; Quality awareness training; Quality management; Resources management; Scanlon plan; Study circles; Suggestion schemes; Total quality management; Zero defects

Quality management

Quality management is not so much a technique as a management philosophy, which is reflected in methods such as quality circles and quality awareness training. The best-known experts associated with the quality management movement are three Americans: J.M. Juran, W. Edwards Deming and Philip Crosby. Juran and Deming taught Japanese managers quality control practices during the American occupation of Japan after the Second World War. Although he did not take part in this initiative, Crosby's concepts of zero defects and quality management have been very influential in American industry.

Crosby's message is that while 'doing things wrong' costs money, it costs nothing to 'do things right'. He argues that simply devoting time and effort to rectifying mistakes increases companies' sales costs by about 25 per cent. According to Crosby's theory of quality improvement, quality is defined as conformance to requirements that can be measured. He notes that traditional quality assurance systems are based on the idea of making something, then checking it. Apart from being labour-intensive and expensive, this approach means that mistakes are not discovered until after the event. Drawing an analogy with safety management, which does not wait for accidents to happen before taking action, but focuses on prevention, he advocates a system which anticipates and detects errors, and takes steps to avoid them. In pursuit of the goal of zero defects, he emphasizes the importance of ensuring that employees understand the requirements of their job by giving them oral and written explanations of the procedures. When a problem occurs, Crosby recommends forming a team to discover its root cause and implement a solution. Finally, rather than relying on means of measurement which only the quality department understands, he suggests framing feedback in simple terms, such as: Mistakes during the last six months have cost the company £500 000.'

Crosby maintains that both senior and middle management have a crucial role to play in ensuring the success of quality improvement programmes. The process should not be left to individuals alone: if it is, then it will fail. Management must understand and be committed to the objectives. It must realize that improvements will demand change, and avoid clinging to habitual working methods.

Bank, J. (1992) *Essence of Total Quality Management*, Prentice-Hall.

Bounds, G. et al. (1994) *Beyond Total Quality Management*, McGraw-Hill.

Crosby, P. (1985) *Quality Without Tears: The Art of Hassle Free Management*, Plume.

Crosby, P. (1979) *Quality is Free: The Art of Making Quality Certain*, Mentor Books.

De Cock, D. and Hipkin, I. (1997) 'TQM and BPR: Beyond the Myth', *Journal of Management Studies*, vol. 34, no. 5, pp. 657–75.

Gartner, W.B. (1993) 'Dr Deming Comes to Class', *Journal of Management Education*, vol. 17, no. 2, pp. 143–8 .

Kanji, G., Dhalgaard, J. and Kristensen, K. (1997) *Fundamentals of Total Quality Management*, Chapman and Hall.

Lock, D. (ed.) (1997) *Gower Handbook of Quality Management* (2nd edn), Gower.

Spencer, B.A. (1995) 'Bringing Total Quality to Business School: The Power of Small Wins', *Journal of Management Education*, vol. 19, no. 3, pp. 367–72.

See also: Customer interface meeting; Excellence training; Involvement teams; Multiple management; Quality awareness training; Quality circles; Study circles; Total quality management; Zero defects

Quality of working life

The quality of working life (QWL) approach had its heyday in the 1970s, although it continued to feature in the literature during the 1980s before being re-labelled (if not transformed into) 'high-performance team-working' and 'empowerment teams'. Originally, QWL was seen as both a goal and a set of initiatives which sought to achieve it. As a goal, QWL reflects a company's desire to improve work conditions by creating more satisfying and attractive jobs and working environments for all its employees. From the employees' point of view, QWL requires that they participate in decisions that affect them, and demonstrate commitment to the organization and its goals in return for a greater sense of personal growth, pride in accomplishment, and job satisfaction. As a change approach, QWL links employees' individual and developmental needs to the organization's goals and its growth. QWL can also be thought of as a management philosophy whose basic premise involves developing a climate which recognizes the dignity of all employees, not only because this is a fundamental human entitlement, but because people are the organization's most important asset.

In some ways, the QWL approach has replaced job enrichment. It encompasses a wide range of change programmes which share certain basic characteristics. These include co-operation between unions and management in planning change, job or task redesign programmes so that each job forms a coherent whole, and introducing workgroups or teams (either autonomous or semi-autonomous) that often take more responsibility than usual for their own supervision and quality control. Because QWL programmes recognize the socio-technical nature of organizations, they often entail redesigning work on the shop floor. In Europe, QWL programmes frequently incorporate an element of democracy by giving employee representatives a seat on the board of directors. In the USA, QWL programmes usually enjoy formal union support, and their objectives explicitly exclude increasing profits or productivity. Some of the most notable QWL programmes, both in Scandinavia and the USA, have been undertaken in response to extreme organizational problems, such as alcoholism, absenteeism, poor timekeeping, labour turnover and grievances.

Cascio, W.F. (1995) *Managing Human Resources: Productivity, Quality of Working Life, Profits*, McGraw-Hill.

Davis, L.E. and Cherns, A.B. (eds) (1975) *The Quality of Working Life* (2 vols), Free Press.

French, W.L. and Bell, C.H. (1994) *Organization Development: Behavioural Science Interventions for Organization Improvement* (5th edn), Addison Wesley Longman .

Guest, R.H. (1982) 'Tarrytown: Quality of Work Life at a General Motors Plant', in Zager, R. and Rostow, M.P. (eds) *The Innovative Organization: Productivity Programmes in Action*, Pergamon, pp. 88–106.

Macy, B.A. (1982) 'The Bolivar Quality of Work Life Programme: Success or Failure?', in Zager, R. and Rostow, M.P. (eds) *The Innovative Organization: Productivity Programmes in Action*, Pergamon, pp. 18–221.

Mills, T. (1978) 'Europe's Industrial Democracy: An American Response', *Harvard Business Review*, vol. 56, no. 6, pp. 143–52.

Stoddart, L. (1986) *Conditions of Work and Quality of Working Life: A Directory*, International Labour Office.

Walton, R.E. (1973) 'Quality of Working Life: What Is It?', *Sloan Management Review*, vol. 15, no. 1, pp. 11–22.

See also: Autonomous workgroups; Job design; Job enlargement; Job enrichment; Participation

Question searching

This approach helps students prepare for their final examinations by setting them the task of finding and articulating their own questions about the course material as it progresses, rather than simply answering those set by the instructor. Presenting well-formed questions demands reflection rather than simply regurgitating information, and provides a number of benefits. Not only does it demonstrate what students have learned, it engages them in a dialogue, it encourages them to link textbook learning to case studies, and it enables them to frame the course content in terms of their own particular interests.

During the course, students meet in groups and

conduct brainstorms to formulate questions about the topics covered, each student eventually drawing up a list of about 50 questions. At the end of the course, groups of four to six students attend a group oral examination lasting one to two hours, where the instructor answers their questions, confining any queries to those essential for clarification, each student submitting a copy of their own list of questions at the end. Students are awarded grades depending on how well they performed and the quality and scope of their questions. The quality of their contributions is judged in terms of whether they demonstrated comprehension of the material, whether their questions were clear and relevant, and whether they displayed adequate integration, conceptual reasoning, synthesis and evaluation skills. The scope is gauged by assessing whether the entire course material was covered, in terms of the various topics and the sources (lectures, reading materials, cases, etc.), and whether the questions drew on ideas from different parts of the course and established links between them.

Cowan, J. and George, J. (1992) 'Case Study: Diminishing Lists of Questions – A Technique for Curriculum Design and Formative Evaluation', *Education and Training Technology International*, vol. 29, no. 2, pp. 118–23.

Van Buskirk, W., Kruger, E. and Hazen, M.A. (1995) 'Finding Your Questions: Final exams for Re-framing Knowledge', *Journal of Management Education*, vol. 19, no. 4, pp. 458–72.

See also: Invitation to discover; Interrogation of experts; Questioning; Question production; Socratic enquiry; Socratic questioning

Question-production

This technique is based on the belief that knowing how to frame questions is an essential learning skill, and the deeper a student's knowledge of a subject, the easier it is for them to construct probing questions about it. White and Gunstone describe five strategies for designing 'thinking questions', which require students to consider content in different ways, shifting perspectives to increase their understanding. The first is to encourage students to phrase questions so that they begin with expressions such as 'What if ', 'Why are ', 'Why does ' or 'How would '. The second strategy involves the tutor providing a stimulus to serve as the basis for questions. In an examination, the stimulus may be an idea, a quotation, data or an event in a novel, and students are asked to respond to it in the way indicated by the examiner, whereas in this approach they are required to formulate questions based on the stimulus. A

simple way to do this is to adapt an existing examination paper which gives information or a set of ideas (e.g., a case study, a map, a table of data or a graph) by removing the original questions and asking students to draw up their own. In the third strategy, the tutor provides an answer, and asks students to devise an appropriate question. The fourth strategy is to ask students to formulate questions about aspects of the course which are puzzling them. The final strategy involves inviting students to play the role of examiner by setting a test to assess individuals' understanding of aspects of the course.

White, R. and Gunstone, R. (1992) *Probing Understanding*, Falmer Press, Chapter 10.

See also: Invitation to discover; Interrogation of experts; Questioning; Socratic enquiry; Socratic questioning

Questioning

Many teaching and learning approaches depend on teachers' ability to ask good questions and train their students to do the same. Indeed, some techniques, such as the case study method, tutorial and seminar, rely almost exclusively on questioning. Good questions do not usually arrive in a flash of inspiration, but need to be prepared in advance. Teachers must know how to vary their questioning in order to maximize their contribution to learning. Questions can be categorized in a variety of ways. For example, Bloom's hierarchy of objectives in the cognitive domain divides them into *low-level* questions, which demand only memorization, comprehension or application, and *high-level* questions, which require the student to demonstrate analysis, synthesis or evaluation.

Andrews conducted research into the effects of different types of questioning, and found that teachers defined a 'good discussion' as one in which a number of different responses were elicited from students as each point was raised, where the majority of students were actively involved, and where students continued to interact for a time without the need for further tutor contribution. This overall level of student response is referred to as *mileage*. Andrews found that the questions with the greatest mileage called for divergent thinking from students, and were high-level, straightforward and structured. He went on to produce a species typology of questions which identified three high-mileage ones (the Playground Question, the Brainstorm Question and the Focal Question) and eight low-mileage ones. We will concentrate on the high-mileage questions as they are the most useful in teaching, but the low-mileage ones will be identified at the end of the entry so that readers understand their pitfalls.

The *Playground Question* ('Is it possible to make any generalizations about the problem described in this case study?') was found to have the highest mileage. The teacher delineated a specific area of interest, but students were given a good deal of freedom in how they could approach the question. In Andrews' terms, this was an invitation to students to explore, and allowed them to choose which theme, concept or category to focus on in their response. Other Playground Question openings included: 'How do you interpret ...?', 'What can you draw from ...?' and 'What are the possible meanings of ...?'

The *Brainstorm Question* ('Suggest as many different ways as possible for the manager in this case to deal with this predicament') had the second-highest mileage. As in the creativity-encouraging technique of brainstorming, the teacher seeks a wide range of ideas and suggestions in response to a specific problem or question. In this type of question, the subject matter is less strictly delineated, all aspects of the case description falling within the scope of the question. However, the issue to be addressed ('deal with this predicament') is specific.

The *Focal Question* involves an issue which requires a decision from a number of alternatives ('Which is the better choice: to raise equity capital or secure a bank loan?'). Although these questions supply the alternatives, they are open because students must select which information to draw on to support their choice. Such questions usually lead to a debate, and taking a stand on a particular decision and defending it demands that students exercise high-order thinking and marshall information to support their view.

The low-mileage questions were found to be either too mechanical, open, narrow or vague, and included the General Invitation ('What did you think about the case?'), the Low-level Divergent Question ('What are the names of some of the other motivation theorists?'), the Analytical Convergent Question ('What was the most important reason why company X went bust?') and the Quiz Show Question ('He developed a five-level hierarchy of human needs: what was his name?'). The others identified by Andrews were the Single Question, the Multiple Consistent Question, the Shotgun Question and the Funnel Question.

Andrews, J.D.W. (1980) 'The Verbal Structure of Teacher Questions: Its Impact on Class Discussion', *Professional and Organizational Development Quarterly*, vol. 2, nos 3 and 4, Fall–Winter, pp. 129–63.
Carin, A.A. and Sund, R.B. (1971) *Developing Questioning Techniques*, Charles E. Merrill.
Dillon, J.T. (1981) 'To Question and Not to Question During Discussion 1: Questioning and Discussion', *Journal of Teacher Education*, vol. 32, no. 5, pp. 51–5.
Dillon, J.T. (1990) *The Practice of Questioning*, Routledge.
Freedman, R.L.H. (1993) *Open Ended Questioning*, Addison Wesley Longman.
Hunkins, F.P. (1976) *Involving Students in Questioning*, Allyn and Bacon.
Hunkins, F.P. (1997) *Teaching Through Effective Questioning*, Christopher-Gordon Publishing.
Kissock, C. (1982) *Guide to Questioning: Classroom Procedures for Teachers*, Macmillan.
Kriger, M. P. (1989–90) 'The Art and Power of Asking Questions', *Organizational Behaviour Teaching Review*, vol. 14, no. 1, pp. 131–42.
Mackay, I. (1997) *Asking Questions*, Institute of Personnel and Development.
Sanders, N.M. (1966) *Classroom Questions: What Kinds?*, HarperCollins.
Wragg, T. (1993) *Questioning*, Routledge.

See also: Invitation to discover; Interrogation of experts; Question production; Socratic enquiry; Socratic questioning

Questionnaires

Questionnaires are used to gather data about the opinions, behaviour, feelings, concerns or problems of a group, team, organization or sector of the population. While they represent an economical way to obtain data, the results tend to be anonymous, ambiguous, cautious and detached. In organizational development, questionnaires are the main tool in survey feedback interventions. However, when management uses them as a data-gathering tool for other purposes, there is no compulsion to publish or feed back the results to those who supplied the data.

Fordyce, J.K. (1979) *Managing With People* (2nd edn), Addison Wesley Longman.
Goode, W.J. and Hatt, P.K. (1972) 'The Collection of Data by Questionnaire', in Margulies, N. and Raia, A.P. (eds) *Organizational Development: Values, Process and Technology*, McGraw-Hill, pp. 16–85.
Margulies, N. and Wallace, J. (1973) *Organizational Change: Techniques and Applications*, Scott Foresman, p. 28 .
Merry, U. and Allerhand, M. (1977) *Developing Teams and Organizations*, Addison Wesley Longman, pp. 2–37.
Schuman, H. and Presser, S. (1996) *Questions and Answers in Attitude Surveys*, Sage.
Walters, M. (ed.) (1996) *Employee Attitude and Opinion Surveys*, Institute of Personnel Development.

See also: Attitude survey; Data-based interventions; Delphi technique; Instrumentation; Nominal group technique; On-going feedback system; Organizational climate analysis; Survey feedback interventions

Re-evaluation counselling

Re-evaluation counselling was developed by Harvey Jackins of Seattle during the 1950s, and the Re-evaluation Counselling Communities continue to train and license Re-evaluation Counsellors. The approach is identical to the less formally accredited co-counselling technique, and focuses on developing participants' autonomy. It helps individuals to re-examine past experiences in an effort to overcome their tendency to react in stereotyped ways to current situations. The result is that they become more spontaneous, and more confident in making creative and unique responses to situations as they arise.

Jackins, H. (1965) *The Human Side of Human Beings: The Theory of Re-evaluation Counselling*, Rational Island Publishers.
Jackins, H. (1973) *Distinctive Characteristics of Re-evaluation Counselling*, Rational Island Publishers.
Jackins, H. (1973) *The Human Situation*, Rational Island Publishers.
Scheff, T. (1972) *Re-evaluation Counselling: Social Implications*, Rational Island Publishers.

See also: Alexander Technique; Bioenergetics; Co-counselling; Coaching; Cognitive behavioural therapy; Counselling; Psychotherapy

Re-writing

Students can gain valuable insights by re-writing a report they have authored in order to tailor it to a certain readership or to serve a specific purpose. For instance, re-writing material for different audiences demonstrates how people's perceptions of the validity of an argument are influenced by the tone and language used in its delivery. To illustrate this, teachers sometimes write or collect examples of articles written in an inappropriate style, such as tabloid newspaper stories written in the style of a learned academic journal, or sensationalist treatments of well-researched and substantiated theories.

A wide variety of exercises can be developed to practise re-writing skills, such as re-writing a technical report on a product to serve as a press release, or as a specification for the company's catalogue. Alternatively, students may be asked to make specific recommendations as how they would adapt the report for publication in the firm's in-house newspaper. They are given the opportunity to discuss and defend their changes, then each produces their own version. A further refinement involves inviting the students to swop their articles, then imagine that they are the editors of the company newspaper. They must decide whether they would accept the contribution, and what editorial changes they would make. This raises the problem of how to communicate their amendments to the writer without giving offence. Many people invest a large amount of emotional capital in their writing and, if expressed in the wrong way, even perfectly valid criticisms may provoke strong negative reactions. Learning to accept constructive feedback is an important aspect of improving writing skills, and the exercise also enables students to practise the management skill of diplomacy.

See also: Book reviewing; Clozure; Data approach method; Dramatic skit; Essay; Language laboratory; Library assignment; Literary criticism; Literature search; Novels for learning; Reading; Reading party; Storytelling; Writing for learning

Reaction panel

This method can be used instead of a symposium or forum meeting if the number of participants is so large that a question-and-answer session would be impracticable. The panel consists of four to six audience members who sit on the stage and listen to the speakers' presentations. They then give their reactions to what has been said, and may question the speakers further on behalf of the audience as a whole.

See also: Audience/reaction watchdog team; Brains Trust; Clinic meeting; Colloquy meeting; Focus group; Forum meeting; Gordon seminar; Interrogation of experts; Listening team

Reaction paper

This type of assignment involves students being asked to read a short article which describes situations or strategic issues currently faced by some well-known organizations. They are set a question to guide their train of thought which serves as the topic of their reaction paper e.g.: 'What are the main factors that might explain company X's actions in this situation?' or 'What in your view were the biggest obstacles to company Y implementing its strategy?' Reaction papers should be short (usually two or three pages long) and clearly focused. Students may be asked to present their papers to the rest of the class to form the basis for a class discussion or debate. Up to ten reaction paper assignments may be set per semester, and the articles and questions are sequenced to ensure that they match the concepts introduced and discussed during the course.

This approach has a number of advantages. It gives students an opportunity to practise their written and oral communication skills, and to develop their skills of analysis, diagnosis and synthesis. It also enhances their understanding and recollection of course concepts by linking them to actual business examples.

Axley, S.R. (1989–90) 'Improving Written and Oral Communication Skills Through Reaction Papers', *Organizational Behaviour Teaching Review*, vol. 14, no. 2, pp. 124–8.

See also: Case live; Case personal history; Case student telling; Management implications paper; Management problems survey method

Reading

Despite forecasts of their demise, books, journals and research papers continue to be the primary information source for most students, although many of them are now also available on the Internet. While most courses rely on works of non-fiction, novels can also provide a thought-provoking stimulus for class discussions. For many students, independent study in the traditional manner is still one of the most fruitful forms of learning. However, they usually need guidance in how to use library facilities, and lecturers have a vital role in providing assistance and stimulation. In any course, students need advice about what to read, what their priorities should be and which books they should buy. They generally find large, unannotated bibliographies daunting and confusing, and prefer booklists which distinguish core reading from supplementary material. Apart from producing reading lists that are broken down into categories such as 'introductory texts' and 'advanced reading', it saves time and effort if lecturers provide full information about the author, title, date and library catalogue number. If students are required to buy a particular book, it is helpful to ensure that the bookshop is forewarned and has sufficient copies in stock.

If the course reading list is extensive, one technique which students will also find useful in their working lives is skim-reading. Unlike speed-reading, which is a different skill that tends to be stressed in some study courses, skim-reading could be described as 'reading with a purpose'. It involves looking for key words in the text, then reading the passage in greater depth when one finds them. One way to gain a quick overview is to read the first sentence in each paragraph, which is usually the topic sentence. A sudden change of subject provides a cue that it is necessary to read that paragraph or the one before it more closely, in order to pick up the thread of the argument.

Forster, G.C.F. (1968) 'Books in University Teaching', in Layton, D. (ed.) *University Teaching in Transition*, Oliver and Boyd.
Maclellan, E. (1997) 'Reading to Learn', *Studies in Higher Education*, vol. 22, no. 3, pp. 277–88.
Mann, P. (1973) *Books and Students*, National Book League.

See also: Book reviewing; Case study method; Historical analysis; Novels for learning; Literature search; Re-writing; Reading aloud; Reading party; Text

Reading aloud (oral reading)

Reading a text aloud to a class is often a more effective teaching method than asking students to read the same material silently, especially if teachers ensure that their delivery is engaging and well modulated. Reading aloud should be distinguished from storytelling, in which the reader relies on memory rather than referring to a text. One example of this approach is the use of poetry for learning, some teachers relying on audio tapes of readings by actors (or even the poet in question), others preferring to develop their own presentation skills.

Barton, B, (1986) *Tell Me Another: Storytelling and Reading Aloud*, Heinemann.
Barton, B. (1990) *Stories in the Classroom: Storytelling and Reading Aloud*, Pembroke Publishers.
Collins, R. and Cooper, P.J. (1996) *The Power of Story*, Holcomb Hathaway.
Stibbs, A. (1983) *Exploring Texts Through Reading and Dramatisation*, Ward Lock Educational.
Trelease, J. (1995) *The Read Aloud Handbook*, Penguin.

See also: Dramatic skit; Playing for learning; Poetry for learning; Reading; Reading party; Storytelling

Reading party (reading club; book club)

Reading parties usually take the form of a retreat extending over a number of days, to allow participants to discuss a topic in depth without distractions. For instance, a teacher or group of teachers may attend to discuss contemporary writings with their students, or the staff of a management department may come together to discuss future strategy. Participants are usually expected to carry out preparatory work such as reading specified texts or preparing discussion papers, but not necessarily on the same topics, since seeking a broad range of contributions is an important feature of this approach.

Beverton, S. et al. (1993) *Running Family Reading Groups*, United Kingdom Reading Association.

Jacobson, R. W. (1994) *The Reading Group Handbook*, Hyperion.

Laskin, D. and Hughes, H. (1995) *The Reading Group Book*, Plume.

Saal. R. (1995) *The New York Public Library Guide to Reading Groups*, Crown Publishing,.

Slezak, E. and Atwood, M. (1995) *The Good Group Book*, Review Press.

See also: Book reviewing; Literature search; Re-writing; Reading; Reading party

Real-life entrepreneurial project

While it was originally developed for management and business studies students, this method can also be applied to planning, law and other subjects. Participants work in project groups rather than individually, and the key element is that the activities should reflect reality as closely as possible. When applied to business management, students may be asked to develop, produce and market a service or product with the intention of making a profit. Because the project parallels the development of a small business whose members have a financial stake in its success, it fosters a sense of reality that would be missing in a business game. The scale of the project is unimportant as long as it gives students experience of the various stages in developing a business. Depending on the level of reality being sought, the local bank manager may be asked to take part and conduct an interview with the students to negotiate a loan, or market research surveys may be conducted to test demand. In other disciplines, such projects have involved town and country planning students meeting real local authority officials to negotiate planning permission for a development, and law students setting up a local community law clinic giving free advice to the public.

A variation of this approach can serve as an in-company developmental activity. The middle managers of a large company which is no longer expanding may be invited to give advice to a newly formed, independent company to help it prepare grant applications to financial institutions, undertake market appraisals, and test and refine product prototypes. Alternatively, managers may be invited to propose an idea for a new small business which they could help develop and in which they could take an equity stake. In addition to providing greater job satisfaction, this would present the opportunity to develop new skills and expertise. However, as with any form of developmental activity, the parent company will wish to ensure that it also benefits from these initiatives.

Chia, R. (1996) 'Teaching Paradigm Shifting in Management Education: University Business Schools and the Entrepreneurial Imagination', *Journal of Management Studies*, vol. 33, no. 4, pp. 409–28.

See also: Action learning; Field project/attachment; Industrial project; Overseas project; Project method; Project-based management development; Project orientation; Reprogramming; Simulated entrepreneurship

Real-time strategic change

Real-time strategic change (RTSC) is a large-group intervention which involves everyone in an organization in planning for change. It was developed by Kathleen Dannemiller and colleagues, including Chuck Tyson and Robert Jacobs. The approach is flexible enough to be used to achieve a wide range of goals, such as developing an organizational vision, restructuring a company, redesigning work, identifying and solving problems, and co-ordinating inter-group activities. RTSC events are customized to address issues that are specific to the individual company. However, all are based on the belief that change only occurs when there is a sufficient dissatisfaction with the current system, when everyone shares a vision of the organization's goals, when the steps to achieving those goals are clear, and when these three elements are strong enough to overcome the resistance to change inherent in the system.

Four features distinguish RTSC from similar methods. First, its authors' commitment to democracy and widespread participation means that RTSC events have been organized which have involved as many as 2 200 people, although numbers between 300 and 900 are more common. This means that RTSC conferences need to be highly structured and well organized. Second, although it demands that senior management accepts input from others, the design allows it to decide how much of its decision-making authority to delegate. Third, because strategic thinking requires that all participants share an understanding of the situation, RTSC events begin with eight-person round table group meetings, representing the company in microcosm. During these meetings, company personnel are brought into contact with outsiders (e.g., customers) they would not normally meet, differences are acknowledged, and participants try to work together, 'acting with one heart and one mind'. Finally, the design encourages a paradigm shift among participants. Participants may arrive uncertain, sceptical or even hostile to proposals for change. However, the process allows them to voice their views and observe management's reactions, and they often end up feeling empowered – more hopeful, more energized and more excited about the possibilities of change.

Bunker, B.B. and Alban, B.T. (1997) 'Real Time Strategic Change', in *Large Group Interventions: Engaging the Whole System for Rapid Change*, Jossey-Bass, pp. 61–76.

Dannemiller, K. and Jacobs, R.W. (1992) 'Changing the Way Organizations Change: A Revolution in Common Sense', *Journal of Applied Behavioural Science*, vol. 28, pp. 480–98.

Jacobs, RW. (1997) *Real Time Strategic Change*, Berrett-Koehler.

See also: Action training and research; Business process re-engineering; Conference Model; Fast-cycle full-participation work design; Future search; Large-group interventions; Open space technology; Participative design; Real-time work design; Search conference; Strategic planning process; Simu-Real; Socio-technical systems design; Work-Out

Real-time work design

Real-time work design (RTWD) is one of several large-group work design methods developed by Kathleen Dannemiller and Paul Tolchinsky. It can complete an organizational design within three to six months, rather than years as might be the case with the traditional socio-technical systems approach, and it also involves a greater number of people. The RTWD design consists of four conferences, two at the beginning and two at the end of the change process, each lasting two or three days. Because all those involved in the change process attend, the conferences may consist of as many as 2 400 participants. RTWD places great reliance on research and design teams, each consisting of eight to twelve members, to guide the whole project. All sectors of the workforce are represented on these (including management and unions), and between each conference they liaise closely with external consultants, reporting to senior management or the sponsors of the redesign in the organization's headquarters.

The whole workforce attends the *launch conference*, which serves three purposes. It informs everyone about the environmental challenges facing the organization, and why the redesign is necessary. It gives them experience of what redesigns can achieve, allowing them to begin reconsidering their own work processes. Finally, it allows shop-floor employees to meet managers and raise any concerns. During the *process conference*, representatives consider how work is currently performed, and the process models drawn up by the research and design teams are used to develop improvements. At the *design conference*, cross-functional representatives meet those who will be affected by the initiatives. The principles that will guide the final design decisions are agreed, and participants prepare an organizational design based on the models prepared by the research and design teams. The final event is the *implementation conference*, which informs all employees about the decisions made so far, and allows them to participate in planning how to implement the new design, individual work units holding their own mini-conferences to decide how to implement it in their sector.

The research and design teams' contribution is crucial to the success of this approach. They assess the outcomes of each conference and plan the next, including any research and analysis that proves necessary. After the process conference, they may create several alternative models of the production process to overcome the problems identified by participants. After the design conference, they decide what support processes will be affected by the proposals. Since inadequate support can easily ruin a new design, they organize a series of separate *deep dive conferences* to address support issues, such as providing adequate training or adjusting the reward system. Finally, at the end of the process, the research and design teams are incorporated into the implementation teams.

Bunker, B.B. and Alban, B.T. (1997) 'Real Time Work Design', in *Large Group Interventions: Engaging the Whole System for Rapid Change*, Jossey-Bass, pp. 123–35.

See also: Action training and research; Business process re-engineering; Conference Model; Fast-cycle full-participation work design; Future search; Large-group interventions; Open space technology; Participative design; Real-time strategic change; Search conference; Simu-Real; Socio-technical systems design; Strategic planning process; Work-Out

Realistic job previews (job previews)

This behavioural intervention technique aims to reduce absenteeism by providing potential employees with an objective view of the organizational climate and what their job would entail. The previews usually take the form of a half hour presentation providing descriptions of both the positive and negative aspects of the job, obtained by means of exit interviews and attitude surveys of current employees. Applicants may also have the opportunity to discuss issues with a former employee. As a result, they should have sufficient information to make an informed decision about whether or not to accept the placement, rather than experiencing disappointment and disillusionment if they find that the job does not live up to their expectations. The technique has been used when engaging part-time checkout operators in a retail food store, technicians in a residential institution for the mentally ill, and telephone operators in a call centre company.

Dugoni, B.L. and Ilgen, D.R. (1981) 'Realistic Job Previews and the Adjustment of New Employees', *Academy of Management Journal*, vol. 24, pp. 579–91.

Ferris, G.R. and Rowland, K.M. (1990) *Organizational Entry*, JAI Press.

Makin, P.J. and Robertson, I.T. (1983) 'Self-assessment, Realistic Job Previews and Occupational Decisions', *Personnel Review*, vol. 12, no. 3, pp. 21–5.

Reilly, R.J., Tenopyr, M.L. and Sperling, S.M. (1979) 'Effects of Job Reviews on Job Acceptance and Survival of Telephone Operator Candidates', *Journal of Applied Psychology*, vol. 64, pp. 218–20.

Reilly, R.R., Blood, M.R., Brown, B.M. and Maletsa, C.A. (1981) 'The Effects of Realistic Job Previews: A Study and a Discussion of the Literature', *Personnel Psychology*, vol. 34, pp. 82–4.

Wanous, J.P. (1977) ' "Organizational Entry": New Comers Moving from Outside to Inside', *Psychological Bulletin*, vol. 84, pp. 601–18.

Wanous, J.P. (1992) *Organizational Entry: Selection and Socialization of Newcomers* (2nd edn), Addison Wesley Longman.

See also: Appraisal; Assessment centre; Induction training; Outplacement counselling; Recruitment

Recognition programmes

Recognition programmes entail giving employees awards for exemplary performance, based on the belief that if a desired behaviour is reinforced by a reward, it is much more likely to be repeated. Examples include *good housekeeping awards* for high standards of tidiness and safety, *exemplary action awards* for outstanding efforts on behalf of the company, and *professional excellence awards* recognizing the contributions of professional and technical staff.

Blanchard, K.H. and Johnson, S. (1983) *The One Minute Manager*, Fontana/Collins.

Boyle, D.C. (1995) *Secrets of a Successful Employee Recognition System*, Productivity Press, USA.

Deeprose, D. (1994) *How to Recognize and Reward Employees*, American Management Association, AMACOM.

Klubnik, J.P. (1995) *Rewarding and Recognizing Employees: Ideas for Individuals, Teams and Managers*, Irwin Professional.

See also: Behaviour modification; Measuring performance; On-going feedback system; Parallel career ladders; Positive feedback; Vendor excellence awards

Recruitment

Recruiting new staff is one of the commonest and most effective ways to change and develop an organization. The selection process is crucial, since the organization must recruit staff with characteristics which will enable it to achieve its goals, whereas candidates must ensure that their post within the organization will satisfy their personal needs.

Arthur, D. (1998) *Recruiting, Interviewing, Selecting and Orienting New Employees*, American Management Association AMACOM.

Christopher, E.M. (1995) *Managing Recruitment, Training and Development*, Kogan Page.

Dale, M. (1995) *Successful Recruitment and Selection*, Kogan Page.

Gatewood, R.D. (1993) *Human Resource Selection*, Harcourt Brace.

Institute of Personnel and Development (1997) *IPD Guide on Recruitment*, IPD.

Land, L. (1995) *Managing Recruitment and Selection*, Quay Books.

Lewis, C.D. (1992) *Employee Selection*, Thornes Publishers.

Oates, D. (1994) *Perfect Recruitment*, Constable.

Robert, G. (1997) *Recruitment and Selection: A Competency Approach*, Institute of Personnel and Development.

Rust, J. and Golombok, S. (1999) *Modern Psychometrics*, Routledge.

See also: Downsizing; MAPS approach; Induction training; Outplacement counselling; Realistic job previews

Reflective learning

Educational techniques place great emphasis on learning from experience, which relies on the process of reflection to extract *meaning* from those experiences. The philosopher and educationalist John Dewey's definition of reflection included consideration of the bases that support our beliefs and knowledge. In management training, the reflective learning (RL) method was developed by Philip Boxer and Richard Boot, who devised techniques to help and support individuals as they think over their past and try to learn from it. Although the term 'reflective learning methods' can be used in a broad sense to refer to any form of assistance to achieve these aims (e.g., certain forms of co-counselling), nowadays it is more usually applied to more formal techniques, often administered by means of computer programs. The reflective learning approach adheres closely to the principles of Kelly's personal construct theory. RL offers a content-free structure that can be used to reflect on any kind of subject matter, acting as a facilitative device that neither draws conclusions nor interprets the data fed in, leaving these activities to its users.

The *Nipper* computer program was among the first to be used with individuals or groups to guide and encourage the process of learning from reflection. The program asked individuals questions, then provided feedback about their patterns of reflections, in a process that resembled certain aspects of Socratic group enquiry. The use of a computer is not essential, but it speeds up the whole process. The method's application parallels the repertory grid technique. Users must first clarify their thoughts in terms of elements and concepts: an *element* is a specific example of a chosen subject area, such as meetings, whereas a *concept* expresses an individual's subjective reaction to an element. For example, in the case of meetings, the concepts might include brevity, decision quality and decision acceptance. The next step is to reflect on the extent to which each concept applies to each of the elements, which serves to clarify the concepts adopted. The feedback about the pattern of reflections can be represented in the form of a tree diagram, or *dendrogram*. In this example, the different types of meetings would be categorized into families, based on a common theme such as satisfactoriness. Users then reflect on these family clusters to check their meaningfulness. It is also possible to search for further underlying concepts.

Bailey, J.R. et al. (1997) 'A Model for Reflective Pedagogy', *Journal of Management Education*, vol. 21 no. 2, pp. 155–67.

Boot, R. and Boxer, P. (1980) 'Reflective Learning', in Beck, J. and Cox, C. (eds) *Advances in Management Education*, Wiley.

Boud, D., Keough, R. and Walker, D. (eds) (1985) *Reflection: Turning Experience into Learning*, Kogan Page.

Boxer, P. (1981) 'Learning as a Subversive Activity', in Boydell, T. and Pedler, M. (eds) *Management Self Development: Concepts and Practices*, Gower.

Brockbank, A. and McGill, I. (1998) *Facilitating Reflective Learning in Higher Education*, Open University Press.

Cowan, J. (1998) *On Becoming an Innovative University Teacher*, Open University Press.

Gould, N. and Taylor, I. (eds) (1996) *Reflective Learning for Social Work*, Ashgate Publishing.

Loughran, J.J. (1996) *Developing Reflective Practice*, Falmer Press.

McKenzie, R.H. (1990) *Prior Learning and Reflection: Analytical Thinking from Experience*, Kendall/Hunt, USA.

Nichol, D. et al (1994) 'Case Study: Improving Laboratory Learning Through Group Working and Structured Reflective Discussion', *Education and Training Technology International*, vol. 31, no. 4, pp. 302–10.

Parker, S. (1997) *Reflective Teaching in the Postmodern World*, Open University Press.

Sooklal, L. (1987) 'Going Down to Hades: The Development of Managerial Introspection', *Journal of Management Development*, vol. 6, no. 4, pp. 53–64.

Whitaker, P. (1995) *Managing to Learn: Aspects of Reflection and Experiential Learning at School*, Cassell Academic.

Wilson, J. and Jan, L.W. (1993) *Thinking for Themselves: Developing Strategies for Reflective Learning*, Heinemann-Butterworth.

See also: Learning conversation; Personalized reflection; Repertory grid; Socratic group enquiry

Reframing

This is a teaching approach which uses different *frames* – images or metaphors – to analyse an example of human behaviour in an organization. The example is presented in one of a number of forms (e.g., as a written case, a novel, a poem or a movie sequence), and students are asked to consider it from a particular perspective. In the first instance, students may focus on the individuals involved, and discuss their perceptions, personality and motivation. Next, the same sequence may be re-analysed from a group perspective, then a structural perspective, then a cultural one, then a political one, and so on.

This approach leads to a number of important insights. The most obvious is that the same situation can be viewed from different perspectives. The chosen perspective determines which questions are asked and which answers are received. Finally, there is usually no single right way or correct answer but, in certain situations, some perspectives are more informative than others.

Bolman, L. and Deal, T.E. (1991) *Reframing Organizations*, Jossey-Bass.

Brown, D.D. (1998) 'Team Frames: The Multiple Realities of the Team', *Journal of Management Education*, vol. 22, no. 1, pp. 95–103.

Dunford, R.W. and Palmer, I.C. (1995) 'Claims About Reframing: Practitioners' Assessment of the Utility of Reframing', *Journal of Management Education*, vol. 19, no. 1, pp. 96–105.

Frost, P.J. et al. (1991) *Reframing Organizational Culture*, Sage.

Gallos, J.V. (1987–8) 'A Need for Reframing the Gulag: A Developmental Perspective', *Organizational Behaviour Teaching Review*, vol. 12, no. 4, pp. 74–6.

Gallos, J.V. (1992) 'Revisiting the Same Case: An Exercise in Reframing', *Journal of Management Education*, vol. 16, no. 2, pp. 257–61.

Gallos, J.V. (1993) 'Teaching About Reframing With Films and Videos', *Journal of Management Education*, vol. 17, no. 1, pp. 127–32.

Huczynski, A.A. (1994) 'Teaching Motivation and Influencing Strategies Using the Magnificent Seven', *Journal of Management Education*, vol. 18, no. 2, pp. 273–8.

Morgan, G. (1986) *Images of Organization*, Sage.

See also: Analogy teaching; Concept attainment model; Contingency approach; Metaphor approach; Neuro-linguistic programming

Reinforcement environment analysis

This approach draws on the model of behaviour modification associated with psychologists such as Pavlov, Watson and Skinner. The underlying theory is that any human behaviour which is rewarded will be reinforced, and hence repeated, whereas any behaviour which is not reinforced, or is punished, will not be repeated. Reinforcement environment analysis applies these ideas to organizational behaviour, examining what behaviours the organization rewards, and how it does so. Every organization has its own reward systems, both formal and informal.

In the case of the formal system, the questions posed by reinforcement environment analysis might include the following: 'Are members rewarded for striving towards organizational goals, or do they receive rewards only when they behave in ways that are actually dysfunctional for the organization as a whole?', 'Does the reward system require employees to emphasize certain goals?', 'Does the system make competitiveness between individuals and sub-units a necessary condition for being rewarded?', 'Does the system obstruct changes in behaviour?' and 'Can the system be broadened to take into account differences between individuals and their preferences for certain forms of reinforcement?'

In examining the informal reward system, different considerations apply. The questions in this case may be answered by observing samples of behaviour, and such observation can identify those who are effective reinforcing agents or influential social models. The issues might include: 'To what extent are the patterns of reinforcement in the informal organizational culture consistent with the goals of the formal organization?', 'Who are the influential people in the informal structure who control the reinforcements?', 'What are the effective reinforcers in the informal structure – space, recognition, privacy, status?', Does the informal reward system encourage inter-personal and inter-departmental rivalry and conflict, and are these dysfunctional to the organization?' and 'Is the informal reward system likely to obstruct or impede current or planned change programmes?'

People in organizations frequently reinforce patterns of dependency and hostility unconsciously, both through their behaviour and as a result of organizational design. Reinforcement environment analysis provides a means of training managers and supervisors to observe their own and others' behaviour in order to identify which aspects of the reward systems need to be modified.

Daniels, A.C. (1994) *Bringing Out the Best in People: How to Apply the Astonishing Power of Reinforcement*, American Society for Training and Development, ASTD Press.

DiClaudio, J. (1991) 'Praise, Pause and More Praise: Designing a Creative Environment in a Health Care Setting, Part 1', *Leadership and Organization Development Journal*, vol. 12, no. 4, pp. 28–31.

DiClaudio, J. (1991) 'Praise, Pause and More Praise, Part 2', *Leadership and Organization Development Journal*, vol. 12, no. 7, pp. 17–20.

Kerr, S. (1975) 'On the Folly of Rewarding A, While Hoping for B', *Academy of Management Journal*, vol. 18, December, pp. 769–83.

Meyers, R.J. and Smith, J.E. Smith (eds) (1995) *Clinical Guide to Alcohol Treatment: The Community Reinforcement Approach*, Guilford Press.

Petersen, D. (1989) *Safe Behaviour Reinforcement*, Aloray.

Villere, M.F. and Hartman, S.S. (1991) 'Reinforcement Theory: A Practical Tool', *Leadership and Organization Development Journal*, vol. 12, no. 2, pp. 27–31.

Zeiler, M.D. and Harzen, F. (1979) *Reinforcement and the Organization of Behaviour*, Wiley.

See also: Behaviour modification; Discipline

without punishment; Positive peer culture; Reward systems; Self-management

Relational diagramming

One way to discover how students discriminate between a particular concept and a related one is to ask them to define the concept. Another way is to ask them to draw a relational diagram. White and Gunstone define a relational diagram as a set of closed figures which shows the pattern of overlap between classes of objects, events or abstractions. Relational diagramming consists of three steps. First, students are asked to draw a large circle or square and label it 'All Plants'. Next, they are asked to draw squares, circles or other shapes on the diagram to represent trees, flowering plants and grasses, showing how they are related to each other and to 'All Plants'. Finally, they are invited to look carefully at their diagram, think about what it represents, and decide whether they want to change any aspect of it.

Proponents of relational diagramming generally make two recommendations. First, *keep the number of terms small*. The example given earlier contains three terms, and relations should ideally consist of clusters of two to four terms, and certainly no more than four. Examples of clusters from different subjects area include: assets/funds, myths/legends/fables, plays/farces/tragedies, equity/debt, hunters/nomads, facts/opinions/beliefs and useful activities/work/teaching. Second, *construct a diagram yourself before asking students to do so*. The chosen terms can take almost any form (emotions, people's names; abstractions, specific objects), but they must stand for classes of things or ideas of a similar nature, so they must be stated in the plural.

White and Gunstone suggest some ways to apply the method. First, after students complete their diagram, ask them to mark where one of more given instances would fit on it (e.g., herbs, mosses). Second, ask students to provide one specific case for each of the areas designated in their diagram (e.g., Tree = birch, Flowering Plant = potentilla, Grasses = millet, Herb = mint). Third, in situations where misunderstandings or errors in drafting diagrams are common, devise cases that force students to reconsider their own relational diagrams in order to compare different

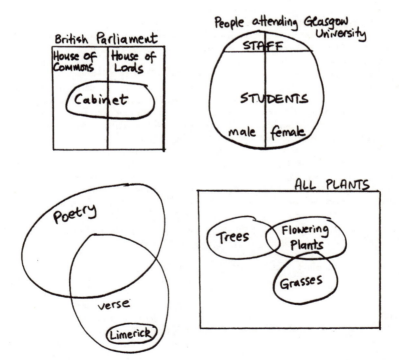

Relational diagrams
Source: adapted from White and Gunstone (1992)

aspects. Fourth, ask them to draw comparative and contrasting diagrams (e.g., representing the relationships between the British and US legislative systems). This makes the basic features – and hence the differences – readily apparent, and is simpler and faster than asking them to write an essay on the similarities and differences between the two. Finally, diagrams can be used to test students' understanding of sorting activities. The categories can be of any type (e.g., long-term/short-term, cheap/expensive, producer-oriented/customer-focused or legal/illegal).

Gunstone, R. and White, R. (1986) 'Assessing Understanding by Means of Venn Diagrams', *Science Education*, vol. 70. pp. 151–8.
White, R. and Gunstone, R. (1992) *Probing Understanding*, Falmer Press, Chapter 8.

See also: Chronology charting; Concept attainment model; Concept formation; Concept mapping; Concept teaching; Concept training; Concept uncovery; Drawing for learning; Posters; Responsibility charting

Relations-by-objectives

Developed in the USA by the Federal Mediation and Conciliation Service, relations-by-objectives (RBO) was an experiment in union–management co-operation which aimed to improve relationships between the parties. The RBO technique draws heavily upon organizational development theory and practice, especially in the area of inter-group conflict-resolution.

Gray, D.A., Sinogropi, A.V. and Hughes, P.A. (1981) 'From Conflict to Co-operation: A Joint Union–management Goal-setting and Problem-solving Programme', *Proceedings of the 34th Annual Meeting*, Industrial Relations Research Association Series, December, pp. 26–32.
Kochan, T.A. and Dyer, L. (1976) 'A Model of Organizational Change in the Context of Union–management Relations', *Journal of Applied Behavioural Science*, vol. 12, January–March, pp. 59–78.

See also: Sensitivity bargaining; Union–management committees

Rent-a-judge

One of the initiatives developed for alternative dispute-resolution, the rent-a-judge scheme was first made available to companies by the California legislature, and has been adopted in the states of New York, Nebraska, Rhode Island, Washington and Oregon. Under the system, the two parties to a dispute jointly ask the court to appoint a referee, possibly one of their own choice, and the procedure differs little from conventional litigation in the US courts. Other than sanctions for contempt of court, the referee has the same powers as a trial judge, and conducts proceedings according to normal court procedures. The referee's judgment is enforceable in the same way as any other, and either party can appeal against it. Although the parties must pay the judge, this cost is more than offset by the benefit of avoiding court costs. In addition, the hearings usually proceed more quickly than in conventional courts, since the parties can choose a referee with experience in their field who will be able to concentrate almost exclusively on their trial, rather than having to divide their time between different hearings, as is often the case with busy judges.

Bevan, A. (1992) *Alternative Dispute Resolution*, Sweet and Maxwell.
Hibbard, P.R. (1996) *Alternative Dispute Resolution in Construction Contracts*, Blackwell Science.
McDermott, E.P. and Berkeley, A.E. (1996) *Alternative Dispute Resolution in the Workplace*, Quorum Books.
York, S. (1996) *Practical Alternative Dispute Resolution*, Longman Law.

See also: Alternative dispute-resolution; Mediation; Mini-trial; Ombudsman; Sensitivity bargaining

Repertory grid

Kelly's theory of personal constructs envisions human beings as scientists, exploring their environment and constructing an individual 'map' of the world which they use to guide their behaviour. The repertory grid technique is used to discover the nature of an individual's map. It has been used in clinical settings for over forty years, and grew in popularity in management training and development during the 1970s. The rationale for its use in this field is that identifying a person's map should help to predict their actions. Training can then be used to alter their map, and hence their behaviour, if necessary.

Kelly's personal construct theory conceives of individual maps as containing *elements* – the objects of thought, such as people or words – and *constructs* – the qualities used to describe these elements. The repertory grid identifies an individual's elements and constructs and analyses them statistically to produce a quantified personal map. When the technique is applied to management training and development, students work in threes, eliciting constructs about a particular subject, such as productivity bargaining or women in management roles. These then serve as a basis for discussion or to help the group consider a problem. An interactive approach is adopted, with the results fed back to the subjects in order to assist in self-development, team-building or organizational development interventions. The technique can also be used in job analysis and career counselling.

Bannister, D. and Fransella, K. (1990) *Inquiring Man: The Theory of Personal Constructs*, Routledge.

Beail, N. (ed.) (1985) *Repertory Grid Techniques and Personal Constructs*, Croom Helm.

Beck, J.E. (1980) 'Changing a Manager's Construction of Reality', in Beck, J. and Cox, C. (eds) *Advances in Management Education*, Wiley.

Drake, J. (1980) 'What is Repertory Grid?', *Leadership and Organizational Development Journal*, vol. 1, no. 1, pp. 33–6.

Easterby-Smith, M. (1977) 'The Repertory Grid as a Personnel Tool', *Management Decision*, vol. 14, no. 5, pp. 239–47.

Easterby-Smith, M. (1980) 'How to Use Repertory Grids in HRD', *Journal of European Industrial Training/International Journal of HRD*, vol. 4, no. 2.

Honey, P. (1979) 'Repertory Grid in Action, Part 1', *Industrial and Commercial Training*, vol. 11, no. 9, pp. 35–9.

Honey, P. (1979) 'Repertory Grid in Action, Part 2', *Industrial and Commercial Training*, vol. 11, no. 10, pp. 407–14.

Honey, P. (1979) 'Repertory Grid in Action, Part 3', *Industrial and Commercial Training*, vol. 11, no. 11, pp. 452–9.

Smith, M. (1980) 'Applications and Use of Repertory Grids in Management Education', in Beck, J. and Cox, C. (eds) *Advances in Management Education*, Wiley.

Smith, M. and Ashton, D. (1975) 'Using Repertory Grid to Evaluate Management Training', *Personnel Review*, vol. 4, no. 4, pp. 15–21.

Stewart, V. (1983) *Business Applications of Repertory Grid*, McGraw-Hill.

See also: Learning conversation; Personalized reflection; Reflective learning

Reprogramming (management by absence)

Reprogramming is sometimes referred to as 'management by absence', and has been adopted by managers in medium-sized companies to change their own role and behaviour within the organization. Clifford and Cavanagh coined the term when describing the case of Parker Montgomery, the chairman of CooperVision, who set up offices for himself in company plants at different ends of the country. Although business considerations prompted this arrangement, it meant that the group of managers at each plant had to work on their own while their boss was absent for two weeks every month, which encouraged them to take on his responsibilities. The approach can be extended to include initiatives such as managers asking others to chair important committees, managing directors deciding not to be present at review meetings they usually attend, and holding departmental and functional meetings in the absence of the director or plant manager. It is argued that this develops a sense of maturity and ownership among those who are left to get on with running the business. It also allows senior executives to take on a new role, attending fewer day-to-day activities and concentrating on dealing with those outside the company.

Clifford, D.K. and Cavanagh, R.E. (1986) *The Winning Performance: How America's Midsize Companies Succeed*, Sidgwick and Jackson, pp. 147–8.

See also: Bottom-up management; Business teams; Independent product teams; Intrapreneurship; Managerial decentralization; Multiple management; Real-life entrepreneurial project; Simulated entrepreneurship

Research assignment

In-company research assignments tend to serve different purposes from those carried out as part of a college or university course. The research topic may be specified by senior staff, and may be designed to assist induction by helping the individual learn about the company, or to address a departmental problem by enlisting the help of an outsider. A manager may be released for a fixed period, perhaps a week, to conduct the study and prepare a verbal or written report. Some preparatory training may be necessary if the manager has no previous experience of research, covering issues such as how to plan and carry out the research.

See also: Acting assignment; Committee assignment; Consulting assignment; Development assignment; Evaluation audit assignment; Library assignment

Research degree

Conducting research, whether for a project, dissertation or thesis, is a form of independent learning which can be very fruitful in developing students' skills, knowledge and experience. Research always involves a certain amount of uncertainty and risk, since it is impossible to know in advance whether all the necessary information will be available, or what, if anything, it will reveal. Students must be prepared to manage the research process themselves. This involves being self-reliant and working independently to set realistic goals, then plan a systematic programme of work to achieve them. It is important to establish a structured approach to identifying problems and solutions, and to show initiative in the methods adopted.

Many regard research as an 'ivory tower' activity. However, although the direct results of research may sometimes appear esoteric, it tends to encourage and develop skills which are necessary for any successful manager. Students develop self-motivation and improve their organizational and creative abilities, learning how to manage the resources of time and materials. Analysing data demands a logical and systematic approach, and the procedures and findings must be presented clearly, precisely and persuasively in the final report.

Allison, B. (1997) *The Student's Guide to Writing Business Theses and Dissertations*, Kogan Page.
Buchanan, D. (1980) 'Gaining Management Skills Through Research Work', *Personnel Management*, vol. 12, no. 4, April, pp. 45–8.
Clardy, A. (1997) *Studying Your Workforce*, Sage.
Easterby-Smith, M., Thorpe, R. and Lowe, A. (1991) *Management Research*, Sage.
Fitzpatrick, J., Secrist, J. and Wright, D.J. (1998) *Secrets for a Successful Dissertation*, Sage.
Graves, N. and Varma, V. (1997) *Working for a Doctorate*, Routledge.
Pearson, R. (1980) 'Higher Degrees as Management Training', *Journal of European Industrial Training*, vol. 4, no. 1, pp. 17–21.
Pearson, R. et al. (1993) 'Employer Demand for Doctoral Social Scientists', *Studies in Higher Education*, vol. 18, no. 1, pp. 95–104.
Remenyi, D. et al. (1998) *Doing Research in Business and Management*, Sage.
Sharp, J.A. and Howard, K. (1996) *The Management of a Student Research Project*, Gower.

See also: Dissertation proposal; Independent study; Literature search; Research proposal; Sabbatical

Residential

A residential is a concentrated period of study, usually lasting a weekend, in which participants work together on a specific task. Residentials are frequently a feature of part-time education programmes, and are a course requirement for some management studies qualifications. Although the time can be devoted to lectures, seminars or similar forms of study, it is more common to adopt more intensive and interactive learning methods, such as protracted role-playing exercises or business games.

Cole, G.A. (1980) 'The Pros and Cons of Residential Weekends', *The Training Officer*, vol. 16, no. 9, pp. 242–5.
Nolan, F. (1985) ' "Residential?", Make the Most of It', *The Training Officer*, March, vol. 21, no. 3, pp. 83–5.

See also: Concentrated study; Mini-course; Module; Retreat; Workshop

Resource centre (multi-media study centre; learning resource centre; resource-based learning)

Resource centres consist of a variety of facilities which enable students to engage in independent, resource-based learning. Many students find that they can learn more effectively by studying on their own outside the classroom, as long as they have access to the materials and equipment required. Resource centres cater for these needs by providing a media library to help students decide how to structure their studies and which methods and materials to use, according to their interests and needs. The facilities they offer usually include books, pamphlets, handouts, videos, audio tapes, multi-media PCs, software and Internet access.

Allowing students to choose for themselves when to study, for how long and with which resources demands that they take responsibility for their own learning. Although this can help to develop autonomy and self-reliance, it is important to ensure that students possess or can develop the necessary skills to cope with such a high degree of freedom and such a wide range of choices. This can be achieved by providing initial assistance from a tutor to clarify students' ideas about what they want to learn and which resources they should use.

Brown, S. and Smith, B. (eds) (1996) *Resource Based Learning*, Kogan Page.
Burke, M. (1999) *Organization of Multimedia Resources*, Gower.
Clark, J. (1982) *Resource Based Learning for Higher and Continuing Education*, Halstead Press.
Davies, K. and Needham, M. (1975) 'Running a Resource Centre Facility for Individuals', *Programmed Learning and Educational Technology*, vol. 12, no. 3, pp. 181–5.
Dorrell, J. (1993) *Resource Based Learning*, McGraw-Hill.
Lopez, M. and Elton, L. (1980) 'A Course Taught Through a Learning Centre: An Evaluation', *Studies in Higher Education*, vol. 5, no. 1, pp. 91–9.

Malone, S.A. (1997) *How to Set Up and Manage a Corporate Learning Centre*, Gower.

Noble, P. (1981) *Resource Based Learning in Post Compulsory Education*, Kogan Page.

Oxford Brooks University Educational Methods Unit (1994) *Course Design for Resource Based Learning Series*, Oxford Brooks University.

Tucker, B. (ed.) (1997) *Handbook of Technology Based Training*, Gower.

Walton, J. (1975) 'The Initiation and Development of a Regional Resource Centre', *Programmed Learning and Educational Technology*, vol. 12, no. 3, pp. 141–50.

See also: Computer-assisted learning; Info bank; Language laboratory

Responsibility charting

When a work team makes a decision, members' roles in carrying it out may be unclear, and implementation sometimes requires the participation of outsiders who do not necessarily share the team's responsibility for the overall task. This means that even relatively straightforward initiatives often become increasingly complex as the number of participants grows, and there is a danger that the core group may lose control of the process. Richard Beckhard and Reuben Harris tried to overcome these difficulties by developing responsibility charting to clarify individuals' roles and responsibilities within the team. This intervention can also identify why decisions taken in the past have not been carried out as intended.

The responsibility chart takes the form of a grid. The types of decisions and classes of actions that need to be taken are arrayed along the vertical axis, and the horizontal axis shows which team members are likely to play a part in decision-making on these issues. The team assigns a function to each member for each issue, and this is entered on the chart. There are four classes of function in this model, which are indicated by the abbreviations R, A-V, S and I. *Responsibility* (R) shows who has primary responsibility for initiating action to ensure that the item is carried out (e.g., it would be the department head's responsibility to initiate the departmental budget). *Approval-Veto* (A-V) indicates which individual has the right to either approve or veto an item. *Support* (S) shows who is responsible for providing logistical support and resources for the item. *Inform* (I) means that someone must be informed about an item, but has no influence over it. If an individual plays no role in a particular item, this is indicated by a dash (–). An example of a responsibility chart is shown below.

Beckhard and Harris provide the following guidance on how to use this technique. They recommend that Responsibility for each item should be assigned to only one person to ensure

Responsibility chart
Source: Beckhard and Harris (1977, Figure 6.1)

clear accountability. They suggest that the number of people with the power of Approval-Veto for each item should be restricted, otherwise progress on the item may be slow, or it may even prove impossible to implement. On the other hand, giving an individual the right of Approval-Veto on too many items may block the decision-making process. The Support function is vital, in that those who provide it expend resources to produce something which is then used by whoever has Responsibility for the item, so the demands of the role need to be clearly specified. Finally, Beckhard and Harris point out that assigning functions to individuals may be difficult at times: for instance, someone may want Approval-Veto on a matter when it is not really necessary; a person may not want to provide Support for an item, but circumstances dictate they should do so, or two people may want Responsibility for a particular issue, but only one of them can have it.

Beckhard, R. and Harris, R.T. (1977) *Organizational Transactions: Managing Complex Change*, Addison Wesley Longman.

French, W.L. and Bell, C.H. (1994) *Organization Development: Behavioural Science Interventions for Organization Improvement* (5th edn), Prentice-Hall.

Melcher, R.D. (1967) 'Roles and Relationships: Clarifying the Manager's Job', *Personnel*, vol. 44, May–June, pp. 33–41.

Raia, A.P. (1974) *Managing by Objectives*, Scott Foresman, pp. 76–81.

See also: Chronology charting; Concept mapping; Drawing for learning; Fortune lining; Illuminative incident analysis; Job descriptions; Management responsibility guide process; Position charter; Poster; Relational diagramming; Role analysis technique; Role-prescription; Storyboarding

Retreat

The word 'retreat' has spiritual connotations, traditionally referring to a period of withdrawal for meditation and personal reflection. Retreats can be a very useful intervention, providing a supportive environment in which a group of participants can escape from the hurly-burly of modern organizational life and re-evaluate their behaviour, lifestyles and work situations, returning refreshed with the resolve to either change direction or pursue their goals with renewed vigour. They are usually residential, lasting a weekend or an entire week, and are often held in relatively secluded locations, perhaps in the country.

Baldwin, J. (1982) *Learning About Retreats*, Mowbray/G. Chapman.

Burns, J. (1997) *Camps, Retreats and Missions*, Regal Books.

Drinkard, G.W. (1998) *Retreats: Handmade Heavens to Refresh the Spirit*, Gibbs M. Smith.

Lederman, E. (1997) *Vacations That Can Change Your Life*, Sourcebooks Inc.

Louden, J. (1997) *A Woman's Retreat Book*, Harper.

Sawyer, K. (1998) *Time Out: Resources for Teen Retreats*, Ave Maria Press.

See also: Concentrated study; Family group team-building meeting; Moral philosophy approach; Residential; Sabbatical

Reward systems (financial compensation)

An organization's reward system should address all aspects of behaviour expected of its employees, and this may encompass both tangible and intangible rewards. Companies usually rely on financial rewards to provide positive reinforcement for satisfactory or outstanding performance, and a recent survey of different productivity improvement methods revealed that incentive payment approaches yielded the highest increase in productivity. Although appropriate reward systems can contribute greatly to organizational health, inappropriate ones may be very counter-productive. Most organizations have problems with their pay structure, and it is important to conduct periodic reviews of what staff behaviour is rewarded, and how this is done. No pay system should be permanent, since organizations must adapt to change.

Lawler argues that the reward system should be the starting point for any organizational change programme. Because pay is so closely related to employees' job satisfaction, motivation and loyalty, this demonstrates that the organization is committed to meaningful change. Also, because pay is closely linked to other organizational systems, addressing this issue may provide a model of how to deal with other problems. However, such change programmes are usually time-consuming, and may take at least six months to design and implement.

Armstrong, M. (1997) *Employee Reward*, Institute of Personnel and Development.

Bloom, M.C. and Milkovich, G.T. (1996) 'Issues in Managerial Compensation Research', in Cooper, C.L. and Rousseau, D.M. (eds) *Trends in Organizational Behaviour, Volume 3*, Wiley, pp. 23–47.

Chingos, P.T. and Marwick, P. (eds) (1997) *Paying for Performance*, Wiley.

Flannery, T.P., Hofrichter, D.A. and Platten, P.E. (1995) *People, Performance and Pay*, Fress Press.

Institute of Personnel and Development (1998) *Rewarding Performance*, IPD.

Lawler, E.E. (1981) *Pay and Organization Development*, Addison Wesley Longman.

Lewis, P. (1998) 'Managing Performance Based Pay', *Human Resource Management Journal*, vol. 8, no. 2, pp. 66–77.

Murlis, H. (1997) *Pay at the Crossroads*, Institute of Personnel and Development.

Patten, T.H. and Fraser, K.L. (1975) 'Using the Reward System as an OD Lever: Case Study of a Data-based Intervention', *Journal of Applied Behavioural Science*, vol. 11, no. 4, December, pp. 457–74.

Pfeffer, J. (1998) 'Six Dangerous Myths About Pay', *Harvard Business Review*, vol. 76, no. 3, pp. 109–19.

Poole, M. and Jenkins, G. (1998) 'Human Resource Management and the Theory of Rewards', *British Journal of Industrial Relations*, vol. 36, no. 2, pp. 227–47.

Schuster, J.R. and Zingheim, P.K. (1996) *The New Pay: Linking Employee and Organizational Performance*, Jossey-Bass.

Wilson, T.B. (1995) *Innovative Reward Systems for the Changing Workplace*, American Society for Training and Development, ASTD Press.

See also: Behaviour modification; Improshare; Productivity sharing; Profit-sharing; Reinforcement environment analysis; Rucker plan; Scanlon plan; Shared ownership

Role analysis technique

Ishwar Dayal and John M. Thomas developed this technique to clarify the roles of top management in a newly established company in India. The authors' aim was to enable individuals to: 'express disagreement with the manner in which a particular role was being defined or currently being performed by the focal role incumbent, particularly in terms of how this performance failed either to meet expectations from others or to convey obligations to others'. Dayal and Thomas's model was based on the work of Brown (1960) and Katz (1964). Some of the concepts adopted include the prescribed and discretionary components of a role, analysis of why a particular role is needed and what purpose it serves in the organization, and the expectations and obligations of related roles. Applied more broadly, the role analysis technique can help team members to clarify their mutual obligations and expectations in order to improve the team's functioning.

The role analysis technique is based on the observation that organizations usually divide tasks into sub-tasks, and these are then grouped into jobs which are allocated to individuals, along with varying degrees of responsibility. Those occupying certain positions in the hierarchy must fulfil specialized roles in order to contribute to the organization's performance. However, individuals may not understand how their contributions affect each others' ability to do this. The role analysis technique can help in these situations. It is particularly suitable for new work teams, but can be used in any team in which there is conflict or ambiguity about the question of roles.

The technique consists of a series of structured activities. At the outset, team members help each role-holder in turn to define and distinguish their role. The individual whose role is being considered is called the *focal person*, and there are five stages in this process. First, the focal person considers their own role, determining what it consists of, how it fits into the organization as a whole, and listing specific duties and activities. These are then discussed by the team members, and the list is amended accordingly until all participants are satisfied with the role definition. Next, the focal person lists what they expect from the other role-holders in order to perform the focal role, and these expectations are discussed and modified by the whole team. In the third stage, team members describe their expectations of the focal person, and these are discussed and amended. The focal person then draws up a written summary of the resulting role definition, known as the *role profile*. This consists of a set of role activities (both prescribed and discretionary), the focal role's obligations to each other role, and other roles' expectations of the focal role. The final stage involves revising this role profile before proceeding to analyse the next role.

Brown, W. (1960) *Explorations in Management*, Heinemann.

Dayal, I. and Thomas, J.M. (1968) 'Operation KPE: Developing a New Organization', *Journal of Applied Behavioural Science*, vol. 4, no. 4, pp. 473–506.

Dunphy, D. C. (1981) *Organizational Change by Choice*, McGraw-Hill, pp. 217–22.

Fonda, N. and Stewart, R. (1994) 'Enactment in Management Jobs: A Role Analysis', *Journal of Management Studies*, vol. 31, no. 1, pp. 83–104.

French, W.L. and Bell, C.H. (1994) *Organization Development: Behavioural Science Interventions for Organization Improvement* (5th edn), Prentice-Hall.

Katz, R.L. et al. (1964) *Organizational Stress: Studies in Role Conflict and Ambiguity*, Wiley.

See also: Functional role analysis; Job description; Management responsibility guide process; Organizational role analysis; Planned renegotiation; Responsibility charting; Role-prescription

Role training (direct role training)

Shortcomings in employees' performance may reflect a lack of the cognitive or emotional skills required to cope with their role. While it is obviously essential to develop the intellectual capacity to cope with a job's demands, many characteristics which are commonly seen as individual personality traits, such as aggressive behaviour, may be attributed to inadequate inter-personal skills among all those concerned. Role training tries to address these problems by identifying areas where there are deficits and providing direct training to remedy them, including extensive use of role-play and techniques drawn from psychodrama.

See also: Interaction management; Job retraining; Organizational role analysis; Personal development laboratory; Psychodrama; Role-playing; Self-development

Role-modelling

The most common and least conscious way in which people learn social and work roles is to observe others performing them, then copying their behaviour. Children's first experience of this is playing 'mothers and fathers', dressing up and mimicking their parents' behaviour. Later in life, pupils adopt role models, both outside school (by emulating certain pop stars or footballers) and inside it (by copying fellow pupils who study diligently, or those who shun hard work). Difficulties arise if the role being modelled is inappropriate, leading to complaints that those in the public eye are 'not setting youngsters a good example'.

In a similar way, employees' behaviour at work, both managerial and non-managerial, is modelled on what they observe among their peers and superiors. In one public sector organization, the quality of first line supervisors was found to be poor because their predecessors, whose management style they had copied, were ineffective. Since role-modelling is such a widespread, unconscious and influential learning method, managers must ensure that new entrants are exposed to desirable models of behaviour. In the area of customer service, for example, poor role models meant that for a time many staff tended to display discourtesy, indifference and poor inter-personal skills when dealing with customers, and remedying this demanded a large investment in time and money among a number of companies. Better role models were presented by showing videos of how customer service staff should behave, coupled with role-playing to reinforce the learning. This can have lasting benefits, since re-establishing a more desirable standard of behaviour means that newcomers quickly develop a clear understanding of what is required.

Day, D. (1989–90) 'Role Modelling of Managerial Behaviour in the Classroom', *Organizational Behaviour Teaching Review*, vol. 14, no. 1, pp. 148–51.
Speizer, J. J. (1981) 'Role Models, Mentors and Sponsors: The Elusive Concepts', *Signs: Journal of Women in Culture and Society*, vol. 6, pp. 692–712.

See also: Behaviour modelling; Mentoring; Organizational citizenship; Organizational role analysis; Playing for learning; Role-playing; Role-reversal

Role-playing

Role-playing is a common technique in social studies, and was first popularized in management training by Norman Maier. It has two main applications: it can be used to rehearse cognitive skills which have been acquired by other methods, and it can help to change individuals' attitudes. Role-playing focuses on real-life issues, and deals with situations participants have already encountered or are likely to face in the future. The emphasis is on problem-solving, and it can provide an alternative or an adjunct to group discussion, allowing students to role-play a variety of solutions. It can be used to achieve a range of objectives, such as practising a skill (e.g., handling grievances), demonstrating a situation for discussion (e.g., 'This is what happened to me last week ...'), trying out proposed actions (e.g., 'You be the boss, and react to my suggestion ...') or giving concrete expression to abstract ideas or processes.

Role-playing can be highly structured or spontaneous, depending on the trainer's objectives. Structured role-plays can be set up to illustrate a particular point by giving each participant a handout describing their role. The realism of the role-play is enhanced if participants portray some of the feelings and attitudes associated with their allotted role. Some trainers insist that participants play a role rather than 'be themselves', to avoid feelings of exposure. Others are less concerned about this, and encourage the spontaneous role-plays which may develop when students try to describe interactions they have experienced. In such cases, the trainer may suggest that individuals play themselves while other course members take on the roles of the other protagonists in the scene.

Bollens, J.C. and Marshall, D.R. (1973) *A Guide to Participation: Field work, Role Playing, Cases and Other Forms*, Prentice-Hall.

Keleman, K.S., Garcia, J.E. and Lovelace, K.J. (1990) *Management Incidents: Role Plays for Management Development*, Kendall/Hunt.

Ladousse, G.P. (1987) *Role Play*, Oxford University Press.

Maier, N.R.F., (1975) *The Role Play Technique*, Pfeiffer/Jossey-Bass.

Melville, A. (1996) *Role Play*, Severn House Publishers.

Quarstein, V.A. and McAfee, R.B. (1993) 'Teaching Business Strategy and Policy Using a Multiple Role Play Technique', *Journal of Management Education*, vol. 17, no. 2, pp. 185–96.

Rueschhoff, M.S. (1989–90) 'Theatre in the OB Classroom: To Role Play or Not to Role Play – That is the Question', *Organizational Behaviour Teaching Review*, vol. 14, no. 3, pp. 105–8.

Tolan, J. and Lendrum, S. (1995) *Case Method and Role Playing in Counselling Training*, Routledge.

Van Ments, M. (1994) *The Effective Use of Role Plays*, Kogan Page.

Yardley-Matwiejczuk, K.M. (1997) *Role Playing: Theory and Practice*, Sage.

Zoll, A.A., (1969) *Dynamic Management Education*, Addison Wesley Longman, Chapters 5–8.

See also: Action training; Apperception-interaction method; Assertiveness training; Behaviour modelling; Case-critical incident analysis; Case with role-play; Character immersion; Dramatic skit; Game; Mini-learning event; Mock trial; Monodrama; Playing for learning; Psychodrama; Role-modelling; Role-rehearsal; Role-reversal; Simu-Real; Skill practice seminar; Sociodrama; Surrogate client

Role-prescription (role-clarification; direct role training; making deals out on the table; meetings for two; role-negotiation; fixed-role therapy)

Role-prescription was developed from George Kelly's fixed-role therapy to provide a definition of how a manager should behave. The method involves collaboration between a manager and their *role reciprocals* (those who interact with the manager in their everyday work role), who act as consultants, working towards a mutually satisfactory role-prescription. This helps to produce a realistic appraisal of the role's requirements as well as fostering a climate of co-operation and commitment.

At the role-prescription meeting, the manager draws up a list of statements which describe the characteristics they would like to exhibit in carrying out their work, while the role reciprocals list their expectations of the manager. The two lists are then compared and discussed. Any unrealistic expectations are discarded, and the participants negotiate compromises until they can agree a provisional role-prescription. This is assessed during a period of role-playing, in which the manager attempts to perform the role according to the prescription. All concerned then discuss how well the provisional prescription worked, the manager may comment on any aspects that seemed awkward or uncomfortable, and the role-prescription is amended accordingly. A second cycle of role-playing, discussion and modification follows, and several such cycles may be necessary before everyone is satisfied. The process is not complete until the role-prescription has been tested in real life and proven satisfactory. A further meeting may be necessary to reassess the role-prescription and decide whether the manager needs training in certain skills required for the role.

Fordyce, J.K. and Weil, R. (1971) *Managing With People*, Addison Wesley Longman, pp. 114–16 and 176–8.

French, W.L. and Bell, C.H. (1984) 'Organization Development: Behavioural Science', in *Interventions for Organization Improvement* (3rd edn), Prentice-Hall.

Golembiewski, R.T. (1979) *Approaches to Planned Change, Part 1: Orienting Perspectives and Micro-level Interventions*, Marcel Dekker Inc.

Harrison, R. (1972) 'Role Negotiation: A Tough Minded Approach to Team Development', in Berger, M.L. and Berger, P.J. (eds) *Group Training Techniques*, Gower.

Harrison, R. (1995) *The Collected Papers of Roger Harrison*, Jossey-Bass, Chapter 4.

Kelly, G.A. (1955) *Psychology of Personal Constructs, Volume 2*, W.W. Norton.

Margulies, N. and Wallace, J. (1973) *Organizational Change: Techniques and Applications*, Scott Foresman, pp. 92–4.

McGivering, I. (1980) 'Facilitating Re-entry Through Role Analysis', in Beck, J. and Cox, C. (eds) *Advances in Management Education*, Wiley.

See also: Behaviour modification; FIDO approach; Functional role analysis; Induction training; Job description; Job support; Learning contract; Management responsibility guide process; Norm clarification; Norm formation; Norm modification; Organizational role analysis; Planned renegotiation; Position charter; Process analysis; Psychological contract; Responsibility charting; Role analysis technique; Role-reversal; Self- with peer appraisal; Team appraisal; Team development

Role-rehearsal

This coaching and mentoring method described by Pascale and Athos resembles the situational interviewing technique, where candidates are presented with a description of a typical work problem the post-holder might face, and asked how they would deal with it. In role-rehearsal, a manager chooses a problem, and a subordinate role-plays how they would handle it. The manager then swops roles with the subordinate to demonstrate how they would have dealt with the situation.

Pascale, R.T. and Athos, A.G. (1986) *The Art of Japanese Management*, Penguin Books, p. 147.

See also: Organizational role analysis; Role analysis technique; Role-modelling; Role-playing; Role-prescription; Role-reversal; Psychodrama

Role-reversal

In this technique, two members of a group are invited to work through a confrontation with each other. Although it can be adopted to resolve tension, conflict, misunderstanding or mistrust between two co-workers, it can also be used in situations where such problems do not exist, simply to enable the participants to gain a deeper appreciation of each other's position.

The two protagonists sit facing each other and outline their differences or develop their distinctive points of view. They then swop chairs and reverse roles, continuing the same discussion but assuming each other's point of view. When this phase has run its course, they swop chairs again and revert to representing themselves in the discussion, drawing on the insights gained by assuming the other's role. The facilitator encourages this to develop into a feedback session between the two, in which they discuss the exercise's impact on their attitudes towards each other. The other group members then offer their observations about the exercise, while the protagonists listen without commenting.

Role-reversal can be combined with role-play. In one variation, a participant re-enacts a situation they have encountered in real life, while another member of the group plays the role of antagonist. Both parts may be role-played if the intention is to explore role conflicts within the organization.

Heron, J. (1973) *Experiential Training Techniques*, Department of Adult Education, University of Surrey, Guildford.
Muney, B.F. and Deutsch, M. (1968) 'The Effects of Role Reversal During Discussion of Opposing Viewpoints', *Journal of Conflict Resolution*, vol. 12, no. 3, pp. 34–56.

See also: Buberian dialogue; Monodrama; Organizational role analysis; Psychodrama; Role-rehearsal; Role-modelling; Role-playing; Role-prescription; Sociodrama

Rotation training

A supervisor's development needs in relation to a particular function may be met by rotation training: assigning them to work with another supervisor who has the necessary experience, and the time and ability to pass on their knowledge. This method is often used to familiarize supervisors with the operations of the whole organization, but it demands thorough planning. The assignment process must be formal in order to ensure that it is clear who is responsible for delivering the training, and those who take on the task must be given adequate support in developing their teaching skills and aids.

A rotation training programme should meet the following criteria. The scheduling of assignments should be controlled by the training department, and should be designed to meet the particular needs of each trainee. There should be a clear pattern of rotation, to avoid departments being overloaded with trainees at any time. Those responsible for providing the training should be guaranteed sufficient time and resources to do so. There is little point in conducting training for training's sake and developing a large pool of trained supervisors if there are too few vacancies for them, so the programme should be geared to the opportunities available within the organization. Finally, although rotation assignments may be purely observational, individuals are more likely to benefit if they are given specific jobs and responsibilities within each function.

See also: Acting assignment; Apprenticeship; Assignment to manager with high development skills; Coaching; Development assignment; Expanding job assignment; Job rotation; Job swop; Manager exchange; Manager shadowing; Mentoring; Parrainage; Sick leave/holiday replacement assignment

Rote learning (memorization)

Rote learning (or 'learning by heart') fell into disrepute during the latter part of the twentieth century because it was felt that it developed students' ability to regurgitate information without necessarily enabling them to understand it. If rote learning were used to the exclusion of all other methods, then this criticism would be valid. However, there are many aspects of education where memorizing items such as facts, figures or formulae is essential, and such learning often serves as the basis for developing higher-order cognitive skills such as analysis and evaluation. For example, although learning the multiplication tables, historical dates or the order of the elements in the periodic table may seem dull in itself, it can enable us to perform mental arithmetic, understand historical developments or grasp the relationships between the elements.

Rote learning's decline in popularity in the classroom has not been mirrored in the business world, where the ability to remember names, decisions and facts without referring to notes is highly valued. There are various techniques which can be used to help students exercise and develop their memories, many of which rely on mnemonics. The most commonly used model emphasizes attention, connections, images and recall. First, students *attend* to the material to be remembered by reflecting on it, listing it or underlining it (e.g., drawing the order of the planets from the Sun). Next, they make it familiar by developing *connections* between the items to be remembered and common objects, using key, substitute or link words (e.g., 'Mars' and 'vase'). The third step is to invent *images* which exaggerate these connections or make them ridiculous (e.g., visualizing the planet Mars resting on the vase on the mantlepiece at home). Finally, students rehearse *recall* of the images until all can be remembered correctly (e.g., the Sun surrounded by a bun, then Mercury stuck in a tree, and so on).

Burley-Allen, M. (1990) *Memory Skills in Business: Basic Techniques*, Kogan Page.

Gruneberg, M.M. and Herrman, D.J. (1998) *Your Memory for Life*, Sterling Publications.

Healey, A.F. and Bourne, L.E. (1995) *Learning and Memorization of Knowledge and Skills*, Sage.

Joyce, B., Weil, M. and Showers, B. (1992) *Models of Teaching*, Allyn and Bacon, Chapter 8.

Levin, M.E. and Levin, J.A. (1990) 'Scientific Mnemonics: Methods for Maximising More Than Memory', *American Educational Research Review*, vol. 27, pp. 301–21.

Pressley, M., Levin, J.R. and Delaney, H.D. (1982) 'The Mnemonic Keyword Method', *Review of Educational Research*, vol. 52, no. 1, pp. 61–91.

Svantesson, I. (1997) *Learning Maps and Memory Skills*, Kogan Page.

See also: Advance organizer; Drill-and-practice method; Mind Mapping; Poetry for learning

Rucker plan

Along with the Scanlon plan and Improshare, the Rucker plan is probably one of the three best-known productivity gainsharing schemes. During the early 1930s, Allan W. Rucker used data collected by the US Census and Surveys of Manufacturers to show that economic productivity had been very stable between 1899 and 1929. It appeared that each industry had its own stable relationship between production and the value added by labour. The concept of value added (the value of production minus the costs of outside purchases such as materials and supplies) has formed the basis for a number of pay schemes. The Rucker plan uses it to calculate the Rucker Standard, which allocates the proceeds from improvements in productivity according to a formula based on the percentage of production value paid out in wages and benefits to certain classes of employees. The formula may include only workers with a close connection to the production process, or it may take into account all the company's personnel. The variable payroll costs are divided by the production value. If the costs are less than the Rucker Standard, a bonus is awarded. Each scheme is overseen by a committee with representatives from the workforce and management, which liaises between the two, considering suggestions, problems and solutions.

See also: Improshare; Productivity sharing; Profit-sharing; Reward systems; Scanlon plan; Shared ownership

Sabbaticals (paid educational leave)

Sabbaticals are periods of paid leave granted to staff after a specified period of service dictated by national legislation and organizational policy. Although this is most common in universities, it has also been adopted by a number of companies, and it has been an established part of employment practice in Australia since 1951. In the UK, one of the most widely known company sabbatical schemes has been operated by the John Lewis Partnership since 1979. Staff who have 25 years of service and who have reached the age of 50 receive six months' fully paid leave. The company does not use sabbaticals as a productivity-enhancing device or as a motivational technique, but to help give 'a fuller life to those entitled to the benefit'. Staff have fulfilled this aim by using their sabbaticals to pursue hobbies or engage in special projects on a full-time basis. Others have chosen to use the time to attend educational courses, engage in charitable activities, or work on home improvements.

Axel, H. (1990) *Redefining Corporate Sabbaticals for the 1990s*, Conference Board, USA.

Dlugozima, H., Scott, J. and Sharp, D. (1996) *Six Months Off*, Henry Holt Publishers.

May, S. (1985) 'Sabbaticals: The John Lewis Experience', in Clutterbuck, D. (ed.) *New Patterns of Work*, Gower, Chapter 9.

McCoy, B.H. (1997) 'Parable of the Sadhu', *Harvard Business Review*, May–June, pp. 54–64.

Shaw, L.A.R. (1995) *Time Off From Work*, Wiley.

Zahorski, K.H. (1994) *The Sabbatical Mentor*, Anker Publishing.

See also: Career life planning; Early retirement; Independent study; Job rotation; Research degree; Retreat

Scanlon plan

The Scanlon plan is one of the most widely known productivity gainsharing schemes, awarding a bonus to every employee in a plant. Unlike the Rucker plan, it does not rely on a standardized formula for calculating productivity bonuses. Instead, it encompasses a wide variety of methods tailored to the circumstances of the individual company. The general approach was developed in the late 1950s by Joseph Scanlon, who was a cost accountant by training. Scanlon drew on his experiences during the Depression, when he led efforts to reorganize a steel mill by the union now known as the United Steel Workers of America. When the mill owner and Scanlon visited the union's Pittsburgh headquarters to talk to regional director Clinton Golden, Golden said that workers at the plant always had ideas about how to increase production, and a way should be found to enlist their support. As a result, Scanlon held talks with the workers, and the plant was saved by applying the ideas he developed. In the USA, the Dana Corporation adopted the Scanlon plan extensively. It requires a show of interest from 80 per cent of a plant's employees before proceeding. Each plan takes eighteen months to two years to install, after which it is usually renegotiated every year.

The Scanlon plan can be applied in any company or plant – unionized or non-unionized, greenfield or conventional. In unionized plants, the productivity sharing agreement is non-negotiable and is separate from the collective bargaining agreement. The plan depends on promoting worker–management co-operation in areas where the two share common objectives. The general aims are to create an organizational climate oriented to increased productivity, and the methods adopted share a number of general features. They establish ways to gauge the performance of the whole company, allowing the effects of labour's contribution to be measured. These are used to calculate a base or normal value as a standard index against which to measure performance, and any savings resulting from increased productivity are distributed to employees, generally in proportion to their salaries. Finally, a formal system for employee participation is introduced by including worker representatives on the committees that develop and review suggested improvements.

The approaches adopted draw on Douglas McGregor's Theory Y assumptions about motivation, emphasizing participation in the belief that all employees are capable of self-directed effort towards organizational goals, as long as their work gives them the opportunity to take responsibility for their actions and use their abilities. Recognizing workers' value as a resource means that management's primary task is to tap their ideas in order to increase production. The Scanlon plan's philosophy rests on a number of principles. It believes that most workers desire participation, so the plan provides an outlet for this through its formal and informal channels. It places emphasis on treating workers as equals, so monetary rewards for improvements are awarded equitably, rather than being used as a motivator. Because it considers that workers' attention should be focused on system-wide improvements rather than on local concerns, performance is measured on company-wide factors. Finally, measuring the performance of individual workers is seen as undignified, so broad, generally available accounting data are used to measure company performance.

Although in theory the Scanlon plan places great emphasis on worker participation, this may not be reflected in the level of participation in practice. Each department elects one or two representatives to gather ideas for improvements from co-workers and present them to joint worker–management production committees. These meet every month, and the representatives' first line supervisor can implement minor or local suggestions, but larger-scale changes or problems must be referred to a higher-level committee. A number of worker representatives are selected from the production committees to sit on a Scanlon plan steering committee, alongside plant managers, staff managers and the local union leaders. This committee reviews suggestions from the production committees, considers major changes or disagreements at the lower levels, and oversees the calculation of the monthly bonus. The bonus is paid to all workers in the organization, from labourer to plant manager, and is usually based on increased productivity, but not necessarily work speed, the motto being: 'Work smarter, not harder.' The plant manager still has formal authority for all production decisions, and retains the traditional management rights under the collective bargaining agreement. The Scanlon committee members do not function as union representatives in grievance procedures. Instead, manufacturing plants usually have two sets of worker representatives, one sitting on the committees, and the other dealing with grievances.

Driscoll, J.W. (1979) 'Working Creatively with a Union: Lessons from the Scanlon Plan', *Organizational Dynamics*, Summer, pp. 61–80.

Frost, C.F. (1982) 'The Scanlon Plan at Herman Miller, Inc.: Managing an Organization by Innovation', in Zager, R. and Rosow, M.P. (eds) *The Innovative Organization: Productivity Programmes in Action*, Pergamon, pp. 63–87.

Frost, C.F. (1996) *Scanlon Plan for Organization Development*, Michigan State University Press.

Lesieur, F. (1958) *The Scanlon Plan: A Frontier in Labour–management Co-operation*, MIT Press.

Lesieur, F. and Packett, E. (1969) 'The Scanlon Plan Has Proved Itself', *Harvard Business Review*, vol. 47, no. 5, September–October, pp. 109–18.

Moore, B.E. and Ross, T.L. (1978) *Improving Productivity Using Scanlon Principles for Organizational Development: A Practical Guide*, Wiley Interscience.

Schuster, M. (1984) 'The Scanlon Plan: A Longitudinal Analysis', *Journal of Applied Behavioural Science*, vol. 20, no. 1, pp. 23–38.

See also: Improshare; Productivity sharing; Profit-sharing; Quality circles; Reward systems; Rucker plan; Shared ownership

Scenario-planning

This technique enables managers to assess the potential impact of a number of alternative future scenarios on their organization's plans, rather than relying on a single best estimate. It is considered particularly relevant in the current turbulent business environment, helping companies to review the assumptions that underpin their corporate planning. There are a number of courses on the subject which provide guidance on the various stages of constructing scenarios. These focus on the role of global forecasts, qualitative and quantitative forecasting methods, computer modelling and environmental scanning.

Collins, J.C. and Parras, J.I. (1997) *Built to Last: Successful Habits of Visionary Companies*, HarperBusiness.

De Geus, A. (1997) *The Living Company*, Harvard Business School Press.

Ringland, G. (1997) *Scenario Planning*, Wiley.

Schwartz, P. (1996) *The Art of the Long View*, Doubleday.

Van der Heijden, K. (1996) *Scenarios: The Art of Strategic Conversation*, Wiley.

See also: Delphi technique; Force field analysis; Goal-setting interface groups; Open systems planning; Policy-formulation; Search conference; Socio-technical systems designs; Strategic management

Scouting

Scouting allows an individual or organizational sub-unit to explore the unknown through continuous information-gathering. The technique involves benchmarking and amassing business intelligence, and applying it demands the development of a goal and a receptive and supportive organizational climate.

Holder, R.J. and McKinney, R. (1994) 'Scouting: A Process for Change Mastering Organizations', *Organization Development Journal*, vol. 12, 1, Spring, pp. 64–74.

See also: Focus groups

Search conference

Search conferences are large-group interventions which use a form of participative democracy to create a desired future vision for a department, company or community. The approach was originated by Fred Emery and Eric Trist in 1959 to assist the merger of the aeronautical engineering companies Bristol and Siddeley, and Merrelyn Emery developed it further in Australia. Each conference lasts a minimum of two-and-a-half days, and involves 35 to 40 participants chosen from the organization because of their expertise, knowledge of the system, influence within it, and their ability to implement any decisions.

The conference is preceded by a thorough briefing to familiarize participants with their roles. The six phases that follow aim to facilitate a community-wide discussion. The first three scan the system's environment – past, present and future. This is a distinctive feature of this intervention, and is based on the theory that it is necessary to be proactive towards environmental change, rather than simply react to it. The first phase, *Discussing our Turbulent Environment*, begins with a brainstorm involving the whole group, identifying perceptions of the significant changes that have occurred over the past five to seven years. Common ground is then established by dividing the conference into sub-groups to analyse these perceptions and look forward a few years, developing ideas for both probable and desirable futures. This process usually reveals shared ideals, such as respect for individual differences. The results of the sub-group discussions are fed back to the whole conference, where they are integrated and provide the guiding principles for later work. The second phase, *Our System's History*, addresses the past. Using storytelling, beginning with the longest-serving participant, the whole conference describes significant events and changes that have occurred in the system, and these may be recorded as a timeline on a wall chart. The third phase, *Our Current System*, considers the present by means of another brainstorm, this time identifying aspects of the current situation that need to be changed or retained. During the fourth phase, *Most Desirable System*, participants again divide into sub-groups, working in parallel to identify what features they would like to see in the system in the future. The sub-groups then report back to the whole conference and integrate their ideas, deciding which visions should be translated into strategic objectives. The fifth phase is *Action Planning*, which takes up a third of the total conference time. Participants select which strategic objectives they wish to work on, and form self-managing teams to develop action plans setting out intermediate aims, time scales and structure, and allocating responsibilities. The teams then report back to the conference, which plans follow-up activities. The final phase is *Implementation*. Participants are expected to realize their own vision of the future, rather than relying on assistance from outside experts. Efforts are made to avoid hierarchical, bureaucratic structures in pursuing these aims, retaining the highly democratic, self-managing community model established during the conference.

In 1995, the Hewlett-Packard Company set up a search conference to enable its manufacturing division to develop strategies and build a shared understanding of the internal and external environments in which staff were working. The conference's aims were to create a future to which they could all commit, to begin action planning, to build a communication plan, and to ensure broad responsibility and commitment to implementation by involving others in the process.

Bunker, B.B. and Alban, B.T. (1997) 'The Search Conference', in *Large Group Interventions: Engaging the Whole System for Rapid Change*, Jossey-Bass, pp. 33–41.

Emery, M. and Purser, R.E. (1996) *The Search Conference: Theory and Practice*, Jossey-Bass.

Weisbord, M. (1987) *Productive Workplaces*, Jossey-Bass.

Williams, T.A. (1979) 'The Search Conference in Active Adaptive Planning', *Journal of Applied Behavioural Science*, vol. 15, no. 4, pp. 470–83.

See also: Action training and research; Business process re-engineering; Conference Model; Delphi technique; Fast-cycle full-participation work design; Force field analysis; Future search; Goal-setting interface groups; Large-group interventions; Open space technology; Open systems planning; Participative design; Real-time strategic change; Real-time work design; Scenario-planning; Socio-technical systems design; Strategic management; Strategic planning process; Simu-Real; Work-Out

Secondment (attachment)

Although being seconded to a department or section of an organization can prove an effective learning method, this is not always the case. Successful secondments need to include four elements: question, contrast, documentation and observation, and report and discussion. Generating a suitable *question* to address during the attachment gives the individual a clear and relevant objective to pursue. The *contrast* or comparison element serves to guide their enquiries, and encourages analytical and critical thinking. Encouraging them to rely on *documentation and observation* means they take up less staff time, and helps to ensure that any questions they ask are well-researched and lead to productive discussions. Finally, the *report and discussion* element means that the individual must clarify their ideas and suggestions in drawing up their report, and test their validity in subsequent discussions.

Preparing for a secondment consists of seven steps. The first involves defining the learning objective of the learning, considering whether the aim should be to increase knowledge, understanding or both. The second is to plan the event, deciding which company activities, procedures or systems should be observed, and which company files and literature should be reviewed. The third step is to visit the department which will be hosting the secondment, ensuring that its managers understand and accept their commitment, and are willing to accept the individual and help them settle in. The fourth step is to brief the individual, giving them names, locations, telephone numbers and e-mail addresses of key staff, and providing timetables, maps and plans if necessary. They should be given clear guidance about what to observe and what data to collect, and asked to classify and summarize their observations, evaluate them critically, then write a report on their findings. In the fifth step, the instructor should accompany the individual to the department and introduce them to the staff in the department they will be studying. In the sixth step, the individual presents their report, and discusses it with the instructor. The final step involves assessing how well the learning objective has been achieved, and what remedial action the instructor should take to overcome any problems.

Clarke, M. (1995) *Breaking Down the Barriers: Inhibitions to Secondment*, LGC Communications.

See also: Accepting positions of responsibility in community associations; Assignment to community organization; Assignment to government body study group; Development assignment; Employee volunteering; Service in professional organization

Selection board assignment

One way to broaden a manager's experience is to assign them to the selection board responsible for interviewing job applicants. Making a satisfactory appointment involves conducting research into the job's requirements, deciding where and how to advertise the vacancy, drawing up a shortlist, interviewing candidates and debating which one should receive the job offer. This develops skills which have wider applications in organizational life.

Hackett, P. (1997) *The Selection Interview*, Institute of Personnel and Development.

See also: Committee assignment; Consulting assignment; Development assignment; Evaluation audit assignment; Proposal team assignment; Staff meeting assignment; Study assignment

Self- with peer appraisal

Although feedback is a vital factor in learning and improving performance, supervisors often feel uncomfortable about providing it. When their work has been unsatisfactory, subordinates tend to regard negative feedback as the allocation of blame rather than as constructive criticism, so it can be counter-productive. On the other hand, providing positive feedback by praising good work can be embarrassing for both parties. To overcome these problems, some companies have attempted to introduce self-appraisal, but this has proven too subjective in practice. A more useful approach is self- with peer appraisal, which provides a structure that enables individuals to identify their own strengths and weaknesses, and develop an action plan to meet their training and development needs. Although the process is more elaborate and time-consuming than traditional forms of assessment, it is more likely to encourage commitment to improving performance. It is less threatening for appraisees, and it gives them more control over their own assessment. It also promotes team development by helping members understand how to provide realistic support for each other. For these reasons, self- with peer appraisal underpins some

of the most popular current approaches to management development, such as action learning and self-development.

First, the appraisee chooses which factors will serve as the basis for their assessment, subject to approval by their line manager. The department running the scheme asks the appraisee to nominate a number of co-workers to serve as peer appraisers, and each is issued with an assessment form, which they complete and return in strictest confidence. The department summarizes the information, and passes it on to the appraisee and their line manager. The appraisee then completes a self-appraisal form, which takes into account the peer appraisal feedback. The line manager draws on both sets of information to arrive at an assessment of the appraisee's performance and the methods that were used to achieve any improvements. This then forms the basis for a discussion between the appraisee and line manager about what has been revealed and what action can be taken to help the appraisee develop further.

Adams, C. and King, K. (1995) 'Towards a Framework for Student Self-assessment', *Innovations in Education and Training International*, vol. 32, no. 4, pp. 336–43.

Boud, D. (1995) *Enhancing Learning Through Self Assessment*, Kogan Page.

Brown, S. (1990) *Self and Peer Assessment*, SCED Publications.

Goedegeburre, L.C.D. (1990) *Peer Review and Performance Indicators*, Lemma B.V. Publishers.

Hancock, R. and Settle, D. (1990) *Practical Teacher's Guide to Appraisal and Self-evaluation*, Blackwell.

Harris, M.M. and Schaubbroeck, J. (1988) 'A Meta-analysis of Self–supervisor, Self–peer and Peer–supervisor Ratings', *Personnel Psychology*, vol. 41, pp. 43–62.

Heron, J. (1981) 'Peer and Self Assessment', in Boydell, T. and Pedler, M. (eds) *Management Self-development: Concepts and Practices*, Gower.

Mabe, P.A. and West, S.G. (1982) 'Validity of Self-evaluation of Ability: A Review and Meta-analysis', *Journal of Applied Psychology*, vol. 67, pp. 280–96.

Smith, R. (1993) *Preparing for Appraisal: Self-evaluation for Teachers*, Framework Press Educational.

Taylor, B. (1995) *Peer Education: Self and Peer Assessment*, Oasis Communications.

See also: Appraisal; Assessment centre; Awareness training; Examination; Goal-setting; Instrumented feedback; Management audit; Management by objectives; Measuring performance; Periodic planning conference; Positive feedback; Role-prescription; Self-criticism; Team appraisal

Self-criticism (public self-criticism)

Self-criticism can serve two purposes. Reflecting in private on one's own decisions and activities and analysing the reasons for success or failure can reveal valuable lessons, and discussing one's mistakes in a group makes those lessons available to others. To be effective, private self-criticism should be structured in some way. For instance, a manager can record events and decisions in a notebook, then read through it periodically, reflecting on what happened, with the benefit of hindsight. In considering how they ran a meeting, the manager might consider whether the meeting's aim was achieved, whether those present benefited from attending it, which parts of the meeting went well and which might be improved, and how well they controlled the direction of the meeting. It may be useful to identify both common errors and unusual ones, and this can be achieved by classifying all the errors made during a period under headings which reveal recurring problems.

Forms of public self-criticism can be found in many teaching approaches. In a problem-solving group, managers may describe problems they have failed to solve, then ask for suggestions or advice. In an experiential exercise, before asking for the observers' views, the instructor may ask participants why they think they failed to achieve the set task. Finally, both the video confrontation technique and the inter-personal process recall method may involve the facilitator asking individuals to comment on their own behaviour.

Bergner, R.M. (1995) *Pathological Self-criticism: Assessment and Treatment*, Plenum Publishing.
Pedler, M. and Boydell, T. (1990) *Managing Yourself*, Gower.
Stone, H. and Stone, S.W. (1993) *Embracing Your Inner Critic: Turning Self-criticism into a Creative Asset*, Harper and Row.
Tompkins, A. (1992) *Criticism and Self-criticism: A Sign of Love and Concern*, Random House.

See also: Inter-personal process recall; Management audit; Personalized reflection; Self- with peer appraisal; Video confrontation

Self-development

Self-development is by no means a new concept, although it was popularized in recent times by the work of Tom Boydell, Mike Pedler and John Burgoyne. It covers such a broad range of activities that it is difficult to define precisely. It underlies many self-teaching approaches, and provides the basis for the design of a number of individual learning events and educational systems. In their writings, Boydell, Pedler and Burgoyne distinguish between development *by* self and development *of* self, the former referring to self-development as a process, and the latter regarding it as a goal.

As a process, self-development allows students to control their own learning, choosing the pace and method of study, the subject content, and so on. Learning approaches which support this form of development include learning communities, action learning, and autonomy labs.

The goal of self-development could be said to be Maslow's 'self-actualized person'. Within organizations, such individuals demonstrate greater competency and effectiveness in their work. However, simply applying specific learning approaches cannot guarantee that this objective will be attained. Pedler and Boydell argue that: 'development is a function of the individual interacting with some part of his environment, either actually or symbolically – there is no development without a developer'. In other words, a self-development experience can be defined as any event in which an individual is able to find significance and personal meaning. The problem is that this learning is unpredictable: a manager may not find any personal meaning in an expensive action learning programme, but may do so while engaged in a hobby at the weekend.

Anderson, A. (1996) *Effective Self-development*, Blackwell.
Boydell, T. and Pedler, M. (1981) *Management Self-development: Concepts and Practice*, Gower.
Burgoyne, J. and Reynolds, M. (eds) (1997) *Management Learning*, Sage.
Megginson, D. and Whitaker, V. (1997) *Cultivating Self-development*, Institute of Personnel and Development.
Pedler, M. (1988) *Applying Self-development in Organizations*, Prentice-Hall.
Pedler, M., Burgoyne J. and Boydell, T. (1994) *A Manager's Guide to Self-Development* (3rd edn), McGraw-Hill.
Sparrow, J. (1998) *Knowledge in Organizations*, Sage.
Stadler, M.A. and Frensch, P.A. (1997) *Handbook of Implicit Learning*, Sage.
Stansfield, L. M. (1996) 'Is Self-development the Key to the Future?', *Management Learning*, vol. 27, no. 4, pp. 429–45.

See also: Context training; Instrumented feedback;

MAPS approach; Personal development laboratory; Role training; Self-improvement programme; Student-planned learning; Tape-assisted learning programme

Self-directed change project

In a self-directed change project, individuals work to change their own behaviours, thoughts and feelings, to bring them closer to a goal that they have set for themselves. This approach is based on two assumptions. The first is that, under proper conditions, proactive forces emerge in individuals which permit them to experiment with new behaviours and strive towards new ideals. In the 1950s, writers such as Rogers, Harlow and White documented the case for the existence of proactive motivation in human beings. The second assumption is that changes in behaviour are most likely to be permanent if individuals feel that the process and outcomes of change are under their own control, rather than that of an external agent. For these reasons, self-directed change projects give individuals responsibility for diagnosing their own problems, setting their own goals, and accomplishing change through their own efforts. First, each participant reflects on their behaviour, and selects a limited but well-defined goal they would like to achieve. Next, they undertake a continuous assessment of their behaviour, thoughts and feelings in areas related to the change goal by keeping objective records of them, which may be displayed in the form of a graph or chart. Finally, they decide on the length of the project.

Two aspects of such projects are particularly important – goal-setting and feedback. *Goal-setting* disrupts the individual's equilibrium, laying them open to the possibility of change. If the new goal is sufficiently valued, they will be motivated to change their behaviour in order to achieve it. *Feedback* takes two forms: self-generated feedback through conscious reflection on progress, and feedback from others. High-quality feedback of either type is essential for successful personal change.

Harlow, H.F. (1953) 'Mice, Monkeys, Men and Motives', *Psychological Review*, vol. 60, pp. 23–32.
Kolb, D.A., Winter, S.K. and Berlew, D.E. (1968) 'Self-directed Changes; Two Studies', *Journal of Applied Behavioural Science*, vol. 4, no. 4, pp. 453–71.
Maslow, A.H. (1954) *Motivation and Personality*, Harper.
White, R. (1959) 'Motivation Reconsidered: The Concept of Competence', *Psychological Review*, vol. 66, pp. 297–333.

See also: Self-discipline; Self-generated scaling; Self-management

Self-directed learning (self-managed learning)

Self-direction in learning can be seen as both a process and a goal. Engaging in life-long learning requires the development of personal autonomy – the willingness and freedom to make choices – and autodidaxy – the motivation, self-discipline and organizational ability to pursue learning independently, outside formal institutional settings. The skills required include comprehension, synthesis and analysis, and the ability to ask questions, think critically and conduct independent research.

Akin, G. (1991) 'Self-directed Learning in Introductory Management', *Journal of Management Education*, vol. 15, no. 3, pp. 295–32.
Areglado, R.J., Bradley, R.C. and Lane, P.S. (1996) *Learning for Life: Creating Classrooms for Self-directed Learning*, Corwin Press.
Boud, D.J. (ed.) (1987) *Developing Autonomy in Student Learning*, Kogan Page.
Boyatzis, R.E. (1994) 'Stimulating Self-directed Learning Through Managerial Assessment and Development Courses', *Journal of Management Education*, vol. 18 no. 3, pp. 304–13.
Candy, P.C. (1991) *Self-direction for Life Long Learning*, Jossey-Bass.
Collier, K.G. (1980) 'Peer Group Learning in Higher Education: The Development of Higher Order Skills', *Studies in Higher Education*, vol. 5, pp. 55–62.
Confessore, G. (1992) *Guideposts to Self-directed Learning*, Organization Design and Development Inc.
Cunningham, I. (1999) *The Wisdom of Strategic Learning* (2nd edn), Gower.
Hammond, M. (1991) *Self-directed Learning: Critical Practice*, Kogan Page.
Kreberic, C. (1998) 'The Relationship Between Self-directed Learning, Critical Thinking and Psychological Type, and Some Implications for Teaching in Higher Education', *Studies in Higher Education*, vol. 23, no. 1, pp. 71–86.
Long, H.B. (1993) *Emerging Perspectives on Self-directed Learning*, Classic Book Distributors, USA.
Long, H.B. (1996) *Current Developments in Self-directed Learning*, Classic Book Distributors, USA.
Ramsey, V.J. and Couch, P.D. (1994) 'Beyond Self-directed Learning: A Partnership Model of Teaching and Learning', *Journal of Management Education*, vol. 18, no. 2, pp. 139–61.
Ryan, G. (1993) 'Student Perceptions About Self-

directed Learning Groups in a Professional Course Implementing Problem-based Learning', *Studies in Higher Education*, vol. 18, no. 1, pp. 53–64.

Taylor, I. and Burgess, H. (1995) 'Orientation to Self-directed Learning: Paradox or Paradigm', *Studies in Higher Education*, vol. 20, no. 1, pp. 87–98.

Taylor, M. (1986) 'Learning for Self-direction in the Classroom; The Pattern of a Transition', *Studies in Higher Education*, vol. 11, no. 1, pp. 55–72.

See also: Autonomous group learning; Creative dialogue; Independent study; Instrumented team learning; Learning through discussion; Media-activated learning group; Tutorium

Self-directed teams (self-regulating work teams; self-managed groups)

Self-directed teams in organizations are distinguished by three characteristics: their members perform inter-dependent work tasks, they are collectively responsible for manufacturing a product or delivering a service; and they regulate their work themselves to a certain extent. Although their level of autonomy varies, they exercise a degree of internal control because the team takes on some of the planning, scheduling, staffing and monitoring tasks which were previously performed by management. Self-directed teams represent one aspect of the trend towards horizontal management. Certain factors are essential if such teams are to be held accountable for their performance. Their tasks should be differentiated and self-contained. Each team should have control over inputs and outputs within its sphere of operation, including the staff budgets. Finally, they should be free to regulate the behaviour of their own members.

Beach, L.R. (1974) 'Self-directed Student Groups and College Learning', *Higher Education*, vol. 3, pp. 187–200.

Cohen, S.G. (1994) 'Designing Effective Self-managing Work Teams', *Advances in Interdisciplinary Studies of Work Teams*, JAI Press.

Flynn, R., McCombs, T. and Elloy, D. (1990) 'Staffing the Self-managing Work Team', *Leadership and Organization Development Journal*, vol. 11, no. 1, pp. 26–31.

Kirkham, B.L. and Shapiro, D.L. (1997) 'The Impact of Cultural Values on Employee Resistance to Teams: Towards a Model of Globalized Self-managing Work Team Effectiveness', *Academy of Management Review*, vol. 22, no. 3, pp. 730–57.

Knowles, M.S. (1975) *Self-directed Learning*, Prentice-Hall.

Kulisch, T. and Banner, D.K. (1993) 'Self-managed Work Teams: An Update', *Leadership and Organization Development*, vol. 14, no. 2, pp. 25–9.

Liden, R.C. and Tewksbury, T.W. (1995) 'Empowerment and Work Teams', in Ferris, G.R., Rosen, S.D. and Barnum, D.T. (eds) *Handbook of Human Resource Management*, Blackwell Business, pp. 386–403.

Mullen, T.P. (1992) 'Integrating Self-directed Teams into the Management Development Curriculum', *Journal of Management Development*, vol. 11, no. 5, pp. 43–54.

Salem, M.A. and Banner, D.K. (1992) 'Self-managing Work Teams: An International Perspective', *Leadership and Organization Development Journal*, vol. 13, no. 7, pp. 3–8.

'Self-managing Teams', special issue of *Human Relations* (1994), vol. 47, no. 1, January.

Todd, F. and Todd, R.C. (1979) 'Talking and Learning: Towards Effective Structuring of Student Directed Learning Groups', *Journal of Further and Higher Education*, vol. 3, no. 2, pp. 52–6.

Wilson, P. (1996) *Empowering the Self-directed Team*, Gower.

Yeatts, D.E. (1998) *High Performing Self-managed Work Teams*, Sage.

See also: Collateral organizations; Greenfield plants; Group technology; Independent product teams; Integrated support functions; Intrapreneurial group; Job enrichment; Job rotation; Likert's level meetings; Matrix designs; Participation; Quality of working life; Socio-technical systems design; Structural interventions

Self-discipline

Self-discipline has developed into a distinct field of research and training, which believes that individuals can be taught how to develop the appropriate mental attitudes and physical steps to guide them towards a goal. In the educational context, this concept is close to self-management, which involves students taking responsibility for the learning process.

Dubrin, A.J. (1997) *Getting It Done: The Transforming Power of Self-discipline*, Petersons Guides.

Strahan, D.B. (1997) *Mindful Learning: Teaching Self-discipline and Academic Achievement*, Carolina Academic Press.

Workman, E.A. and Katz, A.M. (1995) *Teaching Behavioural Self-control to Students*, Pro Ed Publishers.

Zimmerman, B.J., Bonner, S. and Kovach, R. (1996) *Developing Self-regulated Learners*, American Psychological Association.

See also: Self-directed change project; Self-management

Self-efficacy training

'Self-efficacy' has been defined as an individual's judgement of their ability to organize and carry out the courses of action required to achieve certain levels of performance. Associated most closely with Albert Bandura, self-efficacy training was originally applied in clinical psychotherapy, but has been adopted by a number of organizations to address problems such as employee absence and poor time-keeping. An individual's perception of their self-efficacy determines whether or not they will be able to cope with difficult situations, how much effort they will expend, and how long they will persist in trying to overcome obstacles. The more confidence they have in their abilities, the more likely they are to cope, persevere and succeed, so self-efficacy training aims to improve their competencies and self-perception through techniques such as mastery modelling and persuasion.

Bandura, A. (1977) 'Self-efficacy: Toward a Unifying Theory of Behavioural Change', *Psychological Review*, May, pp. 191–215.

Bandura, A. (ed.) (1997) *Self-efficacy in Changing Societies*, Cambridge University Press.

Bandura, A. (1997) *Self-efficacy: The Exercise of Control*, W.M. Freeman & Co.

Gist, M.E. (1987) 'Self-efficacy Implications for Organizational Behaviour and Human Resource Management', *Academy of Management Review*, July, pp. 472–85.

Gist, M.E. and Mitchell, T.R., (1992) 'Self-efficacy: A Theoretical Analysis of its Determinants and Malleability', *Academy of Management Review*, April, pp. 183–211.

Locke, E.A. et al (1984) 'Effect of Self-efficacy, Goals and Task Strategies on Task Performance', *Journal of Applied Psychology*, May, pp. 241–51.

Wood, R., Bandura, A. and Bailey, T. (1990) 'Mechanisms Governing Organizational Performance in Complex Decision Making Environments', *Organizational Behaviour and Human Decision Processes*, vol. 46, pp. 181–201.

Zimmerman, B.J., Bonner, S. and Kovach, R. (1996) *Developing Self Regulated Learners: Beyond Achievement to Self Efficacy*, American Psychological Association.

See also: Achievement motivation training; Assertiveness training; Behaviour modelling; Confidence-building measures

Self-generated scaling

In certain work situations, employees may understand more clearly than management which factors affect performance. When these have been identified and agreed, they can serve as the basis for questionnaires or group-sensing sessions to produce a group or organizational profile. For example, if a team wishes to check how well it is performing, its members can list the factors they think have a significant impact on its functioning. They may identify as many as twenty or thirty items, and the next task is to rate the group's performance on each of them, on a scale of 1 to 10. They then decide what aspects could and should be changed, and how this can be achieved. Once these ideas have been implemented, the same methods may be used to check on progress and identify any aspects that need further attention.

Margulies, N. and Wallace, J. (1973) *Organizational Change: Techniques and Applications*, Scott Foresman, pp. 3–5.

See also: Attitude survey; Employee-designed rules; Instrumented feedback; Polling; Self-generated change project; Survey feedback interventions

Self-help group (support group)

The key characteristic of a self-help group is that members help each other to learn and progress. Participants take responsibility for maintaining the group's norms and processes, and do not rely on expert guidance, although a leader or facilitator may provide assistance in the initial stages. The methods adopted vary from the highly structured to the very open. Self-help groups can be divided into two types. Approaches such as co-counselling are designed to cater for a broad range of people, whereas those adopted in Alcoholics Anonymous and consciousness-raising groups focus on people who have similar experiences or problems.

Bingham, R. and Daniels, J. (1998) *Developing Student Support Groups*, Gower.

Emrick, C.D., Lassen, C.L. and Edwards M.T. (1977) 'Non-professional Peers as Therapeutic Agents', in Gurman, A.S. and Razin, A.M. (eds) *Effective Psychotherapy: A Handbook of Research*, Pergamon.

Garry, A. and Cowan, J. (1992) 'Opinion: Self-help Continuing Professional Development Groups in the Workplace – A Case Study to Determine their Potential and Viability', *Educa-

tion and Training Technology International, vol. 29, no. 1, pp. 64–9.

Kurtz, L.F. (1997) *Self Help and Support Groups*, Sage.

Lieberman, M.A. and Borman, L.D. (1979) *Self Help Groups*, Jossey-Bass.

Messier, G. and Saint Jacques, N. (1975) 'Multimedia: Three Years, Three Phases', *Programmed Learning and Educational Technology*, vol. 12, no. 5, pp. 278–86.

Pancoast, D.L., Parker, P. and Froland, C. (eds) (1983) *Self Help Rediscovered*, Sage.

Wilson, J. (1996) *How To Work With Self Help Groups*, Gower.

See also: Action learning; Co-counselling; Consciousness-raising group; Learning community; Networking

Self-improvement programme

Some employees find it difficult to respond to training programmes devised and directed by others. In such cases, managers can invite them to devise their own self-improvement programmes. This can be achieved by administering a self-assessment questionnaire to stimulate reflection on their medium- to long-term personal and career needs. The questionnaire should address issues such as how the employee feels they are progressing in their career, what their goals are, what skills they have acquired to enable them to work towards these goals, and what additional ones they need to develop. The manager can then discuss the responses with the employee and draw up a jointly agreed programme of developmental activities to meet the needs identified.

Bitton, S. (1981) *This Learning Business: Assignments for Pre-vocational Courses*, McGraw-Hill.

Chapman, E.S. et al. (1996) *Twelve Steps to Self-improvement*, Crisp Publications.

Cohen, A. (1994) *I Had It All the Time: When Self-improvement Gives Way to Ecstasy*, Alan Cohen Publications.

Seligman, M.P. et al (1995) *What You Can Change and What You Can't: The Complete Guide to Successful Self-improvement*, Fawcett Books.

See also: Career life planning; Counselling; Mentoring; Self-development

Self-instructional modules and interactive groups

This method, which has been used to teach biology and similar subjects, combines independent study modules with interactive group activities to reinforce students' learning and develop their problem-solving skills. The modules were originally delivered by means of audio tapes accompanied by study guides and textbooks, with students working individually in carrels in a learning laboratory, but the use of multi-media computers is more common nowadays.

Courses run on these lines do not include lectures or laboratory classes. Instead, students may be asked to complete one module a week during a term, and attend a meeting with a tutor and eight to ten other students for an hour or two every week. Each meeting addresses the previous week's module, beginning with a quiz. Rather than being given the correct answers by the instructor, the group discusses each question in turn, the brief, two- or three-line answers each member has written providing a framework for exploratory interaction. The resulting exchange of opinions helps to expose and resolve any conceptual difficulties, and once the group has reached consensus on what would be an acceptable answer, it moves on to the next question. Individuals mark their own quiz sheets accordingly, and this immediate feedback provides an effective learning experience. At the end of the meeting, the instructor collects their quiz sheets to review them, returning them the following week.

Brewer, I.M. (1974) 'Recall, Comprehension and Problem Solving: An Evaluation of Audio-visual Method of Learning Plant Anatomy', *Journal of Biological Education*, vol. 8, pp. 101–12.

Brewer, I.M. (1977) 'SIMIG: A Case Study of an Innovative Method of Teaching and Learning', *Studies in Higher Education*, vol. 2, no. 1, pp. 33–54.

Brewer, I.M. (1979) 'Group Teaching Strategies for Promoting Individual Skills in Problem Solving', *Programmed Learning and Educational Technology*, vol. 16, no. 2, pp. 111–28.

Brewer, I.M. (1985) *Learning More and Teaching Less: A Decade of Innovation in Self-instruction and Small Group Learning*, Taylor and Francis.

Brewer, I.M. and Tomlinson, J.D. (1981) 'SIMIG: The Effect of Time on Performance with Modular Instruction', *Programmed Learning and Educational Technology*, vol. 18, no. 2, pp. 72–85.

Jones, A. and Kember, D. (1994) 'Approaches to Learning and Student Acceptance of Self-study Packages', *Education and Training Technology International*, vol. 31, no. 2, pp. 93–7.

See also: Audio tutorial method; Autonomous learning group; Construct lesson plan; Data approach method; Guided discussion; Guided group problem-solving; Programmed simulation; Tutorial-tape-document learning package approach

Self-management (behavioural self-management)

Self-management is one of the many behaviour change techniques adopted by organizations to address issues such as absenteeism and poor time-keeping. It demands that employees take responsibility for certain aspects of their behaviour and make efforts to change them. The approach draws on the work of social learning theorists such as Albert Bandura, who noted that people who see themselves as inefficient in coping with environmental demands tend to exaggerate their difficulties. In contrast, efficient people concentrate their attention and their efforts on the demands of the situation, and any obstacles they encounter only spur them on to greater efforts. These problems can be overcome by encouraging the individual to internalize the organization's goals, for example on attendance, and helping them to develop a greater sense of confidence in their abilities to achieve them. In this situation, the satisfaction and self-confidence gained from setting and achieving their own standards of attendance may encourage them to pursue self-improvement in other areas.

Bandura, A. (1982) 'Self Efficacy Mechanisms in Human Ageing', *American Psychologist*, vol. 37, pp. 122–47.

Koroly, P. and Kanfer, F.H. (1982) *Self Management and Behaviour Change*, Pergamon.

Luthans, F. and Davis, T.R.V. (1979) 'Behavioural Self-management - The Missing Link in Managerial Effectiveness', *Organizational Dynamics*, vol. 8, no. 1, Summer, pp. 42–60.

Manz, C.C. (1983) *The Art of Self-leadership*, Prentice-Hall.

Manz, C.C. and Neck, C.P. (1998) *Mastering Self-leadership* (2nd edn), Prentice-Hall.

Manz, C.C. and Sims, H. (1980) 'Self-management as a Substitute for Leadership: A Social Learning Theory Perspective', *Academy of Management Review*, vol. 5, pp. 361–7.

Mills, P.M. (1983) 'Self-management: Its Control and Relationship to Other Organizational Properties', *Academy of Management Review*, vol. 8, pp. 445–53.

Neck, C.P. and Manz, C.C. (1996) 'Thought Self-leadership', *Journal of Organizational Behaviour*, vol. 17, pp. 445–67.

Santamaria, P. (1996) *High Performance Through Self-management*, Rosen Publishing Group.

Thoresen, C.E. and Mahoney, M. (1974) *Behavioural Self Control*, Holt, Rinehart and Winston.

See also: Behaviour modification; Interaction management; Reinforcement environment analysis; Self-directed change project; Self-discipline; Self-efficacy training

Self-service experiment

This variation of programmed learning can be used to teach practical topics. Students are issued with a programmed text which describes the steps in an experiment designed to achieve the chosen learning goal.

O'Connell, S., Penton, S.J. and Boud, D.J. (1977) 'A Rationally Designed Self-service Minicourse', *Programmed Learning and Educational Technology*, vol. 14, no. 2, pp. 154–61.

See also: Programmed learning

Self-tests (quizzes)

Allowing students to mark their own test scripts provides direct feedback which enables them to assess their own progress and identify areas where they need to improve. Students may be allowed to keep their results confidential, or the instructor can use them to assess the individual's or the class's performance. Self-tests can be useful in starting discussions, introducing topics, or summarizing and reinforcing past learning. Setting similar questions at the beginning and end of a course offers two advantages: it allows the instructor to evaluate the results of their teaching, and it enables students to gauge how much they have learned. In preparing a test, the instructor should have a clear idea of the ground to be covered, and the questions should reflect the course objectives. It is best to avoid setting questions which are too open, such as 'What would you do ...?'

See also: Examination; Instrumented feedback; Pre-course learning; Process analysis

Seminar

A seminar is a small-group discussion between an instructor and eight to twelve students, sometimes attended by a guest expert. Attitudes to this teaching method vary. One report on university teaching suggested that it was very popular among students. However, some individuals find learning in groups a highly threatening experience, while others find the sessions boring. Much depends on the skill of the instructor. Some studies report that seminars often degenerate into lectures, leading to poor attendance by students. Instructors must try to weld the individuals into a cohesive group, ensuring that the experience is supportive and emotionally satisfying as well as productive.

Bogardus, E.S. (1947) 'The Seminar as a Research Institution', *Sociological and Social Research*, vol. 31, pp. 389–95.

Broady, M. (1969–70) 'The Conduct of Seminars', *Universities Quarterly*, vol. 24, no. 3, pp. 273–84.

Kahn, M. (1981) 'The Seminar: An Experiment in Humanistic Education', *Journal of Humanistic Psychology*, vol. 21, no. 2, Spring.

McCormick, D. and Kahn, M. (1982) 'Barn Raising: Collaborative Group Process in Seminars', *Exchange: The Organizational Behaviour Teaching Journal*, vol. 7, no. 4, pp. 16–21.

Ruddock, J. (1978) *Learning Through Small Group Discussion: A Study of Seminar Work in Higher Education*, Society for Research into Higher Education.

Watson, W. (1994) *How To Give an Effective Seminar*, Kogan Page.

Watt, I. (1964) 'The Seminar', *Universities Quarterly*, vol. 18, pp. 369–89.

Wilson, A. (1980) 'Structuring Seminars: A Technique to Allow Students to Participate in the Structuring of Small Group Discussions', *Studies in Higher Education*, vol. 5, no. 1, pp. 81–4.

See also: Advanced seminar; Group discussion; Small-group teaching; Structuring seminars; Tutorial; Tutorium

Sensing (organizational sensing; problem-sensing with groups)

Sensing is a diagnostic tool which enables management to identify and prioritize general issues of concern to staff before embarking on more detailed team or organizational activities to address specific problems. There are two main approaches, both of which involve small groups: *vertical sensing* involves interviewing a complete vertical slice of an organization, whereas *horizontal sensing* collects data from no more than three or four levels. In smaller organizations, the groups could include everyone in the organization.

Sensing can be used for a variety of purposes: to collect information as part of a general analysis of the organization, to learn about the problems of specific groups, to check how well employees understand the organization's objectives, and to test their reaction to proposals. It can provide a quick overview of what is going on in the organization, revealing impressions and feelings as well as opinions and ideas, and showing how well the formal communication channels are functioning. However, it will be of limited usefulness if there is a lack of trust between individuals at different levels in the organization. In such circumstances, it may even be counter-productive, as employees may feel that they are being spied on. The success of sensing as an intervention depends on all participants understanding its objectives and likely outcomes. In addition, management must be willing to listen to the messages that emerge, and to act upon them. It should not be seen as a substitute for establishing effective organizational communication channels, and the information must never be used to judge or reprimand employees.

A sensing intervention consists of a series of unstructured group interviews facilitated by a member of the human resources department, a manager or an outside consultant. Each session lasts one-and-a-half to two hours. Beforehand, the facilitator contacts the line managers of the staff members whose views are to be sampled, explaining the purpose of the meeting and emphasizing that there will be no repercussions for the supervisor or staff member as a result of what emerges at the meeting. Each interview begins with a short introduction from the facilitator, explaining the purpose of the exercise and stressing that it is intended to be informal. Participants are forewarned that a senior manager will join them after about half an hour, to listen and ask questions to ensure that what they say has been understood. The proceedings are usually tape-recorded to assist note-taking, but any participant can ask for the recorder to be switched off at any time. Participants are each asked to draw up a list of two or three issues that concern them, then call them out so the facilitator can record them on a flipchart and classify them with the group's assistance. The participants then write the problems on matrix sheets that have been provided, prioritizing them individually by allocating points that add up to a total score of 100. The facilitator marks the scores on the flipchart, and a discussion follows, during which participants are free to change their minds about the priorities or persuade others to do so. The facilitator amends the results accordingly, and the meeting concludes with a discussion about what should be done to address the issues identified.

Dunphy, D.C. (1981) *Organizational Change by Choice*, McGraw-Hill, pp. 66–75.

Margulies, N. and Raia, A.P. (1972) *Organizational Development: Values, Process and Technology*, McGraw-Hill, pp. 131–2.

Margulies, N. and Wallace, J. (1973) *Organizational Change: Techniques and Applications*, Scott Foresman, pp. 29–30.

Merry, U. and Allerhand, M.E. (1977) *Developing Teams and Organizations*, Addison Wesley Longman, pp. 11–18.

See also: Customer interface meeting; Diagnostic activities; External mirror; Family group team-building meeting; Inter-group team-building; Interface groups; Interviewing; Management by walking about; Organizational mirror; Physical representation of organizations; Product familiarization programme

Sensitivity bargaining

Sensitivity bargaining was developed in Canada to provide a clear framework for management–union negotiations in order to speed up the formal bargaining process and improve the prospects of arriving at agreements acceptable to both sides. The approach is useful in dealing with issues where there is a conflict of interests between the two parties, and where the demarcation of jurisdiction is disputed. If the two parties fail to appreciate or accept each other's rights in a certain area (e.g., if management refuses to accept the union's suggestions about how to implement new technology, or the union refuses to give management information about its ballot procedures), negotiations may be sidetracked by efforts to resolve the disagreement, leading to friction and even a breakdown in the collective bargaining relationship. Financial issues can obstruct proceedings even further and, for this reason, sensitivity bargaining enforces a strict separation between non-monetary and monetary issues. It requires each party to be prepared to surrender territorial imperatives and look for a degree of common interest on each issue considered. Both parties must also accept the need to improve the climate of industrial relations, and demonstrate a willingness to discuss any issue that arises.

Sensitivity bargaining consists of seven stages. The *orientation* stage begins by appointing a mutually acceptable neutral chairperson, who briefs the union and management representatives on the procedures that will be followed, and obtains their agreement to exclude monetary items from the initial stages. The second stage calls for both parties to *identify and rank items of interest*, drawing up a list of the issues they wish to address, and rating their level of interest in each one. They then exchange lists so that each party can gauge the other party's level of interest in each item, and copies are given to the chairperson. In the third stage, the two parties *determine their common interest index*. They discuss their common interest ratings, each explaining and justifying the rankings they have given to their items. In phase four, the parties *develop the bargaining framework*, using these ratings to derive majority indices of the degree of management and union interest in the different issues. These form the basis for the collective bargaining framework, indicating how

each issue will be handled. Phase five consists of the *sensitivity bargaining process* itself. Either party can call for a session in order to review the item ranking, or to exercise their bargaining rights on any other matter. If sensitivity bargaining fails to resolve any issue, the sixth stage of *arbitration* may be necessary, and, if this fails to lead to agreement, it may have to be resolved through formal bargaining. The seventh stage consists of the *traditional formal bargaining procedure*, which deals with the unresolved issues. Only at this stage are monetary issues introduced into the discussions.

Smith, I.G. (1975) 'Sensitivity Bargaining: An Alternative to Conflict', *Personnel Review*, vol. 4, no. 2, pp. 17–23.

See also: Alternate dispute-resolution; Mediation; Relations-by-objectives; Rent-a-judge; Union–management committees; Union–management joint participation; Union–management organizations; Union–management problem-solving groups

Sensitivity (T-group) training (group relations training)

Sensitivity training is difficult to define because it has become a generic term embracing a wide variety of techniques. Bradford et al. (1964) trace the birth of the T-group to a workshop held at the State Teachers College in New Britain, Connecticut, in the summer of 1946. The workshop consisted mainly of discussion groups run by trainers, and a research team led by Kurt Lewin attended each meeting. After each day's activities, the trainers and researchers met to compare notes and discuss what had occurred. Some of those participating in the workshop were permitted to attend these debriefing sessions at their own request, where they commented on and sometimes challenged the trainers' and researchers' interpretations of their behaviour.

As practised nowadays, T-groups consist of ten to twelve participants who meet on a part- or full-time basis for a period varying from three days to two weeks in order to explore personal and group dynamics with the help of a trainer who acts as a catalyst and facilitator. Although there may be some formal inputs about inter-personal relations, individual personality theory and group dynamics, the main learning vehicle is the group experience itself, and the data the group discusses arises from its members' interactions and feelings as they develop a mini-society with its own agreed procedures, norms and processes. The technique has three main goals: to make participants more sensitive to others' reactions to their behaviour, to increase their ability to gauge the state of relationships between others, and to develop their social skills in terms of how to behave appropriately in a given situation. There is no fixed agenda for discussion, and events and issues arise spontaneously from the interactions of group members, and are influenced by individual needs, responses and behaviour. The trainer does not lead the discussions, but serves as an interpreter, intervening periodically to explain what is happening in the group. The issues that arise are fairly consistent, including identity ('How am I seen in this group?'), power and influence ('How much influence do I have?'), goals and needs ('What are my needs, and will they be met?') and acceptance and intimacy ('How intimate am I expected to be?'). Although research into the technique is inconclusive, one study found that participants developed a better understanding of themselves, of others in the group, and of group process; exhibited greater openness, receptivity and tolerance of differences; and acquired relationship skills and a greater capacity for co-operation.

T-groups can be differentiated according to which level they focus on – intra-personal, inter-personal, group, inter-group or societal – and also the nature of their membership. *Cousin laboratories* consist of people from the same organization who do not have a working relationship with each other and may not even know each other. *Cluster laboratories* include people from different parts of the same organization, but each group contains clusters of work-related people (e.g., a group of twelve might consist of three groups of four people who interact at work). *Family or functional laboratories* are composed of complete, intact work teams. *Diagonal-slice laboratories* are made up of groups of members from the same company, but from different hierarchical levels and different departments. Finally, *stranger laboratories* consist of people from different organizations.

Back, K.W. (1972) *Beyond Words: Story of Sensitivity Training and Encounter Movement*, Russell Sage Foundation.
Blumberg, A. and Golembiewski, R.T. (1976) *Learning and Change in Groups*, Penguin.
Bradford, L.P., Gibb, J.R. and Benne, K.D. (eds) (1964) *T-group Theory and the Laboratory Method: Innovation and Education*, Wiley.
Brown, J. (1993) 'Reflections on Summer in Bethel', *Management Education and Development*, vol. 24, no. 4, pp. 459–66.
Goldber, C. (1978) *Encounter: Group Sensitivity Training Experience*, Jason Aronson Publisher.
Golembiewski, R.T. (1973) *Sensitivity Training and the Laboratory Approach*, F.E. Peacock Publishers.
Lippitt, G.L. (1975) 'Guides for the Use of Sensitivity Training in Management Development', in Taylor, B. and Lippitt, G.L. (eds) *Management Development and Training Handbook*, McGraw-Hill.
Margulies, N. and Wallace, J. (1973) *Organizational Change: Techniques and Applications*, Scott Foresman, Chapter 5.
Schein, E.H. and Bennis, W.G. (1965) *Personal and Organizational Growth Through Group Methods: The Laboratory Approach*, Wiley.
Schor, S.M. and Sabiers, M. (1995) 'T-groups in the Classroom: Some Examples of Current Practice', *Journal of Management Education*, vol. 19, no. 4, pp. 523–9.

See also: Application discussion group; Basic encounter; Classroom meeting model; Cluster laboratory; Cousin laboratory; Encounter group; Gestalt techniques; Group development laboratory; Group dynamics laboratory; Human relations laboratory; Instrumented laboratory; Laboratory method; Laboratory training; Mini-society; Microlab; Organizational laboratory; Personal development laboratory; Power laboratory; Process analysis; Psychodrama; Team laboratory; Tavistock Conference Method; Transactional Analysis

Service in professional associations

Organizations tend to judge an individual's professional commitment by the degree of interest they show in new developments in their field. One way to keep abreast of current ideas and trends is to join the local branch of the Institute of Management, Institute of Personnel and Development, a legal group or an accounting institution. An additional benefit is that this provides the opportunity to meet professional colleagues working in different organizations.

See also: Accepting positions of responsibility in community associations/university societies; Assignment to community organization; Assignment to customer as representative; Assignment to government study group; Secondment

7-S framework ('The Happy Atom')

In their book, *In Search of Excellence*, Peters and Waterman propose a conceptual framework which has been used by a number of organizations, including the World Bank, to develop diagnostic tools to guide change programmes. The 7-S framework rests on the belief that productive organizational change does not simply depend on interactions between structure, objectives and strategies. It views every organization as a unique

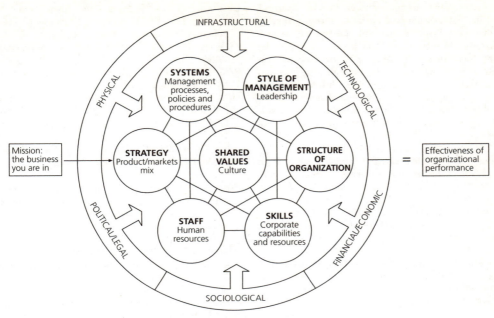

INFRASTRUCTURAL

PHYSICAL

TECHNOLOGICAL

POLITICAL/LEGAL

FINANCIAL/ECONOMIC

SOCIOLOGICAL

SYSTEMS
Management processes, policies and procedures

STYLE OF MANAGEMENT
Leadership

STRATEGY
Product/markets mix

SHARED VALUES
Culture

STRUCTURE OF ORGANIZATION

STAFF
Human resources

SKILLS
Corporate capabilities and resources

Mission: the business you are in

= Effectiveness of organizational performance

THE SURROUNDING ENVIRONMENT

7-S framework (modified)

blend of change variables, among which the authors identify: systems, style, structure, skills, staff, strategy and shared values. *Systems* includes all the formal and informal procedures and processes in an organization that help it to function. *Style* refers to the way management exercises leadership. *Structure* considers how functions are defined and how relationships and accountability are managed in order to co-ordinate and integrate action. *Skills* concerns the expertise the organization possesses, and how well it adapts to different demands. *Staff* refers to the organization's employees. *Strategy* is the art of devising and implementing plans in response to changes in the internal and external environment. Finally, *shared values* refers to the common aspirations which go beyond a company's formal statement of objectives, representing the conceptual foundation on which the organization stands.

The model stresses that these variables are interconnected, and many carefully planned change projects may have failed because one or more of them have been neglected. In addition, the model has no starting point, and it implies no hierarchy. Since no single variable is considered more important than any other, any one or any combination can provide the driving force for organizational

change. Finally, the framework implies that each company's goal will impinge on these variables. If any single variable is crucial, Peters and Waterman believe that this will emerge, since all of them are susceptible to political, economic, ecological, sociological and psychological influences.

Peters, T.J. and Waterman, R.H. (1982) *In Search of Excellence*, Harper and Row.

See also: ACHIEVE model; Assessment of the organization as a system; Benchmarking; Diagnostic activities; Family group diagnostic meeting; Functional administrative control technique; Looking for trouble; Management audit; Organizational analysis; Overhead value analysis

Shadow consultant

When consultants are experiencing problems with a project – perhaps progress is unsatisfactory, they have run out of ideas for possible approaches, or the situation is exceptionally complex – they may enlist the help of a shadow consultant. Although the host consultant or consulting team retain responsibility for the project, the shadow consultant can offer a second opinion, provide feedback on the methods adopted so far, contribute specific skills, and bring a new perspective to events. Shadow consultants need not be more experienced than those they help, but they should be familiar with consulting work in general. Their input should be in sympathy with their hosts' approach, but they may identify a different diagnosis of the problem, reassess the tactics adopted, or examine participants' roles, including the relationship with the client.

Case, T.L., Vandenberg, R.J. and Meredith, P.H. (1990) 'Internal and External Change Agent', *Leadership and Organization Development Journal*, vol. 11, no. 1, pp. 4–15.
Schroder, M. (1974) 'The Shadow Consultant', *Journal of Applied Behavioural Science*, vol. 10, no. 4, pp. 579–94.

See also: Coaching; Consultant network; Consultation; Consulting assignment; Consulting pair; Counselling; Insider-outsider consulting teams; Process consultation

Shared ownership (ESOP)

In recent years, the advance of privatization has led to world-wide economic and political changes. The globalization of production and finance and the diffusion of share ownership have proceeded hand in hand with the promotion of economic and industrial democracy. Initiatives to promote profit-sharing and employee participation in decision-making have taken many forms, including employee share ownership plans (ESOPs). Earlier experiments with fully employee-owned worker co-operatives had met with little success in the UK. The failures of the Meriden motor cycle plant, Kirby Manufacturing and Engineering and the *Scottish Daily News* (formerly the *Scottish Daily Express*) are well documented, although the success of the Mondragon co-operative in Spain's Basque country shows that not all such initiatives are doomed to failure. However, in the 1980s, the UK government's support for ESOPs led to their widespread adoption. Encouraged by tax breaks, some companies distributed shares to their managers and employees, usually as incentive payments. In some cases, management and employees may be major shareholders, in others, they may be only a small element.

Copeman, G. (1991) *Employee Share Ownership*, Kogan Page.
Cornfield, J. (1996) *Stake in the Company*, Institute for Public Policy Research.
Gianaris, N.V. (1996) *Modern Capitalism: Privatization, Employee Ownership and Industrial Democracy*, Praeger.
Leadbeater, C. (1997) *Piece of the Action*, Demos.
McNeish, K. (1997) How to Implement Share Schemes, *People Management*, 24 July, pp. 38–40.
McWhirter, D.A. (1993) *Sharing Ownership*, Wiley.
Reid, D. (1992) *Employee Share Ownership Plans in the UK*, Butterworths.
US Internal Revenue Service (1998) 'Does Employee Ownership Make a Difference in the US?', *IRS Employment Trends*, no. 644, pp. 10–16.
Voets, H. (1995) *Success and Enterprise: Significance of Employee Ownership*, Avebury.

See also: Improshare; Participation; Productivity sharing; Profit-sharing; Reward systems; Rucker plan; Scanlon plan

Short talks by students

The ability to speak in public is essential in many walks of life, especially management. It is also important for students to develop such skills, either to improve their verbal communication in general, or in preparation for vivas. Many people are intimidated by the prospect of public speaking, so it important to introduce the technique in stages. At first, the occasion should be informal, such as asking a syndicate group to nominate a member to report back to the class as a whole, and the presentation should be short, perhaps no longer than two minutes. Over-preparation and speaking too long are common errors which must be avoided. Research has shown that poor-quality presentations are counter-productive. Students tend to learn little new and become resentful, complaining that they expected to learn from the instructor. If the objective is to encourage a climate in which students want to learn from each other, it is important to choose an appropriate topic, and the points made should be reinforced by a follow-up class discussion.

Managers can do much to improve their subordinates' presentation skills, both formally and informally. For example, individuals could first be asked to give a verbal summary of the main points when delivering written reports to their supervisors. Once their confidence has grown, they could be invited to make these presentations in front of a group of listeners, eventually becoming regular contributors when attending in-company or extra-organizational management courses.

Babcock, J.A. (1985–6) 'Encouraging Better Group Presentations Through Peer Evaluation', *Organizational Behaviour Teaching Review*, vol. 10, no. 4, pp. 101–4.
Story, R. (1997) *The Art of Persuasive Communication*, Gower.

See also: Argumentation; Case student telling cases; Confidence-building training; Debate; Jurisprudential model; Learning cell; Staff meeting assignment; Teaching as learning; Visiting speaker

Sick-leave/holiday replacement assignment (fill-in assignment)

In any organization, preparing managers to take on any jobs other than their own is difficult because everyone is usually needed in their own post. However, fill-in assignments provide a means of training employees for promotion or transfer at all levels in the organization without compromising overall efficiency. Some organizations have an explicit policy of assigning temporary replacements to cover for absences due to illness or holiday leave. Staff may be given little notice of these assignments, and the need to quickly come to terms with the key aspects of the job and gauge the ability of new subordinates provides a unique developmental opportunity. Being challenged, motivated and involved can lead to faster, more efficient learning, but guidance and support are essential.

Ideally, the procedure should be planned well in advance to take advantage of any foreseeable absences. Assignees need to be prepared for the experience, since if they do not understand its purposes or advantages, they may view it negatively. They must also be ready to face any jealousies, fears and tensions that may arise among their colleagues as a result of the assignment. The assignment itself may provide a chain of learning opportunities for others, since a subordinate may need to fill the assignee's position, and so on. This not only develops a wide base of experience, but also minimizes disruption to operations. Each assignee's responsibilities in the job they are trying to learn should be clearly defined. Where no reporting relationship exists between the absent manager and their replacement, the assignee may be appointed to the next highest job classification level. Some managers may see subordinates as a threat, so all involved must be convinced that the scheme offers them advantages.

See also: Acting assignment; Assignment to manager with high development skills; Development assignment; Expanding assignment; Exposure to upper management; Job rotation; Job swop; Manager exchange; Manager shadowing; Planned delegation; Rotation training

Simu-Real

Bunker and Alban explain that Simu-Real is the name given to a large-group, whole-system, participative work approach. It allows groups to perform real-time work on current issues, learn about the system, and test future designs. In practice, it is used mainly to analyse and change organizational structure and behaviour, and to test new business processes or structures before they are formally implemented. The approach was devised during the mid-1970s by Donald Klein. It addresses two main problems. First, that organization members typically have a partial view of their whole organization, and neither know nor appreciate the roles of others in the firm. Second, the complexity of organizational life means that they do not understand the things that occur within it. To overcome these difficulties, the Simu-Real design offers a structured simulation that allows members to understand the complexity of the whole system within which they work, see what goes on inside it, and decide what needs to be changed. Before the simulation itself, during its planning phase, agreement is reached as to the objectives of the event. For example, whether the simulation will be used to examine how decisions are made in the company; and whether different decision-making approaches will be explored; and whether all those involved in the simulation will have an equal opportunity to participate and influence the decision processes. More broadly, the planning meeting has to agree whether the decisions that are taken in the simulation will be binding or advisory; and whether implementation of decisions made will be left to company executives, or progressed by representative subgroups.

The Simu-Real meeting resembles a massive role-play involving the entire organization, and tries to condense months of real-life activity into a day. Before the event, a planning committee decides on a decision that will be addressed at the culmination of the session. The meeting begins with *Getting Everyone into the Room*, in which a large space is arranged to represent the company's functional structure in physical terms (e.g, headquarters in the middle of the room, surrounded by each department, represented and staffed by its own members). *Addressing the Task* sets out a problem with implications for all concerned. *Stop Action, Reflection and Analysis* calls for all concerned to work on this issue for an hour, with guidance from consultants. Once they have done this, they reflect on the way the organization functions, and their part in that functioning. As a result, participants often change the way they approach the problem or how they try to solve it. Towards the end of the day, time is allocated to address the decision made earlier. The planning committee could opt for executive decision-making (where executives meet, discuss the outputs of the simulation, and make a real decision for later consideration), ad hoc decision-making (where a pre-selected representative group participates in the decision-making with executives and a consultant) and or choose to adopt a decision-making table. This last experimental and innovative approach to decision-making involves setting out 12 chairs and a table, and establishing the rule that whenever all the chairs are occupied and the group comes to a consensus decision on any topic, that decision becomes binding on the organization. The effect of this approach is to open up opportunities for informal influences.

Bunker, B.B. and Alban, B.T. (1997) 'Simu-Real', in *Large Group Interventions: Engaging the Whole System for Rapid Change*, Jossey-Bass, pp. 159–67.
Klein, D. (1992) 'Simu-Real: A Simulation Approach to Organizational Change', *Journal of Applied Behavioural Science*, vol. 28, no. 4, pp. 566–78.

See also: Action training and research; Business process re-engineering; Conference Model; Fast-cycle full-participation work design; Future search; Large-group interventions; Open space technology; Participative design; Real-time work design; Real-time strategic change; Role-playing; Search conference; Socio-technical systems theory; Strategic planning process; Work-Out

Simulated entrepreneurship (limited-autonomy position)

In this approach, employees are assigned positions which call on them to take an entrepreneurial role, but with limited autonomy within the organization. For example, the managers of United Airlines' stations are given a degree of influence over their future direction. Initially, they are evaluated or assessed not on their overall performance in their jobs, but only on those variables over which they have some control. Regular six-monthly feedback on their performance is provided, expressed as a profit related to their own contribution. Elsewhere, the Dana Corporation adopted the 'store manager' idea, which gives its factory managers a great deal of authority over staff appointments and dismissals, purchasing and financial control systems. Much the same idea can be found in Procter & Gamble (where such staff are known as 'brand managers'), while Schlumberger's simulated entrepreneurs are its 2000 young field engineers who work at isolated locations.

Peters and Waterman explain that simulated entrepreneurship at IBM and Raychem is reflected in the role of the salesperson-as-problem-solver. Those who fill this role must continue to motivate themselves while dealing with everyday issues.

This relieves the organization of the time-consuming management task of creating a mythology and defining role models and heroes to maintain the employee's commitment, but it is still necessary to provide a discreet but firm support system.

Huczynski, A.A. (1985) 'Designing High Performance, High Commitment Organizations', *Technovation*, vol. 3, pp. 111–18.
Peters, T.J. and Waterman, R.H. (1982) *In Search of Excellence*, Harper and Row, pp. 213–14.

See also: Achievement motivation training; Business teams; Corporate culture training; Independent product teams; Intrapreneurship; Line-of-business groups; Managerial decentralization; Multiple management; Real-life entrepreneurial project; Reprogramming

Simulation

A simulation is an instructional activity which reproduces the essential characteristics of a real-life task in a controlled fashion. Whereas games may condense months or years of an organization's life into a few hours, simulations take place in real time. Whether based on commercially available packages or designed by the instructor, simulations aim to give students a carefully structured opportunity to apply what they have learned in their studies. The situations chosen for simulation might range from a jury considering a verdict to an organization dealing with a complex political or economic situation as it unfolds. The participants must experience a sense of reality as they play different roles while facing typical problems in the chosen scenario. Although attention to physical details is crucial (and virtual reality techniques may grow in importance in this respect in years to come), psychological realism is even more vital. For example, although aircraft simulators exploit the latest technology in search of realism, it is the instruction provided and the problems set by the trainer that lead to successful training.

In its simplest form, a simulation can be an extension of an in-basket exercise, with participants sitting at desks, receiving their information, processing it and passing it on just as they would in an actual job. They can also be provided with access to a telephone, fax and e-mail to communicate with others or with the instructor/controller, and be faced with demands for information, decisions or action. The ability to manipulate the simulation means that the instructor can provide direct and immediate feedback on trainees' responses, and the stimuli presented after each response can be chosen to reinforce correct ones and extinguish incorrect ones.

Bailey, D.A. (1990) 'Developing Self-awareness Through Simulation and Gaming', *Journal of Management Development*, vol. 9, no. 2, pp. 38–42.

Drew, S.A.W. and Davidson, A. (1993) 'Simulation-based Leadership Development and Team Learning', *Journal of Management Development*, vol. 12, no. 8.

Duke, R. (ed.) (1978) *Learning With Simulation and Games*, Sage.

Elgood, C. (ed.) (1997) *Handbook of Management Games and Simulations*, Gower.

Ellington, H., Fowlie, J. and Gordon, M. (1998) *Using Games and Simulations in the Classroom*, Kogan Page.

Gillispie, P. (1974) *Learning Through Simulation Games*, Paulist Press.

Gunz, H.P. (1994) 'Learning from a Realistic Simulation: A Case Study', *Journal of Management Education*, vol. 18, no. 1, pp. 45–60.

Gunz, H.P. (1995) 'Realism and Learning in Management Simulations', *Journal of Management Education*, vol. 19, no. 1, pp. 54–74.

Jones, K. (1995) *Simulations: A Handbook for Teachers and Trainers*, Kogan Page.

Keys, B. and Wolfe, J. (1990) 'The Role of Management Games and Simulations in Education and Research', *Journal of Management*, vol. 16, pp. 307–36.

McCormick, J. (1972) 'Simulation and Gaming as a Teaching Method', *Programmed Learning and Educational Technology*, vol. 9, no. 4, pp. 198–205.

Parks, D.M. and Lindstrom, G.I. (1995) 'Achieving Higher Levels of Learning in the Business Policy and Strategy Course Through Integration of a Business Simulation', *Journal of Management Education*, vol. 19, no. 2, pp. 219–27.

Pollard, H.G. and Giacalone, R.A. (1985–6) 'Linking Organizational Behaviour Simulations', *Organizational Behaviour Teaching Review*, vol. 10, no. 2, pp. 19–27.

'Practice Fields for the Learning Organization', special issue of *Journal of Management Development* (1994), vol. 13, no. 8.

Riis, J.O. (ed.) (1995) *Simulation Games in Production*, Chapman and Hall.

Stammers, R.B. (1981) 'Theory and Practice in the Design of Training Simulations', *Programmed Learning and Educational Technology*, vol. 18, no. 2, pp. 67–71.

Thompson, T.A., Purdy, J.M. and Fandt, P.M. (1997) 'Building a Strong Foundation: Using Computer Simulation in an Introductory Management Course', *Journal of Management Education*, vol. 21, no. 3, pp. 418–34.

Towne, D.M., de Jong, T. and Spada, J. (1993) *Simulation-based Experiential Learning*, Springer Verlag.

See also: Action maze; Behavioural simulation; Classroom-as-organization model; Experiential exercise; Game; Guided-design approach; In-basket exercise; Playing for learning; Programmed simulation; Surrogate client

Situational leadership

The Hersey-Blanchard Situational Leadership model is both a prescriptive tool and a diagnostic procedure. Hersey and Blanchard argue that there is no one 'best' way to influence people. The leadership style appropriate for different individuals or groups depends on their *maturity*: their willingness and ability to take responsibility for their own behaviour. In this context, maturity is not considered to be an overall personality characteristic, but a measure of an individual's readiness and ability to perform a specific task. The model classifies managerial behaviour into two categories, task behaviour and relationship behaviour. Hersey and Blanchard offer a prescriptive curve which shows the appropriate style directly above the corresponding level of maturity (see the next page).

Each of the four management styles shown on the prescriptive curve – telling, selling, participating and delegating – is a combination of task behaviour and relationship behaviour. *Task behaviour* refers to how much direction a leader provides for their followers, such as telling them what to do, how to do it, and when. *Relationship behaviour* is the degree of support the leader provides by engaging in two-way communication with them, practising active listening and acting as a facilitator. Hersey and Blanchard propose a continuum of four levels of maturity among followers. The appropriate leadership style for each maturity level depends on the right combination of task behaviour and relationship behaviour: *telling* is appropriate for low-maturity followers, *selling* should be used with followers with low to moderate maturity, *participating* is suitable for those with moderate to high maturity, while *delegating* is reserved for followers of high maturity. Individuals may increase in maturity over time, and leaders should be alert to such developments and do all they can to encourage them.

Gumpart, R.A. and Hambleton, R.K. (1979) 'Situational Leadership: How Xerox Managers Fine-tune Managerial Styles to Employee Maturity and Task Needs', *Management Review*, vol. 68, no. 12, pp. 8–12.

Hersey, P., Blanchard, K. and Johnson, D.E.

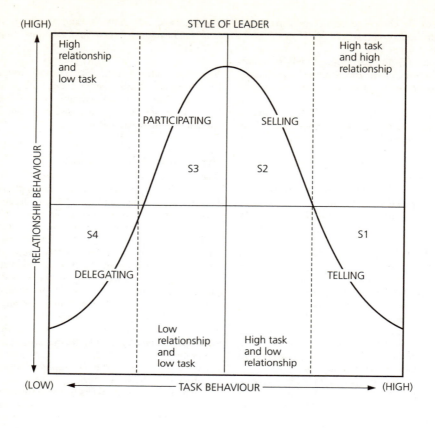

(HIGH)   STYLE OF LEADER

High relationship and low task

High task and high relationship

PARTICIPATING   SELLING

S3   S2

RELATIONSHIP BEHAVIOUR

S4   S1

DELEGATING   TELLING

Low relationship and low task

High task and low relationship

(LOW) ◄——— TASK BEHAVIOUR ———► (HIGH)

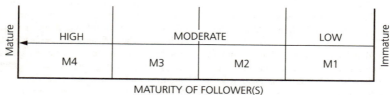

Mature	HIGH	MODERATE		LOW	Immature
	M4	M3	M2	M1	

MATURITY OF FOLLOWER(S)

Situational leadership prescriptive curve

(1996) *Management of Organizational Behaviour: Utilizing Human Resources* (7th edn), Prentice-Hall.

Lueder, D.C. (1985) 'Don't Be Misled by LEAD', *Journal of Applied Behavioural Science*, vol. 21, no. 2, pp. 143–51.

Nicholls, J. (1985) 'A New Approach to Situational Leadership', *Leadership and Organization Development Journal*, vol. 6, no. 4, pp. 2–7.

Nicholls, J. (1986) 'Beyond Situational Leadership: Congruent and Transforming Models for Leadership Training', *European Management Journal*, vol. 4, no. 1, pp. 41–50.

Nicholls, J. (1986) 'Congruent Leadership', *Leadership and Organization Development Journal*, vol. 7, no. 1, pp. 27–31.

Tyler, K. (1993) *Using the Situational Leadership Model as a Training Instrument*, Loughborough University of Technology, Department of Management Studies.

See also: Action-centred leadership; Grid development; Implementing The Organizational Renewal Process; Interaction influence analysis; Interaction management; Likert's level meetings; Managing for productivity; Power management; 3-D management effectiveness seminar

Skill practice session

This approach enables trainees to practise a specific behaviour or skill which they need to improve. To be effective, the session should address the following process: *intention*, isolating and defining a desired behaviour which can serve as a goal; *action*, trying out the behaviour; *feedback of results*, collecting evidence on how the try-out worked, and *desired behaviour*, comparing the results with the goal, in order to correct any mistakes or incorporate improvements. For example, someone attending a course may describe how, during every management meeting at work, another manager continually reacts negatively to all ideas and suggestions. The session could concentrate on developing ways to handle such situations, taking into account the repercussions of confronting the manager's negativity, role-playing possible responses, and assessing their likelihood of success.

Curtis, R.V. and Nestor, D. (1990) 'Interpersonal Skill Building for Instructional Developers', *Education, Training Research & Development*, vol. 38, no. 2, pp. 51–9.

See also: Interactive skills training; Intervisitation; Role-playing; Sociodrama

Skill session

Black devised this type of small-group seminar to develop certain scientific skills. Such sessions may be offered as a whole course, or used occasionally to supplement lectures. They improve students' problem-solving abilities, enable them to practise expressing and substantiating ideas, and give them the opportunity to understand and judge other people's reasoning. At the beginning of the session, participants are offered a 'menu' of problems, forming groups of four to six in order to work on their chosen one for 20 to 30 minutes. The groups may have access to a teacher, who may offer guidance when requested, or may visit the groups to ensure they are making satisfactory headway. Reference books may also be available. Because some groups may progress more quickly than others, supplementary questions can be provided for any that finish well before the deadline. This period is followed by a plenary discussion, during which each group must present their solutions and substantiate the approaches and arguments they relied on. The teacher can draw attention to any neglected aspects and implicit assumptions, and each group can learn from the others' experiences.

In designing the menu of problems, the teacher must take into account the participants' existing level of knowledge, any particular interests they may have, and the time available. The problems can be phrased as either open or closed questions. Black's own questions are aimed to familiarize students with orders of magnitude, helping them to estimate the various influences on a given process and develop a sense of what may be neglected and what not, such as: 'Estimate the total daily income of a town bus.'

Black, P. et al. (1968) 'Group Studies', *Physics Education*, vol. 3, p. 289.
Black, P., Griffith, J.A.R. and Powell, W.B. (1974) 'Skill Sessions', *Physics Education*, vol. 9, pp. 18–22.

See also: Block method; Problem-centred group

Skunkworks

Peters and Waterman define a skunkworks as a group of eight to ten people whose task is to innovate outside the traditional organizational structure. The term was originally used to describe a discrete, innovative research and development unit within the Lockheed Corporation in California. In this case, the organizational and physical barriers between small teams of engineers, technicians, designers and model-makers were removed in order to develop a new product from idea to commercial prototype stage. The idea has been extended to encompass subsidiaries, spin-offs, internal venture capital units or equivalent structures set up within an organization to develop new products. This approach can be adopted by any company which does not possess the infrastructure to encourage or support innovation 'champions', in the form of limited-autonomy positions. Proponents of skunkworks feel that the approach offers a number of advantages. It encourages and brings together entrepreneurs who may be hampered by conventional organizational arrangements and processes. It eliminates bureaucracy, allows fast, unfettered communication, enables experiments to be completed quickly, and produces a high level of group identity and loyalty. It helps the organization to retain entrepreneurial staff who might otherwise seek employment elsewhere, perhaps in small start-up companies. Finally, it enables fledgling ventures to operate without having to comply with organizational policies and procedures.

Peters, T.J. and Waterman, R.H. (1982) *In Search of Excellence*, Harper and Row, pp. 211–14.
Quinn, J.B. (1985) 'Managing Innovation: Controlled Chaos', *Harvard Business Review*, vol. 63, no. 3, May–June, pp. 73–84.

See also: Absenteeism/turnover task force; Collateral organization; Independent product teams; Intrapreneurship; Matrix designs

Small-group teaching

Small-group teaching demands specific strategies beyond those adopted in the lecture method. A large number of approaches have been developed, catering for various learning objectives and different sizes of group, and some of these are described in the references and cross-references for this entry.

Abercrombie, M.L.J. (1969) *The Anatomy of Judgement*, Penguin.

Abercrombie, M.L.J. (1979) *Aims and Techniques of Group Teaching* (4th edn), Society for Research into Higher Education.

Abercrombie, M.L.J. and Terry, P.M. (1978) *Talking to Learn: Improving Teaching and Learning in Small Groups*, Society for Research into Higher Education.

Babbington-Smith, B. and Farrell, B.A. (1979) *Training in Small Groups: A Study of Five Methods*, Pergamon Press.

Bligh, D. (1975) *Teaching Students*, Exeter University Teaching Services.

Daines, J., Daines, C. and Graham, B. (1998) *Adult Learning, Adult Teaching*, Continuing Education Press of Nottingham University.

Lewis, H.A. (1979) 'The Anatomy of Small Groups', *Studies in Higher Education*, vol. 4, no. 2, pp. 269–77.

Webb, G. (1981) 'An Evaluation of Techniques for Analysing Small Group Work', *Programmed Learning and Educational Technology*, vol. 18, no. 2, pp. 64–6.

Wood, A.E. (1979) 'Experiences with Small Group Tutorials', *Studies in Higher Education*, vol. 4, no. 2, pp. 20–39.

See also: Abercrombie method; Advanced seminar; Free discussion method; Group buzz; Group circular interviewing; Group cross-overs; Group discussion; Group five minutes each way; Group line-ups; Group Phillips 66 technique; Group poster tours; Group pyramids; Group rounds; Group syndicate method; Group with ground rules; Large groups as small groups; Seminar

SmartProcess

SmartProcess (SP) is based on an method developed by the US Navy to train officers and enlisted personnel to operate a submarine. 'Smart' is an acronym for: *Self-learning, Motivation, Awareness, Responsibility* and *Technical competence*. Adopting a discovery-guided learning approach which requires individuals to show a great deal of involvement and initiative, it can be used to induct and familiarize newly appointed staff, or as an organizational change technique. A typical task would require the learner to examine the procedure followed in hiring an employee, noting the main steps, the personnel involved, and where they are located, then report on the findings, recommending any improvements that could be made.

The SP programme is guided by a co-ordinator and a review committee consisting of staff at different levels. There are five steps. First, the co-ordinator and the review committee, together with a work unit (e.g., the human resource management department), decide what they think a well-informed organization member should know, and compile a draft SP handbook, consisting of questions and instructions. Next, an existing staff member goes through the process in order to refine and revise the questions. The handbook is then given to the new employee. Completing the tasks set in the handbook usually takes about 80 hours, and demands that the employee talks to people about their jobs, observes processes, gains personal experience of performing certain jobs, finds out information, and so on. In step three, the review committee reads the participant's notebook, holds an oral examination, and conducts a walking tour through the factory or office. In step four, if the employee's performance is satisfactory, they are awarded a certificate. Finally, the review committee asks the employee to prepare two reports: one for the co-ordinator, and one for the review committee. The first report identifies anything that seems to be hindering effective work, and the second contains suggestions for improvements.

While SP's value as a practical individual development programme is obvious, Zierden and Robinson argue that SmartProcess's side-effects mean that it can serve as an organizational change technique. Those who complete the programme become accustomed to meeting and talking to different members of staff within the organization, and this can promote an organizational culture where individuals pursue the common objective of learning about the organization. Being asked to talk about their work means that staff acknowledge its importance. Employees who are required to certify that a trainee has successfully performed a job or task may take a greater interest in training. Some questions may require both the trainee and a job-holder to express a view of a job, which can clarify roles and reduce conflict. As more and more people in an organization complete the SP, technical competence becomes enshrined in the organization's culture. Those who have completed the SP have a common experience which can improve communication and develop mutual respect. Because the technique encourages those involved to communicate across organizational levels and boundaries, it can act as an integrating device. SP can be used regularly to check for misinformation, misunderstanding and improper operating procedures. Finally, the managers and senior staff who participate provide role-models for other staff who might otherwise be reluctant to make the effort to help others learn.

Zierden, W.E. and Robinson, K.M. (1983) 'Smart-Process: A Practical Training Programme and Tool for Change', *Training and Development Journal*, vol. 37, no. 3, March, pp. 62–7.

See also: Induction training; Internship; Job descriptions; Management responsibility guide process; Manager shadowing; On-the-job training; Prompt list; Responsibility charting; Role analysis technique; Role-prescription; Understudy

Socio-technical systems design

Socio-technical systems (STS) is a work design method developed in the UK during the 1950s by Eric Trist and Fred Emery. It has been widely adopted in the USA, and during the 1970s a wide range of different approaches were developed under the banner 'Quality of Working Life'. Drawing on biological systems theory, and acknowledging the ways systems influence and are influenced by their environments, STS analyses an organization's *social system* (its employees' skills and knowledge, experience and relationship networks) and its *technical system* (the way work is carried out in terms of machinery, process layout, procedures, etc.) in an attempt to achieve a good 'fit' between the two. Although technological considerations dictate how work can be organized, companies' social and psychological properties are generally independent of technology. The aim is to optimize company productivity and profits while maintaining a desirable environment for workers, but STS recognizes that these issues cannot be addressed separately, and that trade-offs are necessary. The intervention relies on a change programme drawn up by a team of representatives of the organization's management and workers. Once the team has agreed on a course of action, the next step is to persuade management, unions and workforce to support the programme, and the design process may take a year to complete. Various methods have been adopted, such as creating semi-autonomous workgroups, suggesting changes in payment systems, work structuring and staffing, and encouraging supervisors to spend less time directly supervising staff and more time planning, co-ordinating and training them.

Adler, N. and Docherty, P. (1998) 'Bringing Business into Socio-technical Theory and Practice', *Human Relations*, vol. 51, no. 3, pp. 319–46.

Brown, K.A. (1987–8) 'Integrating Socio-technical Systems into the Organizational Behaviour Curriculum: Discussion and Class Exercise', *The Organizational Behaviour Teaching Review*, vol. 12, no. 1, pp. 35–48.

Bunker, B.B. and Alban, B.T. (1997) 'The Search Conference', in *Large Group Interventions: Engaging the Whole System for Rapid Change*, Jossey-Bass, pp. 33–41.

Cooper, R. and Foster, M. (1971) 'Socio-technical Systems', *American Psychologist*, vol. 26, 467–74.

Mathews, J. (ed.) (1997) 'Organizational Innovation and the Socio-technical Systems Tradition', special issue of *Human Relations*, vol. 50, no. 5, May.

Niepce, W. and Molleman, E. (1998) 'Work Design Issues for a Socio-technical systems Perspective', *Human Relations*, vol. 51, no. 3, pp. 259–88.

Pasmore, W.A. (1988) *Designing Effective Organizations: A Socio-technical System Perspective*, Wiley.

Stebbins, M.W. and Shani, A.B. (1996) 'Organizational Design and the Knowledge Worker', *Leadership and Organization Development Journal*, vol. 16, no. 1, pp. 23–30.

Taylor, J.C. (1975) 'The Human Side of Work: The Socio-technical System Approach to Work System Design', *Personnel Review*, vol. 4, no. 3, pp. 17–22.

Taylor, J.C. and Felten, D.F. (1993) *Performance by Design: Socio-technical Systems in North America*, Prentice-Hall.

'The Tavistock Institute: Past Present and Future', special issue of *Human Relations* (1998), vol. 51, no. 3, March.

Trist, E. and Dwyer, C. (1982) 'Limits of Laissez Faire as a Socio-technical System Strategy', in Zager, R. and Rosow, M.-P. (eds) *The Innovative Organization: Productivity Programmes in Action*, Pergamon, pp. 149–83.

See also: Autonomous workgroup; Conference Model; Fast-cycle full-participation work design; Future search; Industrial dynamics; Inter-group interventions; Job design; Job enrichment; Open space technology; Open systems planning; Participative design; Policy-formulation; Quality of working life; Real-time strategic change; Real-time work design; Scenario-planning; Search conference; Simu-Real; Strategic management; Strategic planning process; Tavistock Conference Method; Work-Out

Sociodrama (dramatization method)

Sociodrama is an unscripted and unrehearsed dramatization in which group members act out the techniques required in specific work situations. It can be seen as a combination of demonstration and discussion, with the participants doing the demonstrating. While the specific actions are unplanned, the facilitator may provide general guidance about the situation and the desired outcomes, and how each actor might move towards accomplishing them. The method can be used to stimulate a group to consider a familiar job technique from a different perspective, or to help participants develop confidence in practising new skills. Sociodrama works best when group members are at ease with each other. A friendly, co-operative atmosphere should exist, so that no one will ridicule the actors or 'ham up' their part. The facilitator should be sensitive to the fact that some individuals may be embarrassed or upset by the need to improvise, and no one should be forced to take part.

The first step is to describe the situation to be dramatized and the desired outcomes as clearly as possible. Next, participants should be selected or asked to volunteer for particular roles. The actors are then allowed a few minutes to discuss in general terms what they want to do, alerting the audience about what points to look for, and asking them to withhold comments until the discussion at the end. The drama is then enacted, ending once the relevant points have been made. The discussion which follows addresses the reasons why the action took the direction it did, whether the desired outcomes were achieved, and how the actors' behaviour influenced the result. These points are then related to the real-life work situation.

Marineau, R.F. (1989) *Jacob Levy Moreno, 1889–1974*, Routledge.

Mickey, T.J. (1996) *Sociodrama: An Interpretive Theory for the Practice of Public Relations*, University Press of America.

Moreno, J.L. (1977) *Who Shall Survive? Foundations of Sociometry, Group Psychotherapy and Sociodrama*, Beacon House.

Moreno, J.L. (1991) *Psychodrama and Sociodrama in American Education*, Beacon House.

Sternberg, A. and Garcia, A. (1989) *Who's In Your Shoes?*, Praeger.

Wiener, R. (1997) *Creative Training: Sociodrama and Team Building*, Jessica Kingsley Publishers.

See also: Case-critical incident analysis; Character immersion; Dramatic skit; Gestalt technique; Hearing; Illuminative incident analysis; Mini-learning event; Monodrama; Psychodrama; Role-playing; Role-reversal; Skill practice session; Surrogate client

Sociometry

Sociometry was developed by Jacob Moreno to determine patterns of human relationships in groups, and can be used to help construct teams and analyse problems in individual and team performance. Relationships depend on personal choice (selection or rejection), and the affective structure of a group – the affinities and distances between individuals or clusters of individuals – can be portrayed in the form of a *sociogram* charting members' responses to certain questions. Each participant is presented with direct questions about the current group, such as 'With whom would you prefer to work?' or 'With whom would you like to study?', and asked to express two preferences. The sociometric term for one person's feeling towards another is *tele*, which may take the form of attraction (positive tele), repulsion (negative tele) or indifference. The sociogram shows who has expressed a preference for whom within the group. A person who was chosen by a large number of members is designated a *star*, those who chose each other are labelled *mutual pairs* or *mutual trios*, and those who were chosen by few or no members are termed *isolates*.

Hale, A.E. (1985) *Conducting Clinical Sociometric Explorations: A Manual for Psychodramatists and Sociometrists*, Royal Publishers.

Jennings, H.H. (1973) *Sociometry in Group Relations*, Greenwood Publishers.

Marineau, R.F. (1989) *Jacob Levy Moreno, 1889–1974*, Routledge.

Moreno, J.L. (1977) *Who Shall Survive? Foundations of Sociometry, Group Psychotherapy and Sociodrama*, Beacon House.

Saris, W.E. and Gallhofer, I.N. (eds) (1988) *Sociometric Research: Data Analysis, Volume 2*, St Martin's Press.

See also: Behavioural analysis; Process analysis

Socratic dialogue

This is a one-to-one version of Socratic questioning. The instructor asks a student to take a position on an issue or to make a value judgement, then challenges the assumptions that underpin that decision by exposing their implications. For example, if the student argues for consumer choice, the instructor may test whether this means that consumers should have free choice even if it means endangering themselves. By probing the position, questioning its relevance, consistency, specificity and clarity, students are forced to develop more complex ideas. Analogies may be used to clarify and challenge general statements. For example, if the student argues that, since students pay university fees they should be able to complain about the service they receive from the university, the instructor might ask whether the student's role in the university is comparable to that of a customer patronizing a shop.

Joyce, B., Weil, M. and Showers, B. (1992) *Models of Teaching* (4th edn), Allyn and Bacon.

See also: Dialogue; Ideological change; Moral philosophy approach; Managerial strategy change; Socratic group enquiry; Socratic questioning

Socratic group enquiry

This is a modified form of Socratic enquiry, in which students draw up questions that arise from reading assignments to serve as the basis for discussions or examinations. Good questions should exhibit characteristics such as scepticism; philosophical understanding of the subject, and concern for the nature of the subject as well as its information base, and the process of devising them entails students addressing issues such as what constitutes a good question, and how existing questions can be improved. Questions which are not discussed during classroom sessions may serve as topics or points of reference for lectures. The method has a number of advantages. It promotes active student involvement, it encourages close reading of carefully chosen material, and students and the instructor can learn from one another through the process of dialogue. However, students should be required to follow a scholarly format in drawing up their questions, citing which page in which text gave rise to them, and avoiding inference, implication and colloquialisms. Questions on a single topic should be grouped together.

One approach is to ask a class to submit a set of questions for the final examination, 25–30 per cent of which may be based on their contributions. The best of these can be duplicated and distributed as study sheets. Alternatively, the instructor can select questions that have been submitted, and present them to the whole class, encouraging members to copy them down for future reference, explaining why they were chosen. This then forms the basis for a group discussion, during which the instructor should restrict their role to clarifying specific points and summarizing students' remarks.

Abbs, P. (1994) *The Educational Imperative: A Defence of Socratic and Aesthetic Learning*, Falmer Press.
Nozick, R. (1997) *Socratic Puzzles*, Harvard University Press.
Seeskin, K. (1986) *Dialogue and Discovery: A Study in Socratic Method*, State University of New York Press.

See also: Interrogation of experts; Invitation to discover; Management problem laboratory; Mystery clue method; One-to-one learning; Question production; Question searching; Questioning; Socratic questioning

Socratic questioning

Socratic questioning is a learning method which examines a student's knowledge of a subject by asking a series of questions. The student must claim that they understand the material, and the questioning sets out to test this claim, revealing areas of misunderstanding or ignorance, and stimulating them to learn more. In this sense, Socratic questioning does not simply check how much students know about a certain subject, but how much they know about themselves. The technique can be applied to any subject matter, and in some cases it may change students' attitudes to learning, but this depends on the individual. Those with low self-esteem are likely to view the experience as public cross-examination. It is most appropriate for strong, self-confident students who feel they have mastered a subject. Such individuals are often eager to display their knowledge. Their sense of self-worth means that they are less likely to be embarrassed or depressed if they cannot answer a question, and more likely to be encouraged to learn more by identifying gaps in their knowledge.

Kasachkoff, T. (ed.) (1997) *In the Socratic Tradition: Essays on Teaching Philosophy*, Rowman and Littlefield.
Whipple, R.D. (1996) *Socratic Method and Writing Instructions*, University Press of America.
Wolfe, E. and Daly, K.R. (1996) *Socratic Selling: How to Ask the Questions and Get that Sale*, Irwin.

See also: Invitation to discover; Interrogation of experts; Question production; Question searching; Questioning; Socratic group enquiry

Staff exchange

Staff exchanges serve two purposes: to transfer know-how, and to develop the individuals concerned. In Japan, such exchanges are common between small and large companies in customer–supplier relationships, and they may be useful to any company which relies on a high percentage of bought-in components that represent a large proportion of its products' costs. The main benefit of this approach is that each company's employees gain a better understanding of the other company's objectives, needs and operations. The staff of the supplier company gain a clearer idea of the contribution their product makes to the customer's output, and why agreed quality levels and timely delivery are essential. On the other hand, the customer company's staff gain an insight into how the supplier company manufactures its products and deals with its own suppliers and its other customers, increasing their awareness of the problems and constraints with which it must contend. Having acquired this information, each company's staff can communicate it to their colleagues, clarifying mutual expectations and improving understanding.

See also: Assignment to customer as representative; Confrontation groups; Criss-cross panels; Customer interface meeting; Inter-group interventions; Intervisitation; Network organizations; Outsourcing; Vendor excellence awards

Staff meeting assignment

Being required to attend too many meetings may drain the energy of even the most ambitious employee. However, the experience of attending meetings may bring a number of benefits, and being exposed to the interplay between different individuals, conflicts of interests, subtleties, agreements or failure to reach agreements can be revealing and stimulating. One way to exploit this for development purposes is to assign a staff member to participate in a meeting they are not usually expected to attend. For instance, an individual who has completed a project may be asked to present the findings at a departmental meeting and take part in the subsequent discussion. This can be particularly useful in renewing an employee's enthusiasm, especially if they have become stale through over-exposure to the same kind of work. The fact that the presentation takes place before peers as well as seniors introduces a competitive element to which moderate performers usually respond well.

Doyle, M. (1996) *How To Make Meetings Work*, Berkeley Publishing.
Janner, G. (1990) *How To Win Meetings*, Gower.
Martin, D. (1995) *Manipulating Meetings*, Pitman.
Payne, J. (1994) *Successful Meetings in a Week*, Hodder and Stoughton.
Tropman, J.E. (1996) *Making Meetings Work*, Sage.

See also: Case student telling; Committee assignment; Development assignment; Evaluation audit assignment; Proposal team assignment; Selection board assignment; Short talks by students; Task force assignment

Step-by-step discussion

This teaching technique combines the functions of a lecture and a follow-up seminar by using a carefully prepared sequence of issues and questions to draw out the required information from students. The aim is to increase students' knowledge of facts and their understanding of logical argument or developmental sequences. The method is of greatest value where a particular set of issues must be covered, since each one can be presented in written form or by means of audio or video tapes, and allocated discussion time.

Brilhart, J.K. (1994) *Effective Group Discussion*, Brown Publishers.
Dillon, J.T. (1994) *Using Discussions in Classrooms*, Open University Press.
Espeseth, M. (1998) *Academic Listening Encounters: Listening, Note Taking and Discussion*, Cambridge University Press.
Van Ments, M. (1991) *Active Talk: The Effective Use of Discussion in Learning*, St Martin's Press.
Wood, J.T. (1994) *Group Discussion Guide*, Harper and Row.

See also: Case study method; Guided discussion; Step-by-step lecture

Step-by-step lecture

Step-by-step lectures usually address three to ten topics, each of which is explained for a few minutes then explored through discussion or other activities. They can be used to impart information and develop problem-solving skills. Because the method allows periodic relaxation from concentrating on the lecture to engage in group discussion, activities, feedback and rehearsal, it can be applied to classes of up to thirty. When a course relies on presenting problems projected on to a screen, a variation of the technique can be adopted by asking students to attempt each question, then discuss their responses to it with the lecturer, before proceeding to the next question. The questions are also supplied as a handout with space for students' notes so that they can maintain a complete record of the course.

McCarthy, W.H. (1970) 'Improving Large Audience Teaching: The Programmed Lecture', *British Journal of Medical Education*, vol. 14, no. 1.

See also: Group buzz; Lecture method; Step-by-step discussion

Story-writing

Story-writing is a variation of the case study method in which students record the case themselves. Conventional case descriptions contain facts, but their story line is often intentionally unclear. In contrast, the descriptions produced by story-writing maintain a clear narrative flow and, because they aim to reflect the tensions of those who are experiencing the events described, they usually include much dialogue and many action sequences.

Preparation for case story-writing resembles that for story-telling, but the approach should be more stringent. Each student should interview a manager, and ask them to describe a problem they have experienced. It is important to ensure that the interview provides sufficient background to set the scene, and there needs to be a strong plot that enables the central character to develop as the sequence of events unfolds. The student's notes should give a clear chronology of events, separate the background from the main occurrences, determine the central character's values and beliefs, and record any characteristic dialogue, especially any jargon, colloquialisms or company-specific terms. The story should be divided into three sections. The first section sets the context. The second consists of an opening passage, a description of the sequence of events, a climax, and a resolution. The final section should explain the story's relevance to some aspect of the course, such as a theory or a research finding.

Boje, D.M. (1991) 'Learning Storytelling: Storytelling to Learn Management Skills', *Journal of Management Education*, vol. 15, no. 3, pp. 279–94.

See also: Case study method; Case with analogue; Learning history; Poetry for learning; Re-writing; Storytelling

Storyboarding

Film and cartoon producers use storyboards – sequences of sketches with notes and comments – to decide which scenes to shoot and how to arrange them. The same technique can be used to summarize and teach topics such as how to manage projects by dividing an A3 sheet of paper or card into boxes or 'frames' which tell a story, usually by means of cartoons and bullet points. Prepared storyboards on certain management and company topics are commercially available (e.g., the 'One Page Coach' series), accompanied by guidance to instructors on how to use them as the basis for simple presentations and workshops.

See also: Drawing for learning; Collages; Exhibit; Fortune lining; Illuminative incident analysis; Poster; Responsibility charting

Storytelling

People have used storytelling since ancient times to pass on knowledge by describing real or imaginary events, and to build a sense of community. A well-told story can arouse emotional responses among listeners, who collectively experience the events described, and learn – or even create – their meaning together. As a teaching method, storytelling provides a means of simplifying complex concepts, bringing them to life and providing a context for later learning. Stories can communicate values, character traits and complex organizational dynamics in a way which grabs the imagination and remains memorable. They are usually more effective if delivered by the instructor, rather than read silently by students. For example, in studying a case, it is often easier to tell a story than to describe a scene, partly because the time sequence gives a clearer idea of how events unfold, and partly because the action of a story tends to attract and hold attention. Storytelling is also an important management skill, since employees often use their manager's stories to make sense of events, to recall precedents that inform choices, and to understand organizational politics. The stories told by customers, vendors and employees contribute greatly to corporate culture. However, like all skills, storytelling improves with practice, and it is best to begin with short descriptions that can be woven into a story.

Boje suggests a method that can help students become better storytellers. Each student should be set the task of asking a manager to describe a problem they have experienced. The students then outline the sequence of events, separating the background from the main occurrences to determine the story's underlying theme, and connecting it to a relevant theory, concept or research finding in their subject. Next, they reframe the narrative by choosing a starting point that will grab the audience's attention. Finally, they recount the story to the rest of the class. These stories could be aired during 'story days', with students telling them to a sub-group or the entire class.

Baker, A. (1996) *Story Telling: Art and Technique*, Bowker.

Bauman, (1986) *Story, Performance and Event*, Cambridge University Press.

Boje, D.M. (1989) 'Postlog: Bringing Performance Back', *Journal of Organizational Change Management*, vol. 2, no. 2, pp. 80–93.

Boje, D.M. (1991) 'Learning Storytelling: Storytelling to Learn Management Skills', *Journal of Management Education*, vol. 15, no. 3, pp. 279–94.

Boje, D.M. (1991) 'The Storytelling Organization: A Performance Study of Stories in an Office Supply Firm', *Administrative Science Quarterly*, vol. 36, pp. 106–26.

Brogida, E. and Nisbett, R. (1977) 'The Differential Impact of Abstract Versus Concrete Information in Decisions', *Journal of Applied Social Psychology*, vol. 7, pp. 258–71.

Coles, R. (1987) 'Storyteller's Ethics', *Harvard Business Review*, March–April, pp. 8–14.

Cooke, E. (1976) *The Ordinary and the Fabulous: An Introduction to Myths, Legends and Fairy Tales*, Cambridge University Press.

Egan, K. (1989) *Teaching as Storytelling*, University of Chicago Press.

Grover, R.A. and Greenberg, J. (1983) 'A Note on the Role and Potency of "War Stories" in Teaching Organizational Behaviour', *Exchange: The Organizational Behaviour Teaching Journal*, vol. 8, no. 4, pp. 38–40.

Martin, J. (1982) 'Stories and Scripts in Organizational Settings', in Hastorf, A.H. and Isen, A.M. (eds) *Cognitive Social Psychology*, Elsevier.

Mason, H. (1996) *Power of Storytelling: A Step by Step Guide*, Sage.

McKay, H. (1996) *About Storytelling*, Hale and Iremonger.

Parkin, M. (1998) *Tales for Trainers: Using Stories and Metaphors to Facilitate Training*, Kogan Page.

Schor, S.M., Sims, R.R. and Dennehy, R.F. (1996) 'Power and Diversity: Sensitizing Yourself and Others Through Self-reflection and Storytelling', *Journal of Management Education*, vol. 20, no. 2, pp. 242–57.

Zemke, R. (1990) 'Storytelling: Back to a Basic', *Training*, March, pp. 44–9.

Zipes, F. (1996) *Creative Storytelling*, Routledge.

See also: Case student telling; Inner dialogue; Learning history; Metaphors; Novels for learning; Playing for learning; Poetry for learning; Reading aloud; Story-writing; Student case telling; Teaching by narration

Strategic management

In recent times, there has been a general move away from an opportunist, crisis-driven management style to one which has a strategic dimension. This involves considering not only the present state of affairs, but possible future developments, and the choice of goals that can be achieved within the organization's environment. It also entails reviewing the capabilities and steps necessary to move from the company's present state towards its future desired state. Beckhard and Harris offer a model which describes practical ways to diagnose an organization's present structure, possible developments in the future, and the changes and mechanisms required to realize a desirable future state. It can be used to consider how organizations can develop, and what they need to do to react to externally triggered change. The steps an organization goes through in drawing up plans can be thought of as a learning process, since it takes note of possible events in its future environment, decides how to adapt in order to cope with them, then reviews the results. Although this may be time-consuming, the process is usually as important as the plans themselves, leading to improved working relationships between peers, incorporating consideration of the future into current decision-making, providing a more open means of dealing with conflicts about which direction to take, improving individuals' understanding of the plans, and as a result engendering greater commitment to them. This intervention demands that the facilitator ensures that group processes do not become entrenched in a single functional discipline, such as finance or marketing. The participative approach broadens the ownership of the plan, and reduces anxiety and resistance since all participants are aware why certain alternatives were discarded. This not only improves commitment, but also increases managers' predictive abilities.

The strategic management meeting is usually run as a two-day residential away from the workplace, where managers work with internal and external consultants. Before the meeting, participants familiarize themselves with the company's financial position, its competition and its socio-environmental situation, in an effort to identify future trends. The meeting begins with a brainstorming session, encouraging participants to look beyond their technical or functional specialities and view the organization as a whole by considering questions such as: 'What would constitute success for the company?', 'Judging by the way we have been managing this organization, what are our objectives?' and 'What are our strengths and weaknesses?' The aim of this exercise is to prepare the way for producing a corporate mission statement. Each participant is asked to produce a 25-word draft which uses action verbs and nouns, and one of these is chosen to be edited and rewritten until it represents a mutually agreed statement of the company's purpose. The session can take up to four hours, and forms the basis of the remainder of the event. Subsequent work deals with identifying and analysing the organization's domains, developing action plans, and devising systems to manage the plans. Domain analysis acknowledges that organizations do not exist in a vacuum, but interact with their environment. Participants are asked to identify what demands are made of the organization, how it currently responds, how these demands might change in the next two to ten years, how the organization is likely to respond during the same time period if no changes are made, and what might be done differently to ensure that the domain makes ideal demands upon the organization. This ideal demand is the company's strategic objective statement and, once it is developed, the consultants work with the managers to clarify how it will be accomplished, focusing on identifying the resources and activities required, scheduling activities, and allocating responsibilities. The consultants then draw up a report based on the outcome. The final stage in the strategic planning process involves establishing a system to manage the plans, focusing on objectives, establishing measurement criteria, agreeing completion dates and then arranging a follow-up review.

Beckhard, R. and Harris, R.T. (1977) *Organizational Transitions: Managing Complex Change*, Addison Wesley Longman.

Channon, D.F. (ed.) (1997) *The Blackwell Encyclopedia of Strategic Management*, Blackwell.

David, F.R. (1997) *Strategic Management*, Prentice-Hall.

Galpin, T. (1997) *Making Strategy Work*, Jossey-Bass.

Rouse, W.B. (1998) *Don't Jump to Conclusions: Thirteen Delusions that Undermine Strategic Thinking and How to Overcome Them*, Jossey-Bass.

Thompson, A. and Strickland, A.J. (1997) *Strategic Management*, McGraw-Hill.

Wright, P., Kroll, M.J. and Parnell, J.A. (1997) *Strategic Management: Concepts* (4th edn), Prentice-Hall.

See also: Contingency approach; Corporate culture training; Delphi technique; Development of a new management/operating philosophy; Force field analysis; Goal-setting interface groups; Industrial dynamics; Nominal group technique; Open systems planning; Policy-formulation; Scenario-planning; Search conference; Socio-technical systems designs; Strategic planning process

Strategic planning process

The strategic planning process was originally developed by the Institute of Cultural Affairs to encourage people to take responsibility for the societies and communities in which they live. It has been adapted to the organizational context, where it serves as a large-group intervention to help a department or company to develop a vision of a desired future. Strategic planning process events usually last between five and seven days; enable participants to consider the data they generate in greater depth and avoid the 'quick-fix' mentality; and may involve 50 to 200 participants. A six-step approach is adopted which allows participants to categorize, prioritize and organize their own data.

In the first step, *Focus on the Question*, consultants work with the steering committee to frame the core question that will be addressed during the

planning process. In the second step, *Map Out a Clear, Practical Vision*, participants spend up to two days developing a vision, assessing its practicality, and setting priorities. The third step, *Analyzing the Underlying Contradictions*, uses brainstorming to consider the obstacles that may prevent participants realizing their vision (e.g., lack of training for staff). The contradictions identified may include procedures that are universally disliked, but are followed because of tradition or inertia. Once all the contradictions are revealed, participants consider how they might change their own behaviour. Step four, *Setting Strategic Directions*, lists the actions necessary to overcome these contradictions, and it is useful to involve outside stakeholders at this stage, since they can provide valuable insights. Step five, *Design the Systematic Action*, identifies the tasks required to achieve the vision, and creates task forces to undertake them. In the final step, *Drawing Up an Agreed-upon Time Line for Implementation*, management allocates tasks and deadlines, decides how frequently to hold follow-up meetings, and asks itself how it will know whether the plans have succeeded.

Bunker, B.B. and Alban, B.T. (1997) 'ICA Strategic Planning Process', in *Large Group Interventions: Engaging the Whole System for Rapid Change*, Jossey-Bass, pp. 77–84.

Fogg, C.D. (1994) *Team Based Strategic Planning*, American Management Association AMACOM.

Spencer, L.J. (1989) *Winning Through Participation*, Kendall/Hunt.

Troxel, J.P. (1993) *Participation Works: Business Cases from Around the World*, Miles River Press.

See also: Business process re-engineering; Conference Model; Fast-cycle full-participation work design; Future search; Issue briefing; Large-group interventions; Open space technology; Participative design; Policy-formulation; Real-time strategic change; Real-time work design; Search conference; Simu-Real; Socio-technical systems design; Strategic management; Work-Out

Stress management

The role of stress in the workplace has been more widely recognized in recent times, and its effects on employees may include poor concentration, absenteeism, or even suicide. Some organizations seek to change their working arrangements to overcome these problems, but since stress is inevitable in many jobs, another approach is to help employees manage their own levels of stress and learn how to cope with the symptoms. Such programmes may be provided by the organization's training department or independent stress consultants, and most involve learning relaxation or visualization techniques. Some follow a sequence of steps, assessing the issues which are affecting an individual's performance, providing advice and counselling to help them increase their self-control and improve their ability to cope, and then training them to use relaxation and deep breathing techniques. One approach derived from clinical psychology aims to de-sensitize the individual by conditioning them to relax in response to adverse stimuli. In another approach, *induced effect*, participants are asked to imagine a stressful situation as vividly as possible, and are then taught coping skills, which include relaxation and the use of self-talk.

Brewer, K.C. (1997) *Managing Stress*, Gower.

Cartwright, S. and Cooper, C.L. (1997) *Managing Workplace Stress*, Sage.

Cooper, C.L. and Kompier, M. (eds) (1999) *Preventing Stress, Improving Productivity*, Routledge.

Dabney, J. (1995) 'Opinion: Stress in Students: Implications for Learning', *Education and Training Technology International*, vol. 32, no. 2, pp. 112–16.

Jex, S.M. (1998) *Stress and Job Performance*, Sage.

Priest, S. and Welch, J. (1998) *Creating a Stress-free Office*, Gower.

Quick, J.C. (1997) *Preventive Stress Management in Organizations*, American Psychological Association.

Schell, B.H. (1997) *A Self-diagnostic Approach to Understanding Organizational and Personal Stressors*, Quorum Books.

'Stress Management', special issue of *Human Relations* (1996), vol. 49, no. 2, February.

See also: Bioenergetics; Coaching; Counselling; Executive Family Seminar; Family communications programme; Inner dialogue; Job support; Outplacement counselling; Psychotherapy; Wellness programmes

Structural interventions (organizational restructuring)

An organization's structure consists of patterns of relationships, especially authority and functional relationships, between its departments and its members, and this is formally expressed in organizational charts and job descriptions, which set out specific policies or instructions. Structural interventions aim to improve the organization's efficiency by means such as altering the number of levels in the hierarchy, expanding or contracting the number of units or departments, changing the composition of teams, or altering responsibilities, authority levels and communication lines. Many companies have adopted such measures in an effort to reduce the complexity of their management structure, broaden spans of control, develop responsibility, increase accountability and create more manageable, self- contained organizational units.

Chris Argyris describes a corporate reorganization intervention in which management played an important part. Managers at all levels diagnosed their organization's existing problems. Groups of functional representatives of roughly equal rank were assembled for a few hours, and took part in brainstorms to identify the problems, but not the solutions. The information generated was fed back to a steering committee consisting of all the managerial ranks, which identified blind spots and unanswered questions. Smaller task forces, made up of staff with the relevant experience, were then formed to answer these questions, and the steering committee drew on their answers to design a new organizational structure.

Ashkensas, R.N. (ed.) (1995) *The Boundaryless Organization: Breaking the Chains of Organizational Structure*, Jossey-Bass.

Cotter, J.J. (1995) *The 20% Solution: Using Rapid Redesign to Create Tomorrow's Organizations Today*, Wiley.

Fritz, R. (1996) *Corporate Tides: The Inescapable Law of Organization Structure*, Berrett-Koehler.

Galbraith, J.R. (1993) *Competing With Flexible, Lateral Organizations*, Addison Wesley Longman.

Galbraith, J.R. (1995) *Designing Organizations: An Executive Briefing on Strategy, Structure and Processes*, Jossey-Bass.

Galbraith, J.R. and Lawler, E.E. (1993) *Organizing for the Future: The New Logic for Managing Complex Organizations*, Jossey-Bass.

See also: Ad hoc committees/task forces; Autonomous workgroups; Business teams; Collateral organization; Flexible staffing; Integrated support functions; Involvement teams; Job descriptions; Job design; Line-of-business groups; Managerial decentralization; MAPS approach; Parallel career ladders; Plural chief executive

Structured social skill seminar

Developed by Lievegoed and colleagues at the Paedagogisk Institut in the Netherlands, this is a less intensive variant of the T-group. In the structured social skill seminar, the learning process is more explicit, and relates more closely to the participants' work situations. Group members prepare by attending a planning session where they work without an observer and agree on a task they wish to tackle. The sessions that follow are held in the presence of an observer, who analyses the interactions that emerge then discusses them with the group, helping them to integrate new insights with the technical and conceptual skills they already possess.

See also: Action training; Coverdale Training; Laboratory method; Micro-lab; Process analysis

Structured tutoring

Structured tutoring adapts the programmed instruction approach for use in one-to-one tutorials. Not only are the instructional materials highly structured, but the approach specifies the nature of the relationship the tutor should establish with the student. The tutor should develop and maintain rapport by expressing empathy, asking questions about activities in which the student is involved, and talking about topics of common interest. It is important to avoid saying 'No' or 'That's wrong' in response to the student's comments, instead providing praise and encouragement, and giving special recognition for outstanding achievements. In the early stages of their studies, students may require a great deal of drill-and-practice work, and they are more likely to tolerate this if they feel they are making progress. For this reason, it is important that the tutor creates opportunities for the student to succeed, and encourages them to become goal-oriented. Because the student's recall may vary from day to day, the approach also includes methods to help them memorize certain material, such as formulae. There are usually about three tutorials per week, during which the tutor sits beside the student and works with them. The first step is to test the student's knowledge or ability before instruction commences, and the tutor plans the rest of the course accordingly, maintaining a record of the student's progress, and conducting regular reviews of what has been learned.

Von Harrison, G. and Guymon, R.E. (1980) *Structured Tutoring*, Instructional Design Library, Volume 34, Educational Technology Publications.

See also: Apprenticeship programme; Assignment to a manager with high development skills; Mentoring; Tutorial

Structuring seminars

Numerous attempts to improve structured group discussions have met with varying degrees of success. If one student within a class is asked to prepare a presentation on a topic, there is no incentive for the others to do their own reading, and the amount they learn depends on the student's presentation skills. Setting every student in a class a reading task may provide a good resource base but, unless there is a degree of overlap between the subject matter of the assignments, subsequent discussion may degenerate into a series of individual student–instructor interactions. Establishing learning contracts for all class members may encourage them to participate, but it does not encourage or enable students to develop an overview of a subject. Based on an approach commonly used to plan essays or exam answers, Wilson developed a way to overcome these problems by enabling students to participate in structuring the discussion.

About a week before the structured seminar, the instructor tells the students a little about the literature of the subject to be discussed next week, giving pointers to the key names and whether sources are grouped into schools of thought. Although no specific reading is allocated, it is emphasized that all are expected to prepare for the seminar by referring to some of the texts. At the beginning of the seminar, the instructor goes round the group, asking each student what they have read, what they thought of it, whether they would recommend it to other members of class, and so on. If any have failed to do some reading, this is tolerated at first. After this exchange of reports on the literature, the next step is to form it into a pattern, which may be drawn on an overhead projector transparency or a board by the lecturer or a student. The topic for the session is placed in the middle, and the instructor asks the students to call out what needs to be examined during the seminar. Whenever a suggestion is made, the instructor asks whether it constitutes a separate item, or whether it could be grouped with an idea that has already been presented. This leads to the creation of main headings and subheadings. As the flow of suggestions dries up, the instructor ask the students to draw lines on the diagram enclosing points that could be dealt with together, and these clusters are then placed in order, ready for discussion. The entire procedure usually takes only ten or fifteen minutes.

Organizing seminars in this way offers a number of advantages. Involving students in structuring the discussion means they are more likely to participate, and the session's structure is clear to all. The process of creating the pattern can also act as an ice-breaking device, since ideas can be thrown in without having to respond to searching questions. The students' contributions help the instructor to choose the appropriate level for the ensuing discussion, and the headings also indicate issues where the instructor should offer an explanation or check students' understanding. Finally, because this initial exercise draws up an agenda, it is easier to plan the allocation of time during the rest of the session.

Wilson, A. (1980) 'Structuring Seminars: A Technique to Allow Students to Participate in the Structuring of Small Group Discussions', *Studies in Higher Education*, vol. 5, no. l, pp. 8l–4.

See also: Agenda method; Construct lesson plan; Data approach method; Discussion guides; Guided group problem-solving; Learning through discussion; Seminar

Student consulting teams (student advisory teams)

In this approach, students work in teams and act as independent management consultants to real-life clients, studying and making recommendations to solve their organizational problems. The people they encounter, the problems they face, the solutions they recommend and the results they obtain give them experience of applying their course knowledge. A number of variations have been developed, but all allow students to experiment with new situations, to take risks, and to use their initiative to make decisions. Having done so, they can then observe what happens, reflect on the process and outcome, and learn and reinforce principles and concepts.

Buller, P.F. (1992) 'Reconceptualizing the Small Business Consulting Course: A Retort to the Porter-McKibben Criticism', *Journal of Management Education*, vol. 16, pp. 56–75.

Congram, C. and LaFarge, V. (1995) 'Student Advisory Teams: A New Approach to Managing Field Projects', *Journal of Management Education*, vol. 19, no. 3, pp. 347–53.

Daly, J.P. and Mitchell, W.B. (1995) 'Synergy on Campus: Student Consulting Teams and the University Library', *Journal of Management Education*, vol. 19, no. 3, pp. 347–53.

Friedman, S.D. (1989–90) 'Education or Service? Coping with Conflicts in Student Consulting Teams', *Organizational Behaviour Teaching Review*, vol. 14, no. 4, pp. 63–77.

Harris, I. (1997) 'Practical Support for Group Student Projects for External Clients', *Innovations in Education and Training International*, vol. 34, no. 4, pp. 233–6.

Mallinger, M.A. (1987–8) 'University as Client', *Organizational Behaviour Teaching Review*, vol. 12, no. 1, pp. 122–4.

Tubbs, S. (1984–5) 'Consulting Teams: A Methodology for Teaching Integrated Management Skills', *Organizational Behaviour Teaching Review*, vol. 9, no. 4, pp. 52–7.

Weil, J. (1985–6) 'The Management Consultation Project', *Organizational Behaviour Teaching Review*, vol. 10, no. 2, pp. 101–3.

See also: Internship; Student-designed companies

Student placement (work placement)

This approach has been particularly popular in secondary schools, where final-year pupils are placed in an organization, ostensibly to help out, but mainly to observe. As always, the effectiveness of this approach depends upon matching the learners' interests with the opportunities available in the local community. Careful assessment is required to avoid situations such as one that was reported, where a girl who expressed an interest in working with animals was assigned to work in a butcher's shop. At university, students may be assigned to an organization and required to complete an applied project, becoming involved in the company's day-to-day activities in the process. Although instructors may provide guidance, they do not programme the students' activities nor evaluate them directly.

Cameron-Jones, M. and O' Hara, P. (1992) 'Making Placement More Successful', *Management Education and Development*, vol. 23, no. 1, pp. 46–53.

French, R.B. (1993) 'All Work is a Placement', *Management Education and Development*, vol. 24, no. 4, pp. 406–14.

Weil, S.W. and McGill, I. (1989) *Making Sense of Experiential Learning*, Open University Press.

See also: Apprenticeship; Co-operative education; Field project attachment; Internship; Manager shadowing

Student-designed companies (students as entrepreneurs)

The idea of incorporating entrepreneurial activities into management courses has been widely adopted, and some government initiatives encourage senior school pupils to create and run companies. However, it is often forgotten that many students already run what are, in effect, small entrepreneurial companies. Each year, officers are elected for student societies, students' unions or representative councils. With titles such as president, secretary or treasurer, the management roles they take on are many and varied, including: advertising what their organization can offer, recruiting members, producing newsletters, organizing events, balancing the books and handing the organization on to the next regime.

Buller, P.F. (1992) 'Reconceptualizing the Small Business Consulting Course: A Retort to the Porter-McKibben Criticism', *Journal of Management Education*, vol. 16, pp. 56–75.

Cousins, R.B., Thorn, R.G. and Benitz, L.E. (1995) 'The Junior Achievement Company as a Living Case', *Journal of Management Education*, vol. 19, no. 2, pp. 228–32.

Starr-Glass, D. (1996) 'Pieces and Patterns: Course Redesign Suggests a Wider Reconsideration of Curriculum', *Journal of Management Education*, vol. 20, no. 2, pp. 236–41.

See also: Junior Achievement company; Student consulting teams; Students as school tutors

Student-planned learning

Student-planned learning combines contract learning and the project method in a long-term, student-designed course which leads to a recognized qualification. Some of the earliest programmes were run by the School of Independent Study at what was then the North East London Polytechnic, and the University of Lancaster. Such programmes aim to develop students' general competence, encourage them to develop transferable skills, and require them to demonstrate their competence in both individual and collaborative situations. These objectives are achieved through independent study, each student working on their specialism, and also through group work involving various project methods and skills workshops. There are several variations on the basic approach. In one version, students plan their learning, and the result is a form of learning contract known as a *learning statement*, which is a formal agreement between the student, the school and a specialized area. The statement includes six appendices: the first three present the student's formulation of the educational problem, the fourth and fifth give the student's detailed proposals for solving it, and the final one states how the outcome will be tested. Each programme is validated in three stages. The student's personal and specialist tutors indicate the extent to which they feel able to support the proposed learning statement. Their views are then considered by the school's internal validation board. Finally, the programme is scrutinized by an external board, which decides whether to approve it.

Benson, P. and Voller, P. (1997) *Autonomy and Independence in Language Learning*, Longman.

Boud, D.J. (ed.) (1981) *Developing Student Autonomy in Learning*, Kogan Page.

Cunningham, I. (1981) 'Self Managed Learning in Independent Study', in Boydell, T. and Pedler, M. (eds) *Management Self-development: Concepts and Practices*, Gower.

Green, A. (1996) *Let Them Show Us the Way: Fostering Independent Learning*, Penguin.

Long, D.G. (1991) *Self Managed Learning*, St Martin's Press.

Percy, K. and Ramsden, P. (1980) *Independent Study: Two Examples from English Higher Education*, Society for Research into Higher Education.

Tait, J. and Knight, P. (eds) (1996) *Management of Independent Learning*, Kogan Page.

Taylor, I. (1997) *Developing Learning in Professional Education: Partnerships for Practice*, Open University Press.

See also: Action learning; Collaboratively designed courses; Course design as learning; Examination; Independent study; Learning community; Learning organization; Project orientation; Self-development

Students as school tutors

This approach uses volunteer university students to assist teachers in local schools, usually for one morning or afternoon per week for about ten weeks. The volunteers work with individuals or with small groups of pupils under the supervision and direction of teachers, helping pupils with their work, and discussing the relationship between the subject being studied and the outside world. Evidence suggests that the majority of student-tutors find their experiences rewarding, stimulating and enjoyable, giving them the opportunity to develop their social, organizational, problem-solving and communication skills. As well as providing a learning experience for student-tutors, the school and its pupils gain from the extra stimulus and assistance. Providing positive role models raises pupils' aspirations and increases their motivation to pursue further education and training. Many companies recognize the value of the experience such programmes provide. For example, British Petroleum has a manager and an office dedicated to identifying and placing student-tutors around the world.

Goodlad, S. (1979) *Learning by Teaching*, Community Service Volunteers Publications.

Goodlad, S. (ed.) (1985) *Study Science: An Examination of Community Service as Method of Study in Higher Education*, NFER-Nelson.

Goodlad, S. (ed.) (1995) *Students as Tutors and Mentors*, Kogan Page.

Goodlad, S. (1997) *Mentoring and Tutoring by Students*, Kogan Page.

Goodlad, S. (1998) *Museum Volunteers: Good Practice in the Management of Volunteers*, Routledge.

See also: Junior Achievement company; Student-designed companies

Study assignment

In a study assignment, a trainee studies a specified company procedure or operation, then writes a report on it. This usually involves consulting documentation, observing administrative procedures, and talking to those who work in the area being studied. In setting such an assignment, the instructor must check that the learner will be able to obtain the information required, and must ensure that the objectives are clear. It is essential that all staff understand the aims and implications of the assignment, and are forewarned that they may be interviewed about their work. Departments must be ready to accept the trainee, and must also be prepared to make their files available for study.

As a developmental tool, study assignments offer numerous advantages. They are practical, since they relate directly to the company's operation, and the content is designed to form part of the individual's job. Used in conjunction with a college course on management, they can help to offset the abstraction and unreality of training methods which rely on role-plays and business games. Each learning programme is individualized, and the onus for making the assignment a success lies with the trainee. Last but not least, they make few demands on the instructor's time while ensuring that trainees make the best use of theirs. Although such assignments are obviously useful for new recruits, the approach can also be applied to different levels of management. For example, the marketing manager may be asked to work alongside the production manager to suggest ways a product might be improved.

Depres identifies four factors which are essential to the success of this method: a good question, the maximum use of documents and observation, an element of contrast and comparison, and writing a report, followed by a discussion. A good question should interest and motivate the trainee, directing their attention and suggesting ways to tackle the task. The reliance on documentation and observation minimizes the disruption other staff will experience as a result of answering the trainee's questions, and helps to ensure that the trainee is well prepared when conducting the interviews. Comparing and contrasting different procedures or work practices encourages the trainee to evaluate what is being studied, rather than just describing it. Writing a report not only clarifies the student's thinking and provides a focus for discussion of the assignment. It also gives practice in producing business reports, and additional skills may be developed if the trainee is asked to summarize the findings verbally. Discussing the report allows the trainee to seek clarification of any areas of uncertainty, and enables the study assignment to be placed in the context of the company as a whole.

Depres, D. (1980) 'A Study Assignment Approach to Training', *Journal of European Industrial Training*, vol. 4, no. 3, pp. 14–16.

Mumford, A. (1980) *Making Experience Pay*, McGraw-Hill.

See also: Committee assignment; Consulting assignment; Development assignment; Evaluation audit assignment; Library assignment; Prompt list; Research assignment; Research degree; Selection board assignment; SmartProcess; Work sheet

Study circles (learning circles; reading circles; supervisory training circles)

During the 1980s, quality circles became a popular method of increasing employees' participation in planning their work and making decisions about their working conditions and practices. Study circles have adapted this concept to develop a positive learning climate in organizations by engaging employees, managers and instructors in a partnership to learn about a topic and develop learning skills, and encouraging them to continue to use these skills in the future. They usually consist of a group of employees, their line manager and an adviser from the company's training department. Although the circles often go beyond organizational concerns to address employees' own educational and social needs, it is felt that they improve communication and lead to increased awareness of common objectives. For this reason, most companies allow study circles to meet during working hours, and some provide support by allocating a member of staff to organize the meetings, arrange speakers and locate study materials requested by the group.

Scriven describes a study circle as an 'ongoing conversation which passes through a number of stages', which he identifies as: exploration, planning, support and evaluation. In the *exploration* phase, group members discuss the gap between their existing level of knowledge and what they need to know in order to function effectively, defining the nature and scope of the learning required, and its relevance to the work of their department. They agree the content to be studied, the time scale, and the standards they wish to achieve, then record these and draw up a learning contract. The *planning* phase concentrates on the learning strategy to be adopted, identifying what information already exists about the subject within the organization. Group members consider which learning materials to use, how to develop their learning skills, what resources may be required, where they might be obtained, and how the materials can be organized. Throughout this process, the adviser assists them by providing self-diagnosis instruments. In the *support* phase, the group selects the materials and organizes them according to group members' learning styles and preferences. It decides how the study circle meetings should be run, and how often they should be held. The group then considers the process and content of the learning, clarifying the support that will be provided by managers and instructors as members work on their study programmes. Each study circle meeting will check on progress, but as the programme nears completion, the group enters the *evaluation* phase, judging whether the learning contract has been fulfilled. Success is measured in terms of both content (Have participants learned what they agreed to learn?) and process (Are participants better able to organize their own learning, and are they more confident about tackling future learning tasks?).

The approach has proven popular in Scandinavia, and is gaining more widespread acceptance in the UK and the USA. De Ridder Thurston Inc. of Rochester, New York, which manufactures graphic arts materials, was one of the first American companies to use study circles. Circle members were challenged to uncover problems and to present recommendations. One circle analysed the company's staff appraisal programme and recommended revisions. At De Ridder, the first study circle established included first-line supervisors, to enable them to understand the process.

Johnson, D., Johnson, R.T. and Holubec, E.J. (1993) *Circles of Learning: Co-operation in the Classroom*, Interaction Book Co.

Olivere, L.P. (1987) *Study Circles: Coming Together for Personal Growth and Change*, Seven Locks Press.

Osborne, K. and Shavat, R. (1982) 'Study Circles', *Management Review*, June, pp. 37–42.

Samway, K.D. and Whang, G. (1995) *Literature Study Circles in a Multicultural Classroom*, Teachers Publishing Group Inc.

Scriven, R. (1984) 'Learning Circles', *Journal of European Industrial Training*, vol. 8, no. 1, pp. 17–20.

Woods, T.L. (1973) 'The Study Group: A Mechanism for Continuing Education and Professional Development', *Clinical Social Work Journal*, vol. 2, no. 2, pp. 120–6.

See also: Educational activities; Informal action group; Instrumentation; Instrumented laboratory; Involvement teams; Learning contract; Quality circles; SmartProcess

Study group

Study groups were developed by the Tavistock Clinic and the Tavistock Institute of Human Rela-

tions, based on experimental work by Wilfred Bion. Each group is facilitated by a consultant who remains detached and non-directive. The group's primary task is to study its own behaviour as it occurs, focusing on the nature of group life, and realizing the costs and benefits of working within a group. Without the distraction of an agenda or intellectual inquiry about external concerns, interpersonal issues come to the fore. According to Bion, this setting reveals the group's 'basic assumption', since it sometimes acts as if it has met to find a leader to gratify its members' shared, primitive needs.

Klein, E.B. and Astrachan, B.M. (1971) 'Learning in Groups: A Comparison of Study Groups and T-Groups', *Journal of Applied Behavioural Science*, vol. 7, no. 6, pp. 659–83.

See also: Basic encounter; Cluster laboratory; Cousin laboratory; Encounter group; Gestalt techniques; Group development laboratory; Group dynamics laboratory; Human relations laboratory; Instrumented laboratory; Laboratory training; Mini-society; Micro-lab; Organizational laboratory; Personal development laboratory; Power laboratory; Psychodrama; Team laboratory; Tavistock Conference Method; Transactional Analysis

Study service (experiential education; service learning)

The term 'study service' was originally used by UNESCO to refer to planned excursions or assignments, in which students visited locations in the Third World to contribute their specialist skills to social, community and national development programmes. In the wider sense, it refers to projects and placements which are intended to be educational for participants, but also provide a service to the host organization, region or country. From the participants' point of view, study service provides an opportunity to practise altruism, based on the view that learning can be productive and contribute to others' well-being. It is a form of experiential education, in which students learn by doing, translating their individual and academic knowledge into practical activities. Contending with challenging real-life problems contributes to their own maturation, widens their perspective and promotes the service ethic.

In the UK, students in secondary or higher education may receive academic credits for performing socially valuable work, normally through course projects and field attachments. For example, dental students may visit schools to teach children about dental care, or secretarial students may carry out research projects for a Social

Services Department. In Salford, secondary school students helped to design aids for the physically disabled in a School Concern Project organized jointly by Community Service Volunteers and Salford Council's Education and Social Services Departments. Examples from elsewhere in the world include Ethiopia's University Year of Service (conducted two-thirds of the way through the course), Iran's Army of Education (an alternative to military service) and Nepal's National Development Service. Some nations also operate programmes to provide assistance in other countries, such as the UK's Voluntary Service Overseas and the US Peace Corps.

Dickson, A. (1979) 'Amelioration, Evasion and Concern', *New Universities Quarterly*, Winter.
Dickson, A. (1980) *Study Service: Problems and Opportunities*, UNESCO.
Holman, R. (1971–2) 'Students and Community Activity', *Universities Quarterly*, vol. 26, pp. 187–94.
Whitley, P. (1980) *Study Service in the United Kingdom: Report Presented to the Department of Education and Science by the Community Service Volunteers*, Community Service Volunteers Publications.

See also: Co-operative education; Internship; Teaching as learning

Study skills training

In recent times, growing numbers of mature students have entered open learning programmes such as the Open University's degree courses. Some have no previous experience of self-directed study, whereas others' experience may have been gained a long time ago. To address their needs, study skills training aims to develop their ability to organize and manage their own study programmes, using three general approaches. In the *resource centre approach*, each student works on their own in a location where they have access to multimedia computers, CD-ROMs, books and learning packages on improving study methods. Another approach is to use *group discussion methods*, where the instructor takes groups of students through a series of structured exercises designed to help them organize their study time better, or to develop skills such as writing essays. Finally, in the *individualized approach*, each student learns about study skills at home by means of CD-ROMs, audio tapes or books. In practice, there is a great deal of overlap between these three approaches.

Drew, S. and Bingham, R. (1998) *The Student Skills Guide*, Gower.

Glenn-Cowan, P. (1995) *Improving Your Reading and Study Skills*, Prentice-Hall.
Langan, J. (1994) *Reading and Study Skills*, McGraw-Hill.
Mayon-White, B. (1990) *Study Skills for Managers*, Chapman.
Van Blerkom, D.L. (1996) *College Study Skills*, Wadsworth.
Wood, N.V. (1995) *College Reading and Study Skills*, Harcourt Brace.

See also: Confidence-building training; Resource centre

Studycade

Studycades allow students to gain first-hand experience of a subject they are studying in the classroom. For instance, if the topic is community development, they may sign up for a studycade programme about community development projects in the surrounding area. In preparation, they are given a reading list, then the group meets several times to discuss what members have read and to identify questions for further study. The group then visits the projects, and this is followed by a series of discussions to consolidate the learning.

See also: Educational visit; Field trip; Outdoor training

Sub-grouping

If a group is proving too large to manage or has reached an impasse, dividing it into sub-groups of two to six persons can improve progress by giving every participant an opportunity to be heard and collecting a broad sample of information, ideas and opinions. Each sub-group may discuss the same topic or focus on different areas. Once they have finished their deliberations, the whole group then reconvenes and the sub-groups usually deliver summaries of their views or conclusions, which form the basis for further discussion.

Facilitators often encounter resistance to dividing into sub-groups, but they should persevere as the experience is usually worthwhile. However, they should be aware that this approach sometimes induces competition between the sub-groups, which may or may not be appropriate. The smaller the group, the greater the intensity of interaction within it. The more homogeneous the group, the easier it is for individuals to talk. However, heterogeneous groups are more likely to reveal a wider range of views, and lead to constructive conflict. Including people from different groups to deal with common issues helps them to work collaboratively on such problems. If it is important to form groups of people who like to work together, then the facilitator should allow them to select their own sub-groups. In other circumstances, membership may be decided according to principles such as ensuring representativeness, a mix of talkative and quiet members, or members from different organizational units. If participants are unhappy about the way the sub-groups have been formed, the facilitator should explain the basis for selection.

When the whole group reconvenes to allow the sub-groups to report back, some of the information may be lost or distorted by being passed on at second hand. There are a number of ways to overcome this. For example, each sub-group may be asked to write a summary of its discussion on a large sheet of paper which can be displayed on the wall or flipcharts for everyone to read and discuss. Another variation is to form cross-representative sub-groups, with members drawn from two or more other sub-groups, for the next stage of proceedings.

Fordyce, J.K. and Weil, R. (1971) *Managing With People*, Addison Wesley Longman, pp. 162–4.

See also: Critiquing; Getting acquainted; Going round the room; Non-verbal encounters; Polling; Process consultation; Self-generated scaling

Suggestion schemes (employee suggestion programmes)

Suggestion schemes encourage employees to recommend improvements for their organization. They mostly involve shop-floor staff, but similar programmes may apply to other employees. Employees receive a payment if their idea is accepted, either a fixed sum or a percentage of the money saved by implementing the suggestion. It would be a mistake to consider suggestion schemes old-fashioned, since many high-tech American multinationals use them, often in imaginative ways. For example, Philip Crosby, the consultant associated most closely with quality management programmes, developed the Buck-a-Day Programme to obtain ideas for improvements from employees in an interesting and entertaining way. Each programme has a time limit of five weeks, during which employees are asked to submit job-related ideas that would save $1 per day by eliminating unnecessary expense. In a large company, the potential annual savings are obviously considerable. Crosby reports that these programmes always succeed, with a return of $100 for each $1 invested. Although the savings are important, Crosby argues that the true benefits come in the form of improved communication and morale within the organization.

Although a great deal of money is saved and distributed to employees through these schemes every year, they need to be well organized to avoid a number of pitfalls. They can cause friction and jealousy among colleagues when one of them receives an award. Employees' suggestions may also cause resentment among supervisors and specialized staff, who may perceive them as criticisms of their expertise or efficiency. Individuals who have identified problems may decide to submit their solutions to the suggestion scheme rather than bringing them to light immediately, while many are likely to be reluctant to suggest more efficient production methods if they fear they may lead to redundancies. A major problem is that most schemes rely on written communication, which is more formal than a face-to-face discussion, and may discourage those who lack practice in writing down what may be complex ideas. Once they have submitted a suggestion, employees are seldom invited to develop or help evaluate their idea, and may hear nothing further until they are informed, often by letter, whether or not it has been accepted.

Bassford, R.L. (1996) *Employee Suggestion Systems*, Crisp Publications.

Japan Human Relations Association (eds) (1997) *Kaizen Teian 1: Developing Systems for Continuous Improvement Through Employee Suggestions*, Productivity Press.

Japan Human Relations Association (eds) (1997) *Kaizen Teian 2: Guiding Continuous Improvement Through Employee Suggestions*, Productivity Press.

Wood, A. (1989) *Ideas Unlimited*, Industrial Society.

See also: Brainstorming; Employee-guided management; Participation; Quality circles

Supervisory counselling

Research suggests that skilled supervisors can bring about and sustain positive behaviour changes in employees. One method that has proven successful in reducing employee absenteeism, for instance, is to train supervisors in counselling skills, relying on a behaviour-modelling approach which uses goal-setting and feedback techniques.

Latham, G.P. and Saari, L.M. (1979) 'The Application of Social Learning Theory to Training Supervisors Through Behaviour Modelling', *Journal of Applied Psychology*, vol. 64, pp. 239–6.

Wexley, K.N. and Nemeroff, W.F. (1975) 'Effectiveness of Positive Reinforcement and Goal Setting as Methods of Management Development', *Journal of Applied Psychology*, vol. 60, pp. 446–50.

See also: Coaching; Counselling; Discipline without punishment; Goal-setting; Interaction management; Stress management

Supervisory methods

One way to change the functioning of workgroups is to focus on how their supervisors perform their jobs. Various strategies have been used to achieve this, including training, appraisal, feedback and management by objectives. Most methods try to promote achievement of the organization's goals by ensuring that the supervisor provides the support and guidance necessary for subordinates to work efficiently. In effect, the supervisor channels the organization's implicit and explicit expectations or demands to employees, indicating how they should behave. However, supervisory interventions need not be top-down, and recent programmes have encouraged the participation of subordinates through the use of representative committees, union–management committees and work forums.

Betts, P.W. (1993) *Supervisory Management*, Pitman.
Bittel, L.R. and Newstrom, J.W. (1992) *What Every Supervisor Should Know*, McGraw-Hill.
Canwell, D. and Sutherland, J.(1998) *Essential Supervisory Management*, Butterworth-Heinemann.
Cartwright, R., Collins, M., Green, G. and Candy, A. (1998) *Managing People: A Competence Approach to Supervisory Management*, Blackwell.
Kaiser, T.L. (1996) *Supervisory Relationships*, Brooks/Cole.
Mosely, D., Megginson, L.C. and Pietri, P.H. (1997) *Supervisory Management*, South-Western.

See also: Interaction management; Management by walking around

Surrogate client (live patient simulation; simulated client; programmed client)

This method was originally developed as a medical teaching aid to overcome the shortage of suitable real cases for study, and to allow more flexibility in training without compromising the care of patients. In that context, Barrows defines a surrogate patient as: 'a person who has been trained to simulate a patient or any aspect of a patient's illness depending upon the educational need.' A similar approach has been adopted in some senior management training courses, where specially trained actors portray clients in role-played interviews when a high degree of realism is desirable.

One of the most important aspects of this approach is that, unlike a real-life interview, if the student is unhappy with how the role-play is progressing, they can call 'time out'. During the break, the student may ask the surrogate client to describe their perceptions and feelings, the two can discuss the impasse, and the client may help the student resolve the problem. The pair then resume their roles, and the interview continues. A group discussion follows, during which the student receives feedback from the surrogate client, other students and the instructor. The technique offers a number of advantages, such as increasing students' awareness of the value of open questions, and emphasizing the importance of non-verbal cues in communication.

Medical students taught by this method felt it gave them more confidence when they came to examine patients without supervision, since they were able to rehearse the same doctor–patient interactions repeatedly, and modify their techniques in response to feedback. Moreover, it allowed the instructor to control the variables in the role-play situation.

Barrows, H.S. (1971) *Simulated Patients (Programmed Patients)*, Charles C. Thomas.
Barrows, H.S. (1987) *Simulated (Standardized) Patients and Other Human Simulations*, Health Sciences Consortium.
Barrows, H.S. and Abrahamson, S. (1964) 'Training of Simulated Patients', *Journal of Medical Education*, vol. 39, pp. 802–7.
Jolly, B. (1982) 'A Review of Issues in Live Patient Simulation', *Programmed Learning and Educational Technology*, vol. 19, no. 2, pp. 99–107.
Kowalski, M.S., Coniglione, P.M. and Jaffe, T.C. (1983) *Clinical Simulations for Students of Medicine*, Year Book Medical Publishers.
Ostrow, D.N. (1980) 'Surrogate Patients in Medical Education', *Programmed Learning and Educational Technology*, vol. 17, no. 2, pp. 82–9.

See also: Character immersion; Simulation; Role-playing; Role-reversal; Sociodrama

Survey feedback interventions (survey-guided development)

Survey feedback interventions collect data from individuals, usually by means of anonymous questionnaires, then provide feedback in a variety of ways. Staff from within and outside the organization may collaborate in designing the survey questions, and analysing and interpreting the data. A number of writers recommend a five-step sequence for this process, with the first three steps constituting the survey element of the approach, and the remaining two representing its workshop aspect. First, senior managers take part in the early planning stages. Second, the data is collected from all the relevant organization members. Third, this data is fed back to the senior managers, and then down the hierarchy to the functional departments. Fourth, the heads of each department meet with their staff to discuss the data. During these meetings, the subordinates may be asked to interpret the data, make plans for constructive changes, and decide how to introduce the data to staff at the next level down in the organization. The fifth step is the survey feedback meeting, which is prepared by a consultant who serves as a resource person to the group as a whole. Follow-up action is usually co-ordinated by an external consultant.

Three different survey designs exist, and these are described below in increasing order of effectiveness. In *data handback*, the information collected by the consultant is returned to the client, who takes part in problem-solving. In *action research, data feedback and action planning*, the information is fed back to clients at a problem-solving meeting which sets goals and plans how implement the proposed changes. In *concept training, data feedback and action planning*, the data is collected and fed back within a structured day-long workshop, during which the participants learn about management theories and the concepts behind the survey, and are helped to develop their problem-solving skills.

Bowers, J.L. and Franklin, J. (1977) *Survey Guided Development I: Data Based Organization Change*, Pfeiffer/Jossey-Bass.

Church, A.H., Margiloff, A. and Coruzz1, C. (1995) 'Using Survey Feedback for Change: An Applied Example in a Pharmaceutical Organization', *Leadership and Organization Development Journal*, vol. 16, no. 4, pp. 3–11.

Clardy, A. (1997) *Studying Your Workforce*, Sage.

Edwards, J.E., Thomas, M.D., Rosenfeld, P. and Booth-Kewley, S. (1996) *How To Conduct Organizational Surveys*, Sage.

Franklin, J. (1977) *Survey Guided Development III: A Manual for Concept Training*, Pfeiffer/Jossey-Bass.

Hausser, D.L., (1977) *Survey Guided Development II: A Manual for Consultants*, Pfeiffer/Jossey-Bass.

Kraut, A.I. (ed.) (1996) *Organizational Surveys: Tools for Assessment and Change*, Jossey-Bass.

Nadler, D.A. (1976) 'Use of Feedback for Organizational Change: Promises and Pitfalls', *Group and Organizational Studies*, vol. 1, June, pp. 177–86.

Nadler, D.A. (1977) *Feedback and Organizational Development: Using Data-Based Methods*, Addison Wesley Longman.

Porras, J. (1979) 'Teaching Survey Feedback in the Classroom', *Exchange: The Organizational Behaviour Teaching Journal*, vol. 4, no. 2, pp. 39–40.

Rosenfeld, P. et al. (1993) *Improving Organizational Surveys*, Sage.

Walters, M. (1996) *Building the Responsive Organization: Using Employee Surveys to Manage Change*, Books Britain.

Walters, M. (1997) *Employee Attitude and Opinion Surveys*, Institute of Personnel and Development.

See also: Attitude survey; Instrumentation; Instrumented laboratory; MAPS approach; On-going feedback system; Questionnaires; Self-generated scaling

Symmetrical communication

Symmetrical communication believes that all participants in a learning situation, whether teachers or students, should be equal partners despite their differences in status and knowledge. Establishing symmetrical communication is one of the first stages in setting up a learning community, but the concept also underlies approaches such as experience-based learning, project orientation and confluent education. Rather than taking on the conventional role of expert, the instructor serves as a facilitator, progressively taking on the role of catalyst as an atmosphere of co-operative learning develops. However, the instructor may briefly provide an expert view if the students specifically request it.

The instructor's first task is to initiate interactions with students which prepare the way for a more equal relationship. This can be achieved in a number of ways, such as asking questions more frequently, and maintaining a period of silence after they have been asked to signal that students are expected to participate. Another approach would be to stress the need for all participants to ensure they understand each other's contributions to discussions before responding themselves. This involves more than developing listening skills, since listening and trying to understand each other implies that participants value both the contribution and the person who makes it. Once a symmetrical communication structure has been established, these overt strategies can be abandoned, since participants are likely to be less reluctant to share their thoughts and feelings. In such a climate of partnership, negotiations can take place regarding the learning aims and strategies.

Brandt, D. (1980) 'Notions and Strategies of Staff

Development Programmes', in *Proceedings of the Sixth International Conference on Improving University Teaching*, University of Maryland, Lausanne, 9–12 July.

Werner, B. and Drexler, I. (1978–9) 'Structures of Communication and Interaction in Courses for Junior Staff Members of the Faculties of Engineering, TH Aachen', *Bulletin of Educational Research*, nos 16 and 17.

See also: Confluent education; Experience-based learning; Learning community; Project orientation

Symposium meeting

A symposium is meeting in which an audience listens to formal presentations from two or more platform speakers. In ancient times, symposia were more participative and less formal, with up to twenty people meeting in someone's home to discuss a topic of mutual interest, often over a meal, as in a modern-day working breakfast or lunch. Nowadays, the audience may be very large, as a true symposium does not involve audience participation. The objective of these events is to present a range of viewpoints on a particular subject, and they are particularly useful when the aim is to introduce a new topic or provide food for thought. Each speaker is allotted only a brief time to give their speech, but this usually encourages them to keep to the point, so it is still possible to identify and explore problems quite thoroughly. The chairperson usually opens the meeting with a few introductory remarks, then calls on each speaker in turn to make their contribution, ensuring that they keep to the time limit. The variety of speakers and the shortness of their speeches reduces the risk of boredom, but the main drawback is the lack of audience involvement. It is difficult to check their understanding, and if one speaker is uninteresting or incompetent, it may jaundice their view of the whole event.

Girling, R.K. (1980) 'Industrial Democracy: Teaching by Symposium', *Exchange: The Organizational Behaviour Teaching Journal*, vol. 5, no. 2, pp. 131–3.

See also: Brains Trust; Colloquy meeting; Forum meeting; Panel discussion

Synectics

Synectics (from the Greek *synektikos*, meaning 'fit for holding together'), the study of inventive and imaginative problem-solving processes, is one of the oldest and most highly developed creativity training approaches. It was developed by W.J.J. Gordon, although George Prince was responsible for founding Synectics Inc., which transformed Gordon's theories into a practical technique to harness creativity in solving technical and theoretical problems. Rational thinking tends to be evaluative, staying within known, safe areas where solutions are produced which 'make sense'. In contrast, synectics training aims to release individuals from these constraints, using structured problem-solving techniques to help them arrive at new ideas and solutions by tapping into emotional, irrational aspects of their personality. Some of the training techniques try to change the climate of the work situation to release creative ability that is normally suppressed, and this can often lead to improved communications, better teamwork, more constructive approaches to conflict-resolution and higher morale. By working at the level of individual transactions, synectics develops basic interpersonal skills, and while it was originally developed to help improve creativity and problem-solving abilities, it can be applied to every kind of interaction between people.

Synectics training programmes are delivered in small, heterogeneous, close-knit groups with a facilitator, whose role is to encourage participants to develop their imaginative abilities, to verbalize their thoughts and feelings, and to keep the group moving through each of synectics's six problem-solving steps. It is important that each group includes participants with a wide range of personalities, skills and interests, since this is more likely to lead to new ideas. The first step is to review the problem being addressed. In the second step, participants re-state the problem, reducing it to its essentials. Next, participants draw a direct analogy between the problem's key element and an object or organization in a completely different field. Following this, each develops a personal analogy, identifying with the analogous object. Participants then imagine how this object might feel. They are encouraged to allow intrinsic contradictions in their descriptions of their perceptions and feelings, and to sum up the conflict in a two-word phrase. Finally, the group returns to the problem stated in the second step, applying the insights gained to obtain a new view of it.

Alexander, J. (1979) 'Synectics, Problem-solving and Interpersonal Skills', *BACIE Journal*, vol. 33, no. l, January.

Alexander, J. (1980) 'Synectics', *Training*, vol. 6, no. 7, pp. 20–2.

Gordon, W.J.J. (1970) *Synectics: The Development of Creative Capacity*, Harper and Row.

Osborn, A.F. (1963) *Applied Imagination*, Charles Scribner's Sons.

Prince, G. (1970) *The Practice of Synectics*, Harper and Row.

Rickards, T. and Freedman, B. (1979) 'A

Reappraisal of Creativity Techniques', *Journal of European Industrial Training*, vol. 3, no. 1.

Roukes, N. (1984) *Art Synectics*, Davis Publications.

Roukes, N. (1988) *Design Synectics*, Davis Publications.

'Synectics', *Industrial Training International* (1973), August, pp. 242–50.

See also: Analogy teaching; Brainstorming; Creativity training; Forcing device; Kepner-Tregoe Approach; Lateral thinking; Nominal group technique; Suggestion schemes; Team action management

Synergogy

Synergogy exploits the notion of synergy – the fact that the output of a team is greater than the sum of its parts – in a number of methods which combine teacher-centred with learner-centred instruction. Because learners benefit from direction and structure, these usually include a series of steps and learning instruments for them to complete, emphasizing teamwork, involvement and participation. In the *team effectiveness design*, team members assess their individual knowledge of a topic by completing a multiple-choice test before discussing it as a team. This design is especially useful where the task demands factual learning and deduction of principles. In the *team member teaching design*, each member is responsible for learning an assigned portion of the subject matter, then teaching it to the others. In the *performance judging design*, individual members take responsibility for helping each other to develop specific skills. Finally, the *clarifying attitude design* uses sentence-completion instruments to address attitudes and personal satisfaction.

Mouton, J.S. (1984) *Synergogy*, Jossey-Bass.

Mouton, J.S. and Blake, R.R. (1984) 'Principles and Designs for Enhancing Learning', *Training and Development Journal*, December, pp. 60–3.

See also: Agenda method; Autonomous learning group; Autonomy lab; Community of enquiry; Guided group problem-solving; Independent study; Instrumented feedback; Instrumentation; Instrumented laboratory; Leaderless group discussion; Learning cell; Learning through discussion; Media-activated learning group; Self-directed learning; Study circles; Tape-assisted learning programme; Transactional Analysis

Talk

Abell argues that lectures can serve a number of functions, such as inspiring and stimulating the audience, but they are an inefficient way to transmit information. He adopts the term 'talk' to refer to a lecture whose main aim is not to convey information, and describes a number of variants. The *come with me* talk describes the process a group of researchers followed in making a discovery. Ideas for such talks can be obtained from books on research projects, research papers or conversations with researchers describing how they went about their studies, what clues they followed, and how they felt. Watson's account of the discovery of the structure of DNA in *The Double Helix* would be a good example. In the *glimpses of great people* talk, a well-known lecturer, manager, industrialist or researcher reminisces before a group of listeners. A video can be shown if they are not available in person. The *flavour of the month* talk is a case study or historical vignette about a company or industry which gives an idea of how it is (or was) managed. In a *dialogue, live interview or debate* talk, up to four people exchange views before an audience, which may or may not participate. For example, two instructors may discuss a topic of interest, such as how new technology was introduced. The underlying thinking here is more important than information about the technology itself. In the *paired antithetical* talk, two speakers with opposing viewpoints take it in turns to make their case. The *challenge* talk presents evidence in support of an erroneous view, such as defending the idea that the earth is flat. A variation of this is the *ring lecture*, in which a series of instructors present differing viewpoints on the same topic from week to week. The *lecture-experiment*, in which the speaker performs an experiment in front of an audience, also has a long tradition. The *analysis of news* talk sets the audience the task of reading a broadsheet newspaper such as *The Sunday Times* or *The Financial Times*, and the speaker then analyses and discusses the news. In a *non-manager's look at management* talk, a group of people from outside the world of management (e.g., priests, musicians and artists) form a panel and discuss the state of management. A *programmed talk* is best conducted in a feedback classroom, which has facilities similar to those used to poll the audience in some television programmes. The speaker asks multiple-choice questions, audience members register their responses, and a central console provides immediate feedback to the instructor and students. If there are a large number of incorrect answers, the speaker can follow a branch in the programme to clarify any points that are giving difficulty. In a *concentrated visual experience* talk, slides or a video tape may be shown, either instead of a talk or with a live commentary, followed by a quiz. Finally, a *multi-sensory experience* talk may bombard the audience with stimuli of various types by means of projectors, bioscopes, audio and video tapes and computer-generated images to integrate perception, emotion and different types of subject matter.

Abell, D. (1970) 'On Lecturing Without Really Lecturing, Part 1', *CUEBS News*, vol. 6, no. 3, February, pp. 7–10.

Carl, J. and O'Brien, N. (1970) 'Classroom Debate', *Journal of Geological Education*, vol. 18, p. 122.

Catt, R. and Eke, J. (1995) 'Classroom Talk in Higher Education: Enabling Learning Through Reflective Analysis of Practice', *Innovations in Education and Training International*, vol. 32 no. 4, pp. 362–9.

See also: Confluent education; Debate; Demonstration-performance method; Feedback classroom; Interactive co-teaching; Lecture; Lecture-building; Lesson-demonstration method; Panel discussion; Preaching; Teach teaching

Talking wall

A talking wall is a large-group feedback device which can cater for as many as 60 participants. It can be used in the middle or at the end of a course, seminar or conference to register participants' reactions to the proceedings in an enjoyable way which involves them actively both as initiators and respondents. It allows opinions to be sampled on a wider range of topics than is usually possible during end-of-event discussions, and the results reflect participants' perceptions of the important aspects of the event, rather than the organizers'.

Before the activity begins, the facilitator writes six or so headings relevant to the event being evaluated (e.g. 'Content', 'Learning Approach', 'Facilities', 'Administration', 'Speakers') on separate cards, and each is affixed above a blank flipchart sheet displayed on the wall. All participants are given a pad of self-adhesive notes and asked to write a statement describing any significant feature of the event on each of them (e.g., 'Guest speaker rotten', 'Food excellent', 'Photocopying facilities crummy'). They then stick each note on the flipchart sheet with the most appropriate heading. Once all the participants have placed their notes and read others' contributions, the facilitator invites them to form groups of roughly equal size around each flipchart sheet, and each group removes the notes from their flipchart and sorts them, identifying any recurring themes. Five or six statements may emerge, and each group writes these on a single flipchart sheet, leaving enough room on the right-hand side for columns headed: 'Strongly Agree', 'Agree', 'Neutral', 'Disagree' and 'Strongly Disagree'. The

groups' flipchart questionnaires are then fixed to the wall, and the participants can wander from chart to chart, reading each statement and indicating their degree of agreement by placing a tick in the appropriate column. Once everybody has completed all the sheets, the groups for each heading reassemble briefly to total the responses. A plenary session follows, at which a representative from each group summarizes their results, which serve as the basis for a general discussion.

See also: Delphi technique; Drawing for learning; Fishbowl; Group poster tours; Illuminative incident analysis; Instrumented feedback; Poster; Process analysis

Tape-assisted learning programme

Programmes where groups of up to twelve students are instructed by audio tapes or CDs have been adopted in a variety of contexts. The approach emphasizes group interaction, which is enhanced by the absence of an instructor, and the aims may include developing active listening, team development, problem-solving and decision-making skills. During the session, participants listen to a recording which describes a structured activity. One of them then stops the recording, and the group carries out the activity. Such programmes usually consist of a dozen sessions or more, and the same group may attend every session.

Berzon, B. and Reisel, J. (1976) *Effective Interpersonal Relationships: A Tape Assisted Learning Programme*, Pfeiffer/Jossey-Bass.

Soloman, L.N. and Berzon, B. (1969) *Encounter Tapes for Employee and Team Development*, Pfeiffer/Jossey-Bass.

See also: Audio for learning; Audio tutorial method; Leaderless group discussion; Learning through discussion; Instrumented team learning; Mastery learning; Media-activated learning group; Self-development; Tape-stop exercise; Micro-lab

Tape-stop exercise

Tape-stop exercises are easy to design, and can be used to train staff in aspects of their daily work activities. The instructor plays an audio tape of a conversation between two people, perhaps a salesperson and a customer, an appraiser and an appraisee or an instructor and a student. A typical conversation might run as follows:

Union Rep: My members are dissatisfied

with the way in which Mr Smith has been treated.

Manager: Mr Smith had been warned about his behaviour in the past.

Union Rep: Past warnings don't give you the right to suspend him!

Manager: ...

At this point, the instructor stops the tape, and the trainees must either write down what they would say next if they were in that position, or give their response verbally if the instructor points to them. The instructor may then either discuss the trainees' suggestions, or play back what the manager actually said and compare it to their responses.

See also: Audio for learning; Inter-personal process recall; Tape-assisted learning programme; Trigger film

Task force assignment (task teams)

In a task force assignment, a group of employees tackles a specific problem that would be difficult to solve within the usual organizational structure, often with a strict deadline. There are many different types of task force, and they can be set up whenever the need arises, then disbanded once they have achieved their objective. Members may be drawn from different departments and levels in the hierarchy. The mix of staff should include those who are most immediately affected by the problem, those with authority to do something about it, and those who possess the skills and knowledge necessary to solve it. Within the task force, participants' relationships differ from their normal work roles, and special ground rules apply.

Peters and Waterman identify a number of factors which characterize a successful task force. Membership should be voluntary, and the group should consist of no more than ten members. Members' reporting level and degree of seniority should be proportional to the importance of the problem. In the examples they studied, there was no formal process of objective-setting, and the documentation produced was informal and often minimal.

Frame, J.S. (1995) *Managing Projects in Organizations*, Jossey-Bass.

George, W.W. (1977) 'Task Teams for Rapid Growth', *Harvard Business Review*, March–April, pp. 71–80.

Lippitt, G.L., Langseth, P. and Mossop, J. (1985) *Implementing Organizational Change*, Jossey-Bass, pp. 57–74.

Peters, T.J. and Waterman, R.H. (1982) *In Search of Excellence*, Harper and Row, pp. 127–32.

Randolph, W.A. and Posner, B.Z. (1991) *Getting the Job Done: Managing Project Teams and Task Forces for Success*, Prentice-Hall.

Williams, P.B. (1996) *Getting a Project Done on Time*, American Management Association AMACOM.

See also: Autonomous workgroup; Business teams; Collateral organization; Committee assignment; Consulting assignment; Development assignment; Evaluation assignment; Independent product teams; Management audit; Multiple management; Plural chief executive; Problem-solving groups; Proposal team assignment; Research assignment; Skunkworks; Staff meeting assignment; Study assignment

Tavistock Conference Method (Bion group)

Tavistock Conferences are educational events which have been run by the Tavistock Institute of Human Relations since 1957. In the USA, they are sponsored by the A.K. Rice Institute. These conferences are sometimes wrongly considered a variant of T-group training. However, their objectives, theoretical base and methodology are unique. Grounded in the psychoanalytical theories of Sigmund Freud and the object relations theory of Melanie Klein, the conference model also owes much to Wilfred Bion's therapeutic community approach to the treatment of psychological casualties during the Second World War. Bion found that groups were helpful in treating psychiatric casualties. Despite this tradition, the conferences aim to achieve learning goals, rather than therapeutic ones. About forty participants take part in a series of small-group, institutional, large-group and inter-group events to enable groups to study their own dynamics. The group is held to face a constant choice between emotionality and work, and the method focuses on the different ways this dilemma is resolved in various contexts, examining the concepts of role, task, authority, boundary and leadership.

There are a number of features which distinguish a Tavistock Conference from other forms of organizational laboratory. Authority relationships are an important part of the learning process. The conference staff are called *consultants*. They dress in formal attire, maintain distance in their relationships with group members, and are very punctual in entering and leaving group meetings. They adopt this role in order to contribute to the group's exploration of relationships within itself, intervening only when they feel it would promote learning. Their statements tend to be metaphorical, and they constantly point out how members seem to be relating to them as consultants. They direct their interventions at the group, rather than individuals. Inter-group relationships are also studied through exercises in which sub-groups negotiate with each other to make a decision or carry out a task.

Astrachan, B.M. and Flynn, H.R. (1976) 'The Intergroup Exercise', in Miller, E.J. (ed.) *Task and Organisation*, Wiley.

Bleandonu, G. (1994) *Wilfred Bion: His Life and Works*, Free Association Press.

Higgin, G. and Bridger, H. (1965) *The Psychodynamics of an Intergroup Experience*, Tavistock Institute of Human Relations, Pamphlet No. 10.

Lawrence, W.G. (ed.) (1979) *Exploring Individual and Organizational Boundaries*, Wiley.

Palmer, B.W.M. (1979) 'The Study of a Small Group in an Organizational Setting', in Babington-Smith, B. and Farrell, B.A. (eds) *Training in Small Groups*, Pergamon.

Symington, J. (1996) *Critical Thinking of Wilfred Bion*, Routledge.

Rice, A.K. (1965) *Learning for Leadership*, Tavistock.

'The Tavistock Institute: Past, Present and Future', special issue of *Human Relations* (1998), vol. 51.

Trist, E.L. and Sofer, C. (1959) *Explorations in Group Relations*, Leicester University Press.

See also: Application discussion group; Basic encounter; Cluster laboratory; Cousin laboratory; Encounter group; Gestalt techniques; Group development laboratory; Group dynamics laboratory; Human relations laboratory; Instrumented laboratory; Laboratory training; Mini-society; Organizational laboratory; Personal development laboratory; Power laboratory; Psychodrama; Sensitivity (T-group) training; Socio-technical systems design; Study group; Team laboratory

Teaching as learning (cross-age tutoring; inter-grade tutoring; peer instruction; youth tutoring; youth, each one teach one)

There is a long tradition of students teaching other students, but this entry will focus on situations in which final-year university students teach younger ones. This approach is based on the theory that students find it easier to learn from those who resemble them in age, experience, general outlook and culture. Conventional tutors are more likely to convey their own preferences and prejudices towards the material being taught, and their behaviour is often constrained by students' expectations of their role. Furthermore, students benefit from the individual attention that student-teachers can provide, in contrast to the normal high staff:student ratio.

In one example of a study service scheme, honours degree students in engineering at London University were given a choice of two projects: they could explore technical questions which were complicated by social, political and economic issues, or they could study social problems which engineers might be able to help to remedy. Twelve students chose to visit a comprehensive school in Pimlico for fifteen weeks during one academic year, to assist in teaching science, their project consisting of evaluating the quality of the tutoring provided. A variety of approaches could have been adopted, ranging from peer teaching (in which pairs of students learn co-operatively) via cross-age, cross-class tutoring (which involves regular meetings between older/abler pupils and younger/less able ones) to monitorial instruction (whereby older students move around a class, assisting where necessary). The student-tutors' experiences and preferences led them to choose a team tutoring approach, where teams of three to five undergraduates moved around the classroom as required, helping individuals or groups under the supervision and direction of the classroom teacher. They were prepared for the project by means of a one-day training session, using video, brainstorming problems and role-playing. The materials they used varied widely, and some were highly structured, relying on programmed texts, textbooks and worksheets. The student-tutors' work included discussing experiments with pupils, answering their queries and posing supplementary questions. As a result, the student-tutors reported that they developed their abilities to communicate scientific ideas in simple terms, and they appreciated the opportunity to get to know pupils from different social backgrounds. Secondary benefits included discovering how others perceived their subject, and a sense that they were doing something useful with their knowledge.

Goodlad, S. (1979) *Learning by Teaching: An Introduction to Tutoring*, Community Service Volunteers.

Goodlad, S. (ed.) (1985) *Study Science: An Examination of Community Service as a Method of Study in Higher Education*, NFER-Nelson.

Goodlad, S. (ed.) (1995) *Students as Tutors and Mentors*, Kogan Page.

Goodlad, S. (1997) *Mentoring and Tutoring by Students*, Kogan Page.

Goodlad, S. (1998) *Museum Volunteers: Good Practice in the Management of Volunteers*, Routledge.

Goodlad, S., Abidi, A., Anslow, P. and Harris, J. (1979) 'The Pimlico Connection: Undergraduates As Tutors in Schools', *Studies in Higher Education*, vol. 4, no. 2, pp. 191–201.

See also: Co-operative learning; Co-op/co-op; Course design as learning; Field project/attachment; Parrainage; Peer teaching; Proctor method; Project orientation; Short talks by students; Study service

Teaching by explaining

It is tempting to regard explanation as a one-way process. However, although the teacher makes the initial effort to convey information, it is important to realize that the process is not complete until learners have linked it to their prior knowledge to arrive at a coherent understanding of the topic. 'Spoon-feeding' students, providing not only facts but also conclusions, is unlikely to promote learning. The effective use of explanation in teaching involves organizing and presenting information in a way that allows learners to participate in the learning process. Providing a complete explanation may sometimes be necessary (e.g., if learners lack the time to discover it for themselves), but it should be a last resort.

The following guidance may be useful in deciding how to explain something. The significant relationships between the facts, situations and activities being presented should be organized into a framework so that the learners can appreciate the context. The explanation should convey the general types of relationships which exist between the items of information and the learners' prior knowledge, to encourage them to discover the links for themselves.

Brown, G. (1982) *Lecturing and Explaining*, Methuen.
Brown, G. (1990) *Effective Teaching and Learning in Higher Education*, Routledge.

See also: Argumentation; Case study method; Discovery method; Teaching by narration

Teaching by narration (teaching by description)

Teaching by description is a method frequently used by managers who act as visiting speakers on university courses. Providing a coherent description of an object, situation or process presents its own difficulties, since the speaker must gauge the audience's level of knowledge, decide where to begin, and judge what degree of detail to include. Narration is in some ways easier, since the element of storytelling involved in recounting a series of events allows greater freedom while providing an overall structure. However, providing a vivid, stimulating, ordered narrative which encourages students to use their imaginations to relive the experiences being recounted demands a high degree of skill and preparation. Speakers must tailor their delivery style to the particular audience and subject matter. They should ensure that they always have a clear idea of the next stage in their story, to avoid rambling or losing the thread. Finally, they need to be sensitive to the audience's reaction, maintaining interest by introducing a sense of suspense, drama or humour on occasions.

Brunner, D.D. (1994) *Inquiry and Reflection: Framing Narrative Practice in Education*, State University of New York Press.
McEwan, H. and Egan, K. (eds) (1995) *Narration in Teaching, Learning and Research*, Teachers College Press.
Roe, E. (1994) *Narrative Policy Analysis: Theory and Practice*, Duke University Press.
Wanner, S.Y. (1994) *On With the Story: Adolescents Learning Through Narrative*, Boyton/Cook.
Witherell, C. and Noddings, N. (eds) (1991) *Stories Lives Tell: Narrative and Dialogue in Education*, Teachers College Press.

See also: Case student telling; Discovery method; Metaphor approach; Playing for learning; Reading aloud; Storytelling; Teaching by explaining

Teaching outside your field

Teaching a subject that falls outside an instructor's normal field can lead to a number of benefits. Coming to terms with an unfamiliar topic can give the instructor insights into the difficulties students are likely to face, and the fact that they are not an acknowledged expert in the field may lead to the development of a more co-operative atmosphere, with the instructor and students forming a learning partnership to explore problems. Whereas an established instructor is likely to favour certain texts or methods, a new instructor is likely to introduce fresh approaches to the subject. The stimulus of discovering new material and finding creative ways to teach it may revitalize the instructor, and this can also benefit the educational institution, since greater interaction across traditional departmental lines may lead to new lines of research and inter-disciplinary interests. However, if the subject is too far removed from the instructor's skills or interests the arrangement is likely to be counterproductive, so the approach is best limited to introductory courses.

Loper, M. and Armor, T. (1978) 'Teaching

Outside Your Field', *Management Education and Development*, vol. 9, no. 3, pp. 197–201.

Stoddart, J. (1975) 'Advance Needed in Business Education', *Higher Education Review*, vol. 7, no. 3.

See also: Interactive co-teaching; Team teaching

Team action leadership

To many managers, the word 'team' refers to the group of individuals on the company board responsible for strategic decisions, or to a functional team, as is found in the sales or the production department. Such groupings reflect the formal hierarchical structure of the organization, and are usually fairly static. However, there is an increasing tendency nowadays to form temporary teams whose membership is based not on the individuals' position or status in the organization, but on their skills or expertise. Team action leadership is one of several approaches which enable the creation of more flexible temporary structures to complement the traditional ones by responding to change and the problems associated with it. For instance, in the USA, 3M introduces over a hundred new products every year by creating a large number of ad hoc teams to develop ideas and market them quickly. Indeed, some individuals find themselves participating in a number of these venture teams simultaneously. Effective team working can be enhanced through team-building and group dynamics interventions. In team-building, a consultant works with the whole team in order to diagnose its working methods and processes, and assess how these affect its performance. Group dynamics approaches usually rely on structured exercises whose aims include assessing how the group influences the individual.

Hastings, C. (1983) 'Team Action Leadership', *Industrial and Commercial Training*, March, pp. 86–9.

Hastings, C., Bixby, P. and Chaudhry-Lawton, R. (1986) *The Superteam Solution: Successful Team Working in Organizations*, Gower.

See also: Autonomous workgroups; Business teams; Collateral organization; Independent product teams; Intrapreneurial group; Matrix designs; Skunkworks

Team appraisal (peer appraisal; colleague appraisal)

Team appraisal involves employees evaluating the performance of other members of their team in order to improve the functioning of both individuals and the team as a whole. The approach can be divided into three stages. The first stage consists of preparation. Each team member writes their own appraisal based on agreed, open-ended questions. They then forward their self-appraisal forms to the team leader, to serve as the basis for an individual performance review meeting. The meeting gives each appraisee the opportunity to discuss the issues raised, and the leader adds their own comments to the appraisee's. In stage two, a consultant develops a straightforward appraisal form which consists of open-ended questions. This is submitted for the team's approval, and it draws up guidelines and procedures for the team appraisal meeting. The third stage consists of the team meeting itself, which takes place away from the workplace in order to avoid interruptions. Team members take it in turns to chair their own appraisal discussion, with advice from the consultant. The team leader is responsible for time-keeping and ensuring that members adhere to the guidelines. The chairperson first delivers a brief summary of their initial self-appraisal document, then the others follow suit. The subsequent discussion focuses on how that team member has helped or hindered others in achieving team objectives, and vice versa, and what action can be taken to remedy any problems. Up to 45 minutes may be allowed for the discussion of any individual's performance, which is usually long enough to ensure a fair hearing, but each chairperson may conclude their section of the meeting at any time by saying that they want to move on to discuss the work of someone else. The team leader takes notes throughout, and is responsible for producing a report of the outcomes.

Abelson, M.A. and Babcock, J.A. (1985–6) 'Peer Evaluation Within Group Projects: A Suggested Mechanism and Process', *Organizational Behaviour Teaching Review*, vol. 10, no. 4, pp. 98–100.

Cederblom, D. and Lounsbury, J.W. (1980) 'An Investigation of User Acceptance of Peer Evaluation', *Personnel Psychology*, vol. 33, no. 3, pp. 567–79.

Cheng, W. and Warren, M. (1997) 'Having Second Thoughts: Student Perceptions Before and After a Peer Assessment Exercise', *Studies in Higher Education*, vol. 22, no. 2, pp. 233–9.

Falchokov, N. (1995) 'Peer Feedback Marking: Developing Peer Assessment', *Innovations in Education and Training International*, vol. 32, no. 2, pp. 175–87.

Ferris, W.P. and Hess, P.W. (1984–5) 'Peer Evaluation of Student Interaction in Organizational Behaviour and Other Courses', *Organizational Behaviour Teaching Review*, vol. 9, no. 4, pp. 74–9.

French, W. and Hollmann, R. (1975) 'Management by Objectives: The Team Approach', *California Management Review*, vol. 17, Spring, pp. 13–22.

Goedebeguure, L.C.J., (1990) *Peer Review and Performance Indicators*, Lemma BV, Netherlands.

Kane, J.S. and Lawler, E.E. (1978) 'Methods for Peer Assessment', *Psychological Bulletin*, vol. 85, pp. 555–86.

Margerison, C. (1983) 'Team Appraisal', *Leadership and Organization Journal*, vol. 4, no. 2, pp. 3–7.

Mowl, G. and Pain, R. (1995) 'Using Self and Peer Assessment to Improve Students' Essay Writing: A Case Study from Geography', *Innovations in Education and Training International*, vol. 32, no. 4, pp. 324–35.

Murrell, K. L. (1984–5) 'Peer Performance Evaluation: When Peers Do It, They Do It Better', *Organizational Behaviour Teaching Review*, vol. 9, no. 4, pp. 83–5.

Pond, K., Ul-Haq, R. and Wade, W. (1995) 'Peer Review: A Precursor to Peer Assessment', *Innovations in Education and Training International*, vol. 32, no. 4, pp. 314–24.

Stefani, L.A. (1994) 'Peer, Self and Tutor Assessment: Relative Reliabilities', *Studies in Higher Education*, vol. 19, no. 1, pp. 69–75.

Watling, B. (1995) *The Appraisal Checklist*, Pitman.

Wisker, G. (1994) 'Assessment: Peer Group and Oral Assessment', *Education and Training Technology International*, vol. 31, no. 2, pp. 104–14.

See also: Appraisal; Assessment centre; Goal-setting; Management by objectives; Measuring performance; Periodic planning conference; Positive feedback; Role-prescription; Self- with peer appraisal

Team briefing (briefing groups; group briefing)

Management has a responsibility to communicate information to employees, to listen to their views, and to act positively in response. Recognizing this, a number of organizations hold regular team briefings for individual work units, enabling shop-floor workers to have a say in decisions such as the layout of the factory, for example. This approach aims to establish a reliable communication network which passes information not only downwards, but also upwards. The network relies on managers, and is designed to support and reinforce their role. Senior management first briefs the departmental heads, who then brief their junior managers, who in turn brief the supervisors below them, who then brief their own teams.

Barker, R.T. and Hall, B.S. (1995) 'Using Business Briefing to Develop Oral Communication Skills', *Journal of Management Education*, vol. 19, no. 4, pp. 513–18.

McGeough, P. (1995) *Team Briefing*, The Industrial Society.

Wintour, P. (1990) *A Briefer's Guide to Team Briefing*, The Industrial Society.

See also: Case student telling; Chairman's forum; Employee letters; Information-sharing meetings; Management information meeting; Open book management; Open forums; Organizational citizenship

Team development (team training)

Teams can be developed by encouraging their members to judge how well they work together, and plan changes to improve their effectiveness. A team may be a *work family* (a manager and immediate subordinates), a *peer group* (a team of managers at the same level of seniority heading different departments) or a *project team* (a group brought together for a limited time or a specific purpose). A range of interventions exist which address issues such as setting group goals, evaluating team working processes and examining the relationships between team members, including some forms of laboratory training.

Cunningham, I. (1994) 'Against Team Building', *Organisations and People*, vol. 1, no. 1, pp. 13–15.

Hardingham, A. (1997) *Working in Teams*, Institute of Personnel and Development.

Harshman, C. (1995) *Team Training: From Startup to High Performance*, McGraw-Hill.

Kinlaw, D. (1998) *Superior Teams*, Gower.

Redman, W. (1996) *Facilitator Skills for Team Development*, Kogan Page.

Silberman, M. (ed.) (1998) *Team and Organizational Development Sourcebook*, McGraw-Hill.

Syer, J. and Connelly, C. (1996) *How Teamwork Works: The Dynamics of Effective Team Development*, McGraw-Hill.

See also: Coverdale training; Grid training; Illuminative incident analysis; Role-prescription; Tavistock Conference Method; Team laboratory

Team laboratory (organizational development group)

One way to examine or improve the functioning of a team is to use a laboratory designed to identify and clarify problems and help members to solve them. Such laboratories offer immediate benefits by refining the group's current operating procedures, but they also have a longer-term value, since they develop members' abilities to deal with similar problems if they arise in the future.

Kuriloff, A.H. and Atkins, S. (1966) 'T-group for Work Teams', *Journal of Applied Behavioural Science*, vol. 2, no. 1, pp. 63–93.

Margulies, N. and Wallace, J. (1973) *Organizational Change: Techniques and Applications*, Scott Foresman, p. 71.

Smith, P.B. (1980) *Group Processes and Personal Change*, Harper and Row.

See also: Cluster laboratory; Cousin laboratory; Encounter groups; Gestalt techniques; Grid training; Group development laboratory; Group dynamics laboratory; Human relations laboratory; Illuminative incident analysis; Instrumented laboratory; Laboratory method; Micro-lab; Mini-society; Organizational laboratory; Personal development laboratory; Power laboratory; Sensitivity (T-group) training; Tavistock Conference Method; Team development; Transactional Analysis

Team learning

The principle of forming individuals into teams to undertake learning tasks is well established, and the approach has grown in popularity to address the problems resulting from the growth in class sizes in higher education. Team learning relies on establishing permanent, heterogeneous student teams of six or seven members each. Members are chosen on the basis of the contribution they can make to the team, taking into account the creative and supportive nature of team working. Unlike more traditional approaches, team learning is not simply a means of following up lectures, but relies on a specific sequence of activities: individual exam, group discussion and exam, instructor input, then an application-oriented session. This sequence places primary responsibility for learning the basic material on the individual, then on the team and instructor. It provides immediate feedback, serves as a context for peer teaching, and enables the instructor to identify which areas require further attention. The method provides teams with information about their members' levels of preparation, and ensures that all students acquire a working knowledge of course concepts before progressing to application-oriented activities, projects or examinations.

Abbot, J.E. (1998) *Quality Team Learning for Schools*, American Society for Quality.

Glacel, B.P. and Emile, A.R. (1996) *Light Bulbs for Leaders: A Guidebook for Team Learning*, Wiley.

Michaelson, L.K. (1983) 'Team Learning in Large Classes', in Bouton, C. and Garth, R.Y. (eds) *Learning in Groups*, Jossey-Bass.

Michaelson, L.K. et al. (1982) 'Team Learning: A Potential Solution to the Problems of Large Classes', *Exchange: The Organizational Behaviour Teaching Journal*, vol. 7, no. 1, pp. 13–22.

Thiagarajan, S. (1995) *Each Teach: Harnessing the Power of Team Learning*, Human Resource Development Press.

Thiagarajan, S. (1996) *Learning Team: Critical Component in Learning Organization*, Human Resource Development Press.

Vennix, J.A.M. (1996) *Group Model Building: Facilitating Team Learning Processes Using System Dynamics*, Wiley.

See also: Guided design approach; Process analysis; Programmed simulation; Synergogy; Team role training

Team learning with informative testing

Informative tests are learning and assessment activities which aim to give each student the benefit of having their own tutor. Ideally, instructors would be able to give each student individualized instruction and feedback, but economic considerations mean it is more likely for teaching to occur in groups of 30 or more. Team learning with informative testing represents a move away from traditional teaching methods and allows personalized teaching within those constraints. It does this by incorporating standard means of teaching, learning and assessment into a sequence of six steps: individual study, individual exam, group exam with immediate marking, preparation of appeals, corrective instructor input, and application-oriented projects or activities.

The *individual study*, *individual exam* and *corrective instructor input* elements ensure that each student gains an adequate understanding of the topic being studied. In the *group exam with immediate marking* step, team members who gave the correct answer to a certain question act as tutors to those who did not, explaining how they arrived at the answer, and identifying where the other student went wrong. This allows those being tutored to receive individualized corrective instruction, while the tutors benefit from learning by teaching. Since team members will usually have given both correct and incorrect answers, they take it in turn to play the two roles. All team members may have given an incorrect answer to certain questions, in which case *preparation of appeals* may enable the team to provide its own corrective instruction. In preparing their appeals, group members re-examine their assigned readings, and use their colleagues as a resource. With the entire group reviewing the reference material, it is likely that many of the errors will have been identified and remedied before *corrective instructor input* is necessary. The final step, *application-oriented projects or activities* involves students working on an undertaking which applies the learning while helping them function as an effective team.

Michaelson, L.K. et al. (1982) 'Team Learning: A Potential Solution to the Problem of Large Classes', *Exchange: The Organizational Behaviour Teaching Journal*, vol. 7, no. 1, pp. 13–22.

Michaelson, L.K. Watson, W.E. and Shrader, C.B. (1984–5) 'Informative Testing: A Practical Approach to Tutoring with Groups', *Organizational Behaviour Teaching Review*, vol. 9, no. 4, pp. 18–33.

Slavin, R.E. and Karweit, N.L. (1981) 'Cognitive and Affective Outcomes of an Intensive Student Team Learning Experience', *Journal of Experimental Education*, vol. 50. no. 1, pp. 29–35.

See also: Audio tutorial method; Autonomous learning group; Guided design approach; Guided group problem-solving; Handout; Mastery learning; Personal system of instruction; Proctor method; Programmed learning; Synergogy; Tutorial-tape-document learning package approach

Team mapping

Team mapping helps managers to understand their own and their team members' work preferences, motivations and relationship styles, enabling them to select and develop teams which have the appropriate balance of abilities, skills and personal attributes. The model was developed from the Margerison-McCann Team Management Index, which is based on Carl Gustav Jung's theory of psychological types. It addresses a number of issues, including how managers establish relationships, gather information and use data, and how they allocate their time and priorities. Margerison and McCann define nine roles that team members can fulfil: Creator-Innovator, Explorer-Promoter, Assessor-Developer, Thruster-Organizer, Concluder-Producer, Controller-Inspector, Upholder-Maintainer, Reporter-Adviser and Linker. Their Team Leadership Wheel relates these roles to two dimensions: an exploring–controlling axis, and an advising–organizing axis. The resulting team map describes which of the roles team members prefer to adopt. Most people have two or three roles they strongly prefer to play, and a number of secondary ones. The information can be useful in drawing up job descriptions, recruiting and selecting staff,

building teams and task forces, and determining training and counselling needs.

Margerison, C. and Lewis, R. (1981) 'Mapping Managerial Styles', *International Journal of Manpower*, vol. 2, no. 1, pp. 2–24.

Margerison, C. and McCann, D. (1984) 'Team Mapping: A New Approach to Managerial Leadership', *Journal of European Industrial Training*, vol. 8, no. 1, pp. 12–16.

Rushmer, R.K. (1996) 'Is Belbin's Shaper Really TMS's Thruster-Organizer? An Empirical Investigation into the Correspondence Between the Belbin and the TMS Team Role Models', *Leadership and Organization Development Journal*, vol. 17, no. 1, pp. 20–6.

See also: Functional role analysis; Interaction influence analysis; Role analysis technique; Role-prescription; Team role training

Team role training

A great deal of work in organizations is carried out through team effort: technical change projects, marketing task forces and appointments committees are just a few examples. The composition of such teams is crucial, since there is no guarantee that members will always work well together and succeed in their task. Team role training is based on the research of R. Meredith Belbin, who suggests that successful teams consist of members who play nine key roles: Co-ordinator, Shaper, Plant, Implementer, Resource Investigator, Monitor-Evaluator, Team Worker, Completer-Finisher and Specialist. This does not mean that every team must have nine members (indeed Belbin favoured teams of four), but that some members may need to take on multiple roles. Team role training enables team members to identify which roles they naturally play and which ones the team lacks, so that the gaps can be filled.

Co-ordinators like organizing people, co-ordinating their activities, mapping their strengths and using them productively. They try to achieve consensus between competing interest groups, making sure everyone has their say. *Shapers* are behind-the-scene facilitators who like to influence group decisions and make their mark in meetings covertly. They are willing to risk unpopularity to get their ideas across. *Plants* are the group's innovators. They are original, independent, imaginative individuals and, although they can sometimes disrupt the team, they can provide new approaches, ideas and strategies. *Implementers* need clear objectives, procedures and direction. They may be uncomfortable with new ideas, but they are solid team members who can turn concepts and ideas into practical working procedures.

Resource Investigators work at the team's boundary, using their networks of personal contacts to bring in people and ideas from outside. *Monitor-Evaluators* take nothing for granted. Often slow and critical, they thoroughly evaluate any new concepts or proposals put forward by the team, placing judgement before feelings. *Team Workers* like to nurture the team and its members. They like people and find it easy to work with them, even when they express ideas with which they disagree. *Completer-Finishers* are highly practical, focusing on meeting targets and deadlines, and can bring the group task to a successful completion. They are perfectionists who notice any mistakes or omissions. *Specialists* provide the team with the information it needs at any point, and are proud of their technical skills and specialized knowledge.

Belbin, R.M. (1991) *Management Teams: Why They Succeed or Fail*, Butterworth-Heinemann.

Belbin, R.M. (1995) *Teams Roles at Work*, Butterworth-Heinemann.

Furnham, A., Steele, H. and Pendleton, D. (1993) 'A Psychometric Assessment of the Belbin Team Role Self-perception Inventory', *Journal of Occupational and Organizational Psychology*, vol. 66, pp. 245–61.

Manning, T. (1997) 'Using Team Role Theory in Management Development', *Organisations and People*, vol. 4, no. 4, pp. 4–10.

McCrimmon, M. (1995) 'Teams Without Roles: Empowering Teams for Greater Creativity', *Journal of Management Development*, vol. 14, no. 6, pp. 35–61.

Parkinson, R. (1995) 'Belbin's Team Role Model: A Silk Purse from a Sow's Ear?', *Organisations and People*, vol. 2, no. 1, pp. 22–5.

Rushmer, R.K. (1996) 'Is Belbin's Shaper Really TMS's Thruster-Organizer? An Empirical Investigation into the Correspondence Between the Belbin and the TMS Team Role Models', *Leadership and Organization Development Journal*, vol. 17, no. 1, pp. 20–6.

Senior, B. (1997) 'Team Roles and Team Performance: Is There Really a Link?', *Journal of Occupational and Organizational Psychology*, vol. 70, pp. 241–58.

See also: Action profiling; Functional role analysis; Interaction influence analysis; Process analysis; Role analysis technique; Role-prescription; Team learning; Team mapping

Team teaching

Team teaching attempts to introduce inter-disciplinary approaches to management education in order to overcome compartmentalization. The term is sometimes used loosely to include interactive co-teaching, where two or more instructors teach a class at the same time. However, this entry deals with situations where two or three instructors from different disciplines take it in turns to teach the same class in successive sessions. The approach has the potential to offer students a greater depth of learning, and the instructors can also benefit by gaining a broader understanding of management problems. However, they must have a good grasp of their own discipline, develop a mutual respect and understanding, and enjoy this mode of teaching. While the team collaborates on the course as a whole, each instructor may choose to hold their own seminars or set and mark their own assignments, the approach's flexibility leading to different types of learning experiences for the students.

Although it is widely used, the approach is not without difficulties. In the initial stages, these may include conflict between instructors over the choice of course material on the one hand, or reluctance to voice disagreements on the other. Preparing the materials and co-ordinating the team members' efforts may be time-consuming, and problems can also arise from inter-personal friction and issues of status. There is also a danger that the need to encompass the instructors' differing views and disciplinary approaches may confuse students and over-complicate the course.

Brumby, S. and Wada, M. (1992) *Team Teaching*, Addison Wesley Longman.

Davis, J.R. (1995) *Interdisciplinary Course and Team Teaching*, Oryx Press.

Easterby-Smith, M. and Olve, N-G. (1984) 'Team Teaching: Making Management Education More Student Centred', *Management Education and Development*, vol. 15, no. 3, pp. 221–36.

Flanagan, M.F. and Ralston, D.A. (1983) 'Intraco-ordinated Team Teaching: Benefits for Both Students and Instructors', *Teaching of Psychology*, vol. 10, no. 2, pp. 116–17.

Frey, J.D. and Nowaczyk, R.H. (1982) 'Combining Research Interests with the Teaching of Undergraduates: A Report on a Team Taught Seminar', *Teaching of Psychology*, vol. 9, no. 4, pp. 220–1.

Fukami, C.V. et al. (1996) 'The Road Less Travelled: The Joys and Sorrows of Team Teaching', *Journal of Management Education*, vol. 20, no. 3, pp. 409–61.

Hanlowski, G., Moyer, S. and Wagner, H. (1968) *Why Team Teaching?*, Charles E. Merrill Publishers.

Lafanci, H. (1970) *Team Teaching at College Level*, Pergamon.

Pitfield, M. and Rees, F.M. (1972) 'Team Teaching: Can It Aid the Integration of Management Education?', *Management Educa-*

tion and Development, vol. 3, no. 2, pp. 98–106.

Pitts, S., Graves, K., Finney, M. and McAllister, B. (1995) *Team Tactics: Innovative Strategies for Teaching and Learning*, J. Western Walch Publisher.

Young, M.B. and Kram, K.E. (1996) 'Repairing the Disconnects in Faculty Team Teaching', *Journal of Management Education*, vol. 20, no. 4, pp. 500–5.

See also: Interactive co-teaching; Talk; Teaching outside your field

Team-based organizations

This organizational structure has its origins in the pioneering research of Tom Burns and Graham Stalker in the 1950s. These authors contrasted the rigid, bureaucratic types of organization structure, which they termed *mechanistic*, with more flexible, responsive designs, which they labelled *organic*. Since then, business school academics have adopted a number of approaches to create sustainable alternative designs to the predominant bureaucratic ones, one of which involves using teams rather than roles as the building blocks for the new structures.

Erb, T.O. and Doda, N.M. (1989) *Team Organization: Promise, Practice and Possibilities*, National Educational Association.

Hansen, D.G. (1997) 'Worker Performance and Group Incentives: A Case Study', *Industrial and Labour Relations Review*, vol. 51, no. 1, pp. 37–49.

Institute of Personnel Management (1997) *IPD Guide to Team Reward*, IPD.

Mears, P. (1994) *Organization Teams: Building Continuous Quality Improvement*, American Society for Training and Development, ASTD Press.

Mohrman, S.A., Cohen, S.G. and Mohrman Jnr, A.M. (1995) *Designing a Team Based Organizations: New Forms for Knowledge Work*, Jossey-Bass.

Mohrman, S.A., Mohrman, A.M., Mohrman Jnr, A.M. and Crocker, C. (1997) *Designing and Leading Team Based Organizations: A Leader's/Facilitator's Guide*, Jossey-Bass.

Mohrman, S.A., Mohrman, A.M., Mohrman Jnr, A.M. and Crocker, C. (1997) *Designing and Leading Team Based Organizations: A Workbook for Organizational Re-design*, Jossey-Bass.

Searle, D. (1979) 'Team Organization in a Construction Firm', in Guest, D. and Knight, K. (eds) *Putting Participation into Practice*, Gower, pp. 114–36.

Sherriton, J. and Stern, J.L. (1996) *Corporate Culture/Team Culture: Removing the Hidden Barrier*, AMACOM.

Stewart, R. (ed.) (1999) *Gower Handbook of Team Working*, Gower.

Zigon, J. (1998) 'Team Performance Measurement', *Association for Quality and Participation*, vol. 21, no. 3, May–June, pp. 48–54.

See also: Family group team-building meeting; Human relations laboratory; Inter-group team-building; Team appraisal; Team laboratory

Team-building activities (team development; internal team development)

Organizational interventions to enhance the functioning of teams may focus on task issues (the way things are done, and the skills needed to accomplish tasks) or on the nature and quality of relationships between team members. Different approaches may be adopted depending on the situation. With a newly established team, team-building involves members developing a common framework and common goals. In the case of existing teams, they can be strengthened by reviewing the recent past, identifying strengths and weaknesses, and developing action plans accordingly.

Although each team-building approach differs, all share certain characteristics, consist of similar stages, and generally aim to improve communication, reduce conflict and improve productivity. The first step is usually to gain top management's commitment to the project, then that of the supervisors. The next step involves holding workshops for teams throughout the organization, identifying problems in team working and helping members understand each other's difficulties. Finally, follow-up meetings are scheduled to help to maintain the momentum of change. The teams may be formal workgroups, committees, temporary task forces or social groups. A wide range of activities may be employed, but such workshops usually include feedback of data, problem-diagnosis and prioritization, and drawing up plans to address the issues identified.

Berger, M. (ed.) (1996) *Cross Cultural Team Building*, McGraw-Hill.

Clark, N. (1994) *Team Building: A Practical Guide for Trainers*, McGraw-Hill.

Coulson-Thomas, C. (1993) *Developing Directors: Building an Effective Boardroom Team*, McGraw-Hill.

Dyer, W.G. (1995) *Team Building: Current Issues and New Alternatives*, Addison Wesley Longman.

Eales-White, R. (1997) *Building Your Team*, Kogan Page.

Fraser, A. and Neville, S. (1993) *Team Building*, The Industrial Society.

Harrison-Mackin, D. (1996) *Keeping the Team Going*, AMACOM.

Kinlaw, D. (1998) *Superior Teams*, Gower.

Moxon, P. (1998) *Building Better Teams*, Gower.

Owen, H. (1995) *Creating Top Flight Teams*, Kogan Page.

Plotkin, H.M. (1997) *Building a Winning Team*, Griffin Publications.

See also: Family group team-building meeting; Human relations laboratory; Inter-group team-building; Process consultation; Team appraisal; Team laboratory

Techno-structural approaches (technical interventions)

Techno-structural approaches draw on the fields of engineering, sociology, psychology, economics and open systems theory to develop interventions which take into account not only an organization's technology (its task methods and processes), but also its structure (relationships and role arrangements within it). Cummings and Worley include formal structure change, differentiation and integration projects, and parallel learning structures in this class of interventions, which may involve redesigning equipment, facilities, work flows or information-processing methods.

Techno-structural approaches can also incorporate socio-technical systems perspectives, job redesign, job enrichment and job enlargement strategies, but these are easier to differentiate in theory than in practice. Socio-technical system designs are a reaction to, and emerge from, scientific management and industrial engineering. They focus on workers' physical environment and physiological requirements. Proponents of socio-technical systems and job design criticize the physical approach for treating social groups and individuals mechanistically, and the psychological approach for either ignoring the organization's technology, or treating it as unchangeable. A further criticism of both approaches is that they treat the organization as a closed system, dealing with inter-organizational issues in a piecemeal fashion while ignoring the important links between an organization and its environment.

Cummings, T.G. and Worley, C.G. (1997) *Organizational Development and Change*, South-Western.

Kilmann, R.H. (1996) 'Designing Collateral Organizations', in Starkey, K. (ed.) *How Organizations Learn*, Routledge, pp 182–98.

Mohrman, S.A. and Cummings, T.G. (1989) *Self-designing Organizations: Learning How to Create High Performance Organizations*, Addison Wesley Longman.

Rubinstein, D. and Woodman, R.W. (1984) 'Spiderman and the Burma Raiders: Collateral Organization in Action', *Journal of Applied Behavioural Science*, vol. 20, no. 3, pp. 1–21.

Stein, B.A. and Kanter, R.M. (1980) 'Building the Parallel Organization: Creating Mechanisms for Permanent Quality of Life', *Journal of Applied Behavioural Science*, vol. 16, no. 3, July–September, pp. 371–86.

Zand, D. (1974) 'Collateral Organizations: A New Change Strategy', *Journal of Applied Behavioural Science*, vol. 10, no. 1, pp. 63–89.

Zand, D. (1981) *Information, Organization and Power*, McGraw-Hill, Chapter 4.

See also: Ad hoc committees/task forces; Autonomous workgroups; Business teams; Collateral organization; Ergonomics; Group technology; Independent product teams; Intrapreneurial group; Job design; Job enlargement; Job enrichment; Matrix designs; Office automation; Parallel career ladders; Parallel organizations; Skunkworks; Team action leadership; Work simplification

Technology-based training

The principle of delivering teaching and training by means of technology rather than human contact is not new – it could even be said that libraries are an example of this approach – but over the past few decades there have been a number of significant advances in this field. The tape–slide programmes and audio-and-text packages which were once so common in study centres and distance learning programmes are being superseded by multi-media PCs, and improvements in communications have led to the development of virtual classrooms, virtual universities and virtual training centres. The Internet, which allows access to video conferencing, asychrononous discussion groups, virtual libraries, virtual cafes and knowledge gardens, is likely to play a far greater role in teaching and learning in future.

Abdul-Wahab, H. et al. (1997) 'Virtual Classrooms and Interactive Remote Instruction', *Education and Training Technology International*, vol. 34, no. 1, pp. 44–50.

Bilimoria, D. (1997) 'Management Educators: In Danger of Becoming Pedestrians on the Information Superhighway', *Journal of Management Education*, vol. 21, no. 2, pp. 232–43.

Cheney, S. and Jarrett, L.L. (eds) (1997) *Excellence in Practice*, ASTD Press.

Ellet, W. (1997) *A Critical Guide to Management Training Media*, ASTD Press.

Grandgenett, N. et al. (1997) 'Integrating IT into Education and Training', special issue of *Innovations in Education and Training International*, vol. 34, no. 3, pp. 252–6.

Hall, B. (1997) *Web-based Training Cookbook*, ASTD Press.

Hall, J.C. (1996) 'Creating Materials for Interactive Television: Winging It Doesn't Work', *Journal of Management Education*, vol. 20, no. 3, pp. 386–98.

Institute for Personnel and Development (1998) *IPD Guide on Training Technology*, IPD.

Jeanquart-Barone, S. (1995) 'Tips for Successful Teaching Through Interactive Television', *Journal of Management Education*, vol. 19, pp. 500–2.

Maier, P. (1997) *Using Technology for Teaching and Learning*, Kogan Page.

Porter, L.R. (1997) *Creating the Virtual Classroom: Distance Learning with the Internet*, Wiley.

Ravat, S. and Layte, M. (1997) *Technology-based Training*, Kogan Page.

Steed, C. (1999) *Web Based Training*, Gower.

Tucker, B. (ed.) (1997) *Handbook of Technology Based Training*, Gower.

'Using the Internet for Teaching and Learning', special issue of *Innovations in Education and Training International* (1998), vol. 36, no. 1.

Warren, A. et al. (1997) *Technology in Teaching and Learning: An Introduction*, Kogan Page.

Young, M.B. and Gilson, C. (1997) 'Management Education with Computer Mediated Communication: Classroom Experiences, Organizational Lessons', *Journal of Management Education*, vol. 21, no. 1, pp. 58–72.

See also: Computer-assisted learning; Distance education; Infobank; Language laboratory; Open learning; Resource centre

Television

A number of television programmes provide material which is relevant to management training and education, but they are seldom broadcast at times convenient for teaching. For this reason they are usually recorded for use at a later date, but it is important to check the copyright rules on this, to avoid infringement. Video tapes of Open University programmes are also available for sale or hire, as are some of the educational programmes screened overnight in the BBC's Learning Zone slot. Many programmes offer case studies suitable for management courses, and in the past *Panorama*, *The Money Programme* and *The Risk Business* have covered topics which would provide excellent teaching material.

Having obtained a recording of a television programme, the question is how to use it. Since programmes are usually self-contained, the easiest approach is to show shorter programmes of 20–25 minutes' duration in full, then discuss some of the issues raised. Longer programmes will probably need to be broken up into smaller sections. It is important to be aware that some programmes lend themselves to this approach better than others. Most people are accustomed to watching television passively for relaxation, and students may find it unexpectedly taxing to adopt the different frame of reference required when viewing a programme for educational purposes. Associations with entertainment may mean that students are unable to take the programme seriously, and production techniques or emotional reactions may reduce the educational impact. For this reason, it is often best to rely on educational broadcasts deliberately designed to serve as learning resources, since they are geared to producing active responses among the audience. They often include prompts which invite viewers to discuss, think or write about an issue, but their pace may be too fast or too slow for individual learners. One way to overcome these difficulties is to make one's own programmes, since video technology is relatively cheap and widely available nowadays. The possibilities are endless. For example, one can produce interactive self-instruction videos, in which short visual sequences are alternated with questions and activities. These can provide useful training in observation and analysis, as well as the type of stimuli provided by trigger films.

Boeckmann, K., Nessmann, K. and Petermandl, M. (1988) 'Effects of Formal Features in Educational Video Programmes on Recall', *Journal of Educational Television*, vol. 14, no. 2, pp. 107–20.

Harris, D. (1975) 'Training Technology', *Industrial Training International*, vol. 10, no. 2, pp. 49–51.

Harris, N.D.C. and Austwick, K. (1973) 'TV or not TV?', *Programmed Learning and Educational Technology*, vol. 10, no. 3, pp. 124–9.

Laurillard, D. (1991) 'Mediating the Message: Television Programme Design and Student Understanding', *Instructional Science*, vol. 20, pp. 3–23.

Pinnington, A. (1995) *Using Video in Training and Education*, McGraw-Hill.

See also: Audio for learning; Film; Movie; Music for learning; Tape-stop exercise; Trigger film, Video

Teleworking (homeworking; remote working; telecommuting)

Teleworking involves employees working from home or from a small satellite office near their home, usually using computer telecommunications technology, rather than commuting to the organization's main location. The advantages for employees include greater flexibility over working hours and the reduction or elimination of the need to travel to work, while the organization benefits from decreased costs for workspace. Despite the widespread media attention it has attracted in recent times, a 1997 survey of European employers revealed that teleworking was the exception rather than the rule in all countries. It was most widely adopted in Sweden and the Netherlands, where 30 per cent of firms used it, and least popular in the UK, France and Germany, where fewer than 10 per cent did so. The survey also revealed that teleworking was not confined to service industries, but was also applied in some manufacturing sectors.

The main advances in this approach have been spurred by the growing numbers of workers who are engaged in organizing and applying information. Through modem links to a central computer, they can perform functions which range from data-processing and computer programming to teaching, engineering design and strategic planning. In fact, almost any task involving the production, manipulation or transfer of data can be carried out in this way. These developments have important implications for management. To allow their output to be monitored, employees usually undertake independent projects within strict deadlines. This means that the teleworking manager must maintain clear channels of communication, set standards and provide feedback. Employees' individual needs for support and recognition need to be identified and met, and the tasks provided should be sufficiently structured and challenging to maintain their motivation and interest.

Apgar, M. (1998) 'The Alternative Workplace: Changes Where and How People Work', May–June, *Harvard Business Review*, vol. 76, no. 3, pp. 121–36.

Baruch, Y. and Nicholson, N. (1997) 'Home Sweet Work: Requirements for Effective Homeworking', *Journal of General Management*, vol. 32, no. 2, pp. 15–30.

Crandell, N.F. and Wallace, M.J. (1998) *Work and Rewards in the Virtual Workplace*, American Management Association AMACOM Press.

Curran, K. and Williams, G. (1997) *Manual of Remote Working*, Gower.

Gray, M., Hodson, N., Gordon, G. and Penny, R. (1993) *Teleworking Explained*, Wiley.

Huws, U. (1997) *Teleworking: Guide to Good Practice*, Institute of Employment Studies.

Incomes Data Services (1996) *Teleworking*, Study No. 616, IDS.

Jackson, P. and Van der Wielen, J. (1998) (eds) *Teleworking: International Perspectives*, Routledge.

Jackson, P. and Van der Wielen, J. (1999) *Virtual Working*, Routledge.

Johnson, M. (1997) *Teleworking ... in Brief*, Butterworth-Heinemann.

Lipnack, J. and Stamps, J. (1997) *Virtual Teams*, American Society for Training and Development, ASTD Press.

Penn, B. (1995) *Complete Guide to Teleworking*, Piatkus.

Piskurich, G.M. (1998) *An Organizational Guide to Telecommuting*, Pfeiffer/Jossey-Bass.

Solomon, N.A. and Templer, A.J. (1993) 'Development of Non-traditional Work Sites: The Challenges of Telecommuting', *Journal of Management Development*, vol. 12, no. 5, pp. 21–32.

Stanworth, C. (1998) 'Telework and the Information Age', *New Technology, Work and Employment*, vol. 13, no. 1, pp. 51–62.

See also: Flexible staffing; Integrated support functions; Intrapreneurial group; Job sharing; Multiple job-holding; Networking; Part-time working

Temporary task forces (temporary systems)

Organizations may set up temporary task forces to explore and develop new ideas or to address specific problems. Their membership is likely to be drawn from several different departments and include staff with diverse skills. They are also known as *temporary systems*, as a result of Miles's early work, and this idea was later elaborated by Bennis and Slater. They define a temporary system as an association of two or more persons for a specific purpose. These persons share an understanding of the temporary nature of the association, and that it will dissolve when its objective has been met, or when it no longer serves its members' interests.

Setting up a temporary task force to solve a problem can be considered a structural intervention: for example, ad hoc committee task forces are often used by those attempting to implement change. Whatever their purpose, there are certain guidelines which should be followed to increase the likelihood of success. Selection should be based on members' competence, rather than their position in the hierarchy. Despite the temporary nature of their assignment, all members should be committed to long-range planning. Members must be open with each other and enjoy mutual trust, to enable ideas to be developed. Task forces do not exist in a vacuum, so they need support from those within the organizational hierarchy, to encourage independent thinking and risk-taking. Next, task-relevant interfacing is necessary, which means involving those who will be affected by the group's work. To avoid isolating itself, the task force needs to involve those who will be affected by its work, preferably at an early stage, since co-operation from others will usually be necessary to implement proposals anyway. Finally, the task force's proposals for change will almost certainly encounter resistance, and this must be confronted openly and directly. Those who raise objections should be seen as potential sources of help to improve the proposals, rather than as obstructions.

Averich, V.A. and Luke, R. (1970) 'The Temporary Task Force: Challenge to Organizational Structure', *Personnel*, May–June.

Bennis, W. and Slater, P. (1968) *The Temporary Society*, Harper and Row.

Chin, R. and Bennis, W. (1985) 'General Strategies for Effecting Changes in Human Systems', in Bennis, W., Benne, K.D. and Chin, R. (eds) *The Planning of Change* (4th edn), Holt, Rinehart and Winston.

Goodman, R.A. (1981) *Temporary Systems: Professional Development, Manpower Utilisation, Task Effectiveness and Innovation*, Praeger.

Luke, R.A. (1975) 'Temporary Task Forces: A Humanistic Problem Solving Structure', in Burke, W.W. (ed.) *New Technologies in Organization Development*, Pfeiffer/Jossey-Bass, pp. 437–92.

Miles, M.B. (1964) 'On Temporary Systems', in Miles, M. B. (ed.) *Innovation in Education*, Bureau of Publications, Teachers College, Columbia University, pp. 437–92.

Waterman, R.H. (1993) *Adhocracy*, W.W. Norton.

See also: Ad hoc committees/task forces; Autonomous workgroups; Business teams; Collateral organization; Evaluation assignment; Independent product teams; Management audit; Multiple management; Plural chief executive; Problem-solving groups; Skunkworks; Task force assignment; Team action leadership

Text

A text is a written resource which has either been chosen or prepared by a tutor for students to study. Most distance learning programmes rely heavily on the use of specially prepared texts. In the past, some of these were accompanied by supplementary materials such as slides, film strips or audio cassettes, but CD-ROM technology has superseded these in most cases. When preparing an instructional text, it is important to include scope for interaction in the form of self tests, activities and feedback, so that isolated learners are required to make decisions and not be passive.

Objectives should be set to clarify each task. The writing style should be clear, interesting and unambiguous, and the layout needs to be well designed. Finally, the text should link to other work.

Gough, J. (1997) *Developing Learning Materials*, Institute of Personnel and Development.

Hartley, J. (1994) *Designing Instructional Text*, Kogan Page.

Lockwood, F. (1992) *Activities in Self-instructional Text*, Kogan Page/Institute of Educational Technology, Open University.

Mayer, R.E. (1995) 'Generative Theory of Textbook Design: Using Annotated Illustrations to Foster Meaningful Learning of Science Text', *Education, Training Research & Development*, vol. 43, no. 1, pp. 31–41.

Race, P. (1994) *The Open Learning Handbook*, Kogan Page.

Rowntree, D. (1990) *Teaching Through Self-instruction*, Kogan Page.

Rowntree, D. (1993) *Preparing Materials for Open, Distance and Flexible Learning*, Kogan Page.

Rowntree, D. (1997) *Making Materials-based Learning Work*, Kogan Page.

Weinstein, K. (1997) *Writing Works: A Manager's Alphabet*, Institute of Personnel and Development.

See also: Guided study; Handout; Pre-course learning; Reading; Tutorial-tape-document learning package approach; Worksheet

Theory-based interventions

In the past, approaches to management teaching tended to regard theories as abstract concepts, rather than principles which managers could absorb and apply to solving real-life issues. Nowadays, teaching emphasizes theories' practical applications, and this demands that students generalize from specific, concrete concerns to develop concepts which can be applied in a variety of situations.

Consultants who use theory-based interventions adopt a nine-step learning strategy. First, they present the client with a typical situation that might occur, and ask what they would do, in order to define their natural response to the problem. Next, the consultant introduces theories relevant to the situation, using whatever learning methods are appropriate, including tests and quizzes. In step three, the client is presented with simulated problems, where arriving at the best solutions demands applying these theories. The next step is to evaluate this exercise, to assess how well the client understands the theory and how it should be applied. This review reveals not only the client's errors, but also the limitations of the theory itself. In step five, the consultant encourages the client to compare the way they would normally deal with a situation with the approach suggested by the theory. This self-confrontation is an important step in understanding the theory in a personally meaningful way, allowing the client to come to terms with their automatic reactions to crisis situations. Applying the theory enables the client to break free from past behaviour patterns and choose a more appropriate course of action. Once the theory has been internalized, the sixth step involves practice sessions to help the client identify situations where the theory can be applied, and improve the skills this requires. In step seven, the client reassesses the approach to the problem identified in step one, in the light of the theory. Step eight consists of making generalizations about this habitual way of responding, to reduce the likelihood of relapsing into it in times of stress. Finally, the consultant provides support to implement the theory-based approaches in the work situation, if necessary.

Butler, J.K. (1987–8) 'Applying Conceptual Models to Problem Analysis: Hardening Up', *Organizational Behaviour Teaching Review*, vol. 12, no. 2, pp. 58–71.

Gumpart, R.A. and Hambleton, R.K. (1979) 'Situational Leadership - How Xerox Managers Fine Tune Managerial Styles to Employee Maturity and Task Needs', *Management Review*, vol. 68, no. 12, pp. 8–12.

Harding, S. and Long, T. (1998) *Proven Management Models*, Gower.

Miner, J.B. (1984) 'The Validity and Usefulness of Theories in an Emerging Organizational Science', *Academy of Management Review*, vol. 9, pp. 296–306.

See also: Achievement motivation intervention; Contingency approach; Grid development; Historical analysis; Interaction management; 7-S framework; Situational leadership; Socio-technical system design; Transactional Analysis

Think tank

A think tank is a group of experts, often from different disciplines, which develops ideas or suggests solutions to problems. Some non-profit-making think tanks provide advice to governments, while others sell their services to clients who have specific problems. Such groups are usually small, restricted to five or so members in order to decrease the scope for inter-personal friction and duplication of effort. They are well suited to considering complex situations where each solution may give rise to a new problem, or addressing

problems that require members to choose a single answer from among a few proposals.

Cockett, R. (1995) *Thinking the Unthinkable*, HarperCollins.

Kandiah, M. and Seldon, A. (eds) (1997) *Ideas and Think Tanks in Contemporary Britain*, Frank Cass.

Smith, J.A. (1993) *The Ideas Brokers: Think Tanks and the Rise of the New Policy Elite*, Prentice-Hall.

Smith, P.S. (1971) *Think Tanks and Problem Solving*, Business Books.

Stone, D. (1996) *Capturing the Political Imagination: Think Tanks and the Policy Process*, Frank Cass.

See also: Brainstorming; Brainwriting; Creativity training; Delphi technique; Down-up-down-up problem-solving method; Evaluation committee method; Kepner-Tregoe Approach; Lateral thinking; Management Oversight and Risk Tree; Mind Mapping; Nominal group technique; Problem-solving cycle; Questioning; Suggestion schemes; Synectics

Think-and-listen session

This is a group activity in which each participant is given a certain amount of time to give their views on a topic. The main ground rule is that other members must devote their attention to the speaker in a supportive way, and must not interrupt.

Brownell, J. (1996) *Listening: Attitudes, Principles and Skills*, Allyn and Bacon.

James, A. and Kratz, D. (1994) *Effective Listening Skills*, Irwin.

See also: Buberian dialogue; Co-counselling; Group with ground rules

Third-party peacemaking interventions

In this approach, an independent third party intervenes either to control a conflict between groups or individuals, or to resolve it. The third party does not serve as a judge, but helps each party to air their grievances, to come to terms with the hidden agendas which may emerge, and to work towards a solution. A key feature of this method is *confrontation*: those involved must be prepared to recognize that conflict exists between them, and that it is affecting their work. In Richard Walton's view, both parties must be equally ready to confront the problems and suggest initiatives, and they must be prepared to devote sufficient time to work through eir antagonisms. The third party's role is to ructure the confrontation and communication ocess, developing norms of openness and uilding trust between the antagonists. The first sk is to clarify the differences that divide them nd address their negative feelings about each ther, then identify what they have in common nd their positive feelings towards each other. The hird party's assistance in this process may be irect or indirect: direct intervention may include tting an agenda; indirect intervention may entail cheduling a meeting on neutral ground, and tting the boundaries of time or topic.

Three other areas have been identified in which hird-party consultation can be useful. The first is n individually focused version of process consul- ncy. When managers are unclear about their ffect on others, or how well they are using their me, they can invite a third party to observe them t work. Afterwards, the consultant discusses the manager's style, and how it might be improved. Third parties can also be invited to sit in on staff meetings, to present observations on how they might be improved. Finally, a third party can be asked to observe as two individuals, usually a manager and a subordinate, try to resolve a diffi- cult situation. Problems often arise when one of them (or perhaps both) is shy or reluctant to confront the other, and finds it difficult to discuss the issue. In such cases, the problem usually stems from the antagonists' attitudes towards each other, rather than from the work itself.

Eiseman, J.W. (1977) 'A Third Party Consultation Model for Resolving Recurring Conflicts Colla- boratively', *Journal of Applied Behavioural Science*, vol. 13, no. 3, pp. 303–14.

Lewicki, R. and Sheppard, B. (1985) 'How To Intervene: Factors Affecting the Use of Process and Outcome Control in Third Party Dispute Resolution', *Journal of Occupational Behaviour*, January, pp. 49–64.

Mitchell, C.R. (1981) *Peacemaking and the Consul- tant's Role*, Gower.

Prein, H. (1987) 'Strategies for Third Party Inter- vention', *Human Relations*, vol. 40, pp. 699–720.

Walton, R.E. (1967) 'Interpersonal Confrontation and Basic Third Party Functions', *Journal of Applied Behavioural Science*, vol. 4, no. 3, pp. 327–44.

Walton, R.E. (1969) *Interpersonal Peacemaking: Confrontations and Third Party Consultation*, Addison Wesley Longman.

Walton, R.E. (1987) *Managing Conflict: Interper- sonal Dialogue and Third Party Roles* (2nd edn), Addison Wesley Longman.

See also: Confidence-building measures; Conflict- resolution techniques; Confrontation groups;

Confrontation meeting; Consultation; Consulting pair; Criss-cross panels; Exchange of persons; FIDO approach; Insider-outsider consulting teams; Negotiation by group members; No-lose conflict-resolution approach; Process consultation; Shadow consultant; Team-building activities

3-D management effectiveness seminar

This change approach is based on the 3-D Theory of Management Effectiveness developed by W.J. Reddin, who argues that the task to be performed and the nature of the relationships between staff are the key elements in management style. Managers may be *task-oriented* – prioritizing achieving goals, and emphasizing planning, organizing and control- ling – or *relationship-orientated* – attaching impor- tance to work relationships built on mutual trust, and respecting subordinates' ideas, suggestions and feelings. Managers may adopt an *integrating style* (using both behaviours together to a high degree), a *dedicated style* (using task orientation alone) or a *separated style* (using each to a small degree), or a *related style* (bringing different behaviours together). Reddin maintains that each style is effective in different circumstances, and introduces a further dimension, *effectiveness*: the extent to which managers achieve the goals required by their posi- tion. 3-D management effectiveness seminars teach managers to read situations and decide which style is most appropriate in a given situation.

The eight management styles are not additional kinds of behaviour, but the terms given to the four basic styles when used appropriately or inap- propriately.

Basic Style	Less effective equivalent	More effective equivalent
Integrative	Compromiser	Executive
Dedicated	Autocrat	Benevolent autocrat
Related	Missionary	Developer
Separated	Deserter	Bureaucrat

Managers are taught to increase their range of behavioural styles in response to different situa- tions. Reddin developed an intervention programme in which groups of managers discuss, in a structured way, their individual and team effectiveness criteria, to improve the way they work as a team. Reddin's programme consists of four stages. Managers are removed from their work colleagues and placed in artificial groups; the work team (boss and subordinates) discuss their roles and how best to operate together; a boss with a single subordinate then consider effectiveness, before the managing director and their team join to discuss working relationships.

Reddin, W.J. (1966) 'The Tri-dimensional Grid',

Canadian Personnel and Industrial Relations Journal, January, pp. 13–20.

Reddin, W.J. (1967) 'The 3-D Management Style Theory', *Training and Development Journal*, April, pp. 8–17.

Reddin, W.J. (1970) *Managerial Effectiveness*, McGraw-Hill.

Reddin, W.J. (1971) *Effective Management by Objectives: The 3-D Method of MBO*, McGraw-Hill.

Reddin, W.J. (1986) '3-D Management Effectiveness Seminar', *Management Education and Development*, vol. 17, no. 3, pp. 159–63.

Reddin, W.J. (1987) *How To Make Your Management Style More Effective*, Gower.

Reddin, W.J. (1989) *The Output Oriented Manager*, Gower.

Reddin, W.J. (1989) *The Output Oriented Organization*, Gower.

See also: Action-centred leadership; Competing values approach; Grid development; Implementing The Organizational Renewal Process; Interaction influence analysis; Interaction management; Kepner-Tregoe Approach; Likert's System 4 Management; LIFO method; Managing for productivity; Power management; Resources management; Situational leadership; Team action management; Theory-based interventions

Three-sixty (360-degree) feedback (360-degree appraisal)

This appraisal technique was originally devised by the National Aeronautics and Space Administration (NASA) to evaluate their space programmes. It involves providing individual employees, supervisors, managers or senior executives with feedback about their performance from all those who have contact with them, including customers and suppliers. The idea is that such a wide range of perspectives will lead to a more comprehensive and objective appraisal.

Bahra, N. (1997) *360 Degree Appraisal*, Financial Times/Pitman.

Edwards, M.R. and Ewen, A.J. (1996) *360 Degree Feedback*, AMACOM.

France, S. (1997) *360 Appraisal*, The Industrial Society.

Jude-York, D. (1997) *Multipoint Feedback: A 360 Catalyst for Change*, Crisp Publications.

Lepsinger, R. (1997) *360 Degree Feedback: Organizing Multinational Corporations*, Jossey-Bass.

Tornow, W.W. (1998) *Maximising the Value of 360 Degree Feedback*, Jossey-Bass.

Waldman, D.A. and Atwater, L.E. (1998) *Power of 360 Degree Feedback*, Gulf Publishing.

Ward, P. (1997) *360-degree Feedback*, Institute of Personnel and Development.

See also: Appraisal; Goal-setting; Goal-setting and planning groups; Management by objectives; Measuring performance; Periodic planning conference; Positive feedback; Self- with peer appraisal; Team appraisal

TORI community experience

The TORI community experience is an organizational intervention derived from the TORI theory of social systems developed by Jack and Lorraine Gibb and their associates. TORI is an acronym for the factors the authors consider essential to the growth of living systems – Trust, Openness, Realization and Interdependence – since they consider that any social system is best understood as a living, growing organism. They identify fear and trust as the primary variables in the system's growth, and maintain that growth occurs in an effort to move away from fear and towards trust. Fear is manifested as strong defences in the form of depersonalization, façade-building and covert strategies, while trust is characterized by weak defences accompanied by self-determining, self-actualizing behaviour. The authors believe that unacknowledged emotions based on norms influence whole organizations. For example, although a manager may express a desire to deal with a shop steward in a mutual problem-solving way, deeply rooted anti-union attitudes may impede this process. The TORI community experience tries to challenge and overcome such nonproductive norms by means of a series of activities in which participants lift and rock each other and walk about blindfolded. This violates norms such as keeping one's distance, being formal and keeping in role, and as these old norms break down, the emotions that come to the surface are discussed. According to Gibb, this emotion-freeing intervention produces deep inter-personal acceptance, with individuals becoming more honest, assertive and direct. Rather than trying to control others, individuals become less intrusive and manipulative, and more collaborative and sharing. In the climate of trust and acceptance generated by these organization-building experiences, he claims it is possible to initiate problem-solving approaches that can be transferred to the work setting.

Gibb, J.R. (1961) 'Defensive Communication', *The Journal of Communication*, vol. 11, no. 3, pp. 141–8.

Gibb, J.R. (1964) 'Climate for Trust Formation', in Bradford, L.P., Gibb, J.R. and Benne, K.D. (eds) *T-group Theory and Laboratory Method*, Wiley.

Gibb, J.R. (1972) 'TORI Theory and Practice', in Pfeiffer, J.W. and Jones, J.E. (eds) *The 1972*

Annual Handbook for Group Facilitators, Pfeiffer/Jossey-Bass.

Gibb, J.R. (1975) 'The TORI Community Experience as an Organizational Change Intervention', in Burke, W.W. (ed.) *New Technologies in Organization Development I*, Pfeiffer/Jossey-Bass, pp. 109–26.

Gibb, J.R. (1978) *Trust: A New View of Personal and Organizational Development*, Guild Tutors Press.

Gibb, J.R. (1991) *Trust: A New Vision of Human Relationships for Business, Education, Family and Personal Living*, Newcastle Publishing, USA.

Gibb, J.R. and Gibb, L.M. (1968) 'Emergence Therapy: The TORI Process in an Emerged Group', in Gazda, G.M. (ed.) *Innovations to Group Psychotherapy*, Thomas Publishers.

Gibb, J.R. and Gibb, L.M. (1969) 'Role Freedom in a TORI Group', in Burton, A. (ed.) *Encounter: The Theory and Practice of Encounter Groups*, Jossey-Bass.

See also: Encounter group; Gestalt techniques; Laboratory training; Norm modification; Tavistock Conference Method

Total quality management (TQM)

Total quality management's aim is to increase customer satisfaction through continuous improvement of every process within an organization which has a bearing on the quality of its products or services. Two Americans, W. Edwards Deming and Joseph Duran, are frequently credited as the originators of the approach, but Japanese companies were the first to embrace and implement it. TQM is based on a number of principles, which have been applied in a variety of ways. It sees all requirements as customer-driven. It considers that all results should be measurable. It adopts a holistic perspective in order to understand how individual processes fit into the overall system. It analyses current processes in order to identify improvements. Finally, best practices are transferred and implemented throughout the organization.

Hang, P. and Keleman, K.S. (1996) 'Introduction of Total Quality Management (TQM) into the Process of Teaching Management: A Discussion of Initial Applications', *Journal of Management Education*, vol. 20, no. 3, pp. 319–40.

Ho, S.K. (1996) 'A TQM Model for Enabling Student Learning', *Innovations in Education and Training International*, vol. 33, no. 3, pp. 178–84.

Jones, O. (1998) 'Changing the Balance: Taylorism, TQM and Work Organization', *New Technology Work and Employment*, vol. 12, no. 1, pp. 13–24.

Kanji, G.K. (1996) *100 Methods for Total Quality Management*, Sage.

Lewis, D. (1996) 'The Organization Culture Saga – From OD to TQM: A Critical Review of the Literature, Part 1 – Concepts and Early Trends', *Leadership and Organization Development Journal*, vol. 17, no. 1, pp. 12–19.

Lewis, D. (1996) 'The Organization Culture Saga – From OD to TQM: A Critical Review of the Literature, Part 2 – Applications', *Leadership and Organization Development Journal*, vol. 17, no. 2, pp. 9–16.

Lock, D. (ed.) (1994) *Gower Handbook of Quality Management* (2nd edn), Gower.

McCabe, D. and Wilkinson, A. (1998) 'The Rise and Fall of TQM: The Vision, Meaning and Operation of Change', *Industrial Relations Journal*, vol. 29, no. 1, pp. 18–29.

Moorhouse, D.L. (1996) *Essentials of TQM*, Gower.

Popplewell, B. and Wildsmith, A. (1995) *Becoming the Best*, Gower.

Waller, J., Allen, D., Burns, A., and English, M. (1995) *The TQM Toolkit*, Kogan Page.

Wilkinson, A. et al. (1998) *Managing With Total Quality Management*, Macmillan.

Zink, K.L. (1997) *Successful TQM*, Gower.

See also: Business process re-engineering; Deming method; Quality awareness training; Quality circles; Quality management; Zero defects

Trainer as consultant

Applying this method demands that organizations' training departments change their perceptions of their function. Rather than simply running courses to meet individual learning objectives, they need to see their role as not only helping individuals to solve their current work problems, but also enabling them to gain personal learning in the process. Such a shift in perspective demands that trainers develop new approaches and skills, and this is likely to provide a learning experience for all those involved. This redefined role emphasizes the contribution of training to achieving the organization's goals.

Cockburn, P., Evans, B. and Reynolds, B. (1992) *Client-centred Consulting: A Practical Guide for Internal Advisors and Trainers*, McGraw-Hill.

Philips, K. and Shaw, P. (1998) *A Consulting Approach for Trainers*, Gower.

Raab, N. (1997) Becoming an Expert in Not Knowing: Reframing Teachers as Consultants', *Management Learning*, vol. 28, no. 2, pp. 161–75.

Robinson, D.G. and Robinson, J.C. (1995) *Performance Consulting: Moving Beyond Training*,

American Society for Training and Development, ASTD Press.

Robinson, D.G. and Robinson, J.C. (1996) *Performance Consulting: Moving Beyond Training*, Berrett-Koehler.

Saunders, M. and Holdaway, K. (1996) *The Inhouse Trainer as Consultant*, Kogan Page.

See also: Case unprepared; Consultant network; Consulting assignment; Consulting pair; Facilitation; Insider-outsider consulting teams; Manager as consultant; Multiple job-holding; Process consultation; Shadow consultant; Student consulting teams

Training evaluation as learning

The results of most management training courses are evaluated by the trainers themselves, but asking participants to undertake this task can provide a valuable learning opportunity. The usual method is to ask for feedback about shortcomings and possible improvements at the end of the course. This can be achieved by dividing participants into sub-groups to discuss the course, by administering questionnaires, or by a combination of these approaches.

Bramley, P. (1996) *Evaluation of Training Effectiveness*, McGraw-Hill.

Institute of Personnel and Development (1997) *Making Training Pay*, IPD.

Reay, D.G. (1994) *Evaluating Training*, Kogan Page.

Rae, L. (1997) *How To Measure Training Effectiveness* (3rd edn), Gower.

Wade, P.A. (1995) *Measuring the Impact of Training*, Kogan Page.

See also: Application discussion group; Appraisal module; Follow-up; Intervisitation; Mini-learning event; Post-course follow-up; Training transfer training

Training transfer training (learning transfer training)

This approach consists of a seminar or a set of activities during a course which aim to help participants apply their learning to their current work. Among the earliest proponents of this approach was Miles, whose 1959 book on group working suggested many activities which could be used to achieve this goal, including running sessions to explore the theory of application, situational diagnosis and planning, problem-centred groups and intervisitation. His ideas have been developed by Huczynski, who has devised a seminar consisting of five-stages: recall, selection, motivation, evaluation and practice. A series of structured activities encourages participants to reflect on their learning experiences and *recall* those which are most significant to them. From these, they *select* several aspects of learning which would be suitable for transfer. Participants then identify factors that *motivate* them to try to transfer their learning. They *evaluate* their work environment, identifying sources of support. The seminar concludes by giving participants an opportunity to *practise* the skills required to enlist others' support for their proposed changes.

Analoui, F. (1993) *Training and Transfer of Training*, Avebury.

Bader, G.E. and Bloom, A.E. (1995) *Making Your Training Results Last*, Kogan Page.

Brethower, D.M. and Smalley, K.A. (1998) *Performance Based Instruction: Linking Training to Business Results*, Pfeiffer/Jossey-Bass.

Broad, M.L. and Newstrom, J.W. (1992) *Transfer of Training: Action Packed Strategies to Ensure High Payoff from Training Investments*, Addison Wesley Longman.

Butterfield, E.C. and Nelson, G.D. (1989) 'Theory and Practice of Teaching for Transfer', *Education, Training Research & Development*, vol. 37, no. 3, pp. 5–38.

Byham, W.C., Adams, D. and Kiggins, A. (1976) 'The Transfer of Modelling Training to the Job', *Personnel Psychology*, vol. 29, pp. 345–9.

Finlay, D.L., Sanders, M.G. and Ryan, A.J. (1996) 'Application of Training Transfer Principles in Developing the High Transfer Training Methodology (HITT)', *Education and Training Technology International*, vol. 33, no. 4, pp. 232–9.

Haskell, R.E. (1998) *Reengineering Corporate Training: Intellectual Capital and Transfer of Learning*, Greenwood Publishing Group, USA.

Huczynski, A.A. (1978) 'The Problems of Learning Transfer', *Journal of European Industrial Training*, vol. 2, no. 1, pp. 26–9.

Huczynski, A.A. and Logan, D.W. (1980) 'Learning to Change: Organizational Change Through Training Transfer Workshops', *Leadership and Organizational Development Journal*, vol. 1, no. 3, pp. 25–31.

Hunter, M. (1995) *Teaching for Transfer*, Corwin Press.

McKeough, A., Lupart, J. and Marini, A. (eds) (1995) *Teaching for Transfer: Fostering Generalization in Learning*, Lawrence Erlbaum Associates.

Robinson, D.G. and Robinson, J.C. (1989) *Training for Impact: How to Link Training to Business Needs and Measure the Results*, Jossey-Bass.

See also: Application discussion group; Follow-up; Intervisitation; Mini-learning event; Post-course follow-up; Training evaluation as learning

Transactional Analysis

Transactional Analysis was invented by Eric Berne, and its principles are widely applied in counselling and group therapy, both as a personal therapy and as an organizational intervention. The central idea is that when people interact with each, they switch between three levels: Parent, Child and Adult. The *Child* aspect manifests itself in behaviour that is usually found in young children (e.g., playfulness, creativity, insecurity, a desire for immediate gratification). The *Parent* aspect reflects attitudes, values and behaviour exhibited by our parents (e.g., authoritarianism, nurturing). The *Adult* is the self-activating aspect of our personality, the rational, mature part that considers each situation anew before deciding how to respond. Problems arise in relationships when these aspects and their associated behaviours are not recognized and responded to appropriately, or when one person in the relationship becomes entrenched in a particular aspect. Berne maintains that we can develop the ability to identify and consciously control these behaviour patterns, switching between them according to the requirements of the situation.

Barker, D. (1978) 'What TA Can Do for You', *Personnel Management*, vol. 10, no. 5, pp. 36–9.

Barker, D. (1980) *TA and Training*, Gower.

Berne, E. (1964) *Games People Play*, Penguin.

Clary, T.C. (1980) 'Transactional Analysis', *Training and Development Journal*, vol. 34, no. 6, pp. 48–54.

Cox, M. and Cox, C. (1980) 'Ten Years of Transactional Analysis', in Beck, J. and Cox, C. (eds) *Advances in Management Education*, Wiley.

Harris, T.A. (1996) *I'm OK, You're OK*, Avon.

Hay, J. (1996) *Transactional Analysis for Trainers*, Sherwood Publishing.

James, M. and Jongewood, D. (1996) *Born to Win: Transactional Analysis with Gestalt Experiments*, Addison Wesley Longman.

Kilcourse, T. (1977) 'Transactional Analysis: Some Concerns', *Journal of European Industrial Training*, vol. 1, no. 2, pp. 1–5.

Kilcourse, T. (1978) 'TA Under Attack', *Personnel Management*, vol. 10, no. 6, pp. 3–5 and 43.

Neath, M. (1995) 'Evaluating Transactional Analysis as a Change Strategy for Organizations', *Leadership and Organization Development Journal*, vol. 16, no. 1, pp. 13–16.

Steiner, C.M. (1990) *Scripts People Live By*, Grove Press.

Stewart, I. (1996) *Developing Transactional Development Counselling*, Sage.

Villere, M.F. (1981) *Transactional Analysis at Work: A Guide for Business and Professional People*, Prentice-Hall.

Villere, M.F. (1983) *Successful Personal Selling Through TA*, Prentice-Hall.

Wellin, M. (1978) 'TA in the Workplace', *Personnel Management*, vol. 10, no. 7, pp. 37–40.

See also: Encounter groups; Gestalt techniques; Interactive skills training; Personal development laboratory; Psychotherapy; Stress management

Trigger film

Trigger films are short, high-impact vignettes specifically designed to excite responses which can be explored in subsequent activities. They usually portray incidents which give rise to an emotional as well as an intellectual reaction in the viewer, encouraging reflection and a sense of personal involvement. The situations they depict are unresolved, and may last between 10 and 30 seconds. Companies producing traditional management training film packages have adopted this idea by including a separate video tape which features the same actors as the main film, but consists of a series of very short excerpts.

Boud, D. and Pearson, M. (1979) 'The Trigger Film: A Stimulus for Affective Learning', *Programmed Learning and Educational Technology*, vol. 16, no. 1, pp. 52–6.

Fisch, A.L. (1972) 'The Trigger Film Techniques', *Improving College and University Teaching*, vol. 20, no. 4.

Mayhew, R. (1984) 'Finger on the Trigger', *Audio Visual*, May, pp. 31–2.

Powell, J.P. (1977) 'The Use of Trigger Films in Developing Teaching Skills', in Elton, L. and Simmonds, K. (eds) *Staff Development in Higher Education*, Society for Research into Higher Education.

See also: Apperception-interaction method; Audio for learning; Confluent education; Film; Interpersonal process recall; Movie; Music for learning; Tape-stop exercise; Television; Video confrontation

Trust exercise

These experiential exercises explore participants' feelings and attitudes towards placing trust in each other. Various structured activities can be used, perhaps the best-known being the Trust Fall and the Trust Walk. In the Trust Fall, a group of students divides into pairs. One stands with their back to the other and gradually falls backwards until their partner catches them. They exchange roles, and once they have completed the activity several times, share their feelings and experiences, first with each other and then with the other group members. In the Trust Walk, a blindfolded student is led around the building (or outside it) by their partner. Like all non-verbal exercises, trust exercises tend to produce strong emotions which can serve as an impetus for further learning.

See also: ExperientiaI exercise; Gestalt technique; Non-verbal exercise

Tutorial

Tutorials have a long historical tradition. William of Wykeham, Bishop of Winchester and founder of New College, Oxford, is credited with originating a method of tuition which involved senior members of his foundation teaching junior members, and this developed into the tutorial system. Whether they involve one-to-one or small-group tuition, the opportunities tutorials offer for individual attention and dialogue make them a very valuable educational method which can serve a variety of purposes. The tutor may offer help with students' difficulties or projects. The group may work through a prepared problem or case study together. It may debate a topic or discuss a paper presented by one or more of the students. Most of the time, the tutor and students will decide together which topics to study, but students generally assume primary responsibility for presenting and sharing ideas with the tutor, who then helps them sharpen their thinking. Various teaching styles may be adopted. Didactic methods are effective when students lack information about the subject and have no foundation on which to build. Socratic methods are appropriate when students have all the information necessary to derive a correct solution to a problem, but need to organize it properly. Problem-solving approaches can be used when the tutor and student both possess some of the same information, but each also has access to information of their own. Tutorials can also fulfil an important pastoral role, since tutors' attitudes and approaches are likely to be modelled by students, and the transactions between them may help students to develop their confidence and abilities. There are a number of variations.

Supervised tutorials are regular meetings between a teacher and a student, during which the student reads an essay they have written, then defends it in argument. These can provide exceptionally able students with excellent opportunities to deepen their understanding of a subject while advancing their mastery of the basic skills of scholarship, but the tutor must be well-informed and sympathetic, and the student must have prepared thoroughly for the encounter. If each student is scheduled to attend a series of supervised tutorials, a more sophisticated approach can be adopted. In the first of the series, the student can negotiate an essay title in a field which interests them. In the second and third tutorials, the tutor and student can explore how to structure and plan the essay. The student then writes the essay, and presents it and debates it during the final tutorial.

Group tutorials mainly arose from the need to make more efficient use of staff time. Unfortunately, few tutors know enough about group dynamics to exploit the full potential of the small-group situation. However, despite the high level of tutor–student interaction in one-to-one tutorials, some students find them intimidating, and need the support of a peer group to overcome their inhibitions and express themselves in the presence of an authority figure. Nevertheless, the fact that some students in the group may be more inclined to contribute than others may present problems. In addition, some research suggests that most tutors monopolize the proceedings, do not give students the opportunity to participate, turn the discussion into a lecture, and generally forget why the students are there. The best approach is to ensure that tutorials are problem-centred rather than competitive. Tutors should act as mentors rather than judges. It is vital that both the students and the tutor prepare beforehand. It is very helpful if the tutor has some knowledge of group processes. In these circumstances, tutorials can achieve high-order cognitive and affective objectives.

Axelroyd, J. (1948) 'The Technique of Group Discussion in the College Class', *Journal of General Education*, vol. 26, pp. 20–7.

Bramley, W. (1977) *Personal Tutoring*, Society for Research into Higher Education.

Bramley, W. (1979) *Group Tutoring: Concepts and Cases*, Kogan Page.

Daines, J., Daines, C. and Graham, B. (1998) *Adult Learning, Adult Teaching*, Continuing Education Press of Nottingham University.

Kowalski, R. (1989) 'Opinion: Some Thoughts on the Role of Tutorials in effective Teaching in Agricultural and Related Subjects', *Education and Training Technology International*, vol. 26, no. 3, pp. 254–61.

McFarland, H.S.N. (1962) 'Education by Tutorial', *Universities Review*, vol. 34, pp. 45–51.

Ogborn, J. (ed.) (1977) *Small Group Teaching in Undergraduate Science*, Heinemann Educational Books.

Wood, A.E. (1979) 'Experiences With Small Group Tutorials', *Studies in Higher Education*, vol. 4, no. 2, pp. 203–9.

See also: Advanced seminar; One-to-one learning; Questioning; Seminar; Small-group teaching; Structuring seminars; Structured tutoring; Team learning with informative testing; Tutorium

Tutorial-tape-document learning package approach

This is a scaled-down version of the Keller plan which can be used by an individual tutor. It was designed by November to allow students to manage their own learning, and consists of five components: audio cassettes, a document file, skeleton notes, exercises and tutorials. The audio cassettes guide students through the course's activities, and may reproduce commentaries on documents, anecdotes and other materials to stimulate learning. The document file is an indexed collection of materials, which may include the aims of the course, diagrams, extracts from journals, cuttings from newspapers or photocopies of book pages. The skeleton notes consist of a series of headings, under which space is provided for the students to take notes. At different points in the course, the audio tape directs the students to complete an exercise, which they then write up in their notes. The tutorials complete the package. Technological developments now permit most of these elements to be provided as an integrated multi-media CD-ROM learning package.

The class is divided into tutorial groups of about five members each. The course content is divided into blocks, and each group attends a weekly meeting with the tutor, to check whether they are making sufficient headway or encountering any problems. The pace of the course is dictated by the skeleton notes the tutor issues at each tutorial. Within each group, members share the tapes and document files, but everyone receives their own copy of the skeleton notes.

November, P. J. (1978) 'The Tape-Tutorial-Document Learning Package', *Studies in Higher Education*, vol. 3, no. 1, pp. 91–5.

See also: Circulated lecture notes; Data approach method; Guided discussion; Guided study; Handout; Personalized system of instruction; Self instructional module and interactive group; Text; Tutorium; Unit box

Tutorium (seminar; tutoring group)

Tutoriums are a weekly one- or two-hour meetings conducted by graduate teaching assistants. They often supplement weekly lectures, checking that the material has been understood, and giving students the opportunity to ask questions, receive feedback and voice opinions. There are several reasons why graduate students are chosen to run these seminars: they are usually closer to the students' age and educational level, the experience may prove useful in their future careers, and they are cheaper to employ than lecturers or professors. They are less likely to be seen as authority figures by the students, who are therefore more likely to ask questions and admit that they have not understood a point. The method has been found to increase students' motivation and the degree of co-operation between them, and to lessen the incidence of competitive behaviour. Both the students and the tutors tend to gain in self-confidence and self-esteem. Since some students may regard even graduate students as authority figures, some experiments have used final-year undergraduate students to deliver tutoriums, and both staff and students generally consider that they perform as well as graduate teaching assistants, and in some cases even better.

Egerton, J. (1976) 'Teaching Learning While Learning to Teach', *Change*, vol. 8, pp. 58–61.

Gartner, A., Kohler, M. and Riessman, F. (1971) *Children Teach Children*, Harper and Row.

Janssen, P. (1976) 'With a Little Help from Their Friends', *Change*, vol. 8, pp. 50–3.

Lincoln, E. (1976) 'Everyman as Psychologist', *Change*, vol. 8, pp. 54–7.

Maas, J.B. and Pressler, V.M. (1973) 'When Students Become Teachers', *Behavioural and Social Science Teacher*, vol. 1, no. 1, pp. 55–60.

Vattano, F.J., Hockenberry, C., Grider, W., Jacobson, L. and Hamilton, S. (1972) 'Employing Undergraduate Students in the Teaching of Psychology', *Teaching of Psychology Newsletter*, March, pp. 9–12.

Wrigley, C. (1973) 'Undergraduate Students as Teachers: Apprenticeship in the University Classroom', *Teaching of Psychology Newsletter*, March, pp. 5–7.

See also: Agenda method; Learning cell; Parrainage; Peer teaching; Proctor method; Self-directed learning; Seminar; Teaching as learning; Tutorial

Understudy

An understudy is a member of staff who is being trained to take over their boss's job when they leave as a result of promotion, retirement or transfer, leading to a smoother transition. Understudies tend to be highly motivated to take advantage of the opportunity to learn by doing. Their managers usually benefit by sharing some of their workload, and the organization is less likely to experience disruption if the executive or supervisor has to leave suddenly. On the other hand, this technique has serious disadvantages. In many cases, the understudy will have been chosen because their way of thinking and acting is similar to that of their boss, in which case, when they fill the post, it is likely that they will perpetuate existing practices – bad as well as good – rather than introducing new ideas and approaches. The other major disadvantage is that the understudy's colleagues may interpret the appointment as an act of favouritism, leading to jealousy and friction, and depressing their morale and motivation.

There are number of ways to choose and develop understudies. The manager who will be leaving may select the individual, provide training and allow them to grapple with some of the problems that characterize the post. The manager may choose several subordinates to act as understudies, allowing them to take it in turns to cover for the manager' absences due to holidays, business trips or illness. Another approach is to designate a subordinate to serve as the manager's administrative assistant, and delegate a progressively wider range of responsibilities. The understudy can be assigned a project, such as investigating long-term problems and drawing up a report suggesting remedies, or appointed to supervise a small task force, which will give them the chance to practise leadership skills. Another method is to ask the understudy to attend important executive meetings, either accompanying or standing in for their boss, and make presentations or proposals to senior management.

See also: Acting assignment; Apprenticeship; Corporate student board of directors; Development assignment; Internship; Manager shadowing; One-to-one learning; Planned delegation; Sick leave/holiday replacement assignment; SmartProcess; Work shadowing

Union observation of management meetings

One division of Standard Telephones and Cable invited employee representatives to attend its regular management meetings as observers. When the union shop stewards realized that this offer was genuine, they responded by inviting management to send representatives to the shop stewards' committee meetings. The company has also held informal, open meetings at its head office, where directors can discuss issues with staff from all levels.

Goldsmith, W. and Clutterbuck, D. (1984) *The Winning Streak*, Penguin Books.

See also: Sensitivity bargaining; Union–manage-ment committees; Union–management joint participation; Union–management organizations; Union–management problem-solving groups

Union–management committees (labour–management committees; study action teams)

Union–management committees are made up of union and management representatives, and technical specialists. In non-unionized organizations, an employees' association takes on the union's role. Some of these committees have proven highly effective in implementing cost-effective programmes, monitoring quality-of-working-life initiatives, helping to eliminate waste, and improving management–employee relationships. They have also been used to find ways to harness employees' skills and new technologies to address economic problems. These committees have been adopted in various forms by some of the largest companies. In pursuit of productivity improvements, they have enabled staff at all levels in the organization to discuss problems outside the collective bargaining framework.

In one case, union and management set up *shop-floor–management problem-solving teams*, which were trained in the required analytical skills. The teams could be seen as forerunners of quality circle groups. They consisted of six employees and one manager, who identified, analysed and solved problems in their work areas, such as eliminating toxic fumes, designing new tools to improve accuracy in installing components, and reducing maintenance costs. Each plant set up a union–management policy and planning committee, which in turn established departmental steering committees to monitor the teams' progress, obtained information for them, and provide support to implement their solutions. Organizational and policy changes were developed to support and sustain these activities.

A variation of the union–management committee concept is the *study action team*, made up of eight members: six shop-floor employees, one manager and one engineer. Unlike problem-solving teams, study action teams consist of full-time members who have no other responsibilities during the team's six-month project. Acting rather like a productivity task force, the team's remit is to find ways to make the company more competitive by improving its delivery times or the quality of its products, thereby securing jobs in future. Team members receive training in accounting, problem-solving, and running meetings and large-group presentations. One study action team's recommendations included redesigning the department, expanding employees' responsibilities, upgrading equipment and eliminating non-essential overhead expenses. Management anticipated that these initiatives would lead to savings of some $3.7 million.

Black, J. and McCabe, D. (1998) 'Jointism and the Role of the Workplace Union in the Autocomponents Industry', *New Technology Work and Employment*, vol. 13, no. 1, pp. 29–42.

Gold, C. (1986) *Labour–management Committee: Confrontation, Co-optation or Co-operation*, ILR Press.

Lazas, P. and Constanza, T. (1983) 'Cutting Costs Without Layoffs Through Union–management Collaboration', *National Productivity Review*, vol. 2, no. 4, pp. 362–70.

Moores, R. (1995) *Joint Consultation*, The Industrial Society.

See also: Ad hoc committees/task forces; Quality circles; Relations-by-objectives; Resources management; Sensitivity bargaining; Union observation of management meetings; Union–management joint participation; Union–management organizations; Union–management problem-solving groups

Union–management joint participation (employee involvement agreements; staff councils)

Joint participation agreements allow union and management to communicate more openly than would be the case with contract negotiations. The agreement may take the form of a letter of understanding or an addendum to the plant's collective bargaining agreement, providing for voluntary participation by the local unions, management and employees. Grievance procedures and the terms of the basic union agreement are unaffected. The aim is to enable the two sides to move from conflict to co-operation, and from authoritarian to participative behaviours in order to improve employee morale, solve production and workplace problems, stabilize employment, and develop training and re-training programmes. Individual plants often set up their own steering committee of management and union representatives to oversee and co-ordinate the employee participation groups, providing group leaders and members with training in problem-solving and communication skills. Where the arrangement applies to a whole company, the participation process is frequently overseen by a national joint committee of senior company managers and top union officials, and each plant can choose whether or not to take part. The experience of joint problem-solving has led many companies to institute quality-of-working-life improvements.

'Agile Production Brings Success for Grundig Satellite Communications Manufacturing', *IRS Employment Trends* (1998), no. 667, pp. 14–16.

Guest, D. and Peccei, R. (1998) *The Partnership Company*, Involvement and Participation Association.

Kochan, T.A. and Dyer, L. (1976) 'A Model of Organizational Change in the Context of Union–management Relations', *Journal of Applied Behavioural Science*, vol. 12, pp. 59–78.

'Staff Councils: Provisioning Two Way Communication at Sainsbury's', *IRS Employment Trends* (1998), no. 668, pp. 13–16.

U.S. Congress, Office of Technology Assessment (1994) *Pulling Together for Productivity: A Union–management Initiative at U.S. West, Inc.*, DIANE Publishing.

Weston, S. and Martinez, L.C. (1998) 'In and Beyond European Possibilities for Trade Union Influence', *Employment Relations*, vol. 20, no. 6, pp. 551–64.

See also: Quality circles; Union observation of management meetings; Union–management committees; Union–management organizations; Union–management problem-solving groups; Sensitivity bargaining

Union–management organizations

These are organizations established to counteract serious difficulties in local industry. They usually consist of about fifteen members from local unions and management, which lobby to attract employment to the area, and promote harmony within and between different companies. They have no paid staff, and their running costs may amount to about $10,000 per year, two-thirds being met by the companies, the other third being contributed by the unions. Many are known by acronyms, such as PRIDE (Productivity and Responsibility Increase and Development of Employment) of St Louis, Michigan, PEP (Planning Economic Progress) of Beaumont, Texas, and MOST (Management and Organized Labour Striving Together) in Columbus, Ohio. In their memorandum, these organizations list among their aims: ending jurisdictional strikes, no limits to production by workers, no restrictions on the use of tools or equipment, and eliminating inefficient work practices. Management is required to supply the necessary equipment and materials promptly, but is free to exercise its rights to manage, hire, fire and lay off staff, which some believe had in the past been usurped by strong-willed union leaders. Customers in their turn pledge to avoid setting unrealistic completion dates which impose high overhead costs.

Cohen-Rosenthal, E. and Burton, C.E. (1993) *Mutual Gains: A Guide to Union–management Co-operation*, ILR Press.

Moores, R. (1990) *Consultative Committees: A Supervisor's Pocket Guide*, The Industrial Society.

Ross, I. (1984) 'A New Spirit of St Louis', *Working Smarter*, Penguin, pp. 128–39.

See also: Flexible staffing; Quality circles; Sensitivity bargaining; Union–management joint participation; Union–management problem-solving groups

Union–management problem-solving groups

This is a structural change intervention in which a hierarchy of problem-solving groups is superimposed on to the existing organizational structure. Union and management representatives meet regularly, lower-level groups dealing with problems specific to their areas, and higher-level groups addressing problems that involve a number of organizational units. The suggestions from such groups have included work-simplification, and the adoption of flexitime and new performance appraisal schemes.

Weekley, T.L., Wilber, J.C. and Creedon, B.R. (1995) *United We Stand: The Unprecedented Story of the GM–AUW Quality Partnership*, McGraw-Hill.

See also: Appraisal; Sensitivity bargaining; Union–management committees; Union–management joint participation; Union–management organizations; Work schedule restructuring; Work-simplification

Unit box approach

The unit box approach involves each student assembling a teaching package built around a commercially available classroom-tested unit of study. It was developed by Batoff at Jersey City State College, USA, for use with schoolteachers, but the idea can also be applied to management training. Commercially available units are used because students' technical knowledge and skill levels would make it impossible for them to write a unit, test it, receive feedback and review it in the time available. Participants therefore devote their spare time during the five or six weeks before the student teaching experience part of their course, to gathering together all the materials necessary to teach the unit. The completed unit box contains a multi-media, multi-sensory, multi-level package of instructional materials designed for in-depth use over a period of four to eight weeks.

Batoff, M.E. (1974) 'The Unit Box Approach: A Novel Facet of Elementary School Science Teacher Preparation', *British Journal of Educational Technology*, vol. 2, no. 5, pp. 88–95.

Conkright, T. (1977) 'Guidelines for the Adoption of Course Materials', *Journal of European Industrial Training*, vol. 1, no. 1, pp. 14–16.

See also: Circulated lecture notes; Data approach method; Guided discussion; Guided study; Keller plan; Personalized system of instruction; Self-instructional module and interactive group; Text

Values-clarification

The values-clarification approach to teaching does not attempt to impose specific values on students, but to help them clarify, appreciate and act upon those they choose to espouse. It is concerned with the process by which learners arrive at their values, not the content of their values. Managers' values impinge on the decisions they make, so the educational experience should include efforts to make these explicit. In addition, the educational process needs to be personalized, emphasizing personal growth as well as intellectual development, to ensure that students are well motivated and receptive to learning. Teacher–student relationships can be improved by developing a climate of trust, acceptance and open communication in the classroom. The classroom itself can be organized to facilitate learning and personal growth. Efforts can be made to tailor the curriculum to ensure that it matches students' values, purposes and goals, but this obviously demands that students have a clear set of values.

Implementing the values-clarification approach involves a process of choosing, prizing and acting. The methods adopted help students to *choose* their values freely from among the alternatives, after weighing the consequences of each one. Having done this, they are encouraged to *prize* their values, sharing and publicly affirming them. Finally, they must *act* according to their values, and do so consistently.

Bargo, M. (1980) *Choices and Decisions: A Guidebook for Constructing Values*, Pfeiffer/Jossey-Bass.

Frey, R. (1994) *Eye Juggling: 31 Values Clarifying Strategies for Daily Living*, University Press of America.

Griseri, P. (1998) *Managing Values*, Macmillan.

Kirschenbaum, H. (1977) *Advanced Value Clarification*, Pfeiffer/Jossey-Bass.

Koberg, G. and Bagnall, J. (1976) *Values Tech: A*

Portable School for Discovering and Developing Decision-making Skills and Self-enhancing Potentials, William Kaufmann Inc.

Simon, S.B. (1990) *Meeting Yourself Halfway*, Values Press.

Simon, S.B., Howe, L.W. and Kirschenbaum, H. (1995) *Values Clarification*, Warner Books.

Smith, M. (1977) *A Practical Guide to Value Clarification*, Pfeiffer/Jossey-Bass.

See also: Argumentation; Apperception-interaction method; Biography; Career life planning; Confluent education; Debate; Gestalt techniques; Ideological change; Jurisprudential model; Managerial strategy change; Moral philosophy approach

Vendor excellence awards (supplier relationships)

Nowadays, as much as 70 per cent of the cost of an assembled product is accounted for by bought-in parts. This means that companies are very dependent on their suppliers, whose performance is as important as that of the companies' own production or assembly operations. For this reason, some companies have developed supply-chain management programmes and vendor training schemes to improve suppliers' understanding of the importance of their products' role and the standards that are required. These often include vendor excellence awards, given to the supplier with the lowest reject rate over a given period, based on regular inspection of the components they supply.

Burns, B. and Dale, B. (eds) (1998) *Working in Partnership: Best Practice in Customer–supplier Relationships*, Gower.

Gattorna, J. (1996) *Managing the Supply Chain: A Strategic Perspective*, Macmillan.

Gattorna, J. (ed.) (1998) *Strategic Supplier Chain Alignment*, Gower.

McIvor, R., Humphreys, P. and McAleer, E. (1997) 'Implications of Partnerships Sourcing on Buyer–supplier Relationships', *Journal of General Management*, vol. 23, no. 1, pp. 53–70.

See also: Excellence training; Network organizations; Outsourcing; Quality circles; Quality management; Recognition programme; Staff exchange; Two-way contracting

Video confrontation (video self-confrontation; video self-review)

Video confrontation allows trainees to observe their own behaviour on a television screen. The technique has proven particularly useful in training managers in public speaking, group dynamics, interviewing and negotiating. The recording is usually replayed immediately after the activity. People are often embarrassed when they hear how they sound on a tape recording, and the experience of seeing themselves performing on video can have a similar effect, so the confrontation needs to take place in a supportive atmosphere. It is essential to provide assistance to interpret and learn from the experience, and to take into account its impact on trainees' self-image and feelings.

Biggs, S. (1980) 'The Me I See: Acting, Participating, Observing and Viewing and Their Implications for Videofeedback', *Human Relations*, vol. 33, no. 8, pp. 575–88.

Chipling, R. (1979) 'Are You Getting Value From Your CCTV?', *Journal of European Industrial Training*, vol. 3, no. 4, pp. 18–20.

Finlayson, D. (1975) 'Self-confrontation: A Broader Conceptual Base', *British Journal on Teacher Education*, vol. 1, pp. 97–103.

Fuller, F.F. and Manning, B.A. (1974) 'Self-confrontation Reviewed: A Conceptualisation, for Video Playback in Teacher Education', *Review of Educational Research*, vol. 43, no. 4, pp. 469–528.

MacLeod, G. (1976) 'Self-confrontation Revisited', *British Journal of Teacher Education*, vol. 2, no. 3.

Nielson, G. (1964) *Studies in Self-confrontation*, Howard Allen Inc.

Perlberg, A. and O'Bryant, D.C. (1970) 'Video-taping and Micro-teaching Techniques to Improve Engineering Education', *Journal of Engineering Education*, vol. 60, pp. 741–4.

Smallwood, R. (1977) 'Using CCTV in Management Training: Part 1', *Journal of European Industrial Training*, in vol. 1, no. 1, p. 6.

Smallwood, R. (1977) 'Using CCTV in Management Training: Part 2', *Journal of European Industrial Training*, vol. 1, no. 2, pp. 15–16.

Smallwood, R. (1977) 'Using CCTV in Management Training: Part 3', *Journal of European Industrial Training*, vol. 1, no. 3, pp. 23–4.

See also: Inter-personal process recall; Micro-teaching; Self-criticism; Trigger film

Vignette analysis

Undergraduate students are often reluctant to express their views in tutorials, either through lack of knowledge or because they fear they might appear foolish in front of the tutor and other students. Vignette analysis tries to overcome these problems by asking students to identify certain aspects of the subject in brief passages of text, and explain their reasoning. Wright and Taylor developed two types of vignettes: specific and integrative. The following *specific* example on perception quoted by Wright and Taylor illustrates, among other things, the concepts of perceptual set, motivated perception, cognitive dissonance and group norms.

The Hunter Who Was Mistaken for a Deer

A group of hunters were out hunting deer just before sunset on an overcast day. One of the hunters, wearing faded red coveralls, got ahead of his colleagues. Not realizing what had happened, one of them mistook him for a deer and shot him. When a policeman later went back to the scene of the accident and observed a man under similar conditions, he had no difficulty in identifying what he saw as a man.

Identify as many psychological processes as you can in the above example.

Integrative vignettes try to break down the boundaries between topics which students study separately, and which they may not otherwise relate. Taylor and Wright developed three types of integrative vignettes: those in which a number of different psychological processes are involved in the same situation, those in which the same behaviour can be described in different terms by various theoretical systems, and those in which the same behaviour can be explained in a variety of ways, depending on which theoretical framework is adopted.

Wright, P.L. and Taylor, D.S. (1981) Vignette Analysis as an Aid to Psychology Teaching', *Bulletin of the British Psychological Society*, vol. 34, pp. 68–70.

See also: Application of principles; Description-prediction-outcome-explanation; Fortune lining; Tutorial

Visiting speaker (guest speaker)

Visiting speakers are a common feature of business school courses and in-company management education and training programmes. They are usually managers themselves, and may make regular contributions during a course. They often supply expert knowledge in subjects where the business school lacks the necessary expertise, such as company law or industrial relations legislation. They can also place the course learning in context, telling students what being a manager entails in practice. During in-company training programmes, the organizers may invite an academic, consultant

or some other outsider to give a talk about a theory, model or framework which may help clarify, contextualize or explain the issues that are being discussed. For the visiting speaker, this can serve as a development opportunity, since the planning and preparation involved in speaking in public draws on skills and knowledge which may be relevant to their work. Some managers are experienced and gifted speakers. Others may have had little or no practice, but they are likely to be keen to perform well, devoting a great deal of time and effort to preparing their talk. They may benefit from coaching provided by their company's training department, other managers or business school staff.

The effective use of visiting speakers demands that their input is integrated into the educational programme. It is essential to brief them in detail about the course as a whole, which topics have already been covered, and which will be dealt with later. Failure to do this may result in the all too common student response: 'Yes, it was interesting, but I'm not sure how it fits in with what we've been doing.'

Barclay, L.A. and Theisen, B.A. (1989–90) 'That's No Guest Speaker ... That's My Other Professor', *Organizational Behaviour Teaching Review*, vol. 14, no. 4 pp. 124–6.

See also: Brains Trust; Confidence-building training; Interrogation of experts; Interview meeting; Short talks by students; Teaching as learning; Teaching by narration; Panel discussion

Wellness programme

In the past, organizations ran fitness programmes to help their employees avoid health problems. Wellness programmes take a more holistic approach, promoting employees' physical, emotional, social, spiritual and intellectual health. The physical aspects include encouraging participants to take regular exercise, lose weight if necessary, eat wholesome food, stop smoking, and learn how to manage stress. Such programmes may be open to all employees or restricted to managers, and they can lead to reductions in health costs, absenteeism and staff turnover. A British plant of an American multi-national corporation introduced a wellness programme for all its employees. It changed the menu in the staff canteen to include more nutritious food and more fibre. Beyond the dining hall, stalls were erected giving information about healthy living, and computers were provided to enable employees to analyse the carbohydrate, mineral and vitamin content of the meal they had just eaten. It also introduced exercise breaks in the production area, accompanied by music and instructions on movement delivered over the public address system.

Bayley-Grant, C. (1997) *Workplace Wellness*, Wiley.
Institute of Personnel and Development (1997) *IPD Guide on Occupational Health and Organizational Effectiveness*, IPD.
Institute of Personnel and Development (1998) *Getting Fit, Staying Fit*, IPD.
Kerr, J., Cox, T. and Griffiths, J. (eds) (1996) *Workplace Health*, Taylor and Francis.
Kogan, H. (ed.) (1997) *The Corporate Healthcare Handbook*, The Industrial Society/Kogan Page.
McPartland, P.A. (1991) *Promoting Health in the Workplace*, Harwood Academic.
O'Donnell, M.O. (1993) *Health Promotion in the Workplace*, Delmar Publications.
Serman, M.T. (1990) *Wellness in the Workplace*, Crisp Publications.
Terborg, J. R. (1986) 'Health Promotion at the Worksite: A Research Challenge for Personnel and Human Resource Management', *Research in Personnel and Human Resources Management*, vol. 4, pp. 225–67.

See also: Alcohol recovery programmes; Counselling; Job support; Psychotherapy; Stress management

Work cards

A work card is a set of instructions mounted on a laminated sheet of board or paper which describes a basic technique or process. Advance trials are usually carried out to ensure that learners can use them without the assistance of a teacher, working either individually, in pairs or in small groups. As well as giving information, they can be designed to stimulate project and discovery work by posing questions or setting tasks.

See also: Poster; Prompt list; Storyboarding; Study assignment; Work-related exercise; Worksheet

Work schedule restructuring (flexible working hours)

Changing employees' work schedules can be considered either as an independent structural intervention within an organization, or as one of a number of approaches in a quality-of-work-life programme. The impact of new technology, employees' choices of how to structure their leisure time and changing trends in family life have led to a growing variety of work patterns, including normal-week working, shift working, part-time working, compressed-hours, annual-hours and zero-hour contracts. Introducing flexible working hours can improve employees' motivation and morale, and reduce absenteeism, since it allows them to strike a better balance between their work and non-work responsibilities. The company also benefits because it is more likely to be able to recruit a higher-quality workforce from a non-traditional labour pool.

Three main types of flexible working programmes have been developed. *Staggered starts and finishes* involve employees observing different but overlapping work schedules. *Flexitime systems* divide work time into core hours during which everyone must work, and flexi-hours when work is optional as long as a quota of hours is completed over a certain period. Finally, in *variable-hour systems*, employees contract to work for specific periods.

Dalton, D.R. and Mesch, D.J. (1990) 'The Impact of Flexible Schedules on Employee Attendance and Turnover', *Administrative Science Quarterly*, June, pp. 370–87.
Golembiewski, R., Hillies, J. and Kagno, M. (1974) 'A Longitudinal Study of Flexi-time Effects: Some Consequences of an OD Structural Intervention', *Journal of Applied Behavioral Science*, vol. 10, no. 4, pp. 503–32.
Ivancevich, J.M. and Lyon, H.L. (1977) 'The Shortened Work Week: A Field Experiment', *Journal of Applied Psychology*, vol. 62, p. 347.
Kush, K.S. and Stroh, L.K. (1994) 'Flextime: Myth or Reality', *Business Horizons*, September–October, p. 53.
Lee, R.A. (1983) 'Hours of Work: Who Controls and How?', *Industrial Relations Journal*, vol. 14, no. 4.
Pierce, J.L. and Newstrom, J.W. Dunham, R.B. and Barber, A.E. (1989) *Alternative Work Schedules*, Allyn and Bacon.
Stredwick, J. and Ellis, S. (1998) *Flexible Working Practices: Techniques and Innovations*, Institute of Personnel and Development.
Torrington, D. and Hall, L. (1998) *Human Resource Management*, Chapter 10, Prentice-Hall.

See also: Core working; Flexible staffing; Homeworking; Intrapreneurial group; Job sharing; Multiple job-holding; Networking; Part-time working; Quality of working life

Work-Out

Work-Out is a large-group, whole-system, participative approach to identifying problems and process improvements at work. It can be seen as a variant of problem-solving groups or quality circles. The technique was developed by General Electric's

Chief Executive Officer, Jack Welch, and Jim Bowman, another executive at the company. Welch had become frustrated at the slow rate of progress in encouraging employees to eliminate outmoded aspects of the company's structure which were having a detrimental effect on performance. The original Work-Outs were led by Welch himself, who invited employee groups of 40–120 to attend an off-site meeting to identify policies and procedures which they considered irrelevant and in need of change. Some of these were visible and easy to address, others were hidden but still had a significant impact on performance. Welch's presence at these meetings, especially when the groups reported back to senior managers, helped to overcome employees' hesitancy or procrastination. The Work-Out model has developed further since then, and now addresses issues of waste, quality and work flow as well as structural blockages. Welch no longer attends the meetings, and they are now held in the plant. The procedure shares several steps with other approaches. Work-Out attempts to overcome structural problems arising from company rules, policies, procedures and bureaucracy without making any major structural changes. It led to a number of changes in General Electric's corporate culture. It improved union–management, cross-level and cross-functional relationships and communications. It involved new people in the problem-solving process and speeded up decision-making. It made senior managers more accountable to the workforce, and persuaded them that those who do the job know best what improvements are necessary. It increased workers' awareness of the complex problems that face managers. Finally, and perhaps most importantly, it challenged existing work practices.

The first step is to choose a troublesome work process for discussion. Next, a cross-functional, cross-level group is formed, and the Work-Out meeting is convened. At the meeting, participants generate recommendations to eliminate work flow problems and any unnecessary work. In Welch's version, blaming and complaining were forbidden, so if workers disliked something, they had to recommend a change, which would be planned and championed by a volunteer or group of volunteers. Senior management must respond to recommendations immediately, although it is acceptable to arrange negotiations and further study if necessary. The final step is to hold follow-up meetings to monitor progress.

Bunker, B.B. and Alban, B.T. (1997) 'Work-Out', in *Large Group Interventions: Engaging the Whole System for Rapid Change*, Jossey-Bass, pp. 169–76.
Tichy, N. and Sherman, S. (1993) *Control Your Destiny or Someone Else Will*, Doubleday.

See also: Action training and research; Business process re-engineering; Conference Model; Fast-cycle full-participation work design; Future search; Large-group interventions; Open space technology; Participative design; Real-time strategic change; Real-time work design; Search conference; Simu-Real; Socio-technical systems design; Strategic planning process

Work-related exercise

Work-related exercises are activities that can be set for business management students who are studying part-time while continuing in their normal jobs. (A similar approach, *work assignments*, can be used with full-time students.) Students are required to conduct research into the relationships between each course concept (e.g., managerial control) and a well-known organizational process (e.g., the appraisal system) or a concrete organizational product (e.g. weekly production figures). This not only provides a context for classroom learning, but also encourages students to become more familiar with their organizations, and more aware of some of their unique features and the assumptions that underpin members' behaviour. To ensure that students can compare the information they have collected, they are issued with a standardized list of questions to answer, which also provides the structure for small-group discussions. For example, if they were set the task of exploring labour turnover statistics, the questions might be: 'Who in your organization is responsible for collecting labour turnover figures?', 'How is the data collected?', 'How is the figure for labour turnover calculated?', 'What is considered the 'normal' turnover rate?' and 'What happens to the information once it is collected?' Similar exercises could be devised to address absenteeism, quality control data, sickness or industrial disputes.

Rendall, J.F. (1977) 'The Activity Record and Its Related Projects', *Management Education and Development*, vol. 8, no. 2, pp. 69–78.

See also: Induction training; Internship; Job descriptions; Management responsibility guide process; Manager shadowing; On-the-job training; Prompt list; Responsibility charting; Role analysis technique; Role-prescription; SmartProcess; Understudy; Work cards; Worksheet

Work-shadowing

This approach allows sixth-formers and undergraduates to sample a career in industry, and to understand how adults spend their working lives. It can also be used to help learners develop observational, listening, inter-personal and communication skills. The students spend between one and five days with a local manager or businessperson, known as a *job guide*, accompanying them through their normal working day, watching everything they do, and finding out why they do it. Teachers find these guides through personal contacts or formal negotiations with firms and organizations. Before the assignment, teachers may help students identify what to look for, and what questions to ask about the job and the subject's attitudes towards it, or they may be given a workbook which gives this information. When matching assignments to students, teachers allocate individuals to areas of work where they have already expressed an interest. After the assignment, the students explore their experiences through open discussions and project work.

Students usually find sharing their experiences with their peer group stimulating, they may gain greater respect from their teachers by being seen to act responsibly in an adult setting, and the assignment and follow-up activities may be taken into account in the exam accreditation system. Problems can arise if students are given menial tasks or insufficient attention during the assignment, but work-shadowing offers a number of advantages compared to work experience. Students can take part at a younger age, allowing longer acquaintance with the world of work. The programme can be more flexible and achieve a wider range of goals. Students can observe executives at work, which might be impossible if they had to fit into a workplace as temporary co-workers. They may be able to gain deeper insights into employees' feelings and attitudes, and explore the relationship between them and other aspects of the organization or firm. Finally, the experience can be concentrated into days, rather than weeks.

Blackledge, R. and Lawson, S. (1991) *European Partnerships Through Work Experience and Work Shadowing*, Industrial Society.
Watts, A.G. (1985) *Work Shadowing: A Report Prepared for the School Curriculum Industry Project*, London.
Watts, A.G. (ed.) (1996) *Rethinking Careers Education*, Routledge.

See also: Acting assignment; Apprenticeship; Corporate student board of directors; Development assignment; Internship; Manager shadowing; One-to-one learning; Planned delegation; Sick leave/holiday replacement assignment; SmartProcess

Work-simplification

Work-simplification is a job redesign technique which aims to streamline the way manual tasks are performed in order to increase efficiency and productivity. The approach was originated by Allan Mogensen during the 1940s and 1950s. Rensis Likert described work-simplification as a unique example of bringing together two management systems: *co-operative motivation*, based on participation and other human relations principles, and *job organization*, by which he meant the industrial or production engineering approach, with its emphasis on work methods analysis. When it was developed, work-simplification's distinguishing feature was that it provided a new way to introduce work method techniques, combining a formal, continuous programme to improve work methods with participation from workers and other non-experts.

Goodwin, one of Mogensen's collaborators, describes three basic elements of a work-simplification programme: appreciation, education and application. *Appreciation* entails stimulating top and middle managers' interest in the programme by explaining the approach, its objectives, and why it is necessary. *Education* involves developing a philosophy, a pattern and a programme within the organization by forming small groups, initially consisting of management personnel, in which members learn about the analytical method by dealing with simulated problems. *Application* includes setting up and co-ordinating project teams which meet regularly to discuss problems brought to light by employees, so that improving work activities becomes a routine managerial function.

The course Mogensen set up was designed for managers rather than workers, and when participants returned to their plants, they initiated their own educational programmes, primarily aimed at managers and shop-floor workers, rather than supervisors. The workers took part in the programme in two main ways: either informally, as the result of the promotional activity and the new company atmosphere, or formally, by selecting some workers to participate directly as members of a project team. Thus, work-simplification was an intervention designed to have limited reach. The initial stages of problem-definition and selection were carried out by management alone, and work-simplification was almost entirely limited to the second phase of the decision-making process: generating alternatives. Management selected the problem and formed the teams without any consultation. The ideal project team was held to consist of four or five people, including the manager directly responsible, their assistant, an outside engineer, and the employee whose work was being studied. The programmes did not offer monetary rewards to those responsible for improvements, although they incorporated a number of non-monetary rewards, which was considered important.

No documented case studies or experiments

concerning work-simplification have appeared in professional journals, so managers have had difficulty in evaluating the effects of this intervention on individual workers and productivity in general. A number of assertions were made in the business magazine *Factory* during the 1950s. Republic Steel claimed to have installed an average of 27 useful ideas for each employee trained in work-simplification. Procter & Gamble started a work-simplification programme in 1946, claiming cost savings of 50–100 per cent, and other companies reported savings of thousands of dollars. The dearth of documentation also extends to the effects of work-simplification on payments-by-results plans. While work-simplification may have produced improvements without offering monetary rewards in certain circumstances, it is not clear what happened when a plant operating a particular type of payment system tried to apply it.

Goodwin, H.F. (1958) 'What Makes Work Simplification Work', *Factory*, July.

Lehrer, R.N. (1957) *Work Simplification*, Prentice-Hall.

Mogensen, A.H. (1963) 'Work Simplification: A Programme of Continuous Improvement', in Maynard, H.B. (ed.) *Industrial Engineering Handbook* (2nd edn), McGraw-Hill, Section 10, Chapter 10, pp. 183–91.

Rowland, A.D. (1984) 'Combining Quality Circles and Work Simplification', *Training and Development Journal*, vol. 38, no. 1, pp. 90–1.

Theriault, P. (1996) *Work Simplification*, Institute of Industrial Engineers, USA.

Uris, A. (1965) 'Mogy's Work Simplification is Working New Miracles', *Factory*, September, pp. 112–15.

Zink, W.C. (1962) *Dynamic Work Simplification*, Van Nostrand Reinhold.

See also: Group technology; Job design; Job enlargement; Job enrichment; Quality circles

Worker-directors (work councils)

Worker-directors are elected by employees to represent them at board meetings, which are usually held three or four times a year. Procedures vary, but they are frequently given access to the company's performance reports and financial data. Little is kept secret from them, with the possible exception of joint ventures and takeovers, and they can discuss any subject except pay. At the meetings, the worker-directors are encouraged to report on the mood of the workforce, to offer suggestions for improving work practices, and to question the company's plans. Many worker-directors see their primary role as detecting general trends, which they communicate to employees by posting reports on noticeboards after every meeting.

Each newly appointed worker-director is given training in interpreting the intricacies of management reports. Their appointment is often part of a wider strategy to encourage openness and communication within the company, and to counter the 'them and us' syndrome. Implementing this idea requires a good deal of care. Management should not interfere in elections, although individuals may be invited to stand for election. Some companies set a minimum response rate of 30 per cent in any election. It is best to ensure that there are at least two worker-directors at any time, preferably serving overlapping two-year terms so that there is always one with a year's experience of serving on the board.

Involvement and Participation Association (1998) *European Works Councils: Moving Forward with Employee Consultation*, IPA.

Kaufman, B.E., Lewin, D. and Adams, R.G. (1995) 'Work-Force Governance', in Ferris, G.R., Rosen, S.D. and Barnum, D.T. (eds) *Handbook of Human Resource Management*, Blackwell Business, pp. 404–24.

Rees, R. (1985) 'Worker Directors Cure "Them and Us" Syndrome', *Works Management*, December, pp. 38–40.

The Industrial Society (1998) *Managing Best Practice No. 49: Works Councils*, IS.

See also: Employee-guided management; Non-executive director; Participation; Suggestion schemes

Worksheet

Worksheets are a very simple, flexible and cheap way to structure learning programmes and provide individualized learning in a variety of educational settings. Many museums now distribute worksheets for visitors to complete as they tour the exhibits, which may include a questionnaire and a series of tasks. In formal educational programmes, worksheets may not necessarily consist of questions, but may give instructions about the nature, number and sequence of the learning tasks students are to undertake.

Ball, S.J. (1980) 'Mixed Ability Teaching: The Worksheet Method', *British Journal of Educational Technology*, vol. 11, no. 1, pp. 36–48.

See also: Block method; Dalton laboratory plan; Library assignment; Prompt list; Study assignment; Tutorial-tape-document learning package approach; Work cards

Workshop (atelier)

Workshops bring together people who are experienced in a particular field to explore issues of mutual interest. Although most workshops are run by one or more facilitators, the participants usually develop their own structures and processes, within certain parameters. It is helpful if they are well informed, self-motivated, and willing to collaborate and learn from each other. The facilitator's role is to establish conditions which promote mutual learning by supplying any materials required, co-ordinating exercises and technical procedures, and offering help and information, either personally or by providing access to learning resources. Experts may also be invited to attend, either to participate or to answer technical or theoretical queries from an information centre. In management education and development, it is common nowadays for any course to be described as a 'workshop', perhaps to attract participants who would not object to sharing experiences with colleagues, but who might be offended by the idea that they need tuition. As long as everyone is clear about what will be involved, this presents no problems, but difficulties arise if participants arrive at a workshop expecting to exchange experiences, only to be subjected to a lecture, or if the facilitator has prepared a structure for mutual learning, but participants expect to be taught.

The sponsoring institution usually specifies the workshop's topic, selects participants, organizes the details and appoints the facilitator, although, ideally, participants should initiate the workshop themselves. Workshops begin with an introductory session, during which the facilitator explains the arrangements that have been made and sets out the general goals. Ice-breaking exercises may be used to help participants learn each others' names and a little about their backgrounds, skills and interests. The next stage is to reach consensus about which areas of the topic to examine, and to draw up an agenda accordingly. The facilitator may suggest that the workshop should aim to do more than merely discuss the issues, perhaps by producing a practical end result, such as an action plan or proposal. For much of the time, workshops consist of sub-groups whose participants are chosen at random or according to their interests and expectations, to work on certain problems, or themes or products. The final stage consists of some form of group evaluation, identifying good and bad points about the workshop and how it was run.

Bates, W.T.G. and Farey, P.R. (1975) 'The Development of a Management Workshop', *Journal of European Training*, vol. 4, no. 3, pp. 162–71.

Chase, P.H. (1972) 'Creative Management Workshop', in *Personnel Journal*, vol. 51, April, pp. 26–9 and 282.

Mack, D. (1979) *The Workshop Way*, CCTUT Occasional Paper No. 1, Report of the Third National Working Conference, Co-ordinating Committee for the Training of University Teachers.

See also: Concentrated study; Learning community; Mini-course; Module; Residential

Writing for learning

The process of committing thoughts to paper in a way that can be understood by others is at the heart of education. Instructors provide access to textbooks, case studies and course notes, and students respond by producing essays, term papers, exam answers, project reports, dissertations and theses. Although writing is obviously important in studying the arts and social sciences, it also plays a crucial role in quantitative subjects such as statistics and accounting, ensuring that students have grasped the ideas and concepts that underlie formulae, rather than simply memorizing them. Instructors can set written tasks to check a student's understanding of a topic, since inability to express ideas clearly in writing usually reflects the fact that they are unclear in the student's mind. Many educators believe that writing and understanding go hand in hand: only when we write about a subject do we truly learn about it, and internalize that learning.

Instructors can set a wide variety of writing tasks, depending on the needs of their students and the demands of the course, including summarizing lecture notes, developing questions about a lecture or a textbook chapter, keeping a weekly diary or reaction journal, preparing a term paper. In deciding which to set and how often to do so, it is important to be clear about the learning objectives. For example, *writing for problem-solving* involves students documenting the mental steps involved in arriving at a solution, and analysing these steps may reveal the source of any difficulties, whereas *writing for interpretation* involves students recording their views of ideas or data, which can also be used to check their understanding and identify problem areas.

Davies, W., Schulte, M.F. and Johnson, V.E. (1995) 'Two Draft Term Papers: Improving the Pedagogical Value of Written Assignments', *Journal of Management Education*, vol. 19 no. 2, pp. 250–3.

Dehler, G.E. (1996) 'Management Education as Intentional Learning: A Knowledge Transforming Approach to Written Composition', *Journal of Management Education*, vol. 20, no. 2, pp. 221–35.

Gregs, L.W. and Steinberg, E.R. (eds) (1980)

Cognitive Processes in Writing, Lawrence Erlbaum Associates.

Kellogg, D.M. (1991) 'Assigning Business Writing to Increase the Learning Potential of Case Courses', *Journal of Management Education*, vol. 15, no. 1, pp. 19–34.

Locke, K. and Brazelton, J.K. (1997) 'Why Do We Ask Them to Write, or Whose Writing Is It Anyway?', *Journal of Management Education*, vol. 21, no. 1, pp. 44–57.

Shibli, A. (1993) 'Opinion: Increasing Learning Through Writing in Quantitative (and Computer) Courses', *Education and Training Technology International*, vol. 30, no. 1, pp. 50–6.

Sommers, D. (1991) 'The Choice of Leader to Write About is not a Random Event', *Journal of Management Education*, vol. 15, no. 3, pp. 359–66.

Webb, G. (1990) 'Case Study: Developing Writing with Peer Discussion and Microcomputers', *Education and Training Technology International*, vol. 27, no. 2, pp. 209–15.

See also: Clozure; Literary criticism; Re-writing; Story-writing

Zero defects (ZD)

Zero defects is a quality management strategy based on the principle that rather than accepting work errors as inevitable and trying to anticipate them, they should be prevented or eliminated. It involves management encouraging employees to aim for zero defects: completing each task properly the first time. Mistakes are caused by lack of knowledge or skill and lack of attention. Lack of knowledge or skill can be measured, but Philip Crosby points out that inattention is a state of mind, and must be dealt with as an attitudinal problem. Each employee must make a personal commitment to improving the quality of their work. Although most individuals respond enthusiastically, Crosby sees zero defects as a performance standard rather than a motivational approach, despite the fact that many organizations use it in that way. Encouraging employees to prevent defects creates a climate which allows them to draw attention to problems without necessarily having to offer solutions, encouraging communication and strengthening relationships between management and the workforce.

Crosby, P.B. (1979) *Quality is Free: The Art of Making Quality Certain*, Mentor Books.

See also: Ideological change; Quality circles; Quality management; Quality awareness training

Appendix: Resources for management development and organizational change

A conscious decision was made to exclude specific learning, training or development materials and programmes of study from the references sections in this encyclopedia, since these are constantly being developed and updated. This appendix gives information about some of the resources that were available at the time of publication.

Management development

Reference works

Interactive Directory of Learning Resources (2nd edn) (1998), compiled by Open Mind, Gower
As the title suggests, this is a CD-ROM-based directory that provides references to over 5000 learning resources produced by 120 different publishers, including CD-ROMs, CDs, computer-based training products, training videos, audio tapes, games, activity manuals and business books. The directory is updated annually.

Bickerstaff, G. (1999) *Which MBA* (10th edn), Financial Times Management/Economist Intelligence Unit; Green, C. and Reingold, J. (1999) *Business Week's Guide to the Best Business Schools* (6th edn), McGraw-Hill
Many different publishers regularly produce a guide to MBA programmes and the business schools that offer them. Most of the business schools teach broadly the same topics, but the methods they adopt vary. The Harvard Business School relies on the case study method, whereas other schools use international student assignments, for example. These guides are updated annually.

International Management Education Directories, EMD Centre, Naarderstraat 296, NL-1272 NT Huizen, The Netherlands
These handbooks give an overview of management training programmes in all major management centres and business schools around the world. Separate directories are available for Western Europe, Central and Eastern Europe, Asia Pacific, and North America. The handbooks are updated regularly.

Sadler, P. (ed.) (1997) *International Executive Development Programmes* (2nd edn), Kogan Page
This directory lists development programmes, open learning programmes, in-house company training programmes, and includes a section on executive MBAs.

Books

Berger, M.L. and Berger, P.J. (eds) (1972) *Group Training Techniques*, Gower
This collection of articles by various authors describes the different applications of group approaches in management education and training.

Boud, D.J. (ed.) (1981) *Developing Student Autonomy in Learning*, Kogan Page
Each chapter is written by a different author, describing how they have attempted to increase students' autonomy in their learning. The book includes descriptions of some approaches that are growing in popularity in management development, such as learning contracts.

Boydell, T. and Pedler, M. (eds) (1981) *Management Self-Development: Concepts and Practices*, Gower
Chapters by different authors describe the varying ways the concept of self-development has been applied in management development programmes, degree courses, entrepreneurship training and other contexts.

Burgoyne, J.G. and Reynolds, M. (eds) (1997) *Management Learning: Integrating Perspectives in Theory and Practice*, Sage
This book introduces the context and history of management learning, providing a framework within which to discuss its objectives, values and methods.

Entwistle, N. (1981) *Styles of Learning and Teaching*, Wiley
This is an educational psychology textbook, but is written in an attractive style. It introduces and illustrates the key concepts in understanding how people learn.

Knowles, M.S. (1970) *The Modern Practice of Adult Education*, Associated Press; Knowles, M.S. (1973) *The Adult Learner: A Neglected Species*, Gulf Publishing; Knowles, M.S. (1975) *Self-Directed Learning: A Guide for Learners and Teachers*, Associated Press, New York
Some of the most comprehensive works on adult education have been written by Malcolm Knowles. Many of his ideas were ahead of their time, and these books reward repeated reading.

Miles, M.B. (1959) *Learning to Work in Groups*, Bureau of Publications, Teachers College, Columbia University, New York
Although written for schoolteachers, this book contains many ideas about the process of learning, and also includes details of group activities and exercises.

Mumford, A. (1995) *Gower Handbook of Management Development*, Gower
This book includes a discussion of how managers learn, and is therefore a useful complement to this encyclopedia.

Rogers, C.R. (1969) *Freedom to Learn*, Charles E. Merrill
One of the all-time educational classics which emphasizes student-centred learning, this book should be read at least once by all educators and trainers, irrespective of whether they agree with Rogers's views.

Runkel, P., Harrison, R. and Runkel, M. (eds) (1969) *The Changing College Classroom*, Jossey-Bass

Although it does not deal explicitly with management education and training, this provocative collection of contributions presents a number of innovative approaches which could be adapted.

Sutherland, P. (1997) *Adult Learning: A Reader*, Kogan Page
Since the majority of management students are likely to be adults, it is important to understand their special characteristics. This book examines various aspects of learning, including informal learning, the effects of age and gender differences, and experiential learning.

Zoll, A.A. (1969) *Dynamic Management Education*, Addison Wesley Longman; Zoll, A.A. (1974) *Explorations in Managing*, Addison Wesley
These books are valuable sources of exercises and activities which can be used in management training. They also give guidance on designing your own case studies, action mazes and role-plays.

Journals

The journals listed below regularly carry articles suggesting practical ideas to improve teaching and learning. Some are specific to management education and development, while others are not.

British Journal of Educational Technology
Continuing Professional Development
Education and Training Technology International
Educational Review
Educational Technology Research and Development
European Journal of Engineering Education
Higher Education
Industrial and Commercial Training
Innovations in Education and Training International
Instructional Science
International Journal of Training and Development
Journal of Co-operative Education
Journal of European Industrial Training
Journal of Experimental Education
Journal of Management Case Studies
Journal of Management Development
Journal of Management Education
Leadership and Organizational Development
Management Learning
Personnel Review
Programmed Learning and Educational Technology
Review of Educational Research
Studies in Higher Education
Teaching at a Distance
Training
Training & Development
Training and Development Journal
Training Journal
Virtual University Journal

Organizational change

Books and journal articles

The author has found these books and articles useful in attempting to understand and implement organizational change. They range from classics in the field (some out of print) to relatively recent publications which have had a dramatic impact on thinking. It is important to re-emphasize that organizational change is not synonymous with organizational development. Many of the current attempts to introduce organizational change totally reject organizational development's values and beliefs. The list below therefore includes works from adherents of both schools of thought.

Argyris, C. (1970) *Intervention Theory and Method*, Addison Wesley Longman.

Beckhard, R. and Harris, R.T. (1987) *Organizational Transitions: Managing Complex Change* (2nd edn), Addison Wesley Longman.

Bennis, W.G., Benne, K.D. and Chin, R. (eds) (1985) *The Planning of Change* (4th edn), Holt, Rinehart and Winston.

Buchanan, D.A. and Badham, R. (1999) *Power Politics and Organizational Change*, Sage.

Buchanan, D.A. and Boddy, D. (1992) *The Expertise of the Change Agent*, Prentice-Hall.

Burke, W.W. (1993) *Organization Development: A Process of Learning and Changing*, Addison Wesley Longman.

Cummings, T.G. and Worley, C.G. (1997) *Organizational Development and Change* (6th edn), South-West Publishing.

Dalton, G.W., Lawrence, P.R. and Greiner, L.E. (1970) *Organizational Change and Development*, Irwin Dorsey.

Dawson, P. (1994) *Organizational Change: A Processional Approach*, Sage.

French, W.L. and Bell, C.H. (1999) *Organization Development: Behavioural Science Interventions for Organization Improvement* (3rd edn), Prentice-Hall.

Huse, E.F. and Cummings, T.G. (1985) *Organizational Development and Change* (3rd edn), West Publishing.

Kotter, J.P. (1996) *Leading Change*, Harvard Business School Press.

Lippitt, G. and Lippitt, R. (1978) *The Consulting Process in Action*, Pfeiffer/Jossey-Bass.

Margulies, N. and Raia, A.P. (1972) *Organizational Development: Values, Process and Technology*, McGraw-Hill.

Margulies, N. and Wallace, V. (1973) *Organizational Change: Techniques and Applications*, Scott Foresman & Co.

Mohrman, A.M. (1989) *Large Scale Organizational Change*, Jossey-Bass.

Paton, R.A and McCalman, J. (1999) *Change Management: A Guide to Effective Implementation* (2nd edn), Sage.

Michael, S.R., Luthans, F., Odiorne, G.G, Burke, W.W. and Hayden, S. (eds) (1981) *Techniques of Organizational Change*, McGraw-Hill.

Neilson, E.N. (1984) *On Becoming an OD Practitioner*, Prentice-Hall.

Porras, J.I. and Robertson, P.J. (1992) 'Organization Development: Theory, Practice and Research', in Dunnette, M.D. and Hough, L.M. (eds) *Handbook of Industrial and Organizational Psychology, Volume 3* (2nd edn), Consulting Psychologists Press, pp. 719–822.

Rothwell, W.J. et al. (1995) *Practising Organization Development: A Guide for Consultants*, Pfeiffer/Jossey-Bass.

Sanzgiri, J. and Gottlieb, J.Z. (1992) 'Philosophic and Pragmatic Influences on the Practice of Organization Development, 1950–2000', *Organizational Dynamics*, vol. 21, no, 2, pp. 57–69.

Senior, B. (1997) *Organisational Change*, Pitman.
Van Eynde, D.F. et al. (eds) (1997) *Organization Development Classics: The Practice of Theory and Change*, Jossey-Bass.

Journals

Sources of new ideas about changing organizations can be found in professional journals and academic publications. The professional journals usually identify and introduce the latest 'good idea', which is studied and evaluated by researchers, and their findings are then published in the academic journals. The number of journals in this field has grown enormously in recent years. Some are available as 'virtual journals' on the Internet or CD-ROMs, as well as in more traditional forms.

Academy of Management Executive
Academy of Management Journal
Academy of Management Review
California Management Review
Employee Relations
Group & Organizational Management
Group and Organizational Studies
Harvard Business Review
Human Behaviour and Organizational Performance
Human Resource Development Quarterly
Human Resource Management
Human Resource Management Journal
Human Resources
Human Resources Management International Digest
Industrial and Corporate Change
International Journal of Human Resource Management
Journal of Applied Behavioural Science
Journal of Human Resources
Journal of Managerial Psychology
Journal of Organizational Behaviour
Journal of Organizational Behaviour Management
Journal of Organizational Change Management
Journal of Workplace Learning
Leadership and Organization Development Journal
National Productivity Review
New Technology Work and Employment
OD Practitioner
Organization Development Journal
Organizational Dynamics
Organizations and People: Successful Development
People Management
Personnel
Personnel Journal
Personnel Review
Team Performance Management: An International Journal
The Learning Organization